BARRON'S

HOW TO PREPARE FOR THE

ACT

ASSESSMENT

12TH EDITION

BARRON'S

HOW TO PREPARE FOR THE

ACT

ASSESSMENT

12TH EDITION

George Ehrenhaft
Former English Department Chairman
Mamaroneck High School, Mamaroneck, New York

Robert L. Lehrman
Former Science Department Supervisor
Roslyn High School, Roslyn, New York

Allan Mundsack
Professor of Mathematics
Los Angeles Pierce College, Los Angeles, California

Fred Obrecht
Professor of English
Los Angeles Pierce College, Los Angeles, California

BARRON'S

All inquiries should be addressed to:
Barron's Educational Series, Inc.
250 Wireless Boulevard
Hauppauge, New York 11788
http://www.barronseduc.com

Library of Congress Catalog Card No. 94-35588

International Standard Book No. 0-7641-1369-0 (book)
0-7641-7399-5 (book/CD-ROM package)

PRINTED IN THE UNITED STATES OF AMERICA

10 9 8 7   (book)
10 9 8 7 6 5 4 3   (book/CD-ROM package)

Contents

PART FOUR MODEL EXAMINATIONS 407

Acknowledgments

The authors acknowledge the kindness of those organizations concerned with the granting of permission to reprint passages. A list of the excerpts used in this book and the works they are from follows:

Page 37, Passage I: Richard L. Worsnop, "Indoor Air Pollution" from *The CQ Researcher*, Congressional Quarterly, Inc. October 27, 1995.

Page 39, Passage II: *Stuttering: Hope Through Research*, U.S. Dept. of Health and Human Services, National Institute of Health Publications 81-2250, GPO, Washington, D.C., May 1981.

Page 41, Passage III: Mario Pei, "Wanted: A World Language," Public Affairs Committee, New York, 1969.

Page 43, Passage IV: Washington Irving, "Buckthorne," *Tales of a Traveller*, Library of America, 1991, pp. 500–502.

Page 121, Passage: Suzanne Britt, "That Lean and Hungry Look," reprinted by permission of the author.

Pages 121–122, Passage: R. Grudin, "Two Views of Time," from *Patterns* by Mary Lou Conlin, © 1994, Houghton Mifflin Company. Reprinted with permission.

Page 122, Passage: Douglas A. Bernstein, et al., "Bonding at Birth," from *Patterns* by Mary Lou Conlin, © 1994, Houghton Mifflin Company. Reprinted with permission.

Page 296, Passage: from *Testing the Current*. Copyright © 1984 by William McPherson. Reprinted by permission of Simon & Schuster, Inc., New York.

Pages 298–300, Passage: Laura Furman, *Watch Time Fly*. Copyright © 1982 by Laura Furman. Viking Penguin, Inc., New York. Reprinted by permission of The Wendy Weil Agency, Inc.

Pages 302–304, Passage: H. E. Bates, "The Good Corn," *The Best of H. E. Bates*, Little, Brown and Co., Boston, 1963, pp. 241–244.

Page 306, Passage: Joseph Machlis, *Johann Strauss*, Music Treasures of the World, New York, 1954.

Pages 306–307, Passage: Miguel de Cervantes, *Six Exemplary Novels*, introduced and translated by Harriet de Onis, Barron's Educational Series, Inc., New York, 1961.

Pages 307–308, Passage: Joseph Machlis, *How to Listen to Music*, Music Treasures of the World, New York, 1954.

Page 308, Passage: Ruth Levin, *Ordinary Heroes: The Story of Shaftsbury*, Shaftsbury Historical Society, Vermont, 1978.

Pages 309–310, Passage: Simon Wilson, *Pop*, Barron's Educational Series, Inc., New York, 1978.

Pages 313–314, Passage: Arnold Sungaard, "Jazz, Hot and Cold," *Essays for Modern Youth*, Globe Book Company, New York, 1960.

Page 316, Passage: Walter J. Wessels, *Economics*, Barron's Business Review Series, Barron's Educational Series, Inc., New York, 1987.

Page 317, Passage: Gerald J. Bean, Jr., Mary E. Stefl, and Stephen R. Howe, "Mental Health and Homelessness: Issues and Findings," © 1987, National Association of Social Workers, Inc. Reprinted with permission from *Social Work*, V 32:5, pg. 411.

Pages 317–318, Passage: "The Right to Keep and Bear Arms," U.S. Senate, Committee on the Judiciary, Report of the Subcommittee on the Constitution, 97th Cong., GPO, Washington, D.C., February 1982.

Pages 319–320, Passage: William A. Korns, "Cults in America and Public Policy," *Editorial Research Reports*, Congressional Quarterly, Washington, D.C., vol. 1, no. 14, April 13, 1979.

Pages 323–324, Passage: Franz Alexander, "Emotional Maturity," *Mental Health Bulletin*, Nov./Dec. 1948, reprinted with permission from the Illinois Society for Mental Hygiene by Hogg Foundation for Mental Health. The University of Texas, Austin TX 78712, 1959.

Pages 326–327, Passage: Maya Pines, "The New Human Genetics: How Gene Splicing Helps Researchers Fight Inherited Disease," U.S. Dept. of Health and Human Services, Public Health Service, Publication 84-662, September 1984.

Pages 327–328, Passage: "Groundwater: A Community Action Guide," Concern, Inc., Washington, D.C., June 1984.

Pages 328–329, Passage: "The Cytoskeleton, the Cell's Physical Props," *Inside the Cell*, US Department of Health and Human Services, Public Health Service, National Institutes of Health, NIH Publication No. 90-1050, p. 41.

Page 329, Passage: Reprinted from *Whale Fishery of New England*, William S. Sullwold Publishing, Inc., Taunton, Massachusetts, 1968.

Page 330–332, Passage: "The Possibility of Intelligent Life in the Universe," U.S. House of Representatives, Report for the Committee on Science and Technology, GPO, Washington, D.C., 1974.

Pages 335–336, Passage: Albert Szent-Györgyi, "Horizons of Life Sciences," in *Ideas in Science,* ed. Oscar H. Fidell, Washington Square Press, New York, 1966.

Page 339, Passage I: Gerald W. Johnson, "Freedom of Inquiry is for Hopeful People," *The First Freedom,* ed. Robert B. Downs, Amer. Library Association (Chicago, 1960).

Pages 340–341, Passage II: Helene L. Baldwin and C.L. McGuinness, *A Primer on Ground Water,* Department of Interior Geological Ground Survey, Washington, D.C., 1963.

Pages 342–343, Passage III: Joachim Miller, "An Old Oregonian in the Snow," *The World Begins Here: An Anthology of Oregon Short Fiction,* ed. Glen A. Love, Oregon State University Press, Corvallis, 1993, pp. 38–40.

Page 344, Passage IV: Wesley Barnes, *The Philosophy and Literature of Existentialism,* Barron's Educational Series, Inc., New York, 1968.

Page 431, Passage I: Theodore Gracyk, *Rhythm and Noise: An Aesthetics of Rock,* Duke University Press, Durham, NC, 1996, pp. 8–10.

Page 433, Passage II: Alan Paton, *Too Late the Phalarope,* Signet, New American Library, 1953, pp. 71–72.

Page 435, Passage III: Peter Coolsen, Michelle Seligson, and James Garbarino, "When School's Out and Nobody's Home," National Committee for Prevention of Child Abuse, Chicago, Illinois, 1986.

Pages 436–437, Passage IV: "The Health Effects of Caffeine," a report by the American Council on Science and Health, New York, March 1981.

Pages 481–482, Passage I: "Characteristics of the Abusive Situation," *Guide to Legal Relief,* Governor's Commission on Domestic Violence, New York, October 1984.

Page 483, Passage II: "Useful Information on Alzheimer's Disease," U.S. Department of Health and Human Services, National Institutes of Health, Rockville, MD.

Pages 484–485, Passage III: Sherwood Anderson, "The Egg," Copyright 1921 by B. W. Huebsch, Inc. Renewed by Eleanor Coperhaver Anderson, 1948.

Page 486, Passage III: Carl Engel, "The Beginnings of Opera," from *From Bach to Stravinski: The History of Music by Its Foremost Critics.* David Ewen, ed. W.W. Norton, 1933.

Page 532–533, Passage I: Emile Zola, *Germinal,* trans. by Stanley and Eleanor Hochman, New American Library, 1970, pp. 114–116.

Page 534, Passage II: Gabriele Sterner, *Art Nouveau: An Art of Transition from Individual to Mass Society,* Barron's Educational Series, Hauppauge, New York, 1982, pp. 87–90.

Pages 535–536, Passage III: Rachel Carson, "The Sunless Seas." *The Sea Around Us,* Oxford University Press, 1989.

Page 537, Passage IV: "Constitutional Rights of Children," Subcommittee on the Constitution of the Committee on the Judiciary of the United States Senate, Government Printing Office, Washington, D.C., 1978.

PART ONE

Preparing for the ACT

Introduction

THE ACT ASSESSMENT

The ACT Assessment is a multiple-choice examination required for admission to many colleges. It takes 2 hours and 55 minutes to complete, and it contains four parts:

TEST	NUMBER OF QUESTIONS	LENGTH
English	75	45 minutes
Mathematics	60	60 minutes
Reading	40	35 minutes
Science Reasoning	40	35 minutes

Performance on the ACT is one of the important items of information that college admissions people consider when deciding whether to accept an applicant. Since the ACT is taken by students all over the country, colleges use the scores to compare the achievement and ability of applicants from a variety of secondary schools. The examination serves as a common standard for predicting students' success in college courses.

Primary Focus of the ACT

Although the ACT is based on subjects studied in high school, the test emphasizes thinking skills. Rather than asking students to recall facts or to remember the content of courses, most of the questions require students to solve problems, draw conclusions, make inferences, and think analytically. Colleges like to know that prospective students have the depth of mind for figuring out answers rather than merely memorizing information.

The Four Parts of the ACT

1. The English Test assesses mastery of the understanding and skills needed to write well. In particular, it tests:

Usage and Mechanics		
Punctuation		10 questions
Grammar and Usage		12 questions
Sentence Structure		<u>18</u> questions
	Total	40
Rhetorical Skills		
Writing Strategy		12 questions
Organization		11 questions
Style		<u>12</u> questions
	Total	35

Satisfactory performance on the English Test tells a college that you know the conventions of standard grammatical English and that you can punctuate and write complete, carefully structured sentences. The test further assesses your understanding of rhetoric, that is, whether you can tell when a piece of writing is unified, well organized, and consistent in style.

On the English Test you are given five prose passages, each about 325 words. Portions of the passage are underlined and numbered. Most of the questions ask you to decide whether the underlined sections are correct, and, if not, which of four alternative choices is the most appropriate substitute. An item may contain an error in punctuation, sentence structure, or some other aspect of grammar and usage. The remaining questions on the English Test, which ask you to judge the quality of expression, unity, clarity, or overall effectiveness of the writing, refer to passages in their entirety or to selected portions of the text.

For the English Test, the ACT reports a total score in addition to two subscores:

    Subscore 1. *Usage/Mechanics*
    Subscore 2. *Rhetorical Skills*

Colleges may use subscores to place you in a suitable English course during your freshman year.

2. The Mathematics Test measures knowledge and understanding of mathematics, in particular.

Pre-Algebra	14 questions
Elementary Algebra	10 questions
Intermediate Algebra	9 questions
Coordinate Geometry	9 questions
Plane Geometry	14 questions
Trigonometry	4 questions

Each of the 60 items presents a mathematical problem that you must solve by using algebra, geometry or trigonometry. The problems are presented in the order of their difficulty. This is not a test of your ability to memorize formulas and techniques or to demonstrate your skill in arithmetic. Accuracy and knowledge are important, of course, but your mathematical reasoning ability is what counts most.

For each problem, you must pick one of five alternative solutions, one of which may be "None of the above." About half the items on the test are application items that require you to perform a sequence of operations. Another eight items require you to analyze the sequence of operations and conditions of the problem. The remaining problems test your basic mathematical proficiency.

The ACT reports your total score on the Mathematics Test as well as three subscores:

    Subscore 1. *Pre-Algebra/Elementary Algebra*
    Subscore 2. *Intermediate Algebra/Coordinate Geometry*
    Subscore 3. *Plane Geometry/Trigonometry*

Subscores reveal your strengths and weaknesses and are often used by college advisors to place you appropriately in college math courses.

3. The Reading Test measures your ability to understand materials similar to those read in college courses. The test consists of four passages, each about 750 words, drawn from four different areas of knowledge:

Prose Fiction: novels, short stories	10 questions
Humanities: art, music, dance, architecture, theater, philosophy	10 questions
Social Sciences: sociology, psychology, economics, political science, history, anthropology	10 questions
Natural Sciences: biology, chemistry, physics, space science, earth science	10 questions

Passages are given in the order of reading difficulty; the first is easiest, the last hardest. On a given ACT any of the four types of passages may be placed first, second, third, or fourth. The order is not announced ahead of time. Passages are taken from books, articles, periodicals, and other publications. Since each passage contains whatever information you need for answering the questions, no additional background or knowledge is required.

The 10 multiple-choice questions about each passage are arranged by level of difficulty, with the easiest first and the hardest last. Each question is followed by four choices. To answer the majority of the questions (26 out of 40) you need to draw inferences from the passage, perceive implications, distinguish the author's intent, separate fact from opinion—show, in short, that you have more than a superficial grasp of the content of the passage. The remaining 14 questions ask about material explicitly stated in the passage.

For the Reading Test, the ACT reports a total score as well as two subscores:

Subscore 1. *Arts/Literature,* which measures your performance on the prose fiction and humanities passages.

Subscore 2. *Social Studies/Sciences,* which indicates how well you read the social sciences and natural sciences passages.

A significant difference between subscores could be useful to both you and your college advisor in making decisions about courses and programs of study. Moreover, a higher subscore in one area may indicate that your interests and talents lean in a particular direction.

4. The Science Reasoning Test assesses your ability to think like a scientist. On the test you must answer questions about seven sets of scientific information presented in three formats:

Data Representation: graphs, tables, other schematics	15 questions
Research Summaries: several related experiments	18 questions
Conflicting Viewpoints: alternative interpretations of scientific matters	7 questions

The sets of information come from biology, chemistry, physics, and the physical sciences, which include earth science and space science. Three of the seven sets of data are presented as graphs, charts, tables, or scientific drawings. Another three are summaries of research, and the seventh is a discussion of a controversial scientific issue.

The key word in this test is *reasoning.* Half the questions ask you to determine the accuracy and validity of conclusions and hypotheses based on the information presented. Another thirteen questions require you to generalize from given data by drawing conclusions or making predictions. The remaining seven questions check your understanding of the information itself. Simple arithmetic or algebra may be necessary to answer some of the questions.

The ACT reports no subscores on the Scientific Reasoning Test.

BEFORE TAKING THE ACT

Choosing a Test Date

Most college-bound students take the ACT during the spring of the junior year or at the beginning of the senior year. Which time you choose works neither for nor against you in the eyes of college admissions officials.

IF YOU TAKE THE ACT AS A:

JUNIOR	SENIOR
1. You will get a clearer picture of your prospects for admission to the colleges you may be considering. As a result, you can make more realistic college plans.	**1.** You are likely to earn higher scores, because you will have had more courses and more experience.

JUNIOR	SENIOR
2. You will have more opportunities to retake the ACT. Hoping to improve scores, students often use the time between exams to prepare themselves more thoroughly.	**2.** You will have the opportunity to retake the ACT but with less preparation time between examination dates.
3. You can apply to a college for an early decision. Deadlines for most early decision applications fall between October 15 and November 15.	**3.** You will easily meet regular college application deadlines, which usually fall between January 1 and March 15 for September admissions.

Ultimately, the date you take the ACT may depend on your college application deadlines. Although most colleges leave the decision to the applicant, some require that you take the ACT at a particular time.

Registering for the ACT

The ACT is given several times a year. The exact dates, times, and testing sites are listed in a free booklet called *Registering for the ACT Assessment,* which is probably available in the guidance office of your school. Or you can contact:

ACT Registration Department
P.O. Box 414
Iowa City, IA 52243-0414
Telephone: 319/337-1270

The booklet comes with a registration form and an explanation of the steps you must take to sign up. The deadline is approximately one month before the exam. After the deadline you may submit a late registration (and a late fee) any time until two weeks before the test date. Register by mail or online at *www.act.org*. Students retaking the test may re-register by phone. Call (319) 337-1270.

Ask also for *Preparing for the ACT Assessment,* an ACT publication containing general test-taking advice, a practice examination, and statistics to help you interpret your score.

Using This Barron's Book to Prepare

This book will help you to do your best on the ACT. It guides you step by step through a program of preparation. Ideally, you should have weeks or months to prepare. The more time, the better, but even if your test date is just around the corner, the book contains enough descriptive material, practical test-taking hints, and sample questions to make it worth your while to spend at least a few hours perusing it. In fact, except for starting high school all over again, working through the pages of this book is the best thing you can do to prepare for the ACT.

Each part has a distinct function and purpose:

Part One—to introduce the ACT Assessment and to get you started.

Part Two—to diagnose the present state of your skills.

Part Three—to prepare you for each of the four tests within the ACT Assessment: English, Mathematics, Reading, and Science Reasoning.

Part Four—to systematically evaluate your growth and progress, using model examinations to be taken under simulated testing conditions.

For the most thorough preparation, start at the beginning of the book and work your way through to the end. But if time is short between now and your test date, you can focus on the parts of the book that deal with the subjects you are most concerned about.

Here are some of the book's features that students find most useful:

1. *Profile of your present academic strengths and weaknesses.*	Start with the Diagnostic Examination in Part Two. Record the results on the charts at the end of the examination. At a glance, you'll know what you do well and what you should spend time on as you get ready for the ACT.
2. *Descriptions of what you are expected to know.*	Each of the four subject areas in Part Three begins with a complete description of the test in that subject. Preparation is more purposeful when you know what you are preparing for.
3. *Long-range preparation strategies.*	Each subject chapter contains several practical, long-range ideas for sharpening skills and building your knowledge of subject matter. If you plan ahead, you'll be better prepared on test day.
4. *Review of skills needed for the English and Mathematics Tests.*	The English and Math chapters in Part Three contain comprehensive review sections to be used for studying and for handy reference while you work on sample questions.
5. *Practice exercises using ACT-type questions*	Each of the subject chapters offers numerous sample questions with suggestions for finding the right answers. Since all answers are fully explained, you learn as you go.
6. *Specific techniques for answering ACT questions.*	In each subject chapter, you'll find test-taking hints for answering questions in that subject. The use of trustworthy test-taking tactics can boost your ACT scores.
7. *Model examinations to be taken under simulated test conditions.*	Turn to Part Four and take Model Examination A. Follow the test directions and time yourself. As you answer the questions, apply the tactics you learned in this book.
8. *Do-it-yourself system for checking growth and progress.*	When you complete each model examination, check your answers and evaluate your work, using the special performance evaluation chart provided. After further study, take another model examination. Again, check the results to bring your self-assessment up-to-date.

To use this book most effectively, try to build ACT preparation time into your daily routine, especially during the several weeks before taking the ACT. For each model examination, set aside three hours. By taking all the examinations, you'll learn to pace yourself and get to know what to expect on test day. Moreover, you can practice many of the test-taking tactics described in the pages of this book. Finding answers to more than two hundred questions takes stamina, so accustom yourself to extended periods of concentrated work. In a sense, you are not unlike an athlete preparing for a big competition. The better your condition, the better you're likely to perform.

Evaluating Your Performance

After taking the full-length diagnostic examination in Part Two or any of the model examinations in Part Three, evaluate your performance by following these steps:

1. Check your answers using the answer key provided after each examination.
2. Turn to the Analysis Chart, and cross out each wrong answer with an **X.** Count the

number of correct answers in each horizontal row, and write the total in the column entitled "Your Score." The sum of your correct answers is your total score on this examination. The percentage of your correct answers is found by dividing your score by the possible score. The completed chart enables you to determine your specific strengths and weaknesses.

3. Evaluate your performance using the chart below. The ratings shown are based on analysis of student performance on past ACT's and on expectations for student performance on the examinations in this book. (The figures do not represent official ACT values, which are standardized for individual examinations.) Examine the rating you earned for each of the four tests. To boost your score in any area, study the appropriate sections of Part Three. Also, identify the types of questions you answered incorrectly. If you find that you consistently missed certain types, review the relevant sections of Part Three.

4. Read the answer explanations for the test you took. Don't skip over explanations for questions you got right because these explanations often contain helpful insights into shorter or different methods of answering questions. For each question you got wrong, be sure you understand why you made an error. That will help you to avoid making a similar mistake in the future.

Performance Evaluation Chart

Rating	English	Mathematics	Reading	Science Reasoning
Excellent	66–75	54–60	35–40	36–40
Very good	54–65	44–53	29–34	29–35
Above average	45–53	30–43	24–28	20–28
Below average	36–44	21–29	19–23	14–19
Weak	25–35	14–20	14–18	9–13
Poor	0–24	0–13	0–13	0–8

TEST TAKING: A GUIDE TO HIGH SCORES

All the studying in the world won't mean a thing on test day unless you know how to take the test. Knowing the basics of test taking offers you the chance to score high on the ACT or any other standardized test. Much of what you need to know is common sense. Anyone who has passed through high school knows, for example, that you should be sure to answer the question being asked, not a similar question or the one you think ought to be asked. Another common-sense tactic is to check regularly that the numbers on the answer sheet correspond with the numbers of the questions. If you put the answer to #9 in the space for #10, every subsequent answer will be in the wrong place.

As the ACT approaches, students sometimes feel apprehensive. They wonder how they'll perform, and they worry about disappointing themselves and others who may be counting on them. It's normal to feel a bit uneasy about an approaching exam. In fact, some degree of tension can help your performance. With your adrenaline pumping, you can push harder toward the peak of your ability and perhaps turn in the performance of your life. If you're basically a fretter, you obviously have to prepare harder to take the ACT than someone who is blessed with a positive attitude. In the long run, however, some anxiety may work in your favor. In contrast, super-confident test takers need to be wary of stumbling over their attitude. A touch of humility wouldn't hurt such people.

Many things must be done to reach the most advantageous frame of mind for taking the ACT, the first of which is being well prepared.

Getting Ready for Test Day

Since the ACT concentrates on four subjects found in all schools, most students are well prepared for the examination by the time they reach eleventh or twelfth grade. If you haven't taken a math course recently, however, or if you don't remember your basic English usage, reviewing the appropriate sections of this books will help. However, studying specifically for the Reading Test or the Science Reasoning Test may not be very fruitful. In fact, it's hard to know exactly what material would be worth studying. It would be smart, however, to know all the terms in the Glossary in the science chapter and to devote considerable time to taking the practice tests in this book.

Overall familiarity with the ACT not only reduces test anxiety but enhances performance. Self-assurance, the feeling that you will do well, helps too, but be wary of overconfidence. Regardless of how ready you think you are, remember that it's impossible to be too well prepared for the ACT.

Beyond that, being prepared depends partly on knowing what to expect when you open your exam booklet and start to work. For example, you can count on finding a specific set of test directions that do not vary from one exam to the next. Read the directions carefully while taking practice exams, and follow them to the letter. Once you've taken a few exams, the directions are likely to become second nature.

Since each section of the ACT is timed literally to the second, pacing is critical. By taking practice examinations, you can adjust the rate at which you answer questions. With experience you can learn to set a comfortable pace, neither too fast nor too slow. Then, on test day you'll have one less thing to worry about.

You have a surprisingly large amount of control over the score you'll earn on the ACT. Some control will grow out of the concentration and practice you devote to the lessons in this book. Still more control, though, will develop from your mastery of common sense test taking tactics. While high scores on college entrance tests come from knowing your material, they also come from knowing yourself and knowing which techniques work best for you. When you take the Reading Test, for example, which should you read first, the passage or the questions? Should you read slowly or quickly? On the English Test, which types of questions do you always get right? Which kind do you stumble over? Are the diagrams on the Science Reasoning Test more comprehensible to you than the charts? Do you coast through algebra problems but get bogged down in trigonometry? The more you know about your personal test taking style, the better you'll do.

On Test Day

Let common sense be your guide on test day. After a good night's sleep, get up early, eat a good breakfast, and arrive at the test site by 8:00 A.M. Latecomers are not admitted. Arrive early if you are not familiar with the location.

Take with you:
- Your ACT ticket of admission.
- Three or more sharpened #2 pencils with erasers.
- Identification—photo, transcripts, or school letter. The photo must be part of an ID document or from a recent yearbook or newspaper and be captioned. Transcripts with photo or a letter on school letterhead are acceptable, with certain restrictions. Please see the ACT document *Registering for the ACT Assessment* for additional requirements regarding transcripts or letters.
- A digital watch; it's faster and easier to read than a conventional watch.
- Calculators (optional). You may use a calculator on the Math Test, but don't use one unless you are accustomed to doing so. Bring one that you are accustomed to using. Don't bring a pocket organizer, a handheld or laptop computer, or electronic

writing pad. Just to be safe, put extra batteries in your pocket so you won't be stuck with a dead calculator halfway through the test.

- Candy or gum, if you feel the need. (Eating snacks or anything more substantial is not permitted during the examination.)

Leave at home:

- Books, notebooks, dictionaries, scrap paper.
- Radios, tape and CD players, beepers, and cell phones.
- Noisy jewelry, including wristwatches that beep.

At the test site, stake out the room before you sit down. In a classroom, choose a seat away from the proctor's desk and away from any other place in the room where there may be distracting activity during the test, such as a water fountain. The same holds true for a gym or cafeteria; pick a seat away from potential distractions, as far as possible from the flow of traffic.

You'll be sitting for about three hours, so wear something comfortable. On an unseasonable Saturday, test sites may be too hot or too cold, so dress for any eventuality. Some candy or gum may give you a boost along the way and is permitted, but be considerate: avoid noisy wrappers or bubble popping.

Throughout the exam, listen attentively to the proctors' announcements. Proctors will distribute test materials, instruct you in test procedures, show you how to fill out the answer sheet, and answer administrative questions. They will also keep order in the exam room, and tell you when to start and stop work. The proctors must also prevent cheating. *During the test, do nothing that might be construed as cheating.* If proctors suspect that you are giving or receiving help, they are obliged to dismiss you from the room and advise the ACT authorities not to score your answer sheet. In addition, don't work on a test after time has been called or before a test has officially begun.

If you need assistance during the exam, raise your hand to summon a proctor. Don't talk to anyone else, and don't leave your seat without a proctor's permission.

Answering the Questions

Easy and hard questions are scattered throughout the English Test. On the Mathematics Test, however, problems are given in order of increasing difficulty from 1 to 60. Passages on the Reading Test are presented in order of difficulty, and the ten questions about each passage are also arranged from easiest to hardest. Similarly, the Science Reasoning Test presents sets of data in order of increasing difficulty, and questions about each set are arranged from the easiest to the hardest.

On the Math, Reading, and Science Reasoning Tests, not everyone will necessarily find question 6 harder than 5, or 9 harder than 8. For this reason, if you are stumped after the first few questions, don't even think of skipping the rest. Because your mind works differently from everyone else's, including ACT test writers', you may often find later questions easier to answer than earlier ones.

Since three of the four tests begin with easy material, you are likely to get off to a quick start. Regardless of how quickly you like to work, however, you must read each question very carefully. Don't read the first few words of the question and presume that the rest follows a familiar pattern. This habit is dangerous. To avoid going astray, read every word of every question. Beware particularly of the presence of absolute words and phrases like *always, never, all of the following EXCEPT* ... and so on. Take such words seriously. A question containing an absolute demands a response that is absolute, too. However, questions that use such words as *mostly, usually,* and *generally,* require a judgment call based on evidence you are given.

If a question stumps you, consider it a temporary stump. Don't panic and don't let it slow you down. (Dawdling over a stubborn question is never a good idea during a timed exam.) Mark it with your pencil and go on to questions that you can answer more easily.

Later, come back to the marked question. When you return you may notice things about the question that you hadn't seen the first time, enabling you to answer it quickly. If you still can't come up with a decent answer, guess. You may get it right. If you are revisiting several knotty questions, keep up your pace; don't use up all your time trying to unravel just one or two.

For each question on the English, Reading, and Science Reasoning Tests, you are given four possible answers, and your task is to choose the best one. Sometimes a choice is partly true. For example, one answer to a reading question may be valid for only part of the reading passage. A better choice would be the answer that pertains to the whole passage. Therefore, it is very important to read all the choices before making your decision. Experts in testing say that the most obvious choice on a difficult question is usually wrong. Consequently, you should *look* for the answer that is most obvious, but you mustn't discount it as a possibility.

Each problem on the Mathematics Test offers five possible answers. You are to choose the only correct one. Before making a choice try to predict the approximate answer. Then scan the choices to see which one comes closest to your prediction. Very often, the best choice is the one you predict. Nevertheless, you should work out the solution to the problem in the space provided in the test booklet.

Each problem on the Mathematics Test offers five possible answers. You are to choose the only correct one. Before making a choice, you may need to work out your own solution to the problem in the space provided in the test booklet. If your solution fails to correspond with any of the choices, pick "None of these" as your answer. But double-check your calculations as well as the question itself, especially if your answer differs radically from any of the choices.

Answer every question on every test, even if you have to guess. You don't lose credit for a wrong answer, and you may make a lucky guess. Before you resort to guessing, though, try to eliminate any outrageous choices. By discarding one choice that you know is way off the mark, the chances of hitting the jackpot are one in three. By eliminating two wrong answers, they jump to fifty-fifty, pretty decent odds in any circumstances.

To complete an item, fill in the oval on your answer sheet that corresponds with the answer you've chosen. If you change your mind later, be sure to erase your original answer completely. Because the scoring machine can't distinguish between your intended answer and the one you changed, press hard on your eraser. Incidentally, studies have shown that it's faster to blacken the ovals on the answer sheet from the center outward than from the perimeter to the center. Try it. You could save a minute or two during the course of the exam—a minute that might be used more productively in finding correct answers.

While working on any of the tests, you may wish to write in the exam booklet. Since there are no restrictions, you may underline, cross out, make any marks you wish. Be mindful, however, that extensive writing takes time. If possible, develop a shorthand system of notations.

Using Time Effectively

Each test on the ACT lasts a prescribed length of time. Once a test is over, you may not return to it. Nor are you permitted to work on a test that has not yet officially begun. After the first two tests, you'll have a 10- to 15-minute break.

To do your best on the ACT, it's useful to know approximately how much time you have to work on each problem or question. With practice, you will soon begin to sense whether you are working at a rate that will allow you to finish each test within its time limit. The following analysis indicates the time allowed for each test.

TEST	CONTENT	AVERAGE LENGTH OF LINE PER QUESTION	COMMENTS
English 75 questions	5 passages, 15 questions each.	30 seconds.	Easy questions should take only a few seconds.
Mathematics 60 questions	Questions increase in difficulty from beginning to end.	1 minute.	Spend as little time as possible on the early questions, to allow more time for the harder ones.
Reading 40 questions	4 passages, 10 questions each.	5 minutes per passage, 4 minutes for 10 questions or 25 seconds per question.	Some passages may take more or less time to completely master.
Science Reasoning 40 questions	7 sets of data with 5 to 7 questions per set; sets increase in difficulty.	5 minutes per set of data.	Try to spend less than 5 minutes on the early, easier questions, allowing more time for the harder ones.

The periods of time allowed for each test are sufficient for almost every student to finish. To answer all the questions, however, you must work deliberately. If you finish a test before the time is up, check your answers, especially those that you're unsure about. Make sure that you've blackened only one oval for each question. If time is about to be called and you haven't finished the test, fill in answers at random on your answer sheet. A lucky guess or two will raise your score.

AFTER THE ACT

On your ACT registration form, you are asked to list the colleges to which you'd like your test results sent. At most colleges ACT scores are regarded as an important detail in your total application package. Whether your ACT performance counts more than or less than your grades in high school, teacher recommendations, extracurricular activities, application essays, or special qualifications depends largely on the college's admissions policies. One thing is certain, however: a high score on the ACT will never hurt your chances of getting into your college of choice.

Although ACT scores are used primarily for admissions, they are sometimes used to place freshmen in remedial, regular, or advanced courses. A college advisor may also use ACT scores to help a student choose a major, schedule realistic course loads, pick extracurricular activities, define educational and career goals, and avoid a variety of potential academic problems. Based on the scores, a student may also be eligible for certain scholarships or part-time campus jobs.

What colleges do with ACT scores is out of your hands, of course, but the test results can be of considerable interest to you as you plan your future. Four to seven weeks after the examination you will receive a report of your scores. Along with your total score on the examination, you will receive separate scores for each of the four tests plus additional subscores in English, Mathematics, and Reading, a total of twelve scores in all. The scores will arrive with an explanation of raw scores, percentiles, and other figures for you to study. You can learn a great deal from the various scores, not only about your academic ability, but also about your chances of being admitted to various kinds of colleges. As a result of your scores, you may decide to aim for more competitive or less competitive colleges.

Instead, you may decide to retake the ACT Assessment, in which case the scores will show you precisely what you need to work on to earn a higher score the next time. Theoretically, you can take the ACT as often as you like. Students who have taken the ACT twice have often raised their scores, although the scores of some students have remained the same or even declined. After taking the ACT twice, it is unusual for scores to rise high enough the third time to make a significant difference to the colleges to which you are applying. In fact, retaking the ACT too often could be counterproductive. If one set of scores was far better than the others, college admissions might regard the best set as an aberration, not a true indication of your academic ability. Moreover, sending more than three sets may tell a college more about the level of your confidence than about the level of your ability as a student. Therefore, it is advisable not to take the ACT repeatedly unless unusual circumstances in your life have prevented you from doing your best.

For better or worse, ACT scores have a bearing on you and your college plans. Like so many of the matters you must attend to during your last year in high school, taking the ACT is one of the rites of passage between childhood and adulthood. It's not unusual to feel stressed, perhaps even overwhelmed, by the challenges of applying to college, keeping up your grades, and maintaining some sort of balance in life between work and play. Remember, though, that millions of students before you have met these challenges successfully. You can, too, particularly if you don't allow the experience to get you down. Grit your teeth if you must; be cheerful if you can. Now turn this page and go to work on the diagnostic test in Part Two. And good luck!

ACT National Test Dates

Registration dates may vary by a day or two; check with ACT at 319-337-1270 if there is a question. Regular registration fee is $24 ($28 in Florida).

REGISTRATION CLOSING DATES	LATE REGISTRATION (PLUS $15 ADDITIONAL FEE— subject to change annually)	TESTING DATES
	2001	
January 5	January 19	February 10
March 2	March 16	April 7
May 4	May 18	June 9
August 17	August 31	September 22*
September 21	October 5	October 27
November 2	November 15	December 8
	2002	
January 4	January 18	February 9
March 1	March 15	April 6
May 3	May 17	June 8

* September test is administered only in Arizona, California, Florida, Georgia, Illinois, Indiana, Maryland, Nevada, North Carolina, Pennsylvania, South Carolina, Texas, and Washington State.

PART TWO

Diagnostic Examination

The purpose of this Diagnostic Examination is to help you identify your strengths and weaknesses. You should take the examination under simulated testing conditions and allow 2 hours and 55 minutes for the entire examination. Each of the four tests should be taken within the time limit stated at the beginning of that test. Mark your answers directly on the detached Answer Sheet.

When you finish the entire examination, check your answers against the Answer Keys and fill in the Analysis Chart for each test. Rate your total score on each specific test by using the Performance Evaluation Chart on page 8. Then, carefully read the Answer Explanations. Pay particular attention to the explanations for questions you got wrong, but don't skip over those for questions you got right; you may pick up some shortcuts or alternative methods.

You can assess your strengths and weaknesses by examining the Question Analysis Charts. Your total scores and ratings indicate your overall performance on the individual tests. The subscores in the last column show how you did on specific passage types or content topics. Special attention should be given to weak areas when you review and do practice exercises in Part Three.

Now you are ready to take the Diagnostic Examination. Find a quiet room, take out your pencils, detach the Answer Sheet, check your watch, and begin.

ᴀɴSWER SHEET—Diagnostic Examination
rections: Mark one answer only for each question. Make the mark dark. Erase completely
y mark made in error. (Additional or stray marks will be counted as mistakes.)

TEST 1

10 Ⓕ Ⓖ Ⓗ Ⓙ	20 Ⓕ Ⓖ Ⓗ Ⓙ	30 Ⓕ Ⓖ Ⓗ Ⓙ	40 Ⓕ Ⓖ Ⓗ Ⓙ	50 Ⓕ Ⓖ Ⓗ Ⓙ	60 Ⓕ Ⓖ Ⓗ Ⓙ	70 Ⓕ Ⓖ Ⓗ Ⓙ
1 Ⓐ Ⓑ Ⓒ Ⓓ	11 Ⓐ Ⓑ Ⓒ Ⓓ	21 Ⓐ Ⓑ Ⓒ Ⓓ	31 Ⓐ Ⓑ Ⓒ Ⓓ	41 Ⓐ Ⓑ Ⓒ Ⓓ	51 Ⓐ Ⓑ Ⓒ Ⓓ	61 Ⓐ Ⓑ Ⓒ Ⓓ	71 Ⓐ Ⓑ Ⓒ Ⓓ
2 Ⓕ Ⓖ Ⓗ Ⓙ	12 Ⓕ Ⓖ Ⓗ Ⓙ	22 Ⓕ Ⓖ Ⓗ Ⓙ	32 Ⓕ Ⓖ Ⓗ Ⓙ	42 Ⓕ Ⓖ Ⓗ Ⓙ	52 Ⓕ Ⓖ Ⓗ Ⓙ	62 Ⓕ Ⓖ Ⓗ Ⓙ	72 Ⓕ Ⓖ Ⓗ Ⓙ
3 Ⓐ Ⓑ Ⓒ Ⓓ	13 Ⓐ Ⓑ Ⓒ Ⓓ	23 Ⓐ Ⓑ Ⓒ Ⓓ	33 Ⓐ Ⓑ Ⓒ Ⓓ	43 Ⓐ Ⓑ Ⓒ Ⓓ	53 Ⓐ Ⓑ Ⓒ Ⓓ	63 Ⓐ Ⓑ Ⓒ Ⓓ	73 Ⓐ Ⓑ Ⓒ Ⓓ
4 Ⓕ Ⓖ Ⓗ Ⓙ	14 Ⓕ Ⓖ Ⓗ Ⓙ	24 Ⓕ Ⓖ Ⓗ Ⓙ	34 Ⓕ Ⓖ Ⓗ Ⓙ	44 Ⓕ Ⓖ Ⓗ Ⓙ	54 Ⓕ Ⓖ Ⓗ Ⓙ	64 Ⓕ Ⓖ Ⓗ Ⓙ	74 Ⓕ Ⓖ Ⓗ Ⓙ
5 Ⓐ Ⓑ Ⓒ Ⓓ	15 Ⓐ Ⓑ Ⓒ Ⓓ	25 Ⓐ Ⓑ Ⓒ Ⓓ	35 Ⓐ Ⓑ Ⓒ Ⓓ	45 Ⓐ Ⓑ Ⓒ Ⓓ	55 Ⓐ Ⓑ Ⓒ Ⓓ	65 Ⓐ Ⓑ Ⓒ Ⓓ	75 Ⓐ Ⓑ Ⓒ Ⓓ
6 Ⓕ Ⓖ Ⓗ Ⓙ	16 Ⓕ Ⓖ Ⓗ Ⓙ	26 Ⓕ Ⓖ Ⓗ Ⓙ	36 Ⓕ Ⓖ Ⓗ Ⓙ	46 Ⓕ Ⓖ Ⓗ Ⓙ	56 Ⓕ Ⓖ Ⓗ Ⓙ	66 Ⓕ Ⓖ Ⓗ Ⓙ	
7 Ⓐ Ⓑ Ⓒ Ⓓ	17 Ⓐ Ⓑ Ⓒ Ⓓ	27 Ⓐ Ⓑ Ⓒ Ⓓ	37 Ⓐ Ⓑ Ⓒ Ⓓ	47 Ⓐ Ⓑ Ⓒ Ⓓ	57 Ⓐ Ⓑ Ⓒ Ⓓ	67 Ⓐ Ⓑ Ⓒ Ⓓ	
8 Ⓕ Ⓖ Ⓗ Ⓙ	18 Ⓕ Ⓖ Ⓗ Ⓙ	28 Ⓕ Ⓖ Ⓗ Ⓙ	38 Ⓕ Ⓖ Ⓗ Ⓙ	48 Ⓕ Ⓖ Ⓗ Ⓙ	58 Ⓕ Ⓖ Ⓗ Ⓙ	68 Ⓕ Ⓖ Ⓗ Ⓙ	
9 Ⓐ Ⓑ Ⓒ Ⓓ	19 Ⓐ Ⓑ Ⓒ Ⓓ	29 Ⓐ Ⓑ Ⓒ Ⓓ	39 Ⓐ Ⓑ Ⓒ Ⓓ	49 Ⓐ Ⓑ Ⓒ Ⓓ	59 Ⓐ Ⓑ Ⓒ Ⓓ	69 Ⓐ Ⓑ Ⓒ Ⓓ	

TEST 2

8 Ⓕ Ⓖ Ⓗ Ⓙ Ⓚ	16 Ⓕ Ⓖ Ⓗ Ⓙ Ⓚ	24 Ⓕ Ⓖ Ⓗ Ⓙ Ⓚ	32 Ⓕ Ⓖ Ⓗ Ⓙ Ⓚ	40 Ⓕ Ⓖ Ⓗ Ⓙ Ⓚ	48 Ⓕ Ⓖ Ⓗ Ⓙ Ⓚ	56 Ⓕ Ⓖ Ⓗ Ⓙ Ⓚ
1 Ⓐ Ⓑ Ⓒ Ⓓ Ⓔ	9 Ⓐ Ⓑ Ⓒ Ⓓ Ⓔ	17 Ⓐ Ⓑ Ⓒ Ⓓ Ⓔ	25 Ⓐ Ⓑ Ⓒ Ⓓ Ⓔ	33 Ⓐ Ⓑ Ⓒ Ⓓ Ⓔ	41 Ⓐ Ⓑ Ⓒ Ⓓ Ⓔ	49 Ⓐ Ⓑ Ⓒ Ⓓ Ⓔ	57 Ⓐ Ⓑ Ⓒ Ⓓ Ⓔ
2 Ⓕ Ⓖ Ⓗ Ⓙ Ⓚ	10 Ⓕ Ⓖ Ⓗ Ⓙ Ⓚ	18 Ⓕ Ⓖ Ⓗ Ⓙ Ⓚ	26 Ⓕ Ⓖ Ⓗ Ⓙ Ⓚ	34 Ⓕ Ⓖ Ⓗ Ⓙ Ⓚ	42 Ⓕ Ⓖ Ⓗ Ⓙ Ⓚ	50 Ⓕ Ⓖ Ⓗ Ⓙ Ⓚ	58 Ⓕ Ⓖ Ⓗ Ⓙ Ⓚ
3 Ⓐ Ⓑ Ⓒ Ⓓ Ⓔ	11 Ⓐ Ⓑ Ⓒ Ⓓ Ⓔ	19 Ⓐ Ⓑ Ⓒ Ⓓ Ⓔ	27 Ⓐ Ⓑ Ⓒ Ⓓ Ⓔ	35 Ⓐ Ⓑ Ⓒ Ⓓ Ⓔ	43 Ⓐ Ⓑ Ⓒ Ⓓ Ⓔ	51 Ⓐ Ⓑ Ⓒ Ⓓ Ⓔ	59 Ⓐ Ⓑ Ⓒ Ⓓ Ⓔ
4 Ⓕ Ⓖ Ⓗ Ⓙ Ⓚ	12 Ⓕ Ⓖ Ⓗ Ⓙ Ⓚ	20 Ⓕ Ⓖ Ⓗ Ⓙ Ⓚ	28 Ⓕ Ⓖ Ⓗ Ⓙ Ⓚ	36 Ⓕ Ⓖ Ⓗ Ⓙ Ⓚ	44 Ⓕ Ⓖ Ⓗ Ⓙ Ⓚ	52 Ⓕ Ⓖ Ⓗ Ⓙ Ⓚ	60 Ⓕ Ⓖ Ⓗ Ⓙ Ⓚ
5 Ⓐ Ⓑ Ⓒ Ⓓ Ⓔ	13 Ⓐ Ⓑ Ⓒ Ⓓ Ⓔ	21 Ⓐ Ⓑ Ⓒ Ⓓ Ⓔ	29 Ⓐ Ⓑ Ⓒ Ⓓ Ⓔ	37 Ⓐ Ⓑ Ⓒ Ⓓ Ⓔ	45 Ⓐ Ⓑ Ⓒ Ⓓ Ⓔ	53 Ⓐ Ⓑ Ⓒ Ⓓ Ⓔ	
6 Ⓕ Ⓖ Ⓗ Ⓙ Ⓚ	14 Ⓕ Ⓖ Ⓗ Ⓙ Ⓚ	22 Ⓕ Ⓖ Ⓗ Ⓙ Ⓚ	30 Ⓕ Ⓖ Ⓗ Ⓙ Ⓚ	38 Ⓕ Ⓖ Ⓗ Ⓙ Ⓚ	46 Ⓕ Ⓖ Ⓗ Ⓙ Ⓚ	54 Ⓕ Ⓖ Ⓗ Ⓙ Ⓚ	
7 Ⓐ Ⓑ Ⓒ Ⓓ Ⓔ	15 Ⓐ Ⓑ Ⓒ Ⓓ Ⓔ	23 Ⓐ Ⓑ Ⓒ Ⓓ Ⓔ	31 Ⓐ Ⓑ Ⓒ Ⓓ Ⓔ	39 Ⓐ Ⓑ Ⓒ Ⓓ Ⓔ	47 Ⓐ Ⓑ Ⓒ Ⓓ Ⓔ	55 Ⓐ Ⓑ Ⓒ Ⓓ Ⓔ	

TEST 3

6 Ⓕ Ⓖ Ⓗ Ⓙ	12 Ⓕ Ⓖ Ⓗ Ⓙ	18 Ⓕ Ⓖ Ⓗ Ⓙ	24 Ⓕ Ⓖ Ⓗ Ⓙ	30 Ⓕ Ⓖ Ⓗ Ⓙ	36 Ⓕ Ⓖ Ⓗ Ⓙ
1 Ⓐ Ⓑ Ⓒ Ⓓ	7 Ⓐ Ⓑ Ⓒ Ⓓ	13 Ⓐ Ⓑ Ⓒ Ⓓ	19 Ⓐ Ⓑ Ⓒ Ⓓ	25 Ⓐ Ⓑ Ⓒ Ⓓ	31 Ⓐ Ⓑ Ⓒ Ⓓ	37 Ⓐ Ⓑ Ⓒ Ⓓ
2 Ⓕ Ⓖ Ⓗ Ⓙ	8 Ⓕ Ⓖ Ⓗ Ⓙ	14 Ⓕ Ⓖ Ⓗ Ⓙ	20 Ⓕ Ⓖ Ⓗ Ⓙ	26 Ⓕ Ⓖ Ⓗ Ⓙ	32 Ⓕ Ⓖ Ⓗ Ⓙ	38 Ⓕ Ⓖ Ⓗ Ⓙ
3 Ⓐ Ⓑ Ⓒ Ⓓ	9 Ⓐ Ⓑ Ⓒ Ⓓ	15 Ⓐ Ⓑ Ⓒ Ⓓ	21 Ⓐ Ⓑ Ⓒ Ⓓ	27 Ⓐ Ⓑ Ⓒ Ⓓ	33 Ⓐ Ⓑ Ⓒ Ⓓ	39 Ⓐ Ⓑ Ⓒ Ⓓ
4 Ⓕ Ⓖ Ⓗ Ⓙ	10 Ⓕ Ⓖ Ⓗ Ⓙ	16 Ⓕ Ⓖ Ⓗ Ⓙ	22 Ⓕ Ⓖ Ⓗ Ⓙ	28 Ⓕ Ⓖ Ⓗ Ⓙ	34 Ⓕ Ⓖ Ⓗ Ⓙ	40 Ⓕ Ⓖ Ⓗ Ⓙ
5 Ⓐ Ⓑ Ⓒ Ⓓ	11 Ⓐ Ⓑ Ⓒ Ⓓ	17 Ⓐ Ⓑ Ⓒ Ⓓ	23 Ⓐ Ⓑ Ⓒ Ⓓ	29 Ⓐ Ⓑ Ⓒ Ⓓ	35 Ⓐ Ⓑ Ⓒ Ⓓ	

TEST 4

6 Ⓕ Ⓖ Ⓗ Ⓙ	12 Ⓕ Ⓖ Ⓗ Ⓙ	18 Ⓕ Ⓖ Ⓗ Ⓙ	24 Ⓕ Ⓖ Ⓗ Ⓙ	30 Ⓕ Ⓖ Ⓗ Ⓙ	36 Ⓕ Ⓖ Ⓗ Ⓙ
1 Ⓐ Ⓑ Ⓒ Ⓓ	7 Ⓐ Ⓑ Ⓒ Ⓓ	13 Ⓐ Ⓑ Ⓒ Ⓓ	19 Ⓐ Ⓑ Ⓒ Ⓓ	25 Ⓐ Ⓑ Ⓒ Ⓓ	31 Ⓐ Ⓑ Ⓒ Ⓓ	37 Ⓐ Ⓑ Ⓒ Ⓓ
2 Ⓕ Ⓖ Ⓗ Ⓙ	8 Ⓕ Ⓖ Ⓗ Ⓙ	14 Ⓕ Ⓖ Ⓗ Ⓙ	20 Ⓕ Ⓖ Ⓗ Ⓙ	26 Ⓕ Ⓖ Ⓗ Ⓙ	32 Ⓕ Ⓖ Ⓗ Ⓙ	38 Ⓕ Ⓖ Ⓗ Ⓙ
3 Ⓐ Ⓑ Ⓒ Ⓓ	9 Ⓐ Ⓑ Ⓒ Ⓓ	15 Ⓐ Ⓑ Ⓒ Ⓓ	21 Ⓐ Ⓑ Ⓒ Ⓓ	27 Ⓐ Ⓑ Ⓒ Ⓓ	33 Ⓐ Ⓑ Ⓒ Ⓓ	39 Ⓐ Ⓑ Ⓒ Ⓓ
4 Ⓕ Ⓖ Ⓗ Ⓙ	10 Ⓕ Ⓖ Ⓗ Ⓙ	16 Ⓕ Ⓖ Ⓗ Ⓙ	22 Ⓕ Ⓖ Ⓗ Ⓙ	28 Ⓕ Ⓖ Ⓗ Ⓙ	34 Ⓕ Ⓖ Ⓗ Ⓙ	40 Ⓕ Ⓖ Ⓗ Ⓙ
5 Ⓐ Ⓑ Ⓒ Ⓓ	11 Ⓐ Ⓑ Ⓒ Ⓓ	17 Ⓐ Ⓑ Ⓒ Ⓓ	23 Ⓐ Ⓑ Ⓒ Ⓓ	29 Ⓐ Ⓑ Ⓒ Ⓓ	35 Ⓐ Ⓑ Ⓒ Ⓓ	

1 1 1 1 1 1 1 1 1 1 1 1

DIAGNOSTIC EXAMINATION
English Test
45 Minutes—75 Questions

DIRECTIONS: The following test consists of 75 under-lined words and phrases in context, or general questions about the passages. Most of the underlined sections contain errors or inappropriate expressions. You are asked to compare each with the four alternatives in the answer column. If you consider the original version best, choose letter **A** or **F**: NO CHANGE. For each question, blacken on the answer sheet the letter of the alternative you think best. Read each passage through before answering the questions based on it.

Passage I

(1)

Typical diseases associated with overweight people are hypertension, or high blood pressure, atherosclerosis, or fatty deposits in blood vessels, which consequently for those reasons restrict the flow of blood, and coronary heart disease. Other diseases occur far more often among the overweight than for those who have ordinary weight, including diabetes, respiratory ailments, gall-bladder and kidney diseases, and some kinds of cancer.

(2)

Most all people who are trying to lose weight are doing so mainly for social reasons. In today's informed society, fat is no longer a symbol of good health and prosperity, as they used to think; and it also keeps a

1. A. NO CHANGE
  B. which therefore in that manner
  C. which
  D. OMIT the underlined portion.

2. F. NO CHANGE
  G. among normal weighted people
  H. others
  J. among persons of normal weight

3. A. NO CHANGE
  B. Among those people
  C. Most people
  D. Most of those people

4. F. NO CHANGE
  G. as it once has been
  H. as was once thought to be
  J. as it once was

GO ON TO THE NEXT PAGE.

1 1 1 1 1 1 1 1 1 1 1

person from looking <u>their</u> best, <u>as do, incidentally,</u>
₅   ₆

<u>underweight.</u> For one thing, <u>to be overweight</u> is
₆   ₇

embarrassing, and even being only slightly overweight

can damage self-esteem, because having a good self-

image <u>has been important</u> to emotional well-being.
₈

Doctors now consider <u>being able to keep one's weight</u> at
₉

a proper level one of the most important aspects of

preventive medicine, which hopes to keep people

healthy by preventing illness.

(3)

About 25 percent of the population is overweight, a

figure that makes obesity "one of the curses of afflu-

ence" <u>and, according</u> to the American Medical Associa-
₁₀

tion, the nation's most crucial health problem.

(4)

Some slightly overweight people never seem to no-

tice their <u>obesity, and they</u> even look attractive to oth-
₁₁

ers. <u>Therefore,</u> mortality rates among even the slightly
₁₂

obese are significantly higher than among persons in

the same age group with normal weights. Insurance

companies are well aware of the seriousness of obesity,

and rank being overweight as a high-risk category. [13]

5. A. NO CHANGE
   B. his
   C. his or her
   D. her

6. F. NO CHANGE
   G. as is, incidentally, underweight
   H. as does incidentally, underweight
   J. as does, incidentally, underweight

7. A. NO CHANGE
   B. being overweight
   C. being burdened with overweight
   D. being several pounds overweight

8. F. NO CHANGE
   G. could be important
   H. is important
   J. will be important

9. A. NO CHANGE
   B. knowing how to keep their weight
   C. knowing that one has kept his weight
   D. keeping one's weight

10. F. NO CHANGE
   G. and according
   H. and according,
   J. and; according

11. A. NO CHANGE
   B. obesity. And they
   C. obesity and they
   D. obesity; and they

12. F. NO CHANGE
   G. However,
   H. For this reason,
   J. Consequently,

13. Choose the sequence of paragraph numbers up to
   this point (paragraphs 1–4) that makes the structure
   of the passage most logical.
   A. NO CHANGE
   B. 1, 4, 3, 2
   C. 2, 3, 4, 1
   D. 4, 3, 1, 2

GO ON TO THE NEXT PAGE.

1   1   1   1   1   1   1   1   1   1   1

An overweight person is likely to be constantly tired and unable to do much. Eventually, obese people are simply unable to be active in any endeavor. Unfortunately, this lack of activity is not the only problem that comes with being overweight. Health problems begin to manifest themselves, especially <u>as a person</u>
₁₄
<u>gets older and eventually approaches middle age.</u>
₁₄

[15]

14. F. NO CHANGE
   G. approaching middle age.
   H. as a person gets older, approaching middle age.
   J. as a person approaches middle age.

15. The writer could most effectively strengthen the passage at this point by adding which of the following?
   A. Reports by life insurance firms linking weight and morbidity
   B. A list of euphemisms for *overweight* like "full-figured" or "pleasingly plump"
   C. A bibliography of diet books
   D. More specific details about what constitutes overweight, including height and weight comparisons

---

Passage II

A convincing way to prove the need for nurses <u>is the</u>
₁₆
<u>long lines in hospital waiting rooms.</u> <u>An additional</u>
₁₆   ₁₇
<u>problem in most hospitals is the terrible food, which is</u>
₁₇
<u>usually prepared by contract service firms.</u> One only has
₁₇
to pick up a newspaper or turn on the radio to be informed about the very critical shortage of skilled nurses. The argument then begins about responsibility for the shortage. [18] <u>Without nurses, a hospital might as</u>
₁₉

<u>well pack away its sheets.</u> <u>Yes, there are many nurses</u>
₁₉   ₂₀

16. F. NO CHANGE
   G. is to point to the long lines in hospital waiting rooms.
   H. are the long lines in hospital waiting rooms.
   J. always has been the long lines in hospital waiting rooms.

17. A. NO CHANGE
   B. Place this sentence at the end of the paragraph.
   C. Place this sentence at the beginning of the paragraph.
   D. OMIT this sentence.

18. A quick scanning of this passage shows it to be a terse summary argument in favor of more training facilities for nurses. In view of this fact, what kind of arguments would be appropriate in the rest of this paragraph?
   F. Detailed, exhaustive explanations
   G. No arguments at all
   H. Short, one-line summary arguments
   J. Long, emotional appeals

19. A. NO CHANGE
   B. OMIT this sentence.
   C. Move this sentence to end of paragraph.
   D. Move this sentence to beginning paragraph.

GO ON TO THE NEXT PAGE.

1   1   1   1   1   1   1   1   1   1   1

licensed who are not in practice, but this tendency of
[20]

nurses to "drop out" has always existed, and, yes,
[20]

health care agencies that employ nurses, particularly

hospitals, could improve, and are improving, working
[20]

conditions but the fact remains that there are more
[20]

vacant positions for nurses than there are available
[20]

applicants.
[20]

[21] Hospitals have had to close wards and they have had
[22]

to tell patients that they are unable to treat them
[22]

because of a lack of nursing staff. [23]

According to the Los Angeles Hospital Council,

there is a 20 percent vacancy for budgeted, registered

nurse positions. Therefore, there is a ready-made job

market for graduates with Associate Degrees in nursing.

20. **F.** NO CHANGE
G. Although there are many nurses licensed who are not in practice, and although this tendency of nurses to "drop out" has always existed, and, yes, health care agencies which employ nurses, particularly hospitals could, and are improving working conditions but the fact remains that there are more vacant positions for nurses than there are available applicants.
H. Yes, there are many nurses licensed who are not in practice, but this tendency of nurses to "drop out" has always existed. Yes, health care agencies that employ nurses, particularly hospitals, could improve, and are improving, working conditions. The fact remains that there are more vacant positions for nurses than there are available applicants.
J. Because there are many nurses licensed who are not in practice, and because health care agencies, particularly hospitals are improving conditions, there are more vacant positions for nurses than there are available applicants.

21. The writer could most effectively strengthen his arguments at this point by adding:
A. a daily log from a critical care nursing station in a large, municipal hospital.
B. a summary of the vacant nurse positions in all of the city's hospitals.
C. testimony from two or three patients in a large hospital.
D. a list of inactive nurses which explains why each nurse is not working.

22. **F.** NO CHANGE
G. turn them out
H. turn away patients
J. tell patients "no go"

23. The first paragraph suggests that it is representing both sides of an "argument." How could the argument be made more fair or even-handed?
A. Bolster the position that there is a critical shortage of nurses by giving statistics, pay scales, etc.
B. Bolster the position that nurses are really in good supply by presenting numbers of nurses now available and of nursing students soon to be graduated.
C. Bolster both positions with testimony of patients that have received adequate hospital care and patients that have received poor care.
D. Bolster the position that nurses are really in good supply by compiling lists of registry applicants who have earned Master's Degrees in nursing.

GO ON TO THE NEXT PAGE.

1   1 1 1 1 1 1 1 1 1   1

The employment and career opportunities are greater

than other community college programs. Students all
_____
24

have jobs before graduation (contingent upon licensure)

if they so desire. This is further demonstrated by the
             ____
             25

waiting lists of applicants for programs. [26]

The Associate Degree nursing programs are appeal-

ing to the disadvantaged individual who could not
                                          _____
                                             27

afford the expenses and other requirements of univer-
_____
27

sity programs. Associate Degree programs attract ethnic

minorities, men, and older students who could not other-
           _____
                    28

wise be served in the educational system. The Associate

Degree nursing program provides disadvantaged

people with a salable skill, thereby enabling them to

enjoy a better way of life while meeting the nursing

shortage that helps all members of the community. The
_____
      29

health care profession has historically been represented

by ethnic minorities, and a program at Los Angeles

Mission College would help to correct this problem. [30]

---

24. **F.** NO CHANGE
  G. than still more
  H. than several more
  J. than those in other

25. **A.** NO CHANGE
  B. This need for more training
  C. This job glut
  D. This excess of jobs

26. Readers are likely to regard the passage as best de-
  scribed by which of the following terms?
  F. Inspirational
  G. Informative
  H. Persuasive
  J. Confessional

27. **A.** NO CHANGE
  B. has not been able to afford
  C. cannot afford
  D. up to now, could not afford

28. **F.** NO CHANGE
  G. men, older students
  H. men; older students
  J. men: older students

29. **A.** NO CHANGE
  B. shortage, a public service that
  C. shortage which
  D. shortage, a philosophy that

30. This passage is probably written for readers who:
  F. are patients in hospitals.
  G. are other community college instructors.
  H. are members of a hospital governing board.
  J. are members of a state licensure panel or other
      group likely to rule on whether a nursing
      school should be opened at L.A. Mission
      College.

Passage III

On the morning of June 8, 1988, Joyce McBride left

her home to attend a garage sale. As she left, McBride

locked her front door with a double dead-bolt lock that

GO ON TO THE NEXT PAGE.

1   1 1 1 1 1 1 1 1 1 1   1

required a key either to open it from inside or outside.
                                     31

    While McBride was away, her next-door neighbor,
Peggy Frobush, looked out her bathroom window and
saw William Goode standing by McBride's front door.
Peggy had known Goode for years; he was a good friend
of her son, Chuck, and had been living in his car parked
outside the Frobushes' home. It had appeared to her that
                          32   33
Goode had just closed McBride's front door behind him.
Thinking a burglary had just taken place, Peggy

screamed, "Police!" She noticed at that moment that
            34

McBride's back door was open. Peggy, by the way, is
                                              35
an extremely attractive woman. 36 The police told
            35
McBride about the burglary upon her return home. Several items were missing, including a guitar, power tools,
and jewelry. Police investigators discovered the

front-door dead-bolt shut and assigned as a cause the
                                          37

back door was the point of entry behind the house.
                                                  38
    Later that morning, Chuck approached a neighbor
of McBride and offered to sell a gold bracelet and
necklace. Chuck left the jewelry with the neighbor, who
returned the articles to McBride. These items were
taken in the burglary. 39

31. A. NO CHANGE
   B. to open it from inside or outside either.
   C. to either open it from inside or outside.
   D. to open it from either inside or outside.

32. F. NO CHANGE
   G. Frobushe's home.
   H. Frobushes's home.
   J. Frobushes home.

33. A. NO CHANGE
   B. has appeared
   C. appeared
   D. appears

34. F. NO CHANGE
   G. screamed "Police"!
   H. screamed, "Police"!
   J. screamed "Police!"

35. A. NO CHANGE
   B. By the way, Peggy is an extremely attractive woman.
   C. Peggy is an extremely attractive woman, by the way.
   D. OMIT this sentence

36. F. NO CHANGE
   G. Begin a new paragraph with the following sentence.
   H. Delete the rest of this paragraph.
   J. Place the rest of this paragraph at the beginning of the passage.

37. A. NO CHANGE
   B. theorized that
   C. laid that fact on
   D. put the saddle on the right horse that

38. F. NO CHANGE
   G. on the nether side of the house.
   H. OMIT the underlined portion.
   J. toward the rear of the house.

39. Is the use of the gold bracelet and necklace effective in this paragraph?
   A. No, because it does not give enough evidence to convincingly accuse Chuck.
   B. Yes, because Chuck had to sell the stolen goods right away in order to buy drugs.
   C. Yes, because this whole passage is about an actual trial and is reporting facts.
   D. No, because a person in Chuck's situation would not sell stolen goods to a neighbor.

GO ON TO THE NEXT PAGE.

1   1 1 1 1 1 1 1 1 1 1   1

On July 15, 1988, Detective Bruno Pilsner interviewed Goode about the burglary. Goode told the detective he had been living in his broken-down car for several weeks, parking it outside the Frobushes' residence. In working on his car, Goode heard Chuck call to him from McBride's house. After walking to the front door, he saw his friend inside the residence. Chuck opened the front door and asked him to help take McBride's property, but Goode refused. He decided to leave when Peggy yelled for the police. 41

After further investigation, Goode was interviewed again. It was with no minor irritation that Detective Pilsner belabored his earlier version because the front door could not have been opened without a key, he accused Goode of planning the burglary with Chuck. Replying, "You are right," Goode told Pilsner the following story: Chuck, needing money to buy drugs, asked for Goode's help in burglarizing the McBride house. Goode agreed. Chuck planned to enter the house from the back and let Goode in through the front, thus he could not open the door. Goode turned to leave when he heard Peggy scream, and fled the area on foot.

At trial, Goode denied participating in the crime. He testified that Chuck approached him that morning, told him he needed money for drugs, and asked for Goode's help in carrying tools from the McBride house. Goode's final version of the story was that he refused to participate. 45

40. F. NO CHANGE
    G. While working
    H. For working
    J. As working

41. Suppose that at this point the writer decided to add more information about the police department in this town. Would this addition be an appropriate one, and, if so, which of the following would be most relevant to the passage as a whole?
    A. A brief biography of Detective Pilsner and his family
    B. A discussion of the structure of the local police department, including the duties of each branch
    C. No addition would be appropriate. This is a very lean summary of a case; additional detail is not required.
    D. A summary of exceptional cases Detective Pilsner has helped to solve

42. F. NO CHANGE
    G. Detective Pilsner was angry about
    H. Detective Pilsner pooh-poohed
    J. This time, Pilsner told Goode he did not believe

43. A. NO CHANGE
    B. a key, he accused
    C. a key. He accused
    D. a key; he accused

44. F. NO CHANGE
    G. but
    H. however
    J. nevertheless

45. This passage was probably written for readers who:
    A. are detective and mystery fiction buffs.
    B. are law enforcement students learning about criminal behavior.
    C. need summary details about this case for a subsequent discussion or determination.
    D. are avid readers and would especially appreciate the technique and style of this author.

GO ON TO THE NEXT PAGE.

1   1 1 1 1 1 1 1 1 1 1   1

Passage IV

(1)

The person or persons suing someone are called the

PLAINTIFFS; the person or persons being sued are

called the DEFENDANTS. Neither plaintiffs <u>nor</u>
₄₆

defendants may bring a lawyer to represent them in

Small Claims Court.

(2)

<u>Having appeared on the Court Calendar,</u> the plain-
₄₇

tiffs simply explain why they feel the defendant owes

them the money they have asked for, and present any

evidence or witnesses they can to help them prove their

case. After <u>having heard</u> from both sides, the judge will
₄₈

decide who is right.

(3)

Any person who is eighteen or older may file suit

in Small Claims Court. A minor may do so only if he or

she has a parent or guardian <u>and who is to come</u> along
₄₉

when the suit is filed. The judges of Small Claims

Courts are members of the Justice and Municipal Courts.

They set aside certain days and times to hold Small

Claims <u>Court which</u> may be different for each county. 51
₅₀

(4)

The Small Claims Court <u>is</u> a special court in which
₅₂

46. F. NO CHANGE
G. or
H. however or
J. and nor

47. A. NO CHANGE
B. When their suit comes before the judge,
C. When the Court Calendar determines the time of the hearing,
D. When the suit is brought before the Court Calendar,

48. F. NO CHANGE
G. they spoke
H. he heard
J. hearing

49. A. NO CHANGE
B. to have come
C. come
D. whom to come

50. F. NO CHANGE
G. Court, which
H. Court that
J. Court, whom

51. The writer could most effectively strengthen the passage at this point by adding which of the following?
A. A visual description of a typical Small Claims Court
B. A description of some of the more unusual small claims suits in recent years
C. A few examples to illustrate the general points being made
D. Testimony from both defendants and plaintiffs of what they think of the Small Claims Court

52. F. NO CHANGE
G. are
H. claims to be
J. was

GO ON TO THE NEXT PAGE.

1   1 1 1 1 1 1 1 1 1   1

an individual can sue anyone who owes him money. By
the same token, the maximum amount of money litigants
₅₄

can collect is $2500. If the suing party's claim is larger,
₅₅

he may either speak to an attorney about taking the case
₅₆

to a higher court, or may accept the $2500 and give up

any claim to the rest.

(5)

In some cases, plaintiffs must file their suit at the

court located in the district where the defendant lives or

works at. If, for example, the complaining party lives in
₅₇

Boston, but the store where a defective vacuum cleaner

was bought is in Worcester, the plaintiff must file suit

in Worcester. [58]

(6)

Unfortunately, there are usually no translators in

Small Claims Court, so if either the plaintiff or the de-

fendant does not speak English, it is advisable to bring

along someone who can act as an interpreter. Also, due
₅₉

to the fact that there are very few night courts, litigants
₅₉

will almost always have to attend court during working

hours. [60]

---

53. A. NO CHANGE
  B. her
  C. him or her
  D. them

54. F. NO CHANGE
  G. However,
  H. Furthermore,
  J. Granted that,

55. A. NO CHANGE
  B. partys'
  C. partys
  D. parties

56. F. NO CHANGE
  G. the defendant
  H. the plaintiff
  J. the judge

57. A. NO CHANGE
  B. has worked
  C. is working at
  D. works

58. Suppose this passage were written for an audience
  that was familiar with the Small Claims Court and
  other legal systems. Which of the following additions would be most relevant to the passage as a
  whole?
  F. A clear, *simple* enactment of a *typical* small
     claims case
  G. A recounting of several typical small claims
     actions, together with decisions rendered
  H. Discussions of fine points of law that have
     made some decisions very difficult to deter-
     mine
  J. A detailed, step-by-step day in the life of a
     small claims judge

59. A. NO CHANGE
  B. owing to the fact that
  C. since
  D. in the light of the fact that

60. Choose the sequence of paragraph numbers that
  makes the structure of the passage most logical.
  F. NO CHANGE
  G. 6, 1, 4, 2, 3, 5
  H. 1, 4, 3, 5, 6, 2
  J. 4, 1, 2, 3, 5, 6

GO ON TO THE NEXT PAGE.

1 1 1 1 1 1 1 1 1 1 1 1 1

Passage V

(1)

Environmental issues appear frequently, especially in states where liberal groups are at odds with the establishment, in Nevada, for example, voters will be asked to withdraw from a five-state nuclear waste compact. Massachusetts will offer a measure that would ban the generation of electricity by nuclear plants that produce radioactive waste. Washington State voters will decide on the issue of whether to impose a tax on hazardous substances to help finance toxic waste cleanup. In general, throughout the nation, environmental initiatives are to be found everywhere, from bottle bills in Montana to surface-mine reclamation in South Dakota.

Many other issues will be brought up by initiatives in this year's general elections. Several states are voting on new minimum wage levels, and at least three are considering measures mandating AIDS testing. Others are deciding such mixed-up issues as personal property taxes, cigarette and beer taxes, mandatory health insurance, tuition tax credits, state park expansion, farm animal abuse, safety inspections, funding of abortions, homeless shelters, gambling, seat belt laws, official language laws, and school financing. 67

(2)

Initiatives are citizen-sponsored ballot measures that circumvent the normal legislative process of placing referendums before the public. Considered by most advocates to be an important and useful safety valve for popular action when citizens are frustrated by state and

61. A. NO CHANGE
   B. establishment. In
   C. establishment in
   D. establishment; In

62. F. NO CHANGE
   G. on a tax
   H. whether a tax
   J. whether to impose a tax

63. A. NO CHANGE
   B. surface mine reclamation
   C. surface, mine reclamation
   D. surface and mine reclamation

64. F. NO CHANGE
   G. Begin new paragraph with this sentence.
   H. OMIT the underlined portion.
   J. Place this sentence at beginning of paragraph as it now exists.

65. A. NO CHANGE
   B. diverse
   C. wildly arrayed
   D. confusing

66. F. NO CHANGE
   G. laws and school
   H. laws, and school,
   J. laws and, school

67. Suppose at this point in the passage the writer wanted to add more information about the diversity of initiative subjects. Which of the following would be most relevant to the passage as a whole?
   A. Several detailed paragraphs about *one* really interesting initiative
   B. A history of the initiative process in England
   C. Two more paragraphs detailing more initiatives to be on ballots this year
   D. A summary of the election results

GO ON TO THE NEXT PAGE.

1 1 1 1 1 1 1 1 1 1 1 1

local legislatures, and which the initiative process has
been a significant factor in elections throughout this nation's history. In the 1970s, for example, the subject of
most initiative propositions was state endorsement of a
national nuclear freeze. During the late '70s and early
'80s, the popular subject for initiatives was the taxpayers' revolt. In contrast, however this year the initiative
targets are very diverse, ranging from automobile insurance and tort liability and they also address mandatory
AIDS testing of prisoners. 71

68. F. NO CHANGE
    G. and the
    H. the
    J. which the

69. A. NO CHANGE
    B. In contrast,
    C. Moreover,
    D. In addition,

70. F. NO CHANGE
    G. to mandatory
    H. they address mandatory
    J. addressing

71. Readers are likely to regard the passage so far as best described by which of the following terms?
    A. Romantic
    B. Journalistic
    C. Fantastic
    D. Persuasive

(3)

Some initiative watchers are alarmed by recent
"judicial activism" that has seen judges nix dozens of
voter-sponsored referendums because petitions used to
place measures on the ballot were not printed in Spanish or other languages that reflect the demographic
makeup of the state, as well as in English. Other
reasons that initiatives have been declared invalid is
that they address more than one subject, they intrude
upon the domain of the legislature, or they bear too
colorful a title. 75

72. F. NO CHANGE
    G. deep-six
    H. pull the plug on
    J. strike down

73. A. NO CHANGE
    B. have been
    C. are
    D. has been

74. F. NO CHANGE
    G. subject; They
    H. subject. They
    J. subject they

75. Choose the sequence of paragraph numbers that makes the structure of the passage most logical.
    A. NO CHANGE
    B. 3, 2, 1
    C. 2, 1, 3
    D. 1, 3, 2

END OF TEST 1
STOP! DO NOT TURN THE PAGE UNTIL TOLD TO DO SO.

2 2 2 2 2 2 2 2 2 2 2

Mathematics Test

60 Minutes—60 Questions

DIRECTIONS: After solving each problem, darken the appropriate space on the answer sheet. Do not spend too much time on any one problem. Make a note of the ones that seem difficult, and return to them when you finish the others. Assume that the word *line* means "straight line," that geometric figures are not necessarily drawn to scale, and that all geometric figures lie in a plane.

1. Which of the following is not a real number?
   A. $\dfrac{0}{5}$
   B. $-\sqrt{23}$
   C. $\dfrac{12}{\sqrt{6}}$
   D. $0°$
   E. π

2. What is the value of $7^2 - 2[3 + 2(5 - 1)]$?
   F. 9
   G. 940
   H. 27
   J. −8
   K. −9

3. What is the solution set of $2x - 5 = 7 - 4x$?
   A. $\{1\}$
   B. $\{2\}$
   C. $\left\{\dfrac{1}{2}\right\}$
   D. $\{-2\}$
   E. $\left\{\dfrac{-1}{3}\right\}$

4. What percent of 24 is 18?
   F. 75%
   G. 150%
   H. 25%
   J. $33\dfrac{1}{3}\%$
   K. $133\dfrac{1}{3}\%$

5. How many curtains can be made from 20 meters of cloth if each curtain requires $2\dfrac{1}{2}$ meters?
   A. 50
   B. 20
   C. 12
   D. 8
   E. 4

6. What is the simplified form of $2x - \{3x - 2[x - (1 - x)]\}$?
   F. $3x - 2$
   G. $-x - 2$
   H. $-4x - 1$
   J. $-x + 2$
   K. $3x - 2x^2$

7. Which of the following numbers is NOT prime?
   A. 43
   B. 51
   C. 73
   D. 97
   E. 101

8. Which of the following is a secant line?

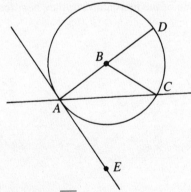

   F. Segment $\overline{BC}$
   G. Segment $\overline{AD}$
   H. Line $\overleftrightarrow{AC}$
   J. Line $\overleftrightarrow{AE}$
   K. Segment $\overline{AB}$

GO ON TO THE NEXT PAGE.

2   **2**   **2**   **2**   **2**   **2**   **2**   **2**   **2**   **2**   **2**

9. If $x = -2$ and $y = 3$, then $-x - xy^2 = ?$
- **A.** 16
- **B.** -34
- **C.** -38
- **D.** 20
- **E.** 144

10. In the circle shown, $\overline{AB}$ is a tangent and $\overline{BD}$ is a secant. If the length of $\overline{AB}$ is 6 and the length of $\overline{BC}$ is 4, what is the length of $\overline{CD}$?

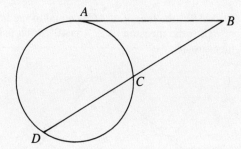

- **F.** $2\sqrt{5}$
- **G.** 8
- **H.** $2\frac{2}{3}$
- **J.** 5
- **K.** 10

11. What is an equivalent expression, in simplest radical form to $\sqrt[3]{4ab^2}\ \sqrt[3]{12a^4b^2}$?
- **A.** $2ab\sqrt[3]{6a^2b}$
- **B.** $\sqrt[3]{48a^5b^4}$
- **C.** $\sqrt[6]{48a^5b^4}$
- **D.** $16a^2b$
- **E.** None of these

12. Which of the following is NOT a quadratic equation in one variable?
- **F.** $3x^2 + 5 = 5x + 7$
- **G.** $x(2x + 5) = 8$
- **H.** $3^2 + 5x = 4^2 + 2x$
- **J.** $x^2 = 16$
- **K.** $(2x - 3)^2 = 5$

13. What is the simplified form of the expression $(3x - 1)^2$?
- **A.** $9x^2 - 1$
- **B.** $9x^2 - 6x + 1$
- **C.** $9x^2 + 1$
- **D.** $9x^2 + 6x + 1$
- **E.** $9x + 1$

14. If 2 less than five times a certain number is 1 more than twice the same number, which equation can be used to find the number?
- **F.** $5(x - 2) = 2(x + 1)$
- **G.** $5x + 1 = 2x - 2$
- **H.** $2 - 5x = 1 + 2x$
- **J.** $5x - 2 = 2x + 1$
- **K.** $5(x - 2) = 2x + 1$

15. The diameter of a circle is one side of a triangle, and the vertex is on the circle. What kind of triangle is formed?
- **A.** Isosceles
- **B.** Right
- **C.** Acute
- **D.** Scalene
- **E.** Equilateral

16. Which of the following is equivalent to $|x - 1| \le 3$?
- **F.** $x \le 4$
- **G.** $x + 1 \le 3$
- **H.** $-2 \le x \le 4$
- **J.** $x \le -2$ or $x \ge 4$
- **K.** $x \le -2$ and $x \ge 4$

17. In the rectangular coordinate system, the point associated with the ordered pair $(-4, 0)$ is located in which quadrant?
- **A.** I
- **B.** II
- **C.** III
- **D.** IV
- **E.** None of these

18. Which of the following ordered pairs satisfies the equation $3x - 2y = 5$?
- **F.** $(-1, -1)$
- **G.** $(1, 1)$
- **H.** $(1, -1)$
- **J.** $(-1, 1)$
- **K.** $(5, -5)$

19. In the diagram, lines m and n in a plane are cut by transversal l. Which statement would allow the conclusion that $m \parallel n$?

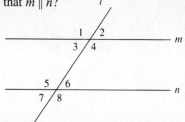

- **A.** $m \angle 2 = m \angle 3$
- **B.** $m \angle 2 = m \angle 6$
- **C.** $m \angle 5 = m \angle 3$
- **D.** $m \angle 2 + m \angle 4 = 180$
- **E.** $m \angle 1 = m \angle 7$

GO ON TO THE NEXT PAGE.

20. If, in $\triangle ABC$, $\overline{BD}$ is drawn so that $AD = DC$, then what is BD?

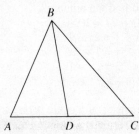

F. An angle bisector
G. An altitude
H. A median
J. A perpendicular bisector of $\overline{AC}$
K. A transversal

21. What is the sum of the fractions $\frac{5}{12}$ and $\frac{7}{18}$?

A. $\frac{3}{5}$

B. $\frac{29}{36}$

C. $\frac{1}{35}$

D. $\frac{1}{18}$

E. $\frac{2}{5}$

22. When completely simplified,

$$\frac{2}{3} - \frac{2 - \frac{5}{6}}{2^3 - 1} \div \frac{1}{2} = ?$$

F. $\frac{1}{3}$

G. 1

H. $\frac{7}{12}$

J. $\frac{-32}{15}$

K. $\frac{5}{18}$

23. What is the value of $\log_3 27$?

A. 3

B. 9

C. $\frac{1}{3}$

D. $\frac{1}{9}$

E. 24

24. If $\sin \theta = \frac{1}{2}$, then $\cos \theta = ?$

F. $\frac{1}{2}$

G. $\frac{-1}{2}$

H. $\frac{\sqrt{3}}{2}$

J. $\frac{-\sqrt{3}}{2}$

K. $\frac{\pm\sqrt{3}}{2}$

25. In $\triangle ABC$, the length of $\overline{AC}$ is equal to the length of $\overline{BC}$. If the measure of $\angle A$ is 40°, what is the measure of $\angle C$?

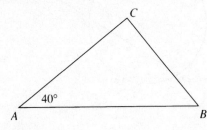

A. 50°
B. 60°
C. 80°
D. 100°
E. 140°

26. Which is the largest of the following numbers?

F. 3.1415926

G. $\frac{22}{7}$

H. 3.14

J. 3.1416

K. All these numbers are equal.

27. If Joan's English assignment is to read 80 pages, and she has read $\frac{4}{5}$ of her assignment, how many pages does she have left to read?

A. 16
B. 20
C. 32
D. 48
E. 64

28. Which of the following is a pure imaginary number?

F. -4
G. $-\sqrt{4}$
H. $\sqrt{-4}$
J. $3 + 2i$
K. 8

GO ON TO THE NEXT PAGE.

2 **2** **2** **2** **2** **2** **2** **2** **2** **2** **2**

29. Which equation corresponds to the accompanying graph?

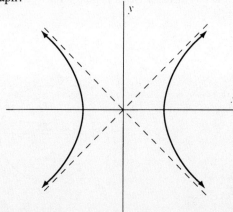

- A. $x^2 - y^2 = 1$
- B. $x^2 + y^2 = 1$
- C. $x^2 + y = 1$
- D. $x - y^2 = 1$
- E. $x + y^2 = 1$

30. What is the solution set of the following system of equations?

$$2x + y = -1$$
$$3x - 2y = -19$$

- F. $\{(2, -5)\}$
- G. $\{(-3, 5)\}$
- H. $\{(-7, -1)\}$
- J. There is no solution.
- K. There are infinitely many solutions.

31. What base ten numeral corresponds to 451 (eight)?
- A. 154
- B. 297
- C. 703
- D. 2,376
- E. None of these

32. Which expression would be appropriate to complete the following equation in order for the equation to illustrate the identity property of addition: $5 + (7 + 0) = ?$
- F. $(7 + 0) + 5$
- G. $5 + (0 + 7)$
- H. $(5 + 7) + 0$
- J. $5 + 7$
- K. 12

33. If $a < b$, then $|a - b| + a + b = ?$
- A. 0
- B. $2a$
- C. $2b$
- D. $2a + 2b$
- E. $a - b$

34. What is the set of prime factors of 6,440?
- F. $\{2, 5, 161\}$
- G. $\{2, 7, 23\}$
- H. $\{2, 5, 7, 23\}$
- J. $\{2, 5, 7\}$
- K. $\{2, 3,220\}$

35. Which of the angles named below are supplementary?

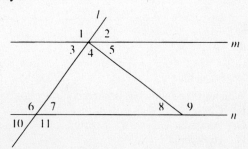

- A. $\angle 6$ and $\angle 11$
- B. $\angle 3, \angle 4,$ and $\angle 5$
- C. $\angle 3$ and $\angle 7$
- D. $\angle 8$ and $\angle 9$
- E. $\angle 2$ and $\angle 7$

36. $13\frac{1}{4} - 7\frac{5}{8} = ?$
- F. $5\frac{5}{8}$
- G. $5\frac{7}{8}$
- H. $6\frac{3}{8}$
- J. $6\frac{1}{2}$
- K. 5

37. What is the degree of the polynomial $3x^2y^3 + 5xy^2 - 7y$?
- A. 0
- B. 2
- C. 5
- D. 8
- E. 9

38. What is the sum of the roots of $4x^2 + 3x - 8 = 0$?
- F. $-\frac{4}{3}$
- G. $\frac{1}{2}$
- H. 2
- J. $-\frac{3}{4}$
- K. $\frac{3}{8}$

GO ON TO THE NEXT PAGE.

39. What is the value of $16^{-3/4}$?

   A. This is undefined.

   B. 8

   C. $\frac{1}{8}$

   D. –8

   E. $-\frac{1}{8}$

40. Which of the following is not a conic section?
   F. Circle
   G. Parabola
   H. Hyperbola
   J. Exponential curve
   K. Ellipse

41. The trigonometric function sin 215° is equal to which of the following?
   A. sin 35°
   B. – cos 35°
   C. – cos 55°
   D. – sin 55°
   E. sin 55°

42. In how many orders can 6 different books be placed on a shelf?
   F. 1
   G. 6
   H. 12
   J. 36
   K. 720

43. What is the value of -2^{-2}?

   A. 4

   B. – 4

   C. $\frac{1}{4}$

   D. $-\frac{1}{4}$

   E. None of these

44. A circle and a semicircle have the same area. If the circle has radius 1, what is the radius of the semicircle?

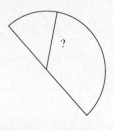

   F. 2
   G. 4
   H. $\sqrt{2}$
   J. $\pi\sqrt{2}$
   K. 2π

45. What is the center of the circle whose equation is $x^2 + y^2 + 4x - 18y + 69 = 0$?
   A. (–2, 9)
   B. (2, – 9)
   C. (4, –18)
   D. (– 4, 18)
   E. (0,0)

46. What is the distance between (5, 3) and (–2, 4)?
   F. $\sqrt{38}$
   G. $2\sqrt{10}$
   H. $\sqrt{58}$
   J. $5\sqrt{2}$
   K. $\sqrt{10}$

47. What is the smallest positive angle that is co-terminal with 846°?
   A. 234°
   B. 126°
   C. 36°
   D. 54°
   E. –234°

48. If a student received a score of 80% on a test in which 60 questions were answered correctly, how many questions were on the test?
   F. 15
   G. 30
   H. 48
   J. 75
   K. 90

49. $7(10^4) + 3(10^3) + 2(10^1) + 9(10^0)$ is the expanded form of what number?
   A. 7,329
   B. 70,329
   C. 73,029
   D. 73,209
   E. 7302.9

GO ON TO THE NEXT PAGE.

2   2 2 2 2 2 2 2 2 2   **2**

50. What is the probability of getting a sum of 8 on one roll of a fair pair of dice?

 F. 5

 G. 36

 H. $\frac{5}{36}$

 J. $\frac{1}{5}$

 K. $\frac{1}{8}$

51. If $\overline{AB}$ is a diameter, $\overline{AD} \parallel \overline{BC}$, and m $\angle BAD = 15°$, what is the measure of arc $\overset{\frown}{BC}$?

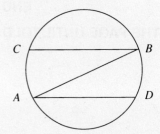

 A. 180°
 B. 165°
 C. 90°
 D. 75°
 E. None of these

52. What is the period of the function
$y = 3 \sin 5 \left(x + \frac{\pi}{12} \right)$?

 F. 3

 G. 5

 H. $-\frac{\pi}{12}$

 J. $\frac{2\pi}{5}$

 K. $\frac{\pi}{5}$

53. What is the y-intercept of the graph of
$y = x^2 - 2x - 8$?
 A. −8
 B. 8
 C. 4 and −2
 D. −4 and 2
 E. There are no y-intercepts.

54. What is the slope of the line whose equation is
$2x - 5y = 7$?

 F. −2

 G. −5

 H. $\frac{5}{2}$

 J. $\frac{2}{5}$

 K. 2

55. In right triangle ABC ($\angle B$ is the right angle), altitude BD is drawn. If $AB = 4$ and $AD = 3$, what is the length of $\overline{AC}$?

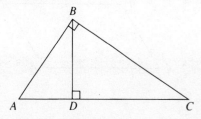

 A. 3

 B. 4

 C. $\frac{9}{4}$

 D. 12

 E. $\frac{16}{3}$

56. What is the sum of the interior angles of a hexagon?
 F. 360°
 G. 540°
 H. 720°
 J. 900°
 K. 1,080°

57. If $\overline{AB}$ is a diameter, m $\angle CEB = 50°$, and m $\overset{\frown}{BC} = 20°$, what is the measure of $\overset{\frown}{DB}$?

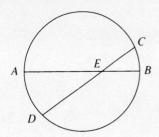

 A. 160°
 B. 130°
 C. 100°
 D. 80°
 E. 70°

58. At a time when a 6-foot-tall man casts a shadow 10 feet long, a tree casts a shadow 85 feet long. What is the height, in feet, of the tree?

 F. 51

 G. 34

 H. $141\frac{2}{3}$

 J. 100

 K. 89

GO ON TO THE NEXT PAGE.

59. In parallelogram *ABCD*, *AD* = 8, *AB* = 6, and m∠*A* = 60°. What is its area?

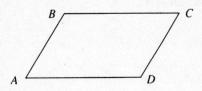

A. 24
B. 28
C. $24\sqrt{3}$
D. 48
E. $12\sqrt{3}$

60. If the measures of the angles of a triangle can be represented by $x + 15$, $3x - 75$, and $2x - 30$, what kind of triangle must it be?
F. Right
G. Equilateral
H. Obtuse
J. Scalene
K. No such triangle exists.

END OF TEST 2

STOP! DO NOT TURN THE PAGE UNTIL TOLD TO DO SO.

3   3 3 3 3 3 3 3 3 3 **3**

Reading Test

35 Minutes—40 Questions

DIRECTIONS: This test consists of four passages, each followed by ten multiple-choice questions. Read each passage and then pick the best answer for each question. Fill in the spaces on your answer sheet that correspond to your choices. Refer to the passage as often as you wish while answering the questions.

Passage I

NATURAL SCIENCE: The following passage is an excerpt from a government report on indoor air pollution.

The Environmental Protection Agency (EPA) says, "the air within homes and other buildings can be more seriously polluted than the outdoor air in even the largest and most industrialized cities."

5 In fact, indoor air is often two-to-five times more polluted than outdoor air and can be up to 1,000 times as dirty. The EPA estimates that most Americans are exposed every day to indoor air contaminants that can lead to serious health problems for some people, including cancer, 10 respiratory ailments, fatigue and headaches.

Moreover, because people spend an estimated 90 percent of their time indoors, the risks to health may be greater due to indoor rather than outdoor air pollution. In addition, the EPA says, people who are most susceptible to 15 indoor pollution are often those who may spend the most time indoors, such as the young, the elderly, and the chronically ill.

Indoor air quality problems can be traced to a variety of sources, including naturally occurring radon gas, 20 poor building design, inadequate building maintenance, structural components and furnishings, consumer products and occupant activities. "Control of these diverse sources of pollution in the air of public and private buildings poses an unprecedented challenge—a challenge that we are only now 25 recognizing," according to pollution experts Jonathan M. Samet and John Spengler.

One of the most visible—and potent—indoor pollutants is environmental tobacco smoke (ETS), or secondhand smoke. According to the American Lung 30 Association, ETS "contains approximately 4,000 chemicals, including 200 known poisons, [such as] formaldehyde and carbon monoxide, and 43 known carcinogens." EPA estimates that secondhand smoke annually causes 3,000

cases of lung cancer in non-smokers and 150,000–300,000 35 cases of lower-respiratory-tract infections in young children.

Indoor air pollution is especially severe in new structures, where glues, carpeting and furniture with foam upholstery emit volatile organic chemicals that can cause cancer and other diseases. But not all indoor pollutants are 40 man-made. Biological contaminants such as pollen and animal dander (tiny scales from hair, feathers or skin that may be allergenic) can reach levels inside houses and buildings that make people sick, especially when distributed by air conditioners and fans.

45 Dirty and poorly maintained ventilation systems themselves are prime breeding grounds for molds and fungi that cause allergic reactions and can release chemical toxins. Sometimes, the buildings must be vacated while the systems are cleaned.

50 Among the organisms that can breed in ventilation components such as cooling towers and humidifiers is Legionella, the bug that causes Legionnaire's disease. The sometimes-fatal disorder usually draws notice when a mass outbreak occurs in a hotel or other public building. Harriet A. Burge, an associate professor at Harvard 55 Medical School, blames dirty humidifiers and home hot-water heaters where the water is not kept hot enough. That enables slime to form inside the tank, which could foster the growth of Legionella.

60 Home humidifiers can also promote the growth of dust mites, which eat molds and human skin scales and thrive in high humidity. Mites and their mite-sized droppings are thought to be a contributing factor in the increasing number of asthma cases in the United States and some 65 European countries.

Sloppy housekeeping aggravates the dust mite problem. "Homes aren't always as clean as they used to be, because working mothers are out working," notes EPA information officer Kristy Miller. "I remember how my 70 grandmother used to beat the rugs and vacuum under every bed once a week. There was an effort to keep the house spotless."

GO ON TO THE NEXT PAGE.

Ironically, families that still strive for the spic-and-span ideal invite another form of indoor air pollution. Many cleaning and home-maintenance products contain volatile chemicals that are harmful when inhaled in excessive amounts or over long periods. The products include oven cleaner, paint remover, wax stripper, furniture polish, disinfectant and bathroom spray cleaner.

Richard L. Worsnop, "Indoor Air Pollution"

1. Based on information in the passage, the EPA is concerned about air quality because:
   A. industrialized cities are losing population.
   B. bad air adversely affects health.
   C. the public is insensitive to air quality.
   D. people are spending too much time indoors.

2. According to the passage, the quality of outdoor air is:
   F. about the same as that of indoor air.
   G. generally worse than that of indoor air.
   H. 1,000 times worse than that of indoor air.
   J. likely to be less polluted than indoor air.

3. Based on information in the passage, air pollution can contribute to the development of all of the following maladies EXCEPT:
   A. asthma.
   B. Legionnaire's disease.
   C. diphtheria.
   D. cancer.

4. The toxic molds and fungi that pollute indoor air are most likely to be found in:
   F. air-conditioning ducts.
   G. the chemicals used in wall paint.
   H. new furniture and carpeting.
   J. de-humidifiers.

5. Based on information in the passage, the population most likely to be harmed by indoor air pollution is:
   A. 0–5 years old.
   B. 15–20 years old.
   C. 30–35 years old.
   D. 45–50 years old.

6. The author of the passage suggests that the problem of indoor air pollution:
   F. is more severe in private than in public buildings.
   G. cannot be solved unless most buildings are redesigned.
   H. has long been a concern of the EPA.
   J. has only recently been identified.

7. According to the passage, the causes of indoor air pollution are:
   A. all natural.
   B. mostly natural.
   C. mostly man-made.
   D. all man-made.

8. Indoor air pollution is more severe today than in the past because:
   F. tobacco consumption is more prevalent today than in the past.
   G. industrialization promotes pollution.
   H. pollution controls are still being developed.
   J. people devote less time to keeping their houses clean.

9. A clean-looking house in itself is no guarantee of clean indoor air because:
   A. the sources of pollution are usually concealed inside walls, ducts, and appliances.
   B. many home-cleaning products release harmful chemicals into the air.
   C. pollution-causing agents are invisible to the naked eye.
   D. no house can be completely germ- and dust-free.

10. Based on the passage, cigarette smoke differs from most other forms of indoor air pollution in all the following ways EXCEPT:
    F. it can be seen by the naked eye.
    G. it is carcinogenic.
    H. it may cause lung cancer in children.
    J. it is laced with toxic chemicals.

GO ON TO THE NEXT PAGE.

3 3 3 3 3 3 3 3 3 3 **3**

Passage II

SOCIAL SCIENCE: This passage is adapted from a publication of the U.S. Department of Health and Human Services titled *Stuttering: Hope Through Research*. The selection describes various symptoms of stuttering.

Stuttering is a disorder in which the rhythmic flow, or fluency, of speech is disrupted by rapid-fire repetitions of sounds, prolonged vowels, and complete stops—verbal blocks. A stutterer's speech is often uncontrollable—
5 sometimes faster, but usually slower than the average speaking rate. Sometimes, too, the voice changes in pitch, loudness, and inflection.

Observations of young children during the early stages of stuttering have led to a list of warning signs that
10 can help identify a child who is developing a speech problem. Most children use "um's" and "ah's," and will repeat words or syllables as they learn to speak. It is not a serious concern if a child says, "I like to go and and and and play games," unless such repetitions occur often,
15 more than once every 20 words or so.

Repeating whole words is not necessarily a sign of stuttering; however, repeating speech sounds or syllables such as in the song "K-K-K-Katy" is.

Sometimes a stutterer will exhibit tension while pro-
20 longing a sound. For example, the 8-year-old who says, "Annnnnnnd—and—thththen I I drank it" with lips trembling at the same time. Children who experience such a stuttering tremor usually become frightened, angry, and frustrated at their inability to speak. A further danger sign
25 is a rise in pitch as the child draws out the syllable.

The appearance of a child or adult experiencing the most severe signs of stuttering is dramatic: As they struggle to get a word out, their whole face may contort, the jaw may jerk, the mouth open, tongue protrude, and
30 eyes roll. Tension can spread through the whole body. A moment of overwhelming struggle occurs during the speech block. ...

While the symptoms of stuttering are easy to recognize, the underlying cause remains a mystery. Hippocrates
35 thought that stuttering was due to dryness of the tongue, and he prescribed blistering substances to drain away the black bile responsible. A Roman physician recommended gargling and massages to strengthen a weak tongue. Seventeenth century scientist Francis Bacon suggested
40 hot wine to thaw a "refrigerated" tongue. Too large a tongue was the fault, according to a 19th century Prussian physician, so he snipped pieces off stutterers' tongues. Alexander Melville Bell, father of the telephone inventor, insisted stuttering was simply a bad habit that could be
45 overcome by reeducation.

Some theories today attribute stuttering to problems in the control of the muscles of speech. As recently as the fifties and sixties, however, stuttering was thought to arise from deep-rooted personality problems, and
50 psychotherapy was recommended.

Stutterers represent the whole range of personality types, levels of emotional adjustment, and intelligence. Winston Churchill was a stutterer (or stammerer, as the English prefer to say). So were Sir Isaac Newton, King
55 George VI of England, and writer Somerset Maugham.

There are more than 15 million stutterers in the world today and approximately 1 million in the United States alone.

Most stuttering begins after a child has mastered the
60 basics of speech and is starting to talk automatically. One out of 30 children will then undergo a brief period of stuttering, lasting 6 months or so. Boys are four times as likely as girls to be stutterers.

Occasionally stuttering arises in an older child or
65 even in an adult. It may follow an illness or an emotionally shattering event, such as a death in the family. Stuttering may also occur following brain injury, either due to head injury or after a stroke. No matter how the problem begins, stutterers generally experience their worst mo-
70 ments under conditions of stress or emotional tension: ordering in a crowded restaurant, talking over the telephone, speaking in public, asking the boss for a raise.

Stuttering does not develop in a predictable pattern. In children, speech difficulties can disappear for weeks or
75 months only to return in full force. About 80 percent of children with a stuttering problem are able to speak normally by the time they are adults—whether they've had therapy or not. Adult stutterers have also been known to stop stuttering for no apparent reason.

80 Indeed, all stutterers can speak fluently some of the time. Most can also whisper smoothly, speak in unison, and sing with no hesitations. Country and western singer Mel Tillis is an example of a stutterer with a successful singing career.

85 Most stutterers also speak easily when they are prevented from hearing their own voices, when talking to pets and small children, or when addressing themselves in the mirror. All these instances of fluency demonstrate that nothing is basically wrong with the stutterer's speech
90 machinery.

U.S. Department of Health and Human Services.
Stuttering: Hope Through Research

GO ON TO THE NEXT PAGE.

3   3   3   3   3   3   3   3   3   3   3

11. According to the passage, stuttering will be a life-long problem for:
    A. males who stuttered in childhood.
    B. males and females who began stuttering in childhood.
    C. only a small percentage of childhood stutterers.
    D. anyone who fails to get help.

12. The passage indicates that during moments of speech blockage, a stutterer may experience all of the following symptoms EXCEPT:
    F. facial distortion.
    G. severe frustration.
    H. body tension.
    J. trembling head and hands.

13. Based on information in the passage, which of the following situations is LEAST likely to occur?
    A. A man begins to stutter after a traumatic divorce.
    B. A schoolgirl temporarily stops stuttering during summer vacation.
    C. An actress stutters off stage but not during performances.
    D. A boy stutters mostly when telling bedtime stories to his baby sister.

14. One can infer from the passage that a parent whose young child repeats the same word over and over while learning to speak would be advised to:
    F. take the child to see a speech therapist.
    G. help the child relax while speaking.
    H. accept the fact that the child will be a stutterer.
    J. keep track of the frequency of repetitions.

15. According to the passage, young children usually begin to stutter:
    A. after learning to speak fluently.
    B. after a severe emotional shock.
    C. during prolonged periods of stress or tension.
    D. when they lack the vocabulary to express themselves.

16. Until the 19th century, authorities apparently regarded stuttering as:
    F. a sign of low intelligence.
    G. an emotional problem.
    H. a physical ailment.
    J. a lack of self-discipline.

17. One can infer from the passage that a stutterer may find relief by:
    A. avoiding situations that typically cause stuttering.
    B. practicing speech in front of a mirror.
    C. preparing what they have to say ahead of time.
    D. speaking more slowly.

18. One may assume that stuttering is NOT caused by a physical disorder of a person's speech apparatus because:
    F. all stutterers speak fluently from time to time.
    G. stuttering sometimes appears and disappears for no apparent reason.
    H. famous people, including athletes, have been stutterers.
    J. highly intelligent people have been known to stutter.

19. The author's main purpose in this passage is to point out that:
    A. treatment is available for stutterers identified early enough in life.
    B. the effects of stuttering are widely known, but uncertainty surrounds its causes.
    C. stutterers should not be held responsible for their speech disorder.
    D. the symptoms of stuttering are confusing and often misunderstood.

20. By pointing out that famous and successful people have been stutterers, the author means to imply all of the following EXCEPT that:
    F. stuttering is not a serious handicap in life.
    G. stuttering is unrelated to I.Q.
    H. the public is generally tolerant of stutterers.
    J. stuttering is not a personality disorder.

GO ON TO THE NEXT PAGE.

3   *3 3 3 3 3 3 3 3 3*

Passage III

HUMANITIES: This passage is adapted from "Wanted: A World Language," by Mario Pei. In this selection, Pei explains the difficulties of developing a single international language.

In the 17th century, French philosopher René Descartes came forth with a revolutionary idea. He proposed the creation of a language that could be used internationally by all sorts of people, peasants as well as
5 scholars.

But Descartes made the mistake of concentrating on the logical aspects of such a language, the progression of ideas from the general to the specific. This logical structure exists in no living language, not even in the great
10 classical tongues of antiquity, which are replete with illogical exceptions and arbitrary features.

While Descartes offered no sample of his ideal constructed language, several of his contemporaries immediately came to the fore with offerings. Some of their
15 suggestions were quite ingenious, but all embodied the principle of logical progression at the expense of familiarity and ease. For example, Bishop John Wilkins' *Essay* of 1668 presents a language in which *Z* indicates animals in general, *Za* indicates fish, and successive consonants
20 and vowels further restrict the concept to particular classes of fish.

But alongside these attempts at constructed languages which had no connection with any existing language, there was also a startlingly modern proposal, one
25 made by the Bohemian scholar Comenius. He suggested the use of existing languages, not on a universal, but on a zonal basis (he actually proposed English and French for use in Western Europe, Russian as a common tongue for Eastern Europe). This type of solution, still widely advo-
30 cated today, is in the nature of a temporary makeshift, because it does not supply us with one universal language, but merely makes the existing linguistic confusion a little easier to bear.

Since the days of Descartes, Wilkins, and Comenius,
35 at least a thousand proposals of one description or another have been advanced. These include several distinct types:
1) The selection and use of an existing language, ancient or modern, such as Latin, French, or English.
2) The combination of two or more existing lan-
40 guages, either in zonal distribution, as advocated by Comenius and, much later, by Stalin; or existing side by side, like the Greek and Latin of antiquity. (The French *Monde Bilingue* organization, for instance, advocates that all English speakers learn French, all French speakers
45 learn English, and all speakers of other tongues learn one or the other. This does not solve the problem of communicating when a Czech who has learned French meets a Japanese who has learned English.)

3) The choice of a modified national language, such
50 as Basic English, which works with a reduced vocabulary made to serve all purposes by a process of substitution and paraphrase (*bush,* for instance, is replaced by *small tree; selfish* is replaced by *without thought of others*); or works with the modification applied not to the vocabulary, but to
55 the system of spelling or the grammatical structure (*thru, filozofi,* would be samples of spelling; *goed, dood, oxes, mouses* instead of the irregular *went, did, oxen, mice* would be examples of grammar).
4) Blends of two or more existing languages, with
60 words and constructions arbitrarily taken from one or another of the constituent languages.
5) Fully constructed languages showing no connection with any known languages (like the American Ro and Suma).
65 6) Constructed languages in which existing languages are freely utilized to supply, or at least to suggest, both vocabulary and grammatical structure, but with concern for component elements familiar to the greatest possible number of people with different language
70 backgrounds (Volapük, Esperanto, Ido, Interlingua).

While many of these projects are impractical and present discouraging features, there are at least as many, of all the types outlined above, that could easily become operational. It is therefore not the lack of suitable schemes
75 that has prevented, up to the time of writing, the adoption of a language for universal use. …

The crux of the problem lies not in the principle, but in its application. *Which* language shall be adopted for international use? There are in existence some 3,000
80 natural languages, including the better-known classical ones, such as Latin and Greek; plus at least 1,000 fully constructed languages, or modified national tongues, that have been presented since the days of Descartes.

Mario Pei, "Wanted: A World Language"

21. For a language to be designated "constructed," it must:
  A. be different from any existing language.
  B. have no connection whatever to any known language.
  C. sound familiar to the greatest number of people, regardless of their native tongues.
  D. combine elements from at least three existing languages.

GO ON TO THE NEXT PAGE.

3 3 3 3 3 3 3 3 3 3 3

22. Which of the following ideas is clearly indicated by the passage?
- F. Speakers of French are unwilling to replace their own tongue with a universal language.
- G. Josef Stalin advocated a language plan that no one had thought of before.
- H. Ancient Latin and Greek are the foundation of most modern languages.
- J. Natural languages are far more common than constructed languages.

23. The author's principal argument is that:
- A. the world has too many languages.
- B. an international language will contribute to the formation of international government.
- C. a single international language will be beneficial to mankind.
- D. a universal language will simplify communications among Eastern and Western European nations.

24. The passage implies that the language proposed by Bishop John Wilkins is a:
- F. blend of two or more existing languages.
- G. type of zonal language.
- H. modified national language.
- J. constructed language.

25. The author of the passage believes that adoption of a universal language:
- A. is not as difficult as it may seem.
- B. will probably never happen.
- C. will occur when the right language is invented.
- D. will take place when linguists agree on which language to use.

26. The passage implies that Descartes' proposal for an international tongue failed because it:
- F. was illogical.
- G. contained too many exceptions to the rules of language.
- H. contradicted a basic principle of language usage.
- J. was too much like old Latin and Greek.

27. By calling Comenius's scheme for an international language "startling modern" (line 24), the author means that:
- A. Comenius devised a plan that could work in today's world.
- B. Comenius's proposal had never been thought of before.
- C. Comenius's ideas parallel the ideas of many 20th-century linguists.
- D. Comenius's language was simple and easy to learn.

28. Which of the following is the most valid generalization about the language types proposed for international use (lines 37 through 70)?
- F. They are simpler to use than most present-day languages.
- G. They are based on universal rules of grammar.
- H. They are rooted in existing languages.
- J. They appeal equally to all nationalities.

29. According to the passage, many proposals for an international language originated during the 17th century because:
- A. Descartes' proposal was incomplete.
- B. it was an enlightened time.
- C. it was a revolutionary era.
- D. international travel began to flourish.

30. The passage implies that, in order to be functional, a constructed language:
- F. must borrow from the widely spoken languages of the world.
- G. may not be based solely on logical principles.
- H. may use the grammar of English or of any other popular language.
- J. must be translatable into several thousand natural languages.

GO ON TO THE NEXT PAGE.

3 3 3 3 3 3 3 3 3 3 **3**

Passage IV

PROSE FICTION: This passage is an excerpt from a short story, "Buckthorne," by the 19th-century American author Washington Irving. The narrator of the passage recalls his boyhood years in a boarding school.

I was sent at an early age to a public school sorely against my mother's wishes; but my father insisted that it was the only way to make boys hardy. The school was kept by a conscientious prig of the ancient system who
5 did his duty by the boys entrusted to his care; that is to say we were flogged soundly when we did not get our lessons. We were put into classes and thus flogged on in droves along the highways of knowledge, in much the same manner as cattle are driven to market, where those
10 that are heavy in gait or short in leg have to suffer for the superior alertness of longer limbs of their companions.

For my part, I confess it with shame, I was an incorrigible laggard. I have always had the poetical feeling, that is to say I have always been an idle fellow and prone
15 to play the vagabond. I used to get away from my books and school whenever I could and ramble about the fields. I was surrounded by seductions for such a temperament. The school house was an old fashioned whitewashed mansion of wood and plaster, standing on the skirts of a
20 beautiful village. Close by it was the venerable church with a tall Gothic spire. Before it spread a lovely green valley, with a little stream glistening along through willow groves; while a line of blue hills bounding the landscape gave rise to many a summer day dream as to the
25 fairy land that lay beyond.

In spite of all the scourgings I suffered at that school to make me love my book I cannot but look back upon the place with fondness. Indeed I considered this frequent flagellation as the common lot of humanity and the reg-
30 ular mode in which scholars were made. My kind mother used to lament over the details of the sore trials I underwent in the cause of learning; but my father turned a deaf ear to her expostulations. He had been flogged through school himself and swore there was no other way of mak-
35 ing a man of parts; though, let me speak it with true reverence, my father was but an indifferent illustration of his theory, for he was considered a grievous blockhead.

My poetical temperament evinced itself at a very early period. The village church was attended every Sun-
40 day by a neighbouring squire; the lord of the manor, whose park stretched quite to the village and whose spacious country seat seemed to take the church under its protection. Indeed you would have thought the church had been consecrated to him instead of to the Deity. The
45 parish clerk bowed low before him and the vergers humbled themselves unto the dust in his presence. He always entered a little late and with some stir, striking his cane

emphatically on the ground; swaying his hat in his hand, and looking loftily to the right and left as he walked
50 slowly up the aisle, and parson, who always ate his Sunday dinner with him, never commenced service until he appeared. He sat with his family in a large pew gorgeously lined, humbling himself devoutly on velvet cushions and reading lessons of meekness and lowliness of
55 spirit out of splendid gold and morocco prayer books. Whenever the parson spoke of the difficulty of a rich man's entering the kingdom of heaven, the eyes of the congregation would turn towards the "grand pew," and I thought the squire seemed pleased with the application.

60 The pomp of this pew and the aristocratical air of the family struck my imagination wonderfully and I fell desperately in love with a little daughter of the squire's, about twelve years of age. This freak of fancy made me more truant from my studies than ever. I used to stroll
65 about the squire's park, and lurk near the house: to catch glimpses of this little damsel at the windows, or playing about the lawns; or walking out with her governess.

I had not enterprise, nor impudence enough to venture from my concealment; indeed I felt like an arrant
70 poacher, until I read one or two of Ovid's Metamorphoses, when I pictured myself as some sylvan deity and she a coy wood nymph of whom I was in pursuit. There is something extremely delicious in these early awakenings of the tender passion. I can feel, even at this mo-
75 ment, the thrilling of my boyish bosom, whenever by chance I caught a glimpse of her white frock fluttering among the shrubbery. I carried about in my bosom a volume of Waller, which I had purloined from my mother's library; and I applied to my little fair one all the compli-
80 ments lavished upon Sacharissa.

At length I danced with her at a school ball. I was so awkward a booby that I dared scarcely speak to her; I was filled with awe and embarrassment in her presence; but I was so inspired that my poetical temperament for the first
85 time broke out in verse and I fabricated some glowing lines, in which I berhymed the little lady under the favourite name of Sacharissa. I slipped the verses, trembling and blushing, into her hand the next Sunday as she came out of church. The little prude handed them to her
90 mamma; the mamma handed them to the squire; the squire, who had no soul for poetry, sent them in dudgeon to the schoolmaster; and the schoolmaster, with a barbarity worthy of the dark ages, gave me a sound and peculiarly humiliating flogging for thus trespassing upon
95 Parnassus.

Washington Irving, "Buckthorne," *Tales of a Traveller*

GO ON TO THE NEXT PAGE.

31. The narrator's father sent his son to a public school mainly:
    A. to toughen him up.
    B. to meet people from the upper class.
    C. because of its excellent curriculum.
    D. because the boy was a trouble maker.

32. The term "poetical feeling" (line 13), as used by the narrator, means that he:
    F. enjoyed writing poetry.
    G. views himself as a budding poet.
    H. was a romantic dreamer.
    J. loved reading poetry more than anything.

33. The speaker attributes his poor record in school to:
    A. too many distractions.
    B. a learning disability.
    C. friends who led him astray.
    D. being unhappy in a boarding school.

34. The narrator compares his schooling to a cattle drive (lines 6–11) in order to make the point that:
    F. students were grouped according to ability.
    G. the students were treated inhumanely.
    H. weak students were punished for their deficiencies.
    J. individuality was discouraged.

35. As a youth, the narrator believed that in order to learn in school you:
    A. should have small classes.
    B. had to be punished.
    C. should study hard.
    D. needed enthusiastic teachers.

36. The boy's attitude toward the country squire was shaped in part by:
    F. the influence of the schoolmaster.
    G. the squire's daughter.
    H. the teachings of the church.
    J. his observation of how others behaved.

37. The narrator introduces the squire into the passage for all of the following reasons EXCEPT:
    A. to explain who the man's daughter was.
    B. to add humor to the passage.
    C. to point out the man's hypocrisy.
    D. to illustrate the evils of England's class structure.

38. The name *Sacharissa* is:
    F. the first name of the girl with whom the narrator falls in love.
    G. a name invented by the narrator because he didn't know the girl's real name.
    H. the woman to whom the poet Waller wrote love poems.
    J. the name of a wood nymph in Ovid's *Metamorphosis*.

39. Which of the following best describes the narrator's feelings about the situations described in the passage?
    A. Amused by the trials of growing up.
    B. Bitter about the way he was treated by adults.
    C. Nostalgic about the days of his boyhood.
    D. Glad that those years are over and done with.

40. At the end of the passage the boy is flogged by the schoolmaster because he:
    F. embarrassed the girl.
    G. fell in love with someone above him.
    H. had illicit thoughts about the girl.
    J. wrote poetry.

END OF TEST 3
STOP! DO NOT TURN THE PAGE UNTIL TOLD TO DO SO.

4 4 4 4 4 4 4 4 4 4 4

Science Reasoning Test

35 Minutes—40 Questions

DIRECTIONS: This test consists of several distinct passages. Each passage is followed by a number of multiple-choice questions based on the passage. Study the passage, and then select the best answer to each question. You are allowed to reread the passage. Record your answer by blackening the appropriate space on the Answer Sheet.

Passage I

In the diagram below, each point represents the average fat intake and rate of death from breast cancer for a particular country.

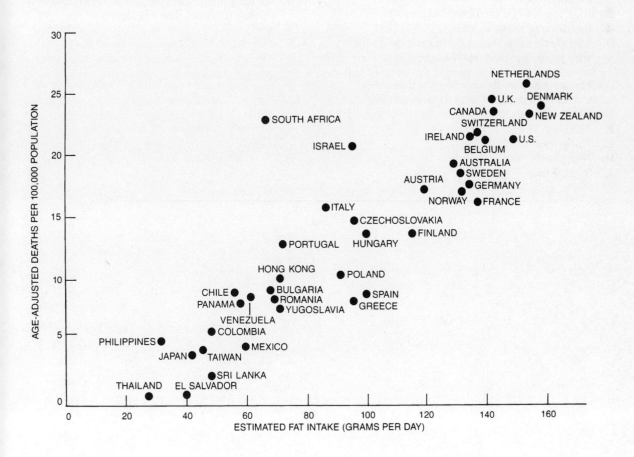

Illustration by Andrew Christie from "Diet and Cancer," by Leonard A. Cohen. Copyright © November 1987 by *Scientific American, Inc.* All rights reserved.

GO ON TO THE NEXT PAGE.

4 4 4 4 4 4 4 4 4 4 4

1. In countries where the death rate from breast cancer is about 13 or 14 per 100,000 of population, the average fat intake is:
   A. 60 g/day.
   B. from 70 to 120 g/day.
   C. from 60 to 90 g/day.
   D. 100 g/day.

2. Of the following pairs, which are two countries with about the same death rate, but drastically different fat intakes?
   F. Israel and Greece
   G. Austria and Germany
   H. France and Mexico
   J. Israel and the United States

3. What inference is suggested by the data?
   A. Consumption of fats is the cause of breast cancer.
   B. Women with breast cancer develop a craving for fatty foods.
   C. High levels of fat intake tend to promote the formation of breast cancers.
   D. Environmental pollution promotes a desire for fatty foods, and therefore, breast cancer.

4. For which country do the data suggest that some factor other than intake of fatty foods is causing many breast cancers?
   F. Thailand
   G. Philippines
   H. Netherlands
   J. South Africa

5. Why are the data points for Greece and Spain slightly below the general trend?
   A. The sunny Mediterranean climate offers some protection against breast cancer.
   B. For many reasons, there is considerable scatter in the points.
   C. Olive oil, rather than animal fats, is used in these countries.
   D. The scatter of the points implies that there is much uncertainty in the data.

6. What additional evidence would tend to show that consumption of dietary fat is a chief contributor to the rate of breast cancer?
   F. Americans who move to Europe develop higher rates of breast cancer.
   G. With an increase in meat consumption, the rate of breast cancer in Japan is increasing.
   H. South Africans have a high level of fat in the diet.
   J. In the United States the rate of breast cancer is higher in whites than in blacks.

GO ON TO THE NEXT PAGE.

4 4 4 4 4 4 4 4 4 4 4 4

Passage II

The chart below is a summary of the weather in New York for the month of July 1988. The large numbers below the temperature graph are dates of the month.

New York's Weather Last Month

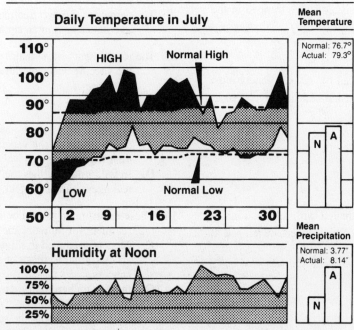

Copyright © 1988 by The New York Times Company. Reprinted by permission.

7. What was the weather like on July 22?
   A. Unusually hot and dry
   B. Humid, but not very hot
   C. Cool and moist in the morning, but very hot later
   D. Comfortably cool and dry all day

8. How many days during the month of July were unusually hot?
   F. 5
   G. 8
   H. 18
   J. 25

9. How would the temperature variation during the month be characterized?
   A. Daily lows were nearly normal, but daily highs were considerably higher than normal.
   B. Daily highs were about normal, but daily lows were considerably above normal.
   C. Both daily highs and daily lows were not much different from normal.
   D. Both daily highs and daily lows were somewhat below normal.

10. How did the humidity variation compare with the temperature variation?
    F. The coolest days had the lowest noon humidity.

G. On the warmest days, humidity increased substantially between noon and dusk.
H. Humidity was about average for the month on days that had the lowest temperature.
J. Humidity at noon was highest on days that did not get unusually hot.

11. Normally, how does the average daily temperature vary during the month of July in New York?
    A. It varies between 77° F and 96° F.
    B. It increases by about 2° F during the month.
    C. It is steady at 76.7° F for the whole month.
    D. It is steady at 79.3° F for the whole month.

12. In comparison with the weather in other Julys, how might the weather in July of 1988 have affected the demand on public utilities?
    F. It probably produced shortages of electricity and water.
    G. It probably relieved the threat of drought and a shortage of natural gas.
    H. There may have been shortages of electric power.
    J. Both electricity and natural gas were probably in plentiful supply.

4 4 4 4 4 4 4 4 4 4 4 4

Passage III

A medical research worker is testing the effectiveness of an experimental vaccine in controlling cancer. His experimental animals are three different groups of mice. Strains A and B are purebred strains of laboratory white mice, whose susceptibility to cancer is well known. The third group consists of mice trapped in the wild.

Experiment 1

All three groups were bred for several generations, and no treatment was given. Skin cancers developed at the following rates:
      Strain A: 8%
      Strain B: 62%
      Wild mice: 3%

Experiment 2

All three groups were treated with applications of benzol, a known carcinogen. Skin cancers developed at these rates:
      Strain A: 59%
      Strain B: 98%
      Wild mice: 14%

Experiment 3

All three groups were treated with benzol, followed by administration of the vaccine. Cancer rates were:
      Strain A: 56%
      Strain B: 61%
      Wild mice: 14%

Experiment 4

All three groups were treated with benzol, followed by treatment with fexadrin, a chemical agent that is now in common use in the treatment of cancer. Cancer rates were:
      Strain A: 32%
      Strain B: 98%
      Wild mice: 3%

13. Unless Experiment 1 were done, the scientist would not know:
   - A. whether mice can develop skin cancer.
   - B. how effective benzol is in producing cancers in these strains.
   - C. whether wild mice can be compared with laboratory mice.
   - D. if all laboratory-bred mice were alike.

14. One clear result of all these tests is the evidence that:
   - F. the vaccine is completely ineffective.
   - G. heredity influences the usefulness of the vaccine.
   - H. there is no way to prevent skin cancer completely.
   - J. neither of the two treatments will be effective in combating human cancers.

15. The experiments show that:
   - A. the vaccine was generally more effective than fexadrin.
   - B. fexadrin was generally more effective than the vaccine.
   - C. where there is a strong hereditary tendency to develop cancer, the vaccine is more effective than fexadrin.
   - D. In wild mice, neither the vaccine nor the chemical agent had any effect.

16. These experiments would be significant in developing treatment for human cancer only if:
   - F. cancers produced in mice by benzol have properties similar to those of spontaneous human cancers.
   - G. there is no hereditary tendency to develop cancer in human beings.
   - H. humans have about the same rate of cancer as wild mice.
   - J. human hereditary endowment is comparable to that of purebred laboratory mice.

17. Which of the following questions would it NOT be worthwhile to pursue further?
   - A. Why do wild mice have such a low rate of cancer?
   - B. Why does the vaccine have such a good effect in a strain with a strong hereditary susceptability to cancer, but not in the other strains?
   - C. Why does fexadrin have such a good effect in Strain A, but not in Strain B?
   - D. How can benzol be altered chemically to increase the rate at which it produces cancer in lines of mice with hereditary susceptibility?

GO ON TO THE NEXT PAGE.

4 **4 4 4 4 4 4 4 4 4 4** **4**

Passage IV

The diagram below shows the results of sampling the stomach contents of 5 species of fish. The data tell what percentage of each species were found to contain each of 6 kinds of food. A dot indicates that a particular species consumed none of the food in question.

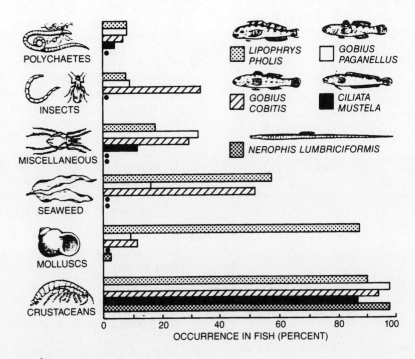

18. In which species did about one third of all individuals contain insects?
   F. *Lipophrys*
   G. *Nerophis*
   H. *G. paganellus*
   J. *G. cobitis*

19. Which statement correctly describes an aspect of the feeding habits of these fishes?
   A. Nonanimal food is used by more *Lipophrys* than by any of the other fishes.
   B. *Nerophis* cannot make any use of molluscs.
   C. *G. paganellus* uses a wider variety of food than any of the others.
   D. *G. cobitis* gets over 90% of its nourishment from crustaceans.

20. The data seem to suggest that:
   F. *G. cobitis* cannot digest plant food.
   G. all members of the genus *Gobius* have identical food choices.
   H. *Lipophrys* has jaws strong enough to crack shells.
   J. a long, thin fish prefers insect food.

21. In what way would a change in the food supply affect the population of the fishes?
   A. If polychaetes were eliminated from the supply, all five fish populations would suffer.
   B. Loss of crustaceans might completely eliminate the *Nerophis* population.
   C. Loss of molluscs might completely eliminate the *Lipophrys* population.
   D. Increase in the availability of insects would increase the population of *G. paganellus*.

22. Which fishes would be most likely to survive if crustaceans were completely wiped out in the ecosystem?
   F. *Nerophis* and *G. cobitis*
   G. *Lipophrys* and *G. cobitis*
   H. *G. paganellus* and *Ciliata*
   J. *Lipophrys* and *Ciliata*

GO ON TO THE NEXT PAGE.

Passage V

A scientist is looking for a general rule that governs the viscous drag that a liquid exerts on a sphere moving through it. The viscous drag is a retarding force, tending to prevent any increase in the velocity of the sphere. If a sphere is dropped into a liquid, it will soon fall at a constant speed, at which the viscous drag is equal to the weight of the sphere.

Experiment 1

Steel spheres of various sizes were dropped into a tank containing a 2% solution of methyl cellulose. When they reached constant velocity, the speed of fall was measured.

Diameter of sphere (cm)	Velocity of fall (m/s)
0.5	0.21
1.0	0.82
1.5	1.80
2.0	3.25
2.5	5.03
3.0	7.25

Experiment 2

Spheres made of materials of different density, but all having a diameter of 1.0 cm, were dropped into a 2% solution of methyl cellulose, and the velocity of fall was measured.

Material	Density (g/cm³)	Velocity of fall (m/s)
Tungsten	14.5	1.54
Lead	11.0	1.14
Brass	9.1	0.93
Steel	8.0	0.80
Gymalloy	5.2	0.48
Aluminum	2.7	0.19
Lignum vitae	1.3	0.03

Experiment 3

The same steel spheres as in Experiment 1 were now dropped through at 4% solution of methyl cellulose.

Diameter of sphere (cm)	Velocity of fall (m/s)
0.5	0.07
1.0	0.27
1.5	0.60
2.0	1.07
2.5	1.65
3.0	2.41

23. If Experiment 1 were repeated using a lead sphere instead of steel, in what way would the readings in the second column compare to those in the second column for steel?
   A. They would all be larger.
   B. They would all be smaller.
   C. They would all be the same.
   D. There is no way to predict the results.

24. Why does a larger steel sphere fall at a higher velocity than a smaller one?
   F. The larger one has a greater surface area, so there is less viscous drag on it.
   G. Since the larger one is heavier, a larger viscous drag is required to keep it from increasing its speed.
   H. The larger sphere generates currents in the liquid that tend to push it along.
   J. The larger sphere has a greater density so it is less buoyant than the smaller one.

25. If a 1.0-cm steel sphere falls at 0.50 m/s through honey, what would be the rate of fall of a 2.0-cm steel sphere?
   A. 0.25 m/s
   B. 0.50 m/s
   C. 1.00 m/s
   D. 2.00 m/s

26. What is a reasonable conclusion obtained by comparing the results of Experiments 1 and 3?
   F. Viscous drag is three times as great in a 2% solution of methyl cellulose as in a 4% solution.
   G. Steel spheres fall three times as fast in a 2% solution of methyl cellulose as in a 4% solution.
   H. Larger steel spheres fall faster than smaller ones in a 4% solution of methyl cellulose.
   J. Doubling the density of a solution of methyl cellulose raises its viscous drag by a factor of 3.

27. Which of the following spheres would probably NOT sink at all if placed in a methyl cellulose solution?
   A. A 1.0-cm sphere of plastic with a density of 1.0 g/cm³
   B. A 0.3-cm brass sphere with a density of 8.0 g/cm³
   C. A 0.1-cm aluminum sphere with a density of 2.7 g/cm³
   D. A 3.0-cm teakwood sphere with a density of 1.3 g/cm³

GO ON TO THE NEXT PAGE.

4 4 4 4 4 4 4 4 4 4 **4**

Passage VI

The egg of a fruit fly hatches into a larva. After some days, the larva forms a shell around itself, turning into a pupa. In the pupa stage, it develops wings and legs and then emerges as an adult fly. The adult lives for some weeks.

Experiment 1

Eggs of a species of fruit fly, *Drosophila A,* were grown at different controlled temperatures, and the average number of days that the developing fly spent in each stage were recorded, as shown in the table below.

Temperature (° C)	Egg stage (days)	Larva stage (days)	Pupa stage (days)	Adult stage (days)
10	5	5	5	15
15	4	7	5	19
20	4	6	5	22
25	3	7	5	20
30	3	5	5	16

Experiment 2

An identical experiment was done with a different species, *Drosophila B:*

Temperature (° C)	Egg stage (days)	Larva stage (days)	Pupa stage (days)	Adult stage (days)
10	6	10	5	28
15	6	9	5	28
20	4	8	5	25
25	3	7	5	20
30	3	6	5	16

Experiment 3

Pupae of both species were moved from the 10° C room to the 25° C room as soon as the pupae formed. Adults of *Drosophila A* survived an average of 15 days, and of *Drosophila B* an average of 28 days.

28. In both species, which of the following effects is produced by higher temperatures?
   F. Faster development occurs through the egg stage.
   G. A larger fraction of the total life span is spent in the pupa stage.
   H. The larva stage is completed more quickly.
   J. Total life expectancy is greater.

29. Which of the following statements applies to both species?
   A. Larvae grow faster and larger at higher temperatures.
   B. The rate at which the egg grows into a larva is independent of temperature.
   C. The rate at which the larva changes into an adult is independent of temperature.
   D. Adults survive longer at lower temperatures.

30. Which of the following statements applies to *Drosophila B* but not to *Drosophila A?*
   F. At higher temperatures, all the early developmental stages are speeded up.
   G. Life expectancy is greatest at the lower temperatures.
   H. The flies that pass through their developmental stages quickest have the longest life spans.
   J. The duration of the pupa stage is the same at all temperatures.

31. Which of the following statements about the probable natural habitat of the two species is suggested by the data?
   A. *Drosophila A* is a tropical species.
   B. *Drosophila B* is a tropical species.
   C. *Drosophila A* is a cold-weather species.
   D. *Drosophila B* is a cold-weather species.

32. Experiment 3 suggests that the life expectancy of a fruit fly depends largely on the temperature during what part of its life cycle?
   F. Pupa
   G. Egg or larva or both
   H. Egg only
   J. Adult

33. Which of the following hypotheses is suggested by all the data?
   A. Fruit flies develop faster at higher temperatures.
   B. Optimum temperatures differ among different species of fruit fly.
   C. Fruit flies that develop faster live longer.
   D. Higher temperatures reduce the life expectancy of fruit flies.

GO ON TO THE NEXT PAGE.

Passage VII

Two scientists disagree on the question of how flight originated in birds.

Scientist 1

What kind of evolutionary process resulted in the flight of birds? The crucial information comes from study of the fossils of the earliest known bird, *Archaeopteryx*. This bird was bipedal, like all birds and also like the small dinosaurs that were its ancestors. We know that it was a very poor flyer, since its breastbone had no keel for the attachment of the wing muscles. This was a creature that lived mostly by running on the ground, like its ancestors. It is most unlikely that *Archaeopteryx* could climb trees, since its hind claw, used by modern birds for grasping limbs, was poorly developed. The long lower leg bone and the short upper one suggest that the bird was more adapted to running than to climbing. The whole skeleton suggests a creature that lived on the ground, running rapidly when necessary. I suggest that the stiff feathers of the wings were first used as a kind of net to trap insects and other small prey. The birds often leaped into the air in pursuit of their prey. Later, the wing feathers took on a second function, that of helping the birds to chase their prey through the air by crude flapping of the wings. As their flying ability improved, they could eventually fly well enough to rise into the trees.

Scientist 2

Evolution presents us with many instances in which vertebrates have acquired the power of flight. We have bats that fly as well as birds. The ability to glide has arisen independently in squirrels, frogs, lizards, the flying lemur, the sugar glider, and even in a snake. In all cases (except flying fish), the animals lived in trees and developed the power of gliding as an aid in getting from one tree to another. I believe the same is true of birds. The hypothesis that the flight feathers were first used as insect traps in a ground-living creature has several flaws. There is no animal that uses its forelimbs as an insect trap in the manner suggested. If it did, it could never learn to fly because the energy needed for an incompetent flyer to chase an insect through the air would be more than the benefit from catching it. Further, the hypothesis does not account for the stiff tail feathers, which have an obvious value in gliding. If the legs and claws of *Archaeopteryx* were imperfectly adapted to climbing, that is surely to be expected in a creature that recently made the transition from running on the ground to climbing in the trees. The tree kangaroo's legs, for example, clearly reflect its ground-living ancestry. If birds are to be considered an exception to the rule that flight originates in gliding, we need much better evidence.

34. What is the strongest argument against the hypothesis of Scientist 1?
    F. *Archaeopteryx* apparently did not live on the ground.
    G. In all other flying vertebrates, flight originated as gliding from tree to tree.
    H. Stiff feathers have no conceivable function in a ground-living bird.
    J. The teeth of *Archaeopteryx* show that it did not eat insects.

35. What property of *Archaeopteryx* is the strongest argument in favor of the hypothesis of Scientist 1?
    A. The shape of the wing feathers shows clearly that they were used for catching insects.
    B. The stiff tail feathers could not have been used to aid in gliding.
    C. The hind claw was clearly adapted for grasping tree limbs.
    D. The legs and claws were like those of a ground-living creature.

36. What is the significance of the anatomy of the tree kangaroo in supporting Scientist 2's position?
    F. It shows that gliding flight develops in tree-living animals.
    G. Although the tree kangaroo lives in trees, the proportions of its leg bones are much like those of a running animal.
    H. The tree kangaroo has fingers adapted for grasping the limbs of trees.
    J. Although the tree kangaroo can climb trees, its anatomy shows that it spends much of its time on the ground.

37. Which of the following discoveries would lend support to the position of Scientist 1?
    A. A lizard that runs and uses flaps of skin on its arms to trap insects
    B. A bird that can climb trees, but spends most of its time on the ground
    C. A fossil bird that had no flight feathers, but only soft body plumage
    D. A fossil dinosaur that was almost identical to *Archaeopteryx,* but had no feathers

38. What additional argument might Scientist 2 bring to refute the theory advanced by Scientist 1?
    F. The structure of the wings and feathers of *Archaeopteryx* shows that this bird could fly.
    G. A broad, flat surface formed by wing feathers would have so much air resistance that it would impede running.
    H. An animal that runs upright on its hind legs would be unable to capture any prey.
    J. There may have been many other kinds of birds whose fossils have never been found.

GO ON TO THE NEXT PAGE.

4 4 4 4 4 4 4 4 4 4 4 **4**

39. What kind of experimental evidence might Scientist 1 bring to refute one of the arguments of Scientist 2?
    A. Measurements showing that large insects are extremely high sources of food energy for birds
    B. A demonstration that gliding flight for tree-living animals takes very little energy
    C. Experiments showing that fast-running lizards are efficient hunters of insects
    D. A study that shows all gliding animals have descended from ground-living creatures

40. Which of the following statements would find the two scientists in disagreement?
    F. The anatomy of *Archaeopteryx* provides the most crucial evidence concerning the dispute.
    G. The earliest birds were descendants of a small dinosaur.
    H. The way the earliest birds developed the ability to fly was different from the process in all other flying vertebrates.
    J. *Archaeopteryx* was a poor and inefficient flyer.

END OF TEST 4

STOP! DO NOT RETURN TO ANY OTHER TEST.

ANSWER KEYS AND ANALYSIS CHARTS

ENGLISH TEST

1.	C	16.	G	31.	D	46.	F	61.	B
2.	J	17.	D	32.	F	47.	B	62.	J
3.	C	18.	H	33.	C	48.	J	63.	A
4.	J	19.	B	34.	F	49.	C	64.	G
5.	C	20.	H	35.	D	50.	G	65.	B
6.	J	21.	B	36.	G	51.	C	66.	F
7.	B	22.	H	37.	B	52.	F	67.	C
8.	H	23.	B	38.	H	53.	C	68.	H
9.	D	24.	J	39.	C	54.	G	69.	B
10.	F	25.	B	40.	G	55.	A	70.	G
11.	A	26.	H	41.	C	56.	H	71.	B
12.	G	27.	C	42.	J	57.	D	72.	J
13.	C	28.	F	43.	C	58.	H	73.	C
14.	J	29.	B	44.	G	59.	C	74.	F
15.	D	30.	J	45.	C	60.	J	75.	C

Analysis Chart

Skills	Questions	Possible Score	Your Score
Usage/Mechanics			
Punctuation	10, 11, 28, 32, 34, 50, 55, 63, 66, 74	10	
Basic Grammar and Usage	4, 5, 6, 24, 25, 29, 46, 49, 56, 59, 70, 73	12	
Sentence Structure	7, 8, 12, 14, 16, 27, 33, 40, 43, 44, 47, 48, 52, 54, 57, 61, 68, 69	18	
Rhetorical Skills			
Strategy	15, 18, 23, 26, 30, 35, 39, 41, 45, 51, 58, 67	12	
Organization	2, 13, 17, 19, 20, 21, 31, 36, 60, 64, 75	11	
Style	1, 3, 9, 22, 37, 38, 42, 53, 62, 65, 71, 72	12	

Total: 75 _____

Percent correct: _____

MATHEMATICS TEST

1.	D	13.	B	25.	D	37.	C	49.	C
2.	H	14.	J	26.	G	38.	J	50.	H
3.	B	15.	B	27.	A	39.	C	51.	E
4.	F	16.	H	28.	H	40.	J	52.	J
5.	D	17.	E	29.	A	41.	C	53.	A
6.	F	18.	H	30.	G	42.	K	54.	J
7.	B	19.	B	31.	B	43.	D	55.	E
8.	H	20.	H	32.	J	44.	H	56.	H
9.	D	21.	B	33.	C	45.	A	57.	C
10.	J	22.	F	34.	H	46.	J	58.	F
11.	A	23.	A	35.	D	47.	B	59.	C
12.	H	24.	K	36.	F	48.	J	60.	G

Analysis Chart

Content Area	Skill Level			Possible Score	Your Score
	Basic Skills	**Application**	**Analysis**		
Pre-Algebra Algebra	1, 7, 17, 21, 26, 32, 34, 49	2, 3, 4, 6, 9, 13, 18, 22, 30, 36, 46, 48	5, 14, 27, 31	24	
Intermediate Algebra Coordinate Geometry	2, 23, 28, 37, 40, 50, 54	11, 16, 29, 38, 39, 43, 53	33, 42, 44, 45	18	
Geometry	8, 15, 19, 20, 35, 56	10, 25, 51, 55, 57, 58, 59, 60		14	
Trigonometry	47, 52	24, 41		4	

Total: 60 _____

Percent correct: _____

READING TEST

1.	B	11.	C	21.	A	31.	A
2.	J	12.	J	22.	J	32.	H
3.	C	13.	D	23.	C	33.	A
4.	F	14.	J	24.	J	34.	H
5.	A	15.	A	25.	D	35.	B
6.	J	16.	H	26.	H	36.	J
7.	C	17.	A	27.	C	37.	D
8.	J	18.	F	28.	H	38.	H
9.	B	19.	B	29.	A	39.	A
10.	H	20.	H	30.	G	40.	J

Analysis Chart

Passage Type	Referring	Reasoning	Possible Score	Your Score
Natural Sciences	3, 4, 8, 9	1, 2, 5, 6, 7, 10	10	
Social Sciences	11, 12, 15	13, 14, 16, 17, 18, 19, 20	10	
Humanities	22, 25, 29	21, 23, 24, 26, 27, 28, 30	10	
Prose Fiction	31, 33, 35, 40	32, 34, 36, 37, 38, 39	10	

Total: 40 _____

Percent correct: _____

SCIENCE REASONING TEST

1.	B	11.	B	21.	B	31.	D
2.	J	12.	H	22.	G	32.	G
3.	C	13.	B	23.	A	33.	B
4.	J	14.	G	24.	G	34.	G
5.	B	15.	C	25.	D	35.	D
6.	G	16.	F	26.	G	36.	G
7.	B	17.	D	27.	A	37.	A
8.	J	18.	J	28.	F	38.	G
9.	A	19.	A	29.	C	39.	A
10.	J	20.	H	30.	G	40.	H

Analysis Chart

Kind of Question	Skill Level			Possible Score	Your Score
	Understanding	**Analysis**	**Generalization**		
Data Representation	1, 2, 7, 18	3, 4, 5, 8, 9, 10, 19, 20	6, 11, 12, 21, 22	17	
Research Summaries	13, 14, 23, 28, 29	15, 24, 25, 30	16, 17, 26, 27, 31, 32, 33	16	
Conflicting Viewpoints	34, 35	36, 37, 48	39, 40	7	

Total: 40 _____

Percent correct: _____

In conducting your review and practice in Part Three, pay particular attention to those areas that need the most work, according to the Analysis Charts above.

Answer Explanations: ENGLISH TEST

1. C The original version (A) and choice B are wordy. The underlined portion cannot be omitted (D) because the pronoun *which* is needed.

2. J Repetition of the preposition *among* creates a phrase that is parallel with *among the overweight*. In choice G *normal weighted* is awkward.

3. C The other options are awkward or wordy.

4. J The only choice that employs the proper pronoun and tense is J. The others either use a pronoun without an antecedent (F), omit a necessary pronoun (H), or use a tense incompatible with the tense of the sentence (G).

5. C The use of *his or her* or any such reflection that there are two sexes is now expected in popular English. The antecedent, *person,* is singular; therefore the pronoun which refers to it must be singular.

6. J The verb (*does*) must agree with its singular subject (*underweight*). In addition, the parenthetical adverb *incidentally* must be set off by two commas.

7. B Actually, choices A and B would be equal options if it were not for the phrase *being … overweight* in the following clause, with which the subject must be parallel. Choices C and D are unnecessarily wordy.

8. H This paragraph is written in the present tense.

9. D The simple gerund phrase *keeping one's weight* is clear and direct; the other choices are wordy or awkward.

10. F The phrase "according to the American Medical Association" is parenthetical and must be set off by commas.

11. A Coordinate clauses need to be separated by a comma. The two clauses are short and closely related and so do not require a stronger mark of separation like a semicolon or a period.

12. G *However* is the only transitional phrase listed that signals the contrasting statement that follows.

13. C Paragraph 2 is clearly an introductory statement. Paragraphs 3, 4, and 1 each become more specific and concrete.

14. J This choice is the most economical; the others are either redundant (F and H) or use an incorrect verb form (G).

15. D More specific details that define overweight would support the general statements made in the passage; the other suggestions are not relevant to the subject.

16. G A *way* to prove the need for nurses is not the long lines, but rather *to point out* the long lines. As this sentence appears (F), the predicate is not compatible with the subject.

17. D While somewhat related, this sentence has no bearing on the main arguments of the passage.

18. H Longer, more detailed, or emotional explanations and arguments would depart abruptly from the concise, one-line strategy of the passage. Obviously, arguments are necessary (G).

19. B This sentence is more remote in relevance than first appears. There is no reference to a hospital without nurses.

20. H Too many data in one sentence can obscure its main point. This is the only choice that presents the facts concisely and logically in keeping with the pattern of the passage.

21. B A summary of unfilled positions is the only information listed here that is appropriate in this paragraph. The other information is at least vaguely off the topic.

22. H The infinitive phrase (*to*) *turn away patients* is economical; the other choices are wordy (F), contain a pronoun without an antecedent (G), or are inappropriate in style (J).

23. B This paragraph really does not represent the opposing opinion very well and should support it with more detail.

24. J The opportunities are not greater than *programs*, but rather greater than opportunities *in* other programs.

25. B The pronoun *this* is almost never adequate alone; an explanatory noun is needed (*this need*). The other options supply nouns that are incompatible with the meaning of the sentence.

26. H From beginning to end, this passage is an attempt to persuade the reader that more nurses must be trained.

27. C The passage is written in the present tense.

28. F Separate three or more items in a series with commas and a conjunction.

Answer Explanations: ENGLISH TEST *(continued)*

29. B The pronoun *that* dangles without a clear antecedent like *service*. Meeting a shortage is not a philosophy (D).

30. J The target of this persuasive attempt to support the opening of another nursing school must be a body that can make such a decision.

31. D The conjunction *either* applies only to the words *inside* and *outside,* and so must be placed just before them.

32. F The plural of the proper name *Frobush* is *Frobushes;* the possessive is formed by adding the apostrophe after the pluralizing *s.*

33. C The tense of this passage is the simple past.

34. F A quotation must be separated from the preceding text by a comma; the exclamation point should be placed *inside* the quotation marks because the quoted utterance is the exclamation.

35. D This sentence has no bearing on the meaning of the passage and should be removed.

36. G A new paragraph begins at this point because a new subject (the police investigation) and line of action begin.

37. B Only the verb *theorized* results in an economical and meaningful sentence; the other options are either wordy or slang.

38. H The prepositional phrase *behind the house* is redundant; the words *back door* already convey that meaning.

39. C The point is that the passage is about a real burglary; among the items taken (jewelry) were a gold bracelet and necklace. We have not been told that Chuck is on drugs (B), and people do not always act sensibly (D).

40. G The phrase *While working* works best; the other options suggest the wrong meaning.

41. C From the outset, this narrative appears to be a very lean summary of a case; embellishment would be inappropriate.

42. J The correct answer maintains the strict, economical style of the passage; the other options are either incompatible in style or misleading in what they say.

43. C Without a period or semicolon, the sentence becomes a comma splice or run-on sentence. The period and new sentence options is most appropriate because of the significant statement made

in the second clause—that is, Goode's being formally accused of a crime.

44. G The conjunction at the beginning of the second clause must logically signal contrast. The words *but* and *however* do just that, but *however,* being a conjunctive adverb, requires a semicolon. *But* is the only possible choice.

45. C Because of its sparse, businesslike style, this passage is clearly one that provides background for a subsequent discussion on a point of law or trial procedure.

46. F The correlative conjunction *neither* means "not one of two," and is followed by *nor; either* means "one of two" and is followed by *or.*

47. B The correct choice presents a concise adverb clause properly modifying the following verb *explain.* There is no need for reference to the court calendar.

48. J Only the gerund *hearing* maintains the sequence of tenses; all other choices confuse the time of the sentence.

49. C Only the infinitive *come,* with the *to* elliptically omitted, sounds natural in this position; the other options are awkward.

50. G The adjective clause *which may be different for each county* is nonrestrictive, modifying *days and times,* and therefore must be set off by a comma.

51. C Some specific details illustrating the plea of a plaintiff, for example, would support the general points made in this passage. The inappropriate alternative answers stray far from the thesis of the passage.

52. F Other options either disagree with the subject in number (G), employ a verb that makes little sense (H), or use the wrong tense (J).

53. C The use of *him and her* or other such recognition that there are two sexes is now expected.

54. G A transitional word signaling contrast is needed here.

55. A A singular noun takes an apostrophe and *s* to indicate possession.

56. H Always use the principal noun enough to establish its presence in the sentence or paragraph.

57. D The correct answer (*works*) is parallel with the preceding verb (*lives*).

Answer Explanations: ENGLISH TEST *(continued)*

58. H Discussion of legal subtleties is compatible with the presence of a trained legal audience; the other options are either trivial or irrelevant.

59. C The correct choice is concise and clear; the others are awkward, wordy, or ungrammatical.

60. J Paragraph 4 begins with a clear, simple sentence explaining the point of the selection.

61. B The two clauses that join at this point contain enough substance to require a full-fledged sentence for each. Options A and C are wrong because they create run-on sentences. In D the word after the semicolon is incorrectly capitalized.

62. J The correct choice is clear and economical; the others are either wordy or result in an incomplete statement.

63. A Hyphenate a compound adjective that precedes the noun it modifies.

64. G The topic abruptly and completely moves from environmental initiatives to other initiatives, mandating a new paragraph.

65. B The adjective *diverse* is in keeping with the style of the passage and the sense of what follows.

66. F The conjunction *and* that marks the end of this long series of nouns needs itself to be preceded by a comma.

67. C Only the correct answer addresses the issue posed in the question. The other options deal with irrelevant material.

68. H The participial phrase preceding the underlined matter of this question is subordinate; *initiative process* is the subject of the sentence, and cannot be introduced by a relative pronoun.

69. B *In contrast* and *however* are both transitions indicating contrast; only one is required. The other options signal addition.

70. G The idiom *ranging from ... to ...* is completed by choice G. The other choices disrupt the structure of the sentence.

71. B The facts presented are simple and sparse; that is, the passage is journalistic.

72. J The phrase *strike down* is the only one compatible with the rest of the passage; the other options represent colloquial usage or slang and are therefore unsuitable.

73. C The subject (*reasons*) is plural, and so the verb must be; options B and D change the tense inappropriately.

74. F The three clauses at the end of this sentence are members of a series and require separation by commas.

75. C Paragraph 2 clearly introduces the subject, and must be the first paragraph in the passage.

Answer Explanations: MATHEMATICS TEST

1. D $0°$ is undefined.

2. H
$$7^2 - 2[3 + 2(5 - 1)] = 7^2 - 2[3 + 2(4)]$$
$$= 7^2 - 2[3 + 8]$$
$$= 7^2 - 2(11)$$
$$= 7^2 - 22$$
$$= 49 - 22 = 27$$
Follow the order of operation rules.

3. B
$$2x - 5 = 7 - 4x \quad \text{Add } 4x \text{ to both sides.}$$
$$6x - 5 = 7 \quad \text{Add 5 to both sides.}$$
$$6x = 12 \quad \text{Divide both sides by 6.}$$
$$x = 2$$

4. F What percent of 24 is 18? P is unknown, $A = 18$, and $B = 24$. The percent proportion is
$$\frac{P}{100} = \frac{18}{24}\left(= \frac{3}{4}\right)$$

5. D The number of curtains, C, can be found by division.
$$C = 20 \div 2\frac{1}{2} = 20 \div \frac{5}{2}$$
$$= \frac{20}{1} \cdot \frac{2}{5} = 8$$

Answer Explanations: MATHEMATICS TEST *(continued)*

6. F $2x - \{3x - 2[x - (1 - x)]\}$
$= 2x - \{3x - 2[x - 1 + x]\}$
$= 2x - \{3x - 2x + 2 - 2x\}$
$= 2x - 3x + 2x - 2 + 2x$
$= 3x - 2$

7. B $51 = (3)(17)$

8. H A secant line intersects a circle in two points. Line $\overleftrightarrow{AC}$ is a secant.

9. D Substituting the given values into $-x - xy^2$ yields
$-(-2) - (-2)(3^2) = -(-2) - (-2)(9)$
$= -(-2) - (-18)$
$= 2 + 18 = 20$

10. J The length of a tangent is the mean proportional between the length of a secant and the length of the external segment of the secant.
$$\frac{4}{6} = \frac{6}{CD + 4}$$
$$4(CD + 4) = 36$$
$$4CD + 16 = 36$$
$$4CD = 20$$
$$CD = 5$$

11. A These radicals can be multiplied since the indices are the same.
$$\sqrt[3]{4ab^2} \sqrt[3]{12a^4b^2} = \sqrt[3]{48a^5b^4}$$
Separate the radicand into cube and noncube factors.
$$= \sqrt[3]{(8a^3b^3)(6a^2b)}$$
$$= 2ab\sqrt[3]{6a^2b}$$

12. H A quadratic equation is one that is equivalent to $ax^2 + bx + c = 0$ for $a \neq 0$. Equation H is equivalent to
$$9 + 5x = 16 + 2x$$
$$3x - 7 = 0$$
This equation is linear.

13. B $(3x - 1)^2 = 9x^2 - 6x + 1$

14. J $5x - 2 = 2x + 1$

15. B Since an inscribed angle is measured by half of the intercepted arc, and the intercepted arc in a semicircle is $180°$, the triangle must be a right triangle.

16. H Using the special rule about absolute value inequalities, we have
$$|x - 1| \leq 3$$
$$-3 \leq x - 1 \leq 3$$
$$-2 \leq x \leq 4$$

17. E Point $(-4, 0)$ is located on the x-axis and is therefore not in any quandrant.

18. H Substitute each ordered pair into the equation.
$(-1, -1)$ $3(-1) - 2(-1)$ $\neq 5$
$(1, 1)$ $3(1) - 2(1)$ $\neq 5$
$(1, -1)$ $3(1) - 2(-1)$ $= 5$
$(-1, 1)$ $3(-1) - 2(1)$ $\neq 5$

19. B If two lines in a plane are cut by a transversal so that a pair of corresponding angles are equal, the lines are parallel. Angles 2 and 6 are corresponding angles.

20. H A segment from a vertex of a triangle to the midpoint of the opposite side is a median. BD is a median.

21. B $\frac{5}{12} + \frac{7}{18} = \frac{15}{36} + \frac{14}{36}$ The LCD is 36.
$$= \frac{29}{36}$$

22. F $\dfrac{2}{3} - \dfrac{2 - \frac{5}{6}}{2^3 - 1} \div \dfrac{1}{2} = \dfrac{2}{3} - \dfrac{2 - \frac{5}{6}}{8 - 1} \div \dfrac{1}{2}$

$= \dfrac{2}{3} - \dfrac{2 - \frac{5}{6}}{7} \div \dfrac{1}{2}$ Multiply by 6.

$= \dfrac{2}{3} - \dfrac{12 - 5}{42} \div \dfrac{1}{2}$

$= \dfrac{2}{3} - \dfrac{7}{42} \div \dfrac{1}{2} = \dfrac{2}{3} - \dfrac{1}{6} \div \dfrac{1}{2} = \dfrac{2}{3} - \dfrac{1}{6} \cdot \dfrac{2}{1}$

$= \dfrac{2}{3} - \dfrac{1}{3} = \dfrac{1}{3}$

23. A Let $x = \log_3 27$.
Then $3^x = 27 = 3^3$
$x = 3$

24. K From the identity $\cos^2 \theta + \sin^2 \theta = 1$, we have
$$\cos^2 \theta + \left(\frac{1}{2}\right)^2 = 1$$
$$\cos^2 \theta + \frac{1}{4} = 1$$
$$\cos^2 \theta = \frac{3}{4}$$
$$\cos \theta = \pm \frac{\sqrt{3}}{2}$$

The $\pm$ sign is appropriate because, if all that is known is that the sine of the angle is $\frac{1}{2}$, the angle may be in either quadrant I or II, and in one of these quadrants the cosine is positive but in the other it is negative.

Answer Explanations: MATHEMATICS TEST *(continued)*

25. D Since $\triangle ABC$ is isosceles, $m\angle A = m\angle B = 40°$. The sum of the angles of any triangle $= 180°$.

$$m\angle C + 40° + 40° = 180°$$
$$m\angle C = 100°$$

26. G Compare the decimal forms of the four numbers.

3.1415926

$\dfrac{22}{7} = 3.\overline{142857}$

3.14

3.1416

Since $\dfrac{22}{7} = 3.\overline{142857}$ has the larger digit in the first position in which the digits differ, it is the largest number.

27. A Joan must read n pages, where

$$n = 80 - \frac{4}{5}(80)$$
$$= 80 - 64 = 16$$

28. H A pure imaginary number is a number of the type bi, where b is a real number and $i = \sqrt{-1}$. $\sqrt{-4} = 2i$.

29. A The graph is a hyperbola. The equations represent
A. Hyperbola   B. Ellipse   C., D., and
E. Parabolas

30. G
$$2x + y = -1$$
$$3x - 2y = -19 \quad \text{Multiply the top equation by 2.}$$
$$4x + 2y = -2$$
$$3x - 2y = -19 \quad \text{Add the two equations.}$$
$$7x = -21$$

$$x = -3 \quad \text{Substitute } -3 \text{ into the top}$$
$$2(-3) + y = -1 \quad \text{equation for } x.$$
$$-6 + y = -1$$
$$y = 5$$

31. B $451_{(eight)} = 4(8^2) + 5(8^1) + 1(8^0)$
$$= 4(64) + 5(8) + 1$$
$$= 256 + 40 + 1 = 297$$

32. J The identity property of addition states symbolically that
$$a + 0 = 0 + a = a$$
Therefore the appropriate right side of the given equation is $5 + 7$.

33. C If $a < b$, then $a - b < 0$ and
$$|a - b| = -(a - b) = b - a$$
So $|a - b| + a + b = b - a + a + b$
$$= 2b$$

34. H $6{,}440 = (2)(2)(2)(5)(7)(23)$

35. D Supplementary angles are two angles whose sum is $180°$. Angles 8 and 9 are supplementary.

36. F
$$13\frac{1}{4} \qquad 13\frac{2}{8}$$
$$= $$
$$-7\frac{5}{8} \qquad -7\frac{5}{8} \quad \text{We must borrow } 1\left(=\frac{8}{8}\right) \text{ from the 13.}$$

$$12\frac{10}{8}$$
$$-7\frac{5}{8}$$
$$\overline{5\frac{5}{8}}$$

37. C The degree of a polynomial is the greatest of the degrees of all of its terms. The degree of each term is the sum of the exponents on the variables in that term. The degrees of the three terms of the given polynomial are 5, 3, 1, respectively.

38. J From the quadratic formula, the sum of the roots of any quadratic equation is $-\dfrac{b}{a}$. In the given quadratic equation, $a = 4$ and $b = 3$, so the sum of the roots is $-\dfrac{3}{4}$.

39. C
$$16^{-(3\backslash4)} = \frac{1}{16^{3\backslash4}}$$
$$= \frac{1}{(\sqrt[4]{16})^3}$$
$$= \frac{1}{2^3} \qquad = \frac{1}{8}$$

40. J Exponential curves are not conic sections.

41. C Since $215°$ is in quadrant III, the value of the sine will be negative, and the reference angle is $215° - 180° = 35°$. So $\sin 215° = -\sin 35°$. But this is not one of the options. Therefore, making use of the rule that states the cofunctions of complementary angles are equal, we have

$$-\sin 35° = -\cos(90° - 35°) = -\cos 55°$$

42. K The question is "How many permutations are there of 6 things taken 6 at a time?"

$$_6P_6 = \frac{6!}{(6-6)!} = \frac{6!}{0!}$$
$$= \frac{6 \cdot 5 \cdot 4 \cdot 3 \cdot 2 \cdot 1}{1}$$
$$= 720$$

43. D The expression -2^{-2} is properly read as "the opposite of 2 to the negative second power." Hence

$$-(2^{-2}) = -\frac{1}{2^2}$$
$$= -\frac{1}{4}$$

Answer Explanations: MATHEMATICS TEST *(continued)*

44. H The area of the circle is $A = \pi r^2 = \pi$, and the area of the semicircle is $A = \frac{1}{2}\pi r^2$. Therefore

$$\frac{1}{2}\pi r^2 = \pi$$
$$\pi r^2 = 2\pi$$
$$r^2 = 2$$
$$r = \sqrt{2}$$

45. A The equation must be put into standard form, $(x - h)^2 + (y - k)^2 = r^2$, by completing the square in each variable.

$$x^2 + 4x \qquad + y^2 - 18y \qquad = -69$$
$$x^2 + 4x + 4 + y^2 - 18y + 81 = -69 + 4 + 81$$
$$(x + 2)^2 + (y - 9)^2 \qquad = 16$$

The center is $(-2, 9)$, and the radius is 4.

46. J This is an application of the distance formula
$$d^2 = (x_1 - x_2)^2 + y_1 - y_2)^2$$

Here
$$\begin{aligned}d^2 &= [5 - (-2)]^2 + (3 - 4)^2 \\ &= 7^2 + (-1)^2 \\ &= 49 + 1 = 50 \\ d &= \sqrt{50} = 5\sqrt{2}\end{aligned}$$

47. B Coterminal angles are found by adding or subtracting multiples of 360°.
$$846° - 2(360°) = 846° - 720° = 126°$$

48. J Rephrasing the problem in the format of a percent problem gives "60 is 80% of what number?" $A = 60$, $P = 80\%$, B is unknown.

$$\frac{80}{100} = \frac{60}{B}$$
$$\frac{4}{5} = \frac{60}{B}$$
$$4B = 300$$
$$B = 75$$

49. C $7(10^4) + 3(10^3) + 2(10^1) + 9(10^0)$

$$\begin{aligned}&= 7(10{,}000) + 3(1{,}000) + 2(10) + 9(1) \\ &= 70{,}000 + 3{,}000 + 20 + 9 \\ &= 73{,}029\end{aligned}$$

50. H The sample space contains 36 pairs of numbers. Among them are 2, 6; 3, 5; 4, 4; 5, 3; and 6, 2. Therefore, 5 out of 36 pairs satisfy the condition of having a sum of 8. P (sum of 8) $= \frac{5}{36}$.

51. E The measures of $\angle BAD$ and $\angle ABC$ are equal because $\overline{AD} \| \overline{BC}$. The measure of an inscribed angle is half of the intercepted arc, so the measure of arc AC is 30°. Since AB is a diameter, the measure of arc ACB is 180°. Therefore

$$m\overset{\frown}{BC} = 180° - 30° = 150°.$$

52. J The period of the sine function
$$y = A \sin B(x - C) \text{ is } \frac{2\pi}{|B|}.$$
The period of the given function is $\frac{2\pi}{5}$.

53. A The y-intercept of a graph is found at the ordered pairs where the x value is 0. Substituting $x = 0$, we find that $y = -8$.

54. J In the slope-intercept form of the equation of a line, $y = mx + b$, m is the slope. Solving the equation for y, we have

$$2x - 5y = 7$$
$$-5y = -2x + 7$$
$$y = \frac{2}{5}x - \frac{7}{5}$$

The slope of the graph is $\frac{2}{5}$.

55. E In a right triangle, the leg $\overline{AB}$ is the mean proportional between its projection on the hypotenuse (the segment AD) and the entire hypotenuse.

$$\frac{3}{4} = \frac{4}{x}$$
$$3x = 16$$
$$x = \frac{16}{3}$$

56. H The sum of the interior angles of any n-gon is
Here
$$\begin{aligned}S &= (n - 2)180° \\ S &= (6 - 2)180° \\ &= 4(180°) = 720°\end{aligned}$$

57. C The measure of an angle formed by the intersection of two chords in a circle is $\frac{1}{2}$ the sum of the measures of the intercepted arcs.

$$50 = \frac{1}{2}(20 + m\overset{\frown}{AD})$$
$$100 = 20 + m\overset{\frown}{AD}$$
$$m\overset{\frown}{AD} = 80$$

Since $\overline{AB}$ is a diameter,

$$m\overset{\frown}{AD} + m\overset{\frown}{DB} = 180$$
$$80 + m\overset{\frown}{DB} = 180$$
$$m\overset{\frown}{DB} = 100$$

Answer Explanations: MATHEMATICS TEST *(continued)*

58. F In similar triangles, the following ratios are equal:

$$\frac{6}{x} = \frac{10}{85}$$
$$10x = 510$$
$$x = 51$$

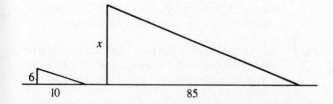

59. C Drawing a segment from $B \perp \overline{AD}$ forms a 30° -60°-90° triangle with hypotenuse 6. Therefore the length of the altitude of the parallelogram is $3\sqrt{3}$. The area of a parallelogram is $A = bh = 8(3\sqrt{3}) = 24\sqrt{3}$.

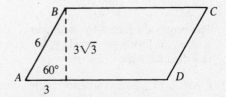

60. G The sum of the angles of a triangle equals 180°.

$$(x + 15) + (3x - 75) + (2x - 30) = 180$$
$$6x - 90 = 180$$
$$6x = 270$$
$$x = 45$$

Substituting 45 into each of the angle measures gives

$$45 + 15 = 60$$
$$3(45) - 75 = 135 - 75 = 60$$
$$2(45) - 30 = 90 - 30 = 60$$

All three angles of the triangle are equal, so the triangle is equilateral.

Answer Explanations: READING TEST

1. B Much of the first part of the passage is devoted to a discussion of the health-related problems caused by dirty air.

2. J The second paragraph states that indoor air is "often two-to-five times more polluted than outdoor air."

3. C All but diphtheria are mentioned in the passage as health problems caused by indoor air pollution.

4. F The prime breeding ground for mold and fungi are unsanitary ventilation systems, according to lines 45–47.

5. A Line 16 indicates that young children, who may spend most of their time indoors, are among the people most susceptible to indoor air pollution.

6. J In the words of EPA experts, the control of indoor air pollution is "a challenge that we are only now recognizing" (lines 24–25).

7. C The causes of indoor air pollution listed in lines 18–26 are mostly man-made. Only radon is a "natural" cause.

8. J Cleaner houses are more apt to contain cleaner air. Because people have less time to devote to home cleaning, indoor air may be dirtier than it was in the past, according to lines 66–72.

9. B Lines 75–79 discuss the effects of using home-maintenance products that have toxic effects.

10. H Although cigarette smoke may cause respiratory problems in children, it won't cause lung cancer until later in life.

11. C Lines 75–77 say that 80 percent of childhood stutterers speak normally by the time they reach adulthood.

12. J Lines 21–32, which discuss signs of stuttering, include all the choices *except* trembling head and hands.

Answer Explanations: READING TEST *(continued)*

13. D Line 85 indicates that stutterers speak easily when talking to small children.

14. J Line 14 suggests that only a high frequency of word repetition should alert parents to a stuttering problem.

15. A Line 60 indicates that stuttering commonly begins after a child has begun to talk automatically.

16. H All the old antidotes for stuttering described in lines 36–45 involve forms of physical therapy.

17. A Lines 65–72 list stressful situations that provoke stuttering.

18. F If stuttering were a physical disorder, stutterers would probably never enjoy moments of speaking freely.

19. B Much of the passage raises questions about the causes of stuttering. Line 34 says that the "underlying cause remains a mystery."

20. H The passage never discusses attitudes toward people who stutter. Therefore, choice H is irrelevant.

21. A Items 5 and 6 at lines 62–70 imply that a constructed language is derived from several existing languages or is built from scratch. Either way, it must differ from any existing language.

22. J Lines 79–82 say that some 3,000 natural languages and at least 1,000 constructed languages exist.

23. C The premise implied throughout the passage is that mankind will be better off with a universal language. Choices A and B are too specific. Choice D refers to Comenius's proposal, which did *not* call for a universal language.

24. J Because the words of Wilkins' language, mentioned in lines 17–21, were newly coined, the language is considered a constructed language.

25. D Lines 79–84 make the point that there are plenty of languages to choose from, but an agreement about which language to use remains the major problem.

26. H Lines 8–10 explain that Descartes' logical scheme failed to reflect the way actual languages are constructed.

27. C Lines 29–30 say that the type of solution proposed by Comenius is "still widely advocated today."

28. H Of the six types of languages listed, four are based on existing languages.

29. A Lines 12–14 state that Descartes' contemporaries offered proposals because Descartes failed to offer an example of his scheme.

30. G Lines 15–17 make the point that languages built on logic alone won't work because they lack the familiarity and ease of natural languages.

31. A The narrator says his father sent him to public school to make him "hardy" (line 3). Later he mentions that flogging was the way to make "a man of parts" (lines 33–34), an expression that means a solid, well-rounded individual.

32. H The narrator defines the phrase in lines 14–15: "I have always been an idle fellow and prone to play the vagabond," that is, someone who likes to wander about aimlessly.

33. A The boy is distracted by "seductions" (line 17) such as the lovely green valley, the little stream, and the blue hills.

34. H Lines 8–11 say that inferior cattle—those that are slow or have short legs—suffer as a result.

35. B In lines 27–29, the narrator says that as a youth he thought flogging was a standard practice in education.

36. J Many details in the paragraph about the squire (lines 37–57) refer to people who humble themselves in the squire's presence.

37. D The passage was not written as a social or political commentary on England. It's more personal and light-hearted.

38. H Line 77 implies that Waller's poems were "lavished upon Sacharissa."

39. A The narrator's point of view throughout the passage is somewhat ironic, as though he is poking fun at the situations and people in his youth.

40. J He is flogged for "trespassing on Parnassus" (line 91), the mythical place where only Gods dwell. By writing poetry, he overstepped the acceptable boundaries of behavior for schoolboys.

Answer Explanations: SCIENCE REASONING TEST

1. B Find the position of 13 on the vertical scale, and move to the right horizontally from there. You will find yourself crossing Portugal, Hungary, and (a little higher) Finland. On the horizontal scale, Portugal is at 75 and Finland is at a little under 120.

2. J Israel and the United States are on the same horizontal line, both with about 20 deaths per 100,000. Their wide separation along this axis shows that they differ greatly in fat intake. Israel and Greece are on the same vertical line, so they have the same fat intake; the separation along this axis shows different death rates. Austria and Germany are not widely separated. France and Mexico are widely separated along both axes, showing that both the death rates and the fat intakes differ greatly.

3. C The general slope of the chart from lower left to upper right shows that there is a broad, general tendency for an increased rate of breast cancer in countries where the average fat intake is greatest. A is wrong because the data do not exclude many other possible causal relationships. B is wrong because the average fat intake in a country is a cultural habit, and the data are taken from the population as a whole, not just women with cancer. D is wrong because no evidence relating either diet or cancer to environmental pollution was presented.

4. J The point for South Africa is far above the general trend, indicating that this country has an extraordinarily high rate of breast cancer compared with its expected rate from the other data. All the other countries named lie within the general trend.

5. B The points of Greece and Spain are no further off the main trend than most of the others; many factors are involved in causing breast cancer. However, there is nothing in the data to implicate either sunshine or olive oil. D is wrong because many of the differences between countries are far too substantial to be blamed on uncertainty in the data.

6. G Although there may be many uncontrolled variables in changing Japan, the whole study seems to show a relationship between fat consumption and breast cancer, and this would be confirmed if the relationship held up in a single country. F is wrong because there is no significant difference between data for the United States and for Europe. H is wrong because this evidence would not represent additional data: South Africa is already on the chart. J is wrong because the chart gives no data distinguishing white from black Americans.

7. B There is a definite dip in the high-temperature limit on this date, and the humidity at noon shown on the graph is around 80%.

8. J Look at all the days in which the high temperature is above normal, shown in black. The only dates on which the temperature did not get above normal were 1, 2, 20, 22, and 23.

9. A Although on most days the low temperature was a little above the normal low, it rarely got very far above. In contrast, there were many days in which the hot part of the day was very hot indeed.

10. J The longest stretch of very high humidity was on July 21 through July 24, coinciding with the period when the daily high temperature was near or below normal. Humidity changes during the day are not given.

11. B Both the normal high and the normal low for the day increase by about 2°F from the beginning of the month to the end, so it is reasonable to assume that the daily average does so also. A describes the full range of temperature for each day, not the daily average. The values given in B and D are monthly averages, not daily averages.

12. H The weather was unusually hot; the use of air conditioning could produce a shortage of electric energy. The precipitation averages show that there was plenty of rainfall. Nothing in the data indicates that there would be any unusual use of gas.

13. B Since it is known at the outset that Strain B is much more likely to develop cancer than Strain A, answer choices A and D are wrong. The effectiveness of benzol in producing cancer in each of the three strains can only be discovered by comparing mice given benzol with mice that do not get it. Nothing prevents comparison with wild mice.

14. G The vaccine did have some effect in all three groups. Although the experiment gives no information about the usefulness of the treatments in humans, there is no reason to doubt that a method for complete prevention will someday be found. The differences among the three groups must be due to differences in heredity, since all received the same treatment.

15. C In Strain B, which has a hereditary cancer defect, the vaccine reduced the incidence of cancer from 98 percent to 61 percent, while fexadrin had no effect. Fexadrin was helpful in wild mice, but not at all in Strain B.

Answer Explanations: SCIENCE REASONING TEST *(continued)*

16. F Whatever the rates of cancer in human beings or the presence of hereditary tendencies, the vaccine might turn out to be of use. However, the experiment was done only on cancers produced in mice by benzol, which might be entirely different from any spontaneous human cancer.

17. D Answers to the questions in F, G, and H might provide valuable information about the causes of cancer and the physiological mechanisms that protect the body. But benzol already gives cancer to nearly all the mice in Strain B, and any increase is not likely to yield useful information.

18. J The bar for insect consumption is much smaller than 33% for all the other species.

19. A The only nonanimal food shown is seaweed, and there the bar for *Lipophrys* is longer than any other. B is wrong because about 3% of the *Nerophis* sample contained molluscs. C is wrong because several of the fishes use food from all 5 groups. D is wrong because the graph shows only how many fishes contained the food, but *not* how much.

20. H Most *Lipophrys* stomachs contain molluscs, while very few of the others do. To get much nourishment out of molluscs, the fish has to break their shells. Note that B is wrong, in part, because only 2 members of the genus have been tested.

21. B *Nerophis* seems to live almost entirely on crustaceans, since very little of any other kind of food is found in its stomach. A is wrong because none of the fishes depends heavily on polychates. C is wrong because *Lipophrys* eats many other kinds of food as well as molluscs. D is wrong because *G. paganellus* eats many kinds of food.

22. G *Lipophrys* and *G. cobitis* eat a wide variety of food, while *Ciliata, Nerophis,* and *G. paganellus* depend very heavily on crustaceans.

23. A Experiment 2 shows that with equal diameters the denser lead sphere falls faster than the steel sphere. It is reasonable to suppose that this would hold true for any lead and steel spheres of equal diameter.

24. G You are told that at constant speed the viscous drag is equal to the weight of the ball. A heavy ball has to be going at a higher velocity to get more viscous drag than a light one. Neither surface area (F) nor density (J) enters the question, and there is no reason to believe that any significant currents (H) are generated.

25. D The data of Experiment 1 show that the velocity of a 2.0-cm ball is four times as great as that of a 1.0-cm ball. There is no reason to believe that the rule would be any different in honey.

26. G Comparing the speeds of any pair of steel spheres in the two different media will reveal that the speed in the 2% solution is three times as great as in the 4% solution. Choice F is wrong because it has the effect reversed; if the speed is greater in the 2% solution, the drag must be smaller, not greater. H is wrong because this effect is seen in either of the two experiments, and no comparison is needed. J is wrong because there is no reason to believe that the density of a 4% solution is twice as great as the density of a 2% solution; in fact, it is not.

27. A Experiment 2 shows that, at any density larger than 1, the ball falls. However, as the density gets closer to 1, the speed of the ball slows up enormously and could be expected to drop to 0 when the density gets to 1.

28. F In both species, the length of time in the egg stage is smallest at higher temperatures. G is wrong because this is true for *Drosophila B,* but not for *Drosophila A,* where life span is maximum at 20°C. H is wrong because the duration of the larva stage for *Drosophila A* does not follow any clear rule. J is wrong because in both species, life is short at the highest temperature.

29. C The larva changes into an adult during the pupa stage, which always lasts just 5 days in both species. A is wrong because, in part, we have no information as to how large the larvae grow. B is wrong because the duration of the egg stage does in fact depend on temperature. D applies to *Drosophila B,* but not to *Drosophila A.*

30. G For *Drosophila B,* there is a clear decrease in duration of the adult stage as the temperature rises. F and J are wrong because these rules apply to both species. H is not true for either species.

31. D *Drosophila B* survives longest in the coldest weather, so it must be a cold-weather species.

32. G For both species, the duration of the adult stage is the same whether the pupae are kept at 10° or they are moved into a warmer room, so the temperature of the adult or pupa stage does not matter. The data show that the life span depends on the temperature in the pre-pupae stages, but do not distinguish between egg and larva stages.

33. B Optimum temperature for *Drosophila A* is about 20° C, and for *Drosophila B* 10° C. The other

Answer Explanations: SCIENCE REASONING TEST *(continued)*

choices are wrong because the data are ambiguous for the larva stage of *Drosophila A*.

34. G With so much precedent, any deviation would have to be backed by extremely persuasive evidence. F is wrong because the evidence for ground-living is highly ambiguous. H is wrong because Scientist 1 has suggested a use for these feathers. J is wrong; whether the first bird ate insects is not a point of contention.

35. D There is no disagreement that the legs of *Archaeopteryx* showed adaptation to life on the ground; the question is whether, as Scientist 2 claims, this is in the process of change. A is wrong because no such evidence is presented. B is wrong because the tail feathers might well be used in gliding. C is wrong because a hind claw adapted for grasping tree limbs would strengthen the case for Scientist 2.

36. G This would be a situation parallel to that envisioned by Scientist 2, in which the legs are in the process of change. None of the other choices has any pertinence.

37. A If such a method of feeding developed once, it might have happened in *Archaeopteryx*. B would be completely ambiguous, supporting neither hypothesis. Either scientist could accept C or D as a precursor of *Archaeopteryx*.

38. G If the feathered wings are slowing the creature down, this would interfere with the method of feeding proposed by Scientist 1. Both scientists agree to F. H is wrong because many lizards feed this way. J is completely immaterial.

39. A This might call into question Scientist 2's claim that the energy expended in catching insects as Scientist 1 suggests would not pay off. B is wrong because it is not this kind of activity that is in question. C does not address the problem of flight. Both scientists would agree that D is true, and has no impact on the argument.

40. H Scientist 1 says that birds evolved from the ground up; Scientist 2 believes that, like other flying vertebrates, they lived originally in trees. They agree on the other three choices.

PART THREE

Review and Practice for the ACT

1 English Review and Practice

DESCRIPTION OF THE ENGLISH TEST

The English Test consists of 75 multiple-choice questions based on five prose passages with portions of their text underlined and numbered. Next to each numbered part are four responses corresponding to the test item. Sometimes the question will attempt to measure your understanding of usage and mechanics. You will have to decide whether to leave the underlined text as it is or substitute one of the choices. Other questions will attempt to measure your understanding of rhetorical skills, such as the order of items within a passage, the organization of a passage, or the appropriateness or consistency of the language. Questions measuring rhetorical skills may ask you to select how a general statement might be better supported or whether a different arrangement of the passage's parts might be more meaningful. You have 45 minutes to complete the 75 items.

Here is a quick view of the test itself. Read this passage and answer the questions. Do not refer to the correct answers (given below each set of choices) until you have tried to answer the questions yourself.

Sample Passage

All creatures in the animal kingdom have the instincts of curiosity and fear. Man alone was endowed with <u>imagination, which</u> was bound to complicate mat-

1
ters for him. Whereas a fox, let us say, was able to shrug off the mysteries of the heavens and such whims of nature as lightning and earthquakes, man <u>had</u>

2
<u>demanded</u> an explanation.

2

And so began the myths, the ancient creeds, witch-craft, astrology, <u>they told fantastic tales</u> of wanderings

3
into the unknown reaches of space and time, the distortions of the mental and physical capabilities of man himself. Evidently, these "explanations" were not enough: Man developed a thirst for something *beyond* the ever-growing knowledge brought to him by empirical scientific research. The French call this *le culte de merveilleux.* We call it science fiction. [4]

1. A. NO CHANGE
   B. imagination; which
   C. imagination, a fact that
   D. imagination, on which

(CORRECT ANSWER: **C**)

2. F. NO CHANGE
   G. had been demanding
   H. demanded
   J. demands

(CORRECT ANSWER: **H**)

3. A. NO CHANGE
   B. fantastic tales
   C. They were told fantastic tales
   D. fireside stories

(CORRECT ANSWER: **B**)

4. If the writer wanted to include more information about the early history of science fiction, which of the following would be most effective for the passage as a whole?
   F. A listing of current science fiction writers
   G. A discussion of recent science fiction movies
   H. A discussion of the "fantastic tales" that were the origin of science fiction
   J. A discussion of witchcraft

(CORRECT ANSWER: **H**)

The *Usage/Mechanics* questions test your understanding of punctuation, grammar, and sentence structure. These questions stress the use of *clear, effective, concise* language. Inappropriate or incorrect choices can often be detected by the way in which they confuse the structure of the sentence or obscure its meaning. A description of the three categories follows, together with the percentage of the test devoted to each.

1. *Punctuation* ✓	13%	These questions concern the use of punctuation marks (apostrophes, colons, commas, dashes, exclamation points, hyphens, parentheses, question marks, quotation marks, and semicolons) and, in particular, their function in clarifying the *meaning of the prose selection*.
2. *Basic Grammar and Usage* ✓	16%	Items in this category test your knowledge and understanding of verbs, adverbs, and adjectives; subject-verb agreement, and agreement of pronoun and antecedent; and the proper use of connectives.
3. *Sentence Structure* ✓	24%	These items deal with the makeup of the sentence, including the relationship of clauses, the correct use and placement of modifiers, parallelism, and consistency in point-of-view and tense.

The *Rhetorical Skills* questions will refer to a specific portion of the text or to the passage as a whole, including the logical sequence of sentences or paragraphs, and the order, appropriateness, or sufficiency of supporting details. You may be asked to choose a term that describes the passage, such as "critical," "emotional," "dispassionate," or "accusatory." Or you may be asked to select a phrase that describes the type of reader for whom the selection is intended. The *Rhetorical Skills* questions are almost equally distributed among three categories: strategy, organization, and style.

1. *Strategy* ✓	16%	Questions on strategy involve examination of some of the options the author has decided upon. Chief among these is the author's choice of supporting material. Is it effective, appropriate, and sufficient in amount and quality? Another author option is the choice of writing vehicle—for example, the descriptive essay, the persuasive essay, the biography, or the comparison-contrast model. You will be asked to make some judgments concerning the writer's handling of these options.
2. *Organization* ✓	15%	Questions on organization will most often involve rearrangement of sentences in a paragraph or paragraphs within a passage. You may also be asked to spot extraneous material that has little or nothing to do with the main idea, and to indicate places where additional material might strengthen the paragraph.
3. *Style* ✓	16%	In these questions, you may be asked to choose an adjective that best describes the style of the prose passage, to select the best phrase of several that have the same words but in a different order, or to choose alternative words. You will be asked to select text that matches the style and tone of the passage, and to choose words or phrases that most concisely express an idea.

LONG-RANGE STRATEGY

As a student planning to take the ACT test, you are already engaged in what is probably the most important of the long-term strategies, that is, learning as much as you can about the test and about the questions you are expected to answer. The English Test questions are quite straightforward, not tricky or devious. They seek to measure your ability to recognize clear and meaningful prose, and to identify word combinations that are either incorrect or less effective than others.

If you feel unsure of your prose "ear" (the language sense you have developed over the years), your best strategy is to review this chapter several times. As you examine each section, think of the materials presented to you as a general review of problem areas, rather than as specific data to memorize or master. The English language has too many options to commit to memory. In each lesson, try to see the general rule and its purpose.

It is a good idea to go over several times any item that you find unfamiliar or difficult. Work on your trouble spots by taking the practice exercises more than once and by reviewing the answers and explanations as often as necessary, since the explanations themselves will help serve as mini-reviews.

More suggestions:

- If you have enough time before you take the actual test, improve your prose "ear" by reading good, informative prose under relaxed conditions, perhaps even on a daily, limited basis. A list of suggested prose reading materials is on pages 288–289.
- Be sure you understand the format of the English Test, the time limitations, the number and types of questions, and the form of the answer sheet.
- Discuss the test frankly with your English teacher. Ask about your strengths and weaknesses in the skills to be tested. Does your teacher see anything in your habits or work that suggests problems you may have with the test? If so, how can you deal with those problems?
- Search out all avenues of help. Perhaps your school counselor has practice tests or other materials on test taking. Also, if there are ACT study groups in your school or community, join one, by all means. The additional practice will give you confidence, and you will find that sharing problems with other prospective test-takers is another good way to build confidence. Consult the on-line help at the *www.act.org* web site.
- Talk with your friends and family about the test and any fears you might have. Keep in mind that the ACT is only one of several means by which you will be evaluated and your admission to a college or university determined. Do not magnify its importance to the degree that you cannot prepare or perform effectively.

Anxiety affects your perception and use of language. Before you take the ACT test, you should come to terms in your own mind that you will do your best and that nobody, including yourself, has a right to ask more of you than that.

Now, look over the Test-taking Tactics that follow, and practice the habits and skills that will help you do your best.

SHORT-RANGE STRATEGY

1. **Concentrate.** On the morning of the test, reduce as many of your distractions, obligations, and plans as possible. Have no social events planned—either before or after the test—so that your full attention is on your answers. Leave adequate time to arrive at the test center. It is better to be a little early.
2. **Work carefully.** Before you arrive, be familiar with the test directions. When the test begins, listen carefully to any directions read to you by a proctor or played on a tape. In marking the answer sheet, be sure to put each answer in the right space. If you skip a question because it is taking too much time, be careful to skip the corresponding space on the answer sheet. Focus only on the test; block out any distractions.

TACTICS

3. **Pace yourself.** You have 45 minutes to answer 75 questions, or roughly nine minutes for each passage and its questions. It is wise to assume that some passages and some questions will be more difficult for you, so that you may wish to complete others that are easier and to return to the more difficult ones before the test ends. Occasionally,

stop to check the time, to be sure you are working at a good pace and will have time both to complete the test and to review your work.

2. **Read with a purpose.** The five passages cover a wide range of topics and are written in different styles. In responding to questions, you should be aware of these differences in writing style. Before you begin to answer the questions, quickly skim the passage. Then, answer each question in light of its context. If you are unsure of a question or your answer, read the sentences immediately before and after the sentence with the underlined part.

3. **Carefully examine the underlined parts.** Think about the principles of usage involved in each question and focus on the one that applies. Many of the questions concern more than one aspect of usage, especially in the answer options. Be sure that the answer you choose does not introduce another error while correcting the first!

4. **Decide on the best answer.** As you approach each question, it is probably best to think how the underlined portion would be expressed in standard written English. If it already seems correct, you should mark NO CHANGE. If your own conversion seems better, check the answers to see if it matches one of them. If it does not, choose the answer you think best. If the choice is too difficult, try substituting each option for the underlined part, being sure to examine it in the context of the question sentence, the preceding sentence, and the following sentence.

USAGE/MECHANICS

Punctuation

The Comma

Among its many functions, the comma is used to set off independent clauses, items in a series, coordinate adjectives, parenthetical expressions, and nonrestrictive phrases or clauses.

Use a comma to separate independent clauses joined by a coordinating conjunction (*and, but, for, or, nor,* or *yet*).

EXAMPLES: He wanted to be a salesman, but no jobs were available.
The people refused to send their children to school, and the school building stood empty the entire year.

Be sure you understand that this rule applies to the joining of *independent clauses,* that is, complete sentences. The use of the coordinating conjunction to join compound subjects (*Bush* and *Gore* debated three times), pairs of phrases (The food at that restaurant is prepared *without care* and *without taste*), compound verbs (Phil *ran* the office and *acted* as athletic director), or the like does not require the comma.

Use commas to separate items in a series.

EXAMPLES: Friendly, small, and innovative are adjectives that accurately characterize this college.
He went to the basement, set the trap, and returned to the kitchen to wait.

Use a comma to separate coordinate adjectives modifying the same noun.

EXAMPLES: He washed his new, black, shiny pickup.
Himalayan cats have long, silky, heavy fur.

To test whether adjectives are coordinate, reverse their order or insert *and* between them. If the phrase still makes sense, they are coordinate adjectives and require a comma.

The first example makes sense using either method: *shiny, black, new pickup,* or *new and shiny and black pickup.*

Non-coordinate adjectives have a special relationship with the nouns they modify. To some degree, they create a word group that itself is modified. They should not be preceded by commas.

EXAMPLE: They all admired the tall, powerful *football player.*

In this sentence, *football* is a non-coordinate adjective, different from the coordinate adjectives *tall* and *powerful.* You cannot put *and* between *powerful* and *football* nor can you move the word *football.* Other examples of non-coordinate adjectives are *doll* house, *art* museum, *computer* science, and *wheat* bread.

Use commas to set off nonrestrictive (amplifying or explanatory) phrases and clauses from the rest of the sentence.

PARTICIPIAL CLAUSE: Having spent his last penny, Luster tried to borrow a quarter from his boss.
PREPOSITIONAL PHRASE: At the beginning of each game, a noted singer gives his rendition of "The Star-Spangled Banner."
ADVERBIAL CLAUSE: When the composer was finished with the prelude, she began work on the first movement.

Use a comma to set off contrasting and nonessential phrases and clauses.

EXAMPLES: Mary Jennings, who was my best friend, dropped the class.
The first offer on the Blake house, which had been on the market for almost a month, was very disappointing.

Be sure to distinguish between these *nonrestrictive* interrupters and the *restrictive modifiers,* which are *not* set off by commas. Nonrestrictive modifiers add information but do not limit or change the meaning of the sentence. Note how the meaning changes when the clause is restrictive.

RESTRICTIVE: The young woman who was my best student dropped the class.

The young woman is now identified as the best student. Here is another example of a nonrestrictive clause:

EXAMPLE: Cardiac patients who have artificial valve implants are required to take anticoagulants for the rest of their lives.

Use a comma to set off nonrestrictive phrases and clauses that follow the main clause.

EXAMPLES: Jessica wanted to see the ice show, not the circus.
Few fans thought the reigning heavyweight champion could win, although he was superior to the challenger in every category.

Use the commas to set off an appositive. An appositive is a noun or noun phrase that renames or explains the noun it follows.

EXAMPLE: The novel, a mystery about a secret island off the Washington coast, was an instant bestseller.

Use commas to set off words in direct address. Words in direct address identify the one being spoken to.

EXAMPLE: Excuse me, Beth, but aren't you late for your tennis lesson?

A comma can take the place of an omitted word or phrase.

EXAMPLE: The Capitol Bank is located in a shopping mall; the Investors Bank, in the heart of town.

A comma is sometimes needed for clarity.

EXAMPLES: Ever since, we have taken the plane rather than the train.
In May, Marcia went to Washington, D.C.

PRACTICE EXERCISE

Decide whether the punctuation is correct or incorrect at each numbered point in the following paragraph. Then place a check in the proper column.

CORRECT   INCORRECT

_____   _____   **1.** When a writer begins a story he must start
                                                1

_____   _____   **2.** the pages smoking right away not bore the
                                                          2

_____   _____   **3.** reader with verbiage about setting
                                                                  3

_____   _____   **4.** characterization, and theme. The
                                             4

_____   _____   **5.** author must present a protagonist, and
                                                              5

_____   _____   **6.** an antagonist and he must also give
                                         6

_____   _____   **7.** them a cause worth arguing over. The
                                              7

_____   _____   **8.** complication, a series of battles the
                                     8

_____   _____   **9.** protagonist always loses, comes next
                                                              9

_____   _____   **10.** just before the crisis, to end all crises. The climax is
                                            10

_____   _____   **11.** the long-awaited, conclusive, high point of the tale.
                                                 11

_____   _____   **12.** There cannot be art without form, and there cannot
                                                         12

                             be form without careful studied, businesslike

_____   _____   **13.** craft. Any writer, who believes art flows
                                         13

_____   _____   **14.** from emotion alone, is not likely to write
                                         14

_____   _____   **15.** the kind of disciplined, organized short
                                                              15

_____   _____   **16.** story, that reflects the real world.
                                     16

ANSWERS AND EXPLANATIONS

1. INCORRECT. An introductory clause is set off by a comma.
2. INCORRECT. Set off a nonrestrictive phrase that follows the main clause.
3. INCORRECT. Use commas to separate items in a series.
4. CORRECT.   See explanation, item 3.
5. INCORRECT. Do not separate pairs of words (here, the compound objects *protagonist* and *antagonist*).

6. INCORRECT. Independent clauses linked by a coordinating conjunction are separated from each other by a comma.

7. CORRECT. The phrase *worth arguing over* is a restrictive (defines *cause*) and should not be separated from the main clause by a comma.

8. CORRECT. Interrupters, in this case a nonrestrictive appositive, are set off by commas.

9. INCORRECT. Nonrestrictive concluding phrases are set off by commas.

10. INCORRECT. The infinitive phrase *to end all crises* is restrictive (defines *crisis*) and should not be set off by a comma.

11. INCORRECT. The adjective *high* in the phrase *high point* is not a coordinate adjective and should not be preceded by a comma.

12. CORRECT. Use a comma to separate independent clauses joined by a coordinating conjunction.

13. INCORRECT. The adjective clause *who believes art flows from emotion alone* restricts the meaning of the word *writer* to those writers who hold the same belief. It should not be set off by commas.

14. INCORRECT. See explanation, item 13. This is the second comma of the pair used mistakenly to set off the adjective clause.

15. CORRECT. The adjective *short* in the phrase *short story* is not a coordinate adjective. It should not be preceded by a comma.

16. INCORRECT. The adjective clause *that reflects the real world* is restrictive (defines *short story*) and should not be set off by a comma.

The Semicolon

The semicolon is generally used to separate coordinate elements in a sentence, that is, items of the same grammatical nature. Most often, it is used between related ideas that require punctuation weaker than a period, but stronger than a comma. In addition, the semicolon divides three or more items in a series when the items themselves contain commas.

Use a semicolon between related independent clauses not joined by a coordinating conjunction.

EXAMPLES: A mature male gorilla may be six feet tall and weigh 400 pounds or more; his enormous arms can span eight feet.
New York has twelve major stadiums; Los Angeles has fifteen.

Use a semicolon between independent clauses joined by a conjunctive adverb.

Frequently, two independent clauses are joined, not by a coordinating conjunction, but by a transitional word (conjunctive adverb) introducing the second clause. A semicolon must be used between the clauses, because these transitional words (*accordingly, also, consequently, finally, furthermore, however, indeed, meanwhile, nevertheless, similarly, still, therefore, thus,* and the like) are *not* connecting words.

EXAMPLE: A female coyote will not bear pups if her diet consists of fewer than fifty rodents a week; thus, Mother Nature achieves a population balance.

Use a semicolon to separate coordinate clauses if the clauses themselves have commas.

EXAMPLE: The warranty on the car covered extensive repairs to the electrical system, front end, transmission, fuel injection system, and valves; but the amount of time and inconvenience involved in returning each time to the dealer cannot be ignored.

Use a semicolon to separate items in a series when the items themselves contain internal punctuation.

Normally, three or more items in a series are set off by commas; however, when they are made more complex by commas and other punctuation, they are separated by semicolons.

EXAMPLE: The trio was composed of a cellist named Grosz, who had been a European virtuoso for many years; a pianist who had won a major music festival in 1954, 1955, and 1958; and a violinist who had studied in Budapest, Vienna, and Munich.

PRACTICE EXERCISE

Each of the following sentences contains a numbered punctuation mark. Decide whether the mark is correct or should be changed to a semicolon. Then check the appropriate space to the left.

CORRECT   INCORRECT

_____ _____   **1.** He hit the ball well, however, he was not much of a
                                                   1
                        fielder.

2. He had played his entire repertoire: a short piece by

Mozart that, in spite of its difficulty, was his

favorite sonata; a prelude by Liszt that once had

caused an audience to erupt in cheers, in spite of the

_____ _____   fact that he was not finished, and finally a mazurka
                                                            2
                        by Chopin that was popular with musicians, com-

                        posers, and the general audience alike.

3. The movie had segments unsuitable for children,

including violent scenes, nudity, and inappropriate

_____ _____   language, but the general theme was inspirational.
                                                   3
_____ _____   **4.** Life is hard work; life can be a pleasure.
                                                   4

ANSWERS AND EXPLANATIONS

1. INCORRECT. When a transitional word (conjunctive adverb) is used between clauses, the clauses must be separated by a semicolon.
2. INCORRECT. This sentence contains a series of items, each a noun modified by an adjective clause, and each containing commas. They should be separated from each other by semicolons.
3. INCORRECT. The general rule is to use a comma to separate independent clauses joined by a coordinating conjunction. However, when the clauses themselves contain a number of commas, a semicolon is used for clarity.
4. CORRECT. A semicolon is used to separate related independent clauses not linked by a coordinating conjunction.

The Colon, Hyphen, and Apostrophe

THE COLON

The colon is a signal that something is to follow: a rephrased statement, a list or series, or a formal quotation. Use a colon in a sentence if you can logically insert *namely* after it.

Use a colon at the end of a complete statement to show anticipation—that is, to show that amplifying details follow, such as a list, a series of items, a formal quotation, or an explanation.

EXAMPLES: Of all the gauges in an airplane cockpit, three are crucial: the altimeter, the gas gauge, and the crash-warning indicator.

After five minutes of silence, the actor uttered those famous words: "To be or not to be; that is the question."

A popover has four common ingredients: flour, milk, salt, and butter.

Problems that occur in the use of the colon usually result from the following lapses:

1. A complete statement (independent clause) does not precede the colon.

INCORRECT: Tasks that I must complete today: mow the lawn, read two chapters of history, and tidy my room.

CORRECT: I must complete several tasks today: mow the lawn, read two chapters of history, and tidy my room.

2. A colon incorrectly separates essential parts of a sentence.

INCORRECT: In updating my computer, I added: a hard disk, a laser printer, and a fine-resolution monitor. (The colon separates the verb from its direct objects.)

CORRECT: In updating my computer, I added some new components: a hard disk, a laser printer, and a fine-resolution monitor.

ALSO CORRECT: In updating my computer, I added a hard disk, a laser printer, and a fine-resolution monitor.

3. There is more than one colon in a sentence.

INCORRECT: The success of the action depended upon three variables: that the weather would hold out, that the supplies would arrive on time, and that the enemy would be short on three things: planes, ammunition, and food.

CORRECT: The success of the action depended upon three variables: that the weather would hold out, that the supplies would arrive on time, and that the enemy would be short on planes, ammunition, and food.

HYPHEN

The hyphen has two main uses: to divide syllables at the end of a line and to link words in certain combinations. It is also used in compound numbers from twenty-one to ninety-nine.

Hyphenate a compound adjective (an adjective made up of two or more words) when it precedes the noun it modifies. The hyphen is ordinarily not used when the words follow the noun.

EXAMPLES: She wore a well-used raincoat.
           BUT
    Her raincoat was well used.
    The past-due bill lay unnoticed behind the couch.
    The bill, past due, lay unnoticed behind the couch.

NOTE: A compound adjective with an adverbial *-ly* modifier is never hyphenated: the *poorly designed* interchange. When the *-ly* modifier is an adjective, a hyphen is properly used: a *friendly-looking* dog.

APOSTROPHE

In addition to indicating possession, the apostrophe is used to take the place of omitted numbers (class of '02) and omitted letters or words in contractions (wasn't [was not], o'clock [of the clock]), and to indicate plurals that might otherwise be confusing (A's [not As]).

Use an apostrophe to show the possessive case of nouns and indefinite pronouns.

1. The possessive case of singular nouns (either common or proper) is indicated by adding an apostrophe and an *s*.

EXAMPLES: George's speech, the senator's campaign, anyone's opinion, the boss's office, Charles's book.

2. The possessive case of plural nouns ending in *s* is formed by adding only the apostrophe.

EXAMPLES: the girls' softball team, the waitresses' union, the Harrisons' antique cars.

NOTE: Irregular plurals, such as *men* or *children,* form the possessive by adding an apostrophe and an *s:* men's, children's.

A common error is to confuse possessive pronouns and contractions, particularly *its* and *it's* (meaning it is) *their* and *they're (they are),* and *whose* and *who's (who is).* Possessive pronouns have no apostrophe.

PRACTICE EXERCISE

Decide whether the punctuation at each numbered point is correct or incorrect. Then place a check in the proper column.

CORRECT   INCORRECT

_____ _____ 1. Into the circus arena paraded all the performers and animals; first the
1

_____ _____ 2. high stepping horses and bareback riders, then the
2
lumbering elephants with their trainers, followed by the cartwheeling clowns and the

_____ _____ 3. brightly costumed trapeze artists.
3

_____ _____ 4. Dennis's expertise at skateboarding amazed his
4
friends.

_____ _____ 5. The long awaited furniture finally
5

_____ _____ 6. arrived at the Jameses house.
6
In saving a threatened species, a basic

_____ _____ 7. step is: the study of it's diet, mating and
7   8

_____ _____ 8. reproductive processes, range patterns, and social behavior.

ANSWERS AND EXPLANATIONS

1. INCORRECT. Use a colon, not a semicolon, to introduce a list after a complete statement.
2. INCORRECT. Hyphenate a compound adjective that occurs *before* the noun.

3. CORRECT. Do not hyphenate a compound adjective if its first member is an adverb ending in *-ly*.
4. CORRECT. To form the possessive, add an apostrophe and an *s* to a singular noun.
5. INCORRECT. See explanation, answer 2.
6. INCORRECT. To form the plural possessive of a proper name, add an apostrophe to the plural (Jameses').
7. INCORRECT. A colon should not be used if it separates essential parts of a sentence (the verb *is* should not be separated from its object, *the study of ...*).
8. INCORRECT. The possessive personal pronoun *its* does not take an apostrophe.

The Dash, Question Mark, and Exclamation Point

DASH

The main function of the dash, like parenthesis, is to enclose information within a sentence. Dashes are generally more forceful and therefore should be used sparingly, since they highlight the ideas and items they enclose.

Use dashes to indicate hesitation, or a sudden break in thought or sentence structure, or to set off appositives and other explanatory or parenthetical elements.

The dash adds emphasis to any part of a sentence that can be separated from the rest of the sentence.

EXAMPLE: The skydiver—in spite of his broken leg—set a new record for endurance.

Some specific uses of the dash are:

1. To interrupt continuity of prose

EXAMPLE: "I really can't tolerate—Well, never mind."

2. To emphasize appositives

EXAMPLE: The items she had asked for in the new car—tape deck, mileage computer, stick shift—were all included.

3. To set off phrases or clauses containing commas

When a modifier itself contains commas, dashes can make its boundaries clear.

EXAMPLE: General Motors—which has manufactured tanks, cannons, and mobile cranes—has always been far more than an automobile assembler.

4. To set off parenthetical elements

EXAMPLE: The child was sitting—actually sprawling—at his desk.

QUESTION MARK

A question mark indicates the end of a direct question. A question mark in parentheses signals doubt or uncertainty about a fact such as a date or a number.

Use a question mark after a direct question.

EXAMPLES: When are we going to eat?
              Ask yourself, what are the odds of winning?
              (It is also correct to capitalize the word *what*.)

A question mark in parentheses may be used to express doubt.

EXAMPLE: The Dean's notes, published in 1774 (?), are considered the novel's origin.

NOTE: The use of the question mark as a mark of irony or sarcasm is not usually considered proper: The superintendent's important (?) announcements took all morning.

The question mark is unlikely to cause you trouble on the English test. Problems mainly occur (a) because of failure to distinguish between *direct* and *indirect* questions (an *indirect* question is always followed by a period: My friend asked why I didn't have my car.) or (b) because of mistaken combination of question marks with other punctuation marks. A question mark should never be combined with a comma, period, exclamation point, or other question mark.

EXCLAMATION POINT

An exclamation point is an indicator of strong *emotional* feelings, such as anger, joy, shock, surprise, or fear. It may also be used to express irony or emphasis. Like the dash, it should be used sparingly.

Use an exclamation point after a command, an interjection, an exclamation, or some other expression of strong emotion.

COMMAND: Stop!

INTERJECTION: Wow! Fire! Help!

EMOTIONAL EXPRESSION: Don't tell me you did it again! How wonderful!

An exclamation point should not be used with commas, periods, other exclamation points, or question marks.

PRACTICE EXERCISE

Decide whether the punctuation at each numbered point is correct or incorrect. Then place a check in the proper column.

CORRECT   INCORRECT

_____ _____ **1.** The tornado headed—no, *hurtled*—our way.
                                                    1

_____ _____ **2.** The doctor—an imposter, actually—cleared his
                                              2
                  throat.

_____ _____ **3.** The book—which was expensive—had been his
                                                          3
                  favorite for many years.

_____ _____ **4.** Don't tell me you're leaving already.
                                                        4

_____ _____ **5.** Is this the building you want to study!
                                                          5

_____ _____ **6.** Mr. Williams asked when I could rake his lawn?
                                                                  6

_____ _____ **7.** Last Tuesday, I'll never forget it, was the first time
                                      7   7
                  we saw Magic Johnson play.

_____ _____ **8.** The famous diva—who had performed in such emi-
                                          8
                  nent opera houses as the Met, LaScala, and Covent
                  Garden—was not willing to sing at our school.

1.	CORRECT.	Dashes can be used to signal a dramatic or emphatic shift in tone.
2.	CORRECT.	Dashes can be used to emphasize an appositive.
3.	INCORRECT.	Commas, not dashes, should be used to set off simple adjective clauses such as this one. Remember, though, that dashes *can* be used to set off adjective and other clauses that contain commas or other marks of punctuation.
4.	INCORRECT.	An exclamation point is called for here, to show dismay.
5.	INCORRECT.	This sentence is a direct question and requires a question mark.
6.	INCORRECT.	An indirect question takes a period, not a question mark.
7.	INCORRECT.	Use dashes to signal an abrupt change of thought.
8.	CORRECT.	Nonrestrictive clauses that are long and contain internal commas can properly be set off by dashes.

Quotation Marks and Parentheses

QUOTATION MARKS

One of the main uses of quotation marks is to signal the exact words of a writer or speaker. Quotation marks are also used to enclose the titles of short literary or musical works (articles, short stories or poems, songs), as well as words used in a special way.

Enclose direct quotations in quotation marks.

EXAMPLE: "We will wage war wherever it takes us," Winston Churchill pledged.

Quotation marks should enclose only the exact words of the person quoted.

EXAMPLE: Winston Churchill pledged that "we will wage war wherever it takes us." (NOT … pledged "that we will …")

NOTE: When a quoted sentence is interrupted by a phrase such as *he said* or *she replied,* two pairs of quotation marks must be used, one for each part of the quotation. The first word of the second part of the quoted material should not be capitalized unless it is a proper noun or the pronoun *I.*

EXAMPLE: "There are two sorts of contests between men," John Locke argued, "one managed by law, the other by force."

Commas and periods *always* belong *inside* quotation marks; semicolons and colons, outside. Question marks and exclamation points are placed inside the quotation marks when they are part of the quotation; otherwise, they are placed outside.

EXAMPLE: What did he mean when he said, "I know the answer already"?
"The case is closed!" the attorney exclaimed.

PARENTHESES

Parentheses, like dashes, are used to set off words of explanation and other secondary supporting details—figures, data, examples—that are not really part of the main sentence or paragraph. Parentheses are less emphatic than dashes and should be reserved for ideas that have no essential connection with the rest of the sentence.

Use parentheses to enclose an explanatory or parenthetical element that is not closely connected with the rest of the sentence.

EXAMPLE: The speech that he gave on Sunday (under extremely difficult circumstances, it should be noted) was his best.

If the parenthetical item is an independent sentence that stands alone, capitalize the first word and place a period inside the end parenthesis. If it is a complete sentence within another complete sentence, do not begin it with a capital letter or end it with a period. A question mark or exclamation point that is part of the parenthetical element should be placed inside the parenthesis.

EXAMPLES: On Easter, I always think of the hot cross buns I used to buy for two cents apiece. (At the time, the year was 1939, and I was three years old.) Congressman Jones (he was the man who once proposed having no entrance standards for community college students) gave a speech decrying the lack of basic skills on campuses today.

The absurd placement of the child-care center (fifteen feet from a classroom building!) was amateur architecture at its worst.

PRACTICE EXERCISE

Decide whether the punctuation or capitalization at each numbered point is correct or incorrect. Then place a check in the proper column.

CORRECT   INCORRECT

_____ _____   **1.** He had said that "he was nobody to fool with."
                      1

_____ _____   **2.** Fred wrote a poem for Barbara, which he entitled

                      "Barbaric Barbara."
                      2

_____ _____   **3.** Joseph Pummell (he was the senator who authored

                      the antifraud bill.) offered to speak at our first
                      3

                      meeting.

_____ _____   **4.** "I knew for sure," she said, "when he didn't ask

                      me to the prom".
                      4

_____ _____   **5.** The measure designed to lower inflationary pres-

                      sures on the economy resulted in a cost-of-living

                      increase of 12 percent (some measure, some reduc-

                      tion!).
                      5

_____ _____   **6.** "There is no doubt," he asserted, "That the enor-
                                            6

                      mous national debt will be a major problem in the

                      next century."

ANSWERS AND EXPLANATIONS

1. INCORRECT. Only the actual words spoken can be in quotation marks. *He was* would not be part of the speaker's words.

2. CORRECT. Quotation marks are used for titles of shorter literary works.

3. INCORRECT. A complete sentence enclosed in parentheses within another sentence does not take a period.

4. INCORRECT. A period always belongs inside the quotation mark.

5. CORRECT. An exclamation point that is part of the parenthetical phrase is placed within the parentheses.

6. INCORRECT. The second part of a quoted sentence interrupted by a phrase like *he asserted* does not begin with a capital unless the first word is a proper noun or *I*.

FOCUS ON THE ACT

The following sample questions represent ways in which the above skills might be tested on your ACT Assessment.

What lies behind the creative genius of our greatest authors has been the subject of speculation over the past two centuries. There is little doubt that many of the worlds creative geniuses experienced miserable lives most often, they suffered a personal and extreme brand of deprivation that profoundly affected the quality of

their daily lives. Almost always, the depth of their misery is related to the greatness of their genius. One who

reads both Emily Bronte's *Wuthering Heights* and the

best known critical discussions about her work cannot

escape the conclusion, that Emily was the product of a

punitive and abusive environment, it is difficult to avoid the further conclusion that the strength and authenticity

of her novel the vulnerabilities and palpable yearnings

of its main characters—are related however, faintly to her personal affliction.

1. **A.** NO CHANGE
   B. authors'
   C. authors,
   D. author's

2. **F.** NO CHANGE
   G. world's
   H. worlds'
   J. world's,

3. **A.** NO CHANGE
   B. lives:
   C. lives;
   D. lives,

4. **F.** NO CHANGE
   G. always;
   H. always—
   J. always:

5. **A.** NO CHANGE
   B. "Wuthering Heights"
   C. Wuthering Heights
   D. Wuthering-Heights

6. **F.** NO CHANGE
   G. best, known
   H. best-known
   J. "best known"

7. **A.** NO CHANGE
   B. conclusion;
   C. conclusion—
   D. conclusion

8. **F.** NO CHANGE
   G. environment;
   H. environment—
   J. environment?

9. **A.** NO CHANGE
   B. novel;
   C. novel—
   D. novel:

10. **F.** NO CHANGE
    G. related; however faintly,
    H. related, however faintly,
    J. related (however faintly)

ANSWERS AND EXPLANATIONS

1. A The noun *authors* is a simple object in this sentence and requires no punctuation.

2. G The plural *geniuses* are a possession of the world and require that it signal that possession with an apostrophe.

3. B The words occurring after *lives* form an independent clause and so must be set off with a stronger mark of punctuation. The colon is the best choice in this context because the following statement gives specific focus to the general statement made in the sentence's introductory clause.

4. F Set off introductory phrases with a comma.

5. A Underline (set in italics) novels and other larger works of literature.

6. H Hyphenate compound adjectives preceding the noun they modify.

7. D The adjective clause following the noun *conclusion* is a restrictive modifier and so does not take separating punctuation.

8. G The clause that follows necessitates a strong mark of punctuation. Since it is closely related in meaning to the previous independent clause, the most appropriate choice is the semicolon.

9. C The dash at the end of this phrase requires a matching dash at the beginning. Dashes are appropriately used to give special emphasis to parenthetical phrases such as this one.

10. H The phrase *however faintly* is parenthetical and must be set off by commas.

Basic Grammar and Usage

Subject-Verb Agreement

Nouns, verbs, and pronouns often have special forms or endings that indicate *number*—that is, whether the word is singular or plural. A verb must agree in number with the noun or pronoun that is its subject.

A verb agrees in number with its subject.

A singular subject requires a singular verb; a plural subject, a plural verb.

SINGULAR	**PLURAL**
The *house has* three bathrooms.	Many *houses have* more than one bathroom.
UCLA is my choice.	*UCLA, Berkeley, and Stanford are* my favorites.
My *cat,* a Persian named Gus, *is* awake all night.	*Cats,* according to this article, *are* almost always nocturnal.
Mandy, together with the other girls, *wants* a pizza for lunch.	*Mandy and the other girls want* a pizza for lunch.

Do not let **intervening words obscure the relationship between subject and verb.** Find the subject and make the verb agree with it.

EXAMPLES: A column of wounded prisoners, townspeople, and exhausted soldiers *was spotted* struggling over the horizon. (*Was spotted* agrees with its subject, *column,* not with the intervening plural nouns.)
She, her brother, and her friends from upstate *have* always *bought* tickets to the rock concert. (The verb agrees with the plural subject.)

Singular subjects followed by such words and phrases as *along with, as well as, in addition to, together with,* **or** *with* **require singular verbs.**

EXAMPLE: The *carrier,* together with three destroyers and two frigates, *was dispatched* to the Mediterranean Sea.

Indefinite pronouns like *anybody, each, either, everyone, neither,* **and** *one* **are always singular, and take a singular verb, regardless of intervening words. Other indefinite pronouns, like** *all, any, none* **or** *some* **may be either singular or plural.** *Both, few, many,* **and** *several* **are always plural.**

EXAMPLES: *Neither* of my children *has* an interest in music.
All is not lost BUT *all* of us *are going.*
Few of the golfers *were* professionals.

Compound subjects joined by *and* **usually take a plural verb.** (An exception is a compound subject that names one person, thing, or idea: *Ham and eggs is* a favorite breakfast.)

EXAMPLES: The *Toyota* and the *Ford are* low on gas.
The *Pendletons,* the *Riveras,* and the *Kleins are coming* to dinner.

In sentences that begin with *there is* **or** *there are,* **the subject follows the verb, and the verb must agree with it.**

EXAMPLES: There *are* (verb) many *reasons* (subject) for the war in the Middle East.

Singular subjects joined by *or* **or** *nor* **take a singular verb. If one subject is singular and the other plural, the verb should agree with the nearer subject.**

EXAMPLES: Either the *vegetable* or the *pan is creating* this awful taste. (Singular subjects)
Either the *pan* or the *vegetables are creating* this awful taste. (The verb agrees with the nearer subject.)

Collective nouns (bunch, committee, family, group, herd, jury, number, team) may be either singular or plural, depending upon whether the group is regarded as a unit or as individuals.

SINGULAR: The *number* of homeless families increases every year.
The *committee has* the serious responsibility of selecting a new dean.

Notice that the same nouns are considered plural when the reference is to individual members of the group.

PLURAL: A *number* of homeless people *were* ill enough to require hospitalization.
The *committee have* not *agreed* on a date for the picnic.

NOTE: A good rule to follow with *number, total,* and similar nouns is that, preceded by *the, number* is singular; preceded by *a,* it is plural. Another test: *A number of* should be treated as plural if it signifies several or many.

Words like *aeronautics, cybernetics, mathematics, physics,* **or** *news* **and** *dollars,* **are plural in form but usually singular in usage.**

EXAMPLES: *Mathematics is* a subject essential to the sciences.
Eighty-five *dollars* for that coat *is* a bargain.

PRACTICE EXERCISE

Decide whether the verb in the following sentences should be singular or plural. Then indicate your answer by placing a check in the appropriate space.

1. Some of us is ( ) are ( ) studying for the test.
2. The Board of Trustees is ( ) are ( ) making a decision about tuition increases this Wednesday.
3. The committee is ( ) are ( ) arriving in Chicago at different times.
4. There is ( ) are ( ) several options available to the opera buff in Chicago.
5. A large shipment of automotive parts has ( ) have ( ) been delayed.
6. Peanuts is ( ) are ( ) high in cholesterol.
7. Neither the mechanics nor the shop manager was ( ) were ( ) able to solve the problem.
8. Hospital expense, as well as doctor's, is ( ) are ( ) skyrocketing.
9. The cat and the dog is ( ) are ( ) getting a flea bath today.
10. Few of us realize ( ) realizes ( ) how much work went into the senior prom.

ANSWERS AND EXPLANATIONS

1. ARE studying. The indefinite pronoun *some* here signifies more than one and consequently requires a plural verb.
2. IS making. The Board of Trustees is a single body acting officially as a legal entity.
3. ARE arriving. The reference is clearly to individual members of the committee; therefore, the verb is plural.
4. ARE. The subject of the sentence is *options,* and the plural verb *are* agrees in number.
5. HAS been delayed. The subject of the sentence, *shipment* requires a singular verb.
6. ARE. The plural subject *peanuts* requires a plural verb.
7. WAS. If a singular subject and a plural subject are joined by *nor,* the verb agrees with the nearer subject ("manager *was*").
8. IS skyrocketing. The singular subject *expense* requires a singular verb.
9. ARE getting. Use a plural verb with two singular subjects joined by *and.*
10. REALIZE. The subject of this sentence is the indefinite pronoun *few,* which requires the plural verb *realize.*

Principal Parts of Verbs

All verbs have four principal parts: the *present* (NOW), the *past* (YESTERDAY), the *present participle* (the -ING form of the verb), and the *past participle* (the form of the verb with HAVE). To find the principal parts of a verb, just remember the clues NOW, YESTERDAY, -ING, and HAVE.

PRESENT: (you) *work* (NOW)
PAST: (you) *worked* (YESTERDAY)
PRESENT PARTICIPLE: (you are) *workING*
PAST PARTICIPLE: (you HAVE) *worked*

PRESENT: (he) *buys* (NOW)
PAST: (he) *bought* (YESTERDAY)
PRESENT PARTICIPLE: (he is) *buyING*
PAST PARTICIPLE: (he HAS) *bought*

Participles are used:

1. as part of the main verb of the sentence

EXAMPLES: Sylvia *was buying* a dress.
Ed *had swum* a mile last Sunday.

2. as an adjective

EXAMPLE: *Protesting* loudly at the podium, Mr. McCracken insisted that an environmental study be held. (The present participle *protesting* modifies the noun *Mr. McCracken.*)

3. As a noun

A gerund is the present participle, or *-ing* form of the verb, used as a noun.

EXAMPLE: SMOKING is indisputably a danger to one's health. (The gerund *smoking* is the subject of this sentence.)

When the main verb is separated from its helping verbs (like *has, have, be, does*) by intervening parts of a sentence, sometimes, through omission, an error in verb formation results. The verb formation *did not swum,* for example, is obviously wrong when seen out of context, but notice how difficult it is to spot in a sentence.

INCORRECT: Florence Chadwick *had swum* the English Channel twice before in treacherously cold weather, but last winter she *did not.*

CORRECT: Florence Chadwick *had swum* the English Channel twice before in treacherously cold weather, but last winter she *did not swim.*

INCORRECT: The rebel groups never *have* and never *will surrender* to any government forces.

CORRECT: The rebel groups never *have surrendered* and never *will surrender* to any government forces.

Another error involving principal parts of verbs results from a confusion of the simple past and the past participle. As in the preceding examples, such errors are more likely to occur in sentences where subject and verb are separated by modifiers. Note the following examples:

EXAMPLES:	PRESENT	PAST	PAST PARTICIPLE
We *saw* (not *seen*) the dog just last week.	see	saw	seen
The Dodgers finally *did* (not *done*) it.	do	did	done
My family had *gone* (not *went*) there for several summers.	go	went	gone
The music *began* (not *begun*) as the ship slid into the sea.	begin	began	begun
Jose Conseco had *broken* (not *broke*) his favorite bat.	break	broke	broken
The guests had *eaten* (not *ate*) before the wedding party arrived.	eat	ate	eaten
The Liberty Bell had *rung* (not *rang*) every Fourth of July for a century.	ring	rang	rung

Verbs like *sit, set, rise, raise, lie,* and *lay* cause trouble because of similarity of form.

EXAMPLES:	PRESENT	PAST	PAST PARTICIPLE
My cats usually *lie* (not *lay*) in the sun.	lie (to recline)	lay	lain
The President *lay* (not *laid*) down for his afternoon rest.	lay (to place)	laid	laid
The wounded soldier had *lain* (not *laid*) on the battlefield for three days.			
If you *lay* (not *lie*) your jacket on the counter, it may become soiled.			
Phillip *laid* (not *lay*) the new sod on the prepared soil.			

EXAMPLES:	PRESENT	PAST	PAST PARTICIPLE
The contractors have recently *laid* (not *lain*) the fresh cement for our new driveway.			
At the sound of "Hail to the Chief," everyone usually *rises* (not *raises*).	rise (to get up or move up)	rose	risen
The flag *rose* (not *raised*) to the strains of "The Marine Hymn."	raise (to cause to rise)	raised	raised
We feel that the faculty and staff have *risen* (not *raised*) to the challenge.			
The college trustees intend to *raise* (not *rise*) student fees.			
The students *raised* (not *rose*) the dress-code issue again.			
The neighbors had *raised* (not *risen*) the third side of the barn by noon.			

Some errors arise from the confusion of the present tense with another principal part. Look at the following examples:

EXAMPLES: The students protested that the test was *supposed* (not *suppose*) to be on Chapter Three.
They *used* (not *use*) to have dinner together every Friday.
Shirley *came* (not *come*) to see how you are.

The following list of principal parts features verbs that sometimes cause trouble in speaking and writing.

PRESENT	PAST	PAST PARTICIPLE
become	became	become
begin	began	begun
bid (offer)	bid	bid
bid (command)	bade	bidden
bite	bit	bit, bitten
blow	blew	blown
break	broke	broken
bring	brought	brought
burst	burst	burst
catch	caught	caught
choose	chose	chosen
come	came	come
dive	dived, dove	dived
do	did	done
drag	dragged	dragged
draw	drew	drawn
drink	drank	drunk
drive	drove	driven
eat	ate	eaten
fall	fell	fallen
fly	flew	flown
forget	forgot	forgot, forgotten
freeze	froze	frozen
get	got	got, gotten
give	gave	given
go	went	gone
grow	grew	grown
hang (suspend)	hung	hung

PRESENT	PAST	PAST PARTICIPLE
hang (execute)	hanged	hanged
know	knew	known
lay	laid	laid
lead	led	led
lend	lent	lent
lie (recline)	lay	lain
lie (speak falsely)	lied	lied
lose	lost	lost
pay	paid	paid
prove	proved	proved, proven
raise	raised	raised
ride	rode	ridden
ring	rang, rung	rung
rise	rose	risen
run	ran	run
see	saw	seen
shake	shook	shaken
shrink	shrank	shrunk
sing	sang, sung	sung
sink	sank, sunk	sunk
speak	spoke	spoken
spring	sprang	sprung
steal	stole	stolen
swim	swam	swum
swing	swung	swung
take	took	taken
tear	tore	torn
throw	threw	thrown
wear	wore	worn
weave	wove	woven
wring	wrung	wrung
write	wrote	written

PRACTICE EXERCISE

Find the verb errors in the following sentences. Not every sentence has an error. Place a check in the appropriate column.

CORRECT   INCORRECT

———— ———— **1.** Within five minutes, the fireman had climbed the ladder, plowed his way through mountains of debris, and did the impossible by putting out the fire.

———— ———— **2.** The play was completely staged by July and began in early August.

———— ———— **3.** She was very weary and simply wanted to lay down until dinner.

———— ———— **4.** The price of football tickets had rose dramatically since 1974.

———— ———— **5.** The New Zealand crew had lost a man overboard and tore the spinnaker.

———— ———— **6.** He had driven his bike to the trail head, run to the lake, and swum to the base camp.

———— ———— 7. When we were down at the lake on weekends, we use to sit on the sand and watch the girls.

———— ———— 8. After my mother removed the sheets from the washer, my sister hanged them on the line.

ANSWERS AND EXPLANATIONS

1. INCORRECT. *Had climbed,* [had] *plowed,* and [had] *done.*
2. INCORRECT. *Was staged* and [was] *begun.*
3. INCORRECT. The infinitive form of the verb *lie* (meaning *to recline*) is *to lie.*
4. INCORRECT. *Rose* is the past tense of the verb *rise;* the past participle required here is *risen.*
5. INCORRECT. *Had lost* and [had] *torn.*
6. CORRECT.
7. INCORRECT. The past tense *used* is needed here.
8. INCORRECT. The past tense of *hang* (to suspend) is *hung.*

Verb Forms and Verbals

A high percentage of verb-related errors occurs because the reader confuses *verb forms*— that is, the different forms that an action word can assume—with entirely different structures known as *verbals*—words formed from verbs but not used as verbs in a sentence. Known as *participles, gerunds,* and *infinitives,* verbals form important phrases within the sentence.

INFINITIVES

An infinitive is ordinarily preceded by *to* and is used as a noun, an adjective, or an adverb.

NOUN: *To err* is human. (Subject)
ADJECTIVE: The survivors had little *to celebrate.* (*To celebrate* modifies the noun *little.*)
ADVERB: *To please* his children, Jerry bought a new pool. (*To please* modifies the verb *bought.*)

Sometimes, infinitives omit the word *to.*

EXAMPLES: Who dares [to] *challenge* a champion?
Please [to] *go.*
Make him [to] turn on the radio.
We saw him [to] leave.

Because both gerunds and participles have an *-ing* ending, they can be harder to distinguish between. However, a sentence that equates the two presents an error in parallel structure. If you understand the function of each in the sentence, you will be sure to spot this error if it occurs on the ACT English test.

GERUNDS

A gerund always ends in *-ing* and functions as a noun.

SUBJECT: *Writing* is very rewarding.
SUBJECTIVE COMPLEMENT: My favorite occupation is *binding* books.
DIRECT OBJECT: He now regrets *resigning.*
OBJECT OF PREPOSITION: After *sealing* the letter, he went for a walk.

PARTICIPLE

A participle acts as an adjective in the sentence.

EXAMPLES: *Growling* threateningly, the gorilla intimidated the crowd. (*Growling* modifies *gorilla.*)

The floor *invaded* by termites was made of oak. (*Invaded* modifies *floor.*)

There are two forms of participles, present and past. Present participles end in *-ing;* past participles assume many different forms (e.g., *bought, granted, shown, heard, hung, hidden, shot, torn*).

Other verb forms that may give trouble are the progressive and the passive. Progressive verb forms are regular action words that emphasize continuing action: "I *am running*" rather than "I *run.*" Passive verbs transform the sentence in such a way that the subject is receiving action instead of performing it: "I *was given*" instead of "I *gave.*"

Note the similarities of form in the following groups:

VERBS: *Simple*—I *hit* the clay target fifty times.
Progressive—I *am hitting* the ball better than ever.
Passive—I *was hit* by a snowball.
VERBALS: *Infinitive*—*To hit* a child is considered criminal.
Gerund—*Hitting* golf balls at a driving range is essential preparation for a match.
Participle—The man *hitting the ball* is also the coach.

PRACTICE EXERCISE

The following items may have errors in the use of verbals and verb forms. Indicate with a check in the proper column, whether the sentence is correct or incorrect.

CORRECT   INCORRECT

_____   _____   **1.** By providing day care will help the working mother, as well as the economy.

_____   _____   **2.** He made me to see this was a mistake.

_____   _____   **3.** Sue is playing golf this morning, having lunch at the clubhouse, and expected home at three.

_____   _____   **4.** Sylvia has traveled often, taking her little sister with her.

_____   _____   **5.** To give underprivileged children gifts at Christmas and serving poor people a meal at this holiday made him happy.

_____   _____   **6.** He wanted to start a cooperative family grocery outlet and selling a variety of household products.

ANSWERS AND EXPLANATIONS

1.   INCORRECT.   Although the gerund *providing* seems to be the subject of the verb *will help,* it is not. It is the object of the preposition *by.* To correct the sentence, omit *by.*

2.   INCORRECT.   Drop the *to* of the infinitive after the verb *make* ("He made me see …").

3.   INCORRECT.   The progressive forms *is playing* and *[is] having* are incorrectly made parallel with the passive form *[is] expected.* The correction is to use the progressive form: "*[is] expecting* to arrive home at three."

4.   CORRECT.   The participle *taking* modifies *Sylvia.*

> **5.** INCORRECT. The infinitive *to give* is not parallel with the gerund *helping* in the compound subject of this sentence. The verbals must both be infinitives or must both be gerunds.
>
> **6.** INCORRECT. The compound direct object of this sentence combines an infinitive (*to start*) and a gerund (*selling*). The elements must be parallel (*to start*) and (*to sell*).

Pronouns

Pronouns are most often employed as substitutes for nouns, but some can also be used as adjectives or conjunctions. To master pronouns and be able to spot errors in their use, you need to understand pronoun *case* (nominative, possessive, objective), pronoun *number* (singular or plural), and pronoun *class* (personal, demonstrative, interrogative, relative, indefinite).

PERSONAL PRONOUNS

A personal pronoun indicates by its form the person or thing it takes the place of: the person speaking (first person), the person spoken to (second person), or the person or thing spoken about (third person).

First-Person Pronouns

	SINGULAR	PLURAL
Nominative case	I	we
Possessive case	my, mine	our, ours
Objective case	me	us

Second-Person Pronouns

Nominative case	you	you
Possessive case	your, yours	your, yours
Objective case	you	you

Third-Person Pronouns

Nominative case	he, she, it	they
Possessive case	his, hers, its	their, theirs
Objective case	him, her, it	them

Some common errors in pronoun case occur frequently in everyday speech and may well appear on the ACT. Study the following applications to see if you have been using the correct forms.

Use the nominative case of a pronoun in a compound subject.

EXAMPLE: Betty and *I* watched the Olympics on television.

Use the nominative case of a pronoun following any form of the verb *to be*. This use may not sound right to you, but it is standard written English, the language of the ACT.

EXAMPLE: It is *she*. The winner was *I*.

Use the objective case when the pronoun is the object of a preposition.

EXAMPLES: This is just between you and *me*.
             Doug looks like *me*. (Like, as well as *but,* can be used as a preposition.)
             Nadine made coffee for Allan, Ken, and *me*.

When there are intervening words, eliminate them to find the correct pronoun to use. "Nadine made coffee for *I* " sounds ridiculous, yet some people might say, "Nadine made coffee for *Allan, Ken, and I.*" Similarly, in the sentence *"We (Us) homeowners want better roads,"* eliminate the word *homeowners* to find the correct word: *"We want better roads."*

Use the objective case when the pronoun is the object of a verb.

EXAMPLE: The noise frightened Karen and *me.*

Use the nominative case for pronouns that are subjects of elliptical clauses (clauses that are incomplete or unexpressed).

As and *than* are subordinating conjunctions that introduce elliptical clauses. Complete the clause to determine the pronoun case.

EXAMPLES: My children are as excited as *I* [am].
She raked more than *he* [raked].

Use a possessive pronoun before a gerund.

Just as you would say *My car,* you would also say *My smoking* bothers her.

EXAMPLE: We have always regretted *her* leaving for California.

DEMONSTRATIVE PRONOUNS

Demonstrative pronouns (*this, that, these, those*) take the place of things being pointed out.

EXAMPLES: *These* are Mary's.
I don't like *this.*

They are called demonstrative adjectives when used before nouns:
These seats are comfortable.

EXAMPLE: *These seats* are comfortable.

INCORRECT: *Them* are the new watches I ordered.
  CORRECT: *Those* are the new watches I ordered. (Demonstrative pronoun)

Do not substitute a personal pronoun for a demonstrative pronoun or a demonstrative adjective.

INCORRECT: Look at *them* diamonds!
  CORRECT: Look at *those* diamonds! (Demonstrative adjective)

INTERROGATIVE PRONOUNS

Interrogative pronouns (*who, whom, whose, which,* and *what*) are used in questions. *Who, which,* and *what* are used as subjects and are in the nominative case. *Whose* is in the possessive case. *Whom* is in the objective case, and, like all objects, it is the receiver of action in the sentence.

The most common error involving interrogative pronouns is the tendency to use *who* instead of *whom.*

When the pronoun is receiving the action, the objective form *whom* must be used.

INCORRECT: *Who* did you contact?
  CORRECT: *Whom* did you contact? (You did contact whom?)

When the pronoun is performing the action, the nominative *who* must be used.

INCORRECT: *Whom* did you say is running the dance?
  CORRECT: *Who* did you say is running the dance? (*Who* is the subject of *is running.*)

RELATIVE PRONOUNS

Relative pronouns (*who, whom, whose, which, what,* and *that*) refer to people and things. When a relative pronoun is the subject of a subordinate clause, the clause becomes an adjective modifying a noun in the sentence.

EXAMPLE: The rumor *that plagued him all his life* was a lie. (*That* [subject] *plagued him all his life* modifies *rumor.*)

That can also act as a conjunction to introduce a subordinate clause.

EXAMPLE: Bob knew *that* Boston would win.

INDEFINITE PRONOUNS

Indefinite pronouns (*all, another, any, both, each, either, everyone, many, neither, one, several, some,* and similar words) represent an indefinite number of persons or things. Many of these words also function as adjectives ("*several* men").

Indefinite pronouns present few problems. One thing to remember:

Use a singular pronoun with an indefinite antecedent like *one, everyone,* and *anybody.*

INCORRECT: Everyone needs to prepare *themselves* for retirement.
CORRECT: Everyone needs to prepare *himself* (or *herself*) for retirement.

And a final caution:

The antecedent of a pronoun should be clear, specific, and close to the pronoun.
Reword the sentence if necessary.

CONFUSING: The coach told Eric that *he* could practice after school.
CLEAR: The coach said that Eric could practice after school.

PRACTICE EXERCISE

Find the pronoun errors in the following sentences. Not every sentence has an error. Place a check in the appropriate column to indicate whether the sentence is correct or incorrect.

CORRECT   INCORRECT

_____   _____   1. Who do you think is coming?

_____   _____   2. I can tell the culprit. It was he.

_____   _____   3. I play more tennis than her, but she has a natural talent.

_____   _____   4. They nominated everybody but Rosa and he.

_____   _____   5. Frank and him have been using the word processor.

_____   _____   6. Everyone must pat themselves on the back once in a while.

_____   _____   7. The broker was surprised at him wanting to buy 5,000 shares of that penny stock.

_____   _____   8. Who did you see in the play?

_____   _____   9. The IRS required Lee, Carlotta, and I to produce more detailed records.

_____   _____   10. Us Chicagoans don't appreciate our city nearly enough.

ANSWERS AND EXPLANATIONS

1. CORRECT. *Who,* the subject of *is coming,* is performing the action.
2. CORRECT. The nominative case is used with all forms of the verb *to be. He* is correct.
3. INCORRECT. To correct this sentence, supply the missing verb: "I play more tennis than *she* [does] ..."
4. INCORRECT. *But* in this sentence is used as a preposition; its object must be in the objective case (*him*), not the nominative.
5. INCORRECT. Use the nominative case for a pronoun in a compound subject (Frank and *he*).
6. INCORRECT. The pronoun should be *himself* (or *herself*) to agree with the singular form *everyone.*
7. INCORRECT. *Wanting to buy stock* is a gerund phrase; it takes the possessive pronoun *his.*
8. INCORRECT. *Whom* is needed, because it is the object of *did see.*
9. INCORRECT. The pronoun *I* should be in the objective case (*me*) because it is a direct object of *required.*
10. INCORRECT. The pronoun *us* should be in the nominative case (*we*) because it modifies *Chicagoans,* the subject of the sentence.

FOCUS ON THE ACT

The following sample questions represent ways in which the above skills might be tested on your ACT Assessment.

Operators and manufacturers of nuclear reactor power facilities are making increased use of robots to improve operations and maintenance, lower operating costs, <u>increasing</u> plant availability and equipment

1. A. NO CHANGE
   B. increases
   C. increase
   D. increased

reliability, <u>enhanced</u> worker safety, and reduce worker exposure to radiation. There is no doubt in the field that

2. F. NO CHANGE
   G. enhancing
   H. enhances
   J. enhance

advanced telerobotic systems <u>can have made</u> more effective use of human operators, expert systems, and

3. A. NO CHANGE
   B. can make
   C. can be made
   D. can be making

intelligent machines; in fact, <u>few</u> of the world's leading
4

nuclear plant designers believe that a facility without

modern robotic and telerobotic systems <u>will have</u>
5

<u>become</u> obsolete in a very few years. The design of
5

future nuclear plants and supporting facilities—

particularly <u>these</u> involving fuel recycling—should
6

incorporate considerations for use of robotic systems.

    A committee of scientists critical of the move

toward robotics <u>believe</u> that existing methods for
7

controlling and preprogramming the typical robot <u>is</u>
8

appropriate for only a limited number of jobs in nuclear

facilities, mainly because <u>it simply require</u> too
9

much supervision. In addition, existing robots are

limited in their ability to sense their surroundings and

<u>interpreting</u> sensor data, a prerequisite for handling
10

unexpected problems during the routine executions of

tasks.

4. F. NO CHANGE
   G. some
   H. one
   J. none

5. A. NO CHANGE
   B. would have become
   C. becomes
   D. will become

6. F. NO CHANGE
   G. they
   H. those
   J. that

7. A. NO CHANGE
   B. believes
   C. believed
   D. have believed

8. F. NO CHANGE
   G. were
   H. are
   J. will be

9. A. NO CHANGE
   B. it simply required
   C. they simply require
   D. it simply requires

10. F. NO CHANGE
   G. interpret
   H. interpreted
   J. has interpreted

ANSWERS AND EXPLANATIONS

1. **C** The verb *increase* needs to be an infinitive to be parallel with the series of infinitive phrases that comprise the end of the sentence.

2. **J** The verb *enhance* needs to be an infinitive to be parallel with the series of infinitive phrases that comprise the end of the sentence.

3. **B** The passage is written in the present tense, and employs the present tense in generally true statements.

4. **G** *Some* is the more logical choice of indefinite pronoun here; the use of *few* in the text renders the sentence meaningless.

5. **D** The future tense is made necessary by the trailing phrase "in a very few years."

6. **H** Demonstrative pronouns take the place of things *being pointed out*. In this case, the word *those* is more appropriate for the antecedent *facilities* because those facilities will be built in the future.

7. **B** The subject of the verb is the singular noun *committee*.

8. **H** The subject of the verb is the plural noun *methods*.

9. **D** The subject of the verb is the singular personal pronoun *it*, the antecedent of which is the noun *robot*.

10. **G** *Interpret* is one of a pair of parallel infinitives (*to sense* and *to interpret*) modifying the noun *ability*.

SENTENCE STRUCTURE

In addition to a NO CHANGE response, the questions on the ACT English Test that deal with sentence structure will offer three alternatives, each one a restructuring of the underlined part. Errors in sentence structure include such items as sentence fragments, run-on sentences, misplaced modifiers, and lack of parallelism. These topics are reviewed in this section.

Sentence Fragments

A sentence fragment is a part of a sentence that has been punctuated as if it were a complete sentence. It does not express a complete thought but depends upon a nearby independent clause for its full meaning. It should be made a part of that complete sentence.

INCORRECT: I was not able to pick up my child at her school. *Having been caught in heavy traffic.* (Participial phrase)

REVISED: Having been caught in heavy traffic, I was not able to pick up my child at her school.

OR

I was not able to pick up my child at her school. I had been caught in heavy traffic.

INCORRECT: The cat sat on the water heater. *Unable to get warm.* (Adjective phrase)

REVISED: Unable to get warm, the cat sat on the water heater.

INCORRECT: The salesman tightened the wire around the burlap feed bag with a spinner. *Which twists wire loops until they are secure.* (Adjective clause)

REVISED: The salesman tightened the wire around the burlap feed bag with a spinner, which twists wire loops until they are secure.

INCORRECT: We will probably try to find another insurance company. *When our policy expires.* (Adverb clause)

REVISED: When our policy expires, we will probably try to find another insurance company.

Run-on Sentences

Probably the most common error in writing occurs when two sentences are run together as one. There are two types of run-on sentences: the *fused* sentence, which has no punctuation mark between its two independent clauses, and the *comma splice,* which substitutes a comma where either a period or a semicolon is needed.

FUSED: Jean had no luck at the store they were out of raincoats.

COMMA SPLICE: She surprised us all with her visit, she was on her way to New York.

To correct a run-on sentence, use a period, a semicolon, or a coordinating conjunction (*and, but, or, nor, for*) to separate independent clauses.

Note the following examples of run-on sentences and the suggested revisions.

FUSED: Eric is a bodybuilder he eats only large amounts of meat.

REVISED: Eric is a bodybuilder; he eats only large amounts of meat.

COMMA SPLICE: He had never seen Alex so prepared, he even had backup copies of his study sheets!

REVISED: He had never seen Alex so prepared. He even had backup copies of his study sheets!

COMMA SPLICE: His father was an artist, his mother was an accountant.

REVISED: His father was an artist, and his mother was an accountant.

PRACTICE EXERCISE

Most of the following items contain sentence fragments or run-on sentences. Place a check in the proper column to indicate whether the item is correct or incorrect.

CORRECT   INCORRECT

_____ _____   **1.** Bert used his manuscript for scratch paper. Having received rejection notices from twelve publishers.

_____ _____   **2.** The bank changed its hours and hired more security officers. After a wave of bank robberies hit the neighborhood.

_____ _____   **3.** We have to leave now it will be dark soon.

_____ _____   **4.** Having been declared fit by his doctor, Cleveland planned a weekend hike to the top of Mount Washington.

_____ _____   **5.** It was an embarrassment to hear Colonel Wilkinson talk about the medals he won with his marching corps. In front of all those wounded veterans!

_____ _____   **6.** Erica played softball for Taft High School, she hit a home run every week.

_____ _____   **7.** Our Himalayan cat Mathilda gave birth to seven beautiful kittens. All little white bundles of purring fluff.

_____ _____   **8.** Boris accidentally stepped on the little girl's foot he felt terrible.

_____ _____   **9.** It is necessary to vacuum around and under your refrigerator at least once a month. To prevent it from overheating.

_____ _____   **10.** Several of us want to give Dr. Kellogg a birthday party. Because he is so kind and generous.

_____ _____   **11.** Human cloning will soon become a reality; people will be able to produce improved versions of themselves.

_____ _____   **12.** Jared was warned, he was offending too many of his superiors.

ANSWERS AND EXPLANATIONS

1. INCORRECT. *Having received rejection notices from twelve publishers* is a participial phrase modifying the proper noun *Bert* and must be attached to the main clause.

2. INCORRECT. The adverb clause *After a wave of bank robberies hit the neighborhood* modifies the verbs *changed* and *hired,* and should be joined to the rest of the sentence.

3. INCORRECT. This is a fused sentence, which needs a period, semicolon, or coordinating conjunction between the words *now* and *it.* If a period is used, the word *it* should begin with a capital letter.

4. CORRECT. The dependent phrases, *Having been declared fit by his doctor* and *to the top of Mount Washington,* have been included in one complete sentence.

5. INCORRECT. *In front of all those wounded veterans* is a prepositional phrase that should be made part of the sentence containing the word it modifies, *talk.*

6. INCORRECT. This sentence is a comma splice; that is, a comma is used where a stronger mark of separation belongs, such as a period, semicolon, or coordinating conjunction.

7. INCORRECT. *All little white bundles of purring fluff* is an appositive phrase modifying *kittens*. It cannot stand alone.

8. INCORRECT. This is a fused sentence, which needs a period, semicolon, or coordinating conjunction between the words *foot* and *he*. If a period is used, the word *he* should begin with a capital letter.

9. INCORRECT. The infinitive phrase *To prevent it from overheating* should be part of the previous sentence.

10. INCORRECT. *Because he is so kind and generous* is a dependent adverb clause that should be attached to the independent clause containing the verb it modifies.

11. CORRECT. The independent clauses are properly separated by a semicolon.

12. INCORRECT. See explanation, item 6.

Connectives

Connectives that join elements of equal rank are called coordinating conjunctions (*and, but, or, nor, for, yet*). Connectives that introduce a less important element are called subordinating conjunctions (*after, although, since, when*).

Coordinating conjunctions link words, phrases, and clauses that are of equal importance.

EXAMPLES: The pilot *and* the crew boarded the plane.
The road ran through the valley *and* along the river.

Compound sentences are formed when coordinating conjunctions link two independent clauses.

EXAMPLE: You can sign the loan papers on Friday, *or* you can sign them on Monday.

Subordinating conjunctions are used in sentences to connect clauses that are not equal in rank—that is, in sentences in which one idea is made subordinate to another. There are many subordinating conjunctions. Some of the important ones are *after, as, because, before, if, in order that, once, since, unless, until, whenever,* and *wherever.*

EXAMPLES: We covered up the newly planted citrus trees *when* the temperature began to drop.
Until I saw her in person, I thought Cher was a tall woman.

Another form of connective is the *conjunctive adverb*. It is actually an adverb that functions as a coordinating conjunction. The principal conjunctive adverbs are *accordingly, also, besides, certainly, consequently, finally, furthermore, however, incidentally, instead, likewise, nevertheless, otherwise, similarly,* and *undoubtedly*. When they join clauses, conjunctive adverbs are usually preceded by a semicolon and followed by a comma.

EXAMPLE: I understand you wish to see a Broadway musical; *undoubtedly,* you'll have to get tickets far in advance for one of the hit shows.

Coordination can be overdone. If every significant idea in every sentence is given equal weight, there is no *main* idea.

FAULTY
COORDINATION: The real power in the company lies with Mr. Stark, and he currently owns 55 percent of the stock; in addition to that, his mother is semiretired as president of the firm.

REVISED: The real power in the company lies with Mr. Stark, who currently owns 55 percent of the stock and whose mother is semiretired as president of the firm.

Notice that subordinating two of the independent clauses tightens the sentence and adds focus.

Subordination of too many parts of a sentence, however, can be just as confusing. Look at the following example:

EXCESSIVE
SUBORDINATION: Standing on the corner were many aliens who had entered the country illegally, and most of whom had applied for amnesty, and even more important to them though, who had families back in Mexico or El Salvador who needed food and shelter.

REVISED: Standing on the corner were many illegal aliens, most of whom had applied for amnesty. Even more important to them, though, was the fact that they had families needing food and shelter back in Mexico or El Salvador.

Notice how proper coordination and subordination helps clarify a confusing stream of excessively entwined modifiers.

You must also keep in mind the *logic* of subordination. What you choose to subordinate in a sentence has to make sense to the reader. For example, the sentence "Sue happened to glance at the sky, amazed to see an enormous flying saucer hovering over the barn" gives greater importance to the fact that Sue glanced at the sky. A more logical version of that sentence is, "Happening to glance at the sky, Sue was amazed to see an enormous flying saucer hovering over the barn."

BACKWARD
SUBORDINATION: She studied medicine with great intensity for fifteen years, becoming a doctor.

LOGICAL REVISION: She became a doctor, having studied medicine with great intensity for fifteen years.

BACKWARD
SUBORDINATION: The pitcher momentarily let the runner on first base take a wide lead, when he stole second.

LOGICAL REVISION: The runner stole second when the pitcher momentarily let him take a wide lead.

BACKWARD
SUBORDINATION: He ran over with a fire extinguisher, saving the driver's life.

LOGICAL REVISION: Running over with a fire extinguisher, he saved the driver's life.

PRACTICE EXERCISE

Most of the following sentences contain either faulty coordination or subordination, or backward subordination. Place a check in the appropriate column to indicate whether the sentence is correct or faulty.

CORRECT   FAULTY

_____ _____   1. I had prepared myself by practicing, and I was able to beat Phil at racquetball.

_____ _____   2. Realizing that the mob does not forgive breaches of security, Lefty went into hiding.

_____ _____   3. As a terrible storm began, we were eating.

_____ _____   4. George found out about the burglary, and he was so shocked at first, and he could not remember his telephone number.

_____ _____   5. Between Big Sur and Carmel, the roads were in very bad condition, because the State Highway Agency is repairing them.

_____ _____   **6.** He bought a secondhand car, which had a sun roof, and it began to leak, so he took the car back to the dealer, who replaced the roof.

_____ _____   **7.** The V-2 Project was manned by prisoners who had no contact with the outside world, because it was completed in total secrecy.

_____ _____   **8.** Janine is a ballet dancer, and her sister is a gymnast.

ANSWERS AND EXPLANATIONS

1. FAULTY. This sentence is an example of faulty coordination. The sentence would be improved by subordinating the less important idea: *Having prepared myself by practicing, I was able to beat Phil at racquetball.*

2. CORRECT. In this sentence, the less important idea is properly subordinated.

3. FAULTY. This sentence is an example of illogical or backward subordination. The important idea is the storm, not the eating: *A terrible storm began as we were eating.*

4. FAULTY. This sentence is an example of faulty coordination. Improve it by subordinating two of the independent clauses: *When George found out about the burglary, he was so shocked at first that he could not remember his telephone number.*

5. FAULTY. This is an example of illogical or backward subordination. The fact that the roads were being repaired is the main idea of the sentence. We know that, because the other clause gives the reason that the roads are being repaired. Revised: *Because the roads between Big Sur and Carmel were in very bad condition, the State Highway Agency is repairing them.*

6. FAULTY. This is an example of both faulty coordination and excessive subordination. Revised: *He bought a secondhand car with a sun roof. When the sun roof began to leak, he took the car back to the dealer, who replaced the roof.*

7. FAULTY. This sentence is an example of illogical subordination. Of the two ideas, *The V-2 Project was manned by prisoners* and *it was completed in secrecy,* the second is the more important one. Revised: *Because the V-2 Project ... world, it ...*

8. CORRECT. This is an acceptable compound sentence, pairing two equal ideas logically.

Modifiers

ADJECTIVES AND ADVERBS

The purpose of adjectives and adverbs is to describe, limit, color—in other words, to *modify* other words. Adjectives modify nouns or pronouns, and generally precede the words they modify. Adverbs describe verbs, adjectives or other adverbs. Some words can be used as either adjectives (He has an *early appointment*) or adverbs (He *arrived early*).

ADJECTIVES: *fuzzy* peach
              impressive view
              sour milk
ADVERBS: He grumbled *loudly.*
              She smiled *broadly.*
              It poured *unmercifully.*

Although most adverbs end in *-ly,* some do not (*fast, hard, long, straight*). A few adjectives also have an *-ly* ending (*lovely* day, *lively* discussion).

ADJECTIVES

Problems that students face with adjectives frequently relate to the use of degrees of comparison. There are three degrees: the *positive*—the original form of the word (*straight*); the *comparative*—used to compare two persons or things (*straighter*); and the *superlative*—used to compare more than two persons or things (*straightest*). If not understood, the spelling and form changes involved can sometimes confuse the unwary student.

1. Most adjectives form the comparative and superlative degrees by adding *-er* and *-est:*

POSITIVE: nice
COMPARATIVE: nicer
SUPERLATIVE: nicest

2. Other adjectives form the comparative and superlative by using *more* and *most:*

POSITIVE: challenging
COMPARATIVE: more challenging
SUPERLATIVE: most challenging

3. Some adjectives change completely as they form the comparative and superlative degrees:

POSITIVE: little
COMPARATIVE: less
SUPERLATIVE: least

Be alert for double comparisons, which incorrectly use *more* or *most* with adjectives that already express a degree: *more softer* or *most strongest.*

Also, watch for the illogical use of the comparative or the superlative with adjectives that cannot be compared, such as *square, round, perfect, unique.* It is meaningless to write *rounder* or *most perfect.*

When comparing only two nouns, use the comparative degree: Mars is the *larger* of the two planets. When comparing more than two, use the superlative: Gibson is the *most dangerous* hitter on their team.

ADVERBS

Adverbs (either as words, phrases, or clauses) describe the words they modify by indicating *when, how, where, why, in what order,* or *how often.*

WHEN: He studied *until 10:00 every night.*
HOW: She testified *with quiet dignity.*
WHERE: Bring the paper *here.*
WHY: They rejected the offer *because it was too little.*
IN WHAT ORDER: *One after another,* the townspeople told the judge their story.

NOTE: *Anywheres, nowheres,* and *somewheres* are incorrect adverb forms. Use *anywhere, nowhere, somewhere.*

The adjectives *good* and *bad* should not be used as adverbs.

NOT
She doesn't sing so *good.*
He wants that job *bad.*
BUT
She doesn't sing so *well.*
He wants that job *badly.*

Standard English requires the use of a formal adverb form rather than a colloquial version.

NOT

This was a *real* good clambake.

He *sure* doesn't look happy.

BUT

This was a *really* good clambake.

He *surely* doesn't look happy.

PRACTICE EXERCISE

Some of the following sentences combine errors in the use of adjectives or adverbs. Determine whether *a* or *b* is the correct word to use. Then place a check in the appropriate column.

a   *b*

_____ _____ **1.** The new Turbo-B ran *real/really* well during the
                                    a   b
          first race.

_____ _____ **2.** Mike is the *more/most* active of the twins.
                              a   b

_____ _____ **3.** I *sure/surely* would like that leather jacket.
                         a   b

_____ _____ **4.** Portia was even more *fussier/fussy* than Elena.
                                            a   b

_____ _____ **5.** These earrings are *unique/most unique!*
                                          a   b

_____ _____ **6.** He had many friends in Chicago, where he lived

          previous/previously.
            a   b

ANSWERS AND EXPLANATIONS

1. *b* The adverb *really* is needed to modify the adverb *well*. (Only adverbs can modify other adverbs.)

2. *a* The comparative degree is used when two are compared.

3. *b* In colloquial speech, the word *sure* is accepted. In the ACT test, as in all secondary school and college writing, the norm is standard English, which requires the adverb *surely* in a construction like this.

4. *b* With the comparative degree *more*, only the positive degree *fussy* is correct. *More fussier* is a double comparison.

5. *a* It is illogical to add degrees to absolutes like *unique*. Something is either unique or not unique.

6. *b* The adverb *previously* is the correct choice to modify the verb *lived*. *Previous*, an adjective, cannot modify a verb.

Probably the most persistent and frustrating errors in the English language involve either *incorrect modification* or else *inexact modification* that is difficult to pin down.

In most cases, if you can keep your eye on the *word or phrase being modified,* it is easier to avoid the following pitfalls.

MISPLACED MODIFIERS

To avoid confusion or ambiguity, place the modifying words, phrases, or clauses near the words they modify.

Misplaced Adverb Modifiers

Adverbs like *scarcely, nearly, merely, just, even,* and *almost* must be placed near the words they modify.

CONFUSED: Last week during the cold spell, I *nearly* lost all of my flowers.
   CLEAR: Last week during the cold spell, I lost *nearly* all of my flowers. (The adverb *nearly* modifies the pronoun *all.*)

CONFUSED: Acme *just* cleaned my rugs last month.
   CLEAR: Acme cleaned my rugs *just* last month. (The adverb *just* modifies the adverbial phrase *last month.*)

Misplaced Phrase Modifiers

CONFUSED: *To plant tomatoes,* it was a good growing year.
   CLEAR: It was a good growing year *to plant tomatoes.*

CONFUSED: *Like a sleek projectile,* the passengers saw the new train approach the station.
   CLEAR: The passengers saw the new train approach the station *like a sleek projectile.*

Misplaced Clause Modifiers

CONFUSED: He packed all of his books and documents into his van, *which he was donating to the library.*
   CLEAR: He packed all of his books and documents, *which he was donating to the library,* into his van.

CONFUSED: The new series of seminars will focus on how to prevent inflation, *which will benefit us all.*
   CLEAR: The new series of seminars, *which will benefit us all,* will focus on how to prevent inflation.

DANGLING CONSTRUCTIONS

A dangling modifier literally hangs in the air; there is no logical word in the sentence for it to modify. Frequently it is placed close to the wrong noun or verb, causing the sentence to sound ridiculous: *Driving through the park, several chipmunks could be seen.*

Dangling Participles

A participle is a form of the verb that is used as an adjective. Unless there is a logical word for it to modify, the participial phrase will dangle, modifying either the wrong noun or none at all.

INCORRECT: Having run out of gas, John was late for dinner.
   REVISED: Because the car ran out of gas, John was late for dinner.

INCORRECT: Driving along the parkway, several deer were spotted.
   REVISED: Driving along the parkway, we spotted several deer.

Dangling Gerunds

A gerund is the *-ing* form of a verb serving as a noun (*Smoking is bad for your health*). When a gerund is used as the object of a preposition ("by *hiding,*" "after *escaping,*" "upon *realizing*"), the phrase can dangle if the actor that it modifies is missing.

INCORRECT: After putting a bloodworm on my hook, the flounders began to bite.
   REVISED: After putting a bloodworm on my hook, I found that the flounders began to bite.

INCORRECT: In designing our house addition, a bathroom was forgotten.
   REVISED: In designing our house addition, we forgot to add a bathroom.

Dangling Infinitives

Unlike the participle and the gerund, the infinitive performs more than one job in a sentence. While the participle acts like an adjective, and the gerund like a noun, the infinitive phrase can take the part of a noun, adjective, or adverb. Note the following examples of dangling infinitive phrases:

INCORRECT: To skate like a champion, practice is essential.
   REVISED: To skate like a champion, one must practice.

INCORRECT: To make a good impression, a shirt and tie should be worn to the interview.
   REVISED: To make a good impression, Jeff should wear a shirt and tie to the interview.

ILLOGICAL COMPARISONS

Occasionally, a writer will mistakenly compare items that are not comparable.

INCORRECT: Her *salary* was lower than a clerk. (The *salary* is incorrectly compared with a *clerk.*)
   CORRECT: Her *salary* was lower than a *clerk's.*

INCORRECT: The cultural *events* in Orlando are as diversified as *any other large city.* *Events* are being compared with a large city.
   CORRECT: The cultural events in Orlando are as diversified as *those in any other large city.*

Another form of illogical comparison results when a writer fails to exclude from the rest of the group the item being compared.

INCORRECT: She is taller than *any girl* in her class.
   CORRECT: She is taller than *any other girl* in her class.

PRACTICE EXERCISE

In the following sentences, find the errors that involve modifiers. Not every sentence has an error. Place a check in the appropriate column to indicate whether the sentence is correct or incorrect.

CORRECT   INCORRECT

_____   _____   **1.** The corn was roasted by the boys skewered on the ends of long, pointed sticks.

_____   _____   **2.** It was still pouring, so Uncle Maurice went out to the sty to feed the hogs with an umbrella.

_____   _____   **3.** Coming nearer to it, the building certainly seemed dilapidated.

_____   _____   **4.** Henry's sales record will be as good as any of the top salespeople.

_____   _____   **5.** Coiled in a corner of the garage and ready to spring, Mrs. Lampert was surprised by a rattlesnake.

_____   _____   **6.** Having been asked to speak at the senior dinner, Fred spent many evenings preparing his speech.

_____   _____   **7.** To be well baked, you have to leave the pork roast in the oven for three hours.

_____   _____   **8.** We saw the impressive Concorde on the porch this morning.

ANSWERS AND EXPLANATIONS

1.   INCORRECT. The participial phrase *skewered on the ends of long, pointed sticks* should be placed closer to corn, the noun it is intended to modify: *Skewered ... sticks, the corn ...*

2. INCORRECT. The prepositional phrase *with an umbrella* is misplaced. It seems to modify the *hogs* or *to feed* but should modify the verb *went*.

3. INCORRECT. This sentence is missing the noun that the participial phrase *Coming nearer to it* is meant to modify. A corrected version might be *Coming nearer to the building, we noticed that it certainly seemed dilapidated.*

4. INCORRECT. This sentence contains an illogical comparison. The correct sentence should include the pronoun *that: Henry's sales record will be as good as that of any of the top salespeople.*

5. INCORRECT. The participial phrase beginning this sentence seems to modify *Mrs. Lampert.* It should modify *rattlesnake.* The correction, of course, is to place the participial phrase close to the word *rattlesnake.*

6. CORRECT. The participial phrase is placed close to *Fred,* the noun it logically modifies.

7. INCORRECT. The infinitive phrase *To be well baked* here incorrectly modifies *you* instead of *roast,* the noun it is intended for.

8. INCORRECT. The Concorde was not on the porch, as this sentence seems to imply. Revised: *As we sat on the porch this morning, we saw the impressive Concorde.*

FOCUS ON THE ACT

The following sample questions represent ways in which the above skills might be tested on your ACT Assessment.

The life of famed watchmaker Abraham-Louis Breguet was, from beginning to end <u>(1747-1823). A</u> steady progression toward fame and fortune. Breguet soon revealed a lively interest that developed into a veritable passion for things mechanical <u>in his stepfather's shop</u>. He studied with the famed jeweler Abbot Marie for twelve <u>years, his vocation</u> was henceforth decided. <u>Living in the Swiss cantons</u> on the French border, watch-making had already been developed on a large scale by refugee French families, <u>because</u> it was limited almost exclusively to inexpensive

1. **A.** NO CHANGE
    B. (1747-1823), a
    C. (1747-1823) a
    D. (1747-1823); a

2. **F.** NO CHANGE
    G. (Place at the beginning of the sentence).
    H. (Place after the verb *revealed*).
    J. (Delete altogether; the phrase is not related).

3. **A.** NO CHANGE
    B. years his vocation
    C. years, then his vocation
    D. years, and his vocation

4. **F.** NO CHANGE
    G. (Place this phrase after *border*).
    H. (Place this phrase after *families*).
    J. (Delete altogether; the phrase is not related).

5. **A.** NO CHANGE
    B. but
    C. even though
    D. however

products. Young Breguet, on the contrary,
                                    6
demonstrating very early a decided disgust for shoddy
                                                6
workmanship, as well as a genius for precision work,
                                              6
had an attitude he never lost.
                6

In 1802, Breguet, receiving the gold medal at an
                               7
exhibition of industrial products, sat at the table of the
                                7
first consul. Throughout his reign, Napoleon's interest
      7
in the works of the watch master, principally those of

high precision, never slackened. The face studded with
                                                      8
brilliant diamonds and rubies, Napoleon acquired
                              8
Breguet's most ambitious creation the day after it was
                          8
completed.
    8

The fall of the empire did not affect either his
                                  9
fortunes adversely or his renown, which had spread
                                          9
throughout Europe. The exhibition of 1819 in which
                  9
Breguet presented a collection of his most important

works was a triumphant compendium of his life,

by then more than seventy years old.
            10

6. **F.** NO CHANGE
   G. Young Breguet, on the contrary, demonstrating very early a decided disgust for shoddy workmanship, as well as a genius for precision work, an attitude he never lost.
   H. Young Breguet, on the contrary, demonstrated very early a decided disgust for shoddy workmanship, as well as a genius for precision work, an attitude he never lost.
   J. Young Breguet, on the contrary, demonstrated very early a decided disgust for shoddy workmanship, as well as a genius for precision work, and had an attitude he never lost.

7. **A.** NO CHANGE
   B. In 1802, Breguet, receiving the gold medal at an exhibition of industrial products, sitting at the table of the first consul.
   C. In 1802, Breguet, received the gold medal at an exhibition of industrial products and sat at the table of the first consul.
   D. In 1802, Breguet sat at the table of the first consul, receiving the gold medal at an exhibition of industrial products.

8. **F.** NO CHANGE
   G. The face studded with brilliant diamonds and rubies, Breguet's most ambitious creation, the day after it was completed, was acquired by Napoleon.
   H. The face studded with brilliant diamonds and rubies the day after it was completed, Napoleon acquired Breguet's most ambitious creation.
   J. Napoleon acquired Breguet's most ambitious creation, the face studded with brilliant diamonds and rubies, the day after it was completed.

9. **A.** NO CHANGE
   B. The fall of the empire did not adversely affect either his fortunes or his renown, which had spread throughout Europe.
   C. Adversely, the fall of the empire did not affect either his fortunes or his renown, which had spread throughout Europe.
   D. The fall of the empire did not affect either his fortunes or his renown adversely, which had spread throughout Europe.

10. **F.** NO CHANGE
    G. (Place this phrase at the beginning of the sentence).
    H. (Place this phrase, bracketed with commas, after the word *Breguet*).
    J. (Delete this phrase; it is not relevant).

ANSWERS AND EXPLANATIONS

1. B This sentence contains the parenthetical interruption "from beginning to end (1747-1823)," which must be set off by commas. Any stronger mark of punctuation after the parentheses results in two fragmented sentences.

2. G The only logical position in this sentence for the prepositional phrase *in his stepfather's shop* is at the beginning of the sentence where it will correctly modify the noun *Breguet.*

3. D A compound sentence is the most appropriate vehicle for these two ideas of equal importance. A comma is used before the coordinating conjunction that joins coordinate clauses.

4. H The only logical position in this sentence for the participial phrase *Living in the Swiss cantons* is next to the noun it logically modifies, *families.*

5. B Only a connective signaling contrast like *but* makes sense in this context, especially in the light of the next sentence.

6. H This choice allows the main clause to emphasize the major characteristic of the subject, and correctly subordinates the parenthetical phrase, "an attitude he never lost."

7. C The act of receiving the gold medal is logically as important as sitting with the first consul, and should not be subordinated in a participial phrase.

8. J The phrase *The face studded with brilliant diamonds and rubies* modifies the noun *creation* and so must be placed next to it.

9. B The adverb *adversely* logically modifies only the verb *affect* and should be place near it.

10. H The phrase *By then more than seventy years old* appropriately modifies the noun *Breguet* and should be placed next to it, set off by commas since it is a parenthetical addition.

Consistency and Tense

VERBS IN SUBORDINATE CLAUSES

Because *tense* indicates the time of the action and *voice* indicates whether the subject is the agent of the action (*active:* Tom *saw*) or the recipient of the action (*passive:* Tom *was seen*), both of these verb forms are central to the consistency of a sentence or passage.

Tense

A verb in a subordinate clause should relate logically in tense to the verb in the principal clause. Avoid any unnecessary shift.

INCORRECT: As the wedding *began* [past], the bride's mother *starts* [present] to cry.
  CORRECT: As the wedding *began* [past], the bride's mother *started* [past] to cry.

INCORRECT: He *had intended* [past perfect] to finish his third novel by the end of the year, but he *has been very sick* [present perfect] until Thanksgiving.
  CORRECT: He *had intended* [past perfect] to finish his third novel by the end of the year, but he *was very sick* [past] until Thanksgiving.

INCORRECT: By the time the fire *had been extinguished* [past perfect], the priceless paintings *had been destroyed* [past perfect].
  CORRECT: By the time the fire *was extinguished* [past], the priceless paintings *had been destroyed* [past perfect]. (The past perfect expresses action that took place before the simple past.)

Voice

A verb in a subordinate clause should relate logically in voice to the verb in the main clause. It is generally better to avoid voice shifts within a sentence.

INCORRECT: Sighs of appreciation *could be heard* [passive] as the waiters *brought* [active] huge trays of roast beef and Yorkshire pudding.

  REVISED: The guests *sighed* [active] with appreciation as the waiters *brought* [active] huge trays of roast beef and Yorkshire pudding.

INCORRECT: If the fishing boat *had been reached* [passive] in time, the Coast Guard *might have saved* [active] it with floats. (Note that the subject shifts as well as the voice.)

  CORRECT: If it *had reached* [active] the fishing boat in time, the Coast Guard *might have saved* [active] it with floats.

THE PRESENT INFINITIVE

Always use the present infinitive (to run, to see), after a perfect tense (a tense that uses some form of the helping verb **have** or **had**).

EXAMPLES: He *has decided to order* the Jaguar Model S-1. (Present Perfect + Present Infinitive)

   They *had hoped to hold* a spring picnic. (Past Perfect + Present Infinitive)

Keep in mind that the ACT test offers three substitute choices for each underlined part. Frequently, even though you may not remember the grammatical terms involved, your prose sense will lead you to the right answer.

Look at the following set of responses. Which is correct?

A. Fran would of wanted to see the show.
B. Fran would have wanted to had seen the show.
C. Fran would have wanted to have seen the show.
D. Fran would have wanted to see the show.

Choice **D** is correct. If you selected this answer, did you apply the grammatical principle involved (use the present infinitive after a perfect tense), or were you guided by your prose "ear"? Chances are that it may have been your own language sense that suggested this answer. The point is that you already possess language sense that should help you on the test. With more preparation, you should do even better.

THE SUBJUNCTIVE MOOD

Verbs may be expressed in one of three moods: the *indicative,* used to declare a fact or ask a question; the *imperative,* used to express a command; and the *subjunctive,* generally used to indicate doubt or to express a wish or request or a condition contrary to fact. The first two moods are fairly clear-cut.

INDICATIVE: This cake is tasty. Who baked it?
IMPERATIVE: Please leave now. Go home.

NOTE: The imperative mood has only one subject (*you*) and one tense (the present).

The subjunctive mood presents more of a problem. It suggests *possibilities, maybes, could have beens,* or *wishes that it had been,* and its uses are sometimes more difficult to understand. The subjunctive mood appears more frequently in formal English than in standard written English.

Notice the following uses, including some traditional ones:

EXAMPLES: I insist that the new road *be started* this spring.
   The company requires that the check *be certified.*
   Had she been certain of her facts, she would have challenged the teacher.
   If need *be,* we can use our pension money.
   Should the swarm *reappear,* I will call a beekeeper.
   If he *were* honest, he would return all the money.
   I move that the budget *be accepted.*
   Far *be* it from me to suggest that he is lying.
   Would that I *were* sixteen again!
   I wish I *were* on a plane to Tahiti.

NOTE: Today, the subjunctive is most often used to express doubt, wishes, or conditions contrary to fact. However, the indicative can also be used for some of these same feelings.

SUBJUNCTIVE MOOD: If it *be* true, I will be delighted.
INDICATIVE MOOD: If it *is* true, I will be delighted.

SPECIAL USE OF THE PRESENT TENSE

Use the present tense to express universally true statements or timeless facts.

EXAMPLES: Ice *forms* at 32° F.
The rainy season seldom *arrives* in California.
She told the campers that mosquitos *are* part of nature.

THE HISTORICAL PRESENT

In writing about a poem or describing events in fiction or plays, use the present tense.
This convention is called the *historical present.*

EXAMPLE: In *A Tale of Two Cities,* Dr. Manette *is restored* to his daughter after twenty years in jail.

PRACTICE EXERCISE

In the following sentences, find any errors in mood or tense. Not every sentence has an error. Place a check in the appropriate column to indicate whether the sentence is correct or incorrect.

CORRECT   INCORRECT

_____ _____ 1. If I knew about winning the lottery, I would not have sold my boat.

_____ _____ 2. In his poem "In Memoriam," Tennyson speaks of his sorrow at the death of his friend Arthur Henry Hallam.

_____ _____ 3. They have decided to have gone on a trip.

_____ _____ 4. By the time the tide had covered the sand castles, we had already put the children to bed.

_____ _____ 5. Groans and catcalls could be heard as the opposing team took the field.

_____ _____ 6. When the earthquake struck, we all run out of our houses.

_____ _____ 7. If I was you, I would take the job.

_____ _____ 8. If we reach an accord by Monday, we will offer it to the membership by Monday night.

ANSWERS AND EXPLANATIONS

1. INCORRECT. The past tense *knew* does not go back in time far enough to permit the use of the present perfect tense later in the sentence. The correction is to change *knew* to *had known* (the past perfect).

2. INCORRECT. Use the historical present for statements about literary works (*Tennyson ... speaks*).

3. INCORRECT. Use the present infinitive after a perfect tense.

4. INCORRECT. Watch the sequence of tenses: The children had been put to bed *before* the tide covered the sand castles. *Covered* is the correct tense.
5. INCORRECT. Both the subject and the voice shift in this sentence. Revised: *The opposing team heard groans and catcalls as they took the field.*
6. INCORRECT. Maintain a consistent verb tense: *When the earthquake struck* [past], *we all ran* [past] *out of our houses.*
7. INCORRECT. Use the subjunctive mood for a condition contrary to fact: *If I were you ...*
8. CORRECT. There are no awkward shifts of subjects or voice in this sentence. The sequence of tenses is also correct.

Predication

Predication refers to the process of joining the *naming* part of the sentence (the *subject*) to the *doing* or *describing* part of the sentence (the *predicate*).

SUBJECT	PREDICATE
People	are buying more fish.
Cecelia	is a counselor.

It is not likely that a writer or reader will have trouble linking the subjects and predicates of sentences as short as these. It is in the use of longer, more detailed sentences that predication errors come about. Illogical predication equates unlike constructions and ideas. Look at the following incorrect examples.

INCORRECT: By working at such technical plants as Lockheed and Bendix gives the engineering students insight into what will be expected of them. (*By working* does not give them insight; *working* does.)

According to one authority, the ages of thirty to forty are subject to the most pressures concerning self-identity. (The *ages* are not subject to the pressures, but rather the *people* of those ages.)

The sheer simplicity of frozen food may soon replace home-cooked meals. (*Simplicity* will not replace the meals; *frozen food* will, *because* of its simplicity of preparation.)

Paying bills on time causes many worries for young families. (*Paying* bills does not cause worries, but *not paying* them does.)

IS WHEN, IS WHERE, IS BECAUSE

The use of *is when, is where, is because* is always incorrect. The reason is simple: *when, where,* and *because* introduce adverbial clauses; and a noun subject followed by a form of the verb *to be* must be equated with a noun structure, not with an adverb clause.

INCORRECT: Lepidopterology *is where you study butterflies and moths.*
CORRECT: Lepidopterology *is the study of butterflies and moths.* (Here, the adverb clause *where you study ...* has been changed to a subject complement: *lepidopterology = study.*)
INCORRECT: The reason they won *is because they had better coaching.*
CORRECT: The reason they won *is that they had better coaching.* (The noun clause *that they had better coaching* equates with the noun *reason.*)
OR
They *won because* they had better coaching. (The adverb clause modifies the verb *won.*)

PRACTICE EXERCISE

In the following sentences, find any errors in predication. Not every sentence has an error. Place a check in the appropriate column to indicate whether the sentence is correct or incorrect.

CORRECT   INCORRECT

_____   _____ 1. By building a more efficient engine will save fuel.

_____   _____ 2. Maintaining a healthy weight causes problems for many millions of Americans.

_____   _____ 3. Vertigo is when people become dizzy and are unable to maintain their balance.

_____   _____ 4. Heart failure results from the inability of the heart to pump enough blood to maintain normal bodily functions.

_____   _____ 5. Niagara Falls is an inspiring experience.

_____   _____ 6. The reason that our team did not win was because our key players had injuries.

ANSWERS AND EXPLANATIONS

1. INCORRECT. *Building* a more efficient engine may save fuel, but not *by building.*
2. INCORRECT. The problem does not lie in *maintaining* a healthy weight. It lies in *not maintaining* a healthy weight.
3. INCORRECT. *Is when* is always incorrect. Revised: *Vertigo is a condition in which ...*
4. CORRECT. This sentence has no errors in predications.
5. INCORRECT. A place (*Niagara Falls*) cannot be an experience.
6. INCORRECT. Equate a noun (*reason*) with a noun structure (the clause *that our key players had injuries*).

Parallelism

Parallel ideas in a sentence should be expressed in the same grammatical form. If they are not, the sentence will be unbalanced.

A series of coordinated elements should be parallel in form.

INCORRECT: He enjoys *plays, exhibitions,* and *to walk* every morning. (An infinitive is paired with two nouns.)
CORRECT: He enjoys *going* to plays, *visiting* exhibitions, and *walking* every morning.
       OR
He enjoys *plays, exhibitions,* and morning *walks.*

INCORRECT: The union wanted *pay increases for every employee* and *that there would be shorter working hours.* (A noun is paired with a noun clause.)
CORRECT: The union wanted *pay increases* and shorter *working hours* for every employee.

The constructions that follow correlative conjunctions (*both-and, either-or, neither-nor, not only-but also, whether-or*) should be parallel in form.

INCORRECT: He was *neither qualified* to lead this country *nor was he willing.*
CORRECT: He was *neither qualified nor willing* to lead this country.

Do not use *and* before *which* or *who* unless the sentence has a previously expressed *which* or *who* clause with which to be parallel.

INCORRECT: She is a well-known surgeon from New York, and who has written many books on brain surgery.

CORRECT: She is a well-known surgeon from New York, who has lectured at many medical schools and who has written many books on brain surgery.

NOTE: A sentence may lack parallelism even though its parts are *grammatically* parallel. If the ideas are not logically equal, then the flow of ideas is not parallel.

INCORRECT: The dean introduced new faculty members, explained some curriculum strategies, began an exploratory discussion of the accreditation process, *spilled coffee on his tie,* reviewed the budget for the fiscal year, and *went to lunch with Don Love.* (Although the italicized phrases are grammatically parallel, they are not parallel with the other ideas expressed.)

PRACTICE EXERCISE

In the following sentences, find any errors in parallelism. Not every sentence has an error. Place a check in the appropriate column to indicate whether the sentence is correct or incorrect.

CORRECT   INCORRECT

_____   _____   **1.** William Faulkner wrote *As I Lay Dying, The Sound and the Fury, Sartoris,* and he was also the author of *The Reivers.*

_____   _____   **2.** Cluster secretaries answer calls about special programs, file important papers, sort mail, and they do typing and stuffing envelopes.

_____   _____   **3.** He bought a new scooter with an electric starter, and which has dual pipes and a digital clock.

_____   _____   **4.** My sister's tamale pie is made with ground meat, chili seasoning, olives, and it has onions and beans as well.

_____   _____   **5.** Playing racquetball is more taxing than to jog or play basketball.

_____   _____   **6.** The union stood firm on its demands for a realistic wage, a better health plan, and a more generous pension package.

_____   _____   **7.** The pool is eighteen feet in length and twelve feet wide.

_____   _____   **8.** Most citizens felt gas rationing to be a necessity and fair.

ANSWERS AND EXPLANATIONS

1. INCORRECT. *Made parallel:* William Faulkner wrote *As I Lay Dying, The Sound and the Fury, Sartoris,* and *The Reivers.* (*He was also the author of* is unnecessary.)

2. INCORRECT. *Made parallel:* Cluster secretaries answer calls about special programs, file important papers, sort mail, type, and stuff envelopes.

3. INCORRECT. *Made parallel:* He bought a new scooter with an electric starter, dual pipes, and a digital clock. (A sentence that contains *and which* is not parallel unless it has a previously expressed *which* clause.)

4. INCORRECT. *Made parallel:* My sister's tamale pie is made with ground meat, chili seasoning, olives, onions, and beans.
5. INCORRECT. *Made parallel:* Playing racquetball is more taxing than jogging or playing basketball. (In the original, the infinitives *to jog* and [*to*] *play* are not parallel with the gerund phrase *playing racquetball*.)
6. CORRECT. The structures in this sentence—*wage, plan,* and *package*—are parallel.
7. INCORRECT. *Made parallel:* The pool is eighteen feet long and twelve feet wide. (Or match the phrase *in length* with the phrase *in width*.)
8. INCORRECT. *Made parallel:* Most citizens felt gas rationing to be necessary and fair. (In the original sentence, an adjective, *fair*, is paired with a noun, *necessity*.)

Transitional Words and Phrases

Words of transition are clues that help the reader to follow the writer's flow of ideas. Confusion can result, however, when an illogical or incorrect connective is used. The following list includes more commonly used transitional words and phrases, and the concepts they suggest. For a more comprehensive list, turn to pages 125-126 of this chapter.

CONCEPT

Addition	also, furthermore, moreover, similarly, too
Cause and Effect	accordingly, as a result, consequently, hence, so, therefore, thus
Concession	granted that, it is true that, no doubt, to be sure
Conclusion	in short, that is, to conclude, to sum up
Contrast	although, but, however, nevertheless, on the contrary, on the other hand
Example	for example, for instance

Watch for errors in logical use of transitional words. For example:

INCORRECT: At many gas stations, drivers have to pump their own gasoline; *therefore,* at Ken's Union Station, full service is still the rule.

CORRECT: At many gas stations, drivers have to pump their own gasoline; *however,* at Ken's Union Station, full service is still the rule.

PRACTICE EXERCISE

In the following sentences, find any transition errors. Not every sentence has an error. Place a check in the appropriate column to indicate whether the sentence is correct or incorrect.

CORRECT   INCORRECT

1. Her apple pie won a blue ribbon at the county fair; nevertheless, we all wanted the recipe.
2. Bud and Jake climbed to the top of the falls, and Jake had a fear of heights.
3. I have been meaning to learn more about electronics, so I just bought a book on the subject.
4. I have just finished preparing my tax return after four weeks of figuring and frustration; furthermore, I refuse to fill out any other forms for at least a month!

5. Maria has spent almost twelve years of her academic life studying medicine; however, she feels well qualified to treat sick people.

ANSWERS AND EXPLANATIONS

1. INCORRECT. The connective *nevertheless* is obviously illogical here, with its implication of contrast. A better transitional word might be *consequently*.

2. INCORRECT. A contrast like *although* is needed in this sentence.

3. CORRECT. This is a typical cause-and-effect sentence, correctly using the word *so*.

4. INCORRECT. The speaker refuses to fill out another form *because of* his work on the tax return. Needed here is a causal transition like *as a result*.

5. INCORRECT. The connective *however* does not make sense here because it implies contrast. A causal word like *accordingly* is required.

FOCUS ON THE ACT

The following sample questions represent ways in which the above skills might be tested on your ACT Assessment.

Crime and Punishment by Fyodor Dostoevsky is a topical novel dealing with philosophical doctrines, political, and social issues widely discussed in Russia
1

just after the 1861 reforms. By most critical essays,
2

treating Dostoevsky's work has employed
3

psychological or biological points of view. Because *Crime and Punishment* is a passionate, masterly portrayal of internal psychological conflict, a general assumption has evolved in the general critical world that the author wrote, at least in part, from personal experience. Nevertheless, Dostoevsky's biography has
4

been endlessly probed, explored, and it was thoroughly
5
analyzed.
5

1. A. NO CHANGE
   B. politically
   C. politics
   D. that are political

2. F. NO CHANGE
   G. Because of most critical essays
   H. Most critical essays,
   J. Most critical essays

3. A. NO CHANGE
   B. have employed
   C. should employ
   D. employ

4. F. NO CHANGE
   G. Hence,
   H. On the contrary,
   J. Furthermore

5. A. NO CHANGE
   B. and being analyzed.
   C. and analyzed.
   D. subject to analysis.

In 1849, Dostoevsky was convicted of consorting

with known radical <u>factions; however, he was sentenced</u>
₆

to a four-year prison term. Many critical commentaries

on *Crime and Punishment* consider this experience

formative and essential, certainly a major source of the

creative impulses that eventually resulted in the

execution of the novel. The epilogue of the novel

<u>had been set</u> in Siberia, where he was imprisoned.
₇

When <u>talking</u> to his fellow prisoners, he must have
₈

focused on crime and guilt and thought about the

psychology of the criminal mind <u>granted that</u> he lived
₉

among hardened convicts. One must ask, though, why

he waited until 1865 to write *Crime and Punishment*.

One possible answer <u>is because</u> he wrote the novel in
₁₀

part to speak against foreign ideas adopted by the Russ-

ian radicals of the 1860s.

6. **F.** NO CHANGE
   G. factions, yet, he was sentenced
   H. factions and was sentenced
   J. factions; moreover, he was sentenced

7. **A.** NO CHANGE
   B. is set
   C. was set
   D. has been set

8. **F.** NO CHANGE
   G. having talked
   H. he had talked
   J. having been talking

9. **A.** NO CHANGE
   B. as he
   C. knowing that
   D. considering that

10. **F.** NO CHANGE
    G. is when
    H. is where
    J. is that

ANSWERS AND EXPLANATIONS

1. **C** A noun is necessary in this position to be parallel with the other noun objects in this series, *doctrines* and *issues*.

2. **J** As it stands, this sentence contains an error in predication, beginning with one construction, *By most critical essays,* and continuing with a different one, *treating Dostoevsky's work has employed ... points of view.* It is incorrect to separate a subject from its verb, as in choice H.

3. **D** The verb must agree with its plural subject *essays* and maintain the established present tense.

4. **G** The logic of the sentence requires a cause/effect transitional marker like *Hence,* not the contrast or addition markers suggested by the alternative choices.

5. **C** The parallel series of past participles in this sentence requires this option: *has been probed, explored, and analyzed.*

6. **H** The logic of this sentence requires a transitional word suggesting either *cause* or *addition.* Since the acts of *conviction* and *sentencing* seems to be of equal weight, the conjunction *and* is a sound choice.

7. **B** Use the historical present tense when relating events that occur in fiction.

8. **F** The present participle is used for an action going on at the same time as the main verb.

9. **B** The use of the subordinating conjunction *as* is a sound choice in this position because it creates an adverb clause that modifies the verbs *focused* and *thought.* The other choices create modifiers of the subject to little effect.

10. **J** Only the use of the words *is that* in this spot forms a noun structure that equate with the noun *answer.* The other choices form adverb clauses that cannot equate with the noun.

RHETORICAL SKILLS

Strategy

Some questions on the English ACT Assessment will ask you to choose the most effective introductions and conclusions, both of paragraphs and essays. Others will ask you to select the most logical transitions between sentences or between paragraphs. You will most likely be asked if a passage is appropriate for a particular audience or what kind of supporting details should be added to strengthen a paragraph. You may be asked whether a particular sentence or paragraph is relevant to the selection. A good way to prepare for such questions is to look over writing strategies and some of the principles that apply to each.

Description

Descriptive writing usually relies on sense impressions—records of what the eye sees, the ear hears, the nose smells, the tongue tastes, and the skin feels. If you are asked how a descriptive selection can be strengthened, be sure to consider the addition of more specific sense impressions, if that is an option you are given.

In addition to sense impressions, descriptive writing often employs a *dominant impression* at the outset of the selection, a controlling idea that helps unify the passage and place the specific details employed.

Narration

Narration is usually a series of events presented in chronological sequence, all of which have one purpose: *to tell what happened.* Narration, primarily used in storytelling, biographical histories, diaries, and journals, is a fundamental strategy in all writing. To be effective, narration requires coherent order and also a good deal of rich, descriptive detail.

It is probable that any ACT test choices dealing with the structure of the narrative passage will focus on the *order* of events that make up the narrative. The exact chronological relationships among the events are signaled by tenses, transitions, and time markers. Notice how the author of the following selection uses each of these cues to establish coherent order.

> In the past, this type of literature—whether in books or magazines— was published under such titles as *Travel Adventures, Wonder Stories, Fantastic Tales,* or *Mysteries of the Universe.* It took garish "head-lines" like these to draw attention to the special nature of this material.
>
> In 1929, Hugo Gernsback, a New York magazine publisher and one of the great pioneers in the field we are exploring here, provided the much-needed common denominator by coining the inspired term *science fiction.*
>
> Instantly and universally, science fiction was defined and accepted as a form of literature distinct and apart from all others, a form that imposed on the writer none of the shackles that confine traditional writing to the limits of so many rules and precedents.
>
> Comfortably settled under the aegis of its brand-new generic name, science fiction prospered in spite of a worldwide depression and World War II. Other entertainment media contributed their share. The movies gave us Boris Karloff as Frankenstein's monster and Fredric March as Dr. Jekyll. In 1938, a science fiction radio program about Martian invaders threw the East Coast of the United States into a panic.

Note that the events in the development of science fiction are carefully presented in a clear, coherent sequence and include cues that leave no doubt about the order in which these events took place. For instance, the use of *in the past, this type of literature ... was published* in the first paragraph establishes the fact that science fiction existed in some form *before* the events described in the subsequent paragraphs. In the next three paragraphs, such transitions and time markers as *in 1929, instantly and universally, comfortably settle under ... brand-new ... name, worldwide depression, World War II,* and *in 1938* firmly establish the relative order of events.

Explanation of a Process

Explaining a process is, in some ways, similar to narration; however, you have to be even more careful with the sequence of events. Narration adheres *in general* to a sequence; a process depends *exactly* on a sequence, one that can be repeated time after time with the same results. In explaining a process, the use of transitional signals such as *after, before, next, immediately, while the [glue] is still [wet],* and *when [this] is done,* to indicate the sequence of steps, is an essential writing strategy. To evaluate the sequence of steps in a process passage, pay careful attention to transitional words and phrases.

> I would like to explain a process by which some doctors in Kaiser Permanente Hospital in Woodland Hills helped me to breathe normally again. My problems began during the last week in October 2000 when I found I could barely breathe. Dr. Norman Mundsack, who was the first to see me in the emergency room, noted that my face was gray, my breathing was shallow, and that my EKG and monitor display indicated a significantly reduced flow of blood from my left ventricle. He prescribed *lasix,* a diuretic to improve the ability of the kidneys to eliminate the excess fluids that were building up throughout my body tissues, particularly my lungs, and *digitalis,* a drug that strengthens ventricular contractions and corrects irregular heartbeats. This immediate treatment was important, because it enabled my breathing and circulation to stabilize so that the doctors had time to perform more exhaustive diagnostic tests.

Classification and Division

Classification is the sorting of a group of similar items, like boys, girls, cars, or hair styles into like subdivisions. For example, the group *boys* might be classified into these categories: *surfers, greasers, nerds, jocks,* and *scholars.* Classification helps organize detailed material into different groups so that it can be dealt with in steps or stages, can be seen more clearly, or can be explained or illustrated in all its diversity. *Division* is the breaking down of *one* item, such as a team, a uniform, a style of dress, or a kind of behavior, into its component parts or characteristics. Classification and division are often used together. Frequently, a writer begins by dividing a topic—for example, the topic *California,* which might be divided into *deserts, mountains, coastal regions,* and *forests*—and then by classifying the divisions according to some common principle, in this case perhaps recreational activities available in each region.

Classification helps organize detailed material into different groups so that it can be dealt with in steps or stages, can be seen more clearly, or can be explained or illustrated in all its diversity.

Suppose that you are a newspaper writer who specializes in restaurants and that you want to do an article on international food available in a certain town. You might divide the restaurants in the following way:

ETHNIC FOOD SOLD IN ENCINO, CALIFORNIA

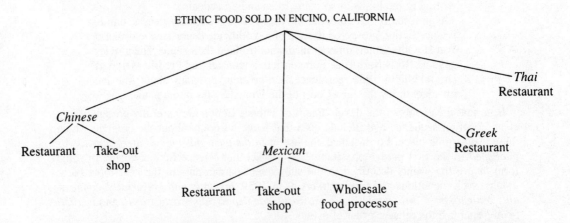

Each division and subdivision of a subject must make sense, that is, it must be necessary for the writer's purpose and also understandable to the reader. The division must be based upon some clear principle: in the diagram of ethnic food sales in Encino, for instance, each ethnic group heads a category. Restaurants, take-out shops, and a wholesale food processor are placed in a subdivision.

Definition

A definition usually takes the form of one or more paragraphs within a larger piece of writing. The writer has decided at that point in the essay that an explanation is needed of the nature or essential qualities of something.

A definition begins by placing the term being defined into a *class;* then it lists the details by which the term can be *distinguished* from other members of that class. For example, a blender is in the class of small kitchen appliances; it can be distinguished from other members of that class—like toasters, can openers, and waffle irons—by the fact that it blends liquids. Here are some other examples:

TERM BEING DEFINED	CLASS TO WHICH IT BELONGS	DISTINGUISHING CHARACTERISTICS
A stove is	a kitchen appliance	designed to heat and cook food.
Freedom is	a political condition	without restraints or limitations.
A lion is	a feline animal	that inhabits wide plains areas.
Psychiatry is	the medical field	dealing with physical and behavioral disorders of the mind.

> Freud defines wish-fulfillment as a dream that represents a fulfilled wish. This does not mean that these dreams are meaningless or absurd, but actually that they have complete validity. He claims that dreams express the unfulfilled wishes of the individual. When discussing wish-fulfillment, Freud gives a variety of different examples of dreams, not only from his own family but from his patients, too. For example, he claims that his eating anchovies or olives in the evening causes him to be thirsty in his dream and that in his dream he is aware of his craving. After identifying what he wished for, in this case a glass of water, he actually dreams that he is getting a glass of water and drinking it. Obviously, dreaming that he satisfied his craving did not satisfy his physical need, just his mental need.

An extended definition begins with this simple form and builds upon it, using any of the techniques common to other strategies.

Comparison and Contrast

A common way to explain something is to show how it is *similar to* or *different from* something else—in other words, to *compare* or *contrast.* You have two main options in comparing and contrasting: (a) you can present the similarities or differences point by point, turning first to one subject and then to the other each time, or (b) you can treat each subject as a whole, finishing with one during the first half of the essay, and then with the other.

Point-By-Point Format

> Some people say the business about the jolly fat person is a myth, that all of us chubbies are neurotic, sick, sad people. I disagree. Fat people may not be chortling all day long, but they're a hell of a lot *nicer* than the wizened and shriveled. Thin people turn surly, mean, and hard at a young age because they never learn the value of a hot-fudge sundae for easing tension. Thin people don't like gooey soft things because they themselves are neither gooey nor soft. They are crunchy and dull, like carrots. They go straight to the heart of the matter while fat people let things stay all blurry and hazy and vague, the way things actually are. Thin people want to face the truth. Fat people know there is no truth. One of my thin friends is always staring at complex, unsolvable problems and saying, "The key thing is...." Fat people never say that. They know there isn't such a thing as the key thing about anything.

Separation Format

> Imagine that you spent your whole life at a single house. Each day at the same hour you entered an artificially lit room, undressed and took up the same position in front of a motion-picture camera. It photographed one

frame of you per day, every day of your life. On your seventy-second birth-day, the reel of film was shown. You saw yourself growing and aging over seventy-two years in less than half an hour (27.4 minutes at sixteen frames per second). Images of this sort, though terrifying, are helpful in suggest-ing unfamiliar but useful perspectives of time. They may, for example, symbolize the telescoped, almost momentary character of the past as seen through the eyes of an anxious or disaffected individual. Or they may sug-gest the remarkable brevity of our lives in the cosmic scale of time. If the estimated age of the cosmos were shortened to seventy-two years, a human life would take about ten seconds.

But look at time the other way. Each day is a minor eternity of over 86,000 seconds. During each second, the number of distinct molecular functions going on within the human body is comparable to the number of seconds in the estimated age of the cosmos. A few seconds are long enough for the revolutionary idea, a startling communication, a baby's conception, a wounding insult, a sudden death. Depending on how we think of them, our lives can be infinitely long or infinitely short.

In either case, strict organization of the specific differences and similarities between one item and the other is essential. In addition, there has to be some balance and some sense of equal treatment of each subject to establish coherence.

Cause and Effect

Cause-and-effect essays can be immensely complicated and, as a result, require more careful organization than any other strategic approach. The cause-and-effect essay or para-graph usually begins with a clear, detailed examination of the *effect* that is the essay sub-ject (such as the slow death of Monterey pine trees around Lake Arrowhead in Southern California) and then proceeds to discuss each of the causes in detail, usually in order of importance.

What can be more troublesome about cause-and-effect essays is that both causes and effects are usually multiple; there are frequently not only several causes, but also primary *and* secondary effects as well. What is more, there is a progression of importance among the causes.

In 1976 a book called *Maternal-Infant Bonding* was published. It changed the way that newborn infants are treated from the moment of birth. The authors, pediatricians Marshall Klaus and John Kennell, had observed mothers and their newborns and found that, during the first hour or so after birth, babies are usually awake and will gaze at the mother's face while the mother gazes at and touches the infant. The importance of this early con-tact was demonstrated by Klaus and Kennell's experiments on the effect of leaving mothers and newborns together for the hour after birth or giving them extra opportunities to be together during their hospital stay. They found that women who were given early and extended contact with their babies were later more emotionally attached to them than mothers given only the routine contact allowed by usual hospital procedures. Further, mothers given early and extended contact with their infants felt more com-petent and were more reluctant to leave their infants with another person. They stayed closer to their infants, often gazing into their eyes, touching and soothing them, and fondling and kissing them. This difference occurred in the hospital and lasted for a year or more.

Any item on the English Test that deals with a cause-and-effect passage will usually concern the organization of the essay, perhaps questioning the orderly and coherent arrangement of supporting facts.

Persuasion

For our purposes, the term *persuasion* refers to either argument (usually defined as an appeal to logic) or persuasion (defined as an appeal to emotion or ethics). In a persuasion paper, the writer hopes to *convince* the reader and attempts to do so through a series of steps: (1) gain the reader's attention, (2) outline the problem or situation, (3) anticipate or recognize opposing points of view, and (4) appeal to both reason and emotion (in the choice of examples and details).

> We in the United States have made great progress in lowering our birth rates. But now, because we have been responsible, it seems to some that we have a great surplus. There is, indeed, waste that should be eliminated, but there is not as much fat in our system as most people think. Yet we are being asked to share our resources with the hungry peoples of the world. But why should we share? The nations having the greatest needs are those that have been the least responsible in cutting down on births. Famine is one of nature's ways of telling profligate peoples that they have been irresponsible in their breeding habits.
>
> Naturally we would like to help, and if we could, perhaps we should. But we can't be of any use in the long run—particularly if we weaken ourselves.
>
> Until we have a couple of years' supply of food and other resources on hand to take care of our own people and until those asking for handouts are doing at least as well as we are at reducing existing excessive population-growth rates, we should not give away our resources—not so much as one bushel of wheat. Certainly we should not participate in any programs that will increase the burden that mankind is already placing on the earth. We should not deplete our own soils to save those who will only die equally miserable a decade or so down the line—and in many cases only after reproducing more children who are inevitably doomed to live and die in misery.

PRACTICE EXERCISE

Identify the appropriate writing strategy for developing a paragraph on each of the following topics. Choose your answer from the following list and write the letter of your choice in the space to the left.

A. Description
B. Narration
C. Explanation of a Process
D. Classification and Division
E. Definition
F. Comparison and Contrast
G. Cause and Effect
H. Persuasion

WRITING
STRATEGY   TOPIC

_____ **1.** Types of diets
_____ **2.** An inspiring moment
_____ **3.** American students and Japanese students
_____ **4.** Why so many high school students drop out
_____ **5.** My grandmother's kitchen
_____ **6.** How to install a three-way switch
_____ **7.** The meaning of commitment
_____ **8.** Don't let them cut the homeowner's tax deduction.

ANSWERS AND EXPLANATIONS

1. D *Classification and Division.* Whenever a plural topic (diets) is to be broken down into subtypes, the written material will be detailed and will require classification, division, and subdivision.

2. B *Narration.* The word *moment* is an important clue. Obviously something happened to make that moment memorable. Narration presents a series of events.

3. F *Comparison and Contrast.* A topic with such clear polarity has to fall into this strategy. When two items are being discussed, it is almost impossible to avoid a discussion of similarities and differences.

4. G *Cause and Effect.* The effect is the dropout rate; the cause is the main substance of a paper on this topic (*why* such a phenomenon occurs). It is clearly a complicated topic, with multiple causes and effects.

5. A *Description.* Grandmother's kitchen is full of smells and visual impressions that can only be approached *through a descriptive essay.*

6. C *Explanation of a Process.* The words *How to* signal a process paper, a paper that explains the exact and repeatable steps to take to achieve the same result each time—in this case, an operating three-way switch.

7. E *Definition.* Definition writing is required when a word must be placed in a class—in this case, a class of philosophical stances—and then distinguished from other members of that class, to achieve a clear and understandable definition.

8. H *Persuasion.* The very form of this topic ("Don't let them …") indicates that it is a form of argument in which the writing is meant to convince the reader.

Organization

The Main Idea

If a passage of prose can be viewed as a liquid and boiled in a pan until just one drop is left, that one drop can be considered the *essence* or *main idea* of that passage. It is essential to realize that every piece of writing that can stand on its own has one *main idea* from which the entire work, no matter how large or small, is derived.

It should not be too difficult to discover the central idea in each of the short selections that generally make up the ACT English Test. If you get in the habit of formulating the main idea as you read each passage, you will find that the rhetorical questions, especially those concerning organization, can be answered more easily. Remember that the main idea must always be a complete sentence, not a word or a topic. Only a sentence is able to express the *idea* of the passage.

For example, a passage might be about exercise (the *topic*). But what does it state about exercise? If the selection points out that exercise makes a person more alert, more fit, more productive, and more likely to live longer, the central idea is probably something similar to "Exercise is essential to a healthy, productive life." On the other hand, if statements are made concerning bruised heel bones, pulled hamstrings, shinsplints, and muscle pain, then the main idea might be something similar to "Exercise can do more harm than good."

Whatever sentence you decide expresses the main idea of the passage, you must test it to make sure it really does represent the thrust of the entire selection. For example, you can ask, "In what way can exercise do more harm than good?" Or, "In what way is exercise essential to a healthy, productive life?" If every sentence and paragraph in the passage pertains to the main idea you have chosen, then you know your choice is sound. However, if you find that the passage contains sentences and paragraphs that support other ideas, then you need to start over and formulate another main idea.

Questions that test your ability to determine the central idea can be expressed in a number of ways:

The main point the author makes is …
The author seems chiefly concerned with …
The main idea of this passage is …
Which of the following titles could best be used for this selection?
Which of these statements best expresses the idea of the passage?

Supporting Material

The supporting material that makes up the larger portion of most selections (often called the *body of the writing*) contains the essential material of the work—specific details, anecdotes, allusions, references, or reasons—by which a writer substantiates the main thought.

Keep in mind that supporting material may vary considerably from one context to another. The specific details in a report on a scientific discovery, for example, may be very different from the kind of detail needed in a biographical selection.

Try to be continually mindful of the logical order of paragraphs within a selection, and of the logical order of sentences within each paragraph. Transitional words and phrases usually highlight paragraph or essay coherence, and should be of great help when you are asked whether or not a sentence or paragraph is out of place.

At times, the English Test will include a question about the readers or audience for whom the selection is intended. The relative quality and sophistication of the supporting details will supply the basis for the answer to such questions. For example, a selection intended for children would probably include simple explanations and supporting details that would be unnecessary or inappropriate for adult readers.

Transition

Transitional words and phrases make clear the relationship between phrases, clauses, and sentences, and lend coherence to the sequence of paragraphs.

A transitional paragraph is used to link the main parts of an essay. Such a paragraph may be just a single sentence that eases the progression from one idea to the next:

EXAMPLE: Sometimes a solution is based upon a study of the past. Let us review what has taken place in new architecture so far this century.

Most of the time, however, transitions are individual words or phrases that provide transition while signaling a concept like addition, contrast, example, or time. The following list will show you the functions of some transitions.

CONCEPTS	TRANSITIONS
Addition and continuation	also, and, another, besides, finally, likewise, furthermore, in addition, indeed, moreover, similarly, then, too
Cause and effect	accordingly, as, as a result, because, consequently, for this reason, since, then, therefore, thus
Concession	certainly, granted that, it is true that, no doubt, of course, still, to be sure
Conclusion or repetition	in other words, in particular, in short, in summary, once again, that is, to repeat
Contrast or limitation	although, but, however, if, in contrast, instead, nevertheless, on the contrary, on the other hand, otherwise, provided that, still, yet
Example	for example, for instance, in particular, likewise, specifically, that is, to illustrate
Place	above, behind, below, elsewhere, here, in back of, north of, on this side, there, to the right of, underneath
Time	afterward, before, earlier, eventually, immediately, later, meanwhile, next, now, since, soon, until

Openings and Closings

Being able to spot beginning and ending paragraphs is important when you are asked on the ACT to rearrange paragraphs that are obviously scrambled. The beginning paragraph will often include signals that will help you determine the proper order of subsequent paragraphs.

The *opening paragraph* is crucial. In a few words, the author must make clear the central purpose of the work and also persuade the reader to continue reading. Sometimes, authors will use the opening paragraph to establish their authority for the task or to create a question in the reader's mind that he or she needs or hopes to have answered—by continuing to read.

The land that became the United States was in colonial times an extension of the Old World into the New. Through the centuries, the descendants of the original colonists blended their European heritage into the new Nation that evolved. But for the courage and resourcefulness of the Europeans who first explored and settled the unknown wilderness, that evolution would not have been possible.

The simplest *closing paragraphs* summarize the gist of the entire passage in a sentence or two. Others invite or challenge the reader to engage in further research on the topic. A good concluding paragraph will complete the passage logically and clearly, leaving the reader with the certainty that the main idea has been adequately developed.

The amalgamation of such rich and diverse national, cultural, and racial elements into a free and democratic society has created the United States of America—a blending of cultures, languages, and traditions that mirrors the hopes and aspirations of all mankind.

PRACTICE EXERCISE

The sentences in the following paragraphs have been deliberately rearranged so that the thoughts are not coherent. You will find, however, that they contain enough key words and ideas for you to identify the central idea and then rearrange the sentences to form a well-crafted, coherent paragraph. In the space at the left, indicate the correct sequence of sentence numbers.

Paragraph I

(1) More flowed at Concord, and much more along the route of the British as they retreated to Boston, harassed most of the way by an aroused citizenry. (2) About 77 militiamen confronted the redcoats when they plodded into Lexington at dawn. (3) What once had been merely protest had evolved into open warfare; the War for Independence had begun. (4) After some tense moments, as the sorely outnumbered colonials were dispersing, some blood was shed.

Paragraph II

(1) It was not just the Iranian hostage crisis or the Soviet invasion of Afghanistan, but the fear, felt by many of our friends, that America could not, or would not, keep her commitments. (2) We need to remember where America was five years ago. (3) Other nations were saying that it was dangerous—deadly dangerous—to be a friend of the United States. (4) We need to recall the atmosphere of that time—the anxiety that events were out of control, that the West was in decline, that our enemies were on the march. (5) Pakistan, the country most threatened by the Afghan invasion, ridiculed the first offer of American aid as "peanuts."

Paragraph III

(1) Finally, and probably most important, inflation must be brought under control so that the country can enjoy a period of disciplined growth. (2) Another would be to increase investment in human capital, particularly skilled workers and technical personnel, through training in the workplace and in institutions of higher education. (3) The U.S. government can do much to create an environment in which the innovative capacity of American business and labor can be maximized. (4) It is clear that it would

be impossible for the United States to emulate the much-vaunted Japanese form of industrial policy. (5) To do so would require a very different system for allocating capital investments, a different government-business-labor relationship, and perhaps a different set of cultural institutions. (6) Yet there are some lessons to be learned from the successes of Japan, as well as from those of other industrial countries. Increasing the level of investments and savings would be a desirable goal.

ANSWERS AND EXPLANATIONS

The sentences have been rearranged in the logical order.

PARAGRAPH I: 2, 4, 1, 3. About 77 militiamen confronted the redcoats when they plodded into Lexington at dawn. After some tense moments, as the sorely outnumbered colonials were dispersing, some blood was shed. More flowed at Concord, and much more along the route of the British as they retreated to Boston, harassed most of the way by an aroused citizenry. What once had been merely protest had evolved into open warfare; the War for Independence had begun.

Commentary: Note that the second, third, and fourth sentences of the rearranged paragraph begin with the transition clues that place them after a key statement in the previous sentence. For example, in the second sentence, the phrase *After some tense moments* clearly belongs after the event described in the initial sentence. Similarly, the word *More* in the next sentence has as its antecedent the word *blood* in the sentence before, and the summation of the last sentence applies to the paragraph as a whole.

PARAGRAPH II: 2, 4, 1, 5, 3. We need to remember where America was five years ago. We need to recall the atmosphere of that time—the anxiety that events were out of control, that the West was in decline, that our enemies were on the march. It was not just the Iranian hostage crisis or the Soviet invasion of Afghanistan, but the fear, felt by many of our friends, that America could not, or would not, keep her commitments. Pakistan, the country most threatened by the Afghan invasion, ridiculed the first offer of American aid as "peanuts." Other nations were saying that it was dangerous—deadly dangerous—to be a friend of the United States.

Commentary: Again, each sentence has a clue to help you determine where it belongs. The first sentence has the phrase *We need,* echoed by the second sentence, which then goes on to speak of events out of control. The next sentence actually lists events out of control and also mentions the fear, on the part of our friends, that we would not meet our commitments. Then these "friends," Pakistan and other nations, are identified in the next two sentences.

PARAGRAPH III: 4, 5, 6, 7, 2, 3, 1. It is clear that it would be impossible for the United States to emulate the much-vaunted Japanese form of industrial policy. To do so would require a very different system for allocating capital investments, a different government-business-labor relationship, and perhaps a different set of cultural institutions. Yet there are some lessons to be learned from the successes of Japan, as well as from those of other industrial countries. Increasing the level of investments and savings would be a desirable goal. Another would be to increase investment in human capital, particularly where skilled workers and technical personnel, through training in the workplace and in institutions of higher education. The U.S. government can do much to create an environment in which the innovative capacity of American business and labor can be maximized. Finally, and probably most important, inflation must be brought under control so that the country can enjoy a period of disciplined growth.

Commentary: The key to unraveling this set of sentences is the phrase *To do so* in the second sentence. A cursory look at all of the sentences in the paragraph reveals that only one (the sentence beginning *It is clear that ...*) makes sense in an earlier position. The other sentences occur naturally in order from that point on. The contrast indicator *yet* signals a departure from the "it is impossible to emulate" position of the first two sentences, with the sentence it begins stating that "there are some lessons to be learned." The next two sentences list two of those lessons, and the last two sentences add two more steps that could be taken by the U.S. government.

Style

As you read each passage on the test, it is important to be aware of the author's style of writing. You may be asked a question about style, and its characteristics, or about a portion of the test that departs from that style. A fundamental principle of writing is that style should remain consistent throughout any writing selection. If there is an obvious shift in style in one of the ACT selections, you will probably be questioned about it.

There are several levels of formality in the prose that most secondary and post-secondary students encounter: formal, informal, popular, elevated, and esoteric.

Formal Writing Style

Formal style is characterized by long and complex sentences, a scholarly vocabulary, and a consistently serious tone. Grammatical rules are observed, and the subject matter is substantial. The selection may include references to literary works or allusions to historical and classical figures. Absent are contractions, colloquial expressions, and an identified speaker, with the impersonal *one* or *the reader* frequently used as the subject.

> The California coast, endowed with a wonderful climate and peopled by docile Indians, was ideally suited for the pastoral mission system by which New Spain had been slowly extending her northern frontiers. Elsewhere in the present United States the system had either failed or met with only moderate success; in California it thrived and reached perfection. Nevertheless, California was the last area in the United States to be penetrated by Spain—and not until the frontier lay virtually dormant elsewhere. Located as it was so far out on the lifelines of the Spanish Empire in the New World, California was sparsely populated and neglected.

Explorers and Settlers, Government Printing Office

A formal writing style is used in serious essays, research papers, and legal documentation. Although this type of writing is not likely to appear on the ACT test, you should be prepared to identify it.

Informal Writing Style

Informal style uses the language of everyday speech, characterized by contractions, colloquialisms, and occasional slang. The topics are often light, and the approach, or tone, is conversational. Sentences are usually uncomplicated, and the writer makes no attempt to distance himself from the reader, frequently using *I* or *we* as the subject.

> Animals talk to each other, of course. There can be no question about that; but I suppose there are very few people who can understand them. I never knew but one man who could ... This was Jim Baker. According to Jim Baker, some animals have only a limited education, and use only very simple words, and scarcely ever a comparison or a flowery figure; whereas, certain other animals have a large vocabulary, a fine command of language and a ready and fluent delivery; consequently these latter talk a great deal; they like it; they are conscious of their talent, and they enjoy "showing off."

Mark Twain, *A Tramp Abroad*

Popular Writing Style

The popular style is the writing style most students use in school work. Less colloquial and relaxed than the informal, the popular style consists of longer sentences, with no contractions but some colloquialisms when necessary for clarity and immediacy. Usually the tone of the work is serious, and the content is substantial and informative. The popular style is characteristic of the language used in newspapers, magazines, and contemporary literature. Look at the following student essay, written in popular style.

Fishing has always been an art form to the practitioner of the sport. The techniques involved in outsmarting fish are passed down from generation to generation. Sometimes this information is related in the form of direct instruction or through the use of illustrated books, but most neophytes learn by watching others fish or by being asked to "mind my pole." That is usually the time when the best fish of the day is caught. Such an occurrence can and does drive expert anglers to distraction, causing them to mutter under their breath and cast sidelong glances at a youngster who is doing everything wrong but still manages to bring in a whopper.

Elevated Writing Style

The elevated style is poetic in tone and is intended for certain solemn occasions that exist infrequently today—for example, addressing a king or memorializing a national hero. Heightened funeral orations or eulogies now seem inappropriate, most expressions of grief or commemoration being couched in more popular styles. Literary allusions, biblical phrases, figures of speech, ornate language, graveness of tone—all are characteristic of the elevated style. Although this type of writing is not likely to appear on the ACT English Test, it is a good idea to be familiar with it, in case you are asked to differentiate it from another style of writing. The following excerpt is from a eulogy that appeared in a July 1852 newspaper.

Alas! who can realize that Henry Clay is dead! Who can realize that never again that majestic form shall rise in the council-chambers of his country to beat back the storms of anarchy which may threaten, or pour the oil of peace upon the troubled billows as they rage and menace around?

Esoteric Writing Style

The word *esoteric* refers to knowledge that is limited to a small group. This writing style uses technical or specialized phraseology (sometimes referred to as jargon) characteristic of a particular profession, trade, or branch of learning. Groups employing such language include medical personnel, astronauts, air traffic controllers, jazz musicians, and a variety of others. The following excerpt is from a medical journal.

Morphologic changes in the myocardium are caused by coronary obstruction leading to infarction and hemorrhaging within the wall of the sclerotic coronary vessel.

PRACTICE EXERCISE

Identify the following items according to the writing style used: formal (F), elevated (EL), informal (I), popular (P), or esoteric (ES). Put the correct letter in the space to the left of each item.

_____ 1. If gold were the first valuable product to be found in America, wood of the *Caesalpina* species, known in English as brazilwood, or simply logwood, had become the second by 1510.

_____ 2. Before the sale started, I spotted an old beat-up table, drop-leaf style, that was pure cherry, as far as I could see.

_____ 3. Parry made the crucial connection between this "formulaic" diction and the possibility, long speculated on, that Homer was an oral bard rather than a literate writer.

_____ 4. The essential difference between capitalizing with discount rates, GRMs, and overall capitalization rates is that specific forecasting of periodic cash flows is required when using discount rates.

_____ 5. Of course, this man was an eccentric. In fact, an eccentric among eccentrics. Most furniture forgers use old wood. And where do these crooks get two-hundred-year-old wood? The answer's simple. From two-hundred-year-old houses.

_____ **6.** Alas, in those dark hours, which, as they come in the history of all nations, must come in ours—those hours of peril and dread which our land has experienced, and which she may be called to experience again—to whom now may her people look up for that counsel and advice, which only wisdom and experience can give?

_____ **7.** Second-rate matadors lived at that pension because the address on the Calle San Jeronimo was good, the food was excellent, and the room and board was cheap.

ANSWERS AND EXPLANATIONS

1. **F** Note the factual approach, the scholarly tone and vocabulary.
2. **I** This sentence is colloquial and conversational, and uses the subject *I*.
3. **F** Phrases like *"formulaic" diction* and *oral bard,* as well as the scholarly tone and subject matter, indicate the writing style.
4. **ES** It is easy to identify this style by the specialized vocabulary and technical approach.
5. **I** Informal style uses colloquialisms, slang, contractions, and short, uncomplicated sentences.
6. **EL** Extravagant sentiment and ornate phrases mark the elevated style.
7. **P** The popular style has no contractions or slang and is less colloquial than the informal style.

Word Choice

Diction

Some of the questions on the English Test will require you to decide the appropriateness of a word in its context. In a technical passage about the development of the transistor, for example, the use of a flowery or ornate word or phrase would stand out as inappropriate. Similarly, words that are illiterate or colloquial, or used in spoken English, for the most part, are not appropriate in a formal literary passage.

A word is *appropriate* if it fits the reader, occasion, and purpose for which the writing is intended. In general, most language can be categorized as either formal, informal (colloquial), or popular.

FORMAL DICTION

Formal diction is seldom used in everyday conversation and writing. It is found in writing that serves a serious purpose (for example, a research paper) and concerns weighty or substantial topics, such as death, crime, philosophy, scholarship, science, and literature.

Formal language employs a more scholarly vocabulary than popular English (*eccentric* for *strange, extenuation* for *excuse, immaculate* for *clean, tantamount* for *equivalent,* and so on). Another characteristic is grammatical exactness.

INFORMAL DICTION

Informal diction is *colloquial* language, that is, the language of everyday conversation. It includes contractions (always improper in formal writing), slang, colloquialisms, dialect and turns of phrase peculiar to local areas (*provincialisms*), and shortened word forms (*TV* for *television, phone* for *telephone, CD* for *compact disc,* for example).

POPULAR DICTION

Popular diction lies somewhere between formal and informal (colloquial) diction. It is not as free as colloquial, nor does it include slang or provincialisms, but it relaxes many of the rules and restrictions of formal written English. Generally, popular diction is the language of mass-media publications. Its aim is to appeal to and communicate clearly with the average reader.

The following expressions have no place in formal prose.

Cool it.	yeah
guys	turn-on
high (intoxicated)	guts
spaced-out (on drugs)	I've had it!
for sure	stuck-up
creep (obnoxious person)	an awful lot
macho	screwball

This list contains some common misspellings, provincialisms, illiterate expressions, and incorrect forms to be avoided.

NOT	BUT
aggravate	annoy; exasperate
a half an hour	a half hour *or* half an hour
alot	a lot
alright	all right
and etc.	etc. or et cetera
anywheres	anywhere
being that, being as how	as, because, since
can't seem to	seem unable to
considerable sick	quite sick
dark-complected	dark-complexioned
different than	different from
hadn't ought	ought not
heighth	height
irregardless	regardless, irrespective
no-account; no-good	worthless
off of	off, from
out loud	aloud
outside of	except; beside
should of, would of	should have, would have
the reason is because	the reason is that
tote	carry
try and give	try to give
use to	used to
visit with	visit
won him	beat him

Some colloquialisms and short forms are appropriate in everyday conversation and informal writing, but should not be used in formal written English.

NOT	BUT
ad	advertisement
at about; at around	about; around
can't help but	cannot help but
center around	center on
get going	go
guess so, reckon so	think, suppose
has got to go	has to go
he is liable to be there	he is likely to be there
hold on	wait
kids	children
kind of a, sort of a	kind of, sort of
mighty hard	very hard
okay	all right

out loud	aloud
packs quite a punch	delivers a strong blow
phone	telephone
show up	appear to be superior
TV	television
wait a bit	wait

Here is a list of frequently misused or confused words. Be sure you can distinguish their meanings.

accept: to receive; to agree to
except: to exclude
except: a preposition meaning *but, other than*

affect: to influence
effect: to bring about
effect: a noun meaning *result*

allusion: indirect reference
illusion: false perception or image

all ready: everything is ready
already: by this time

alumna: a female graduate
alumnae: two or more female graduates
alumnus: a male graduate
alumni: two or more male graduates; also,
   a universal term for college graduate

amount: used for noncountable bulk or weight (an amount of milk)
number: used for things that can be counted as
   individual units (a number of gallons of milk)

compare: to deal with similarities
contrast: to deal with differences

complement: to complete or strengthen
compliment: to praise

continual: frequently repeated
continuous: without interruption; never ending

emigrate: to move out of a country or region
immigrate: to move into a country or region

fiancé: engaged man (plural: fiancés)
fiancée: engaged woman (plural: fiancées)

former: first
latter: last

healthful: giving health
healthy: having good health

imply: to suggest or hint by word or manner (He *implied,* by the way he ignored me,
   that he did not want to talk to me.)
infer: to gain an opinion or understanding from what one reads or hears (I *inferred*
   from the mayor's announcement that he was going to run.)

incredible: unbelievable (A story is *incredible.*)
incredulous: unwilling or unable to believe (That person is *incredulous.*)

less: used with noncountable items (We had *less* information about the earthquake than they did.)

fewer: used with countable items (There were *fewer* students every year.)

principal: main, most important; a sum of money; a school official

principle: a rule of conduct; a general truth

than: a conjunction used to express a comparison

then: at that time; therefore

Imagery and Figurative Language

Writers in search of clear, vivid, and forceful prose often use devices called figures of speech to gain a desired effect. Note the image conveyed by Phillip Wylie's description of a very thin woman as "a trellis for varicose veins." Among the important figures of speech are *simile, metaphor, synecdoche, metonymy,* and *personification.* Inappropriate expressions that you may need to *rule out* on the English Test could involve misuse of these figures of speech.

SIMILE

A simile is a figure of speech that uses *like* or *as* to compare two dissimilar things.

EXAMPLES: "… mountains like thirsty giants"—*National Geographic*
"a complexion like the belly of a fish"—*Charles Dickens*

Some similes have been used so much that they are no longer effective and are considered clichés.

INEFFECTIVE SIMILES: old as the hills
dull as dishwater
American as apple pie
teeth like pearls

METAPHOR

A metaphor is a figure of speech that suggests a likeness between two ideas or objects. *As* or *like* is not used.

EXAMPLES: This monstrous human error, the megalopolis …
"She is the rose, the glory of the day."—Edmund Spenser

As with similes, some metaphors have become trite through overuse.

INEFFECTIVE METAPHORS: the black sheep of the family
a wolf in sheep's clothing
a sea of troubles

A mixed metaphor results when metaphors occurring in the same sentence or paragraph create ludicrous images. If a woman is said to be a rose, and her arms petals, then she cannot be a jewel in the next sentence.

EXAMPLES: The floodgates of atheism and permissiveness are stalking arm in arm throughout the land. (Floodgates cannot stalk.)
The harvest sown by the crooked politicians came home to roost. (Two mixed metaphors here: *seeds,* not a *harvest,* are sown, and *chickens,* not a *harvest,* come home to roost.)

SYNECDOCHE

Synecdoche uses the part to represent the whole: ranch hands, for example, for a group of men performing labor with their hands, or *daily bread* for food. Here are a few more synecdoches:

EXAMPLES: The pen [writing] is mightier than the sword [fighting].
Five hundred souls [people] were lost.

METONYMY

Metonymy substitutes something closely related for the thing actually meant. The *White House* stands for the President, for example; *the Blue and the Gray,* for the Union and Confederate forces.

EXAMPLES: "Scepter and crown [the king] must tumble down."
The Dodgers need to add more bats [good hitters] to their team.
I'm going to complain directly to City Hall.

PERSONIFICATION

Personification is a form of metaphor in which an inanimate object or abstract idea—for example, a car, or a quality like love—is treated as if it has human characteristics, feelings, or actions.

EXAMPLES: "I have seen the ambitious ocean swell and rage and foam."
—*William Shakespeare*
Justice hung her head.

We use personification often in daily conversation when we speak of the "bitter wind," "nasty weather," "gentle breeze," "cruel sea," "unforgiving clock," or "bountiful Mother Nature."

Errors involving these figures of speech on the ACT English Test will most probably consist of mixed or confused examples, so be alert for any absurd, illogical, or meaningless expressions or comparisons.

PRACTICE EXERCISE

Most of the following sentences contain errors in diction, imagery, or logical expression. Place a check in the appropriate space to indicate whether the sentence contains appropriate diction and sound expressions, or uses faulty language or flawed expressions. Note that all sentences should be in standard written English.

	FAULTY	
CORRECT	OR FLAWED	

_____   _____   **1.** It was a near perfect day to have a picnic.

_____   _____   **2.** Quick as a flash, the horse and rider jumped the gun and sailed around the track at full steam.

_____   _____   **3.** Paul excepted the invitation to compete in the biathlon.

_____   _____   **4.** The college has finally untangled itself from the briar bush of debt and is now in smooth water.

_____   _____   **5.** I was tickled pink to discover that the Senate had passed the revised income tax legislation.

_____   _____   **6.** He use to be a catcher for the Mets.

_____   _____   **7.** You hadn't ought to aggravate the Doberman!

_____   _____   **8.** Though the other political party keeps dragging the national debt red herring across our path, it misfires every time.

_____   _____   **9.** The issue of increased subway fares has become a political football.

_____   _____   **10.** They discovered a large amount of gold coins.

ANSWERS AND EXPLANATIONS

1. FAULTY. This is a colloquial use of *near* (an adjective), instead of *nearly* (an adverb), to modify *perfect*.
2. FLAWED. This sentence contains two overused expressions (the simile *Quick as a flash* and the metaphor *jumped the gun* and a mixed metaphor (*sailed ... at full steam*).
3. FAULTY. The correct word to use here is *accepted* (agreed), not *excepted* (excluded from).
4. FLAWED. The college is likened first to an animal or person becoming tangled in a bush, then to a ship at sea.
5. FAULTY. *Tickled pink* is a colloquial expression.
6. FAULTY. *Use to* should be changed to *used to*.
7. FAULTY. Use *ought not*, not *hadn't ought. Annoy* is a better word choice than *aggravate*.
8. FLAWED. A red herring cannot fire (or misfire) like a gun.
9. CORRECT. The metaphor presents a clear, vivid picture of an unpopular issue that is being tossed back and forth by politicians.
10. FAULTY. *Number* is used for a countable noun like *coins*. (But it would be correct to use *a large amount of gold*.)

Wordiness

To avoid wordiness, eliminate language that either duplicates what has already been expressed or adds nothing to the sense of the statement.

WORDY: At the present time, you can call up the library on the telephone if you want to receive that particular information.
REVISED: Now you can call the library for that information.

WORDY: A factor in the cause of the decline in stock prices was unwarranted growth.
REVISED: One cause of the decline in stock prices was unwarranted growth.
OR
A factor in the decline in stock prices ...

WORDY: As a pet, the llama is easygoing in its habits and has a friendly personality.
REVISED: As a pet, the llama is easygoing and friendly.

Expressions like *there are* and *it is* can add unnecessary words to your sentences.

EXAMPLES: [There are] several people at school [who] have promised to help with the gardening at the new campus.
[It is] the way you swing the club [that] amazes me.

A *redundant* expression is characterized by unnecessary repetition. To say *adequate enough* is to be redundant, because *adequate* and *enough* have nearly the same meaning.

EXAMPLES: The two clubs joined [together] to feed the poor at Christmas.
They circled [around] the field.
For a list of ski areas in the state, refer [back] to page 25.

Avoid redundancies and roundabout phrases (*circumlocutions*) like the following:

WORDY	CONCISE
advance planning	planning
contributing factor	factor
due to the fact that	because
during the course of	during
exact same symptoms	same symptoms; exact symptoms
for the purpose of	for
in the event that	if

in the near future	soon
large in size	large
past experience	experience
past history	history
revert back	revert
sufficient enough	sufficient; enough

Omissions

A common error in written English is the careless omission, especially the omission acceptable in speech but not in writing. Some of the errors on the ACT test are likely to be such omissions.

THE CARELESS OMISSION

Do not omit a needed verb, preposition, or conjunction.

FAULTY: The Coast Guard always has and always will assist boaters in distress.
CORRECT: The Coast Guard always has *assisted* and always will assist boaters in distress.

FAULTY: Carol will graduate high school in June.
CORRECT: Carol will graduate *from* high school in June.

FAULTY: Liza was both allergic and fond of cats.
CORRECT: Liza was both allergic *to* and fond of cats.

FAULTY: He eats as much or more than anyone else in the family.
CORRECT: He eats as much *as* or more than anyone else in the family.

THE INCOMPLETE COMPARISON

Include every word needed to make a complete comparison.

It may seem obvious to state that a comparison expresses a relationship between *two* things: for example, *Johnny is older than Sue.* A surprisingly common error, however, is the incomplete comparison.

INCOMPLETE: Our new lawn requires less water.
REVISED: Our new lawn requires less water *than our old one did.*

INCOMPLETE: A subcompact's mileage is better than a large sedan.
REVISED: A subcompact's mileage is better *than that of* a large sedan.

INCOMPLETE: He wanted that medal more than his competitors. (Did he want the medal or the competitors?)
REVISED: He wanted that medal more than his competitors *did* [want].

THE MISSING TRANSITION

Without logical transitions, the flow of ideas can lack natural progression and unity. Note the following.

WITHOUT TRANSITION: He wanted so much to do well on the test; he had not studied enough.

REVISED: He wanted so much to do well on the test, *but* he had not studied enough.

WITHOUT TRANSITION: The multimillionaire Getty lived in London; most of his holdings were in the United States.

REVISED: The multimillionaire Getty lived in London, *although* most of his holdings were in the United States.

Sexist Language

Throughout most of the history of the English language, masculine pronouns have been used to represent either sex. In addition, women have been routinely excluded from many nouns intended to represent humanity. Still worse, traditional use of sexist language tends to place men and women in stereotyped roles.

It is not necessary to begin using awkward terms to avoid sexist language. Terms like *mail carrier, firefighter,* or *police officer* are reasonable alternatives to *mailman, fireman,* and *policeman.*

The use of the sexist pronoun is more difficult to avoid. One alternative is to use the plural: instead of *A voter must do his duty,* say, *Voters must do their duty.* An occasional use of *he* or *she* is acceptable, though the phrase tends to be cumbersome.

EXAMPLE: When a person is called by the IRS for an audit, *he or she* should go over last year's return.

You can avoid the construction by rewording the sentence.

EXAMPLE: A person called by the IRS for an audit should go over the past year's return.

PRACTICE EXERCISE

Most of these sentences are either wordy or incomplete in some way. Place a check in the appropriate column to indicate whether the sentence is correct or faulty.

CORRECT   FAULTY

_____ _____   **1.** His appeal was his good looks as well as his natural charm.

_____ _____   **2.** Mexican food is as well liked by Europeans as Americans.

_____ _____   **3.** Because of the likely possibility that rain will occur this weekend, we will not venture to have the canoe race.

_____ _____   **4.** The teacher impatiently repeated the answer again.

_____ _____   **5.** Is it true that snow tires are safer?

_____ _____   **6.** She always let her cat out at 5 A.M. in the morning.

_____ _____   **7.** The comma, semicolon, and colon are punctuation marks used to separate components of a sentence.

_____ _____   **8.** New materials to construct long-lasting batteries have and continue to be developed by Bell scientists.

_____ _____   **9.** In my opinion, I think the autobiography of her life would make a good movie.

_____ _____   **10.** I admire Dylan more than Cherie does.

_____ _____   **11.** The baby was crying as if she were hungry; she had been fed only an hour ago.

_____ _____   **12.** The motion picture *Gone With the Wind* is a movie that still has great audience appeal.

ANSWERS AND EXPLANATIONS

1. FAULTY.   Revised: His appeal was *due* to his good looks and natural charm.

2. FAULTY.   Revised: Mexican food is as well liked by Europeans as *it is by* Americans.

3. FAULTY.   Revised: Because of the possibility of rain this weekend, we will not have the canoe race. (Excessive words omitted.)

4. FAULTY.   *Repeated ... again* is redundant.

5. FAULTY.   Revised: Is it true that snow tires are safer *than other types of tires?*

6. FAULTY.   *In the morning* is unnecessary with A.M.

7. CORRECT.   This sentence is neither wordy nor incomplete.
8. FAULTY.   Revised: New materials to construct long-lasting batteries have *been* and continue to be developed by Bell scientists.
9. FAULTY.   *In my opinion* and *I think* express the same idea. Also, *autobiography of her life* is a redundant phrase.
10. CORRECT.   The thought in this sentence is complete.
11. FAULTY.   A transitional word like *yet* is needed in this sentence.
12. FAULTY.   Revised: The motion picture *Gone With the Wind* still has great audience appeal.

FOCUS ON THE ACT

The following sample questions represent ways in which the above skills might be tested on your ACT Assessment.

(1)

Modern literary criticism is a literary specialty composed of many varying and inharmonious parts. There are, however, five major trends in contemporary criticism that take into account almost every significant critical essay written in the twentieth century. It is the critics' differing opinions on the purpose of literature that create the divisions or schools of modern criticism. These schools or approaches to literature are the moral, the psychological, the sociological, the formalistic, and the archetypal. ⬚1

(2)

The oldest view, the moral approach, originated with Plato when he ordered Homer banished from his fictional utopian republic. "Poetry," said Plato, "by its very nature appeals to the emotions rather than to the intellect and is, therefore, potentially dangerous." Here is the first expression of concern over the effect of literature on life, and this concern becomes the primary concern of the moral critic, who gauges all literature by its ability to aid and comfort man, and convey a higher ideal of life. ⬚2

1. This entire passage was probably written for readers who are:
   A.   college or college-bound literature students.
   B.   poor readers who require supplemental material.
   C.   interested in the scientific method.
   D.   foreign students preparing for an English proficiency test.

2. Which of the following statements is best supported by the details supplied in paragraph number 2?
   F.   The moral view is the most important by far.
   G.   The moral approach is really a religious view.
   H.   The moral approach is the oldest and most noble of the critical modes.
   J.   The moral critical view requires rigid standards of behavior of its adherents.

(3)

As you can imagine, the psychologists got into the
                                                3
act and started linking novels with Freud and Jung and
                                                    3
that crowd and their theories that man is a victim of
                                              3
society and his own biological drives. Psychological
                        3
critics argue that literature that advocates chastity, gen-

tility, and other virtues is frustrating to the normal

drives of man and is therefore unhealthy.

The psychological school studies the author's life as a
                                                      4
means of understanding his writings, the characters and
                                                      4
their motivation in the literature itself, and the creative
                                            4
process as a psychological evolution.
                    4

(4)

Looking at what it is that makes folks tick when
                                            5
they get together in towns and the like is what the
                                          5
sociological critic does. A literary work is studied in
          5
order to discover the degree to which it acts as a mirror

of society through contemporary social theory and

practice. $\boxed{6}$

---

3. Which of the suggested sentences below make the best introduction to paragraph 3 and the best transition from 2?
- **A.** NO CHANGE
- **B.** In contrast to this idea is the psychological approach to literature, a school that originated with Freud and his theory that man is a victim of both the repressive mores of society and his own biological compulsions.
- **C.** The psychological approach to literature is our next mode of criticism.
- **D.** Next, we have the psychological school of criticism, a hands-on way of looking at the nitty-gritty of an author's life.

4. Suppose at this point in the passage the author wanted to revise the third paragraph so that it is more appropriate for younger students? Which of the following revisions of this sentence would accomplish that purpose most effectively?
- **F.** NO CHANGE
- **G.** The Freudian and post-Jungian school focuses upon the subject's experiential past as a means of explicating his creative output, personality projections, and basic drives, as well as the genesis of the creative process.
- **H.** This way of talking about a book we have read lets us think about the author's life to see if it is related to the story, to think about the characters in the story and decide whether or not they make sense, and to ask why the author wrote the book.
- **J.** Psychological criticism tells us to look at the authors first, as if the author's life really always tells you that much. Anyway, you study the author's life and supposedly learn more about the book from an analytical, what-makes-us-tick point of view.

5. A. NO CHANGE
- **B.** As the boy's choir did in William Golding's novel *The Lord of the Flies,* man tends to organize his ruling bodies according to his inner drives.
- **C.** When people get together, whether they are savages or yuppies, they form social units. This process is what the sociological critic studies.
- **D.** The study of man's drives when he is organized into a state is the province of the sociological critic.

6. What kind of supporting details could strengthen this paragraph?
- **F.** A list of American states and major cities.
- **G.** A list of authors that have written "sociological novels."
- **H.** Examples of ways a novel can mirror contemporary society.
- **J.** A consistent way to gauge the quality of life.

(5)

Used as an isolated method, each approach to literary commentary has serious drawbacks, leading to narrow and restrictive readings. Used collectively, however, the five approaches can deal with every facet of a work, enabling a balanced and complete interpretation of literature. ⬚7

(6)

The most influential method of contemporary criticism, however, is the formalistic, or "new" criticism. Assuming that literature has intrinsic meaning, the school advocates the close study of texts themselves, rather than extrinsics such as society or the author's biography. The primary route by which a formalistic critic reveals and expresses his views on a classic work of literature is by means of a very ambitious and comprehensive examination and scrutiny of the text of the novel itself.

(7)

The archetypal approach studies literature in its relation to all men, assuming a "collective unconscious" that binds all men from all time. The archetypal critic eyeballs a work in an attempt to disclose its reliance on either a specific myth or a universal pattern of thought, both of which might reveal a man's subconscious attempt to link himself with all humanity, past and present. ⬚10

7. This paragraph is organized according to which of the following schemes?
   A. A general statement followed by a number of specific examples.
   B. A narrative structure controlled by the events being described.
   C. A typical classification/division format where the topic is broken down into groups and labeled.
   D. A simple contrasting paragraph, with the point of the first sentence contrasting sharply with the next.

8. F. NO CHANGE
   G. A close, in-depth examination of a work's structure and language is the primary characteristic of this highly analytical mode of commentary.
   H. A close, in-depth examination in which scholars scrutinize very minutely the actual text of a work of literature is the main primary characteristic of this highly analytical mode of commentary.
   J. The main way a critic reports on a book is really by looking very closely at the words and sentences.

9. A. NO CHANGE
   B. peruses
   C. ponders
   D. studies

10. Choose the sequence of paragraph numbers that makes the structure of the passage most logical.
    F. 1, 3, 5, 6, 7, 4, 2.
    G. 1, 2, 4, 3, 7, 6, 5.
    H. 1, 2, 3, 4, 6, 7, 5.
    J. 1, 2, 7, 6, 5, 4, 3.

ANSWERS AND EXPLANATIONS

1. A The subject and tone of the passage clearly addresses serious students of literature.

2. H The details supplied in paragraph 2 bear out solely this statement.

3. B This choice highlights the obvious contrast between the critical schools described in the two paragraphs, and effectively introduces the topic that is supported in the paragraph. The other choices either fall short of introducing the paragraph topic or depart markedly from the style and tone of the passage.

4. H This choice is written for a younger reading level, yet roughly covers the main points of the original sentence. The other choices (G and J) either do not communicate the main points of the original sentence, or are not written for young readers.

5. D Only this choice concludes the paragraph clearly and effectively, while maintaining the style of the passage.

6. H The original paragraph *does* lack specific examples of literary works that mirror their contemporary society. The information conveyed in the other choices is off the topic of the paragraph.

7. D The paragraph does, indeed, contain two sentences, one contrasting sharply with the other.

8. G This choice is the only one that expresses the primary characteristics of the formalistic critic with economy of language and in a style consistent with that of the passage. The other choices are either wordy or lacking in content or compatible style.

9. D The word *studies* is consistent with the tone of the passage. The other choices suggest activities that are other than scholarly.

10. H The paragraphs in this passage are linked to each other by means of transitional statements, and by means of the controlling order established near the end of paragraph 1.

SAMPLE ENGLISH TEST

The ACT English Test consists of five prose passages and 75 questions, with a 45-minute time limit. The test is designed to measure your ability to discern and remedy errors and awkwardness in punctuation, grammar and usage, and sentence structure. You will also find questions about the prose—for whom the passage is intended, for example, or how the paragraph or sentence might be improved with reorganization or additional material.

The following two practice passages are intended to familiarize you with questions that approximate those on the ACT. Each passage is accompanied by 30 multiple-choice questions. These passages are approximately double the length of the ones on the actual test. If you wish to time yourself, allow 18 minutes to read each passage and answer the question.

DIRECTIONS: The following test consists of 60 items. Some concern underlined words and phrases in context; others ask general questions about the passages. Most of the underlined sections contain errors or inappropriate expressions. You are asked to compare each with the four alternatives in the answer column. If you consider the original version best, choose letter **A** or **F**: NO CHANGE. For each question, select the alternative you think best. Read each passage through before answering the questions based on it.

NOTE: Answers and explanations can be found at the end of each passage.

Passage I

A peaceful oasis in the midst of the bustling San

Fernando Valley, San Fernando Mission has been

declared a historic cultural monument by the City of

Los Angeles, according to a bronze plaque at the

entrance to the mission. In addition to being an active

religion center, many tourists come to the mission
1   2

1. A. NO CHANGE
   B. religions
   C. religious
   D. more religious

each year to stroll through the well-tended grounds and
2

2. F. NO CHANGE
   G. many tourists are invited to the Mission each year
   H. it is a place where many tourists come each year
   J. people come

they admire the unique architecture of the restored
3
mission buildings.

3. A. NO CHANGE
   B. they were admiring
   C. admiring
   D. admire

The entrance to the mission quadrangle opens onto
4

4. F. NO CHANGE
   G. out into
   H. wide into
   J. for

the east garden, a large, <u>grass covered</u> courtyard in the
₅
middle of which is a flower-shaped fountain modeled

after one that stands in Cordova, Spain. Wind rustles

through the branches of the trees, and water tinkles in

the fountain, <u>also</u> the sounds of traffic outside the walls
₆
only accentuate the tranquility of the setting. Strolling

about the grounds, the smell of spring flowers scenting

the air and the sunlight warm upon your back, <u>one can</u>
₇
<u>easily</u> imagine being back two hundred years during the
₇
time of the founding of the mission. The present-day

mission compound, however, with its air of serenity and

unhurried repose, is nothing like the mission in its

heyday, when it was the scene of bustling activity and

<u>the labor was diligent</u> by hundreds of Indians under the
₈
direction of a few Spanish Franciscan padres.

San Fernando Mission, founded in 1779 by

Padre Fermin Lasuen and named for a saintly king of

thirteenth-century Spain, <u>it was</u> the seventeenth of
₉

California's twenty-one missions <u>stretching</u> in a chain
₁₀
from San Francisco to San Diego. The purpose of the

mission chain was to create centers of Christian

civilization <u>who would want</u> to convert the California
₁₁
Indians and prepare them for Spanish citizenship.

Mission San Francisco was established <u>centrally</u>
₁₂
between the missions of San Buenaventura and San

Gabriel, at a distance of one day's journey from each.

The <u>site chosen</u> for the <u>mission—land</u> that had been
₁₃   ₁₄
used by Don Francisco Reyes, first mayor of the Pueblo

de Los Angeles, to graze cattle—was rich in water, in

5. A. NO CHANGE
B. grass-covered
C. grass covering
D. grass, covered

6. F. NO CHANGE
G. while
H. moreover,
J. furthermore,

7. A. NO CHANGE
B. you can easily
C. it seems easy to
D. one easily

8. F. NO CHANGE
G. diligent labor
H. the labor was industrious
J. labor that was diligent

9. A. NO CHANGE
B. it had been
C. it will be
D. was

10. F. NO CHANGE
G. and it stretched
H. that was stretching
J. widely stretched out

11. A. NO CHANGE
B. which was hoping
C. seeking
D. needing

12. F. NO CHANGE
G. in a great spot
H. well within and
J. OMIT the underlined phrase.

13. A. NO CHANGE
B. cite chosen
C. sight chose
D. site choosed

14. F. NO CHANGE
G. Mission: land
H. Mission; land
J. Mission. Land

fertile, arable soil, and it had an Indian population, all

15

necessary elements for a successful mission.

The chapel—an exact replica of the original, which

was built between 1804 and 1806 and destroyed by the

1971 earthquake—is long and narrow, with adobe walls

decorated by frescoes of native designs. The overall

effect of the frescoes, the colorful Spanish altar hang-

ings, and the Stations of the Cross are, as one writer put

16

it, "a glorious, if barbaric spectacle!"

Although there is a number of windows on the

17

south wall of the chapel, there is only one window on

the north wall. It is not known whether this architec-

tural detail was meant to keep out cold winds from the

nearby mountains or as a defense against a potential

18

attack by hostile Indians.

18

Behind the chapel is a cemetery, where many of the

natives and other early settlers attached to the mission

were buried. Only a few wooden crosses and there is

19

one large gravestone mark the final resting places of

19

approximately 2,000 persons buried there. Beyond the

burial grounds is a fountain: fed by a small stream and

20

surrounded in foliage and a flower garden.

21

Across the compound, stands the "convento"—the

22

largest original mission building in California—with its

famous corridor of twenty-one Roman arches that today

front San Fernando Mission Road. Two stories high,

23

with four-foot-thick adobe walls that keeps the inside

24

15. **A.** NO CHANGE
    B. there also were Indians,
    C. it had Indians,
    D. in an Indian population,

16. **F.** NO CHANGE
    G. was
    H. is
    J. will have been

17. **A.** NO CHANGE
    B. were a number of
    C. are a number of
    D. should be a number of

18. **F.** NO CHANGE
    G. hostile Indians.
    H. defending against an Indian attack.
    J. an attack against hostile Indians.

19. **A.** NO CHANGE
    B. one large gravestone
    C. there might have been a gravestone
    D. there most likely is a gravestone

20. **F.** NO CHANGE
    G. fountain. Fed
    H. fountain; fed
    J. fountain fed

21. **A.** NO CHANGE
    B. overhead in the
    C. about with
    D. by

22. **F.** NO CHANGE
    G. Across the compound, stood
    H. Across the compound stands
    J. Across the compound, is standing

23. **A.** NO CHANGE
    B. fronts
    C. fronting
    D. fronted

24. **F.** NO CHANGE
    G. walls, that keep
    H. , walls that keep
    J. walls, that keeps

cool on even the hottest summer <u>day. It</u> served as living
₂₅
quarters for the missionaries and visitors in the early

1800's. <u>Tourists taking pictures inside the mission</u>
₂₆
<u>should bring high-speed color film.</u>
₂₆

      Just inside the entrance hall <u>an atmosphere is able</u>
₂₇
<u>to be felt</u> of great age, perhaps due in part to the still-
₂₇
ness that seems to echo within the brick-floored rooms.

Then again, this feeling might be due to the <u>odor,</u>
₂₈
<u>emanating</u> from the nearby wine cellar, a musty smell
₂₈
that grows stronger as one moves slowly down the

whitewashed <u>stairs—past</u> a deep tub cut from rock
₂₉
where grapes were once pressed underfoot. | 30 |

25. **A.** NO CHANGE
    B. day, it
    C. day—it
    D. day: it

26. **F.** NO CHANGE
    G. Retain the position of this sentence in the passage but place it in its own paragraph.
    H. Move this sentence to the beginning of the paragraph.
    J. OMIT the underlined sentence.

27. **A.** NO CHANGE
    B. may be feeling an atmosphere
    C. one feels an atmosphere
    D. an atmosphere can be felt

28. **F.** NO CHANGE
    G. odor; emanating
    H. odor. Emanating
    J. odor emanating

29. **A.** NO CHANGE
    B. stairs, passed
    C. stairs; passed
    D. stairs, past

30. Is the mention of the odor appropriate and effective at the end of this passage?
    F. No, because it introduces a new element at the end of the passage.
    G. Yes, because the musty odors of old buildings and old wine presses appropriately reflect the age of this historic mission.
    H. Yes, because the description of the odor is somewhat suspenseful, and mentioning it gives a mysterious quality to the passage.
    J. No, because an odor is generally perceived as offensive.

Answer Key

1.	C	6.	G	11.	C	16.	H	21.	D	26.	J
2.	H	7.	B	12.	J	17.	C	22.	H	27.	C
3.	D	8.	G	13.	A	18.	G	23.	B	28.	J
4.	F	9.	D	14.	F	19.	B	24.	H	29.	D
5.	B	10.	F	15.	D	20.	J	25.	B	30.	G

ANSWER EXPLANATIONS

1. C The underlined word is intended to modify the noun *center* and so must be an adjective.

2. H The introductory phrase *In addition to being an active [religious] center* clearly refers to the mission, not the tourists. Therefore, the main clause must begin with the word *mission* or with the referent pronoun *it.*

3. D The infinitive *to admire* is parallel in construction with *to stroll,* with which it is paired: *to stroll ... and [to] admire.*

4. F No other choice is idiomatically correct.

5. B Hyphenate a compound adjective that precedes the noun it modifies.

6. G Conjunctive adverbs (such as *also, moreover,* and *furthermore*) used to join clauses must be preceded by a semicolon. *While,* a subordinating conjunction used to introduce an adverb clause, is properly preceded by a comma.

7. B Avoid a shift in point of view, from the second person *your* to the third person *one.* Choice C incorrectly makes *it* the word modified by the introductory participial phrase.

8. G The prepositional phrase *of bustling activity* requires a parallel object, *diligent labor.* Choice J is wordy.

9. D The sentence has two subjects: *San Fernando/it. It* is unnecessary.

10. F The participial phrase *stretching in a chain ...* correctly modifies the noun *missions.* Choice G incorrectly uses *it* to refer to the plural word *missions.* H also incorrectly uses a singular form, *was,* which does not agree with *missions,* the antecedent of *that.* J is wordy.

11. C The other options either carry meanings inappropriate to the sense of the passage or contain faulty grammar.

12. J *Centrally* repeats the idea of *at a distance of one day's journey from each. In a great spot* is too colloquial for this passage. Choice H is wordy.

13. A The correct word to use here is *site,* meaning location. The verb forms *chose* and *choosed* in choices C and D are incorrect.

14. F A pair of dashes precedes and follows an interrupting parenthetical element.

15. D Only this option is parallel with the other prepositional phrases: *in water, in ... soil,* and *in ... population.*

16. H The singular subject *effect* requires the singular verb *is.* The predominant tense of the passage is the present.

17. C The phrase *a number of* is plural in meaning and takes the plural verb *are.* Choice B is wrong, since the predominant tense of the passage is the present. D changes the meaning of the clause.

18. G The infinitive phrase *to keep out* needs a parallel second object: *to keep out cold winds ... or hostile Indians.*

19. B A simple noun is needed to form the other half of the compound subject: *crosses and ... gravestone.*

20. J The participial phrase *fed by a small stream* is a restrictive modifier and should not be separated from the noun it modifies, *fountain,* by a punctuation mark. Choice G introduces a sentence fragment.

21. D The correct idiom is *surrounded by.*

22. H In an inverted sentence, do not use a comma to separate a short adverb construction from the verb it modifies.

23. B The subject of the verb *front* is the relative pronoun *that,* which refers to the singular noun *corridor,* not the plural *arches.* Thus, the correct verb form is *fronts.* Choice C is a participle, not a verb form. D shifts to the past tense.

24. H The subject of the verb *keep* is the relative pronoun *that,* which refers to the plural noun *walls.* Do not use a comma to separate a restrictive clause from the word it modifies (G and J).

25. B A comma is used to separate the introductory phrase *two stories high ... day* from the main clause of the sentence. Choice A creates a sentence fragment.

26. J This sentence has no bearing on the topic of the passage.

27. C As a rule, it is better to avoid the passive voice. The active voice is more direct and forceful.

28. J The participial phrase *emanating from the nearby wine cellar* is a restrictive modifier and cannot be set off by commas. Choice H introduces a sentence fragment.

29. D A comma is called for at this point for clarity. A dash is too great a mark of separation. Choices B and C incorrectly substitute the verb form *passed* for the preposition *past*.

30. G This descriptive paragraph adds a meaningful sense impression to the passage.

Passage II

Each of the paragraphs in this passage is numbered, but may not be in the most logical position. The last question asks you to select the correct number.

---

(1)

Sometime around the middle of January, after reading about standard organic gardening techniques, prospective home gardeners should make a list of the vegetables most enjoyed by their families. Sitting down with a few seed catalogs, preferably those from local companies such as Santa Rosa Gardening Co. or Burbank Farms,—whose catalogs contain detailing
$_1$ $_2$
planting instructions for Southern California, including the proper planting dates for each of the distinct climatic regions—they should review the directions for growing vegetables, narrowing the choices to crops easy to grow. And although January is an ideal time here to plant such winter vegetables such as beets,
$_3$
broccoli, peas, lettuce, and swiss chard, novice gardeners might do well to plan a spring garden as a first effort. For one thing, summer vegetables like tomatoes, zucchini, and beans are easy to grow, they
$_4$
require little in the way of additional care once they
$_4$
have been planted and are growing well. And for another, spring—traditionally a time of renewal—seems the right time of year to begin a gardening project.

1. A. NO CHANGE
   B. Farms—whose
   C. Farms; whose
   D. Farms. Whose

2. F. NO CHANGE
   G. details of
   H. detailed
   J. in detailed

3. A. NO CHANGE
   B. like
   C. such as;
   D. as

4. F. NO CHANGE
   G. grow. Since these vegetables require
   H. grow. Requiring
   J. grow, requiring

(2)

These differences make it impossible <u>that gardeners</u>
₅

in Southern California to follow <u>in an explicit way</u> the
₆

advice given in nationally circulated magazines and

books on organic gardening. Instead, these methods

<u>must be adopted</u> to the particular climate in this area.
₇

Some suggestions follow that may be helpful to fellow

gardeners in the San Fernando Valley region.

(3)

Just as organic gardening differs from gardening

with the help of a chemical <u>company. Gardening</u> in
₈

Southern California differs dramatically from gardening

in almost every other part of the country. For one thing,

crops <u>will be planted</u> here almost any time during the
₉

year, whereas spring gardens are the rule in most other

parts of the country. Diversity of weather systems

within the relatively small area that <u>encompassing</u>
₁₀

Southern California is another distinction. For instance,

coastal communities experience cool, damp weather for

much of the year, while the San Fernando and San

Gabriel valleys are blistering hot in summer and cold in

<u>winter—some</u> inland valleys even encounter frost and
₁₁

freezing temperatures! Thus, although these areas

<u>separate</u> by fewer than fifty miles, the climates are dis-
₁₂

parate, necessitating the use of distinct gardening tech-

niques for each locale.

(4)

After deciding what vegetables to grow, <u>a rough</u>
₁₃

<u>draft is made</u> of the garden, which should be located in
₁₃

an area of <u>flat well-drained</u> ground that <u>has gotten</u> at
₁₄ ₁₅

least six full hours of sun daily. Taller-growing crops

should be put on the north side of the garden so that

5. **A.** NO CHANGE
   B. to be a gardener
   C. to go on being a gardener
   D. for gardeners

6. **F.** NO CHANGE
   G. explicitly
   H. in a more explicit way
   J. explicitly and definitely

7. **A.** NO CHANGE
   B. should be adopted
   C. must be adapted
   D. must adopt

8. **F.** NO CHANGE
   G. company; gardening
   H. company, gardening
   J. company: gardening

9. **A.** NO CHANGE
   B. can be planted
   C. have been planted
   D. ought to be planted

10. **F.** NO CHANGE
    G. encompassed
    H. has encompassed
    J. encompasses

11. **A.** NO CHANGE
    B. winter;—some
    C. winter—Some
    D. winter, some

12. **F.** NO CHANGE
    G. are separated
    H. must be separated
    J. were separated

13. **A.** NO CHANGE
    B. a rough draft should be made
    C. the gardener should make a rough draft
    D. it is necessary to make a rough draft

14. **F.** NO CHANGE
    G. flat, well-drained
    H. flat, well drained
    J. flat and well drained

15. **A.** NO CHANGE
    B. will have gotten
    C. got
    D. gets

they do not shade any low-growing <u>vegetables; except</u>

those that cannot survive the intense summer sun. The

latter include lettuce and many other greens. The rows,

or beds, should be wide enough to accommodate the

<u>particular kind of a</u> crop to be grown. The wider the

rows, of course, the more crops the garden <u>will have</u>

<u>produced.</u> <u>This</u> is known as "intensive gardening" and

is ideal for small backyard gardens. One suggestion is

to make the beds three feet wide, with enough space

between them to allow easy access for cultivating,

weeding, and <u>to harvest</u> mature plants. However, two-foot

beds are also <u>okay.</u>

(5)

After the plan has been drawn up and the seeds <u>will</u>

<u>be ordered,</u> the next step is to prepare the soil <u>properly,</u>

<u>one</u> of the most important procedures in insuring a suc-

cessful harvest. Testing the soil for deficiencies is a

<u>must; soil-testing</u> kits are available from most home

improvement stores and gardening centers. The organic

gardening books and magazines mentioned earlier go

into <u>heavy detail</u> regarding soil composition, testing,

and preparation. Following their recommendations will

contribute <u>for the success</u> of the gardening project.

16. F. NO CHANGE
    G. vegetables except
    H. vegetables: except
    J. vegetables. Except

17. A. NO CHANGE
    B. kind of a
    C. kinds of a
    D. OMIT the underlined words.

18. F. NO CHANGE
    G. would of produced.
    H. will produce.
    J. is producing.

19. A. NO CHANGE
    B. This close spacing
    C. Which
    D. This here

20. F. NO CHANGE
    G. harvesting
    H. to be harvesting
    J. so we can harvest the

21. A. NO CHANGE
    B. alright.
    C. all right.
    D. allright.

22. F. NO CHANGE
    G. should be ordered,
    H. were ordered,
    J. have been ordered,

23. A. NO CHANGE
    B. properly. One
    C. properly; one
    D. properly, it is one

24. F. NO CHANGE
    G. must, as soil-testing
    H. must, soil-testing
    J. must because soil-testing

25. A. NO CHANGE
    B. much detail
    C. exquisite detail
    D. alot of detail

26. F. NO CHANGE
    G. in the success
    H. to the success
    J. for the successfulness

(6)

Once the condition of the soil is ascertained by the
                                                    27
person doing the gardening, deficient elements (such as
                                                    27
phosphorus, potassium, magnesium, or sulphur) can be
                                                    27

added. In addition to these minerals; however, enough
 27   28
fertilizer to get the seedlings off to a good start should

be incorporated into the soil. [29] [30]

27. **A.** NO CHANGE
    B. Once the condition of the soil is ascertained by the gardener, elements that are lacking in sufficient quantity (such as phosphorus, potassium, magnesium, or sulphur) can be added by the gardener.
    C. Once the gardener ascertains the condition of the soil, he or she can add deficient elements (such as phosphorus, potassium, magnesium, or sulphur).
    D. Once, the gardener ascertains the condition of the soil, deficient elements (such as: phosphorus, potassium, magnesium, or sulphur) can be added.

28. **F.** NO CHANGE
    G. minerals however,
    H. minerals, however—
    J. minerals, however,

29. This passage is most likely directed to readers who:
    A. are experts in gardening and need little advice.
    B. are residents of Southern California and have never had a garden.
    C. are residents of Freeport, Maine, and are just curious about gardening in a warmer state.
    D. have gardened so much that they hope never to see another bud.

30. Select the correct order of the numbered paragraphs so that the passage will read in logical sequence.
    F. NO CHANGE
    G. 3, 2, 1, 4, 5, 6
    H. 1, 2, 4, 5, 3, 6
    J. 4, 2, 3, 1, 5, 6

Answer Key

1.	**B**	6.	**G**	11.	**A**	16.	**G**	21.	**C**	26.	**H**
2.	**H**	7.	**C**	12.	**G**	17.	**D**	22.	**J**	27.	**C**
3.	**D**	8.	**H**	13.	**C**	18.	**H**	23.	**A**	28.	**J**
4.	**J**	9.	**B**	14.	**G**	19.	**B**	24.	**F**	29.	**B**
5.	**D**	10.	**J**	15.	**D**	20.	**G**	25.	**B**	30.	**G**

ANSWER EXPLANATIONS

1. **B** A pair of dashes is used to separate a parenthetical element from the rest of the sentence; a comma is not used with the dash. Choice D introduces a sentence fragment.

2. **H** The correct choice is the past participle *detailed,* which acts as an adjective to modify the noun phrase *planting instructions.* The present participle *detailing* carries meaning that does not apply to this sentence. Choice J adds a word that does not make sense in the structure of the sentence.

3. **D** The sentence already contains the word *such (such winter vegetables as).* Choice B offers an ungrammatical construction, *such ... like.*

4. **J** This is the only correct option. The other choices produce sentence fragments or a comma splice.

5. **D** Idiomatic English requires the construction *impossible for gardeners ... to follow.*

6. **G** The other choices are wordy or redundant.

7. **C** The correct word here is *adapted,* meaning modified to suit. *Adopted* means taken as is.

8. **H** Use a comma to separate an introductory adverb clause from the main clause.

9. **B** The verb phrase *can be planted* also means *are planted* in the context of this sentence. The other options do not carry this essential additional meaning.

10. **J** Use the present tense to express generally true statements.

11. **A** A dash is used for emphasis to separate a parenthetical comment from the rest of the sentence. It is not used together with a semicolon. Choice C incorrectly capitalizes the word *some.* D introduces a comma splice.

12. **G** The passive voice is required when the subject is acted upon. The present tense is consistent with the rest of the passage.

13. **C** Without a logical noun to modify (*gardener,* for example), the introductory phrase would dangle.

14. **G** Place a comma between coordinate adjectives. The compound adjective *well-drained* takes a hyphen when it precedes the noun it modifies.

15. **D** The predominant tense in this passage is the present.

16. **G** Do not use a punctuation mark to separate a restrictive phrase from the word if modifies. The phrase beginning *except those …* limits *low growing vegetables.* Choice J would create a sentence fragment.

17. **D** The other choices are unnecessarily wordy and also introduce an error. (*Kind of a* is not idiomatic English.)

18. **H** The simple future tense, showing expectation, is appropriate here, because the passage is set in the present tense. *Would of* is incorrect grammatically.

19. **B** The pronoun *This* needs a specific antecedent for clear reference. Since there is none, the meaning

of *this* has to be clarified. Choice C introduces a sentence fragment. D is redundant, as *here* repeats the meaning of *this.*

20. **G** The gerund *harvesting* is required, to be parallel with the other gerunds, *cultivating* and *weeding.*

21. **C** Choice A is colloquial. B and D are misspellings.

22. **J** The verb must agree in tense with *has been drawn.*

23. **A** Set off a nonrestrictive appositive phrase with a comma. Choice B introduces a sentence fragment; D, a comma splice.

24. **F** A semicolon is used to separate clauses that are closely related. The transitional words in Choices G and J change the meaning. H creates a comma-splice sentence.

25. **B** The other options are either inappropriate or incorrect.

26. **H** The correct idiom is *contribute to.*

27. **C** The passive voice (*is ascertained* and *can be added*) is less forceful and usually results in more wordy sentences than the active voice. Choice D incorrectly places a comma after the conjunction *Once* and a colon after *such as.*

28. **J** The word *however* is used here as an adverb, not as a conjunctive adverb introducing a clause, and so should be set off by commas as a simple parenthetical word.

29. **B** The references to the southwestern climate, to aids for novice gardeners, and to gardening techniques indicate that this article is addressed primarily to first-time gardeners in Southern California.

30. **G** Paragraph (3) is clearly the introduction to this passage; it makes general statements about the topic that are supported by data in subsequent paragraphs. The phrase *These differences* that begins paragraph (2) directly relates to the ending of paragraph (3). The step-by-step process begins with paragraph (1) and continues in order with paragraphs (4), (5), and (6).

2 Mathematics Review and Practice

DESCRIPTION OF THE MATHEMATICS TEST

The ACT test in mathematics is a 60-minute test designed to evaluate your mathematical achievement in courses commonly taught in high school. This test includes questions from the areas of pre-algebra, algebra, plane geometry, intermediate algebra, coordinate geometry, and trigonometry.

The 60 questions on the test are classified by topic and skill level according to the following chart:

Topic	Basic Skills	Application	Analysis	Total
Pre-Algebra Algebra	8	12	4	24
Intermediate Algebra Coordinate Geometry	7	7	4	18
Plane Geometry	6	8	0	14
Trigonometry	2	2	0	4

The questions in the Basic Skills category cover recognition and simple application of elementary concepts such as subsets of real numbers, terms and relationships concerning operations, and axioms of the real number system. The Application questions require you to apply one or two concepts to the solution of a problem. The questions in the Analysis category usually require the application of several concepts to obtain the solution. Frequently this type of question is posed as a typical "word problem."

The emphasis in this test is on your ability to reason with numbers and mathematical concepts. No very complicated formulas or procedures will be involved in the solution of the problems.

For each question five potential answers are given, only one of which is correct. The answers may be designated as **A, B, C, D, E** or **F, G, H, J, K.** For some questions the last choice (either **E** or **K**) may be "None of the above." (In this book the alternative form "None of these" is used.)

STRATEGY

To be in the best position to do well on the ACT mathematics test, a review of the mathematics material covered on the test should be planned. Included in this chapter is a review that should be read with a pencil in hand. There are many examples of problems with detailed commentary on their solutions, as well as many practice exercises. The practice exercises also have complete solutions and explanations. The best plan is to work each practice problem on your own, and then check your solution with the one given in this book. If your answer is the same, you can be reasonably sure you did the problem correctly, even though your procedure may be different. There is no claim that there is only one way to do any given problem. Also, the chapter is intended to be review, not a textbook on mathematics. No attempt is made to prove most statements; they are merely presented as facts. If you want justification for a given statement or if you want more practice on a particular topic, consult a textbook that covers the material in a nonreview manner.

A reasonable time period to review the material in the mathematics section of this book may be 2 or 3 months. This would leave time to search for additional help if you find that you need it.

The best long-range strategy for preparation for this or any other test is to do well in the courses that you take in school. Although the ACT test is not necessarily like the tests that you had in these courses, much of the same material is covered; and if you have retained the fundamental concepts, you should be able to do well on the ACT test. As in many skills, however, the level of mathematics ability decreases with time if one does not practice continuously. Therefore, even if you have done very well in course work, it would be wise to spend time on this review chapter.

TACTICS

After you have reviewed the mathematics chapter and done the practice exercises, you should be ready to take the mathematics tests in this book. The following techniques will be helpful in taking model or actual ACT mathematics tests:

Pace yourself. The ACT mathematics test is a 60-question, 60-minute test to determine your mathematical achievement. Keep in mind as you take the test that the average amount of time allotted to each question is 1 minute. This means that you must work quickly and use the time that remains to try the more difficult questions again.

Know the directions. The ACT directions state that figures are not necessarily drawn to scale. You may also assume that geometric figures lie in a plane and that the word *line* means a straight line. Keep these directions in mind during the test. Mark your answer carefully on the appropriate answer sheet.

Work efficiently. You should work through each question, taking each step in order, rather than try to answer the question by working backward from the proposed answers; usually too much time is required to eliminate incorrect responses. Once you have an answer, try to locate it among the response choices. If it is there, mark the answer sheet quickly but accurately and go on to the next question. If your answer is not among the choices there are three possibilities:

1. You misread or misunderstood the question. Reread the question carefully. Be sure that you answer the question that was asked.
2. You made a mistake in the solution of the problem. Quickly review your steps, looking for errors. Perhaps your answer is equivalent to one of the choices by a simple manipulation.
3. You solved the problem correctly, and the correct answer is "None of the above."

If the search for a correct answer takes too much time, mark the question so that you can return to it after you have answered all of the others.

Evaluate your method. If you find that a question involves a very complicated computation or a very involved procedure for its solution, you should re-evaluate your method. The problems on the ACT do not require lengthy computations or proofs. In many cases computations can be done more easily if products are left in factored form until the very last step in order to make use of cancellation. (This is particularly true in the evaluation of combinations and permutations.)

Draw on your knowledge. Although the questions do not require the application of complicated formulas, you should know certain basic formulas such as those for the areas of squares, rectangles, triangles, and so on, perimeters, simple interest, uniform motion ($d = rt$), and the Pythagorean theorem. You should also know the definitions of terms and operations, such as prime numbers, composite numbers, union of sets, intersection of sets, axioms of the real number system, the axioms of equality and inequality (used to solve equations and inequalities), the trigonometric functions, and some of the simpler identities.

Guess when necessary. When you return to questions that you abandoned temporarily because they took too much time, consider eliminating any response that is not reasonable, given the proper interpretation of the problem. If then the solution still eludes you, guess. There is no penalty for guessing.

Check if possible. If time remains when you have finished the test to your satisfaction, go back to see that you have answered each question, and check your answers.

USE OF CALCULATORS

Some calculators may be used on the ACT. No questions on the ACT require the use of any calculator, but if you are accustomed to using a calculator in your classes or while doing your homework, you may bring your calculator to the test and use it to assist you on any question or to verify your answer. Be sure that you are very familiar with any calculator that you plan to use. Do not purchase one the day before the test and expect it to do you any good.

Any calculator may be used with the exception of the following:

- no pocket organizers or electronic notepads with pen-input devices
- no laptop or similar computers
- no device with a standard typewriter keyboard
- no calculator with symbolic algebra ability
- no calculator with the ability to communicate with another calculator unless the communication port is disabled
- no calculator that requires a power cord
- no calculator that has a sound function unless the sound function is disabled

The following calculators are some specific models that are not allowed.

Texas Instruments	TI-89
Texas Instruments	TI-92
Casio	CFX-9970G
Casio	ALGEBRA FX-2.0
Hewlett-Packard	HP-49G

Because the introduction of new models occurs regularly, a comprehensive list of disallowed models is given. Use the above guidelines to determine whether a specific calculator will be allowed. The supervisors of the test will give the final word on the acceptability of the calculator you bring to the test.

Four-function, scientific, and graphing calculators are acceptable if they meet the guidelines above. Be sure that any calculator you plan to use is in good repair with adequate batteries (bring extras if you wish). You may not store any test data in your calculator. You may not share a calculator with another test-taker, and it may be used only on the mathematics portion of the test.

ARITHMETIC/PRE-ALGEBRA

Sets

A well-defined set is one whose members or elements can be determined. The set of all people on earth is well-defined; however, the set of all intelligent people on earth is not well-defined. There is no common agreement about what constitutes intelligence.

There are two ways of conveniently identifying the elements of a set:

1. In the *roster* method, each element of the set is listed between braces separated by commas. The set of odd whole numbers less than 10 is {1, 3, 5, 7, 9}. A set may be named, usually by a capital letter: $T = \{1, 3, 5, 7, 9\}$. Do you see the difference

between T and $\{T\}$?

If a set has many elements, one can establish a pattern and use three dots to indicate that the pattern should continue: $M = \{1, 2, 3, \ldots, 99\}$. (A finite set).

$$N = \{1, 2, 3, \ldots\} \text{ (An infinite set).}$$

2. In *set-builder* notation, the same set T as above may be written as $T = \{x | x \text{ is an odd whole number less than } 10\}$. The symbols $\{x | \ldots\}$ are read "the set of elements x such that ..."

The statement "7 is an element of set T" may be written as $7 \in T$.

The statement "Zero is not an element of set T" may be written $0 \notin T$.

PRACTICE EXERCISES

State whether each of the following is true or false:
1. The set of planets in the solar system is a well-defined set.
2. The set of friendly dogs is a well-defined set.
   Questions 3, 4, and 5 pertain to the set $A = \{0, 1, 4, 9, 16, 25\}$.
3. $A = \{9, 0, 25, 1, 16, 4\}$
4. $36 \in A$
5. $25 \in \{A\}$
6. $49 \notin A$

SOLUTIONS

1. True
2. False. A certain dog may be friendly to one person and not to another.
3. True. The order of elements in a set is not important.
4. False. The number 36 is not found inside the braces of A.
5. False. The set $\{A\}$ has only one element, namely A. Note that A differs from $\{A\}$.
6. True.

Subsets

B is a subset of A ($B \subseteq A$) if and only if each element of B is also an element of A. Let $A = \{1, 2, 3, \ldots, 99)$ and $B = \{2, 4, 6, \ldots, 98\}$. Then $B \subseteq A$.

The Empty Set and the Universal Set

The *empty set* or the *null set* is designated by a special symbol, $\{ \} = \emptyset$. Note that $\emptyset \neq \{\emptyset\}$.

A set chosen to be large enough to include all possible elements in a certain discussion is called a *universal set, U*.

PRACTICE EXERCISES

State whether each of the following is true or false. (Let $A = \{1, 2, 3, \ldots, 99\}$ and $B = \{2, 4, 6\}$.)

1. $A \subseteq A$
2. $15 \notin B$
3. $\emptyset \in A$
4. $\emptyset \subseteq B$
5. The universal set for this group of five questions may be
   $$U = \{x | x \text{ is a whole number less than } 100\}$$

SOLUTIONS

1. True. Certainly every element of A is in A. Every set is a subset of itself.
2. True. 15 is not an element of B.

3. False. Whatever appears to the left of the symbol ∈ must appear in the set on the right. The symbol ∅ is not one of the elements of A.
4. True by default. The empty set is a subset of every set.
5. True.

Operations on Sets

There are three set operations, whose definitions follow:

$A \cup B = \{x | x \in A \text{ or } x \in B\}$ The union of sets A and B.
$A \cap B = \{x | x \in A \text{ and } x \in B\}$ The intersection of A and B.
$A' = \{x | x \notin A \text{ and } x \in U\}$ The complement of A. (Others may use $\sim A$ or $\overline{A}$ or not A to represent the complement of set A.)

Venn Diagrams

A *Venn diagram* is a device to visually depict sets and their relationships to each other. For example:

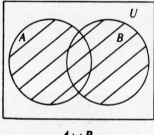
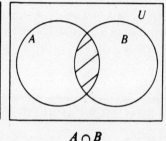
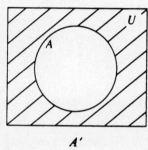

$A \cup B$ $A \cap B$ A'

Real Numbers

The set of real numbers has several very important subsets:
$N = \{1, 2, 3, \ldots\}$ Natural (or counting) numbers.
$W = \{0, 1, 2, 3, \ldots\}$ Whole numbers.
$J = \{\ldots, -3, -2, -1, 0, 1, 2, 3, \ldots\}$ Integers.

$Q = \{x | x \text{ can be written in the form } \frac{p}{q}, p \text{ and } q \in J, q \neq 0\}$ Rational numbers.

$I = \{x | x \in R \text{ and } x \notin Q)$ Irrational numbers.
$R = Q \cup I$ Real numbers.

The set of rational numbers is the set of all numbers that can be written as fractions. The irrational numbers are the real numbers that cannot be written as fractions. The real numbers are all those, rational and irrational, that are found on a number line.

The following Venn diagram shows the relationships among the subsets of real numbers:

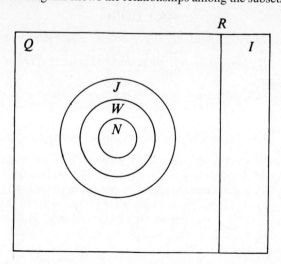

It is important to be able to categorize numbers according to the subsets above. All integers are rational numbers because any integer can easily be written as a fraction by placing the integer in the numerator and the number 1 in the denominator. $-3 = \dfrac{-3}{1}$

Real numbers that are written in decimal form fall into two basic types:

1. There are those that terminate. (One may think of this type as having an infinitely long string of zeros after the last nonzero digit.) All such decimals represent rational numbers. For example, 23.346 is twenty-three and three hundred forty-six thousandths. Therefore an appropriate fraction would be $23\dfrac{346}{1000}$ or $\dfrac{23346}{1000}$.

2. Some decimals do not terminate, and these fall into two types:
   a. Some nonterminating decimals repeat. All such repeating decimals represent rational numbers. For example:
   - $\dfrac{1}{3} = 0.3333\ldots = 0.\overline{3}$
   - $\dfrac{5}{6} = 0.83333\ldots = 0.8\overline{3}$
   - $\dfrac{3}{11} = 0.27272727\ldots = 0.\overline{27}$
   b. Other nonterminating decimals do not repeat. A number of this type cannot be written as a fraction and is therefore irrational. For example:
   - $\sqrt{2} = 1.414213\ldots$
   - $\sqrt[3]{7} = 1.912931\ldots$
   - $\pi = 3.1415926\ldots$

PRACTICE EXERCISES

1. Change $\dfrac{7}{8}$ to decimal form.

2. Change $\dfrac{8}{7}$ to decimal form.

3. Find a fraction equivalent to 0.21.
4. Find a fraction equivalent to $0.\overline{21}$.
5. Categorize each of the following numbers. Choose the appropriate letter(s) from the following list: N, W, J, Q, I, R.

   a. $\dfrac{5}{9}$

   b. -5

   c. $\sqrt{5}$

   d. $\sqrt{64}$

   e. $\sqrt{-9}$

   f. 3.1416

   g. $3.\overline{1416}$

SOLUTIONS

1. $\dfrac{7}{8} = 0.875$ This is merely a division problem; divide the denominator into the numerator. The zero to the left of the decimal point is optional.

2. $\dfrac{8}{7} = 1.\overline{142857}$

3. $0.21 = \dfrac{21}{100}$

4. $0.\overline{21} = \dfrac{21}{99} = \dfrac{7}{33}$ If the repeating block consists of one digit, place the repeating digit over 9; if the repeating block has two digits, place the repeating digits over 99; if the repeating block has three digits, place the repeating digits over 999; etc. If the repeating part does not begin immediately after the decimal point, first multiply by an appropriate power of 10 to place the decimal point immediately at the left of the repeating block. Follow the directions above, and then divide by the same power of 10.

For example: $2.3\overline{7} = \left(\dfrac{1}{10}\right)23.\overline{7}$

$$= \left(\dfrac{1}{10}\right)\dfrac{214}{9}$$

$$= \dfrac{214}{90} = \dfrac{107}{45}$$

5. a. *Q, R*
    b. *J, Q, R*
    c. *I, R*
    d. *W, N, J, Q, R* ($\sqrt{64} = 8$)
    e. $\sqrt{-9}$ is not a real number.
    f. *Q, R* (3.1416 is a rational approximation for π.)
    g. *Q, R*

Numeration Systems

A *numeration system* is a method of using symbols to represent numbers. Throughout history many different numeration systems have been developed. The old numeration systems, however, lacked two of the most important characteristics of the numeration system that is used today throughout the world: zero and place value.

Our current numeration system, called the Hindu-Arabic numeration system, utilizes 10 symbols: 0, 1, 2, 3, 4, 5, 6, 7, 8, 9. Beginning at the decimal point in any numeral, each digit is multiplied by the place value of its position in the numeral. Each place value is 10 times the place value of the position to its right. The place values are as follows:

...	10^6	10^5	10^4	10^3	10^2	10^1	10^0
...	1,000,000	100,000	10,000	1,000	100	10	1

Thus the 7 in the numeral 56,719 represents 10 times more than the value of the 7 in 56,179.

If human beings had evolved with only eight fingers instead of ten, our numeration system may very well have been based on 8 rather than 10. In other words, the place values would have been as follows:

...	8^6	8^5	8^4	8^3	8^2	8^1	8^0
...	262,144	32,768	4,096	512	64	8	1

In base 8 the only symbols used would be 0, 1, 2, 3, 4, 5, 6, and 7, and one would count in the following fashion:

1, 2, 3, 4, 5, 6, 7, 10, 11, 12, . . . , 76, 77, 100, . . .

The numeral $10_{(eight)} = 8_{(ten)}$, and $100_{(eight)} = 64_{(ten)}$.

The base eight numeral $2534_{(eight)} = 2(8^3) + 5(8^2) + 3(8^1) + 4(8^0)_{(ten)}$

$$= 2(512) + 5(64) + 3(8) + 4(1)_{(ten)}$$
$$= 1024 + 320 + 24 + 4_{(ten)}$$
$$= 1372_{(ten)}.$$

Numeration systems patterned after the Hindu-Arabic system exist with many different bases. Three of the common systems are these:

Octal—base 8   Hexadecimal—base 16
Binary—base 2

PRACTICE EXERCISES

1. What basic set of symbols would one normally use in base:
   a. 2?
   b. 5?
   c. 16?
2. Determine the corresponding base ten numeral for each of the following:
   a. $357_{(eight)}$
   b. $101110_{(two)}$
   c. $a5c_{(sixteen)}$
3. Convert $325_{(ten)}$ to a corresponding numeral in base:
   a. 8.
   b. 16.
   c. 5.

SOLUTIONS

1. a. {0, 1}
   b. {0, 1, 2, 3, 4}
   c. {0, 1, 2, 3, 4, 5, 6, 7, 8, 9, a, b, c, d, e, f} Since we don't have a single symbol to represent the number $10_{[ten]}$, we must invent one. Most commonly the symbols are chosen as indicated in the set to represent 10 through 15.
2. a. $3(64) + 5(8) + 7(1) = 239$
   b. $32 + 8 + 4 + 2 = 46$
   c. $10(256) + 5(16) + 12 = 2652$
3. a. $505_{(eight)}$ $325 \div 8 =$ 40 remainder 5
                                           $40 \div 8 = 5$ remainder 0
   b. $145_{(sixteen)}$ $325 \div 16 = 20$ r 5 ← (this is the rightmost digit.)
                                     $20 \div 16 = 1$ r 4
   c. $2300_{(five)}$ $325 \div 5 = 65$ r 0
                                     $65 \div 5 = 13$ r 0
                                     $13 \div 5 = 2$ r 3

Axioms of the Real Number System

An axiom (or assumption or postulate) is a statement that is accepted without proof. For the algebra of real numbers, we have the following set of axioms:

- **Closure.** The set of real numbers is closed under both addition and multiplication. Closure means that, if you choose any two real numbers and then perform the operation on these numbers, the answer is always found also in the set of real numbers. (For all a, $b \in R$, both $a + b \in R$ and $ab \in R$.)

- *Commutative.* For all real numbers a and b,

$$a + b = b + a \quad \text{and} \quad ab = ba \text{ (order change)}$$

- *Associative.* For all real numbers a, b, and c,

$$a + (b + c) = (a + b) + c \quad \text{and} \quad a(bc) = (ab)c \text{ (grouping change)}$$

- *Identity.* There exists a real number, 0, such that, for all real numbers a,

$$a + 0 = 0 + a = a \text{ (0 is the additive identity)}$$

There exists a real number, 1, such that, for all real numbers a,

$$a \cdot 1 = 1 \cdot a = a \text{ (1 is the multiplicative identity)}$$

- *Inverse.* For each real number a there exists another real number, $-a$, such that

$$a + (-a) = (-a) + a = 0 \ (-a \text{ is the additive inverse or opposite of } a)$$

For each real number, a, $a \neq 0$, there exists another real number, $\dfrac{1}{a}$, such that

$$a\left(\frac{1}{a}\right) = \left(\frac{1}{a}\right)a = 1$$

The inverse for multiplication is also called the *reciprocal*. In general, the reciprocal of $\frac{a}{b}$ is $\frac{b}{a}$.

- *Distributive*. For all real numbers a, b, and c,

$$a(b + c) = ab + ac$$

PRACTICE EXERCISES

Name the axiom that is illustrated in each of the following:

1. $7 + (6 + 8) = (6 + 8) + 7$
2. $7 + (6 + 8) = (7 + 6) + 8$
3. $7 + (6 + 8) = 7 + (8 + 6)$
4. $7 + (6 + 0) = 7 + 6$
5. $7(6 + 8) = 7 \cdot 6 + 7 \cdot 8$
6. $7(6 \cdot 8) = (7 \cdot 6)8$
7. $7 + 6\left(\dfrac{1}{6}\right) = 7 + 1$
8. $[7 + (-7)] + 8 = 0 + 8$
9. $[7 + (-7)] + (8 + 6) = 7 + [(-7) + (8 + 6)]$
10. $7 + 6 = 13$

SOLUTIONS

1. Commutative axiom of addition (order change)
2. Associative axiom of addition (grouping change)
3. Commutative axiom of addition
4. Identity axiom of addition
5. Distributive axiom (There's only one. It's not necessary to specify an operation.)
6. Associative axiom of multiplication
7. Inverse axiom of multiplication
8. Inverse axiom of addition
9. Associative axiom of addition
10. Closure axiom of addition (The real number 13 is assigned to 6 and 7.)

Three meanings of the symbol "−"

Many students have problems with this symbol: −. The reason these problems occur is that the symbol actually has three distinct meanings. A clear understanding of these three meanings can go a long way toward correcting errors made with signs.

1. When this symbol appears between two numbers, it always means "subtract." Thus $7 - 4$ can be read either as "7 subtract 4" or "7 minus 4."
2. When the symbol appears to the left of a numeral, it is properly read as "negative." Thus, -8 is read as "negative 8." The word *negative* means that the number is located to the left of zero on the number line.
3. In any other position, however, the symbol "−" should be read as "opposite." In particular:

   $-x$ means the opposite of x.

   $-(-9)$ means the opposite of negative 9.

   $-(a + b)$ means the opposite of the sum of a and b.

   $-[-(-8)]$ means the opposite of the opposite of negative 8.

   -5^2 means the opposite of 5 squared.

Order of Operation Rules

So that there is no ambiguity about an expression like

$$1 + 3 \cdot 4 \qquad \text{or} \qquad -2^2$$

the order in which operations are to be performed must be defined.

ORDER OF OPERATION RULES

1. Perform all operations inside grouping symbols first. Grouping symbols include parentheses: ( ), brackets: [ ], braces: { }, and a bar (vinculum): $\frac{2+3}{7}$.
2. Do all roots and exponents in order from left to right.
3. Do all multiplications and divisions in order from left to right. (This rule does NOT say, "Do all multiplications and then do all divisions.")
4. Do all additions and subtractions (and opposites) in order from left to right.

Operations with Signed Numbers

Absolute Value

The absolute value of any number is its distance from the origin on a number line. The symbol for this operation is $|x|$. An alternative (and more algebraic) definition of absolute value is

$$|x| = \begin{cases} x \text{ if } x \geq 0 \\ -x \text{ if } x < 0 \end{cases}$$

Addition

If the two numbers are either both positive or both negative, add the absolute values of the numbers and prefix the answer with the sign that is common to the original numbers.

$$(-2) + (-5) = -7 \qquad 5 + 3 = 8 \qquad -4 + (-6) = -10$$

If the two numbers have opposite signs, subtract the absolute values of the numbers (the smaller from the larger) and prefix the answer with the sign of the original number that has the larger absolute value.

$$-7 + 9 = 2 \qquad 4 + (-3) = 1 \qquad 5 + (-9) = -4$$

Subtraction

The definition of subtraction is

$$a - b = a + (-b)$$

This definition says, "a minus b equals a plus the opposite of b." In other words, to subtract, add the opposite of the number following the subtraction sign.

- $2 - 5$
  $= 2 + (-5)$
  $= -3$

  Change the operation to addition and replace the number following the subtraction sign by its opposite. Follow the rules for addition.

- $5 - (-3)$
  $= 5 + 3$
  $= 8$

  Change to addition, replace second number by its opposite. Add.

- $-7 - 8$
  $= -7 + (-8)$
  $= -15$

  Change to addition, replace second number by its opposite. Add.

- $-2 - (-4)$
  $= -2 + 4$
  $= 2$

Multiplication

To multiply two numbers, multiply their absolute values and prefix the answer with a sign determined by the following rule:

If the two numbers have the same sign, the product is positive, +. If the two numbers have opposite signs, the product is negative, –.

$$(-3)(4) = -12 \qquad (-5)(-4) = 20 \qquad 3(-7) = -21$$

Division

The rule for division is similar to the rule for multiplication. Divide the absolute values of the numbers, and prefix the answer with a sign determined by the following rule:

If the two numbers have the same sign, choose +. If the two numbers have opposite signs, choose –.

Exponentiation

The following equation defines exponentiation:

$$x^n = x \cdot x \cdot x \cdot \ldots \cdot x \qquad (n \text{ factors of the base } x)$$

It is important to remember that any exponent always refers only to the symbol immediately to its left. Thus:

$$5^3 = 5 \cdot 5 \cdot 5 = 25 \cdot 5 = 125$$

$$-2^4 = -(2 \cdot 2 \cdot 2 \cdot 2) = -16 \ (-2^4 \text{ is read as "the opposite of 2 to the fourth power."})$$

$$2(-3x)^2 = 2[(-3x)(-3x)] = 2(9x^2) = 18x^2 \text{ (In this expression the symbol immediately to the}$$
left of the exponent is the parenthesis and parentheses come in pairs.)

Roots

The definition is

$$a \text{ is the } n\text{th root of } b \text{ if and only if } a^n = b$$

An immediate consequence of the definition is that there are no real nth roots of negative numbers when n is an even number because any real number raised to an even power is always positive. Also, any positive real number has two real square roots, one positive and the other negative.

The radical sign is used in the context of roots. However, in the case of nth roots when n is even, the symbol represents the *principal* nth root. The principal nth root is always the positive root. Thus:

$$\sqrt{9} = 3 \qquad (\text{and not } -3)$$

Odd roots, on the other hand, do not have this problem—the odd root of a positive number is positive, and the odd root of a negative number is negative.

PRACTICE EXERCISES

Perform the indicated operations.

1. $3 - 5 \cdot 7$
2. $-2(3 - 4)^3 - 2$
3. $5\{2[3(4 + 1) - 3] - 2\} - 7$
4. $\dfrac{3(-4)}{2} + (-2)^2(3) - (-3)(-3)^2 + \dfrac{-5}{-1}$
5. $\sqrt{(-3)^2 + 4^2}$
6. -5^2
7. $(-5)^2$

SOLUTIONS

1. $\mathbf{3 - 5 \cdot 7} = 3 - 35 = 3 + (-35) = -32$
2. $\mathbf{-2(3 - 4)^3 - 2} = -2[3 + (-4)]^3 - 2$
   $\qquad = -2(-1)^3 - 2$
   $\qquad = -2(-1) - 2 = 2 - 2$
   $\qquad = 2 + (-2) = 0$
3. $\mathbf{5\{2[3(4 + 1) - 3] - 2\} - 7}$ (These steps show excruciating detail.
   $\quad = 5\{2[3(5) - 3] - 2\} - 7$ Many steps may be omitted by experienced
   $\quad = 5\{2[15 - 3] - 2\} - 7$ students.)
   $\quad = 5\{2[15 + (-3)] - 2\} - 7$
   $\quad = 5\{2[12] - 2\} - 7$
   $\quad = 5\{24 - 2\} - 7$

$$= 5\{24 + (-2)\} - 7$$
$$= 5\{22\} - 7 = 110 - 7$$
$$= 110 + (-7) = 103$$

4. $\dfrac{3(-4)}{2} + (-2)^2(3) - (-3)(-3)^2 + \dfrac{-5}{-1}$

$$= \dfrac{3(-4)}{2} + 4(3) - (-3)(9) + \dfrac{-5}{-1}$$

$= \dfrac{-12}{2} + 12 - (-27) + 5$ (All multiplications and divisions are done before any additions or subtractions).

$$= -6 + 12 - (-27) + 5$$
$$= -6 + 12 + 27 + 5$$
$$= 6 + 27 + 5$$
$$= 33 + 5 = 38$$

5. $\sqrt{(-3)^2 + 4^2} = \sqrt{9 + 16}$ (The bar is a grouping symbol.)

$$= \sqrt{25} = 5$$

6. -5^2 means "the opposite of five squared"
   $-5^2 = -(5 \cdot 5) = -25$

7. $(-5)^2$ means "negative five, squared"
   $(-5)^2 = (-5) \cdot (-5) = 25$

Divisibility

There are four relationships between a and b in the equation $a = bc$, where a, b, and c are whole numbers: For example: $12 = 3 \cdot 4$ so

1. a is a *multiple* of b.	12 is a multiple of 3
2. a is *divisible* by b.	12 is divisible by 3
3. b is a *factor* of a.	3 is a factor of 12
4. b is a *divisor* of a.	3 is a divisor of 12

Many times it is important to know whether or not a number is divisible by another. For the whole numbers 1 through 11, there are specific tests for divisibility:

1. Every whole number is divisible by 1.
2. Every even number is divisible by 2.
3. A whole number is divisible by 3 if the sum of the digits of the number is divisible by 3.
4. A whole number is divisible by 4 if the two rightmost digits constitute a number that is divisible by 4.
5. A whole number is divisible by 5 if the rightmost digit is either 0 or 5.
6. A whole number is divisible by 6 if it is divisible by both 2 and 3.
7. A whole number is divisible by 7 if the result of the repeated process of doubling the final digit and subtracting it from the number obtained by deleting the final digit is divisible by 7. For example, 3766 is divisible by 7 if

$$\begin{array}{r|l} 376 & 6 \\ -12 & \\ \hline 364 & \end{array}$$ Double the last digit and subtract from 376.

$$\begin{array}{r|l} 36 & 4 \\ -8 & \\ \hline 28 & \end{array}$$ Again, double the last digit and subtract.

    Since 28 is divisible by 7, so is 3766.

8. A whole number is divisible by 8 if the rightmost three digits constitute a number divisible by 8.
9. A whole number is divisible by 9 if the sum of the digits is divisible by 9.
10. A whole number is divisible by 10 if the rightmost digit is 0.
11. A whole number is divisible by 11 if the absolute value of the difference between the sum of the digits in positions whose place values are even powers of 10 and the sum

of the digits in positions whose place values are odd powers of 10 is divisible by 11. (Add every other digit; add the remaining ones; subtract. If the answer is divisible by 11, then so is the original number.) Consider, for example the number 72,406,037.

$$\underline{72,4\underline{06},\underline{037}}$$

Add the underlined digits: 9.
Add the remaining digits: 20
Subtract: -11.
Take the absolute value: $|-11| = 11$.
Since 11 is divisible by 11, the number 72,406,037 is also divisible by 11.
The use of a calculator can make all of these divisibility rules unnecessary.

PRACTICE EXERCISE

Which numbers from the following set:

$$\{1, 2, 3, 4, 5, 6, 7, 8, 9, 10, 11\}$$

divide the given number?

1. 2520
2. 59,049
3. 7203

4. 2197
5. 24,167

SOLUTIONS

1. 1, 2, 3, 4, 5, 6, 7, 8, 9, 10
2. 1, 3, 9
3. 1, 3, 7

4. 1
5. 1, 11

Prime and Composite Numbers

A whole number is *prime* if and only if it has exactly two factors.
A whole number greater than 1 is *composite* if and only if it is not prime.
Both of these definitions involve whole numbers, so examine each whole number.

Number	Factors	Conclusion
0	0, 1, 2, . . .	Neither prime nor composite
1	1	Neither prime nor composite
2	1, 2	Prime
3	1, 3	Prime
4	1, 2, 4	Composite
5	1, 5	Prime
6	1, 2, 3	Composite
7	1, 7	Prime
8	1, 2, 4, 8	Composite

A prime number must first be a whole number, and then it must have exactly two factors. It is a good idea to memorize the primes up to 20. They are 2, 3, 5, 7, 11, 13, 17, and 19. There are an infinite number of primes, but it is very difficult to determine whether a very large number is prime.

The tests for divisibility in the preceding section will be useful for determining whether a particular number is prime or composite. Every whole number has 1 as a factor, and every whole number is a factor of itself; therefore each whole number greater than 1 has at least two factors. The task then is to determine whether there is another factor in addition to the number 1 and the number itself. If there is another factor, then the number greater than 1 is not prime; it is composite. Consider these examples:

- 51 has 1 and 51 as factors. Examining other whole numbers to determine divisibility, we find that 0 is not a factor, 2 is not, 3 is a factor; therefore 51 is composite.

- 61 has 1 and 61 as factors. Examining other whole numbers:

0 is a factor of 0 only. (Don't bother with 0.)

2 is not a factor; 2 divides even numbers only.

3 is not. The sum of the digits is 7.

4 is not. If 4 were a factor, then 2 would also be a factor and 2 has already been tested. Don't bother with 4.

5 is not.

6 is not. If it were, then both 2 and 3 would also be factors. *Test the prime numbers only.*

7 is not.

11 is not.

Must all the prime numbers up to 61 be tested? No, you must test only those up to the approximate square root of the number. The square root of the number is passed when the quotient is smaller than the divisor. If no other factor has been found, the number is prime. If another factor is found, the number is composite.

Since $\frac{61}{11} = 5 +$ and 5 is smaller than 11, the conclusion is that 61 is prime.

Here's another example. To determine whether or not 97 is prime, only the primes up to 11 need to be tested as factors.

2 is not a factor.

3 is not.

5 is not.

7 is not.

11 is not, and the quotient is less than 11.

Therefore 97 is prime.

To categorize any number as prime or composite up to 200, only the primes up to 13 need to be tested, and the tests from the preceding section can be applied.

PRACTICE EXERCISES

Determine whether each of the following numbers is prime or composite:

1. 143   **2.** 151   **3.** –5   **4.** 79   **5.** 1

SOLUTIONS

1.   Composite   (The factors are 1, 11, 13, 143.)

2.   Prime

3.   Neither   (According to the definitions, both prime and composite numbers are whole numbers.).

4.   Prime

5.   Neither

Prime Factorization

It is important to be able to express a whole number as a product of prime factors. For example, $12 = 2 \cdot 2 \cdot 3 = 2^2 \cdot 3$. There are two useful methods to accomplish this task.

Method 1: Factor tree. Find the prime factorization of 72. First name any two factors of 72 (not necessarily prime), say 8 and 9. Each of these numbers can be factored. Continue this until all factors are prime. It is convenient to arrange these numbers in a tree.

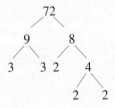

$$72 = 2 \cdot 2 \cdot 2 \cdot 3 \cdot 3$$

Method 2: Repeated division by primes. Determine the prime factorization of 120. First name any prime number that divides 120, and perform the division; then repeat the process with the quotient until the last quotient is also prime. The factorization consists of all the prime divisors and the last quotient.

$$
\begin{array}{r}
5 \\
3\overline{)15} \\
2\overline{)30} \\
2\overline{)60} \\
2\overline{)120}
\end{array}
$$

$$120 = 2 \cdot 2 \cdot 2 \cdot 3 \cdot 5$$

Therefore the prime factorization is $120 = 2 \cdot 2 \cdot 2 \cdot 3 \cdot 5 = 2^3 \cdot 3 \cdot 5$.
You may find that this is easy with a calculator.

PRACTICE EXERCISES

Determine the prime factorization of each of the following numbers:
1. 50 **2.** 300 **3.** 73 **4.** 1617 **5.** 243

SOLUTIONS

1. $50 = 2 \cdot 5^2$
2. $300 = 2^2 \cdot 3 \cdot 5^2$
3. 73 is prime, so there is no prime factorization. In particular, the answer is not $1 \cdot 73$.
4. $1617 = 3 \cdot 7^2 \cdot 11$
5. $243 = 3^5$

Greatest Common Factors and Lowest Common Multiples

The list of factors of any whole number is always finite, and the list of multiples is infinite. For example, the factors of 12 are 1, 2, 3, 4, 6, and 12, whereas the multiples of 12 are 12, 24, 36, 48, . . .

Given any two natural numbers, it is frequently necessary to find the lowest (or least) common multiple (LCM).

To find the LCM of 54 and 60, first find the prime factorizations:

$$54 = 2 \cdot 3^3 \qquad 60 = 2^2 \cdot 3 \cdot 5$$

Use each factor the greater number of times that it appears in either factorization. In other words, use the factor 2 twice, the factor 3 three times, and the factor 5 once. Therefore the LCM of 54 and 60 is $2^2 \cdot 3^3 \cdot 5 = 540$.

Sometimes it is necessary to find the largest number that is in the list of factors of two numbers, that is, the greatest common factor (GCF) (also called greatest common divisor, GCD). This operation could also become difficult without the following factorization process:

To find the GCF of 96 and 108, first find the prime factorizations:

$$96 = 2^5 \cdot 3 \qquad 108 = 2^2 \cdot 3^3$$

Any factor that occurs in both lists is a common factor, so to find the GCF use each common factor the smaller number of times that it appears in either factorization. Thus the GCF of 96 and 108 is $2^2 \cdot 3 = 12$.

Tests for the divisibility of many composite numbers can be developed easily. For example, a number is divisible by 15 if it is divisible by both 3 and 5; a number is divisible by 18 if it divisible by both 2 and 9. A number is not necessarily divisible by 18 if it is divisible by both 3 and 6, however, because the GCF of 3 and 6 is not 1. The rule is to find two factors of the number whose GCF is 1. (Such numbers are said to be *relatively prime*.)

PRACTICE EXERCISES

Find the lowest common multiple of each of the following groups of numbers:
1. 28 and 70
2. 72 and 150
3. 24, 48, and 60

Find the greatest common factor of each of the following groups of numbers:
4. 70 and 120
5. 180 and 300
6. 24, 54, and 72
7. 108 and 245

Devise a test for divisibility for each of the following numbers:
8. 30
9. 36
10. 60

SOLUTIONS

1. $28 = 2^2 \cdot 7$ and $70 = 2 \cdot 5 \cdot 7$
   Choose 2 twice, 5 once, and 7 once.
   The LMC is $2^2 \cdot 5 \cdot 7 = 140$.
2. $72 = 2^3 \cdot 3^2$ and $150 = 2 \cdot 3 \cdot 5^2$
   Choose 2 three times, 3 twice, and 5 twice.
   The LCM is $2^3 \cdot 3^2 \cdot 5^2 = 1800$.
3. $24 = 2^3 \cdot 3$, $48 = 2^4 \cdot 3$, and $60 = 2^2 \cdot 3 \cdot 5$
   The LCM is $2^4 \cdot 3 \cdot 5 = 240$.
4. $70 = 2 \cdot 5 \cdot 7$ and $120 = 2^3 \cdot 3 \cdot 5$
   Choose 2 once and 5 once.
   The GCF is $2 \cdot 5 = 10$.
5. $180 = 2^2 \cdot 3^2 \cdot 5$ and $300 = 2^2 \cdot 3 \cdot 5^2$
   Choose 2 twice, 3 once, and 5 once.
   The GCF is $2^2 \cdot 3 \cdot 5 = 60$.
6. 6
7. 1 These numbers are relatively prime.
8. A number is divisible by 30 if it is divisible by both 5 and 6 or by both 3 and 10 or by both 2 and 15 (and a number is divisible by 15 if it is divisible by both 3 and 5).
9. A number is divisible by 36 if it divisible by both 4 and 9. But 3 and 12 would not work. Why not?
10. A number is divisible by 60 if it is divisible by both 5 and 12 (5, 3, and 4) or 3 and 20 or 4 and 15. But 6 and 10 would not work. Why not?

FOCUS ON THE ACT

The following sample questions represent ways in which the reviewed skills might be tested on your ACT Assessment.

1. Which of the following is not a rational number?
   A. 3.14
   B. $7.\overline{4}$
   C. 0
   D. $-\sqrt{4}$
   E. $\sqrt{5}$

2. $-2 - [-3^2 + (-1)^2] = ?$
   F. -12
   G. 6
   H. 16
   J. -18
   K. 8

3. Which of the following numbers is prime?
   A. 51
   B. 52
   C. 53
   D. 54
   E. 55

4. What is the greatest common factor (GCF) of 48 and 90?
   F. 6
   G. 8
   H. 9
   J. 480
   K. 720

5. What is the lowest common multiple (LCM) of 24 and 42?
   A. 6
   B. 24
   C. 42
   D. 168
   E. 1008

ANSWERS AND EXPLANATIONS

1. **E** Each of the other numbers can be written as a fraction.

$$3.14 = \frac{314}{100}$$

$$7.\overline{4} = 7\frac{4}{9} = \frac{67}{9}$$

$$0 = \frac{0}{1}$$

$$-\sqrt{4} = -2 = \frac{-2}{1}$$

There is no fraction equivalent to $\sqrt{5}$.

2. **G** $-2 - [-3^2 + (-1)^2]$
$= -2 - [-9 + 1]$
$= -2 - [-8]$
$= -2 + 8$
$= 6$

3. **C** Only 53 has exactly two factors, namely 1 and 53.
$51 = 1 \cdot 51 = 3 \cdot 17$
$52 = 1 \cdot 52 = 2 \cdot 26 = 4 \cdot 13$
$54 = 1 \cdot 54 = 2 \cdot 27 = 3 \cdot 18 = 6 \cdot 9$
$55 = 1 \cdot 55 = 5 \cdot 11$

4. **F** $48 = \underline{2} \cdot 2 \cdot 2 \cdot \underline{3}$ Choose the prime factors in both lists.
$90 = \underline{2} \cdot \underline{3} \cdot 3 \cdot 5$ $2 \cdot 3 = 6$ is the GCF.

5. **D** $24 = \underline{2 \cdot 2 \cdot 2} \cdot 3$ Use each prime factor the
$42 = \underline{2} \cdot \underline{3} \cdot \underline{7}$ greater number of times it appears in either list. $2 \cdot 2 \cdot 2 \cdot 3 \cdot 7 = 168$ is the LCM.

Fractions

A rational number can always be expressed as a fraction in which the numerator (the top number) is an integer and the denominator is a natural number. (Notice that zero is not a natural number.) If the absolute value of the numerator is greater than or equal to the denominator, the fraction is called *improper;* otherwise it is a *proper* fraction. Two fractions are *equivalent* if they represent the same number. An easy way to tell whether two fractions are equivalent is to cross-multiply. If the products are equal, then the fractions are equivalent and the rational numbers are equal:

$$\frac{a}{b} = \frac{c}{d} \quad \text{if and only if} \quad ad = bc, \quad b, d \neq 0$$

The Fundamental Principle of Fractions states that any fraction is equivalent to a fraction obtained by multiplying the numerator and denominator by the same nonzero number:

$$\frac{a}{b} = \frac{ak}{bk}, \quad b, k \neq 0$$

This property is used to reduce fractions to lowest terms:

$$\frac{12}{18} = \frac{2 \cdot 6}{3 \cdot 6} = \frac{2}{3}$$

$$\frac{90}{108} = \frac{45}{54} \ (k = 2) \qquad \text{(This reduction can be done in stages.)}$$

$$= \frac{5}{6} \ (k = 9)$$

This same property is used to rewrite a fraction so that it has a specific denominator:

$$\frac{5}{9} = \frac{?}{63} = \frac{35}{63} \quad (k = 7)$$

$$\frac{5}{8} = \frac{?}{120} = \frac{75}{120} \quad (k = 15)$$

PRACTICE EXERCISES

Reduce each fraction to lowest terms.

1. $\dfrac{20}{50}$

2. $\dfrac{18}{30}$

3. $\dfrac{60}{84}$

4. $\dfrac{108}{162}$

Rewrite each fraction so that it has the specified denominator.

5. $\dfrac{4}{5} = \dfrac{?}{70}$

6. $\dfrac{5}{8} = \dfrac{?}{96}$

7. $\dfrac{7}{12} = \dfrac{?}{180}$

SOLUTIONS

1. $\dfrac{2}{5} \ (k = 10)$

2. $\dfrac{3}{5} \ (k = 6)$

3. $\dfrac{5}{7} \ (k = 12)$

4. $\dfrac{2}{3} \ (k = 54)$

5. $\dfrac{56}{70} \ (k = 14)$

6. $\dfrac{60}{96} \ (k = 12)$

7. $\dfrac{105}{180} \ (k = 15)$

Proper and Improper Fractions and Mixed Numbers

If the absolute value of the numerator is not smaller than the denominator, the fraction is improper, and it can be changed to a mixed number or a whole number. A mixed number is a special form that represents the sum of a whole number and a proper fraction:

$$\frac{7}{5} = 1 + \frac{2}{5} = 1\frac{2}{5}$$

To determine the mixed number that is equivalent to an improper fraction, divide the denominator into the numerator. The quotient becomes the whole number part of the mixed number, and the remainder becomes the numerator of the fraction part of the mixed number.

PRACTICE EXERCISES

Change each improper fraction to a corresponding mixed number.

1. $\dfrac{23}{5}$

2. $\dfrac{87}{13}$

3. $\dfrac{105}{7}$

4. $\dfrac{72}{16}$

Change each mixed number to a corresponding improper fraction.

5. $7\dfrac{3}{4}$

6. $12\dfrac{3}{7}$

7. $5\dfrac{11}{12}$

SOLUTIONS

1. $4\dfrac{3}{5}$

2. $6\dfrac{9}{13}$

3. 15 (not a mixed number)

4. $4\dfrac{1}{2}$ (Be sure to reduce the fraction to lowest terms.)

5. $7\dfrac{3}{4} = \dfrac{31}{4}$ (The numerator is 7(4) + 3 = 31.)

6. $\dfrac{87}{7}$

7. $\dfrac{71}{12}$

Operations with Fractions

Addition and Subtraction

The rules for addition and subtraction of fractions are as follows:

$$\frac{a}{b} \pm \frac{c}{b} = \frac{a \pm c}{b}, \quad b \neq 0$$

These rules are very easy to apply; however, difficulty with these operations comes in four areas:

1. If the fractions do not have the same denominators, they must first be changed so that there is a common denominator. For example:

- $\dfrac{3}{4} + \dfrac{1}{8} = \dfrac{6}{8} + \dfrac{1}{8} = \dfrac{7}{8}$ The lowest common denominator (LCD) is the lowest common multiple of the denominators.

- $\dfrac{5}{12} + \dfrac{7}{16} = \dfrac{20}{48} + \dfrac{21}{48} = \dfrac{41}{48}$ The LCM of 12 and 16 is 48.

2. If the numbers to be added or subtracted are given as mixed numbers, there are two methods of performing the operations. For example:

- $3\dfrac{2}{3} + 5\dfrac{1}{2} = 3\dfrac{4}{6} + 5\dfrac{3}{6}$ Add the fraction parts and whole number parts separately.

$= 8\dfrac{7}{6}$ Since the fraction part is an improper fraction, the answer must be expressed in simplest

$= 8 + 1\dfrac{1}{6} = 9\dfrac{1}{6}$ form.

OR

- $3\dfrac{2}{3} + 5\dfrac{1}{2} = \dfrac{11}{3} + \dfrac{11}{2}$ Write each mixed number as an improper fraction and then add according to the rule.

$= \dfrac{22}{6} + \dfrac{33}{6}$

$= \dfrac{55}{6} = 9\dfrac{1}{6}$ Change the answer back to a mixed number:

3. The answers must normally be expressed in simplest form.

$\dfrac{1}{6} + \dfrac{1}{2} = \dfrac{1}{6} + \dfrac{3}{6} = \dfrac{4}{6} = \dfrac{2}{3}$ The answer has been reduced.

4. In subtraction of mixed numbers, borrowing or regrouping must be done carefully.

$5\dfrac{2}{3} - 1\dfrac{3}{4} = 5\dfrac{8}{12} - 1\dfrac{9}{12}$ Borrow 1 from the 5 and add it to the fraction part of the mixed number

$= 4\dfrac{20}{12} - 1\dfrac{9}{12}$ $\left(1 + \dfrac{8}{12} = \dfrac{20}{12}\right)$.

$= 3\dfrac{11}{12}$

Some calculators will perform operations with fractions.

PRACTICE EXERCISES

Add or subtract as indicated, and express the answer in simplest form.

1. $\dfrac{4}{9} + \dfrac{2}{9}$ 6. $8 - 5\dfrac{5}{8}$

2. $\dfrac{5}{7} + \dfrac{2}{21}$ 7. $3\dfrac{2}{5} - 1\dfrac{3}{4}$

3. $\dfrac{3}{7} - \dfrac{1}{9}$ 8. $6\dfrac{7}{8} + 2\dfrac{2}{3}$

4. $\dfrac{7}{20} + \dfrac{3}{16}$ 9. $\left(-2\dfrac{3}{5}\right) + 1\dfrac{1}{2}$

5. $4\dfrac{1}{2} - 2\dfrac{1}{3}$ 10. $\left(-17\dfrac{8}{9}\right) - 5\dfrac{11}{12}$

SOLUTIONS

1. $\dfrac{4}{9} + \dfrac{2}{9} = \dfrac{6}{9} = \dfrac{2}{3}$

2. $\dfrac{5}{7} + \dfrac{2}{21} = \dfrac{15}{21} + \dfrac{2}{21} = \dfrac{17}{21}$

3. $\dfrac{3}{7} - \dfrac{1}{9} = \dfrac{27}{63} - \dfrac{7}{63} = \dfrac{20}{63}$

4. $\dfrac{7}{20} + \dfrac{3}{16} = \dfrac{28}{80} + \dfrac{15}{80}$ LCM of 20 and 16 is 80.

$= \dfrac{43}{80}$

5. $4\dfrac{1}{2} - 2\dfrac{1}{3} = 4\dfrac{3}{6} - 2\dfrac{2}{6} = 2\dfrac{1}{6}$

6. $8 - 5\dfrac{5}{8} = 7\dfrac{8}{8} - 5\dfrac{5}{8}$ Borrow 1 from 8.

$= 2\dfrac{3}{8}$

7. $3\dfrac{2}{5} - 1\dfrac{3}{4} = 3\dfrac{8}{20} - 1\dfrac{15}{20}$ Borrow 1 from 3 and add to the fraction part.

$= 2\dfrac{28}{20} - 1\dfrac{15}{20}$

$= 1\dfrac{13}{20}$

8. $6\dfrac{7}{8} + 2\dfrac{2}{3} = 6\dfrac{21}{24} + 2\dfrac{16}{24}$

$= 8\dfrac{37}{24} = 8 + 1\dfrac{13}{24}$

$= 9\dfrac{13}{24}$

9. $\left(-2\dfrac{3}{5}\right) + 1\dfrac{1}{2}$

All rules of signs that apply to positive and negative integers apply also to fractions.

$= \left(-2\dfrac{6}{10}\right) + 1\dfrac{5}{10}$

$= -1\dfrac{1}{10}$

10. $\left(-17\dfrac{8}{9}\right) - 5\dfrac{11}{12} = \left(-17\dfrac{8}{9}\right) + \left(-5\dfrac{11}{12}\right)$

$= \left(-17\dfrac{64}{72}\right) + \left(-5\dfrac{66}{72}\right)$

$= -22\dfrac{130}{72}$

$= -\left(22 + 1\dfrac{62}{72}\right) = -23\dfrac{31}{36}$

Multiplication

The rule for multiplication of fractions is as follows:

$$\dfrac{a}{b} \cdot \dfrac{c}{d} = \dfrac{ac}{bd}, \quad b, d \neq 0$$

This rule states that, to multiply any two fractions, one must multiply the numerators and denominators separately.

Division

The rule for division is as follows:

$$\dfrac{a}{b} \div \dfrac{c}{d} = \dfrac{a}{b} \cdot \dfrac{d}{c}, \quad b, c, d \neq 0$$

This rule states that, to divide fractions, one must replace the divisor with its reciprocal and change the operation to multiplication. Here are some examples:

- $\dfrac{2}{3} \cdot \dfrac{5}{7} = \dfrac{10}{21}$

- $\dfrac{3}{4} \cdot \dfrac{8}{9} = \dfrac{24}{36} = \dfrac{2}{3}$ All answers must be reduced. The common factors in the numerators and denominators are normally divided out before actually multiplying. This is called *canceling*.

- $\dfrac{5}{12} \cdot \dfrac{8}{9} = \dfrac{5}{\overset{}{\underset{3}{\cancel{12}}}} \cdot \dfrac{\overset{2}{\cancel{8}}}{9} = \dfrac{5}{3} \cdot \dfrac{2}{9} = \dfrac{10}{27}$

- $2\dfrac{1}{2} \cdot 3\dfrac{5}{6} = \dfrac{5}{2} \cdot \dfrac{23}{6}$ Mixed numbers must be changed to improper fractions before multiplying.

  $= \dfrac{115}{12} = 9\dfrac{7}{12}$

- $\left(-3\dfrac{4}{5}\right) \cdot \left(-6\dfrac{1}{3}\right) = \left(\dfrac{-19}{5}\right) \cdot \left(\dfrac{-19}{3}\right)$ The same rules of signs apply.

  $= \dfrac{361}{15} = 24\dfrac{1}{15}$

- $\dfrac{2}{5} \div \dfrac{3}{8} = \dfrac{2}{5} \cdot \dfrac{8}{3}$ The reciprocal of $\dfrac{3}{8}$ is $\dfrac{8}{3}$.

  $= \dfrac{16}{15} = 1\dfrac{1}{15}$

- $7\dfrac{1}{4} \div \left(-2\dfrac{3}{5}\right) = \dfrac{29}{4} \div \left(\dfrac{-13}{5}\right)$ Change to improper fractions.

  $= \dfrac{29}{4} \cdot \left(\dfrac{-5}{13}\right)$ Replace divisor by reciprocal, and change operation to multiplication.

  $= \dfrac{-145}{52} = -2\dfrac{41}{52}$

Exponents with Fractions

It is important to recall that an exponent always applies only to the immediately preceding symbol. Thus, to raise any fraction to a power, parentheses are necessary. For example:

$$\left(\dfrac{2}{3}\right)^2 = \dfrac{4}{9} \qquad \dfrac{2^2}{3} \neq \dfrac{4}{9}$$

Complex Fractions

If the numerator or the denominator, or both, themselves contain fractions, the expression is called a *complex fraction*. There are two methods to simplify complex fractions:

1. Treat the complex fraction as a division-of-fractions problem. For example:

$$\dfrac{\dfrac{2}{3} + \dfrac{3}{4}}{2 - \dfrac{5}{6}} = \dfrac{\dfrac{8}{12} + \dfrac{9}{12}}{\dfrac{12}{6} - \dfrac{5}{6}} = \dfrac{\dfrac{17}{12}}{\dfrac{7}{6}}$$

$$= \dfrac{17}{12} \cdot \dfrac{6}{7} = \dfrac{17}{\underset{2}{\cancel{12}}} \cdot \dfrac{\overset{1}{\cancel{6}}}{7} \quad \text{(Cancel the 6.)}$$

$$= \dfrac{17}{14} = 1\dfrac{3}{14}$$

2. Multiply the numerator and denominator by the lowest common denominator of the fractions within both numerator and denominator. For example:

$$\frac{\dfrac{5}{6}+\dfrac{1}{2}}{\dfrac{7}{8}-\dfrac{3}{4}}=\frac{24\left(\dfrac{5}{6}+\dfrac{1}{2}\right)}{24\left(\dfrac{7}{8}-\dfrac{3}{4}\right)}\qquad\text{(24 is the LCD.)}$$

$$=\frac{20+12}{21-18}=\frac{32}{3}=10\frac{2}{3}$$

This is usually the more efficient method.

PRACTICE EXERCISES

Find the reciprocal of each of the following rational numbers:

1. $7\dfrac{3}{5}$

2. $\dfrac{-2}{5}$

3. $\dfrac{1}{8}$

4. 6

5. 0

Perform the indicated operations, and express the answers in simplest form.

6. $-2\dfrac{4}{9}\cdot 4\dfrac{1}{2}$

7. $3\dfrac{1}{3}\div 1\dfrac{3}{7}$

8. $\dfrac{3}{7}\div\dfrac{3}{14}$

9. $\dfrac{\dfrac{1}{4}+\dfrac{1}{2}}{\dfrac{1}{3}+\dfrac{1}{4}}$

10. $\dfrac{3-\dfrac{3}{4}}{-4+\dfrac{1}{2}}$

SOLUTIONS

1. $7\dfrac{3}{5}=\dfrac{38}{5}$ so the reciprocal is $\dfrac{5}{38}$.

2. $\dfrac{-5}{2}=-2\dfrac{1}{2}$

3. $\dfrac{8}{1}=8$

4. $\dfrac{1}{6}$

5. Zero is the only real number that has no reciprocal. This is part of the reason that 0 may not be chosen as the divisor.

6. $-2\dfrac{4}{9} \cdot 4\dfrac{1}{2} = \dfrac{-22}{9} \cdot \dfrac{9}{2}$ Cancel both 2 and 9.

$$= \dfrac{\overset{-11}{\cancel{-22}}}{\underset{1}{\cancel{9}}} \cdot \dfrac{\overset{1}{\cancel{9}}}{\underset{1}{\cancel{2}}} = -11$$

7. $3\dfrac{1}{3} \div 1\dfrac{3}{7} = \dfrac{10}{3} \div \dfrac{10}{7}$ Change to improper fractions.

$$= \dfrac{10}{3} \cdot \dfrac{7}{10}$$ Replace divisor.

$$= \dfrac{\overset{1}{\cancel{10}}}{3} \cdot \dfrac{7}{\underset{1}{\cancel{10}}}$$ Cancel.

$$= \dfrac{7}{3} = 2\dfrac{1}{3}$$

8. $\dfrac{3}{7} \div \dfrac{3}{14} = \dfrac{3}{7} \cdot \dfrac{14}{3}$

$$= \dfrac{\overset{1}{\cancel{3}}}{\underset{1}{\cancel{7}}} \cdot \dfrac{\overset{2}{\cancel{14}}}{\underset{1}{\cancel{3}}} = 2$$ Cancel.

9. $\dfrac{\dfrac{1}{4} + \dfrac{1}{2}}{\dfrac{1}{3} + \dfrac{1}{4}}$

$$= \dfrac{12\left(\dfrac{1}{4} + \dfrac{1}{2}\right)}{12\left(\dfrac{1}{3} + \dfrac{1}{4}\right)}$$ (LCD is 12.)

$$= \dfrac{3 + 6}{4 + 3} = \dfrac{9}{7} = 1\dfrac{2}{7}$$

10. $\dfrac{3 - \dfrac{3}{4}}{-4 + \dfrac{1}{2}}$

$$= \dfrac{4\left(3 - \dfrac{3}{4}\right)}{4\left(-4 + \dfrac{1}{2}\right)}$$ (LCD is 4.)

$$= \dfrac{12 - 3}{-16 + 2}$$

$$= \dfrac{9}{-14} = \dfrac{-9}{14}$$

FOCUS ON THE ACT

The following sample questions represent ways in which the reviewed skills might be tested on your ACT Assessment.

1. $3\frac{1}{2} + 7\frac{3}{4} = ?$

  A. $10\frac{5}{4}$

  B. $11\frac{1}{4}$

  C. $10\frac{2}{3}$

  D. 11

  E. None of these.

2. $5 - 3\frac{3}{5} = ?$

  F. $2\frac{3}{5}$

  G. $2\frac{2}{5}$

  H. $1\frac{2}{5}$

  J. $1\frac{3}{5}$

  K. None of these.

3. $1\frac{2}{3} \cdot 2\frac{1}{4} = ?$

  A. $2\frac{1}{6}$

  B. $\frac{20}{27}$

  C. $1\frac{1}{6}$

  D. $3\frac{3}{4}$

  E. None of these.

4. $7\frac{1}{2} \div 5 = ?$

  F. $35\frac{1}{2}$

  G. $37\frac{1}{2}$

  H. $1\frac{1}{2}$

  J. $\frac{2}{3}$

  K. None of these.

5. $\dfrac{3 - \frac{1}{2}}{\frac{2}{3} + \frac{3}{4}} = ?$

  A. $1\frac{13}{17}$

  B. $\frac{17}{30}$

  C. $\frac{-3}{17}$

  D. $3\frac{1}{2}$

  E. None of these.

ANSWERS AND EXPLANATIONS

1. B $3\frac{1}{2} + 7\frac{3}{4}$ Rewrite with common denominators.

      $= 3\frac{2}{4} + 7\frac{3}{4}$ Add whole numbers and fractions.

      $= 10\frac{5}{4} = 10 + 1 + \frac{1}{4} = 11\frac{1}{4}$ Simplify.

2. H $\quad 5 - 3\frac{3}{5}$ $\qquad$ Borrow (regroup) $1\left(\frac{5}{5}\right)$ from the 5.

$\quad = 4\frac{5}{5} - 3\frac{3}{5}$ $\qquad$ Subtract whole numbers and fractions separately.

$\quad = 1\frac{2}{5}$

3. D $\quad 1\frac{2}{3} \cdot 2\frac{1}{4}$ $\qquad$ Rewrite as improper fractions.

$\quad = \frac{5}{3} \cdot \frac{9}{4}$

$\quad = \frac{5}{\cancel{3}} \cdot \frac{\cancel{9}^{3}}{4}$ $\qquad$ Cancel common factors.

$\quad = \frac{15}{4} = 3\frac{3}{4}$

4. H $\quad 7\frac{1}{2} \div 5$ $\qquad$ Rewrite as improper fractions.

$\quad = \frac{15}{2} \div \frac{5}{1}$ $\qquad$ Invert and multiply.

$\quad = \frac{15}{2} \cdot \frac{1}{5}$ $\qquad$ Cancel.

$\quad = \frac{\cancel{15}^{3}}{2} \cdot \frac{1}{\cancel{5}_{1}} = \frac{3}{2} = 1\frac{1}{2}$ $\qquad$ Multiply and simplify.

5. A $\quad \dfrac{3 - \dfrac{1}{2}}{\dfrac{2}{3} + \dfrac{3}{4}}$ $\qquad$ The LCM of the denominators is 12.

$\quad = \dfrac{12\left(3 - \dfrac{1}{2}\right)}{12\left(\dfrac{2}{3} + \dfrac{3}{4}\right)}$ $\qquad$ Multiply top and bottom by the LCM.

$\quad = \dfrac{36 - 6}{8 + 9} = \dfrac{30}{17} = 1\dfrac{13}{17}$

Operations with Decimals

Addition and Subtraction

For addition and subtraction, the decimal points are aligned vertically and the operation is performed as if the decimal points weren't there. The decimal point in the answer is in the same vertical column as in the numbers being added or subtracted.

For example: $2.3902 + 13.006$

$$\begin{array}{r} 2.3902 \\ +13.006 \\ \hline 15.3962 \end{array}$$

Multiplication

To multiply decimal numbers, one ignores the decimal points until after the usual multiplication procedure is completed. The decimal point is located in the answer so that the number of decimal places (digits to the right of the decimal point) is the same as the sum of the number of decimal places in the factors.

For example: (1.023)(15.6)

$$
\begin{array}{r}
1.0\,2\,3 \\
1\,5.6 \\
\hline
6\,1\,3\,8 \\
5\,1\,1\,5 \\
1\,0\,2\,3 \\
\hline
1\,5.9\,5\,8\,8
\end{array}
$$

(total of four decimal places)

(four decimal places)

Division

In division of decimals it is important to be very careful in the placement of the digits. The rule states that the decimal point in the divisor must be moved to the far right (make the divisor a whole number). The decimal point in the dividend is moved the same number of places to the right. The division is then completed as usual, and the decimal point in the quotient is located immediately above the decimal point in the dividend.

For example: 3.036 ÷ 1.32

$$
1.32\sqrt{)}\overline{3.03\,6}^{2.3}
$$

PRACTICE EXERCISES

1. Why must the decimal points be aligned in addition and subtraction? Perform the indicated operations.
2. 5.3 + 2 + 0.125
3. −73.8 + 15.73
4. 27.72 ÷ (−15.4)
5. (8.1)(7.3) + 4.2
6. 0.2³
7. [2.4 + (−1.8)]²
8. 24 ÷ 1.5

SOLUTIONS

1. Each decimal position represents a fraction with a certain power of 10 in the denominator. Since addition and subtraction require common denominators, the decimal points are aligned to place digits with the same place value in the same columns.

2.
$$
\begin{array}{r}
5.3 \\
2. \\
125 \\
\hline
7.425
\end{array}
$$
(A whole number has a decimal point after the rightmost digit.)

3.
$$
\begin{array}{r}
73.8 \\
-15.73 \\
\hline
58.07
\end{array}
$$
(Follow the same rules of signs as those given for integers.) Since −73.8 has the larger absolute value, the answer is −58.07.

4. Divide 154 into 277.2 (Make the divisor a whole number.) When the rule of signs for division is followed, the answer is −1.8.

5. (8.1)(7.3) + 4.2   (Multiplication must be done before addition.)
   = 59.13 + 4.2 = 63.33

6. $0.2^3 = (0.2)(0.2)(0.2) = (0.04)(0.2) = 0.008$

7. $[2.4 + (-1.8)]^2 = 0.6^2 = 0.36$

8. 24 ÷ 1.5 = 240 ÷ 15 = 16

Percents

The word *percent* literally means hundredths, so 25% means $\frac{25}{100}$, which reduces to $\frac{1}{4}$. Since "hundredths" could also be interpreted as divided by 100, and dividing by 100 can most efficiently be accomplished by moving the decimal point two places to the left, 25% is also 0.25. Therefore we have two rules:

1. To change a percent to a fraction, omit the percent sign, divide by 100, and reduce the fraction.

2. To change a percent to a decimal, omit the percent sign and move the decimal point two places to the left.

To change either a fraction or a decimal to a percent, the rules above are reversed:
1. To change a fraction to a percent, (do the division to get a decimal) multiply by 100 and attach a percent sign.
2. To change a decimal to a percent, move the decimal point two places to the right and attach a percent sign.

Examples:
Change each percent to both a fraction and a decimal.

1. 78%   Fraction: $\dfrac{78}{100} = \dfrac{39}{50}$ Decimal: 0.78

2. 8%   Fraction $\dfrac{8}{100} = \dfrac{2}{25}$ Decimal: 0.08

3. 2.5%   Fraction: $\dfrac{2.5}{100} = \dfrac{25}{1000}$ (Multiply numerator and denominator by 10.)

$= \dfrac{1}{40}$

Decimal: 0.025

4. $3\dfrac{1}{3}\%$ Fraction: $\left(3\dfrac{1}{3}\right) \div 100 = \dfrac{10}{3} \div 100 = \dfrac{10}{3} \cdot \dfrac{1}{100} = \dfrac{1}{3} \cdot \dfrac{1}{10} = \dfrac{1}{30}$

Decimal: $3\dfrac{1}{3}\% = 3.333 \ldots \% = 0.0\overline{3}$

5. $86\dfrac{2}{3}\%$ Fraction: $\left(86\dfrac{2}{3}\right) \div 100 = \dfrac{260}{3} \div 100 = \dfrac{260}{3} \cdot \dfrac{1}{100} = \dfrac{13}{3} \cdot \dfrac{1}{5} = \dfrac{13}{15}$

Decimal: $86\dfrac{2}{3}\% = 86.666 \ldots \% = 0.8\overline{6}$

Change each fraction or decimal to a percent.

6. $\dfrac{4}{5}$ $\dfrac{4}{5}(100\%) = \dfrac{400}{5}\% = 80\%$

7. 7 $7(100)\% = 700\%$

8. $\dfrac{3}{8}$ $\dfrac{3}{8}(100)\% = \dfrac{3}{8}\left(\dfrac{100}{1}\right)\%$

$= \dfrac{3}{2}\left(\dfrac{25}{1}\right)\% = \dfrac{75}{2}\% = 37\dfrac{1}{2}\%$ or 37.5%

9. 0.34 $0.34 = 0.34(100)\% = 34\%$
10. 0.005 $0.005 = 0.005(100)\% = 0.5\%$

PRACTICE EXERCISES

Change each percent to both a fraction and a decimal.
1. 53%
2. 129%
3. $12\dfrac{1}{2}\%$
4. 0.1%
5. 200%

Change each number to a percent.
6. 0.8
7. $\dfrac{5}{8}$

8. $\dfrac{3}{5}$

9. 0.003

10. $\dfrac{3}{11}$

SOLUTIONS

1. Fraction: $\dfrac{53}{100}$

   Decimal: 0.53

2. Fraction: $\dfrac{129}{100} = 1\dfrac{29}{100}$

   Decimal: 1.29

3. Fraction: $12\dfrac{1}{2} \div 100 = \dfrac{25}{2} \cdot \dfrac{1}{100}$

   $\qquad\qquad = \dfrac{1}{2} \cdot \dfrac{1}{4} = \dfrac{1}{8}$

   Decimal: $0.12\dfrac{1}{2} = 0.125$

4. Fraction: $\dfrac{0.1}{100} = \dfrac{1}{1000}$

   Decimal: 0.001

5. Fraction: $\dfrac{200}{100} = 2$

   Decimal: 2

6. $0.8 = 0.8(100)\% = 80\%$

7. $\dfrac{5}{8} = \dfrac{5}{8}(100\%) = \dfrac{500}{8}\% = 62\dfrac{1}{2}\% \ or \ 62.5\%$

8. $\dfrac{3}{5} = \dfrac{3}{5}(100)\% = \dfrac{300}{5}\% = 60\%$

9. $0.003 = 0.003(100)\% = 0.3\%$

10. $\dfrac{3}{11} = \dfrac{3}{11}(100)\% = \dfrac{300}{11}\% = 27.\overline{27}\% = 27\dfrac{3}{11}\%$

Applications of Percent

Most percent applications are variations of this sentence:

$$A \text{ is } P \text{ percent of } B.$$

In this sentence, A is the amount (or percentage), P is the percent (or rate), and B is the base. The key to solving a percent problem is to translate the problem into the form of the sentence above. Consider the following example:

The enrollment in an algebra class dropped from 30 students to 27. What percent of the class dropped out?

In this problem we are asked to find the percent, P.

The base is always the quantity before any change, 30.

The number of students that dropped out is the amount (or percentage), 3. Hence the sentence is

$$3 \text{ is } P \text{ percent of } 30.$$

Once the problem has been written in the proper form, there are two methods of solving the problem:

1. An equation may be written:

$$A = (P\%)B$$

Of course a percent sign is not written in the equation, so the percent must first be changed to either a fraction or a decimal.

If the unknown in the equation is A, multiply (P%) times B.

If the unknown is either (P%) or B, divide A by the other quantity.

2. A proportion may be written.

$$\frac{P}{100} = \frac{A}{B}$$

To solve any proportion, $\frac{x}{y} = \frac{z}{w}$, first cross-multiply, and then divide by the coefficient of the unknown.

In the problem above, $\frac{P}{100} = \frac{3}{30}$, $\begin{array}{l} 30P = 300 \\ P = 10 \end{array}$ 10% of the students dropped.

Examples:

1. What is 22% of 1086?

A is unknown, P = 22%, and B = 1086. Substituting into the percent equation gives

$$A = (0.22)(1086) = \underline{238.92}$$

2. Find 12% of 350.

A is unknown, P = 12%, and B = 350. Substituting into the percent proportion gives

$$\frac{12}{100} = \frac{A}{350}$$
$$100A = 4200 \qquad \text{Cross-multiply.}$$
$$A = \underline{42} \qquad \text{Divide by 100.}$$

3. 4 is what percent of 80?

A = 4, P is unknown, and B = 80.

$$4 = P(80)$$
$$P = 4 \div 80 = 0.05 = \underline{5\%}$$

4. What percent of 75 is 90?

A = 90, P is unknown, and B = 75.

$$\frac{P}{100} = \frac{90}{75}$$
$$75P = 9000$$
$$P = 120 \qquad \text{The answer is } \underline{120\%}.$$

5. 35.1 is 78% of what number?

A = 35.1, P = 78%, and B is unknown.

$$35.1 = (0.78)B \qquad \text{Divide by 0.78.}$$
$$B = \underline{45}$$

6. A student got a grade of 85% on a test in which she answered 3 questions incorrectly. How many questions were on the test?

The 3 wrong answers represent 15% (100%–85%) of the questions on the test. Therefore we have this question: 3 is 15% of what number?

A = 3, P = 15%, and B is unknown.

$$3 = (0.15)B \qquad \text{Divide by 0.15.}$$
$$B = 20$$

There were $\underline{20}$ questions on the test.

7. A house worth $120,000 is in an area where real estate is increasing in value at the rate of 8% per year. How much will the house be worth in 1 year?

The amount that the house will increase in value in 1 year is 8% of the original value of the house. Hence the amount of increase is 8% of $120,000.

A is unknown, P = 8%, and B = 120,000.

$$A = (0.08)(120,000) = 9600$$

The value of the house in 1 year will be $120,000 + 9600 = \underline{\$129,600}$.

This problem could also be done by the following method:

The value in 1 year will be 108% of the present value. Hence the new value is 108% of $120,000.

$$A = 1.08(120,000) = 129,600$$

When approached in this manner, the problem is called a *percent-increase* type. If an amount decreases over time, the problem can be approached similarly, but it is then called a *percent-decrease* type. For example:

On a diet James's weight decreased 10%. If he now weighs 126 pounds, what was his original weight?

James's new weight is 90% (100% − 10%) of his original weight. Therefore 126 is 90% of the original weight.

$A = 126$, $P = 90\%$, and B is unknown.

$$\frac{90}{100} = \frac{126}{B}$$
$$90B = 12600$$
$$B = 140$$

James originally weighed <u>140 pounds</u>.

PRACTICE EXERCISES

Solve the following proportions:

1. $\dfrac{x}{4} = \dfrac{8}{15}$

2. $\dfrac{5}{9} = \dfrac{t}{12}$

3. $\dfrac{7.2}{12} = \dfrac{5.4}{z}$

   Write both the percent equation and the percent proportion for each sentence. It is not necessary to solve the problem.

4. What number is 30% of 58?

5. 24 is what percent of 33?

6. 1.8 is 80% of what number?

Solve the following percent problems:

7. How much interest is earned in 1 year on an investment of $25,000 at 12% annual interest?

8. Last month Dale's paycheck was $840.00. If she is to receive a raise of 5% on this month's check, what should be the amount of this month's check?

9. In the fall semester Alice enrolled in 20 units. If she wants to decrease her load 15% in the spring semester, how many units should she take?

10. Jon paid $24.00 for a sweater that was advertised on sale at 10% off. What was the original price of the sweater?

SOLUTIONS

1. $\dfrac{x}{4} = \dfrac{8}{15}$

   $15x = 32$

   $x = 2\dfrac{2}{15}$

2. $\dfrac{5}{9} = \dfrac{t}{12}$

   $9t = 60$

   $t = 6\dfrac{2}{3}$

3. $\dfrac{7.2}{12} = \dfrac{5.4}{z}$

$7.2z = 64.8$

$z = 9$

4. Equation: $A = 0.3(58)$

Proportion: $\dfrac{30}{100} = \dfrac{A}{58}$

5. Equation: $24 = P(33)$

Proportion: $\dfrac{P}{100} = \dfrac{24}{33}$

6. Equation: $1.8 = 0.8B$

Proportion: $\dfrac{80}{100} = \dfrac{1.8}{B}$

7. Interest is 12% of $25,000.

A is unknown, $P = 12\%$, and $B = 25,000$

$A = 0.12(25,000) = 3000$

The interest is $3000.

8. This is a percent-increase type of problem.

Dale's new salary is 105% (100% + 5%) of her old salary.

The new salary is 105% of $840.

A is unknown, $P = 105\%$, $B = 840$.

$A = 1.05(840) = 882$

Dale's new salary is $882.

9. This is a percent-decrease type of problem.

The spring semester load is 85% of the fall semester load.

The spring load is 85% of 20.

A is unknown, $P = 85\%$, and $B = 20$.

$A = 0.85(80) = 17$

The spring load is 17 units.

10. The sale price is 90% of the original price.

$A = 24$, $P = 90\%$, B is unknown.

$24 = 0.9B$

$B = 26.66\dfrac{2}{3}$

The original price was $26.67.

Statistics

Scientists frequently need to interpret data that arise from an experiment. The data are usually obtained in random fashion and are presented in a large array of numbers. The purpose of statistics is to "make sense" of such an array. There are three basic characteristics of data that are most helpful:

1. Where is the middle? The middle is a measure of central tendency, also called the average.
2. How are the data spread out? The spread is represented by a measure of dispersion.
3. What do the data look like graphically?

In the following discussion, examples will be based on this sample of data:

$$4, 7, 2, 8, 7, 4, 8, 10, 1, 4$$

For many applications of statistics, it is helpful to have the data ranked from the smallest to largest:

$$1, 2, 4, 4, 4, 7, 7, 8, 8, 10$$

Averages

The statistic that most people refer to as the average is the *mean*. The mean is found by dividing the sum of the data by the number of items in the data set. For example, the mean of the sample data given above is

$$\frac{1+2+4+4+4+7+7+8+8+10}{10} = \frac{55}{10} = 5.5$$

Most scientific calculators have an automatic mean function. It may be worth your time to study your calculator's manual to learn to do this efficiently. This function is usually designated by the symbol $\bar{x}$.

The item of data that occurs most frequently is called the *mode*. In our sample data, the number 4 occurs three times, more than any other item, so 4 is the mode. If no one item of data occurs more than any other, the set of data has no mode. If two items of data occur with equal frequency, greater than any other, the data set is said to be bimodal.

The number that lies exactly in the middle of the ranked data is called the *median*. If the data set contains an odd number of items, the median is the middle number at the $\frac{n+1}{2}$ position, where n is the number of items of data. If the data set has an even number of items, the median is the mean of the two data items in the middle. Since our sample data has ten items and the two items in the middle are 4 and 7, the median is $\frac{4+7}{2} = 5.5$

Measures of Dispersion

The difference between the largest item of data and the smallest is called the *range*. In our sample data 10 is the largest item and 1 is the smallest, so the range is $10 - 1 = 9$. Other measures of dispersion, such as average deviation, standard deviation, and variance, will not be reviewed here.

Graphic Displays of Data

Information about a collection of data can be gained easily from a graphical display. Graphs of data can take many forms. Bar charts, histograms, pie charts, and broken-line graphs are a few of the types of graphs commonly used in statistics.

PRACTICE EXERCISES

Given this set of data: 6, 5, 4, 6, 1, 6, 6, 1, 5.
  1. Find the mean.
  2. Find the median.
  3. Find the mode.
  4. Find the range.
     Given the following frequency distribution:

Data Item	Frequency
5	2
6	5
7	8
8	3
9	1
10	1

  5. Find the mode.
  6. How many items of data are in this data set?
  7. Find the mean.
  8. Find the median.
  9. Find the range.

SOLUTIONS

First, rank the data: 1, 1, 4, 5, 5, 6, 6, 6, 6.

1. Add the data and divide by 9: $\dfrac{40}{9} = 4\dfrac{4}{9}$.
2. Since there is an odd number of items of data, the middle number is the median. The fifth number from either end is 5.
3. The most frequently occurring item of data is 6.
4. The range is $6 - 1 = 5$.
5. The most frequently occurring item of data is 7; it occurs eight times.
6. The number of items of data is the sum of the frequencies: 20.
7. Since 5 occurs twice, 6 occurs five times, etc., it is easy to find the sum of the products of the classes and their frequencies and then divide by 20:

Class	Frequency	Product
5	2	10
6	5	30
7	8	56
8	3	24
9	1	9
10	1	10
	Sum of products =	139

The mean is $\dfrac{139}{20} = 6.95$.

8. The median is the mean of the tenth and eleventh items of data, counting from either direction. Since both of these numbers are in the 7 class, the median is 7.
9. The range is $10 - 5 = 5$.

Probability

Probability is a number assigned to the likelihood of an event's occurrence. The probability of an event that is sure to happen is 1, and the probability of an event that is sure not to happen is 0. All other probabilities are numbers between 0 and 1. The probability of event A is denoted by P(A).

An experiment is any procedure that has a random output, i.e., the results of the experiment occur randomly. The *sample space* of an experiment is the set of all possible outcomes. For example:

The sample space for the experiment of tossing two coins and noting heads (H) or tails (T) of each coin is:

$$\{HH, HT, TH, TT\}$$

The sample space for the experiment of rolling one die and noting the number of spots on top is:

$$\{1, 2, 3, 4, 5, 6\}$$

The probability of any event is the fraction $\dfrac{a}{b}$ where a is the count of the number of items in the sample space that show the given event and b is the number of items in the sample space.

If A is the event of both coins showing heads (HH), then the probability of event A, $P(A) = \dfrac{1}{4}$ (the number of outcomes in the sample space that show 2 heads divided by the number of items in the sample space).

If B is the event of a number less than 3 showing when a die is rolled, then $P(B) = \dfrac{2}{6} = \dfrac{1}{3}$.

PRACTICE EXERCISES

Find the sample space for each experiment.

Experiment **1.** Tossing three coins.

Experiment **2.** Rolling two dice.

Experiment **3.** Drawing one card from a standard deck of 52 cards.

Experiment **4.** Flipping one coin and then rolling one die.

Determine the probability of each event.

5. Experiment 1.:
    a. A, the event that all three coins show T.
    b. B, the event that at least two coins show T.
    c. C, the event that all three coins land on edge.

6. In Experiment 2.:
    a. D, the event that both dice show even number of spots.
    b. E, the event that the sum of spots showing is 5.
    c. F, the event that the sum of spots showing is 1.

7. Experiment 3.:
    a. G, the event that the ace of hearts is drawn.
    b. H, the event that an ace is drawn.
    c. I,   the event that a heart is drawn.
    d. J,   the event of drawing a red card.

8. In Experiment 4.:
    a. K, the event of head on the coin and even number on the die.
    b. L, the event of tail on the coin and a number less than 6 on the die.

SOLUTIONS

1. {HHH, HHT, HTH, THH, HTT, THT, TTH, TTT}

2. The sample space is the set of all ordered pairs of numbers 1 through 6. Consider a table:

	Second die					
	1	2	3	4	5	6
1	11	12	13	14	15	16
2	21	22	23	24	25	26
First 3	31	32	33	34	35	36
die 4	41	42	43	44	45	46
5	51	52	53	54	55	56
6	61	62	63	64	65	66

There are 36 items in this sample space.

3. This sample space consists of the set of all 52 cards.

4. {H1, H2, H3, H4, H5, H6, T1, T2, T3, T4, T5, T6}

5. a $P(A) = \dfrac{1}{8}$

    b. $P(B) = \dfrac{4}{8} = \dfrac{1}{2}$

    c. $P(C) = 0$ (Well, maybe.)

6. a. $P(D) = \dfrac{9}{36} = \dfrac{1}{4}$

    b. $P(E) = \dfrac{9}{36} = \dfrac{1}{9}$

    c. $P(F) = 0$

7.   a. $P(G) = \dfrac{1}{52}$

   b. $P(H) = \dfrac{4}{52} = \dfrac{1}{13}$

   c. $P(I) = \dfrac{13}{52} = \dfrac{1}{4}$

   d. $P(J) = \dfrac{26}{52} = \dfrac{1}{2}$

8.   a. $P(K) = \dfrac{3}{12} = \dfrac{1}{4}$

   b. $P(L) = \dfrac{5}{12}$

FOCUS ON THE ACT

The following sample questions represent ways in which the reviewed skills might be tested on your ACT Assessment.

1. Which of the following is not equivalent to the others?
   A. $\dfrac{3}{8}$
   B. 0.375
   C. $37\dfrac{1}{2}\%$
   D. 375%
   E. $\dfrac{15}{40}$

2. $(0.2)^3 = ?$
   F. 0.8
   G. 0.6
   H. 0.0008
   J. 0.008
   K. $\dfrac{3}{5}$

3. What is 15% of 40?
   A. 600
   B. 60
   C. 6
   D. $266\dfrac{2}{3}$
   E. 25

4. Corey received 10 toys for his birthday and 12 toys for Christmas. By what percent did the number of toys increase?
   F. 10%
   G. 12%
   H. 20%
   J. 2%
   K. $16\dfrac{2}{3}\%$

5. A card is drawn from a standard, well-shuffled deck of 52 cards. What is the probability that it is a face card (J, Q, or K)?
   A. $\dfrac{12}{52} = \dfrac{3}{13}$
   B. $\dfrac{1}{3}$
   C. $\dfrac{3}{10}$
   D. $\dfrac{4}{52} = \dfrac{1}{13}$
   E. None of these.

ANSWERS AND EXPLANATIONS

1. D   All of the others are equivalent to $\dfrac{3}{8}$. Only 375% is different. It is equivalent to $\dfrac{375}{100} = \dfrac{15}{4}$.

2. J $(0.2)^3$
      $= (0.2)(0.2)(0.2)$ Keep track of the decimal places.
      $= (0.04)(0.2)$
      $= 0.008$

3. C   "What is 15% of 40?" translates to a proportion as follows:

   $\dfrac{15}{100} = \dfrac{A}{40}$ Cross multiply.

   $100A = 600$ Divide by 100.
   $A = 6$

4. H Corey received 2 more toys at Christmas than he received at his birthday. Therefore the question is "2 is what percent of 10?"

$$\frac{P}{100} = \frac{2}{10} \qquad \text{Cross multiply.}$$

$10P = 200$ Divide by 10.
$P = 20$ Be sure to attach a % sign.

Corey received 20% more toys at Christmas.

5. A There are 12 face cards in a standard deck. Twelve outcomes in the event divided by 52 items in the sample space give a probability of $\frac{12}{52} = \frac{3}{13}$.

ALGEBRA AND COORDINATE GEOMETRY

Constants and Variables

Symbols that represent numbers may be constants or variables. If the replacement set for a symbol contains only one element, the symbol is a *constant*. If the replacement set contains more than one element, the symbol is a *variable*. Examples of constants are 1, -56, $\frac{5}{8}$, $\sqrt{7}$, and π. Variables are usually letters of the English alphabet: x, y, t, a, etc., but other symbols may be used as well, such as the Greek letters, $\alpha, \beta, \ldots$. It is important to remember that, when an expression contains variables, these variables represent numbers. When numerical values are known for variables, the constant may be substituted for the variable with no change in the meaning in the expression:

If $a = b$, then b may be substituted for a in any expression with no change in meaning. Examples:

Evaluate each expression if $a = 3$, $b = -2$, and $c = -5$. (The rules for order of operations given previously are important.)

1. $a + b - c$ $\qquad 3 + (-2) - (-5) = 3 + (-2) + 5$
$\qquad\qquad\qquad\qquad\qquad = 1 + 5 = 6$

2. ab^2c $\qquad\qquad 3(-2)^2(-5) = 3(4)(-5)$
$\qquad\qquad\qquad\qquad\qquad = 12(-5) = -60$

3. $ab + ac - bc$ $\qquad 3(-2) + 3(-5) - (-2)(-5) = -6 + (-15) - 10$
$\qquad\qquad\qquad\qquad\qquad\qquad\qquad\qquad = -6 + (-15) + (-10)$
$\qquad\qquad\qquad\qquad\qquad\qquad\qquad\qquad = -21 + (-10) = -31$

Any of these may be done using a calculator.

PRACTICE EXERCISES

If $x = -2$, $y = 4$, and $z = -3$, evaluate the following expressions:

1. $x - yz$
2. $7(x + y + z)$
3. $\dfrac{x - y}{z}$
4. $xy + yz$
5. xyz^2

SOLUTIONS

1. $x - yz = -2 - 4(-3)$
$\qquad\qquad = -2 - (-12)$
$\qquad\qquad = -2 + 12 = 10$

2. $7(x + y + z) = 7[(-2) + 4 + (-3)]$
$\qquad\qquad\qquad = 7[2 + (-3)]$
$\qquad\qquad\qquad = 7(-1) = -7$

3. $\dfrac{x - y}{z} = \dfrac{(-2) - 4}{-3}$
$\qquad\quad = \dfrac{(-2) + (-4)}{-3}$
$\qquad\quad = \dfrac{-6}{-3} = 2$

4. $xy + yz = -2(4) + 4(-3)$
$= -8 + (-12) = -20$

5. $xyz^2 = -2(4)(-3)^2$
$= -2(4)(9)$
$= -8(9) = -72$

Similar Terms and Simplification

In an algebraic expression, *terms* are the parts separated by plus and minus signs. The numerical factor of any term is called its *coefficient*. Similar terms are terms that have exactly the same variable part (including exponents). Since multiplication is commutative, the order in which the variables appear is not important. Expressions with similar terms may be simplified by combining the coefficients and keeping the same variable factors. For example:

$$2x + 3y + 5x - 2y = 7x + y$$
$$-3xy^2 + 7x^2 - 5x^2 - 4xy^2 = -7xy^2 + 2x^2$$

Equations

An equation is almost any meaningful mathematical sentence that contains an equal sign. Some equations are true, some are false, and some are open or conditional.

$5 = 5$	True
$\dfrac{2}{3} = \dfrac{2}{3}$	True
$x + 1 = x + 1$	True for every replacement of x
$7 = 9$	False
$x + 3 = x + 1$	False for every replacement of x
$x + 2 = 5$	Open; true if $x = 3$ only

The set of numbers that makes an open equation true when substituted for the variable is called the *solution set*. The numbers themselves are called the *solution*. (The solution set of the equation $2x + 1 = 7$ is {3}.)

Equations that have the same solution set are called *equivalent* equations. There are two basic rules to use in order to solve equations. The application of either rule guarantees that an equivalent equation will result.

Addition Axiom of Equality

1. If $a = b$, then $a + c = b + c$ for any number c.

Multiplication Axiom of Equality

2. If $a = b$, then $ac = bc$ for any number $c \neq 0$.

The process of solving an equation is to produce a sequence of equivalent equations, the last one of which looks like

$$x = \text{constant}$$

from which the solution set can easily be found.

Since subtraction can be done by adding the opposite of the second number, there is no need for a subtraction axiom of equality. And division can be done by multiplying by the reciprocal of the divisor, so there is no need for a division axiom of equality.

Examples:
Solve each of the following:

1. $3x - 15 = 9$
$3x - 15 \underline{+ 15} = 9 \underline{+ 15}$ Rule 1. Add 15 to both sides of equation.
$3x = 24$

$3x\left(\dfrac{1}{3}\right) = 24\left(\dfrac{1}{3}\right)$ Rule 2. Multiply both sides by $\dfrac{1}{3}$.
$x = 8$

The solution set is {8}.

2. $\quad 4z + 2 = -2(z + 2)$ First use distributive property to simplify.

$\quad\quad 4z + 2 = -2z - 4$

$4z + 2 \underline{+ 2z} = -2z - 4 \underline{+ 2z}$ Add $2z$ to both sides.

$\quad\quad 6z + 2 = -4$

$\quad 6z + 2 \underline{- 2} = -4 \underline{- 2}$ Add -2 to both sides.

$\quad\quad\quad 6z = -6$

$\quad 6z\left(\dfrac{1}{6}\right) = -6\left(\dfrac{1}{6}\right)$ Multiply both sides by $\dfrac{1}{6}$.

$\quad\quad\quad\quad z = -1$

The solution set is $\{-1\}$.

3. Solve for x: $3x - 2y = 7$

$\quad\quad 3x - 2y + 2y = 7 + 2y$

$\quad\quad\quad\quad\quad 3x = 7 + 2y$

$\quad\quad 3x\left(\dfrac{1}{3}\right) = (7 + 2y)\left(\dfrac{1}{3}\right)$

$\quad\quad\quad\quad\quad x = \dfrac{7 + 2y}{3}$

This is called a *literal* equation (an equation with more than one letter), and its solution is another equation, not a set.

PRACTICE EXERCISES

Solve the following equations:

1. $2x - 5 = 3$
2. $5x - 6 = 2x + 9$
3. $4(x + 3) = 2(3x - 5) + 4$
4. $2x + 2(3x + 2) - 9 = (3x - 9) + 3$
5. $3(m - 4) - (4m - 11) = -5$
6. $1.2(x + 5) = 3(2x - 8) + 23.28$
7. $\dfrac{2x + 1}{3} + \dfrac{1}{4} = \dfrac{2x - 1}{6}$
8. $\dfrac{3y - 1}{5} - \dfrac{2y + 1}{4} = 1$
9. Solve for x: $3x + 7y = 5$
10. Solve for b: $A = \dfrac{1}{2}(b + B)h$

SOLUTIONS

1. $\mathbf{2x - 5 = 3}$ Add 5 to both sides.

    $\quad\quad 2x = 8$ Multiply by $\dfrac{1}{2}$. (This is the same as dividing by 2.)

    $\quad\quad\quad x = 4$ Solution set is $\{4\}$.

2. $\mathbf{5x - 6 = 2x + 9}$ Add $-2x$ to both sides.

    $3x - 6 = 9$ Add 6 to both sides.

    $\quad 3x = 15$ Divide by 3.

    $\quad\quad x = 5$ Solution set is $\{5\}$.

3. $\mathbf{4(x + 3) = 2(3x - 5) + 4}$ Use distributive property.

    $4x + 12 = 6x - 10 + 4$ Combine similar terms.

    $4x + 12 = 6x - 6$ Subtract $4x$ from both sides.

    $\quad\quad 12 = 2x - 6$ Add 6 to both sides.

    $\quad\quad 18 = 2x$ Divide by 2.

    $\quad\quad\ 9 = x$ Solution set is $\{9\}$.

4. $\mathbf{2x + 2(3x + 2) - 9 = (3x - 9) + 3}$ Use distributive property.

    $2x + 6x + 4 - 9 = 3x - 9 + 3$ Combine similar terms.

    $\quad\quad\ 8x - 5 = 3x - 6$ Subtract $3x$ from both sides.

    $\quad\quad\ 5x - 5 = -6$ Add 5 to both sides.

    $\quad\quad\quad\ 5x = -1$ Divide by 5.

    $\quad\quad\quad\ x = -1$ Solution set is $\left\{\dfrac{-1}{5}\right\}$.

5. $3(m - 4) - (4m - 11) = -5$

$3m - 12 - 4m + 11 = -5$

$-m - 1 = -5$

$-m = -4$

$m = 4$ Solution set is $\{4\}$.

6. $1.2(x + 5) = 3(2x - 8) + 23.28$ Multiply by 100.

$120(x + 5) = 300(2x - 8) + 2328$

$120x + 600 = 600x - 2400 + 2328$

$120x + 600 = 600x - 72$

$600 = 480x - 72$

$672 = 480x$

$x = \dfrac{672}{480} = 1.4$ Solution set is $\{1.4\}$.

7. $\dfrac{2x + 1}{3} + \dfrac{1}{4} = \dfrac{2x - 1}{6}$ Multiply by 12.

$4(2x + 1) + 3 = 2(2x - 1)$

$8x + 4 + 3 = 4x - 2$

$8x + 7 = 4x - 2$

$4x + 7 = -2$

$4x = -9$

$x = -\dfrac{9}{4}$ Solution set is $\left\{\dfrac{-9}{4}\right\}$.

8. $\dfrac{3y - 1}{5} - \dfrac{2y + 1}{4} = 1$ Multiply by 20.

$4(3y - 1) - 5(2y + 1) = 20$

$12y - 4 - 10y - 5 = 20$

$2y - 9 = 20$

$2y = 29$

$y = \dfrac{29}{2}$ Solution set is $\left\{\dfrac{29}{2}\right\}$.

9. $3x + 7y = 5$

$3x = -7y + 5$

$x = \dfrac{-7y + 5}{3}$

10. $A = \dfrac{1}{2}(b + B)h$ Multiply by 2.

$2A = (b + B)h$

$2A = bh + Bh$

$2A - Bh = bh$

$\dfrac{2A - Bh}{h} = b$ $b = \dfrac{2A}{h} - B$ is also correct.

Inequalities

The rules for solving linear inequalities with one variable are similar to those used to solve equations.

Addition Axiom of Inequality

1. If $a < b$, then $a + c < b + c$. Any number may be added to both sides of an inequality without changing the sense of the inequality.

Multiplication Axiom of Inequality

2. If $a < b$, then:
   a. $ac < bc$ if $c > 0$.
   b. $ac > bc$ if $c < 0$.
   If both sides of an inequality are multiplied by a positive number, the sense of the inequality is not changed.
   If both sides of an inequality are multiplied by a negative number, however, the sense of the inequality must be reversed.

PRACTICE EXERCISES

Solve the following inequalities:

1. $3x + 1 > 16$
2. $\dfrac{3x - 2}{4} > 2$
3. $\dfrac{3x - 2}{-5} \geq 4$
4. $2(3x - 5) + 7 > x + 12$
5. $-6 \leq 2x + 4 \leq 12$

SOLUTIONS

1. **$3x + 1 > 16$**   Add -1 to both sides.

   $3x > 15$ Multiply by $\dfrac{1}{3}$ (or divide by 3).

   $x > 5$

   --–|–|–|–|–|–|–|–|–|–|–|–|–
   -1 0 1 2 3 4 5 6 7 8

Often it is convenient to show the solution set, $\{x \mid x > 5\}$, on a number line. An open circle at 5 indicates that 5 is not included in the solution set. A closed circle would indicate that a particular number is included.

2. **$\dfrac{3x - 2}{4} > 2$**   Multiply by 4.

   $3x - 2 > 8$ Add 2 to both sides.

   $3x > 10$ Divide by 3.

   $x > \dfrac{10}{3}$

   --–|–|–|–|+|–|–|–|–|–|–|–
   0 1 2 3 4

   $\dfrac{10}{3}$

3. **$\dfrac{3x - 2}{-5} \leq 4$**   Multiply by -5. Reverse sense of inequality.

   $3x - 2 \geq -20$

   $3x \geq -18$

   $x \geq -6$

   --–|–|–|–|–|–|–|–|–|–|–|–
   -6   0

4. **$2(3x - 5) + 7 > x + 12$**   Simplify first.

   $6x - 10 + 7 > x + 12$

   $6x - 3 > x + 12$ Subtract x from both sides.

   $5x - 3 > 12$

   $5x > 15$

   $x > 3$

   --–|–|–|–|–|–|–|–|–|–|–|–
   -1 0 1 2 3 4

5. **$-6 \leq 2x + 4 \leq 12$**   Subtract 4 from all three parts, then divide each part by 2.

   $-10 \leq 2x \leq 8$

   $-5 \leq x \leq 4$

   --–|–|–|–|–|–|–|–|–|–|–|–
   -5   0   4

Polynomials

A *monomial* is any constant or any variable or any product of constants or variables:

$$5, \quad -78, \quad \frac{2}{3}, \quad \sqrt{3}, \quad x, \quad t, \quad 2y, \quad -7x^4yz^5$$

The following are NOT monomials:

$$\frac{1}{x}, \quad x + y, \quad \sqrt{x}$$

A *binomial* is any sum or difference of two monomials:

$$x + y, \quad 2t^2 - 3, \quad -4x^2y + 5xy^2$$

A *trinomial* is the sum or difference of three monomials:

$$x^2 + 2x + 1, \quad a + b - c$$

Monomials, binomials, and trinomials are all members of a class of objects called *polynomials*. A polynomial is either a monomial or the sum or difference of monomials.

The *degree of a monomial in a specified variable* is the exponent on that variable in the monomial. The *degree of a monomial* is the sum of the degrees of the monomial in all of its variables. The degree of any nonzero constant is 0. (Zero has no degree.) The *degree of a polynomial* is the greatest of the degrees of all of its terms.

For example, the degree of the monomial $-32x^3y^5z$:

$$\text{in } x \text{ is } 3,$$

$$\text{in } y \text{ is } 5,$$

$$\text{in } z \text{ is } 1.$$

The degree of this monomial is $3 + 5 + 1 = 9$.
Consider the trinomial $3^2xyz^2 - 5xy^2z^2 + 8$.

The degree of the first term is 4.

The degree of the second term is 5.

The degree of the third term is 0.

The degree of this trinomial is 5.

PRACTICE EXERCISES

Find the degree of each term and the degree of the polynomial.
1. $x^2 + 3x - 5$.
2. $7^3pt^3 - 3p^2t^2 + 4pt$
3. $\dfrac{-2}{3}$
4. 0
5. $\dfrac{1}{x + y}$

SOLUTIONS

1. 2, 1, 0; 2
2. 4, 4, 2; 4
3. 0
4. No degree
5. This is not a polynomial, so the word *degree* does not apply.

Operations on Polynomials

Addition and Subtraction

To add or subtract polynomials, first use the distributive property as needed to get rid of parentheses and then combine similar terms. Usually the terms of a polynomial are arranged in the order of descending degree in a specified variable. For example:

$$(3x^2 + 5x - 4) + (2x^2 - 7x - 3) = 3x^2 + 5x - 4 + 2x^2 - 7x - 3$$
$$= 5x^2 - 2x - 7$$
$$(2x^2 - 6xy + 3y^2) - (x^2 - xy + 2y^2) = 2x^2 - 6xy + 3y^2 - x^2 + xy - 2y^2$$
$$= x^2 - 5xy + y^2$$

Multiplication

Multiplication of a monomial by a polynomial of several terms is merely an extension of the distributive property.

$$-2a(3a^2 - 5a + 8) = -6a^3 + 10a^2 - 16a$$

Multiplication of two polynomials of more than one term each is also an extension of the distributive property. It is easier, however, to follow the rule "Multiply each term of one polynomial by each term of the other polynomial and then simplify."

$$(a + b - c)(2a - b + c) = a(2a - b + c) + b(2a - b + c) - c(2a - b + c)$$
$$= 2a^2 - ab + ac + 2ab - b^2 + bc - 2ac + bc - c^2$$
$$= 2a^2 + ab - ac - b^2 + 2bc - c^2$$

Multiplication of two binomials is such a common operation that a special procedure has been devised to make it easy to do mentally.

Consider the product of two binomials:

Call A and C the First terms of the binomials.
Call A and D the Outer terms.
Call B and C the Inner terms.
Call B and D the Last terms.
The product can be found by following the acronym FOIL.
For example, to multiply $(2x + 3)(x + 4)$;

Multiply the First terms: $(2x)(x) = 2x^2$.
Multiply the Outer terms: $(2x)(4) = 8x$.
Multiply the Inner terms: $(3)(x) = 3x$.
Multiply the Last terms: $(3)(4) = 12$.

Since the Outer product and the Inner product are similar terms, combine them and write the answer:

$$2x^2 + 11x + 12$$

Three products occur frequently and deserve special attention:

Sum and difference binomials: $(A + B)(A - B) = A^2 - B^2$
Binomial square: $(A \pm B)^2 = A^2 \pm 2AB + B^2$
Binomial cube: $(A \pm B)^3 = A^3 \pm 3A^2B + 3AB^2 \pm B^3$

PRACTICE EXERCISES

Perform the indicated operations. Express each answer in the order of descending degree in some variable.

1. $(5x + 3xy - 8y) - (y - 6yx + 2x)$
2. $(2x - 3) - [(4x + 7) - (5x - 2)]$
3. $-3ab(4a^2 - 5ab + 2b^2)$
4. $(2x - 3)(4x^2 + 6x + 9)$
5. $(x + 3)(x - 5)$
6. $(3x + 1)(2x + 5)$
7. $2x(x - 8)(2x - 5)$
8. $(3x + 8)(3x - 8)$
9. $(3x + 5)^2$
10. $(x - 2)^3$

SOLUTIONS

1. $(5x + 3xy - 8y) - (y - 6yx + 2x)$
$= 5x + 3xy - 8y - y + 6yx - 2x$
$= 3x + 9xy - 9y$

2. $(2x - 3) - [(4x + 7) - (5x - 2)]$ Do inner grouping symbols first.
$= (2x - 3) - [4x + 7 - 5x + 2]$
$= 2x - 3 - 4x - 7 + 5x - 2$
$= 3x - 12$

3. $-3ab(4a^2 - 5ab + 2b^2)$
$= -12a^3b + 15a^2b^2 - 6ab^3$

4. Multiply each term of the second polynomial first by $2x$ and then by -3:
   $(2x - 3)(4x^2 + 6x + 9)$
   $= 8x^3 + 12x^2 + 18x - 12x^2 - 18x - 27$
   $= 8x^3 - 27$

5. $(x + 3)(x - 5)$ Use FOIL.
   $= x^2 - 5x + 3x - 15$ Try not to write this line.
   $= x^2 - 2x - 15$

6. $(3x + 1)(2x + 5)$ Use FOIL. Do the Outer and Inner mentally.
   $= 6x^2 + 17x + 5$

7. $2x(x - 8)(2x - 5)$ Multiply the binomials first.
   $= 2x(2x^2 - 21x + 40)$
   $= 4x^3 - 42x^2 + 80x$

8. $(3x + 8)(3x - 8)$ This is an example of sum and difference binomials,
   $= 9x^2 - 64$ one of the special types.

9. $(3x + 5)^2$ This is a binomial square. The middle term is 2 times
   $= 9x^2 + 30x + 25$ the product of the terms of the binomial.

10. $(x - 2)^3$ This is a binomial cube. The second term, for example,
    $= x^3 - 6x^2 + 12x - 8$ is found by squaring the first term, multiplying by the
         second term, and then multiplying by 3.

Division

We can interpret the rule for addition and subtraction of fractions as a method of dividing a polynomial by a monomial.

$$\frac{a \pm b}{c} = \frac{a}{c} \pm \frac{b}{c}$$

The rule means that each term of the polynomial in the numerator is to be divided by the monomial in the denominator. (Sometimes the rule for division of exponential expressions is needed:

$$\frac{x^m}{x^n} = x^{m-n}$$

The rule and others will be reviewed in the section entitled Exponents and Radicals, page 216. Here are two examples:

- $\dfrac{4x - 8}{2} = \dfrac{4x}{2} - \dfrac{8}{2} = 2x - 4$

- $\dfrac{3x^3 - 6x^2 + 9x}{-3x} = -x^2 = 2x - 3$

The procedure for dividing a polynomial by a binomial (or other polynomial) is similar to that for whole number division. Consider the division problem

$$x - 3 \overline{) 2x^2 + 5x - 1}$$

Divide the first term of the divisor into the first term of the dividend, x into $2x^2$. Place the quotient above the first term of the dividend.

$$\begin{array}{r} 2x \\ x - 3 \overline{) 2x^2 + 5x - 1} \end{array}$$

Multiply $2x$ times $x - 3$, place the product under $2x^2 + 5x$, and subtract. Remember to follow the rule for subtraction; change the sign of the subtrahend (the bottom expression) and add.

$$\begin{array}{r} 2x \\ x - 3 \overline{) 2x^2 + 5x - 1} \\ \underline{2x^2 - 6x } \\ 11x \end{array}$$

Bring the next term down from the dividend, and repeat the process. Divide x into $11x$. Then multiply and subtract.

$$
\begin{array}{r}
2x + 11 \\
x - 3\overline{)2x^2 + 5x - 1} \\
\underline{2x^2 - 6x} \\
11x - 1 \\
\underline{11x - 33} \\
32
\end{array}
$$

The answer may be written as either

$$2x + 11 \text{ remainder } 32 \qquad \text{or} \qquad 2x + 11 + \frac{32}{x - 3}$$

When the divisor in algebraic division is of degree greater than 1, the signal to stop the division process comes when the degree of the remainder is smaller than the degree of the divisor.

A polynomial can be easily divided by a first-degree binomial of the type $x - a$ by a procedure called *synthetic division*. To demonstrate, we will consider the division problem done above. The coefficients of the dividend are aligned in descending degree. (The variables are not written.) The constant term of the divisor is written with the opposite sign to the left of the coefficients of the dividend. In this problem, 3 is placed to the left of the row of numbers, 2 5 –1:

$$
3 \,\big|\, \begin{array}{ccc} 2 & 5 & -1 \end{array}
$$

The procedure is as follows:

1. Bring the first coefficient of the dividend down to the bottom row under the line.

2. Multiply the number on the left of the top row, that is, the divisor, by the number on the bottom row.

3. Place this product above the line and under the next number to the right.

4. Add the numbers in that column, place the sum under the line, and repeat steps 2, 3, and 4.

In the bottom row, the last number is the remainder, and the others are the coefficients of the quotient in order of descending degree.

$$
\begin{array}{r|rrr}
3 & 2 & 5 & -1 \\
& & 6 & 33 \\
\hline
& 2 & 11 & 32
\end{array} \rightarrow 2x + 11 \text{ remainder } 32
$$

Here is another example: $(2x^3 - 5x + 7) \div (x + 2)$.

$$
\begin{array}{r|rrrr}
-2 & 2 & 0 & -5 & 7 \\
& & -4 & 8 & -6 \\
\hline
& 2 & -4 & 3 & 1
\end{array} \rightarrow 2x^2 - 4x + 3 \text{ remainder } 1
$$

PRACTICE EXERCISES

1. $(-48x^2y^3z) \div (-16xy^2z)$
2. $(25x^3 - 10x^2 + 5x) \div (5x)$
3. $(2x^2 + 13x + 21) \div (2x + 7)$
4. $(8x^3 + 1) \div (2x + 1)$
5. $(12x^3 - 17x^2 + 30x - 10) \div (3x^2 - 2x + 5)$

Use synthetic division to find the quotient and the remainder in each of the following problems:

6. $(x^2 - 3x - 18) \div (x - 6)$
7. $(x^3 - x^2 + 3x + 1) \div (x - 3)$
8. $(2x^3 - 3x^2 + 5) \div (x + 2)$

SOLUTIONS

1. $3xy$
2. $5x^2 - 2x + 1$
3. $(2x^2 + 13x + 21) \div (2x + 7)$

$$\begin{array}{r} x + 3 \\ 2x + 7\overline{)2x^2 + 13x + 21} \\ \underline{2x^2 + 7x} \\ 6x + 21 \\ \underline{6x + 21} \\ 0 \end{array}$$

The 0 remainder indicates that $(2x + 7)$ and $(x + 3)$ are factors of $2x^2 + 13x + 21$.

4. $(8x^3 + 1) \div (2x + 1)$

$$\begin{array}{r} 4x^2 - 2x + 1 \\ 2x + 1\overline{)8x^3 + 0x^2 + 0x + 1} \\ \underline{8x^3 + 4x^2} \\ -4x^2 + 0x \\ \underline{-4x^2 - 2x} \\ 2x + 1 \\ \underline{2x + 1} \\ 0 \end{array}$$

5. $(12x^3 - 17x^2 + 30x - 10) \div (3x^2 - 2x + 5)$

$$\begin{array}{r} 4x - 3 \\ 3x^2 - 2x + 5\overline{)12x^3 - 17x^2 + 30x - 10} \\ \underline{12x^3 - 8x^2 + 20x} \\ -9x^2 + 10x - 10 \\ \underline{-9x^2 + 6x - 15} \\ 4x + 5 \end{array}$$

The answer is $4x - 3$ remainder $4x + 5$.

6. $(x^2 - 3x - 18) \div (x - 6)$

$$\begin{array}{r} 6 \,| \; 1 \quad -3 \quad -18 \\ \underline{\quad\; 6 \quad\;\; 18} \\ 1 \quad\; 3 \quad\;\;\; 0 \end{array}$$

The answer is $x + 3$.

7. $(x^3 - x^2 + 3x + 1) \div (x - 3)$

$$\begin{array}{r} 3 \,| \; 1 \quad -1 \quad 3 \quad\; 1 \\ \underline{\quad\;\; 3 \quad\; 6 \quad 27} \\ 1 \quad\;\; 2 \quad 9 \quad 28 \end{array}$$

The answer is $x^2 + 2x + 9$ remainder 28.

8. $(2x^3 - 3x^2 + 5) \div (x + 2)$

$$\begin{array}{r} -2 \,| \; 2 \quad -3 \quad\;\; 0 \quad\;\;\; 5 \\ \underline{\quad\quad\;\; -4 \quad 14 \quad -28} \\ 2 \quad -7 \quad 14 \quad -23 \end{array}$$

The answer is $2x^2 - 7x + 14$ remainder -23.

Factoring

The process of factoring involves changing an expression from addition or subtraction to multiplication—creating factors. The property underlying all factoring rules is the distributive property:

$$ab + ac = a(b + c)$$

Notice that on the left there is the *sum* of terms, while on the right is the *product* of factors.

If an expression has a *common factor* other than 1 in all of its terms, application of the distributive property serves to factor it. Here are some examples:

- $4ab^2 + 2a^2b = 2ab(2b + a)$

- $39x^5y^3 - 26x^7y^2 + 52x^8y^5 = 13x^5y^2(3y - 2x^2 + 4x^3y^3)$ The common factor chosen should be the greatest common factor of the terms. Choose the exponent on each variable to be the smallest exponent on that variable in the expression.

- $-25x^3y^2 - 20x^4y^3 + 15x^5y^4 - 50x^6y^2 = -5x^3y^2(5 + 4xy - 3x^2y^2 + 10x^3)$ If the first term is negative, choose a negative common factor.

- $(x + 5)(x - 6) + (x + 5)(x - 1) = (x + 5)[(x - 6) + (x - 1)]$ The common factor is the binomial $(x + 5)$.
  $$= (x + 5)(2x - 7)$$

- $pq + 3rq + pm + 3rm = (pq + pm) + (3rq + 3rm)$ The trick is to rearrange and group so that each group has a common factor.
  $$= p(q + m) + 3r(q + m)$$
  $$= (q + m)(p + 3r)$$

- $8x^2 + 6xy - 12xy - 9y^2 = (8x^2 + 6xy) - (12xy \boxed{+} 9y^2)$ Be very careful of signs.
  $$= 2x(4x + 3y) - 3y(4x + 3y)$$
  $$= (4x + 3y)(2x - 3y)$$

PRACTICE EXERCISES

Factor completely,

1. $8x^3y^3 - 12x^2y^2$
2. $28a^2b - 14ab^2 + 7ab$
3. $-6a^5b^5 - 8a^4b^4 - 4a^3b^2$
4. $7m^3n^3 + 6$
5. $9x(3x + 2y) - 5y(3x + 2y)$
6. $5x^2y^2 + 10x^2 - 7y^2 - 14$
7. $6x^2y^2 - 6xy - 24xy^2 + 24y$

SOLUTIONS

1. $4x^2y^2(2xy - 3)$
2. $7ab(4a - 2b + 1)$ The 1 is easy to miss but very important.
3. $-2a^3b^2(3a^2b^3 + 4ab^2 + 2)$
4. The terms of this binomial have no common factor other than 1. It is not factorable. A nonfactorable polynomial is said to be prime.
5. $(3x + 2y)(9x - 5y)$
6. $5x^2y^2 + 10x^2 - 7y^2 - 14$
   $(5x^2y^2 + 10x^2) - (7y^2 + 14)$ Group, being careful of signs.
   $= 5x^2(y^2 + 2) - 7(y^2 + 2)$
   $= (y^2 + 2)(5x^2 - 7)$
7. $6x^2y^2 - 6xy - 24xy^2 + 24y$
   $6y(x^2y - x - 4xy + 4)$ $6y$ is a common factor.
   $6y[x(xy - 1) - 4(xy - 1)]$ Group in pairs and find common factors in each.
   $6y(xy - 1)(x - 4)$

Difference of Squares and Sum and Difference of Cubes

The following products are the bases for factoring special types of binomials:

$$(a + b)(a - b) = a^2 - b^2 \quad \text{Difference of squares.}$$
$$(a + b)(a^2 - ab + b^2) = a^3 + b^3 \quad \text{Sum of cubes.}$$
$$(a - b)(a^2 + ab + b^2) = a^3 - b^3 \quad \text{Difference of cubes.}$$

Here is an example of each type:
- $25 - 49x^2 = (5 + 7x)(5 - 7x)$ Difference of squares.
- $x^3 + 8 = (x + 2)(x^2 - 2x + 4)$ Sum of cubes. Watch signs carefully.
- $125x^3 - 64y^3 = (5x - 4y)(25x^2 + 20xy + 16y^2)$ Difference of cubes.

Factoring Trinomials of the Type $x^2 + Bx + C$

When two binomials of the type $(x + a)(x + b)$ are multiplied, a trinomial of the type $x^2 + Bx + C$ results, in which C is the product of a and b and B is the sum of a and b. To factor such a trinomial, look for two factors of C whose sum is B.
Examples:
  Factor each of the following:

1. $x^2 + 7x + 12$ Search the factors of 12 to find a pair whose sum is 7. The factors of 12 in pairs are 1, 12; 2, 6; and 3, 4. The sum is 7. The answer is $(x + 3)(x + 4)$.
2. $x^2 - 8x + 15$ The factors of 15 are 1 and 15 or 3 and 5. The answer is $(x - 3)(x - 5)$.
3. $x^2 - 3x - 40$ Since the sign of the third term is negative, the signs in the two binomials are different, and the middle term is the sum of two numbers with different signs. Search for a pair of factors so that the difference is 3, and adjust signs. The answer is $(x - 8)(x + 5)$.
4. $x^2 + 5x - 66$ Look for two factors of 66 whose difference is 5: 6, 11. The answer is $(x - 6)(x + 11)$.

Factoring Trinomials of the Type $Ax^2 + Bx + C$

The leading coefficient of this type of polynomial is always something other than 1. The procedure is to multiply the coefficients of the first and third terms and look for a pair of factors of that number whose sum or difference is the second coefficient. Rewrite the second term using those numbers, then group and factor.
Examples:

1. $2x^2 + 5x - 12$ Multply 2 times 12.
                                     Look for two factors of 24 whose difference (because the 12 is negative) is 5.
   $24 = (3)(8)$
   $2x^2 + 8x - 3x - 12$ Rewrite $5x$ using the numbers above.
   $(2x^2 + 8x) - (3x + 12)$ Group.
   $2x(x + 4) - 3(x + 4)$ Factor out the common factor in each group.
   $(x + 4)(2x - 3)$ Factor out the common factor $(x + 4)$.

2. $24x^2 - 14x - 3$ $24 \cdot 3 = 72$
   $24x^2 - 18x + 4x - 3$ $72 = 18 \cdot 4$
   $(24x^2 - 18x) + (4x - 3)$
   $6x(4x - 3) + 1(4x - 3)$
   $(4x - 3)(6x + 1)$

3. $24x^2 - 34x + 5$ $24 \cdot 5 = 120$
   $24x^2 - 4x - 30x + 5$ $120 = 30 \cdot 4$
   $(24x^2 - 4x) - (30x - 5)$
   $4x(6x - 1) - 5(6x - 1)$
   $(6x - 1)(4x - 5)$

This type of trinomial can also be factored by a method best described as "trial and error." Given a trinomial of the appropriate type, begin with either the first or third term (whichever one has fewer factors). Look for obvious factors of that number to place in the binomial factors.

4. $6x^2 + 19x + 10$ There are two possibilities for the first terms of the binomials. Guessing that the correct choice is $2x$ and $3x$, list
   $(2x \quad)(3x \quad)$
         2 5 the factors of 10 and check them, adding the outer and
         5 $2 \leftarrow$ inner products in the hope of getting $19x$. The answer is
         1 10 $(2x + 5)(3x + 2)$.
       10 1

5. $8x^2 - 2x - 3$ There are two possibilities for the first terms of the binomials and only one for the second terms, so begin there,
   $(\quad 1)(\quad 3)$
      $2x$ $4x \leftarrow$ and list the factors of $8x$. Since the sign of the third term
      $4x$ $2x$ is negative, substract the outer and inner products in the
        x $8x$ hope of getting $2x$. Then adjust the signs to make the
      $8x$ x middle term negative. The answer is $(2x + 1)(4x - 3)$.

Perfect Square Trinomials

If the first and last terms of a trinomial are squares, it is worth considering the special form of a perfect square trinomial:

$$a^2 + 2ab + b^2 = (a + b)^2$$

For example, $x^2 + 10x + 25$ is a perfect square trinomial. The correct factorization is $(x + 5)^2$. [The factorization $(x + 5)(x + 5)$ is also correct.]

General Strategy for Factoring a Polynomial
  1. If a polynomial has a common factor, *always* factor that first.
  2. If there is no common factor (or if the common factor has already been factored out):
     a. factor a binomial according to the rule for the difference of squares or the sum or difference of cubes;
     b. factor a trinomial according to the appropriate rule;
     c. consider factoring by grouping if there are more than three terms.
  3. Look for tricks.

Here are some examples:

- $250x^3 + 54y^3 = 2(125x^3 + 27y^3)$
  $$= 2(5x + 3y)(25x^2 - 15xy + 9y^2)$$

  There is a common factor of 2. In the parentheses is a sum of cubes. Be sure the common factor appears in the answer.

- $u^8 - v^8 = (u^4 + v^4)(u^4 - v^4)$
  $$= (u^4 + v^4)(u^2 + v^2)(u^2 - v^2)$$
  $$= (u^4 + v^4)(u^2 + v^2)(u - v)(u + v)$$

  This is a difference of squares. The second factor is also the difference of squares.
  And again.

- $-288x^2 + 8y^4 = -8(36x^2 - y^4)$
  $$= -8(6x - y^2)(6x + y^2)$$

  The common factor is –8. In the parentheses is the difference of squares.
  By reversing the terms, a correct answer would also be obtained:
  $8(y^2 - 6x)(y^2 + 6x)$.

- $4x^4 - 5x^2 + 1 = (4x^2 - 1)(x^2 - 1)$
  $$= (2x - 1)(2x + 1)(x - 1)(x + 1)$$

  There is no common factor. Factor the trinomial. Now each binomial is the difference of squares.

- $9x^2y^2 - 6xy + 1 = (3xy - 1)^2$

  This is a perfect square trinomial.

- $3ab + a - 3b^2 - b = (3ab + a) - (3b^2 + b)$
  $$= a(3b + 1) - b(3b + 1)$$
  $$= (3b + 1)(a - b)$$

  Try grouping.

- $x^2 - y^2 + 6x - 6y = (x^2 - y^2) + (6x - 6y)$
  $$= [(x - y)(x + y)] + 6(x - y)$$
  $$= (x - y)[(x + y) + 6]$$
  $$= (x - y)(x + y + 6)$$

  Here's a trick. The common factor is $(x - y)$. Simplify the second factor.

- $x^4 + x^2 + 1$
  $=x^4 + x^2 + x^2 + 1 - x^2$
  $= x^4 + 2x^2 + 1 - x^2$
  $= (x^4 + 2x^2 + 1) - x^2$
  $= (x^2 + 1)^2 - x^2$
  $=[(x^2 + 1) - x][(x^2 + 1) + x]$
  $= (x^2 - x + 1)(x^2 + x + 1)$

  Here's another trick. Add and subtract x^2.

  This is a difference of squares.

PRACTICE EXERCISES

Factor completely.
  1. $5x^2y^2 - 10xy$
  2. $x^2 - 4x - 21$
  3. $2x^2 - x - 10$
  4. $-5x^2 - 15xy + 50y^2$
  5. $8a^3 - b^3$
  6. $6y^2 + y - 40$
  7. $9x^2 + 30xy + 25y^2$
  8. $16u^4 - v^4$

9. $6x^2 - 14xy - 21xy + 49y^2$
10. $x^{2n} - 6x^n + 5$

SOLUTIONS

1. $5x^2y^2 - 10xy = 5xy(xy - 2)$
2. $x^2 - 4x - 21 = (x - 7)(x + 3)$
3. $2x^2 - x - 10$ Multiply 2 times 10. Look for factors of 20 whose difference is 1. Rewrite $-x$ using those two numbers. Group and find common factors in each group.
   $2x^2 - 5x + 4x - 10$
   $x(2x - 5) + 2(2x - 5)$
   $(2x - 5)(x + 2)$
4. $-5x^2 - 15xy + 50y^2 = -5(x^2 + 3xy - 10y^2)$ -5 is the common factor.
   $\qquad\qquad\qquad = -5(x + 5y)(x - 2y)$
5. $8a^3 - b^3 = (2a - b)(4a^2 + 2ab + b^2)$ Difference of cubes.
6. $6y^2 + y - 40$ Multiply first and last coefficients. $6 \cdot 40 = 240 = 16 \cdot 15$,
   $= 6y^2 + 16y - 15y - 40$ factors whose difference is 1. Rewrite the middle term,
   $= 2y(3y + 8) - 5(3y + 8)$ group and factor.
   $= (3y + 8)(2y - 5)$
7. $9x^2 + 30xy + 25y^2 = (3x + 5y)^2$ A perfect square trinomial.
8. $16u^4 - v^4 = (4u^2 + v^2)(4u^2 - v^2)$
   $\qquad\qquad = (4u^2 + v^2)(2u + v)(2u - v)$ Two layers of difference of squares.
9. $6x^2 - 14xy - 21xy + 49y^2 = (6x^2 - 14xy) - (21xy - 49y^2)$ Grouping.
   $\qquad\qquad\qquad\qquad = 2x(3x - 7y) - 7y(3x - 7y)$
   $\qquad\qquad\qquad\qquad = (3x - 7y)(2x - 7y)$
10. $x^{2n} - 6x^n + 5 = (x^n - 5)(x^n - 1)$

Quadratic Equations

An equation is called *quadratic* if it is equivalent to

$$ax^2 + bx + c = 0, \quad a \neq 0$$

An equation in this form is said to be in *standard* form.

An important rule used in the solution of quadratic equations is sometimes called the Zero Product Principle (ZPP):

$$\text{If } AB = 0, \quad \text{then } A = 0 \quad \text{or} \quad B = 0.$$

Examples:
Solve each of the following:

1. $\qquad x^2 + 8x + 15 = 0$ Factor.
   $\qquad (x + 5)(x + 3) = 0$ ZPP
   $x + 5 = 0 \quad \text{or} \quad x + 3 = 0$
   $\qquad x = -5 \text{ or} \qquad x = -3$
   The solution set is $\{-5, -3\}$.

2. $\qquad 3x^2 + 5 = 2x$
   $\qquad 3x^2 - 2x + 5 = 0$ Standard form.
   $(3x - 5)(x + 1) = 0$ Factor.
   $3x - 5 = 0 \quad \text{or} \quad x + 1 = 0$ ZPP
   $\qquad x = \dfrac{5}{3} \quad \text{or} \quad x = -1$ Solve each linear equation.
   The solution set is $\left\{\dfrac{5}{3}, -1\right\}$.

If the coefficient of the linear term in the standard form of the quadratic equation is zero ($b = 0$), it is easier to solve the equation by isolating x^2 and taking the square root of both sides, remembering that there are two solutions to such an equation—one positive and the other negative.

Examples:
   Solve each of the following:

1. $x^2 - 49 = 0$
   $x^2 = 49$ Isolate x^2.
   $x = \pm 7$ Take the square root of
              each side.

   The solution set is $\{7, -7\}$.

2. $2x^2 - 10 = 0$
      $2x^2 = 10$
       $x^2 = 5$
       $x = \pm \sqrt{5}$.
   The solution set is $\{\sqrt{5}, -\sqrt{5}\}$.

The Quadratic Formula

A quadratic equation that cannot be solved by factoring can always be solved by using the quadratic formula:

$$x = \frac{-b \pm \sqrt{b^2 - 4ac}}{2a}$$

The radicand of the quadratic formula, $b^2 - 4ac$, is called the *discriminant*. The discriminant allows one to describe the nature of the solution of the equation without actually solving it. The following rules apply if the coefficients are rational:

If the discriminant is:	then the solution is:
0	one rational number
positive square	two unequal rationals
positive nonsquare	two unequal irrationals
negative	two unequal complex numbers (conjugates; see page 244)

An immediate consequence of the quadratic formula is the following theorem:
If r_1 and r_2 are the roots of the quadratic equation

$$ax^2 + bx + c = 0$$

then

$$r_1 + r_2 = \frac{-b}{a} \quad \text{and} \quad r_1 \cdot r_2 = \frac{c}{a}$$

These relationships are useful for checking the solution to a quadratic equation.

PRACTICE EXERCISES

Solve the following quadratic equations:
   1. $x^2 - 3x - 4 = 0$
   2. $x^2 + 9 = 6x$
   3. $2x^2 + 5x = 0$
   4. $3x^2 - 75 = 0$
   5. $x^2 - 2x - 5 = 0$

Use the discriminant to describe the roots of these equations:
   6. $3x^2 - 2x + 4 = 0$
   7. $2x^2 + 11x - 40 = 0$
   8. $x^2 = x + 1$

Without solving, find the sum and product of the roots of these equations:
   9. $2x^2 + 9x - 35 = 0$
   10. $7x^2 + \frac{1}{2}x = 0$
   11. $x^2 + 7x + 6 = 0$

SOLUTIONS

   1. $x^2 - 3x - 4 = 0$
   $(x - 4)(x + 1) = 0$ Factor the left side.
   $x - 4 = 0$ or $x + 1 = 0$
   $x = 4$ $x = -1$ Set each factor equal to zero.
                        Solve each equation.
   The solution set is $\{4, -1\}$.

   2. $x^2 + 9 = 6x$
   $x^2 - 6x + 9 = 0$ The equation is in standard form.
   $(x - 3)^2 = 0$ Factor.
   $x - 3 = 0$ Set factor equal to zero.
   $x = 3$ Solve.
   The solution set is $\{3\}$.

3. $2x^2 + 5x = 0$
$2x(x + 5) = 0$ Factor.
$2x = 0$ or $x + 5 = 0$ Set each factor equal to zero.
$x = 0$ $x = -5$ Solve.
The solution set is $\{0, -5\}$.

4. $3x^2 - 75 = 0$
$3(x^2 - 25) = 0$
$3(x - 5)(x + 5) = 0$ Factor.
$x - 5 = 0$ or $x + 5 = 0$ Set each variable factor equal to zero.
$x = 5$ $x = -5$ Solve.
The solution set is $\{5, -5\}$.

5. The left side is not factorable, so use the quadratic formula.

$$x^2 - 2x - 5 = 0$$
$$a = 1, b = -2, c = -5$$

$$x = \frac{-b \pm \sqrt{b^2 - 4ac}}{2a}$$

$$= \frac{2 \pm \sqrt{(-2)^2 - 4(1)(-5)}}{2(1)}$$

$$= \frac{2 \pm \sqrt{4 - (-20)}}{2} = \frac{2 \pm \sqrt{24}}{2}$$

$$= \frac{2 \pm 2\sqrt{6}}{2} = 1 \pm \sqrt{6}$$

6. The discriminant is

$$(-2)^2 - 4(3)(4) = 4 - 48 = -44 < 0$$

Therefore there are two unequal complex solutions.

7. The discriminant is

$$(11)^2 - 4(2)(-40) = 121 - (-320) = 441$$

which is a positive square ($441 = 21^2$).
Therefore there are two unequal rational solutions.

8. The equation must first be in standard form:
$x^2 - x - 1 = 0$. The discriminant is

$$(-1)^2 - 4(1)(-1) = 1 - (-4) = 5$$

which is a positive nonsquare.
Therefore the solution set consists of two unequal irrational numbers.

9. Sum: $\dfrac{-b}{a} = \dfrac{-9}{2}$ Product: $\dfrac{c}{a} = \dfrac{-35}{2}$

10. Sum: $\dfrac{-b}{a} = \dfrac{-\frac{1}{2}}{7} = \dfrac{-1}{14}$ Product: $\dfrac{c}{a} = \dfrac{0}{7} = 0$

11. Sum: $\dfrac{-b}{a} = \dfrac{-7}{1} = -7$ Product: $\dfrac{c}{a} = \dfrac{6}{1} = 6$

Fractions

Algrebraic fractions can be reduced by using the Fundamental Principle of Fractions:

$$\frac{a}{b} = \frac{ak}{bk}, b, k \neq 0$$

Multiplication and Division

Multiplication and division of fractions are merely extensions of the same procedure. It is important to factor all expressions first and to cancel only common *factors* from any numerator and any denominator. Most errors are made by attempting to cancel *terms*, not factors.

Examples:

1. Reduce: $\dfrac{15x + 7x^2 - 2x^3}{x^2 - 8x + 15}$

$\dfrac{x(5 - x)(3 + 2x)}{(x - 3)(x - 5)}$ Factor.

$\dfrac{-x(3 + 2x)}{(x - 3)}$

The factors $(x - 5)$ and $(5 - x)$ are not equal, but they are opposites. Therefore, when canceled, these factors yield -1.

2. Multiply: $\dfrac{a^3 + a^2b}{5a} \cdot \dfrac{25}{3a + 3b}$

$\dfrac{a^2(a + b)}{5a} \cdot \dfrac{25}{3(a + b)}$ Cancel a, $(a + b)$, and 5.

$\dfrac{\cancel{a^{a}}^{}(a + b)}{\cancel{5a}} \cdot \dfrac{\cancel{25}^{5}}{\cancel{3(a + b)}}$

$\dfrac{5a}{3}$

3. Divide: $\dfrac{x - y}{4x + 4y} \div \dfrac{x^2 - 2xy + y^2}{x^2 - y^2}$

$\dfrac{x - y}{4(x + y)} \div \dfrac{(x - y)^2}{(x - y)(x + y)}$ Factor.

$\dfrac{\cancel{x - y}}{4(x + y)} \cdot \dfrac{\cancel{(x - y)}(x + y)}{\cancel{(x - y)^2}}$ Invert second fraction and cancel.

$\dfrac{1}{4}$

Addition and Subtraction

The same rules for addition and subtraction that are used in arithmetic apply to the addition and subtraction of algebraic fractions.

$$\frac{a}{b} \pm \frac{c}{b} = \frac{a \pm c}{b}, b \neq 0$$

Examples

1. Add: $\dfrac{3}{5x} + \dfrac{5 - 6x}{10x^2}$

First find the lowest common denominator.

$5 \cdot x$ Use each factor the greater number of

$2 \cdot 5 \cdot x \cdot x$ times it appears. The LCD is $10x^2$

Rewrite each fraction so that the denominators of the fractions are the same. Then add the numerators and reduce, if possible.

$$\frac{6x}{10x^2} + \frac{5 - 6x}{10x^2} = \frac{6x + (5 - 6x)}{10x^2}$$

$$= \frac{5}{10x^2} = \frac{1}{2x^2}$$

2. Subtract: $\dfrac{3}{x^2 - 5x + 6} - \dfrac{2}{x^2 - x - 2}$

Factor each denominator: $(x - 2)(x - 3)$
                              $(x - 2)(x + 1)$

Therefore the LCD is $(x - 2)(x - 3)(x + 1)$. The numerator and denominator of the first fraction must be multiplied by the factor $(x + 1)$, and those in the second fraction by $(x - 3)$,

$$\frac{3(x + 1)}{(x - 2)(x - 3)(x + 1)} - \frac{2(x - 3)}{(x - 2)(x - 3)(x + 1)} = \frac{3(x + 1) - 2(x - 3)}{(x - 2)(x - 3)(x + 1)}$$

$$= \frac{3x + 3 - 2x + 6}{(x - 2)(x - 3)(x + 1)}$$

$$= \frac{x + 9}{(x - 2)(x - 3)(x + 1)}$$

Fractional Equations

An equation that has a variable in a denominator is a *fractional* equation. In addition to the usual procedure for solving equations, care must be exercised to see that the proposed solution set does not contain numbers that would make any denominator zero. The proposed solution set must be checked, and the extraneous solutions omitted.

Example:

Solve:
$$2 + \frac{4}{x-2} = \frac{8}{x^2 - 2x} \qquad \text{Multiply both sides by the LCD: } x(x-2)$$

$$x(x-2)\left(2 + \frac{4}{x-2}\right) = \left(\frac{8}{x^2-2x}\right)x(x-2) \qquad x \neq 0, 2$$

$$2x(x-2) + 4x = 8$$
$$2x^2 - 4x + 4x = 8$$
$$2x^2 - 8 = 0$$
$$2(x-2)(x+2) = 0$$
$$x - 2 = 0 \qquad x + 2 = 0$$
$$x = 2 \qquad x = -2$$

But $x \neq 0, 2$, so the only solution is $\{-2\}$.

Solve:
$$\frac{7}{z-5} - \frac{6}{z+3} = \frac{48}{z^2 - 2z - 15}$$
$$7(z+3) - 6(z-5) = 48 \qquad \text{Multiply by } (z-5)(z+3),\ z \neq 5, -3.$$
$$7z + 21 - 6z + 30 = 48$$
$$z + 51 = 48$$
$$z = -3 \qquad \text{But } -3 \text{ makes the second denominator zero, so the solution set is empty.}$$

PRACTICE EXERCISES

Perform the indicated operations and simplify.

1. $\dfrac{x^2 - 16}{x} \cdot \dfrac{3}{4-x}$

2. $\dfrac{z^2 - z - 6}{z - 6} \cdot \dfrac{z^2 - 6z}{z^2 + 2z - 15}$

3. $\dfrac{a^3 - b^3}{a^2 - b^2} \div \dfrac{a^2 + ab + b^2}{a^2 + ab}$

4. $\dfrac{2}{x+1} + \dfrac{6}{x-1}$

5. $\dfrac{2x}{2x^2 - x - 1} - \dfrac{3x}{3x^2 - 5x + 2}$

6. $\dfrac{\dfrac{3}{x} - 5}{6 + \dfrac{1}{x}}$

7. $\dfrac{\dfrac{3}{x} - \dfrac{2}{y}}{9y^2 - 4x^2}{xy}$

Solve each equation.

8. $\dfrac{5y}{y+1} - \dfrac{y}{3y+3} = \dfrac{-56}{6y+6}$

9. $\dfrac{2}{x-3} - \dfrac{3}{x+3} = \dfrac{12}{x^2 - 9}$

SOLUTIONS

1. $\dfrac{(x-4)(x+4)}{x} \cdot \dfrac{3}{4-x}$

$= \dfrac{-1(x+4)}{x} \cdot \dfrac{3}{1} \qquad (x-4) \text{ and } (4-x) \text{ are opposites.}$

$= \dfrac{-3(x+4)}{x}$

2. $\dfrac{(z-3)(z+2)}{z-6} \cdot \dfrac{z(z-6)}{(z+5)(z-3)}$

$= \dfrac{z+2}{1} \cdot \dfrac{z}{z+5}$

$= \dfrac{z(z+2)}{z+5}$

3. $\dfrac{(a-b)(a^2+ab+b^2)}{(a-b)(a+b)} \cdot \dfrac{a(a+b)}{a^2+ab+b^2}$

$= \dfrac{1}{1} \cdot \dfrac{a}{1} = a$

4. The LCD is $(x+1)(x-1)$.

$\dfrac{2(x-1)}{(x+1)(x-1)} + \dfrac{6(x+1)}{(x+1)(x-1)}$

$= \dfrac{2x-2+6x+6}{(x+1)(x-1)}$

$= \dfrac{8x+4}{(x+1)(x-1)}$

5. Factor each denominator:

$$(2x+1)(x-1)$$
$$(3x-2)(x-1)$$

The LCD is $(2x+1)(3x-2)(x-1)$.

$\dfrac{2x(3x-2)}{(2x+1)(3x-2)(x-1)} - \dfrac{3x(2x+1)}{(2x+1)(3x-2)(x-1)}$

$= \dfrac{2x(3x-2) - 3x(2x+1)}{(2x+1)(3x-2)(x-1)}$

$= \dfrac{6x^2 - 4x - 6x^2 - 3x}{(2x+1)(3x-2)(x-1)}$

$= \dfrac{-7x}{(2x+1)(3x-2)(x-1)}$

6. Multiply the numerator and denominator by the LCD, which is x.

$$\dfrac{3-5x}{6x+1} \quad \text{(Complex fraction; see page 174.)}$$

7. Multiply the numerator and denominator by the LCD, which is xy.

$\dfrac{3y-2x}{9y^2-4x^2} = \dfrac{3y-2x}{(3y-2x)(3y+2x)}$

$= \dfrac{1}{3y+2x}$

8. Multiply both sides of the equation by the LCD, which is $6(y+1)$.

$30y - 2y = -56$
$28y = -56$
$y = -2$

The solution set is $\{-2\}$. The only restricted value is -1.

9. Multiply by the LCD, which is $(x-3)(x+3)$. The restricted values are 3 and -3.

$2(x+3) - 3(x-3) = 12$
$2x + 6 - 3x + 9 = 12$
$-x + 15 = 12$
$-x = -3$
$x = 3$

Because 3 is a restricted value, the solution set is empty.

FOCUS ON THE ACT

The following sample questions represent ways in which the reviewed skills might be tested on your ACT Assessment.

1. Find the solution set: $1 - \dfrac{2x-1}{6} = \dfrac{3x}{8}$
   A. $\{28\}$
   B. $\left\{\dfrac{28}{17}\right\}$
   C. $\left\{\dfrac{7}{5}\right\}$
   D. $\left\{\dfrac{20}{17}\right\}$
   E. $\{\ \}$

2. Solve: $4(x-3) > 9(x+2)$
   F. $\{x|x < -1\}$
   G. $\{x|x > -1\}$
   H. $\{x|x > -6\}$
   J. $\{x|x < -6\}$
   K. $\left\{x|x > \dfrac{-6}{5}\right\}$

3. Divide: $(2x^3 - x + 4) \div (x - 2)$
   A. $2x^2 + 4x + 7$ remainder 18
   B. $2x + 3$ remainder 10
   C. $2x - 5$ remainder 14
   D. $2x^2 - 4x + 7$ remainder -10
   E. $2x^2 + 3x + 6$ remainder 16

4. Factor completely over integers: $4x^2 - 4x - 15$
   F. $(2x - 5)(2x - 3)$
   G. $(4x + 5)(x - 3)$
   H. $(2x + 3)(2x - 5)$
   J. $(2x - 15)(2x + 1)$
   K. $(2x - 3)(2x + 5)$

5. Solve: $(x - 1)(x + 9) = 11$
   A. $\{-10, 2\}$
   B. $\{10, -2\}$
   C. $\{12, 2\}$
   D. $\{1, -9\}$
   E. $\{-1, 9\}$

ANSWERS AND EXPLANATIONS

1. B
$$1 - \frac{2x-1}{6} = \frac{3x}{8}$$
$$24\left(1 - \frac{2x-1}{6}\right) = \left(\frac{3x}{8}\right)24$$
$$24 - 4(2x - 1) = 9x$$
$$24 - 8x + 4 = 9x$$
$$24 - 8x + 4 = 9x$$
$$28 - 8x = 9x$$
$$28 = 17x$$
$$x = \frac{28}{17} \quad \text{The solution set is } \left\{\frac{28}{17}\right\}.$$

2. J
$$4(x - 3) > 9(x + 2)$$
$$4x - 12 > 9x + 18$$
$$-5x - 12 > 18$$
$$-5x > 30 \quad \text{Reverse sense of inequality when}$$
$x < -6$ dividing by a negative number.
The solution set is $\{x|x < -6\}$.

3. A Use synthetic division:
$$2\underline{|2\ \ 0\ -1\ \ 4}$$
$$\underline{\ \ \ \ 4\ \ \ 8\ \ 14}$$
$$2\ \ 4\ \ \ 7\ \ 18$$

The quotient is $2x^2 + 4x + 7$ remainder 18.

4. H $4x^2 - 4x - 15$
$= 4x^2 + 6x - 10x - 15$
$= 2x(2x + 3) - 5(2x + 3)$
$= (2x + 3)(2x - 5)$

Multiply the first and last coefficients.
$4 \cdot 15 = 60 = 6 \cdot 10$
Factors of 60 whose difference is 4.

5. A $(x - 1)(x + 9) = 11$
$$x^2 + 8x - 9 = 11$$
$$x^2 + 8x - 20 = 0$$
$$(x + 10)(x - 2) = 0$$
$$x + 10 = 0 \qquad x - 2 = 0$$
$$x = -10 \qquad x = 2$$
The solution set is $\{-10, 2\}$.

Word Problems

In this section, certain typical word problems of the kind found in most algebra courses will be solved in detail with hints given to aid in their solution.

Here is a general strategy:

---

1. *Read the problem carefully,* often several times until the meaning of the problem is clear.
2. *Make a sketch or diagram* if it would help make the problem clear.
3. *Choose a variable* to represent an unknown quantity in the problem.
4. *Represent all other unknown quantities* in terms of the chosen variable.
5. *Write an equation.* Many times a well-known formula can be used. Other times a literal translation of the problem leads to the equation. This is the most difficult step in the procedure.
6. *Solve the equation.*
7. *Answer the question.*

Example 1: Uniform motion problem.

One train starts from Des Moines and travels toward Dallas at 40 miles per hour at the same time that a second train starts from Dallas and travels toward Des Moines on a parallel track. If the distance between Dallas and Des Moines is 1080 miles on these tracks and the trains pass each other in 12 hours, what is the speed of the second train?

Solution:

A diagram may help organize the information in the problem.

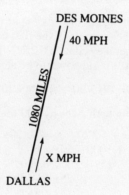

In all problems involving uniform motion, the following formula applies:

$$d = rt$$

A chart constructed with the aid of this formula will help to find an equation that can be used to answer the problem. Let us choose to let the variable represent the speed of the second train. When all else fails, put the variable in the chart where the question is.

	d	$=$	r	$\cdot$	t
To Dallas			40		12
From Dallas			x		12

When two boxes in any row are filled in, let the formula fill in the third box. In this case the formula indicates that the distances traveled by each train are $40(12) = 480$ and $12x$.

	d	$=$	r	$\cdot$	t
To Dallas	480		40		12
From Dallas	$12x$		x		12

As is common with this type of problem, one piece of information did not get into the chart—the total distance between the cities, 1080 miles. Use this information to write the equation:

$$\text{Total distance} = 1080 \text{ miles}$$

The sum of the entries in the d column total 1080

$$480 + 12x = 1080$$

Solve this equation.

$$12x = 600$$
$$x = 50$$

Therefore the speed of the second train is 50 miles per hour.

Example 2: Mixture problem
   A nurse needs 20 ml of a 30% alcohol solution. The only solutions available are 25% and 50%. How many milliliters of each should be mixed in order to obtain the required solution?

Solution:
   A diagram of the physical situation will be helpful. Draw three containers, two whose contents will be mixed together to obtain the third. Under each container describe the contents, and inside the containers label the quantity that it holds.

$$\frac{|x \text{ ml}|}{25\%} + \frac{|(20-x) \text{ ml}|}{50\%} = \frac{|20 \text{ ml}|}{30\%}$$

The amount of alcohol does not change in the process of mixing. This is the basis of the equation. Twenty-five percent of the contents of the first container is alcohol; 50% of the second container is alcohol. Together they contain $0.25x + 0.5(20 - x)$ ml of alcohol. Thirty percent of the final mixture [0.3(20)] is supposed to be alcohol, so the equation is:

$$0.25x + 0.5(20 - x) = 0.3(20)$$

To solve this equation, first multiply both sides by 100 to get rid of the decimal numbers.

$$25x + 50(20 - x) = 30(20)$$
$$25x + 1000 - 50x = 600$$
$$-25x + 1000 = 600$$
$$-25x = -400$$
$$x = 16$$

The nurse must mix 16 ml of the 25% solution with 4 ml of the 50% solution in order to obtain 20 ml of a solution that is 30% alcohol.

Example 3: Consecutive integer problem
   The sum of three consecutive odd integers is 87. Find the integers.
   If the problem is about consecutive integers, let the integers be represented by

$$x$$
$$x + 1$$
$$\text{and} \quad x + 2$$

If the problem is about consecutive even or consecutive odd integers, let them be represented by

$$x$$
$$x + 2$$
$$\text{and} \quad x + 4$$

Solution:
   The sum of three consecutive odd integers is represented by

$$x + (x + 2) + (x + 4)$$

The problem states that this sum is equal to 87. Therefore the equation is

$$x + (x + 2) + (x + 4) = 87$$

To solve this equation first simplify the left side.

$$3x + 6 = 87$$
$$3x = 81$$
$$x = 27$$

The three consecutive integers are

$$x = 27$$
$$x + 2 = 29$$
$$\text{and } x + 4 = 31$$

Example 4: Geometric problem

The length of a rectangle is 4 more than 5 times its width. Find the dimensions of the rectangle if its perimeter is 68 meters.

Solution:

Always draw a diagram for geometric type problems.

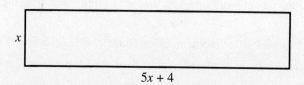

$$5x + 4$$

If x represents the width of the rectangle then the length is $5x + 4$. One must know certain formulas that apply to geometric figures. In this case the relevant formula regards the perimeter of a rectangle: $P = 2l + 2w$. Therefore the equation is:

$$68 = 2(5x + 4) + 2x$$

To solve this equation, first simplify the right side.

$$68 = 10x + 8 + 2x$$
$$68 = 12x + 8$$
$$60 = 12x$$
$$5 = x$$

Then $5x + 4 = 29$.

The width of the rectangle is 5 meters and its length is 29 meters.

Example 5: Age problem

Lisa is now six years older than Cheryl. In two years, Lisa will be twice as old as Cheryl. How old is each girl now?

Solution:

A chart will aid in organizing this problem. Make a chart with one row for each person and the first column headed "Now." Since the problem makes a statement about two years from now, let the other column heading be "2 years hence."

	Now	2 years hence
Lisa	$x + 6$	
Cheryl	x	

Let the column heading fill in the second column—add 2 to each value of the first column.

	Now	2 years hence
Lisa	$x + 6$	$x + 8$
Cheryl	x	$x + 2$

Now Lisa's age in two years ($x + 8$) is twice Cheryl's age in two years ($x + 2$). Therefore the equation is:

$$x + 8 = 2(x + 2)$$

To solve this equation, first simplify the right side.

$$x + 8 = 2x + 4$$
$$8 = x + 4$$
$$4 = x$$

Cheryl is now 4 years old and Lisa is 10 years old.

Example 6: Work problem

Diana can type a batch of 100 form letters in six hours. When Frankie helps, they can do the job together in four hours. How long will it have taken Frankie to do the job if he worked alone?

Solution:

The formula that applies to this type of problem states that the amount of work accomplished is equal to the rate of work times the amount of time spent working.

$$w = rt$$

A chart will help to organize this problem. Since Diana can do the job in 6 hours, she can do $\frac{1}{6}$ of the job in one hour—her rate of work is $\frac{1}{6}$ of the job per hour. Let the amount of time that it would take Frankie to do the job be x, then his rate is $\frac{1}{x}$ part of the job per hour.

Both work for 4 hours. (The 100 is extra information not needed in the solution of the problem.)

	w	$=$	r	$\cdot$	t
Diana			$\frac{1}{6}$		4
Frankie			$\frac{1}{x}$		4

Let the formula fill in the third column of the chart.

	w	$=$	r	$\cdot$	t
Diana	$\frac{2}{3}$		$\frac{1}{6}$		4
Frankie	$\frac{4}{x}$		$\frac{1}{x}$		4

Diana does $\frac{2}{3}$ of the work, and Frankie does $\frac{4}{x}$ part of the work. A completed job in this type of problem is always represented by the number 1 (*one* completed job.)
The equation therefore is:

$$\frac{2}{3} + \frac{4}{x} = 1$$

To solve this equation, first multiply by the common denominator, $3x$.

$$2x + 12 = 3x$$
$$12 = x$$

It would take Frankie 12 hours to do the job alone.

Example 7: Time problem

Elizabeth agreed to do a certain job for $48.00. She was able to finish the job in two hours less time than she had anticipated it would take. As a result she earned $2 per hour more than she would have if the job had taken the anticipated amount of time. How long did she anticipate that the job would take to complete?

Solution:

Let x represent the amount of time she had anticipated it would take her to complete the job. Then $x - 2$ represents the amount of time it actually took her to do the job. Let's organize the information:

	Total price	Number of hours	Price per hour
Anticipated	$48	x	$\dfrac{48}{x}$
Actually	$48	$x - 2$	$\dfrac{48}{x - 2}$

The problem states that she actually earned $2 per hour more than she had anticipated. The equation is therefore

$$\frac{48}{x - 2} = \frac{48}{x} + 2 \qquad \text{Multiply both sides by } x(x - 2).$$
$$48x = 48(x - 2) + 2x(x - 2)$$
$$48x = 48x - 96 + 2x^2 - 4x$$

This equation is quadratic, so write it in standard form and factor.

$$0 = 2x^2 - 4x - 96$$
$$0 = 2(x^2 - 2x - 48)$$
$$0 = 2(x - 8)(x + 6)$$
$$x - 8 = 0 \qquad x + 6 = 0$$
$$x = 8 \qquad x = -6$$

The solution set is $\{8, -6\}$.

The solution -6 is obviously extraneous. The answer is:

Elizabeth anticipated that it would take her 8 hours to do the job.

PRACTICE EXERCISES

1. An airplane has just enough fuel for a five-hour flight. How far can it fly on a round trip on which, during the first leg of the trip, it flies with the wind at 225 miles per hour and, during the return trip, it flies against the wind at 180 miles per hour?

2. A race car needs a fuel mixture that is 20% alcohol. How many liters of a 10% alcohol fuel mixture must be combined with 100 liters of a 40% alcohol mixture in order to obtain the required percentage of alcohol?

3. Find four consecutive even integers whose sum is 100.

4. Find the dimensions of a rectangle whose perimeter is 38 m and whose area is 84 square meters.

5. Diane was 24 years old when her daughter Heidi was born. In how many years will Diane be four years less than five times Heidi's age?

6. One pipe can fill a tank in four hours; another pipe can fill the same tank in three hours. If both pipes flow at the same time, how long will it take to fill the tank?

7. Clarice purchased some very breakable items for sale in her shop. She paid $100 for these items, but she discovered that three of the items had broken and could not be sold. When she sold the remaining items for $5 more per item than she paid for them she discovered that her total profit turned out to be only $5. How many items did she purchase?

SOLUTIONS

1. Create a chart. Let x be the one way distance traveled.

	d	$=$	r	$\cdot$	t
With wind	x		225		
Against wind	x		180		

Let the formula fill in the third box in each row of the chart, that is, $t = \dfrac{d}{r}$.

	d	$=$	r	$\cdot$	t
With wind			x	225	$\dfrac{x}{225}$
Against wind			x	180	$\dfrac{x}{180}$

The sum of the times of the two legs of the trip must be five hours:

$$\frac{x}{225} + \frac{x}{180} = 5$$

Multiply both sides by the common denominator, 900.

$$4x + 5x = 4500$$
$$9x = 4500$$
$$x = 500$$

The one-way distance is 500 miles; therefore the total round-trip distance is 1000 miles.

2. Set up a diagram of containers.

$$\frac{\lfloor x \rfloor}{10\%} + \frac{\lfloor 100 \rfloor}{40\%} = \frac{\lfloor x + 100 \rfloor}{20\%}$$

The amount of alcohol did not change in the mixing process. Therefore the equation is:

$$.1x + .4(100) = .2(x + 100)$$

To solve this equation, first multiply by 10 to get rid of the decimals.

$$x + 4(100) = 2(x + 100)$$
$$x + 400 = 2x + 200$$
$$400 = x + 200$$
$$200 = x$$

One must use 200 liters of the 10% alcohol fuel mixture.

3. The equation is:

$$x + (x + 2) + (x + 4) + (x + 6) = 100$$
$$4x + 12 = 100$$
$$4x = 88$$
$$x = 22$$

The four consecutive even integers are 22, 24, 26, and 28.

4. Draw a diagram.

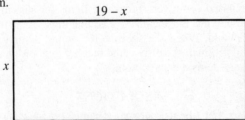

Since the perimeter is 38, then the sum of one length and one width must be half of 38. Therefore if the width is represented by x then the length is $19 - x$.

The equation is therefore:

$$x(19 - x) = 84$$
$$19x - x^2 = 84$$
$$0 = x^2 - 19x + 84$$
$$0 = (x - 12)(x - 7)$$
$$x - 12 = 0 \text{ or } x - 7 = 0$$
$$x = 12 \qquad x = 7$$

If 12 were the width then the length would be 7 (the length is $19 - x$). The width is always the smaller dimension of a rectangle, so 12 is an extraneous solution of the equation.

The width of the rectangle is 7 m and the length is 12 m.

5. Create a chart.

	Age at birth	x years hence
Diane	24	$24 + x$
Heidi	0	x

According to the words of the problem. Diane's age in the future must be 4 less than 5 times Heidi's age then. Therefore the equation is:

$$24 + x = 5x - 4$$
$$24 = 4x - 4$$
$$28 = 4x$$
$$7 = x$$

Therefore this condition will happen in 7 years from Heidi's birth, that is when Heidi is 7 years old.

6. Create a chart.

	w	$=$	r	$\cdot$	t
Pipe 1			$\dfrac{1}{4}$		x
Pipe 2			$\dfrac{1}{3}$		x

Let the formula fill in the third box in each row.

	w	$=$	r	$\cdot$	t
Pipe 1	$\dfrac{x}{4}$		$\dfrac{1}{4}$		x
Pipe 2	$\dfrac{x}{3}$		$\dfrac{1}{3}$		x

The sum of the amounts of work done is always one, therefore the equation is:

$$\frac{x}{4} + \frac{x}{3} = 1$$

Multiply by the common denominator.

$$3x + 4x = 12$$
$$7x = 12$$
$$x = \frac{12}{7} = 1\frac{5}{7}$$

The tank will be filled in $1\frac{5}{7}$ hours.

7. Organize the information.

	Price	No. of items	Price per item
Items purchased	$100	x	$\dfrac{100}{x}$
Items sold	$105	$x - 3$	$\dfrac{105}{x - 3}$

The selling price is $5 more per item than the purchasing price. The equation is therefore:

$$\frac{105}{x - 3} = \frac{100}{x} + 5 \qquad \text{Multiply both sides by } x(x - 3).$$

$$105x = 100(x - 3) + 5x(x - 3)$$
$$105x = 100x - 300 + 5x^2 - 15x$$
$$0 = 5x^2 - 20x - 300$$
$$0 = 5(x^2 - 4x - 60)$$
$$0 = 5(x - 10)(x + 6)$$
$$x - 10 = 0 \qquad x + 6 = 0$$
$$x = 10 \qquad\quad x = -6$$

The solution set is $\{10, -6\}$.

The solution -6 is obviously extraneous. The answer is:

Clarice purchased 10 items originally.

Exponents and Radicals

The following laws of exponents apply to all real-number exponents:

1. $x^m \cdot x^n = x^{m+n}$
2. $(x^m)^n = x^{mn}$
3. $(xy)^m = x^m \cdot y^m$
4. $\dfrac{x^m}{x^n} = x^{m-n}, \; x \neq 0$
5. $\left(\dfrac{x}{y}\right)^m = \left(\dfrac{x^m}{y^m}\right), \; y \neq 0$
6. $x^0 = 1, \; x \neq 0$
7. $x^{-m} = \dfrac{1}{x^m}, \; x \neq 0$

   a. $\left(\dfrac{x}{y}\right)^{-m} = \left(\dfrac{y}{x}\right)^m, \; x,y \neq 0$

   b. $\dfrac{a}{x^{-m}} = ax^m, \; x \neq 0$

Here are some examples:

- $x^{5/3} \cdot x^{-2/3} = x^{3/3} = x^1 = x$
- $(x^{3/2})^4 = x^6$
- $(x^3 y)^3 = x^9 y^3$
- $\dfrac{x^5}{x^6} = x^{-1} = \dfrac{1}{x^1} = \dfrac{1}{x}$
- $\dfrac{a^3 b}{a^{-2} b^2} = a^{3-(-2)} \, b^{1-2} = a^5 b^{-1} = \dfrac{a^5}{b}$
- $\left(\dfrac{x^2}{y^4}\right)^{-3} = \left(\dfrac{y^4}{x^2}\right)^3 = \dfrac{y^{12}}{x^6}$
- $\dfrac{3^{-2}}{3^{-3}} = 3^{-2-(-3)} = 3^1 = 3$

PRACTICE EXERCISES

Simplify and write without negative exponents.

1. $\dfrac{x^{10}}{x^4}$

2. $\left(\dfrac{4x^3}{y^2}\right)^3$

3. $\left(\dfrac{a^2b^3}{2a^{-2}b}\right)^{-2}$

4. $\dfrac{2}{a^{-7}}$

5. $\left(\dfrac{3}{2}\right)^0$

6. $3x^0$

SOLUTIONS

1. $\dfrac{x^{10}}{x^4} = x^{10-4} = x^6$

2. $\left(\dfrac{4x^3}{y^2}\right)^3 = \dfrac{4^3x^9}{y^6} = \dfrac{64x^9}{y^6}$

3. $\left(\dfrac{a^2b^3}{2a^{-2}b}\right)^{-2} = \left(\dfrac{2a^{-2}b}{a^2b^3}\right)^2 = \dfrac{2^2a^{-4}b^2}{a^4b^6}$

   $= 4a^{-4-4}b^{2-6} = 4a^{-8}b^{-4} = \dfrac{4}{a^8b^4}$

4. $\dfrac{2}{a^{-7}} = 2a^7$

5. $\left(\dfrac{3}{2}\right)^0 = 1$

6. $3x^0 = 3(1) = 3$ An exponent applies only to the immediately preceding symbol.

*n*th Root

The definition of an *n*th root is as follows:

a is an *n*th root of b if and only if $a^n = b$.

The symbol for the *n*th root of b is $\sqrt[n]{b}$. The number in the notch of the radical, n, is the index, and b is the radicand. According to the definition, this is the number that, when raised to the *n*th power, yields b. If n is even and b is negative, the *n*th root of b is not a real number. The laws of exponents apply to all real-number exponents, and $(b^{1/n})^n = b^1 = b$. Since both $\sqrt[n]{b}$ and $b^{1/n}$ give the same result when raised to the *n*th power, they are defined to be equal: $\sqrt[n]{b} = b^{1/n}$.

FRACTIONAL EXPONENTS

The definition of a fractional exponent is as follows:

$a^{p/q} = \sqrt[q]{a^p} = \left(\sqrt[q]{a}\right)^p$ for all real numbers a and integers p and q for which p and q have no common factor and a is not negative if q is even. All of the previous laws of exponents apply to fractional exponents also.

Example 1: $8^{2/3} = \left(\sqrt[3]{8}\right)^2 = 2^2 = 4$

Example 2: $(-125)^{-1/3} = \dfrac{1}{(-125)^{1/3}} = \dfrac{1}{\sqrt[3]{-125}} = \dfrac{1}{-5} = \dfrac{-1}{5}$

Example 3: $\dfrac{\sqrt{3}}{\sqrt[3]{3}} = \dfrac{3^{1/2}}{3^{1/3}} = 3^{1/2-1/3} = 3^{1/6} = \sqrt[6]{3}$

Simplest Radical Form

A radical expression is said to be in simplest radical form (SRF) if the following conditions are met:

1. The radicand has no perfect nth-power factors.
2. There are no fractions in the radicand.
3. There are no radicals in a denominator.
4. The index is as low as possible.

Here are some examples of these rules:

- $\sqrt{12}$ is not in simplest radical form because the radicand has $4 = 2^2$ as a factor. To put $\sqrt{12}$ in SRF, factor the radicand so that one factor is the largest square factor of the radicand. Then use the rule of radicals.

$$\sqrt[n]{xy} = (\sqrt[n]{x})(\sqrt[n]{y}) \text{ for all defined radicals.}$$

The square factor can be extracted from the radical.

$$\sqrt{12} = \sqrt{4 \cdot 3} = \sqrt{4} \cdot \sqrt{3} = 2\sqrt{3}$$

- $\sqrt[3]{32x^3y^8} = \sqrt[3]{(8x^3y^6)(4y^2)}$ Separate the radicand into cube and noncube factors.
  $= \sqrt[3]{8x^3y^6} \cdot \sqrt[3]{4y^2}$
  $= 2xy^2\sqrt[3]{4y^2}$

- $\sqrt{\dfrac{5}{8}}$ is not in SRF because of rule 2 above. To simplify, multiply the numerator and denominator by some number in order to make the denominator a perfect square. Then use the rule of radicals

$$\sqrt[n]{\frac{x}{y}} = \frac{\sqrt[n]{x}}{\sqrt[n]{y}} \text{ for all defined radicals.}$$

$$\sqrt{\frac{5}{8}} = \sqrt{\frac{5 \cdot 2}{8 \cdot 2}} = \sqrt{\frac{10}{16}} = \frac{\sqrt{10}}{\sqrt{16}} = \frac{\sqrt{10}}{4}$$

- $\dfrac{7}{\sqrt[3]{12}}$ is not in SRF because of rule 3 above. To simplify, multiply the numerator and denominator by an appropriate radical to make the bottom radicand a perfect nth power.

$$\frac{7}{\sqrt[3]{12}} = \frac{7\sqrt[3]{18}}{\sqrt[3]{12}\sqrt[3]{18}} = \frac{7\sqrt[3]{18}}{\sqrt[3]{216}} = \frac{7\sqrt[3]{18}}{6}$$ Since $12 = 2 \cdot 2 \cdot 3$, one more 2 and two 3's are needed to make a perfect cube. Multiply by $2 \cdot 3 \cdot 3 = 18$ in the radical.

- $\dfrac{2}{3 - \sqrt{2}}$ is not in SRF because of rule 3 above. To simplify, multiply by an appropriate radical expression, sometimes called the *conjugate* of the denominator. In this case, multiply the numerator and denominator by $3 + \sqrt{2}$.

$$\frac{2(3 + \sqrt{2})}{(3 - \sqrt{2})(3 + \sqrt{2})} = \frac{2(3 + \sqrt{2})}{9 - 2} = \frac{2(3 + \sqrt{2})}{7} = \frac{6 + 2\sqrt{2}}{7}$$

- $\sqrt[6]{x^4}$ is not in SRF because of the rule 4 above. To simplify, use the rule of radicals

$$\sqrt[n]{\sqrt[m]{x}} = \sqrt[mn]{x}$$

Then

$$\sqrt[6]{x^4} = \sqrt[3]{\sqrt{x^4}} = \sqrt[3]{x^2}$$

PRACTICE EXERCISES

Simplify. Assume all variables are nonnegative.

1. $2^{1/3} \cdot 2^{1/4}$

2. $\dfrac{1}{8^{-4/3}}$

3. $\sqrt{500}$

4. $\sqrt{20x^6}$

5. $\sqrt[4]{x^5y^7}$

6. $\sqrt{\dfrac{5}{12}}$

7. $\dfrac{6}{\sqrt{3}}$

8. $\dfrac{4}{\sqrt{6}-4}$

9. $\sqrt[8]{4x^6y^{10}}$

SOLUTIONS

1. $2^{1/3} \cdot 2^{1/4} = 2^{1/3\,+\,1/4} = 2^{7/12}$

2. $\dfrac{1}{8^{-4/3}} = 8^{4/3} = (\sqrt[3]{8})^4 = 2^4 = 16$

3. $\sqrt{500} = \sqrt{(100 \cdot 5)} = \sqrt{100} \cdot \sqrt{5} = 10\sqrt{5}$

4. $\sqrt{20x^6} = \sqrt{(4x^6)(5)} = \sqrt{4x^6}\sqrt{5} = 2x^3\sqrt{5}$

5. $\sqrt[4]{x^5y^7} = \sqrt[4]{(x^4y^4)(xy^3)}$

   $= \sqrt[4]{x^4y^4} \cdot \sqrt[4]{xy^3} = xy\sqrt[4]{xy^3}$

6. $\sqrt{\dfrac{5}{12}} = \sqrt{\dfrac{15}{36}}$ Multiply by $\dfrac{3}{3}$ to make the denominator a square.

   $= \dfrac{\sqrt{15}}{\sqrt{36}} = \dfrac{\sqrt{15}}{6}$

7. $\dfrac{6}{\sqrt{3}} = \dfrac{6\sqrt{3}}{\sqrt{9}}$ Multiply by $\dfrac{\sqrt{3}}{\sqrt{3}}$ to make the denominator a square.

   $= \dfrac{6\sqrt{3}}{3} = 2\sqrt{3}$

8. $\dfrac{4}{\sqrt{6}-4}$

   $= \dfrac{4(\sqrt{6}+4)}{(\sqrt{6}-4)(\sqrt{6}+4)}$ Multiply the numerator and denominator by the conjugate of the denominator.

   $= \dfrac{4(\sqrt{6}+4)}{6-16}$

   $= \dfrac{4(\sqrt{6}+4)}{-10} = \dfrac{-2(\sqrt{6}+4)}{5} = \dfrac{-2\sqrt{6}-8}{5}$ Reduce the fraction.

9. $\sqrt[8]{4x^6y^{10}} = \sqrt[4]{\sqrt{4x^6y^{10}}} = \sqrt[4]{2x^3y^5} = \sqrt[4]{y^4 \cdot 2x^3y} = \sqrt[4]{y^4} \cdot \sqrt[4]{2x^3y} = y\sqrt[4]{2x^3y}$

Operations with Radicals

All of the following discussion assumes that the radicals represent real numbers, that is, there are no even roots of negative numbers.

Any radicals with the same index may be multiplied or divided according to the following rules:

$$\sqrt[n]{x}\,\sqrt[n]{y} = \sqrt[n]{xy} \quad \text{and} \quad \frac{\sqrt[n]{x}}{\sqrt[n]{y}} = \sqrt[n]{\frac{x}{y}}$$

Radicals may be added and subtracted only if both the indices and the radicands are the same.

$$a\sqrt[n]{x} \pm b\sqrt[n]{x} = (a \pm b)\sqrt[n]{x}$$

PRACTICE EXERCISES

Perform the indicated operations and simplify. Assume all variables are nonnegative.

1. $5\sqrt{8} - 3\sqrt{72} + 3\sqrt{50}$
2. $6\sqrt[3]{128m} - 3\sqrt[3]{16m}$
3. $\sqrt{2}(\sqrt{32} - \sqrt{9})$
4. $(\sqrt{7} + \sqrt{3})(\sqrt{7} - \sqrt{3})$
5. $(4\sqrt{5})^2$
6. $(\sqrt{6} - \sqrt{2})^2$
7. $\dfrac{\sqrt{3} + 1}{\sqrt{5} + \sqrt{3}}$

SOLUTIONS

1. $\mathbf{5\sqrt{8} - 3\sqrt{72} + 3\sqrt{50}}$
    Simplify each radical first.
    $5\sqrt{8} = 5 \cdot 2\sqrt{2} = 10\sqrt{2}$
    $3\sqrt{72} = 3 \cdot 6\sqrt{2} = 18\sqrt{2}$
    $3\sqrt{50} = 3 \cdot 5\sqrt{2} = 15\sqrt{2}$
    $10\sqrt{2} - 18\sqrt{2} + 15\sqrt{2} = 7\sqrt{2}$

2. $\mathbf{6\sqrt[3]{128m} - 3\sqrt[3]{16m}}$
    $6\sqrt[3]{128m} = 6\sqrt[3]{(64)(2m)}$
    $\qquad = 6 \cdot 4\sqrt[3]{2m} = 24\sqrt[3]{2m}$
    $3\sqrt[3]{16m} = 3\sqrt[3]{(8)(2m)}$
    $\qquad = 3 \cdot 2\sqrt[3]{2m} = 6\sqrt[3]{2m}$
    $24\sqrt[3]{2m} - 6\sqrt[3]{2m} = 18\sqrt[3]{2m}$

3. $\mathbf{\sqrt{2}(\sqrt{32} - \sqrt{9})}$ Apply the distributive property.
    $= \sqrt{64} - \sqrt{18}$
    $= 8 - \sqrt{9 \cdot 2} = 8 - 3\sqrt{2}$

4. $\mathbf{(\sqrt{7} + \sqrt{3})(\sqrt{7} - \sqrt{3})}$
    $= \sqrt{49} - \sqrt{9}$ This is the same FOIL for binomials.
    $= 7 - 3 = 4$

5. $\mathbf{(4\sqrt{5})^2} = 16\sqrt{25}$ Square each factor.
    $\qquad = 16 \cdot 5 = 80$

6. $\mathbf{(\sqrt{6} - \sqrt{2})^2}$
    $= \sqrt{36} - 2\sqrt{12} + \sqrt{4}$ Use the same pattern as squaring a binomial. Then
    $= 6 - 4\sqrt{3} + 2 = 8 - 4\sqrt{3}$ simplify.

7. $\dfrac{\sqrt{3} + 1}{\sqrt{5} + \sqrt{3}}$

    $= \dfrac{(\sqrt{3} + 1)(\sqrt{5} - \sqrt{3})}{(\sqrt{5} + \sqrt{3})(\sqrt{5} - \sqrt{3})}$ Multiply the numerator and denominator by the conjugate of the denominator.

    $= \dfrac{\sqrt{15} - \sqrt{9} + \sqrt{5} - \sqrt{3}}{\sqrt{25} - \sqrt{9}}$

    $= \dfrac{\sqrt{15} + \sqrt{5} - \sqrt{3} - 3}{2}$

Radical Equations

The procedure for solving radical equations is to raise both sides of the equation to the nth power at an appropriate point. This does not always assure that equivalent equations will result; therefore the potential solutions must be checked in the original equation. Solutions are not lost in the process, but frequently extraneous solutions are introduced and must be eliminated.

Examples:
  Solve each of the following:
  1. $\sqrt{3x+1} - 4 = 0$ Isolate the radical term first, if possible.
    $\sqrt{3x+1} = 4$ Square both sides. This eliminates the radical on the left.
    $3x + 1 = 16$
    $3x = 15$
    $x = 5$
  Check: $\sqrt{3 \cdot 5 + 1} - 4 = \sqrt{16} - 4 = 0$
  The solution set is {5}.

  2. $x = \sqrt{x^2 - 4x - 8}$ Square both sides.
    $x^2 = x^2 - 4x - 8$
    $0 = -4x - 8$
    $4x = -8$
    $x = -2$
  Check $-2 \neq \sqrt{(-2)^2 - 4(-2) - 8} = \sqrt{+4 - (-8) - 8} = \sqrt{4} = 2$
  Since $-2 \neq 2$, -2 is not a solution.
  The solution set is empty.

  3. $\sqrt{x^2 - 3x + 3} = x - 1$ Be sure to square the binomial on the right.
    $x^2 - 3x + 3 = x^2 - 2x + 1$
    $-3x + 3 = -2x + 1$
    $3 = x + 1$
    $2 = x$
  Check: $\sqrt{2^2 - 3 \cdot 2 + 3} = 2 - 1$
    $\sqrt{4 - 6 + 3} = 1$
    $\sqrt{1} = 1$
  The solution set is {2}.

  4. $\sqrt{x+6} - \sqrt{x-2} = 2$ Separate the radicals.
    $\sqrt{x+6} = \sqrt{x-2} + 2$ Carefully square both sides.
    $x + 6 = x - 2 + 4\sqrt{x-2} + 4$
    $6 = 2 + 4\sqrt{x-2}$
    $4 = 4\sqrt{x-2}$
    $1 = \sqrt{x-2}$
    $1 = x - 2$ Square again.
    $3 = x$
  Check $\sqrt{3+6} - \sqrt{3-2} = \sqrt{9} - \sqrt{1} = 3 - 1 = 2$
  The solution set is {3}.

PRACTICE EXERCISES

Solve.
  1. $\sqrt{5x-1} + 3 = 0$
  2. $\sqrt{y^2 - 4y + 9} = y - 1$
  3. $\sqrt{5x+6} + \sqrt{3x+4} = 2$

SOLUTIONS

  1. $\sqrt{5x-1} + 3 = 0$
    $\sqrt{5x-1} = -3$ Square both sides.
    $5x - 1 = 9$
    $5x = 10$
    $x = 2$
  Check: $\sqrt{5 \cdot 2 - 1} + 3 = \sqrt{9} + 3$
    $= 3 + 3 = 6 \neq 0$
  The solution set is empty.

  2. $\sqrt{y^2 - 4y + 9} = y - 1$ Square both sides.
    $y^2 - 4y + 9 = y^2 - 2y + 1$
    $8 = 2y$
    $4 = y$
  Check: $\sqrt{4^2 - 4 \cdot 4 + 9} = 4 - 1$
    $\sqrt{16 - 16 + 9} = 3$
    $\sqrt{9} = 3$
  The solution set is {4}.

3. $\sqrt{5x + 6} + \sqrt{3x + 4} = 2$ Separate the radicals.

$\sqrt{5x + 6} = 2 - \sqrt{3x + 4}$ Square both sides.

$5x + 6 = 4 - 4\sqrt{3x + 4} + 3x + 4$

$2x - 2 = -4\sqrt{3x + 4}$

$x - 1 = -2\sqrt{3x + 4}$ Square again.

$x^2 - 2x + 1 = 4(3x + 4) = 12x + 16$

$x^2 - 14x - 15 = 0$

$(x - 15)(x + 1) = 0$

$x - 15 = 0$ or $x + 1 = 0$

$x = 15$ or $x = -1$

Check 15: $\sqrt{5 \cdot 15 + 6} + \sqrt{3 \cdot 15 + 4}$

$= \sqrt{81} + \sqrt{49}$

$= 9 + 7$

$= 16 \neq 2$

15 is not a solution.

Check 1: $\sqrt{5(-1) + 6} + \sqrt{3(-1) + 4}$

$= \sqrt{1} + \sqrt{1}$

$= 1 + 1 = 2$

The solution set is $\{-1\}$.

FOCUS ON THE ACT

*The following sample questions represent ways in which the reviewed skills might
be tested on your ACT Assessment.*

1. Which equation could be used to solve the following problem?

The sum of the squares of two consecutive whole numbers is 85. Find the whole numbers.
A. $[x + (x + 1)]^2 = 85$
B. $x^2 + x^2 + 1 = 85$
C. $x^2 + (x + 2)^2 = 85$
D. $x^2 + (x + 1)^2 = 85$
E. None of these.

2. Simplify: $-2x^{-2}$

F. $\dfrac{1}{4x^2}$

G. $\dfrac{-1}{4x^2}$

H. $\dfrac{-1}{2x^2}$

J. $\dfrac{-2}{x^2}$

K. $4x^2$

3. Express in simplest radical form: $\dfrac{-12}{\sqrt{20}}$

A. $\dfrac{-6}{\sqrt{5}}$

B. $\dfrac{-6\sqrt{5}}{5}$

C. $\dfrac{-3\sqrt{20}}{5}$

D. $\dfrac{-3}{\sqrt{5}}$

E. $\dfrac{-3\sqrt{5}}{5}$

4. Simplify: $2\sqrt{18} - \sqrt{50}$
F. 1
G. 60
H. $\sqrt{2}$
J. $-7\sqrt{2}$
K. None of these.

5. Solve: $\sqrt{x - 1} = x - 3$
A. $\{5, 2\}$
B. $\{2\}$
C. $\{-5, -2\}$
D. $\{ \}$
E. $\{5\}$

ANSWERS AND EXPLANATIONS

1. D Two consecutive whole numbers may be represented by x and $x + 1$.
Therefore the sum of their squares is $x^2 + (x + 1)^2$.

2. J Any exponent applies only to the immediate preceding symbol.

3. B $\dfrac{-12}{\sqrt{20}}$ To make the radicand in the denominator

$\dfrac{-12}{\sqrt{20}} \cdot \dfrac{\sqrt{5}}{\sqrt{5}}$ a perfect square, multiply top and bottom

$\dfrac{-12\sqrt{5}}{\sqrt{100}}$ by $\sqrt{5}$.

$\dfrac{\overset{-6}{\cancel{-12}}\sqrt{5}}{\underset{5}{\cancel{10}}}$ Reduce.

4. H $2\sqrt{18} - \sqrt{50}$
$= 2\sqrt{9 \cdot 2} - \sqrt{25 \cdot 2}$
$= 2 \cdot 3\sqrt{2} - 5\sqrt{2}$
$= 6\sqrt{2} - 5\sqrt{2} = \sqrt{2}$

5. E $\sqrt{x - 1} = x - 3$ Square both sides.
$x - 1 = x^2 - 6x + 9$
$0 = x^2 - 7x + 10$
$(x - 5)(x - 2) = 0$
$x - 5 = 0 \qquad x - 2 = 0$
$x = 5, x = 2$
2 is extraneous. The solution set is $\{5\}$.

Graphing

Two number lines perpendicular to each other and intersecting at their respective origins form the Cartesian, or rectangular, coordinate system. The number line that is oriented horizontally is called the *horizontal axis,* or the *x-axis,* and the other one is the *vertical axis,* or the *y-axis.* The axes separate the plane into four regions called *quadrants I, II, III,* and *IV,* beginning in the upper right and proceeding counterclockwise.

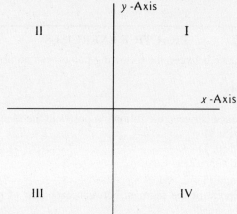

There is a one-to-one correspondence between ordered pairs of real numbers and points in the rectangular coordinate system. The points are located by moving horizontally from the origin according to the first number in the ordered pair and then vertically according to the second number.

The ordered pairs are usually obtained from solutions to equations in two variables. For example, the ordered pair $(2, -1)$ is a solution of the equation $3x + y = 5$. Other solutions may be obtained by choosing a number for x (or for y) and solving for the other variable. If -1 is chosen for x, then $3(-1) + y = 5$ and $y = 8$, so that a solution is the ordered pair $(-1, 8)$. When a sufficient number of points have been located for a particular equation so that a smooth curve can be drawn through them, the equation is said to be graphed.

Distance Formula

The distance between any two points on a number line can be found by taking the absolute value of the difference of the coordinates.

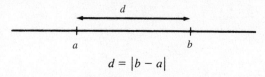

$$d = |b - a|$$

The distance between any two points (x_1, y_1) and (x_2, y_2) in the plane can be found by the distance formula, which is a result of the Pythagorean Theorem.

$$d = \sqrt{(x_2 - x_1)^2 + (y_2 - y_1)^2}$$

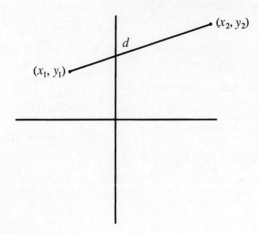

Midpoint Formula

The midpoint of the segment between two points $A\ (x_1, y_1)$ and $B\ (x_2, y_2)$ is found by averaging the x-coordinates and the y-coordinates

$$\text{midpoint of } \overline{AB}: \left(\frac{x_1 + x_2}{2}, \frac{y_1 + y_2}{2} \right)$$

PRACTICE EXERCISES

1. Find the distance between the following points on a number line:
    a. 6 and 15
    b. –3 and –11
    c. –5 and 12
2. Find the distance between the following points in the plane:
    a. (2, 5) and (5, 9)
    b. (–4, 8) and (6, 1)
    c. (0, –5) and (–3, –2)
    d. $(\sqrt{2}, -1)$ and $(3\sqrt{2}, -5)$
3. Find the midpoint of the segment between each pair of points in problem 2 above.
4. Determine if the triangle with vertices at $A\ (-1, 1)$, $B\ (1, 3)$, and $C\ (6, -2)$ is a right triangle or not.

SOLUTIONS

1. a. $|15 - 6| = 9$
    b. $|-11 - (-3)| = |-8| = 8$
    c. $|12 - (-5)| = |17| = 17$
2. a. $d = \sqrt{(5 - 2)^2 + (9 - 5)^2} = \sqrt{3^2 + 4^2} = \sqrt{9 + 16} = \sqrt{25} = 5$
    b. $\sqrt{[6 - (-4)]^2 + (1 - 8)^2} = \sqrt{10^2 + (-7)^2} = \sqrt{100 + 49} = \sqrt{149}$
    c. $\sqrt{(-3 - 0)^2 + [-2 - (-5)]^2} = \sqrt{(-3)^2 + 3^2} = \sqrt{9 + 9} = \sqrt{18} = 3\sqrt{2}$
    d. $\sqrt{(3\sqrt{2} - \sqrt{2})^2 + [-5 - (-1)]^2} = \sqrt{(2\sqrt{2})^2 + (-4)^2} = \sqrt{8 + 16} = \sqrt{24} = 2\sqrt{6}$
3. a. $\left(\frac{2 + 5}{2}, \frac{5 + 9}{2} \right) = \left(\frac{7}{2}, 7 \right)$
    b. $\left(1, \frac{9}{2} \right)$

c. $\left(\dfrac{-3}{2}, \dfrac{-7}{2}\right)$

d. $(2\sqrt{2}, -3)$

4. Find the length of each side:

$AB = \sqrt{[1 - (-1)]^2 + (3 - 1)^2} = \sqrt{2^2 + 2^2} = \sqrt{8} = 2\sqrt{2}$

$BC = \sqrt{(6 - 1)^2 + (-2 - 3)^2} = \sqrt{5^2 + (-5)^2} = \sqrt{50} = 5\sqrt{2}$

$AC = \sqrt{[6 - (-1)]^2 + [-2 - 1]^2} = \sqrt{7^2 + (-3)^2} = \sqrt{58}$

Then check to see whether or not these lengths satisfy the Pythagorean Theorem.

$$(2\sqrt{2})^2 + (5\sqrt{2})^2 \overset{?}{=} (\sqrt{58})^2$$
$$8 + 50 = 58$$

Therefore, yes, $\triangle ABC$ is a right triangle.

Linear Equations

A graphing calculator may help with this topic.

The graph of every linear equation is a line in the rectangular coordinate system. A linear equation is one that is equivalent to $Ax + By = C$ in which not both A and B are zero. A linear equation written in the form $Ax + By = C$ is in *standard form*.

The two ordered pairs obtained by choosing each variable in turn to be 0 are the coordinates of the intercepts of the graph of a linear equation, that is, by choosing $x = 0$, one obtains the ordered pair $(0, b)$, which identifies the y-intercept. The ordered pair $(a, 0)$ identifies the x-intercept.

For any two ordered pairs (x_1, y_1) and (x_2, y_2) on the graph of a linear equation, the following is called the *slope formula:*

$$m = \frac{y_2 - y_1}{x_2 - x_1} \text{ if } x_1 \neq x_2$$

If $x_1 = x_2$, then the line is vertical, and it has no slope. If $y_1 = y_2$, then the line is horizontal, and it has slope 0. Zero slope is very different from no slope.

Slopes of parallel lines are equal. The product of the slopes of perpendicular lines is -1. Of course neither of these statements is true if either line is vertical because vertical lines have no slope. But on the other hand, all vertical lines are parallel to each other and every vertical line is perpendicular to every horizontal line.

A linear equation written in the form

$$y = mx + b$$

is said to be in *slope-intercept* form because the coefficient of x is the slope of the line m and b is the y-intercept. This form is most useful for determining the slope of a line, given its equation.

We derive the *point-slope* form of the equation of the line from the slope formula:

$$y - y_1 = m(x - x_1)$$

in which m is the slope and (x_1, y_1) is a given fixed point on the line. This form is most useful for determining the equation of a line with certain given characteristics.

PRACTICE EXERCISES

Graph.
1. $x + 2y = 3$
2. $5x - 2y = 7$
3. $x + 2 = 0$

Find the slope of the line:
4. through $(2, 3)$ and $(-1, 5)$
5. with equation $2x - 3y = 5$
6. perpendicular to the line with equation $4x - 3y = 8$.

Find the standard form of the equation of the line:

7. through $(-3, 4)$ with slope $m = \dfrac{5}{8}$

8. through $(-8, 1)$ and $(3, 5)$

SOLUTIONS

1. It is a good idea to find three ordered pairs for each linear equation; the third one serves as a built-in check. Three ordered pairs: $(1, 1)$ $(3, 0)$, $(-3, 3)$.

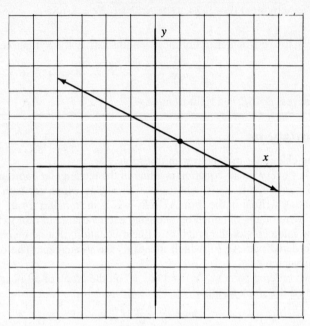

2. Three ordered pairs: $(1, -1)$, $(3, 4)$, $(-1, -6)$, (It is actually more likely that ordered pairs like $\left(2, \dfrac{3}{2}\right)$ would show up. No matter; fractions are OK.)

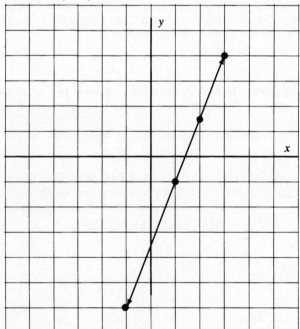

3. Because the *y*-variable is not in the equation, its value may be chosen to be any convenient number as long as $x = -2$. Three ordered pairs: $(-2, 0)$, $(-2, 3)$, $(-2, -4)$.

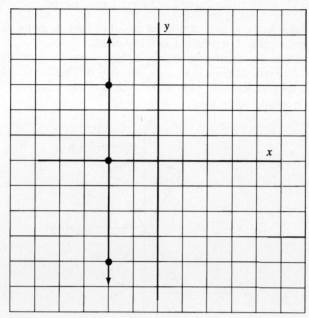

4. $\dfrac{y_2 - y_1}{x_2 - x_1} = \dfrac{5 - 3}{-1 - 2} = \dfrac{2}{-3} = \dfrac{-2}{3}$

5. Solve the equation for *y:* $y = \dfrac{2}{3}x - \dfrac{5}{3}$.

   The slope is the coefficient of *x:* $\dfrac{2}{3}$.

6. The slope of the line whose equation is $4x - 3y = 8$ is $\dfrac{4}{3}$. Then the slope of the line perpendicular to that line is $-\dfrac{3}{4}$.

7. Plug the slope and the coordinates of the fixed point into the point-slope form:

   $y - 4 = \dfrac{5}{8}[x - (-3)]$

   $y - 4 = \dfrac{5}{8}(x + 3)$ \qquad Multiply by 8.

   $8y - 32 = 5(x + 3)$
   $8y - 32 = 5x + 15$
   $-5x + 8y = 47$
   or
   $5x - 8y = -47$ \qquad If both sides are multiplied by -1.

8. First find the slope: $m = \dfrac{5 - 1}{3 - (-8)} = \dfrac{4}{11}$.

   Choose either ordered pair, and plug into the point-slope form:
   $y - 5 = \dfrac{4}{11}(x - 3)$
   $11y - 55 = 4(x - 3)$
   $11y - 55 = 4x - 12$
   $-4x + 11y = 43$
   or
   $4x - 11y = -43$

Conic Sections

If an equation of the type

$$Ax^2 + Bxy + Cy^2 + Dx + Ey + F = 0$$

has a graph, the graph is a conic section (or one of its degenerate forms). A *conic section* is either a circle, an ellipse, a parabola, or a hyperbola.

A circle is obtained by cutting the cone by a plane perpendicular to the axis of the cone. If the cutting plane cuts the cone at an angle less than 90°, the cut is an ellipse. A parabola results from a cut parallel to the side of the cone, and a hyperbola is obtained when the cutting plane is parallel to the axis.

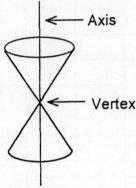

If any of the planes cuts the cone at the vertex, the result is one of the degenerate forms. The degenerate form of each conic section is:
- a point (from a circle or an ellipse)
- a line (from a parabola)
- two intersecting lines (from a hyperbola)

Circle

The equation of the circle in the plane comes from the distance formula:

$$(x - h)^2 + (y - k)^2 = r^2$$

For an equation in this form the center of the circle is *(h, k)*, and its radius is *r*.

Ellipse

An ellipse is defined by an equation of the type

$$\frac{x^2}{a^2} + \frac{y^2}{b^2} = 1 \qquad \text{or} \qquad \frac{x^2}{b^2} + \frac{y^2}{a^2} = 1$$

Center at the origin. The larger denominator is always a^2.

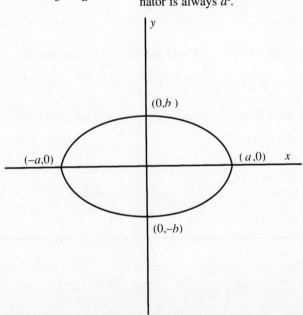

The major axis is a segment of length 2a, and the minor axis is 2b. The foci are located along the major axis at a distance $c = \sqrt{a^2 - b^2}$ from the center.

If the center is not at the origin, the equation of an ellipse with major axis oriented horizontally is

$$\frac{(x - h)^2}{a^2} + \frac{(y - k)^2}{b^2} = 1$$

If the larger denominator is under the variable y, then the major axis is vertical, and the foci are located c units from the center in a vertical direction.

Parabola

The equation of a parabola is either

$$y - k = a(x - h)^2 \qquad \text{or} \qquad x - h = a(y - k)^2$$

In both cases the vertex is at the point (h, k). In the first case the parabola is oriented vertically, so that there is a maximum or a minimum point, depending on whether a is negative or positive, respectively. In the second case the parabola is oriented horizontally, and there is a point farthest to the left or farthest to the right depending on whether a is positive or negative.

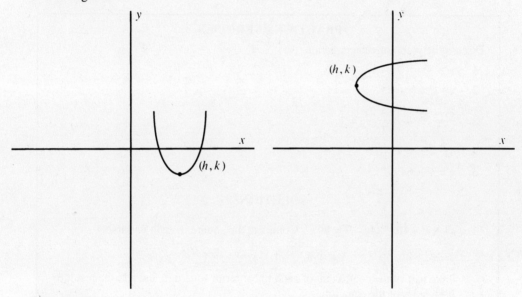

Hyperbola

A hyperbola is defined by an equation of the type

$$\frac{x^2}{a^2} - \frac{y^2}{b^2} = 1 \qquad \text{or} \qquad \frac{y^2}{a^2} - \frac{x^2}{b^2} = 1$$

Center at the origin. The positive term identifies a^2. It is not the larger value as with an ellipse.

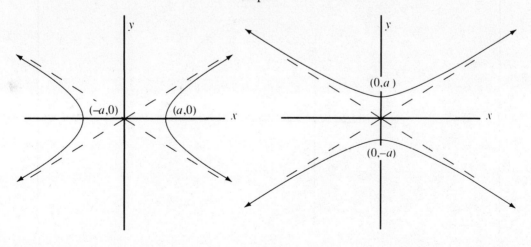

The segment of length $2a$ between the intercepts is called the *transverse axis*. The segment perpendicular to the transverse axis at its midpoint (the center of the hyperbola) of length $2b$ is called the *conjugate axis*.

If the positive term contains the y-variable, then the transverse axis is vertical and the conjugate axis is horizontal.

The foci of the hyperbola are located along the line containing the transverse axis at a distance $c = \sqrt{a^2 + b^2}$ from the center.

The asymptotes of a hyperbola with a horizontal transverse axis are two lines that intersect at the center of the hyperbola and have equations

$$\frac{x}{a} + \frac{y}{b} = 0 \qquad \text{and} \qquad \frac{x}{a} - \frac{y}{b} = 0$$

If the center is not at the origin [at some point (h, k)], then the equation of a hyperbola with a horizontal transverse axis is

$$\frac{(x - h)^2}{a^2} - \frac{(y - k)^2}{b^2} = 1$$

PRACTICE EXERCISES

Discuss the graph of each equation.

1. $x^2 + y^2 - 10x - 4y - 7 = 0$

2. $x - 2 = (y - 1)^2$

3. $\dfrac{(x - 3)^2}{25} + \dfrac{(y + 4)^2}{16} = 1$

4. $4x^2 - 25y^2 = -100$

5. $y = x^2 - 6x + 2$

SOLUTIONS

1. $x^2 + y^2 - 10x - 4y - 7 = 0$ Complete the square in each variable:

$$x^2 - 10x \quad + y^2 - 4y \quad = 7$$

Take half of the coefficient of each linear term, square it, and add the result to both sides of the equation.

$$x^2 - 10x + 25 + y^2 - 4y + 4 = 7 + 25 + 4$$

$$(x - 5)^2 + (y - 2)^2 = 36 \qquad \text{Standard form.}$$

The graph is a circle with center at $(5, 2)$ and radius 6.

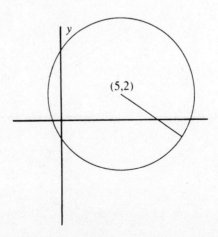

(5,2)

2. Written as $x - 2 = (y - 1)^2$, this equation is the standard form of the equation for a parabola oriented horizontally with a vertex at (2, 1), which happens to be the point farthest to the left. Locating a couple of other points gives the graph.

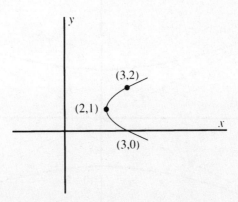

3. $\dfrac{(x-3)^2}{25} + \dfrac{(y+4)^2}{16} = 1$ This is the standard form of an equation of an

ellipse with major axis horizontal, of length $2a = 10$, minor axis of length $2b = 8$, and center at point (3, –4).

The foci are located $c = \sqrt{5^2 - 4^2} = \sqrt{9} = 3$ units horizontally from the center, (3 + 3, –4) and (3 – 3, –4).

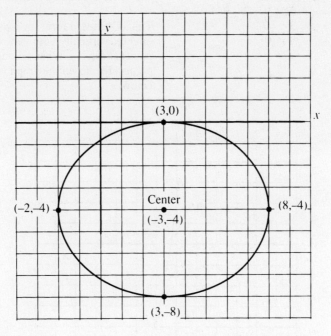

4. $4x^2 - 25y^2 = -100$ To obtain the standard form, divide both sides by –100:

$\dfrac{y^2}{4} - \dfrac{x^2}{25} = 1$

The graph of this equation is a hyperbola with center at the origin and with transverse axis vertical, of length $2a = 4$, and conjugate axis horizontal, of length $2b = 10$. The asymptote equations are

$\dfrac{y}{2} + \dfrac{x}{5} = 0$ and $\dfrac{y}{2} - \dfrac{x}{5} = 0$

The foci are located $c = \sqrt{2^5 + 5^2} = \sqrt{29}$ units from the center along the line containing the transverse axis, that is, at $(0, \sqrt{29})$ and $(0, -\sqrt{29})$.

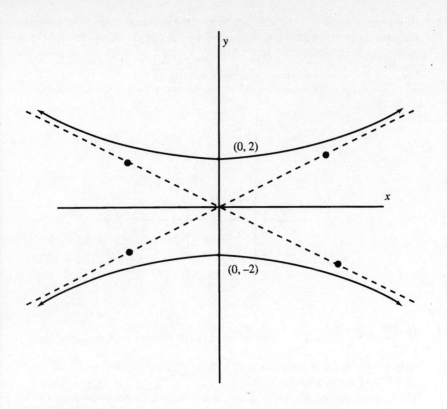

5. $y = x^2 - 6x + 2$
   $y = x^2 - 6x \underline{+ 9} + 2 \underline{- 9}$
   $y = (x - 3)^2 - 7$
   $y + 7 = (x - 3)^2$

Complete the square in x.

This is standard form for a parabola oriented vertically with vertex (minimum point) at $(3, -7)$. When a couple of other points are chosen the graph is as shown below.

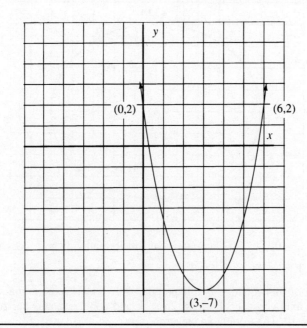

FOCUS ON THE ACT

The following sample questions represent ways in which the reviewed skills might be tested on your ACT Assessment.

1. Find the distance between $(-2, 1)$ and $(5, -4)$.
   A. $2\sqrt{6}$
   B. $\sqrt{74}$
   C. $3\sqrt{2}$
   D. $\sqrt{82}$
   E. $2\sqrt{5}$

2. Find the slope of the line through $(5, -2)$ and $(-1, -5)$.
   F. $\dfrac{-7}{4}$
   G. 2
   H. $\dfrac{-1}{2}$
   J. $\dfrac{1}{2}$
   K. -2

3. Find the standard form of the equation of the line through $(4, -8)$ with slope $\dfrac{-3}{5}$.
   A. $3x + 5y = -28$
   B. $3x + 5y = 28$
   C. $5x - 3y = -4$
   D. $3x + 5y = -4$
   E. None of these.

4. Which equation's graph is a parabola?
   F. $4x^2 + 2y^2 = 25$
   G. $3x^2 - 5y^2 = 15$
   H. $5x + 2y = 7$
   J. $y = -3x^2 + 2x + 1$
   K. $x^2 + y^2 = 5$

5. What is the center of the circle with equation $x^2 + y^2 - 2x + 4y - 5 = 0$?
   A. $(2, -4)$
   B. $(-2, 4)$
   C. $(1, -2)$
   D. $(-1, 2)$
   E. $\sqrt{10}$

ANSWERS AND EXPLANATIONS

1. B Apply the distance formula
$$d = \sqrt{(x_2 - x_1)^2 + (y_2 - y_1)^2}.$$
$$d = \sqrt{(5 - (-2))^2 + (-4 - 1)^2}$$
$$\sqrt{7^2 + (-5)^2} = \sqrt{49 + 25} = \sqrt{74}$$

2. J Apply the slope formula $m = \dfrac{y_2 - y_1}{x_2 - x_1}$.
$$m = \frac{-5 - (-2)}{-1 - 5} = \frac{-3}{-6} = \frac{1}{2}$$

3. A Apply the point-slope form of the equation of the line.
$$y - (-8) = \frac{-3}{5}(x - 4)$$
$$5(y + 8) = 5\left[\frac{-3}{5}(x - 4)\right]$$
$$5y + 40 = -3(x - 4)$$
$$5y + 40 = -3x + 12$$
$$3x + 5y = -28$$

4. J The graphs of the others given are: F. ellipse G. hyperbola H. line K. circle

5. C Complete the square in both x and y:
$$x^2 + y^2 - 2x + 4y - 5 = 0$$
$$(x^2 - 2x \quad) + (y^2 + 4y \quad) = 5$$
$$(x^2 - 2x + 1) + (y^2 + 4y + 4) = 5 + 1 + 4$$
$$(x - 1)^2 + (y + 2)^2 = 10$$
Add the square of half of the coefficients of x and y to both sides. The center is $(1, -2)$.

Functions

A function is a set of ordered pairs of real numbers in which no two ordered pairs have the same first component.

An example of a function according to this definition is

$$f = \{(1, 1), (2, 4), (3, 9), (4, 16), (5, 25)\}$$

The equation $f(x) = y$, read as "f of x equals y," is special notation for functions to indicate that the ordered pair, $(x, y,)$ is in the function. In the example, $f(4) = 16$ conveys the same information as $(4, 16) \in f$.

The *domain* of a function is the set of all first components of the ordered pairs in the function. The *range* is the set of all second components of the ordered pairs. In the example:

$$\text{Domain} = \{1, 2, 3, 4, 5\}$$
$$\text{Range} = \{1, 4, 9, 16, 25\}$$

Many times a function is given by the rule that generates the ordered pairs, rather than by the ordered pairs themselves. For example, $g(x) = x^2$. The domain in this case should always be chosen to be the largest set of real numbers for which the defining rule makes sense—no division by 0 or square roots of negative numbers. The range is usually a more difficult question; it can be determined by examining the rule itself or by observing the graph of the function.

Consider the defining rules for functions f and g:

$$f(x) = x^2 \quad \text{and} \quad g(x) = \frac{1}{x - 1}$$

Domain of f: R (all real numbers)
Range of f: $\{y | y \geq 0\}$
Domain of g: $\{|x \in R \text{ and } x \neq 1\}$
Range of g: $\{y | y \in R \text{ and } y \neq 0\}$ (A graph is the best tool to determine this.)

Other functions can also be created by the usual operations of addition, subtraction, multiplication, and division. For example:

$$(f + g)(x) = f(x) + g(x) = x^2 + \frac{1}{x - 1}$$

or

$$\left(\frac{f}{g}\right)(x) = \frac{f(x)}{g(x)} = \frac{x^2}{\frac{1}{x - 1}} = x^2(x - 1) \text{ if } x \neq 1$$

The domain of all functions is the intersection of the domains of the original functions except for the quotient. The domain of the quotient also omits numbers for which the second function value is 0.

Another useful combination of functions is called the *composite function*:

$$f \circ g(x) = f(g(x)) = f\left(\frac{1}{x - 1}\right) = \left(\frac{1}{x - 1}\right)^2$$

or

$$g \circ f(x) = g(f(x)) = g(x^2) = \frac{1}{x^2 - 1}$$

The domain of $f \circ g$, for example, consists of all numbers in the domain of g such that their function values $g(x)$ are contained in the domain of f.

Domain of $f \circ g$: same as domain of g
Domain of $g \circ f$: $\{x | x \in R \text{ and } x \neq \pm 1\}$

PRACTICE EXERCISES

Find the domain and range of each function (1–3).
1. $f(x) = x^2 + 1$
2. $g(x) = \frac{1}{x}$

3. $h(x) = \sqrt{x-1}$
4. Determine the composition function $f \circ g$ and its domain for the functions given in exercises 1 and 2.
5. Determine the difference function $g - h$ and its domain for the functions given in exercises 2 and 3.

SOLUTIONS

1. Domain: R
   Range: $\{y \mid y \in R \text{ and } y \geq 1\}$
2. Domain: $\{x \mid x \in R \text{ and } x \neq 0\}$
   Range: $\{y \mid y \in R \text{ and } y \neq 0\}$
3. Domain: $\{x \mid x \in R \text{ and } x \geq 1\}$
   Range: $\{y \mid y \in R \text{ and } y \geq 0\}$
4. $(f \circ g)(x) = f(g(x)) = f\left(\dfrac{1}{x}\right) = \left(\dfrac{1}{x}\right)^2 + 1$

   Domain: $\{x \mid x \in R \text{ and } x \neq 0\}$
5. $(g - h)(x) = g(x) - h(x) = \dfrac{1}{x} - \sqrt{x-1}$

   Domain: $\{x \mid x \in R \text{ and } x \geq 1\} = D_g \cap D_h$

Systems of Equations

The graphs of two linear equations may intersect at one point, be parallel, or coincide. The solution set of a system of two linear equations in two variables will therefore be either:

1. $\{(a, b)\}$ if the graphs intersect at a single point, (a, b). The equations are classified as independent and consistent.
2. $\{\ \}$ if the graphs are parallel lines. The equations are classified as inconsistent.
3. $\{(x, y) \mid (x, y)$ is any point on the line$\}$ if the lines are coincident. The equations are classified as dependent and consistent.

There are several methods of solving systems of two linear equations with two variables. One method is to graph both equations on the same coordinate axes and observe the point where they intersect. This method is effective, however, only if the point of intersection is some point near the origin with integer coordinates.

The elimination or addition method will work for all 2 by 2 systems. In this method, after suitably manipulating the coefficients of one or both of the equations, the equations are added—left side to left side and right side to right side—so that one of the variables is eliminated. The resulting equation is then solved, and the solution is substituted into one of the original equations to find the value of the other variable.
Example:
Solve:
$$2x + 3y = -1$$
$$3x + y = 2$$
Multiply both sides of the second equation by -3.

$$
\begin{array}{ll}
2x + 3y = -1 & \\
\underline{-9x - 3y = -6} & \text{Add the left and right sides of the equations.} \\
-7x \quad\;\; = -7 & \\
x \quad\;\; = 1 & \text{Substitute 1 into either equation, and solve.} \\
3(1) + y = 2 & \\
3 + y = 2 & \\
y = -1 &
\end{array}
$$

The solution set is $\{(1, -1)\}$.
The substitution method is useful when one of the equations is easy to solve for one of its variables.

Example:
Solve:

$$5x - 4y = 9$$
$$3 + x = 2y$$

Solve the second equation for x and substitute into the first equation.

$$x = 2y - 3$$
$$5(2y - 3) - 4y = 9$$
$$10y - 15 - 4y = 9$$
$$6y - 15 = 9$$
$$6y = 24$$
$$y = 4 \qquad \text{Substitute 4 into either equation.}$$
$$3 + x = 2(4)$$
$$3 + x = 8$$
$$x = 5$$

The solution set is $\{(5, 4)\}$.

PRACTICE EXERCISES

Solve by any method.
1. $2x + 3y = 10$
   $-3x + 2y = 11$
2. $3x + 5y = 2$
   $x + 3y = 4$
3. $2x = y + 6$
   $y = 5x$

SOLUTIONS

1. Multiply both sides of the first equation by 3 and of the second by 2.
   $$3(2x + 3y) = (10)3$$
   $$2(-3x + 2y) = (11)2$$
   $$6x + 9y = 30$$
   $$\underline{-6x + 4y = 32} \qquad \text{Add the left and right sides of the equations.}$$
   $$13y = 52$$
   $$y = 4 \qquad \text{Substitute 4 into one of the original equations.}$$

   $$2x + 3(4) = 10$$
   $$2x + 12 = 10$$
   $$2x = -2$$
   $$x = -1$$

   The solution set is $\{(-1, 4)\}$.

2. This system of equations could reasonably be solved by either method. Using the elimination method, we multiply both sides of the second equation by -3.
   $$3x + 5y = 2$$
   $$\underline{-3x - 9y = -12} \quad \text{Add the left and right sides of the equations.}$$
   $$-4y = -10$$
   $$y = \frac{5}{2}$$

   Since this number is not easy to substitute, redo the problem by eliminating the other variable.
   $$3(3x + 5y) = (2)3$$
   $$-5(x + 3y) = (4)(-5)$$
   $$9x + 15y = 6$$
   $$\underline{-5x - 15y = -20}$$
   $$4x = -14$$
   $$x = \frac{-7}{2}$$

   The solution set is $\left\{ \left(\frac{-7}{2}, \frac{5}{2} \right) \right\}$.

3. Use the substitution method. Replace y in the first equation by $5x$ from the second.

$$2x = y + 6$$
$$y = 5x$$
$$2x = 5x + 6$$
$$-3x = 6$$
$$x = -2 \qquad \text{Substitute } -2 \text{ into the equation used to substitute.}$$
$$y = 5(-2)$$
$$y = -10$$

The solution set is $\{(-2, -10)\}$.

Nonlinear Systems

If one equation in a system is linear and the other is not, the substitution method is usually the only reasonable method to use.

Consider this nonlinear system:

$$y = x^2 - 4x + 4 \qquad \text{A parabola.}$$
$$x + y = 2 \qquad \text{A line.}$$

Replace y in the second equation by $x^2 - 4x + 4$ from the first equation.

$$x + (x^2 - 4x + 4) = 2$$
$$x^2 - 3x + 2 = 0$$
$$(x - 2)(x - 1) = 0$$

$x = 2 \quad$ or $\quad x = 1 \qquad$ These are the first components of the two

$(2,) \qquad\qquad (1,) \qquad$ ordered pairs at the points of intersection.

$2 + y = 2 \qquad 1 + y = 2$

$\quad y = 0 \qquad\quad y = 1$

The solution set is $\{(2, 0), (1, 1)\}$.

Exponential and Logarithmic Functions

An *exponential function* is any function of the type

$$f(x) = a^x \qquad \text{for any positive number } a,\ a \neq 1.$$

The following is a definition of a *logarithmic function:*

$$y = \log_a x \qquad \text{if and only if} \qquad x = a^y.$$

Logarithmic functions are inverses of exponential functions. The inverse of a function, if it exists, is found by reversing all of the ordered pairs in the function. The same effect can be achieved by reversing the roles of x and y in the equation. Consequently, the graphs of inverse functions are always symmetric to the line $y = x$.

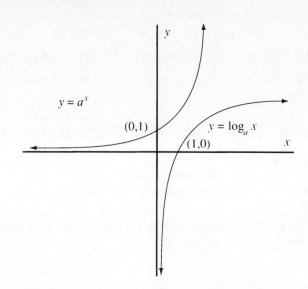

Six fundamental properties of logarithms are easily derived from the definition given above:

1. $\log_a(xy) = \log_a x + \log_a y$ The logarithm of a product is the sum of the logarithms.
2. $\log_a\left(\dfrac{x}{y}\right) = \log_a x - \log_a y$ The logarithm of a quotient is the difference of the logarithms.
3. $\log_a x^n = n \log_a x$ The logarithm of a power is that power multiplied by the logarithm.
4. $\log_a a^x = x$ and $a^{\log_a x} = x$
5. $\log_a 1 = 0$
6. $\log_a a = 1$

When no base is indicated, the base is understood to be 10. Base 10 logarithms are called common logs.

Examples:
1. Write as a logarithmic equation: $2^5 = 32$.
$$\log_2 32 = 5$$

2. Write as an exponential equation: $\log_2 \dfrac{1}{8} = -3$.
$$2^{-3} = \dfrac{1}{8}$$

Evaluate the following logarithms:
3. $\log_8 64$ Let the value of the logarithm be x, and change to the corresponding exponential form.
$$x = \log_8 64$$
$$8^x = 64$$

The answer is easily seen to be 2. So $\log_8 64 = 2$

4. $\log_5 \dfrac{1}{25} = x$
$$5^x = \dfrac{1}{25} = 5^{-2} \quad \text{So } x = -2.$$

5. $\log_6 \sqrt{6^3} = x$
$$6^x = \sqrt{6^3} = (6^3)^{1/2} = 6^{3/2} \quad \text{So } x = \dfrac{3}{2}.$$

Solve each equation.
6. $\log_x 9 = \dfrac{1}{2}$ Change to exponential form.
$x^{1/2} = 9$ Square both sides.
$x = 81$

The solution set is $\{81\}$.

7. $\log_{1/2} x = -3$
$$x = \left(\dfrac{1}{2}\right)^{-3}$$
$$x = 2^3 = 8$$

The solution set is $\{8\}$.

8. $4^x = 7$ Take the logarithm of each side.
$\log_a 4^x = \log_a 7$ Any convenient base will do.
$x \log_a 4 = \log_a 7$
$$x = \dfrac{\log_a 7}{\log_a 4}$$ It would require a calculator or tables to continue to find a decimal answer.

9. $\log x + \log (3x - 5) = \log 2$ Apply the first rule of logarithms to the left side.
$\log[x(3x - 5)] = \log 2$ If $a = b$, then $10^a = 10^b$.
$x(3x - 5) = 2$
$3x^2 - 5x - 2 = 0$
$(3x + 1)(x - 2) = 0$
$x = \dfrac{-1}{3}$ or $x = 2$

Each potential solution must be checked.

Check $\dfrac{-1}{3}$: $\log\left(\dfrac{-1}{3}\right)$ does not exist. There are no logarithms of negative numbers. Eliminate $\dfrac{-1}{3}$.

Check 2: $\log 2 + \log(3 \cdot 2 - 5)$ $= \log 2 + \log 1$ $\log_a 1 = 0$ in any base
$= \log 2 + 0 = \log 2$

The solution set is $\{2\}$.

10. Write as a single logarithm:

$$2 \log x + \frac{1}{2} \log y - \frac{3}{2} \log z - 3 \log a$$

Applying property 3 of logarithms gives:

$$\log x^2 + \log y^{1/2} - \log z^{3/2} - \log a^3$$

Applying rules 1 and 2, together with properties of radicals, we have

$$\log \frac{x^2\sqrt{y}}{a^3\sqrt{z^3}}$$

PRACTICE EXERCISES

1.   Write as a logarithmic equation:
$8^{-(1/3)} = \dfrac{1}{2}$

2.   Write as an exponential equation:
$\log_{1/4} 16 = -2$

Evaluate.

3. $\log_3 \dfrac{1}{9}$

4. $\log_3 \sqrt{3^5}$

5. $\log_3 27^{1/2}$

Solve (6–9).

6. $\log_x 125 = -3$

7. $\log_x 4 = 1$

8. $\log_5 x = 0$

9. $\log_2 (x + 5) - \log_2 (x - 1) = \log_2 3$

10. Write as a single logarithm:
$\log_b 2 + 2 \log_b 3 - \log_b 5$

SOLUTIONS

1. $\log_8 \dfrac{1}{2} = -\dfrac{1}{3}$

2. $\left(\dfrac{1}{4}\right)^{-2} = 16$

3. $\log_3 \dfrac{1}{9} = x$

   $3^x = \dfrac{1}{9} = 9^{-1} = (3^2)^{-1} = 3^{-2}$ So $x = -2$.

4. $\log_3 \sqrt{3^5} = x$

   $3^x = \sqrt{3^5} = (3^5)^{1/2} = 3^{5/2}$ So $x = \dfrac{5}{2}$.

5. $\log_3 27^{1/2} = x$

$3^x = 27^{1/2} = (3^3)^{1/2} = 3^{3/2}$ So $x = \dfrac{3}{2}$.

6. $\log_x 125 = -3$ Write the equation in exponential form.

     $x^{-3} = 125$ Raise both sides to the $\dfrac{-1}{3}$ power.

     $x = 125^{-(1/3)}$

     $= \sqrt[3]{\dfrac{1}{125}} = \dfrac{1}{5}$

7. $\log_x 4 = 1$ $x^1 = 4$ A rule is $\log_b b = 1$. The logarithm of the base is
                    $x = 4$ always 1.

8. $\log_5 x = 0$ $5^0 = x$ A rule is $\log_b 1 = 0$. The logarithm of 1 in any base
                    $x = 1$ is 0.

9. $\log_2(x + 5) - \log_2(x - 1) = \log_2 3$

         $\log_2 \dfrac{x+5}{x-1} = \log_2 3$ Apply rule 2.

            $\dfrac{x+5}{x-1} = 3$ If $a = b$, then $2^a = 2^b$.

            $x + 5 = 3(x - 1)$ Multiply by $x - 1$.

            $x + 5 = 3x - 3$

                $5 = 2x - 3$

                $8 = 2x$

                $4 = x$

Check 4: $\log_2 9 - \log_2 3 = \log_2 \dfrac{9}{3}$

                         $= \log_2 3$

The solution set is $\{4\}$.

10. $\log_b \dfrac{2 \cdot 3^2}{5} = \log_b \dfrac{18}{5}$

Sequence and Series

A *sequence* (also called a *progression*) is a function whose domain is the set of natural numbers, $N = \{1, 2, 3, \ldots\}$. For the sequence 1, 4, 9, ..., whose terms are the squares of the natural numbers, it is common to use subscripts and write $a_1 = 1$, $a_2 = 4$, $a_3 = 9$, ... instead of $a(1) = 1$, $a(2) = 4$, $a(3) = 9$, ..., as in other functions. The general or nth term for this function is $a_n = n^2$.

If any term of a sequence is obtained by adding a constant to the preceding term, the sequence is called *arithmetic*. The terms of an arithmetic sequence therefore are:

$a_1 = a$
$a_2 = a + d$ The constant d is the *common difference*.
$a_3 = a + 2d$
$a_4 = a + 3d$
$\ldots$

$a_n = a + (n - 1)d$ This is the formula for the nth term of an arithmetic sequence.

The sequence of the sums of the first n terms of an arithmetic sequence is called the *series* associated with the given sequence. The following are formulas for the sum of the first n terms of an arithmetic sequence.

$$S_n = \frac{n}{2}[2a + (n - 1)d] \quad \text{or} \quad S_n = \frac{n}{2}(a_1 + a_n)$$

$$S_n = \sum_{i=1}^{n} a_i$$

A sequence is *geometric* if any term is obtained by multiplying the preceding term by a nonzero constant. The terms of geometric sequence then are as follows:

$a_1 = a$

$a_2 = ar$ The constant r is called the *common ratio*.

$a_3 = ar^2$

$a_4 = ar^3$

$\cdots$

$a_n = ar^{n-1}$ This is the formula for the nth term of a geometric sequence.

The sum of the first n terms of a geometric sequence is:

$$S_n = \frac{a - ar^n}{1 - r} = \sum_{i=1}^{n} a_i$$

If $|r| < 1$, then the sum of the infinite sequence can be found:

$$S_\infty = \frac{a}{1 - r}$$

PRACTICE EXERCISES

Write the first five terms of each of the following sequences, whose nth term is given:

1. $a_n = 2n - 1$
2. $a_n = n^2 + n$
3. $a_n = 3^n$
4. Which of the above sequences is arithmetic?
5. Which of the above sequences is geometric?
6. Find the 25th term of the sequence whose nth term is $a_n = 3n + 2$.
7. Find the eighth term of the sequence whose first three terms are 4, 2, 1.
8. Find the sum of this series:

$$\sum_{i=1}^{50} (2i - 1) = 1 + 3 + 5 + \cdots + 99$$

9. Find the sum of the first 20 terms of the sequence whose nth term is $a_n = (-2)^n$.
10. Find the sum: $0.9 + 0.09 + 0.009 + \cdots$.

SOLUTIONS

1. 1, 3, 5, 7, 9
2. 2, 6, 12, 20, 30
3. 3, 9, 27, 81, 243
4. $a_n = 2n - 1$ is arithmetic. The common difference is 2.
5. $a_n = 3^n$ is geometric. The common ratio is 3.
6. $a_n = 3n + 2$ is arithmetic with first term 5 and common difference 3. The 25th term is

   $a_{25} = 5 + 24(3) = 5 + 72 = 78$

7. **4, 2, 1,** ... is geometric with first term 4 and common ratio $\frac{1}{2}$. The eighth term is $a_8 = 4\left(\frac{1}{2}\right)^7 = 4\left(\frac{1}{128}\right) = \frac{1}{32}$

8. $\sum_{i=1}^{50} (2n - 1) = 1 + 3 + 5 + \cdots + 99$ is arithmetic with first term 1 and common difference 2. Using the formula, we obtain

$$S_{50} = \frac{50}{2}[2(1) + 49(2)] = 25(2 + 98)$$

$$= 25(100) = 2500$$

9. $a_n = (-2)^n$ is geometric with first term -2 and common ratio -2. The series of the first 20 terms is

$$S_{20} = \frac{(-2) - (-2)(-2)^{20}}{1 - (-2)}$$

$$= \frac{(-2) - (-2)(1,048,576)}{3}$$

$$= \frac{(-2) - (-2,097,152)}{3}$$

$$= \frac{(-2) + 2,097,152}{3}$$

$$= \frac{2,097,150}{3}$$

$$= 699,050$$

10. $0.9 + 0.09 + 0.009 + \cdots$ is geometric with first term 0.9 and common ratio 0.1. Since the common ratio is between -1 and 1, the formula for an infinite geometric series applies:

$$S_\infty = \frac{0.9}{1 - 0.1} = \frac{0.9}{0.9} = 1$$

The Binomial Theorem

The expression $n!$ (read as "n factorial") is defined as follows:

$$n! = n(n - 1)(n - 2)(n - 3) \cdots 2 \cdot 1$$
$$1! = 1$$
$$0! = 1$$

Factorials allow easy counting of certain arrangements (or permutations) and combinations. The number of permutations of n things taken r at a time is

$$_nP_r = \frac{n!}{(n - r)!} \qquad \text{(The notation } P_{n,r} \text{ is also used.)}$$

For example, if one has 20 different books and a shelf that will hold 8 of them, how many different arrangements of those books on the shelf are possible?

$$_{20}P_8 = \frac{20!}{(20 - 8)!} = \begin{array}{l} 20 \cdot 19 \cdot 18 \cdots \cdot 13 \\ = 5,079,110,400 \end{array}$$

The number of combinations of n things taken r at a time is

$$_nC_r = \frac{n!}{r!(n - r)!} \qquad \text{(The notation } C_{n,r} \text{ and } \binom{n}{r} \text{ are also used.)}$$

The difference is that permutations are concerned with order, whereas combinations are not. For example, the number of different combinations of the 20 books on the shelf that will hold 8 books is

$$_{20}C_8 = \frac{20!}{8!12!}$$

$$= 125,970$$

Most scientific calculators have combination and permutation functions. You may want to familiarize yourself with them.

The combination numbers turn out to be useful in the formula to raise a binomial to a power. This formula is known as the Bionomial Theorem.

$$(a + b)^n = {}_nC_0 a^n + {}_nC_1 a^{n-1}b^1 + {}_nC_2 a^{n-2}b^2 + \cdots + {}_nC_r a^{n-r}b^r + \cdots + {}_nC_n b^n$$

The coefficients of the terms in the Binomial Theorem are found in the nth row of Pascal's triangle, an array of numbers in which each entry other than the 1 at the end of each row is found by adding the two numbers immediately above it.

$$\begin{array}{c}
1 \\
1 \quad 1 \\
1 \quad 2 \quad 1 \\
1 \quad 3 \quad 3 \quad 1 \\
1 \quad 4 \quad 6 \quad 4 \quad 1 \\
1 \quad 5 \quad 10 \quad 10 \quad 5 \quad 1 \\
1 \quad 6 \quad 15 \quad 20 \quad 15 \quad 6 \quad 1
\end{array}$$

PASCAL'S TRIANGLE

Row 0
Row 1
Row 2

Using Pascal's triangle, we can easily write the expansion of $(x + y)^6$ as follows:

$$(x + y)^6 = 1x^6 + 6x^5y + 15x^4y^2 + 20x^3y^3 + 15x^2y^4 + 6xy^5 + 1y^6$$

PRACTICE EXERCISES

Evaluate.

1. $7!$
2. $_8P_3$
3. $_{10}C_4$
4. In how many ways can the 3 officers of a club—president, vice president, and secretary—be chosen from a membership of 12 people?
5. How many 4-member committees can be selected from a club that has 16 members?
6. Expand $(12x - 3)^4$.
7. What is the fifth term of the binomial expansion of $(x - 2)^6$?

SOLUTIONS

1. $7! = 7 \cdot 6 \cdot 5 \cdot 4 \cdot 3 \cdot 2 \cdot 1 = 5040$

2. $_8P_3 = \dfrac{8!}{(8 - 3)!}$

   $= \dfrac{8 \cdot 7 \cdot 6 \cdot 5 \cdot 4 \cdot 3 \cdot 2 \cdot 1}{5 \cdot 4 \cdot 3 \cdot 2 \cdot 1}$

   $= 8 \cdot 7 \cdot 6 = 336$

3. $_{10}C_4 = \dfrac{10!}{4!(10 - 4)!}$

   $= \dfrac{10!}{4!6!}$ Cancel 6!.

   $= \dfrac{10 \cdot \overset{3}{\cancel{9}} \cdot 8 \cdot 7}{\cancel{4} \cdot \cancel{3} \cdot \cancel{2} \cdot 1}$ Cancel common factors.

   $= 10 \cdot 3 \cdot 1 \cdot 7 = 210$

4. This question concerns order, so the correct answer is

   $$_{12}P_3 = \dfrac{12!}{(12 - 3)!} = 12 \cdot 11 \cdot 10 = 1320$$

5. Order on a committee is not important, so this is a combination question.

   $$_{16}C_4 = \dfrac{16!}{4!(16 - 4)!}$$

   $= \dfrac{16 \cdot 15 \cdot 14 \cdot 13}{4 \cdot 3 \cdot 2 \cdot 1}$ Cancel.

   $= 4 \cdot 5 \cdot 7 \cdot 13 = 1820$

6. Use the fourth row of Pascal's triangle.

$$(2x - 3)^4 = 1(2x)^4 + 4(2x)^3(-3) + 6(2x)^2(-3)^2 + 4(2x)(-3)^3 + 1(-3)^4$$
$$= 16x^4 - 96x^3 + 216x^2 - 216x + 81$$

7. The coefficients of the expansion of $(x - 2)^6$ are the numbers in the sixth row of Pascal's triangle. They are also the combination numbers. The fifth one is $_6C_4$, so the fifth term is

$$_6C_4(x)^2(-2)^4 = 15x^2(16) = 240x^2$$

[Notice that the exponent on the second factor, (-2), is the same as the number on the right of the combination symbol.]

Complex Numbers

A complex number is any number in the form $a + bi$, in which a and b are real numbers and $i = \sqrt{-1}$. The real number a is called the *real* part of the imaginary number, and the real number b is called the *imaginary* part. Complex numbers are equal if and only if the real parts are equal and the imaginary parts are equal.

$$a + bi = c + di \quad \text{if and only if} \quad a = c \text{ and } b = d$$

The following are the definitions of the operations on complex numbers:
- *Absolute value:* $|a + bi| = \sqrt{a^2 + b^2}$. (Note that i is not used in the radicand.) The absolute value of a complex number is called its modulus.
- *Conjugate:* The conjugate of $a + bi$ is $a - bi$. (Change the sign of the imaginary part.)
- *Addition:* $(a + bi) + (c + di) = (a + c) + (b + d)i$ (Add the real parts and add the imaginary parts separately.)
- *Subtraction:* $(a + bi) - (c + di) = (a - c) + (b - d)i$ (Subtract the real parts and subtract the imaginary parts.)
- *Multiplication:* $(a + bi)(c + di) = (ac - bd) + (ad + bc)i$ (Rather than use the definition, it is common to treat the complex numbers like binomials and multiply by the FOIL method.)
- *Division:* $\dfrac{a + bi}{c + di} = \dfrac{(a + bi)(c - di)}{(c + di)(c - di)}$ (Multiply the numerator and denominator by the conjugate of the denominator.)

Here are some examples:
- $(2 + 3i) + (-5 + 7i) = -3 + 10i$
- $(7 - 8i) - (-6 - 3i) = 13 - 5i$
- $i^2 = -1$ (So i is definitely not a real number.)
- $i^3 = -i$
- $i^4 = 1$
- $i^{27} = (i^4)^6(i^3) = 1^6(-i) = -i$ (The easy method is to divide the exponent by 4. Match the remainder with the exponents in the first four powers of i:

$$i^1 = i, \ i^2 = -1, \ i^3 = -i, \ i^4 = i^0 = 1)$$

- $(2 + 5i)(-3 + i) = -6 + 2i - 15i + 5i^2$
$$= -6 - 13i + 5(-1)$$
$$= -6 - 13i - 5 = -11 - 13i$$

- $(5 + 6i)(5 - 6i) = 25 - 36i^2$ (The outer and inner products cancel out.)
$$= 25 - 36(-1)$$
$$= 25 + 36 = 61$$

- $\dfrac{4 + 3i}{3 - i} = \dfrac{(4 + 3i)(3 + i)}{(3 - i)(3 + i)}$
$$= \dfrac{9 + 13i}{10} = \dfrac{9}{10} + \dfrac{13}{10}i$$

- $\dfrac{1}{i} = \dfrac{1(-i)}{i(-i)} = \dfrac{-i}{-i^2} = \dfrac{-i}{-(-1)} = \dfrac{-i}{1} = -i$

The graph of a complex number is a point in the complex plane on which is drawn a horizontal real axis and a vertical imaginary axis. It looks like the usual rectangular coordinating system, and points are located in the same way. The complex number $a + bi$ is located at the same place that the ordered pair (a, b) is located in the rectangular plane. The absolute value of a complex number is its distance from the origin of the complex plane.

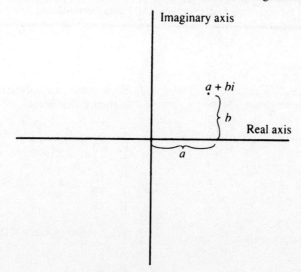

PRACTICE EXERCISES

Perform the indicated operations. Express answers in the standard form, $a + bi$.

1. $\sqrt{-125}$
2. $\sqrt{-9} \cdot \sqrt{-36}$
3. $(-3 + 2i) + (4 + 5i)$
4. $(-3 - 4i) - (-1 - i)$
5. $2i(4 - 3i)$
6. $(7 + 3i)(-5 + i)$
7. $(-5 + 2i)^2$
8. $\dfrac{4i}{1 - i}$
9. i^{98}
10. $\left| 2 + 5i \right|$

SOLUTIONS

1. $\sqrt{-125} = \sqrt{(-1)(25)(5)} = \sqrt{-1} \cdot \sqrt{25} \cdot \sqrt{5} = i \cdot 5 \cdot \sqrt{5} = 5i\sqrt{5}$
2. $\sqrt{-9} \cdot \sqrt{-36} = (3i)(6i) = 18i^2 = 18(-1) = -18$

    (The rule from algebra, $\sqrt{ab} = \sqrt{a}\,\sqrt{b}$, does not apply to this problem because the factors are not real numbers.)
3. $(-3 + 2i) + (4 + 5i) = 1 + 7i$
4. $(-3 - 4i) - (-1 - i) = -2 - 3i$
5. $2i(4 - 3i) = 8i - 6i^2 = 8i - 6(-1)$
    $= 8i + 6 = 6 + 8i$
6. $(7 + 3i)(-5 + i) = -35 + 7i - 15i + 3i^2$
    $= -35 - 8i + 3(-1)$
    $= -35 - 8i - 3 = -38 - 8i$
7. $(-5 + 2i)^2 = 25 - 2(5)(2i) + 4i^2$ Use the rule for squaring a binomial.
    $= 25 - 20i + 4(-1)$
    $= 21 - 20i$
8. $\dfrac{4i}{1 - i} = \dfrac{4i(1 + i)}{(1 - i)(1 + i)} = \dfrac{4i - 4}{1 - i^2}$
    $= \dfrac{-4 + 4i}{2} = -2 + 2i$
9. $i^{98} = i^2 = -1$ Divide 98 by 4. The remainder is 2.
10. $\left| 2 + 5i \right| = \sqrt{2^2 + 5^2} = \sqrt{29}$

FOCUS ON THE ACT

The following sample questions represent ways in which the reviewed skills might be tested on your ACT Assessment.

1. Solve: $\begin{pmatrix} x + 5y = -2 \\ 3x - 4y = -25 \end{pmatrix}$

   A. $\{(1, -7)\}$
   B. $\{(7, -1)\}$
   C. $\{(-1, 7)\}$
   D. $\{(-7, 1)\}$
   E. $\{\ \}$

2. What is the value of $\log_4 8$?

   F. $\dfrac{2}{3}$

   G. $\dfrac{3}{2}$

   H. 2

   J. $\dfrac{1}{2}$

   K. $(\sqrt{4})^3$

3. If $\log_b 2 = x$ and $\log_b 3 = y$, express $\log_b 12$ in terms of x and y.

   A. $x^2 + y$
   B. $2xy$
   C. $2x + y$
   D. $x + 2y$
   E. $x^2 y$

4. What is the fifteenth term of the arithmetic sequence that begins:

   $$0, 3, 6, 9, \ldots?$$

   F. 42
   G. 45
   H. 15
   J. 39
   K. 48

5. What is the product of $2 + i$ and $3 - 2i$?

   A. 8
   B. $4 - i$
   C. $4 - 7i$
   D. $6 - 2i$
   E. $8 - i$

ANSWERS AND EXPLANATIONS

1. D Multiply both sides of the first equation by -3 and add:

$$\begin{pmatrix} -3x - 15y = 6 \\ 3x - 4y = -25 \end{pmatrix}$$

$$-19y = -19$$

   $y = 1$ Substitute $y = 1$ into either
   $x + 5(1) = -2$ original equation, say the first.
   $x = -7$ The solution set is $\{(-7, 1)\}$.

2. G Call the value x: $\log_4 8 = x$ Rewrite in expo-
   $\quad\quad\quad\quad\quad 4^x = 8$ nential form.
   $\quad\quad\quad (2^2)^x = 2^3$ Express both sides
   $\quad\quad\quad\quad 2^{2x} = 2^3$ with a common
   $\quad\quad\quad\quad 2x = 3$ base. Set the
   $\quad\quad\quad\quad\quad\quad\quad$ exponents equal.
   $\quad\quad\quad\quad\ x = \dfrac{3}{2}$

3. C $\log_b 12 = \log_b 2^2 \cdot 3 = 2 \log_b 2 + \log_b 3 = 2x + y$

4. F The nth term of any arithmetic sequence is given by the formula $a_n = a_1 + (n - 1)d$ in which a_1 is the first term and d is the common difference between successive terms.

   $$a_{15} = 0 + (15 - 1)3 = 0 + 14 \cdot 3 = 42$$

5. E Multiply them as you would multiply binomials, but remember that $i^2 = -1$.

   $$(2 + i)(3 - 2i) = 6 - 4i + 3i - 2i^2 =$$
   $$6 - i - 2(-1) = 6 - i + 2 = 8 - i.$$

GEOMETRY

Lines

A *line* is a set of points that extends infinitely in both directions, and it is always straight.

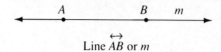

Line $\overleftrightarrow{AB}$ or m

A *line segment* consists of two points and all of the points between.

C •————————————————• D

Line segment $\overline{CD}$
of length CD

A *ray* consists of a point (called the *endpoint*) and all of the points in one direction.

Ray $\overrightarrow{EF}$

Parallel lines are two lines in a plane that do not intersect.

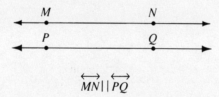

$\overleftrightarrow{MN} \| \overleftrightarrow{PQ}$

If segments have the same measure, they are called *congruent.* The point between the endpoints of a segment that separates the segment into two congruent segments is called the *midpoint* of the segment. A ray, a line, or a segment that contains the midpoint of a segment is called the *bisector* of the segment.

Angles

An *angle* is the union of two rays with a common endpoint.

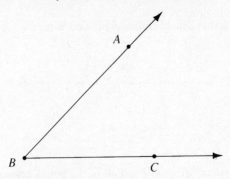

The angle shown above consists of $\overrightarrow{BA}$ and $\overrightarrow{BC}$. The common endpoint *B* is called the *vertex*.

Two angles that have the same measure are called *congruent*.

Angles can be classified according to their measure.

- The measure of an *acute angle* is between 0° and 90°.
- A *right angle* measures 90°.
- The measure of an *obtuse angle* is between 90° and 180°.
- A *straight angle* measures 180°.
- The measure of a *reflex angle* is greater than 180° but less than 360°.

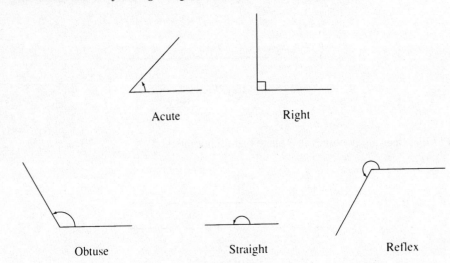

| Acute | Right |

| Obtuse | Straight | Reflex |

Two angles are called *adjacent* if they have a common side and the interiors of the angles do not intersect.

A segment, a ray, or a line that contains the vertex of an angle such that it forms two congruent adjacent angles with the sides of the angle is called the *angle bisector.*

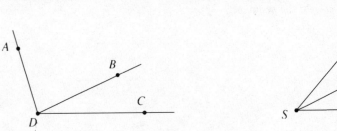

Angles *ADB* and *BDC* are adjacent.

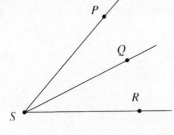

$\overrightarrow{SQ}$ is the bisector of ∠*PSR*.

There are always two pairs of *vertical angles* formed by the intersection of two lines. In the figure shown below, angles *AEB* and *DEC* are vertical angles, and angles *AED* and *BEC* are also vertical angles.

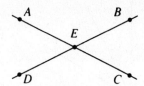

Angles *AED* and *BEC*
are vertical angles.

Two angles are *complementary* if their sum is 90°. Two angles are *supplementary* if their sum is 180°. Notice that both definitions specify two angles. These definitions do not apply to three or more angles.

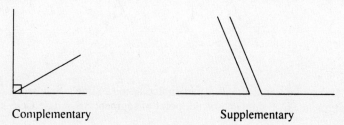

Complementary   Supplementary

Perpendicular lines are two lines that intersect to form a right angle. Of course, if there is one right angle, then there must be four of them.

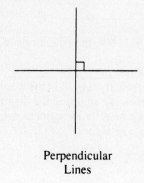

Perpendicular
Lines

If two parallel lines are intersected by a third line (called the *transversal)*, then the following angles are congruent:

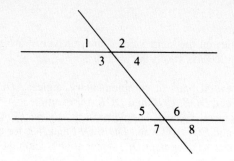

Corresponding angles: 1 and 5, 2 and 6, 3 and 7, 4 and 8
Alternate interior angles: 3 and 6, 4 and 5
Alternate exterior angles: 1 and 8, 2 and 7
Vertical angles: 1 and 4, 2 and 3, 5 and 8, 6 and 7
Interior angles on the same side of the transversal are supplementary. Angles 4 and 6 are supplementary, and 3 and 5 are supplementary. Exterior angles on the same side of the transversal are also supplementary: 2 and 8, 1 and 7.

PRACTICE EXERCISES

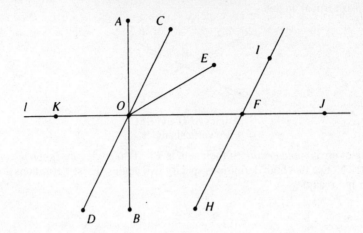

In the diagram, segment $\overline{AB}$ is perpendicular to ($\perp$) line l. Segment $\overline{CD}$ is parallel to ($\parallel$) segment $\overline{FH}$. Point O is the midpoint of segment AB. Angle COE and $\angle EOF$ are congruent.

1. The measure of $\angle AOF$ is _____.
2. Angle AOC and $\angle$ _____ are vertical angles.
3. Angle COF and $\angle$ _____ are alternate interior angles.
4. Angle HFJ and $\angle DOF$ are _____ angles.
5. If the measure of $\angle COF$ is 80°, then the measure of $\angle OFI$ is

   _____.
6. Angle DOB and $\angle BOF$ are _____ angles.
7. Name a pair of complementary angles in the diagram.
8. Name a pair of supplementary angles in the diagram.
9. _____ is a bisector of segment $\overline{AB}$.
10. _____ is a bisector of $\angle COF$.

SOLUTIONS

1. Since segment $\overline{AB} \perp l$, the measure of $\angle AOF$ is 90°.
2. Angle DOB.
3. Angle OFH.
4. Corresponding.
5. Interior angles on the same side of the transversal are supplementary, so the measure of $\angle OFI$ is 180° − 80° = 100°.
6. Adjacent.
7. There are several pairs of complementary angles: AOC and COF, AOE and EOF, KOD and DOB, COF and DOB, for example.
8. There are several pairs of supplementary angles: KOA and AOF, KOC and COF, KOE and EOF, AOD and DOB, OFI and IFJ, for example.
9. Either segment $\overline{KF}$, segment $\overline{OC}$, segment $\overline{OD}$, segment $\overline{OE}$, line l, or ray $\overline{OF}$, for example.
10. Segment $\overline{OE}$.

Polygons

A *polygon* is the union of three or more segments connected in pairs at their endpoints. The endpoints of the segments are called the *vertices*. The polygon is called *convex* if the lines containing the sides of the polygon do not intersect the interior of the polygon. If, however, at least one such line does intersect the interior of the polygon, then the polygon is called *concave*.

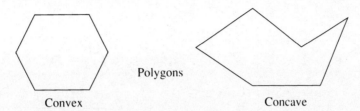

Polygons

Convex   Concave

If two polygons have their angles congruent in sequence and their corresponding sides have the same ratio, then the polygons are similar.

If two polygons have the same size and shape (that is, they would coincide if one was placed on top of the other), they are congruent. Congruent polygons are also similar, and the ratio of corresponding sides is 1.

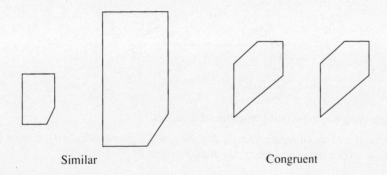

Similar   Congruent

If all of the angles of a polygon are congruent and the sides are also congruent, the polygon is regular.

A diagonal of a polygon is a segment with endpoints at two nonadjacent vertices. The only polygons with no diagonals are triangles.

Triangles

A *triangle* is a polygon with three sides. Triangles may be classified according to the lengths of their sides.

- An *equilateral triangle* has three congruent sides.
- An *isosceles triangle* has at least two congruent sides.
- A *scalene triangle* has no two congruent sides.

A triangle may also be classified according to the measure of its angles.
- An *equiangular triangle* has three congruent angles.
- An *acute triangle* has all acute angles.
- A *right triangle* has one right angle.
- An *obtuse triangle* has one obtuse angle.

An *altitude* of a triangle is a segment from a vertex perpendicular to the opposite side (the base). Each triangle has three altitudes, and the lines that contain all three intersect at a point. The area of any triangle is $\frac{1}{2}$ of the product of the length of an altitude and the length of the base to that altitude:

$$A = \frac{1}{2}bh$$

An *angle bisector* of a triangle is a segment that bisects one of the angles of the triangle. The three angle bisectors of a triangle intersect at a point. This point is the center of a circle that is inscribed in the triangle.

A *median* of a triangle is a segment with one endpoint at a vertex and the other endpoint at the midpoint of the opposite side. The three medians of a triangle intersect at a point.

The three perpendicular bisectors of the sides of a triangle meet at a point. This point is the center of a circle circumscribed about the triangle.

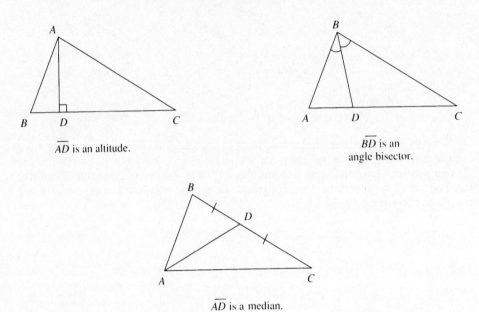

$\overline{AD}$ is an altitude.

$\overline{BD}$ is an angle bisector.

$\overline{AD}$ is a median.

The following are important properties of triangles:

1. Base angles of an isosceles triangle are congruent. (If two sides are the same length, then the angles opposite those sides are congruent.)

If $AB = BC$, then $m\angle A = m\angle C$.

2. The sum of the measures of the angles of any triangle is 180°. Therefore the sum of the measures of the angles of an n-sided polygon is $(n - 2)(180°)$.
3. The angles of an equilateral triangle are congruent. They each have measure 60°.
4. If two sides of a triangle are unequal, then the angles opposite those sides are unequal in the same order.
5. The sum of the lengths of any two sides of a triangle must be greater than the length of the third side.
6. The sum of the exterior angles of a triangle (taking one at each vertex) is 360°. An exterior angle is formed by extending one side of a triangle through the vertex.
7. If the sides of a right triangle have lengths a, b, and c (c is the length of the hypotenuse), then these numbers satisfy the Pythagorean Theorem:

$$a^2 + b^2 = c^2$$

8. If an altitude is drawn from the right angle of a right triangle, it separates the hypotenuse into two segments.

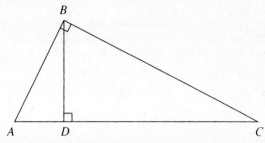

The following are true because of similarity of the three triangles: $\triangle ABC$, $\triangle ADB$, and $\triangle BDC$.

a. The altitude is the mean proportional between the two segments of the hypotenuse.

$$\frac{AD}{BD} = \frac{BD}{DC}$$

b. Either leg is the mean proportional between the hypotenuse and the nearer segment of the hypotenuse.

$$\frac{AD}{AB} = \frac{AB}{AC}, \qquad \frac{DC}{BC} = \frac{BC}{AC}$$

9. In an isosceles right triangle, the legs are congruent and the length of the hypotenuse is $\sqrt{2}$ times the length of a leg.

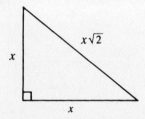

10. In a 30°-60°-90° right triangle, the length of the hypotenuse is twice the length of the shorter leg, and the length of the longer leg is $\sqrt{3}$ times the length of the shorter leg.

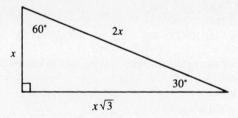

PRACTICE EXERCISES

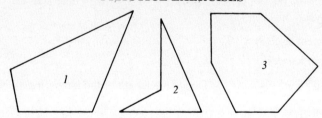

1. Which, if any, of the polygons in the diagram is (are) convex?
2. Which, if any, of the polygons is (are) concave?
3. What is the sum of the interior angles of the first polygon?
4. What is the sum of the exterior angles (taking one at each vertex) in the first polygon?

5. What is another name for a regular polygon having:
   a. four sides?
   b. three sides?
6. How many diagonals can be drawn in a polygon of seven sides?
7. In each case below, the length of one side of a 30°-60°-90° triangle is given. Find the lengths of the other two sides.

	Shorter Leg	Longer Leg	Hypotenuse
a.	8		
b.		3	
c.			12

8. In each case below, the length of one side of a 45°-45°-90° triangle is given. Find the length of the other sides.

	Legs	Hypotenuse
a.	9	
b.	$8\sqrt{3}$	
c.		16
d.		$5\sqrt{5}$

9. For right triangle *ABC*, in which altitude $\overline{CD}$ is drawn, find the indicated part for the given information in each question.

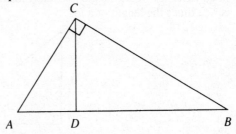

   a. *AD* = 4, *BD* = 12
      i. Find *AC*.
      ii. Find *CD*.
      iii. Find *BC*.
   b. *BC* = 12, *AB* = 13
      i. Find *AC*.
      ii. Find *BD*.
      iii. Find *CD*.

SOLUTIONS

1. Polygons 1 and 3 are convex.
2. Polygon 2 is concave.
3. The sum of the interior angles of any polygon is $(n - 2)180°$.
   $(4 - 2)180° = 2(180°) = 360°$
4. The sum of the exterior angles (taking one at each vertex) for any polygon is always 360°.
5. a. Square
   b. Equilateral triangle
6. In a polygon of 7 sides, four diagonals can be drawn from one vertex, then four more from an adjacent vertex, three from another, two from another, and finally 1 from the last vertex. So $4 + 4 + 3 + 2 + 1 = 14$ diagonals can be drawn in a polygon of seven sides.
7. a. Hypotenuse: $2(8) = 16$
      Longer leg: $8\sqrt{3}$
   b. Shorter leg: $\frac{3}{\sqrt{3}} = \sqrt{3}$ Divide the length of the longer leg by $\sqrt{3}$.
      Hypotenuse: $2\sqrt{3}$
   c. Shorter leg: 6 Divide by 2.
      Longer leg: $6\sqrt{3}$
8. a. Hypotenuse: $9\sqrt{2}$
   b. Hypotenuse: $(8\sqrt{3})\sqrt{2} = 8\sqrt{6}$
   c. Legs: $\frac{16}{\sqrt{2}} = 8\sqrt{2}$
   d. Legs: $\frac{5\sqrt{5}}{\sqrt{2}} = \frac{5\sqrt{10}}{2}$

9. a. i. *AC* is the mean proportional between the hypotenuse and the nearer segment of the hypotenuse.

$$\frac{4}{AC} = \frac{AC}{16}$$
$$AC^2 = 64$$
$$AC = 8$$

ii. *CD* is the mean proportional between the two segments of the hypotenuse.

$$\frac{4}{CD} = \frac{CD}{12}$$
$$CD^2 = 48$$
$$CD = \sqrt{48} = 4\sqrt{3}$$

iii. $$\frac{12}{BC} = \frac{BC}{16}$$
$$BC^2 = 192$$
$$BC = \sqrt{192} = 8\sqrt{3}$$

b. i. The Pythagorean Theorem applies.

$$AC^2 + 12^2 = 13^2$$
$$AC^2 + 144 = 169$$
$$AC^2 = 25$$
$$AC = 5$$

ii. 12 is the mean proportional between *BD* and 13.

$$\frac{BD}{12} = \frac{12}{13}$$
$$13BD = 144$$
$$BD = \frac{144}{3} = 11\frac{1}{13}$$

iii. Since $BD = \frac{144}{13}$, $AD = \frac{25}{13}$, and *CD* is the mean proportional between the two segments of the hypotenuse.

$$\frac{\frac{25}{13}}{CD} = \frac{CD}{\frac{144}{13}}$$

$$CD^2 = \frac{25}{13} \cdot \frac{144}{13}$$

$$CD = \frac{5 \cdot 12}{13} = \frac{60}{13} = 4\frac{8}{13}$$

Quadrilaterals

A *quadrilateral* is a polygon with four sides. The following are definitions of certain quadrilaterals with special characteristics:

• A *trapezoid* has one pair of opposite sides parallel.

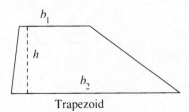

Trapezoid

- A *parallelogram* has both pairs of opposite sides parallel.

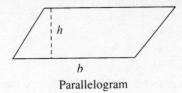

Parallelogram

- A *rectangle* is a parallelogram with a right angle (and, hence, four right angles).

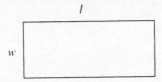

Rectangle

- A *square* is an equilateral rectangle or a regular quadrilateral.

Square

- A *rhombus* is an equilateral parallelogram.

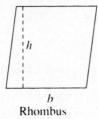

Rhombus

Areas of Quadrilaterals

The following are area formulas for the quadrilaterals defined above:

Trapezoid: $A = \frac{1}{2}h(b_1 + b_2)$

Parallelogram: $A = hb$

Rectangle: $A = lw$

Square: $A = s^2$

Rhombus: $A = hb = \frac{1}{2}$ (product of diagonals)

The diagonals of a parallelogram bisect each other, and the diagonals of a rhombus are perpendicular bisectors of each other.

PRACTICE EXERCISES

State whether each of the following is true or false:
1. All squares are rectangles.
2. All rhombuses are squares.
3. All rectangles are quadrilaterals.
4. All trapezoids are polygons.
5. All parallelograms are rhombuses.
6.

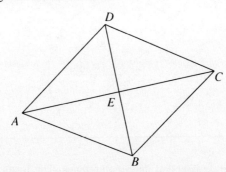

Given: Rhombus $ABCD$, length of $\overline{DB}$ = 8, length of $\overline{AC}$ = 12.

Find: a. DE.
     b. AE.
     c. Area of rhombus $ABCD$.
     d. DC.

7.

Given: Trapezoid $ABCD$, $\overline{AB} \parallel \overline{DC}$, $\overline{AD} \perp \overline{DC}$, $AB = 5$, $DC = 8$, $AD = 3$.

Find: a. Area of trapezoid $ABCD$.
     b. Perimeter of trapezoid $ABCD$.

SOLUTIONS

1. True
2. False
3. True
4. True
5. False
6.   a. $DE = \dfrac{1}{2}DB = 4$

    b. $AE = 6$

    c. Area of rhombus $= \dfrac{1}{2}$ (product of diagonals)

$$= \dfrac{1}{2}(8)(12) = 48$$

    d. $DC = \sqrt{4^2 + 6^2}\ = \sqrt{16 + 36} = \sqrt{52} = 2\sqrt{13}$

7.   a. Area of trapezoid $= \dfrac{1}{2}h\,(b_1 + b_2)$

$$= \dfrac{1}{2}(3)(5 + 8)$$

$$= \dfrac{39}{2} = 19\dfrac{1}{2}$$

    b. Since the triangular portion of the trapezoid is a 45°–45°–90° triangle, the length of the slanted side is $3\sqrt{2}$, and the perimeter is
$5 + 3 + 8 + 3\sqrt{2} = 16 + 3\sqrt{2}$

Circles

A *circle* is the set of points in a plane that are a given fixed distance from a given point. The given distance is called the *radius* and the fixed point is the *center.* A segment whose endpoints are on the circle is called a *chord.* A chord that also contains the center is a *diameter* (the longest chord). A line that contains a chord of a circle is a *secant line.* A line that contains only one point of a circle is a *tangent line.*

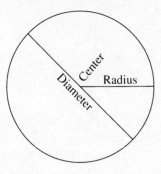

The length around a circle is called its *circumference.* The formula for the circumference is

$$C = \pi d \ (\pi \text{ times diameter}) \qquad \text{or} \qquad C = 2 \pi r \ (2\pi \text{ times radius})$$

The area formula for a circle is

$$A = \pi r^2$$

A *central angle* is an angle with its vertex at the center of a circle. The measure of a central angle is the same as the measure of its intercepted arc. Thus there are 360° of arc in a circle.

An *inscribed angle* is an angle formed by two chords of a circle; its vertex is on the circle. The measure of an inscribed angle is one-half the measure of its intercepted arc.

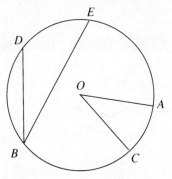

Angle *AOC* is a central angle.
Angle *DBE* is inscribed.

If two chords intersect inside a circle, the measures of the angles formed are one half of the sum of the measures of the intercepted arcs.

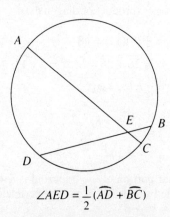

$$\angle AED = \frac{1}{2}(\overarc{AD} + \overarc{BC})$$

If secant lines intersect outside a circle, the measure of the angle formed is one half of the difference of the measures of the intercepted arcs.

If a secant and a tangent line intersect outside a circle, the measure of the angle formed is one half of the difference of the measures of the intercepted arcs.

If two tangent lines intersect outside a circle, the measure of the angle formed is one half of the difference of the measures of the intercepted arcs.

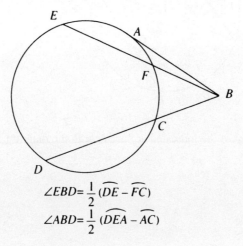

$$\angle EBD = \frac{1}{2}(\widehat{DE} - \widehat{FC})$$
$$\angle ABD = \frac{1}{2}(\widehat{DEA} - \widehat{AC})$$

The measure of the angle formed by a tangent line and a chord from the point of tangency is one half of the measure of the intercepted arc.

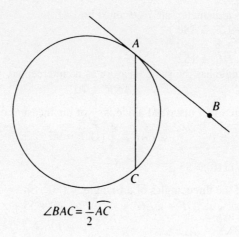

$$\angle BAC = \frac{1}{2}\widehat{AC}$$

Concentric circles are circles in a plane that have the same center.

PRACTICE EXERCISES

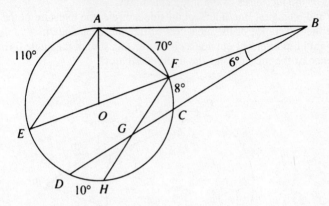

Find the measure of the indicated arc or angle in the diagram.

1. $\overset{\frown}{DE}$
2. $\overset{\frown}{DC}$
3. $\angle AOF$
4. $\angle EAF$
5. $\angle EFA$
6. $\angle OAF$
7. $\angle ABE$
8. $\angle BAF$
9. $\angle FGC$

SOLUTIONS

1. $6 \overset{\circ}{=} \dfrac{1}{2}(\overset{\frown}{DE} - 8)$

    $12 \overset{\circ}{=} \overset{\frown}{DE} - 8$

    $\overset{\frown}{DE} \overset{\circ}{=} 20$

2. Since $\overline{EF}$ is a diameter, arc EDF must be $180°$.

    $\overset{\frown}{DE} + \overset{\frown}{DC} + \overset{\frown}{CF} \overset{\circ}{=} 180$

    $20 + \overset{\frown}{DC} + 8 \overset{\circ}{=} 180$

    $\overset{\frown}{DC} \overset{\circ}{=} 152$

3. A central angle has the same measure as its intercepted arc.

    $\angle AOF \overset{\circ}{=} 70$

4. The measure of an inscribed angle is $\dfrac{1}{2}$ of the measure of the intercepted arc.

    $\angle EAF \overset{\circ}{=} \dfrac{1}{2}(180) = 90$

5. $\angle EFA \overset{\circ}{=} \dfrac{1}{2}(110) = 55$

6. The sum of the three angles of a triangle is $180°$. So

    $\angle AOF + \angle EFA + \angle OAF \overset{\circ}{=} 70 + 55 + \angle OAF$

    $\overset{\circ}{=} 125 + \angle OAF \overset{\circ}{=} 180$

    $\angle OAF \overset{\circ}{=} 55$

7. The measure of an angle formed by a tangent and a secant line is $\dfrac{1}{2}$ of the difference of the measures of the intercepted arcs.

    $\angle ABE \overset{\circ}{=} \dfrac{1}{2}(110 - 70) = \dfrac{1}{2}(40) = 20$

8. The measure of an angle formed by a tangent and a chord intersecting at the point of tangency is $\dfrac{1}{2}$ of the measure of the intercepted arc.

    $\angle BAF \overset{\circ}{=} \dfrac{1}{2}(70) = 35$

9. The measure of an angle formed by the intersection of two chords in a circle is $\dfrac{1}{2}$ of the sum of the measures of the intercepted arcs.

    $\angle FGC \overset{\circ}{=} \dfrac{1}{2}(8 + 10) = \dfrac{1}{2}(18) = 9$

Relationships among Chords, Secants, and Tangents

If two chords intersect in a circle, the product of the lengths of the segments of one chord is equal to the product of the lengths of the segments of the other.

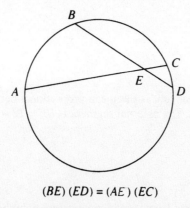

$$(BE)(ED) = (AE)(EC)$$

If a tangent and a secant intersect outside a circle, the length of the tangent is the mean proportional between the length of the secant and the length of its external segment.

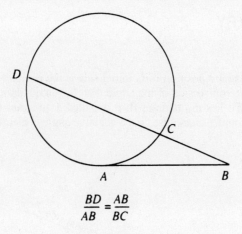

$$\frac{BD}{AB} = \frac{AB}{BC}$$

If two secants intersect outside a circle, the product of the length of one secant and the length of its external segment equals the product of the length of the other secant and the length of its external segment.

PRACTICE EXERCISES

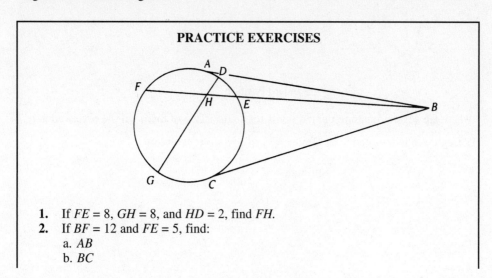

1. If $FE = 8$, $GH = 8$, and $HD = 2$, find FH.
2. If $BF = 12$ and $FE = 5$, find:
   a. AB
   b. BC

SOLUTIONS

1. Let the length of one segment of chord $\overline{FE}$ be x; then the other segment is $8 - x$. The product of the lengths of the segments of one chord equals the product of the lengths of the segments of the other.

$x(8 - x) = 8(2)$
$8x - x^2 = 16$
$0 = x^2 - 8x + 16$
$0 = (x - 4)^2$
$x - 4 = 0$
$x = 4$ So $FH = 4$.

2. a. The length of a tangent is the mean proportional between a secant and its external segment. The external segment is $BE = 12 - 5 = 7$.

$$\frac{12}{AB} = \frac{AB}{7}$$

$AB^2 = 84$

$AB = \sqrt{84} = 2\sqrt{21}$

b. Tangents to a circle from a common external point have the same length.
$AB = BC = 2\sqrt{21}$

TRIGONOMETRY

Angles

An angle is in standard position if its initial side is the positive x-axis and the vertex is at the origin. If the terminal side of the angle then lies in quadrant I, the angle is called a quadrant I angle: if it lies in quadrant II, it is called a quadrant II angle; etc. A positive angle is measured counter-clockwise, and a negative angle is measured clockwise from the positive x-axis.

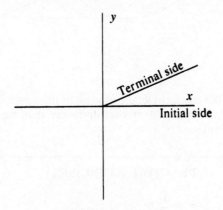

Standard Position

There are several measurement systems for angles. Two of them will be reviewed here.

1. Degree-minute-second: 1 degree $= 1° = \dfrac{1}{360}$ of a revolution

$$1 \text{ minute} = 1' = \frac{1}{60}°$$

$$1 \text{ second} = 1'' = \frac{1}{60}'$$

2. Radians: 1 radian is the central angle subtended by an arc equal in length to the radius of the circle.

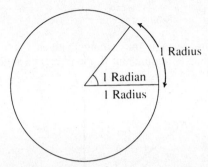

The formula for the circumference of a circle, $C = 2\pi r$, shows that there are 2π radii in the circumference of a circle. Therefore there are 2π radians in one complete revolution.

2π radians = 360°   (The equal sign is used here to mean that the two numbers measure the same angle.)

Therefore:

$$\pi \text{ radians} = 180°$$
$$\frac{\pi}{2} \text{ radians} = 90°$$
$$\frac{\pi}{3} \text{ radians} = 60°$$
$$\frac{\pi}{4} \text{ radians} = 45°$$
$$\frac{\pi}{6} \text{ radians} = 30°$$

Most angles of interest are multiples of these five, so these should be memorized.

Generally, to convert an angle measurement from degrees to radians, multiply the number of degrees by $\frac{\pi}{180}$. The measurement of an angle in radians is commonly expressed in terms of π. ($1° = \frac{\pi}{180}$ radians.)

To convert an angle measurement from radians to degrees, multiply the number of radians by $\frac{180}{\pi}$. The π normally cancels. (1 radian = $\frac{180°}{\pi}$.)

Any statement made below, even though it may be phrased with the angles measured in degrees, will be true also if the angles are measured in radians.

If two different angles in standard position have the same terminal side, the angles are called *coterminal*. Coterminal angles can be found by adding or subtracting multiples of 360° or 2π to or from the original angle.

The acute angle formed by the terminal side of the angle and the nearer portion of the *x*-axis is called the *reference* angle.

Examples:
Convert from degree measure to radian measure.

1. $150° = 150\left(\frac{\pi}{180}\right) \text{ radians} = \frac{5\pi}{6} \text{ radians}$

2. $-240° = -240\left(\frac{\pi}{180}\right) \text{ radians} = \frac{-4\pi}{3} \text{ radians}$

Convert from radian measure to degree measure.

3. $\frac{11\pi}{6} \text{ radians} = \frac{11\pi}{6}\left(\frac{180}{\pi}\right)° = 330°$

4. $\frac{-3\pi}{4} \text{ radians} = \frac{-3\pi}{4}\left(\frac{180}{\pi}\right)° = -135°$

Find the smallest positive angle that is coterminal with each of the following:

5. 832° $832° - 2(360)° = 832° - 720° - 112°$

6. -1058° $-1058° + 3(360)° = -1058° + 1080° = 22°$

7. $\dfrac{23\pi}{4}$ $\dfrac{23\pi}{4} - 2(2\pi) = \dfrac{23\pi}{4} - \dfrac{16\pi}{4} = \dfrac{7\pi}{4}$

8. $\dfrac{-11\,\pi}{3}$ $\dfrac{-11\pi}{3} + 2(2\pi) = \dfrac{-11\pi}{3} + \dfrac{12\pi}{3} = \dfrac{\pi}{3}$

Determine the reference angle for each angle given.

9. 140°   For an angle, θ, in quadrant II, the reference angle is 180° − θ.
    180° − 140° = 40°

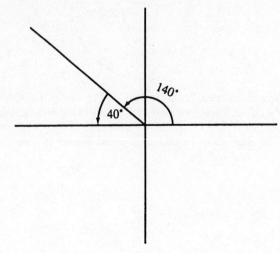

10. 215°   For an angle, θ, in quadrant III, the reference angle is θ − 180°.
    215° − 180° = 35°

11. 307°   For an angle, θ, in quadrant IV, the reference angle is 360° − θ.
    360° − 307° = 53°

12. $\dfrac{-7\pi}{3}$ If necessary, first find the smallest positive angle that is coterminal with the original angle. Then use the rules above with radians instead of degrees.

$$\dfrac{-7\pi}{3} + 2(2\pi) = \dfrac{-7\pi}{3} + \dfrac{12\pi}{3} = \dfrac{5\pi}{3} \text{ (quad. IV)}$$

Reference angle is $2\pi - \dfrac{5\pi}{3} = \dfrac{6\pi}{3} - \dfrac{5\pi}{3} = \dfrac{\pi}{3}$.

PRACTICE EXERCISES

Convert from degree measure to radian measure.
1. 210°
2. −540°

Convert from radian measure to degree measure.
3. $\dfrac{5\pi}{4}$
4. $\dfrac{7\pi}{9}$

Find: a. The smallest positive angle that is coterminal with the given angle
     b. The reference angle
5. 478°
6. −815°
7. $\dfrac{11\pi}{3}$
8. $\dfrac{-17\pi}{6}$

SOLUTIONS

1. $210\left(\dfrac{\pi}{180}\right) = \dfrac{7\pi}{6}$

2. $-540\left(\dfrac{\pi}{180}\right) = -3\pi$

3. $\dfrac{5\pi}{4}\left(\dfrac{180}{\pi}\right) = 225$

4. $\dfrac{7\pi}{9}\left(\dfrac{180}{\pi}\right) = 140$

5. a. $478 - 360 = 118$
   $118°$ is in quad. II.
   b. $180 - 118 = 62$

6. a. $-815 + 3(360) = -815 + 1080 = 265$
   $265°$ is in quad. III.
   b. $265 - 180 = 85$

7. a. $\dfrac{11\pi}{3} - 2\pi = \dfrac{11\pi}{3} - \dfrac{6\pi}{3} = \dfrac{5\pi}{3}$
   $\dfrac{5\pi}{3}$ is in quad. IV.

   b. $2\pi - \dfrac{5\pi}{3} = \dfrac{6\pi}{3} - \dfrac{5\pi}{3} = \dfrac{\pi}{3}$

8. a. $\dfrac{-17\pi}{6} + 2(2\pi) = \dfrac{-17\pi}{6} + \dfrac{24\pi}{6} = \dfrac{7\pi}{6}$
   $\dfrac{7\pi}{6}$ is in quad. III.

   b. $\dfrac{7\pi}{6} - \pi = \dfrac{\pi}{6}$

Definitions of Trigonometric Functions

Choose a point, (x, y), on the terminal side of an angle, θ, in standard position. The distance from the origin is $r = \sqrt{x^2 + y^2}$

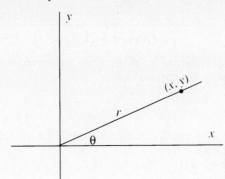

$\sin \theta = \dfrac{y}{r}$		Sine
$\cos \theta = \dfrac{x}{r}$		Cosine
$\tan \theta = \dfrac{y}{x},$	$x \neq 0, \theta \neq 90° \pm 180n°$	Tangent
$\csc \theta = \dfrac{r}{y},$	$y \neq 0, \theta \neq \pm 180n°$	Cosecant
$\sec \theta = \dfrac{r}{x},$	$x \neq 0, \theta \neq 90° \pm 180n°$	Secant
$\cot \theta = \dfrac{x}{y},$	$y \neq 0, \theta \neq \pm 180n°$	Cotangent

In each case above, $n = 0, 1, 2, \ldots.$

For an angle, θ, in quadrant I, both of the coordinates of a point on the terminal side of θ are positive; and since r is always positive, all of the six trigonometric functions have positive values.

In quadrant II the value of x is negative and both y and r are positive, so the values of the functions sine and cosecant are positive while the other four are negative.

In quadrant III the values of both x and y are negative, so the values of the tangent and cotangent are positive while the other four are negative.

In quadrant IV the values of x and r are positive and y is negative, so the values of the functions cosine and secant are positive while the other four are negative.

This information should be memorized for the four quadrants:

I:	**A**ll positive.
II:	**S**ine and cosecant positive, others negative.
III:	**T**angent and cotangent positive, others negative.
IV:	**C**osine and secant positive, others negative.

(ASTC is a helpful mnemonic aid.)

The domains of the six trigonometric functions are sets of angles in standard position.

Domain of sine: All angles

Domain of cosine: All angles

Domain of tangent: All angles except those coterminal with 90° or 270°

Domain of cosecant: All angles except those coterminal with 0° or 180°

Domain of secant: Same as for tangent

Domain of cotangent: Same as for cosecant

The ranges of the trigonometric functions are subsets of real numbers.

Range of sine: $\{y \mid -1 \le y \le 1\}$

Range of cosine: $\{y \mid -1 \le y \le 1\}$

Range of tangent: R(All real numbers)

Range of secant: $\{y \mid y \le -1 \text{ or } y \ge 1\}$

Range of cosecant: Same as for secant

Range of cotangent: R

The following useful rule can easily be derived:

A function of any angle is equal to ± the same function of the reference angle. The sign of the function value is determined by ASTC.

PRACTICE EXERCISES

Name the six trigonometric function values for the angle θ in standard position with the given point on the terminal side.

1. $(-3, 4)$

2. $(-2, -6)$

Name the quadrant in which the angle θ must lie for the following to be true:

3. $\sin \theta > 0$ and $\tan \theta < 0$

4. $\cos \theta < 0$ and $\csc > 0$

5. $\cot \theta > 0$ and $\sec \theta < 0$

6. $\sec \theta > 0$ and $\sin \theta < 0$

Find the remaining five function values, given the following information:

7. $\tan \theta = \dfrac{1}{2}$ and $\sin \theta$ is negative

8. $\sec \theta = \dfrac{-\sqrt{2}}{5}$ and $\tan \theta < 0$

9. $\sin \theta = \dfrac{-\sqrt{3}}{5}$ and $\cos \theta > 0$

10. Express each function as a function of its reference angle.
    a. sin 223°
    b. tan (–57°)
    c. $\cos \dfrac{5\pi}{6}$
    d. sec 680°

SOLUTIONS

1. First $r = \sqrt{(-3)^2 + 4^2} = \sqrt{25} = 5$

   $\sin \theta = \dfrac{4}{5} \qquad \csc \theta = \dfrac{5}{4}$

   $\cos \theta = \dfrac{-3}{5} \qquad \sec \theta = \dfrac{-5}{3}$

   $\tan \theta = \dfrac{-4}{3} \qquad \cot \theta = \dfrac{-3}{4}$

2. $r = \sqrt{(-2)^2 + (-6)^2} = \sqrt{40} = 2\sqrt{10}$

   $\sin \theta = \dfrac{-6}{2\sqrt{10}} = \dfrac{-3\sqrt{10}}{10}$

   $\cos \theta = \dfrac{-2}{2\sqrt{10}} = \dfrac{-\sqrt{10}}{10}$

   $\tan \theta = \dfrac{-6}{-2} = 3$

   $\csc \theta = \dfrac{2\sqrt{10}}{-6} = \dfrac{-\sqrt{10}}{3}$

   $\sec \theta = \dfrac{-2\sqrt{10}}{2} = -\sqrt{10}$

   $\cot \theta = \dfrac{-2}{-6} = \dfrac{1}{3}$

3. ASTC indicates that the sine is positive in quads.
   I and II, while the tangent is negative in quads.
   II and IV. Both are true only in quad. II.

4. $\cos \theta < 0$ in II and III
   $\csc \theta >$ in I and II
   Both are true only in quad. II.

5. $\cot \theta > 0$ in I and III
   $\sec \theta < 0$ in II and III
   Both are true only in quad. III.

6. $\sec \theta > 0$ in I and IV
   $\sin \theta < 0$ in III and IV
   Both are true only in quad. IV.

7. Since $\tan \theta = \dfrac{1}{2}$ (>0) and $\sin \theta < 0$, angle θ must be in quad. III. And since

   $$\tan \theta = \frac{y}{x} = \frac{1}{2} = \frac{-1}{-2}$$

   choose a point (–2, –1) on the terminal side of θ.

   $$r = \sqrt{2^2 + 1^2} = \sqrt{5}$$

   $\sin \theta = \dfrac{-1}{\sqrt{5}} = \dfrac{-\sqrt{5}}{5}$

   $\cos \theta = \dfrac{-2}{\sqrt{5}} = \dfrac{-2\sqrt{5}}{5}$

   $\tan \theta$ is given.

   $\csc \theta = \dfrac{\sqrt{5}}{-1} = -\sqrt{5}$

   $\sec \theta = \dfrac{-\sqrt{5}}{2}$

   $\cot \theta = \dfrac{2}{1} = 2$

8. The secant is given as $\dfrac{-\sqrt{2}}{5}$, which is not in the range of the secant function. There is no angle that satisfies the conditions given; therefore there are no function values.

9. Here $\sin \theta = \dfrac{-\sqrt{3}}{5}$ (< 0) and $\cos \theta > 0$, which occurs only in quad. IV. Since

$$\sin \theta = \frac{y}{r} = \frac{-\sqrt{3}}{5}$$

choose a point $(x, -\sqrt{3})$ with $r = 5$. Substitute into the distance formula to find x:

$$5 = \sqrt{x^2 + (-\sqrt{3})^2} = \sqrt{x^2 + 3}$$
$$25 = x^2 + 3$$
$$22 = x^2$$
$$\pm \sqrt{22} = x$$

Choose the positive sign because the point is in quad. IV: $x = \sqrt{22}$.
$\sin \theta$ is given.

$$\cos \theta = \frac{\sqrt{22}}{5}$$

$$\tan \theta = \frac{-\sqrt{3}}{\sqrt{22}} = \frac{-\sqrt{66}}{22}$$

$$\csc \theta = \frac{5}{-\sqrt{3}} = \frac{-5\sqrt{3}}{3}$$

$$\sec \theta = \frac{5}{\sqrt{22}} = \frac{5\sqrt{22}}{22}$$

$$\cot \theta = \frac{\sqrt{22}}{-\sqrt{3}} = \frac{-\sqrt{66}}{3}$$

10. a. 233° is in quad. III and the reference angle is 233 − 180 = 53. So

$$\sin 233° = -\sin 53°$$

b. −57° is in quad. IV and the reference angle is 57°. So

$$\tan(-57°) = -\tan 57°$$

c. $\dfrac{5\pi}{6}$ is in quad. II and the reference angle is $\pi - \dfrac{5\pi}{6} = \dfrac{\pi}{6}$. So

$$\cos \frac{5\pi}{6} = -\cos \frac{\pi}{6}$$

d. 680° is coterminal with 320°, which is in quad. IV and its reference angle is 360 − 320 = 40. So

$$\sec 680° = \sec 40°$$

Trigonometric Function Values of Special Angles

The values of the trigonometric functions in the following table occur frequently enough that they should be memorized.

Angle	sin	cos	tan
0°	0	1	0
30°	$\dfrac{1}{2}$	$\dfrac{\sqrt{3}}{2}$	$\dfrac{\sqrt{3}}{3}$
45°	$\dfrac{\sqrt{2}}{2}$	$\dfrac{\sqrt{2}}{2}$	1
60°	$\dfrac{\sqrt{3}}{2}$	$\dfrac{1}{2}$	$\sqrt{3}$
90°	1	0	undef.

The function values of angles in other quadrants for which the reference angle is 30°, 45°, or 60° may be found by using the rule that a function of any angle is equal to ± the same function of the reference angle, the sign being determined by ASTC.

Here are some examples:

- $\tan 240° = \tan 60° = \sqrt{3}$
- $\sin 330° = -\sin 30° = \dfrac{-1}{2}$
- $\cos(-210°) = -\cos 30° = \dfrac{-\sqrt{3}}{2}$

PRACTICE EXERCISES

Determine each function value.

1. $\sin 225°$
2. $\tan 480°$
3. $\sec(-300°)$
4. $\cos \dfrac{11\pi}{6}$
5. $\sin 270°$

SOLUTIONS

1. $\sin 225° = -\sin 45° = \dfrac{-\sqrt{2}}{2}$

2. $\tan 480° \quad = \tan 120° \quad$ 120° is the smallest positive coterminal angle.
   $= -\tan 60° \quad$ 60° is the reference angle.
   $= -\sqrt{3}$

3. $\sec(-300°) = \sec 60° \quad$ 60° is the smallest positive coterminal angle and the reference angle.

   $= \dfrac{1}{\cos 60°}$

   $= \dfrac{1}{\dfrac{1}{2}}$

   $= 2$

4. $\cos \dfrac{11\pi}{6} = \cos \dfrac{\pi}{6}$

   $= \dfrac{\sqrt{3}}{2} \quad$ Since $\dfrac{\pi}{6} = 30°$.

5. Since **270°** is not in a quadrant, the rule does not apply. Instead, choose a point on the terminal side of 270°.

   The point $(0, -1)$ is on the terminal side and $r = 1$. So

   $$\sin 270° = \frac{y}{r} = \frac{-1}{1} = -1$$

Application

Right triangles may be solved by trigonometric means by interpreting the definitions as ratios of the lengths of the sides.

$$\sin A = \frac{\text{length of side opposite } A}{\text{length of hypotenuse}} = \frac{\text{opp}}{\text{hyp}}$$

$$\cos A = \frac{\text{length of side adjacent to } A}{\text{length of hypotenuse}} = \frac{\text{adj}}{\text{hyp}}$$

$$\tan A = \frac{\text{opp}}{\text{adj}}$$

$$\csc A = \frac{\text{hyp}}{\text{opp}}$$

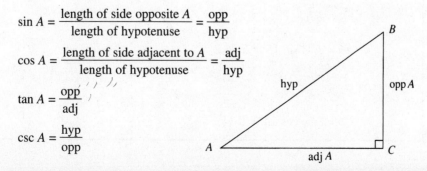

$$\sec A = \frac{\text{hyp}}{\text{adj}}$$

$$\cot A = \frac{\text{adj}}{\text{opp}}$$

Since the acute angles of a right triangle are always complementary, the following rule applies:

> Cofunctions of complementary angles are equal.

Here are some examples:

- $\sin 83° = \cos (90 - 83)° = \cos 7°$

- $\tan 27° = \cot (90 - 27)° = \cot 63°$

- $\csc \dfrac{\pi}{5} = \sec \left(\dfrac{\pi}{2} - \dfrac{\pi}{5}\right) = \sec\dfrac{3\pi}{10}$

Given right triangle ABC with right angle C, $\angle B = 33°$, and side $b = 12.5$. (The sides of a triangle are labeled with the lower case letter of the angle opposite.)

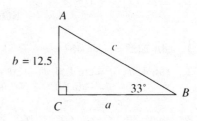

- $\angle A = (90 - 33)° = 57°$

- $\tan 33° = \dfrac{\text{opp}}{\text{adj}} = \dfrac{12.5}{a}$

   $a = \dfrac{12.5}{\tan 33°} = 19.2$ (by calculator)

- $\sin 33° = \dfrac{\text{opp}}{\text{hyp}} = \dfrac{12.5}{c}$

   $c = \dfrac{12.5}{\sin 33°} = 23.0$ (by calculator)

A scientific calculator is indispensable in trigonometry.

PRACTICE EXERCISE

Solve right triangle ABC using the following information: Given right angle C, $\angle A = 15°$ and side $c = 8.74$.

SOLUTION

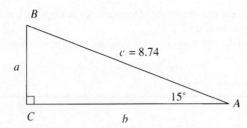

$\angle B = (90 - 15)° = 75°$

$\sin 15° = \dfrac{a}{8.74}$

$a = 8.74 \sin 15° = 2.26$

$\cos 15° = \dfrac{b}{8.74}$

$b = 8.74 \cos 15° = 8.44$

Graphs

Each of the trigonometric functions is periodic. A *periodic function f* is any function for which the following is true for some number p:

$$f(x + p) = f(x) \text{ for all } x \text{ in the domain}$$

If p is the smallest number for which this equation is true, then p is called the *period*.

Since $\sin(\theta + 2\pi) = \sin\theta$:

$\cos(\theta + 2\pi) = \cos\theta$,   These all show that the functions are periodic with period 2π.

$\csc(\theta + 2\pi) = \csc\theta$,

$\sec(\theta + 2\pi) = \sec\theta$.

Since $\tan(\theta + \pi) = \tan\theta$:   The period of tangent and cotangent is π.

$\cot(\theta + \pi) = \cot\theta$.

The following are the graphs of one period of each trigonometric function:

$y = \sin x$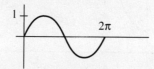

$y = \cos x$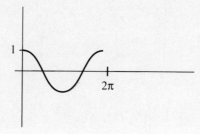

$y = \tan x$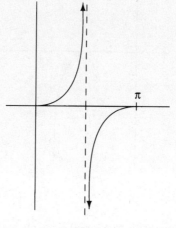

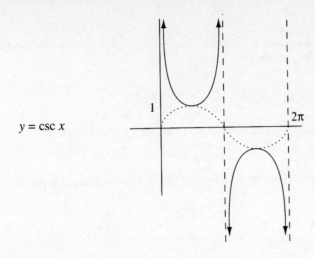

$y = \csc x$

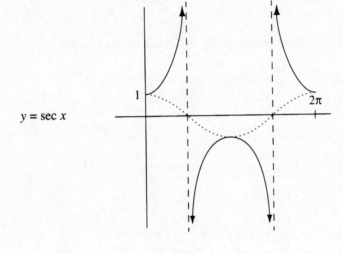

$y = \sec x$

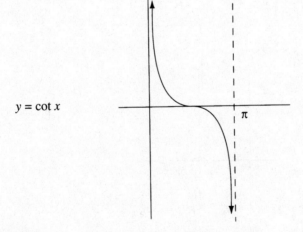

$y = \cot x$

Identities

An *identity* is an equation that is true for all elements in the domains for which the functions involved are defined. There are many identities in trigonometry, and the following
list should be memorized:

- *Reciprocal identities*

$$\sin x = \frac{1}{\csc x} \qquad \csc x = \frac{1}{\sin x}$$

$$\cos x = \frac{1}{\sec x} \qquad \sec x = \frac{1}{\cos x}$$

$$\tan x = \frac{1}{\cot x} \qquad \cot x = \frac{1}{\tan x}$$

- *Quotient identities*

$$\tan x = \frac{\sin x}{\cos x} \qquad \cot x = \frac{\cos y}{\sin x}$$

- *Pythagorean identities*

$$\sin^2 x + \cos^2 x = 1 \qquad \text{Note that } \sin^2 x = (\sin x)^2.$$
$$\tan^2 x + 1 = \sec^2 x$$
$$1 + \cot^2 x = \csc^2 x$$

- *Sum and difference identities*

($\pm$ and $\mp$ are different; if one is $-$, the other is $+$.)
$$\cos(A \pm B) = \cos A \cos B \mp \sin A \sin B$$
$$\sin(A \pm B) = \sin A \cos B \pm \sin B \cos A$$
$$\tan(A \pm B) = \frac{\tan A \pm \tan B}{1 \mp \tan A \tan B}$$

- *Double-angle identities*

$$\sin 2A = 2 \sin A \cos A$$
$$\cos 2A = \cos^2 A - \sin^2 A = 2 \cos^2 A - 1 = 1 - 2 \sin^2 A$$
$$\tan 2A = \frac{2 \tan A}{1 - \tan^2 A}$$

- *Half-angle identities*

$$\sin \frac{A}{2} = \pm \sqrt{\frac{1 - \cos A}{2}}$$

$$\cos \frac{A}{2} = \pm \sqrt{\frac{1 + \cos A}{2}}$$

$$\tan \frac{A}{2} = \pm \sqrt{\frac{1 - \cos A}{1 + \cos A}} = \frac{\sin A}{1 + \cos A} = \frac{1 - \cos A}{\sin A}$$

PRACTICE EXERCISES

Use the identities above to find each function value.
1. $\cos 15°$
2. $\tan 75°$
3. $\sin 195°$
4. $\cos \dfrac{\pi}{8}$
5. $\sin 2A$, given that $\sin A = \dfrac{3}{4}$ and a is in quadrant I.
6. $\tan 2A$, given that $\sin A = \dfrac{-2}{5}$ and A is in quadrant III.

SOLUTIONS

1. Find two angles whose difference is 15° (45° and 30° will do).
$$\mathbf{\cos 15°} = \cos(45 - 30)°$$
$$= \cos 45 \cos 30 + \sin 45 \sin 30$$
$$= \left(\frac{\sqrt{2}}{2}\right)\left(\frac{\sqrt{3}}{2}\right) + \left(\frac{\sqrt{2}}{2}\right)\left(\frac{1}{2}\right)$$
$$= \frac{\sqrt{6}}{4} + \frac{\sqrt{2}}{4}$$
$$= \frac{\sqrt{6} + \sqrt{2}}{4}$$

2. Several choices are possible. Choose the half-angle tangent formula.

$$\tan 75° = \tan \frac{1}{2}(150°) = \frac{\sin 150°}{1 + \cos 150°}$$

$$= \frac{\dfrac{1}{2}}{1 + \dfrac{-\sqrt{3}}{2}}$$

$$= \frac{1}{2 - \sqrt{3}} = 2 + \sqrt{3}$$

3. $\sin 195° = \sin(150 + 45)°$

$$= \sin 150 \cos 45 + \sin 45 \cos 150$$

$$= \left(\frac{1}{2}\right)\left(\frac{\sqrt{2}}{2}\right) + \left(\frac{\sqrt{2}}{2}\right)\left(\frac{-\sqrt{3}}{2}\right)$$

$$= \frac{\sqrt{2}}{4} + \frac{-\sqrt{6}}{4} = \frac{\sqrt{2} - \sqrt{6}}{4}$$

4. $\cos \dfrac{\pi}{8} = \cos \dfrac{\left(\dfrac{\pi}{4}\right)}{2} = \dfrac{\pm\sqrt{1 + \cos\left(\dfrac{\pi}{4}\right)}}{2}$

$$= \pm\sqrt{\frac{1 + \dfrac{\sqrt{2}}{2}}{2}}$$

$$= \pm\sqrt{\frac{2 + \sqrt{2}}{4}} \quad \text{Choose the positive sign because } \frac{\pi}{8} \text{ is in quad. I.}$$

$$= \frac{\sqrt{2 + \sqrt{2}}}{2}$$

5. Since $\sin A = \dfrac{3}{4}$ and A is in quad. I,

$$\sin^2 A + \cos^2 A = 1$$

$$\left(\frac{3}{4}\right)^2 + \cos^2 A = 1$$

$$\frac{9}{16} + \cos^2 A = 1$$

$$\cos^2 A = \frac{7}{16}$$

$$\cos A = \frac{\sqrt{7}}{4} \quad \text{Choose the positive sign.}$$

So

$$\sin 2A = 2 \sin A \cos A = 2\left(\frac{3}{4}\right)\left(\frac{\sqrt{7}}{4}\right) = \frac{3\sqrt{7}}{8}.$$

6. Since $\sin A = \dfrac{-2}{5}$ and A is in quad. III,

$$\cos A = -\sqrt{1 - \sin^2 A}$$

$$= -\sqrt{1 - \left(\frac{-2}{5}\right)^2}$$

$$= -\sqrt{1 - \frac{4}{25}} = -\sqrt{\frac{21}{25}} = \frac{-\sqrt{21}}{5}$$

So

$$\tan A = \frac{\sin A}{\cos a} = \frac{\dfrac{-2}{5}}{\dfrac{-\sqrt{21}}{5}} = \frac{2}{\sqrt{21}} = \frac{2\sqrt{21}}{21}$$

Then

$$\tan 2A = \frac{2 \tan A}{1 - \tan^2 A}$$

$$= \frac{2\left(\dfrac{2\sqrt{21}}{21}\right)}{1 - \left(\dfrac{2\sqrt{21}}{21}\right)^2}$$

$$= \frac{\dfrac{4\sqrt{21}}{21}}{1 - \dfrac{4}{21}} = \frac{4\sqrt{21}}{17}$$

Inverse Trigonometric Functions

Since all six trigonometric functions are not one-to-one, inverse functions do not exist for them without modifications. The usual plan is to restrict the domain of each function to a portion upon which it is one-to-one, so that the inverse will be a function. The inverses for sine, cosine, and tangent will be reviewed. Only degree measurements will be used here, but all statements could be made with radian measures as well.

● The notation arcsin x is the same as $\sin^{-1}x$.

On the interval $\{x \mid -90° \leq x \leq 90°\}$, the sine is one-to-one and the equations $y = \sin x$ and $x = \sin^{-1} y$ have the same meaning. In other words, the equation $x = \sin^{-1} y$ can be interpreted as meaning "x is the angle whose sine is y" as long as the answer is found in quadrant I or IV and, if it is in quadrant IV, it must be measured negatively. The notation arcsin x is the same as $\sin^{-1} x$.

Exactly the same argument can be made for the other functions, given the following intervals upon which they are one-to-one:

$y = \cos x$ and $x = \cos^{-1} y$ mean the same on the interval $\{x \mid 0° \leq x \leq 180°\}$, quadrants I and II.

$y = \tan x$ and $x = \tan^{-1} y$ mean the same on the interval $\{x \mid -90° < x < 90°\}$, quadrants I and IV.

Here are some examples:

● $\sin^{-1} \dfrac{1}{2} = 30°$ because $\sin 30° = \dfrac{1}{2}$

● $\sin^{-1} \left(\dfrac{-1}{2}\right) = -30°$ because $\sin(-30°) = \dfrac{-1}{2}$. (Note that this must be $-30°$ and *not* $330°$

or any other angle.)

● $\cos^{-1} \left(\dfrac{-1}{2}\right) = 120°$ (in quadrant II)

● $\tan^{-1} (-\sqrt{3}) = -60°$

PRACTICE EXERCISES
Find the value of each of the following:
1. $\cos^{-1}(-1)$

2. $\sin^{-1}\dfrac{\sqrt{2}}{2}$

3. $\sin^{-1}\left(-\dfrac{\sqrt{2}}{2}\right)$

4. $\tan^{-1}(-1)$

5. $\cos^{-1}\left(-\dfrac{\sqrt{3}}{2}\right)$

6. $\sin^{-1}(\sin 25°)$

7. $\cos^{-1}(\cos 300°)$

8. $\sin^{-1} 2.5$

SOLUTIONS

1. $180°$
2. $45°$
3. $-45°$
4. $-45°$
5. $150°$
6. $25°$ Because sin and $\sin^{-1}$ are inverses of each other, they *undo* each other.
7. The answer is not $300°$, because $300°$ is not in the range of the inverse cosine function. The question is really, "What is the angle, in the appropriate interval, that has the same value as cos $300°$?" The answer is $60°$.
8. This is undefined because 2.5 is not in the domain of the inverse sine function.

Solution of Nonright Triangles

The Law of Sines says that in any triangle the ratio of the sine of an angle to the length of the opposite side is constant.

$$\frac{\sin A}{a} = \frac{\sin B}{b} = \frac{\sin C}{c}$$

This law is useful in the solution of a triangle in which the given information is in the order ASA (Angle, Side, Angle), AAS, or SSA (the ambiguous case).

The Law of Cosines is useful in the solution of triangles for which the data are given in the order SAS or SSS.

$$a^2 = b^2 + c^2 - 2bc \cos A$$
$$b^2 = a^2 + c^2 - 2ac \cos B$$
$$c^2 = a^2 + b^2 - 2ab \cos C$$

PRACTICE EXERCISES

1. Solve $\triangle ABC$, given: $A = 25°$, $B = 70°$, $c = 3.7$ cm.
2. Find the largest angle of a triangle with sides 51 cm, 35 cm, and 72 cm.

SOLUTIONS

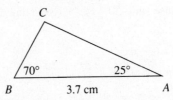

1. The data given are of the type ASA (the side is between the two angles.) The Law of Sines applies:
First find C: $C = 180 - (25 + 70) = 85$

$$\frac{\sin 25°}{a} = \frac{\sin 70°}{b} = \frac{\sin 85°}{3.7}$$

Solve two proportions:

$$a = \frac{3.7 \sin 25°}{\sin 85°} = 1.57 \text{ (by calculator)}$$

$$b = \frac{3.7 \sin 70°}{\sin 85°} = 3.49 \text{ (by calculator)}$$

2. The largest angle of a triangle is opposite the longest side. The Law of Cosines may be written in the alternative form for finding an angle.

$$\cos A = \frac{b^2 + c^2 - a^2}{2bc}$$

$$= \frac{51^2 + 35^2 - 72^2}{2(51)(35)}$$

$$= -0.3804$$

So

$$A \doteq 112 \quad [\cos^{-1}(-0.3804) \doteq 112]$$

FOCUS ON THE ACT

The following sample questions represent ways in which the reviewed skills might be tested on your ACT Assessment.

1. If, in the right triangle ABC, $m\angle A = 60°$ and $AB = 12$, what is BC?
   A. 12
   B. 6
   C. $6\sqrt{3}$
   D. $6\sqrt{2}$
   E. $4\sqrt{3}$

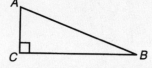

2. If $m\overarc{AB} = 105°$ and $\overline{AC}$ is a diameter, find the measure of $\angle ADB$.
   F. 15°
   G. 30°
   H. 45°
   J. $7\frac{1}{2}°$
   K. $52\frac{1}{2}°$

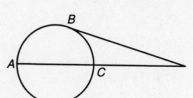

3. Chords $\overline{AB}$ and $\overline{CD}$ intersect in a circle such that $CE = 4$ and $DE = 2$. If $BE = 1$, what is AE?
   A. 6
   B. 8
   C. 4
   D. 9
   E. 10

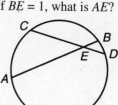

4. What is the smallest positive angle that is coterminal with −815°?
   F. 85°
   G. −95°
   H. 625°
   J. 265°
   K. None of these.

5. If $\sin A = x$ and x is in quadrant I, what is the value of $\sin 2A$?
   A. $2x$
   B. $\frac{x}{2}$
   C. $x^2 + 1$
   D. $\sqrt{1 - 2x^2}$
   E. $2x\sqrt{1 - x^2}$

ANSWERS AND EXPLANATIONS

1. C In a 30-60-90° triangle the shorter leg is half of the hypotenuse and the longer leg (BC) is $\sqrt{3}$ times the shorter leg.

2. F The angle formed by a tangent line and a secant line intersecting outside a circle has measure equal to half of the difference of the intercepted arcs. Since arc AB is given to be 105°, then arc BC must be

$$75°(= 180° - 105°). \frac{1}{2}(105 - 75) = \frac{1}{2}(30) = 15.$$

3. B The product of the segments of two intersecting chords in a circle must be equal.
$$(CE)(DE) = (AE)(BE)$$
$$(4)(2) = (AE)(1)$$
$$8 = AE$$

4. J Coterminal angles are found by adding or subtracting multiples of 360°. −815 + 3(360) = −815 + 1080 = 265.

5. E Apply the double angle identity $\sin 2A = 2\sin A \cos A$ and the Pythagorean identity $\cos A = \pm\sqrt{1 - \sin^2 A}$, choosing the positive sign because A is in quadrant I. $\sin 2A = 2x\sqrt{1 - x^2}$.

SAMPLE MATHEMATICS TEST

The following test is representative of the ACT mathematics tests except that it is half as long. All content areas and skill levels are presented in approximate proportions to the actual test. Allow yourself 30 minutes to do the 30 questions. Try to simulate actual test conditions.

DIRECTIONS: Do not spend too much time on any one problem. Make a note of the ones that seem difficult, and return to them when you finish the others. Assume that the word *line* means "straight line," that geometric figures are not necessarily drawn to scale, and that all geometric figures lie in a plane.

1. What is the value of $5 \cdot 3^2 - 3(4 + 2 \cdot 3)$?
   A. 195
   B. 171
   C. 150
   D. 15
   E. –9

2. Which of the following is NOT an irrational number?
   F. π
   G. $\sqrt{2}$
   H. 3.1416
   J. 3.101001000100001 . . .
   K. $\sqrt[3]{9}$

3. If a student received a score of 85% on a test on which he got six questions wrong, how many questions were on the test?
   A. 5
   B. 40
   C. 90
   D. 510
   E. None of these

4. On the diagram, which of the following is a chord?

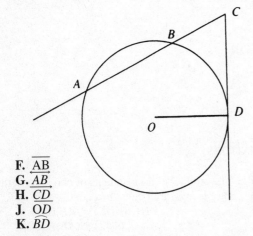

   F. $\overline{AB}$
   G. $\overleftrightarrow{AB}$
   H. $\overline{CD}$
   J. $\overrightarrow{OD}$
   K. $\overparen{BD}$

5. What is the solution of $5 - 2[3x - (x - 2)] = 1 - x$?
   A. {0}
   B. {1}
   C. $\left\{\dfrac{8}{3}\right\}$
   D. $\left\{\dfrac{-5}{7}\right\}$
   E. $\left\{\dfrac{-21}{19}\right\}$

6. What base two numeral corresponds to $29_{(ten)}$?
   F. $141_{(two)}$
   G. $701_{(two)}$
   H. $11101_{(two)}$
   J. $10111_{(two)}$
   K. $11111_{(two)}$

7. $2\dfrac{7}{8} + 5\dfrac{5}{12} = ?$
   A. 8
   B. $8\dfrac{7}{24}$
   C. $2\dfrac{13}{24}$
   D. $3\dfrac{1}{2}$
   E. $7\dfrac{3}{5}$

8. Which of the following is a polynomial of degree 3?
   F. $3x + 1$
   G. $4x^2 + x + 1$
   H. $(2x^2 + 1)^3$
   J. $\dfrac{1}{x^2}$
   K. $5x^3 - 2x^2 + x - 3$

9. What is the simplified form of $x - \{5 - 3[2x - 3(x + 2)]\}$?
   A. $-8x - 3$
   B. $16x - 23$
   C. $-2x - 23$
   D. $-2x + 13$
   E. $-9x - 12$

10. Which expression would be appropriate to complete the following equation in order for it to illustrate the associative property of multiplication: $(ab)(c + d) = ?$
    F. $(ba)(c + d)$
    G. $abc + abd$
    H. $(c + d)(ab)$
    J. $a[b(c + d)]$
    K. $(ab)(d + c)$

11. What is the expanded form of $(5x - 2)^2$?
    A. $25x^2 + 4$
    B. $25x^2 - 20x + 4$
    C. $25x^2 + 10x + 4$
    D. $5x^2 - 4$
    E. $25x + 4$

12. Which of the following numbers is prime?
   F. –5
   G. 0
   H. 1
   J. 51
   K. None of these

13. Jack is 4 years older than Jill. If 3 years ago Jack was 2 years less than twice Jill's age then, what equation can be used to determine how old each person is now?
   A. $2(x - 3) - 2 = x + 1$
   B. $2(x + 1) - 2 = x - 3$
   C. $2(x - 3) = (x + 1) - 2$
   D. $2(x + 1) = (x - 3) - 2$
   E. $x + 1 = 2(x - 3)$

14. What is the slope of the line whose equation is $x + 2y = 5 - (x + y)$?
   F. $\dfrac{5}{3}$

   G. -2

   H. $\dfrac{-2}{3}$

   J. $\dfrac{-3}{2}$

   K. -1

15. What is the solution set of $x(x - 3) = 18$?
   A. $\{0, 3\}$
   B. $\{18, 21\}$
   C. $\{-6, 3\}$
   D. $\{6, -3\}$
   E. $\{9\}$

16. What is the center of the ellipse whose equation is $\dfrac{(x - 2)^2}{9} + \dfrac{(y + 4)^2}{25} = 1$?
   F. The origin
   G. $(3, 5)$
   H. $(2, -4)$
   J. $(-2, 4)$
   K. $(9, 25)$

17. What is an equivalent expression, in simplest radical form, to $\sqrt[3]{\dfrac{16a^4}{b^2c}}$?
   A. $\dfrac{4a^2\sqrt{c}}{bc}$

   B. $2a\sqrt[3]{\dfrac{2a}{b^2c}}$

   C. $\dfrac{\sqrt[3]{16a^4bc^2}}{bc}$

   D. $\dfrac{2a\sqrt[3]{2abc^2}}{bc}$

   E. $\dfrac{4a^2\sqrt[3]{c}}{bc}$

18. In which quadrant does the terminal side of angle θ lie if $\sin \theta > 0$ and $\tan \theta < 0$?
   F. I
   G. II
   H. III
   J. IV
   K. None of these

19. If $\overline{CD}$ is a diameter, $\overline{CD} \parallel \overline{AB}$, and m∠$BCD$ = 50°, the measure of arc $\overset{\frown}{AB}$ = ?

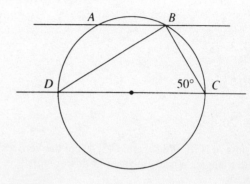

   A. 100°
   B. 50°
   C. 25°
   D. 20°
   E. 10°

20. How many 4-person committees can be formed from a club of 12 people?
   F. 11,880
   G. 495
   H. 48
   J. 3
   K. 1

21. What is the graph of the solution set of $|x - 1| \le 5$?

   A.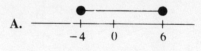

   B.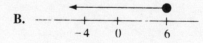

   C.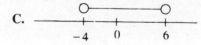

   D.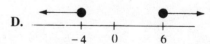

   E.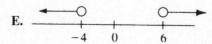

22. If $\triangle ABC \sim \triangle DEF$, and the sides have the measures indicated, what is the length of $\overline{BC}$?

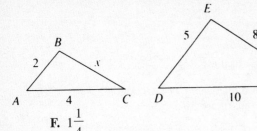

F. $1\frac{1}{4}$

G. 3

H. $3\frac{1}{5}$

J. 5

K. 20

23. Points $A(1, 0)$, $B(8,0)$, and $C(3, 4)$ are the vertices of a triangle. What is the area of this triangle?

A. 5

B. $10\frac{1}{2}$

C. 14

D. 16

E. 28

24. If
$A = \{1, 3, 5, \ldots\}$
and
$B = \{x \mid x = 2n - 1, n \in \{1, 2, 3, 4, 5\}\}$
which of the following statements is true of sets A and B?

F. $A \subseteq B$

G. B is an infinite set.

H. $A \cap B = \phi$

J. $A \cup B = A$

K. $A \cap B = A$

25. Given that tangent $\overline{AB}$ is 4 cm and radius $\overline{CD}$ is 3 cm, the length of segment $\overline{BC} = ?$

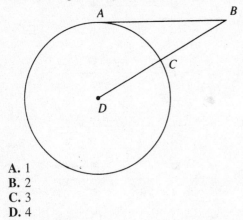

A. 1

B. 2

C. 3

D. 4

E. 5

26. What is the probability of exactly one head showing when two coins are tossed?

F. $\frac{1}{4}$

G. $\frac{3}{4}$

H. 1

J. $\frac{1}{2}$

K. 0

27. Working alone, Bill can paint a room in 12 hours. When Tom helps him, the job takes only 8 hours. How many hours would it take Tom to do the job alone?

A. 4

B. 10

C. 20

D. 24

E. 48

28. In $\triangle ABC$, $m\angle B = 30°$, $m\angle A = 60°$, and $AC = 4$ cm. What is the length of $\overline{AB}$?

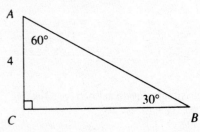

F. $4\sqrt{3}$

G. 8

H. $4\sqrt{2}$

J. $\frac{4\sqrt{3}}{3}$

K. $\frac{8\sqrt{3}}{3}$

29. Which of the following statements is false?

A. Every rectangle is a quadrilateral.

B. Every square is a rhombus.

C. Every trapezoid is a parallelogram.

D. Every rhombus is a parallelogram.

E. None of these statements is false.

30. If $\tan 25° = 0.4663$, then $\tan 875° = ?$

F. 0.4663

G. –0.4663

H. $\frac{1}{0.4663}$

J. $-\frac{1}{0.4663}$

K. 35(0.4663)

Answer Key

1.	**D**	6.	**H**	11.	**B**	16.	**H**	21.	**A**	26.	**J**
2.	**H**	7.	**B**	12.	**K**	17.	**D**	22.	**H**	27.	**D**
3.	**B**	8.	**K**	13.	**A**	18.	**G**	23.	**C**	28.	**G**
4.	**F**	9.	**C**	14.	**H**	19.	**D**	24.	**J**	29.	**C**
5.	**A**	10.	**J**	15.	**D**	20.	**G**	25.	**B**	30.	**G**

ANSWER EXPLANATIONS

1. D Follow the order of operation rules.

$$\begin{aligned} 5 \cdot 3^2 - 3(4 + 2 \cdot 3) &= 5 \cdot 3^2 - 3(4 + 6) \\ &= 5 \cdot 3^2 - 3(10) \\ &= 5 \cdot 9 - 3(10) \\ &= 45 - 30 = 15 \end{aligned}$$

2. H $3.1416 = \dfrac{31,416}{10,000}$

3. B If 85% were correct, then $100\% - 85\% = 15\%$ were wrong, and 6 is 15% of the total number of questions on the test. $A = 6$, $P = 15\%$, and B is unknown. The percent proportion is

$$\frac{15}{100} = \frac{6}{B}$$
$$15B = 600$$
$$B = 40$$

4. F By definition.

5. A
$$\begin{aligned} 5 - 2[3x - (x - 2)] &= 1 - x \\ 5 - 2[3x - x + 2] &= 1 - x \quad \text{Simplify the left side.} \\ 5 - 6x + 2x - 4 &= 1 - x \\ -4x + 1 &= 1 - x \\ -3x + 1 &= 1 \quad \text{Add } x \text{ to both sides.} \\ -3x &= 0 \quad \text{Add } -1 \text{ to both sides.} \\ x &= 0 \quad \text{Divide both sides} \\ & \qquad \text{by } -3. \end{aligned}$$

6. H
$$\begin{aligned} 29 \div 2 &= 14 \text{ remainder } 1 \\ 14 \div 2 &= 7 \ \text{ remainder } 0 \\ 7 \div 2 &= 3 \ \text{ remainder } 1 \\ 3 \div 2 &= 1 \ \text{ remainder } 1 \end{aligned}$$

The answer is the last quotient and the remainders in reverse order: $11101_{\text{(two)}}$.

7. B
$$\begin{aligned} 2\frac{7}{8} + 5\frac{5}{12} &= 2\frac{21}{24} + 5\frac{10}{24} \\ &= 7\frac{31}{24} \\ &= 7 + 1 + \frac{7}{24} = 8\frac{7}{24} \end{aligned}$$

8. K The largest exponent on the variable in K is 3.

9. C
$$\begin{aligned} x - \{5 - 3[2x - 3(x + 2)]\} \\ = x - \{5 - 3[2x - 3x - 6]\} \\ = x - \{5 - 6x + 9x + 18\} \\ = x - 5 + 6x - 9x - 18 \\ = -2x - 23 \end{aligned}$$

10. J Regrouping the multiplication gives

$$(ab)(c + d) = a[b(c + d)]$$

11. B Following the pattern for squaring a binomial, we have

$$(a + b)^2 = a^2 + \underline{2ab} + b^2$$
$$(5x - 2)^2 = 25x^2 - 20x + 4$$

12. K Prime numbers are whole numbers that have exactly two different factors. Of the answer choices: -5 is not a whole number.
0 has many factors.
1 has only one factor.
$51 = (1)(52) = (3)(17)$

13. A

	Now	3 Years Ago
Jack	$x + 4$	$x + 1$
Jill	x	$x - 3$

Since Jack's age 3 years ago was 2 less than twice Jill's age then, $x + 1 = 2(x - 3) - 2$.

14. H To find the slope of a line from its equation, put the equation in slope-intercept form, $y = mx + b$.

$$\begin{aligned} x + 2y &= 5 - (x + y) \\ &= 5 - x - y \\ 3y &= -2x + 5 \\ y &= \frac{-2}{3}x + \frac{5}{3} \end{aligned}$$

15. D
$$\begin{aligned} x(x - 3) &= 18 \\ x^2 - 3x &= 18 \\ x^2 - 3x - 18 &= 0 \\ (x - 6)(x + 3) &= 0 \quad \text{Set each factor equal to 0.} \\ x - 6 = 0 \quad & x + 3 = 0 \\ x = 6 \quad & \ \ x = -3 \end{aligned}$$

16. H The center of an ellipse whose equation is

$$\frac{(x - h)^2}{a^2} + \frac{(y - k)^2}{b^2} = 1$$

is (h, k). The given equation's graph has its center at $(2, -4)$.

17. D First multiply the numerator and denominator of the radicand by bc^2 to make the denominator a perfect cube.

$$\sqrt[3]{\frac{16a^4 \cdot bc^2}{b^2c \cdot bc^2}} = \frac{\sqrt[3]{16a^4bc^2}}{\sqrt[3]{b^3c^3}}$$

$$= \frac{\sqrt[3]{16a^4bc^2}}{bc} \quad \text{Now separate the radicand into cube and noncube factors.}$$

$$= \frac{\sqrt[3]{8a^3 \cdot 2abc^2}}{bc}$$

$$= \frac{2a\sqrt[3]{2abc^2}}{bc}$$

18. G The value of the sine function is positive in quadrants I and II, and the tangent function is negative in quadrants II and IV. Both of these conditions are satisfied only in quadrant II.

19. D Since $\overline{CD}$ is a diameter, $\angle DBC = 90°$. Therefore $\angle BDC = 40°$ and arc $\overarc{BC} = 2(40°) = 80°$. Parallel lines cut off equal arcs in a circle, so arc $\overarc{AD} = 80°$ also. Therefore

$$\text{arc } \overarc{AB} = 180° - [2(80°)] = 180° - 160° = 20°$$

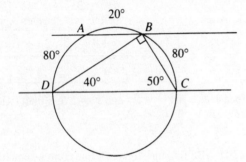

20. G Order in a committee is not important, so this is a combination, not a permutation, problem.

$$_{12}C_4 = \frac{12!}{4!(12-4)!} = \frac{12!}{4! \cdot 8!}$$

$$= \frac{12 \cdot 11 \cdot 10 \cdot 9}{4 \cdot 3 \cdot 2 \cdot 1}$$

$$= \frac{1 \cdot 11 \cdot 5 \cdot 9}{1} = 495$$

21. A Using the special rule for absolute value inequalities, we have $|x - 1| \le 5$ equivalent to

$$-5 \le x - 1 \le 5 \quad \text{or} \quad -4 \le x \le 6$$

22. H In similar triangles, corresponding sides have the same ratio.

$$\frac{2}{5} = \frac{x}{8}$$

$$5x = 16$$

$$x = 3\frac{1}{5}$$

23. C The length of the base of the triangle is 7, and the length of the altitude is 4. Therefore the area is

$$A = \frac{1}{2}bh = \frac{1}{2}(7)(4) = 14$$

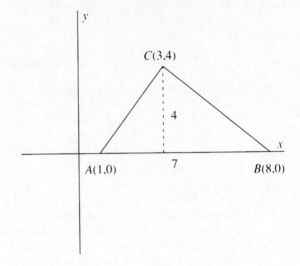

24. J $A = \{1, 3, 5, \ldots\}$ and $B = \{1, 3, 5, 7, 9\}$. The only statement that is true is $A \cup B = A$.

25. B The length of a tangent is the mean proportional between the length of a secant and the length of the external segment of the secant.

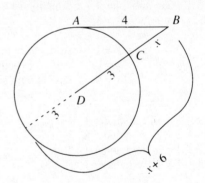

$$\frac{x}{4} = \frac{4}{x+6}$$

$$x(x+6) = 16$$

$$x^2 + 6x - 16 = 0$$

$$(x+8)(x-2) = 0$$

$$x + 8 = 0 \qquad x - 2 = 0$$

$$x = -8 \qquad x = 2$$

26. J The sample space is {HH, HT, TH, TT}. Among the four elements in the sample space are two that have exactly one head. P (exactly one head) $= \frac{2}{4} = \frac{1}{2}$.

27. D Create a chart in which the data always apply to what the workers do *together*. Since Bill can do the job *alone* in 12 hours, his rate of work is $\frac{1}{12}$ of the job per hour. Suppose it takes Tom x hours to do the job alone; then his rate is $\frac{1}{x}$ part of the job per hour.

W	$=$	r	$\cdot$	t
Bill	$\frac{2}{3}$	$\frac{1}{12}$		8
Tom	$\frac{8}{x}$	$\frac{1}{x}$		8

The total of the (W) column is 1 (one job completed).

$$\frac{2}{3} + \frac{8}{x} = 1 \qquad \text{Multiply both sides by } 3x.$$
$$2x + 24 = 3x$$
$$x = 24$$

28. G In a $(30\text{-}60\text{-}90)°$ triangle, the length of the hypotenuse is twice the length of the shorter leg, so $AB = 8$.

29. C A trapezoid is not a parallelogram.

30. G The smallest positive angle that is coterminal with $875°$ is $155°$, which is in quadrant II. The reference angle for $155°$ is $(180 - 155)° = 25°$. In quadrant II the value of the tangent is negative. The rule is "The function of any angle is equal to the same function of the reference angle except for a sign that is determined by ASTC." Therefore

$$\tan 875° = -\tan 25° = -0.4663.$$

3 Reading Review and Practice

DESCRIPTION OF THE READING TEST

Knowing the variety and the amount of reading that await you in college, the writers of the ACT have included a 35-minute Reading Test in the examination. Answering the questions gives you an opportunity to show your ability to read and understand the kind of materials required in college coursework. The ACT Reading Test contains four kinds of reading:

Content Area	Subject	# of Questions	% of Test
1. Prose Fiction	novel or short story	10	25
2. Humanities	art, music, dance, architecture, theater, or philosophy	10	25
3. Social Sciences	sociology, psychology, economics political science, or anthropology	10	25
4. Natural Sciences	biology, chemistry, physics, earth science, or space science	10	25

Scoring: Two subscores reported:
    1) Prose fiction and Humanities   – 20 questions
    2) Social Sciences and Natural Sciences   – 20 questions

Each passage is about 750 words, or roughly two pages of a typical book. The passages are arranged by level of reading difficulty, with the easiest passage first and the hardest, last. On a given ACT, the prose fiction passage may be first, second, third, or fourth. The same holds true for the other passages. The order is not announced ahead of time.

The passages are meant to be comprehensible to college-bound high school students. They aren't supposed to stump, trick, or frustrate you. On the other hand, they aren't totally transparent. To grasp them you'll have to read carefully and thoughtfully, being ever alert to all the facts and ideas they contain. Everything you need to know to answer the questions is right in the passage, although you may have a slight advantage if you happen to know something about the topic.

Each passage is followed by 10 multiple-choice questions—40 questions in all. Fourteen of the questions test what the passages say explicitly. These are what the ACT calls *referring* questions, because they "refer" precisely to what is stated in the passages.

Many more of the questions—almost twice as many, in fact—ask what the passage implies or suggests. The ACT calls these *reasoning* questions, because they call for answers that you must reason out by interpreting ideas, making generalizations, and drawing inferences and conclusions.

The ten questions about each passage are arranged according to level of difficulty, the easiest question being first and the hardest, last. The focus of the questions is objective—on what the author of the passage thinks and says—not on what readers believe the author ought to think or say.

In addition to the total score, two subscores are reported. One is for Prose Fiction and Humanities, the other for the Social Sciences and Natural Sciences reading passages.

STRATEGY

Whatever your reading style, it can be changed if you're not satisfied with it. For example, you can learn to increase your reading speed as well as your comprehension in a fairly short time. Doing so won't be easy, but if you have the determination to alter habits that keep you from getting the most out of reading, you can do it. By trying out some of the ideas that follow, you could make changes in your reading that will stay with you for the rest of your life.

1. **Developing a positive, aggressive attitude.** *Get psyched for success.* Maybe it sounds simpleminded, but you can go far if you think positively. Successful people often attribute success to their positive mental attitude. Set a reading goal for yourself, one that's attainable in the time between now and the ACT. Specify what you will do: read 200 pages a week, take a book to bed with you every night, meet a daily reading quota. State your goal in short-term measurable quantities, in time and in numbers of pages to be read or books to finish.

2. **Finding time for reading.** *Add reading time to your daily life.* If you set aside about 30 minutes a day for reading, one year from today you will have read over thirty books. Look at the figures. An average-size book contains about 75,000 words. Reading at an average rate of 250 words a minute, a rate that's neither slow nor fast, you can read 7500 words in 30 minutes. At that rate, you'd finish a book every ten days. In a month you'd read three books, in a year three dozen.

   Let's be realistic, though. Some books are long and hard, and on some days you won't have half an hour to read. Conservatively, then, during the next twelve months you can read more than twenty books. Keep a book at your side wherever you go, and you'll be surprised how easily you'll fill up vacant minutes with reading.

   If you're committed to add reading to your life, 30 minutes a day will suffice, but if you want to become a reader in the fullest sense of the word, don't set a time limit. Just read, read, read, and enjoy yourself.

3. **Reading more than books.** *In addition to books, include high-quality magazines and newspapers in your reading diet.* Growth in reading power doesn't depend on the size of the page or the style of type. It does, however, depend on the quality of the material you read. Turn to the well-written, first-rate articles you invariably find in such magazines as *U.S. News & World Report, The New Yorker, Esquire, Time,* and *The Atlantic,* and in such newspapers as *The New York Times, Washington Post, Los Angeles Times,* and *Christian Science Monitor.* Regular reading of any of these publications is superb preparation for the ACT. In fact, don't be surprised to find passages on the ACT that first appeared in one of these highly regarded publications.

4. **Improving your reading.** *Check your reading ability for deficiencies.* Everybody's reading can be improved. The fact is that most people don't read as well as they think they do, especially when the reading material bores them. Even if you read a lot, do well on tests, and feel confident that you understand almost everything you read, you may be missing some of the contents without realizing it. One way to check yourself, regardless of how well you think you read, is to read aloud for several minutes into a tape recorder. Pick something hard, something written in a mature style with difficult words and long sentences, something a lot more demanding, for example, than your daily newspaper. Read it with expression, as though you want to tell an audience something important. When you play back the tape, follow the text and listen carefully to the way you read. Still better, get someone to listen with you and to help you answer the following self-assessment questions:

   Did you stumble or hesitate?
   Did you fail to pause between any sentences?
   Did your voice fail to drop slightly at the end of each sentence?
   Did you misread any of the numbers?
   Did you skip parenthetical material?
   Did you omit any individual words in your reading?
   Did you accidentally substitute one word for another?
   Did you invert words?
   While reading, did you ever lose track of where you were in the passage?

While reading, did you ever stop concentrating, even for an instant, and think about something else—about your voice, your pronunciation, or anything else?

A yes answer to any of these self-assessment questions could suggest a weakness in your reading, but not one that you necessarily need to be concerned about. Omitting a word here and there, for instance, usually doesn't signify a problem. Readers often skip words with their eyes but their minds fill in the blank space. You need to attend only to those reading errors that interfere noticeably with your comprehension of the passage.

At the same time, several yes responses on the self-assessment can indicate that your reading needs considerable improvement, that you are not getting the most out of what you read. An imperfect reading of one difficult passage, however, doesn't prove that you have a "reading problem." Before you draw such a conclusion, tape yourself reading several passages with varying degrees of difficulty. If you have trouble with easy-to-read material, ask a reading specialist to check your reading.

On the other hand, maybe all you need to improve your reading is to change your reading habits. For example, instead of doing all your reading just before bedtime, the time when your mind is usually least alert, read earlier in the day. Instead of slouching in an easy chair, sit at a table. Turn off the TV and CD player while you read. If necessary, get out of the house and find a quiet place, the library, for instance. If your eyes bother you after reading for a while, get a stronger light or have your vision checked. You may need reading glasses. In short, treat reading like something that really matters.

You should also get a good college-level dictionary to keep by your side as you read. Look up unfamiliar words that can't be figured out from the context. An unfamiliar word might be crucial to a full understanding of what you are reading. Reading builds vocabulary, and reading with a dictionary improves the odds of your remembering new words.

5. **Developing reading speed.** *Train yourself to pick up the pace of your reading.* Anyone can read faster by following a few basic principles of rapid reading and by learning to skim. On tests, where speed matters, rapid reading and skimming will save you lots of time.

First, you need to know that different kinds of material require different reading speeds. Many students read everything at the same speed, usually at a deliberate word-by-word pace, which covers perhaps 200 to 250 words per minute and sometimes less. The appropriate speed depends not only on the nature of the material but on your reason for reading it. Clearly, reading something on which you'll be tested requires more care than reading something only for pleasure.

You may know people who, without realizing it, move their lips as they read. Mouthing words slows them down because they read no faster than their lips can move. To prevent your lips from moving, hold a finger to your mouth as you read.

Watch the eyes of slow readers. Then watch the eyes of fast readers. You'll notice that the eyes of slow readers stop several times as they cross a line of print. They might stop as often as the number of words in the line, nine, twelve, maybe fifteen times. In contrast, the eyes of fast readers make few stops, no more than three or four per line.

Fast readers take in groups of words at a time, while slow readers plod along word by word. In actuality, when you are reading at a fast rate, your eyes often skip words. But your mind grasps the meaning nevertheless.

Fortunately for one-word-at-a-time readers, grouping words into meaningful clusters is fairly simple. And it's equally simple for faster readers to expand the size of their groupings. A reader whose eyes stop only twice while traversing a line of text can read up to 33 percent faster than a reader whose eyes make three stops.

Skimming takes you across the surface of a passage at a still higher speed, perhaps three to five times your normal reading rate. While skimming, your eyes are taking in large quantities of print in one fell swoop. Skilled skimmers can glance at an ACT reading passage for a few seconds and tell you generally what it's about. They can also pick out answers to specific detail questions with little apparent effort. Although they'll take somewhat longer to find specific ideas in a passage, they can do that, too—a great deal more rapidly than someone who hasn't learned to skim.

The good news is that there's nothing mysterious about skimming. It's a simple technique, easy to master and easy to use. Moreover, skimming rates climb with only a little bit of practice. Skimming isn't meant for serious reading, of course. But for people who want a little bit of information in a hurry, it's a valuable technique.

6. **Concentrating.** *Force yourself to pay close attention to what you are reading.* Most reading errors come from a lack of concentration. The obvious remedy, then, is to figure out ways to help you stay focused on the material. Here's an example of a quick lesson in concentration: Suppose that you're in the middle of a gripping adventure novel. On page 164, the author digresses from the story and describes in great detail how Ace Harris, the hero, lands his Piper Cub in a storm. By the time you've read three sentences you are lost. So you skim the rest of the page and resume reading on page 165. A week later you happen to be a passenger in a private Piper Cub when the pilot suffers a coronary attack. Your life is at stake. You turn to page 164 of your novel, but this time you don't get lost after three sentences. You follow Ace Harris step by step through the landing process, and you bring the aircraft safely down to earth. Bravo!

What made the difference! Obviously, you focused on the passage this time because your life literally depended on it. The example is extreme, but the message is clear: force yourself to concentrate on what you read. How you build the power of concentration is up to you, but the most obvious way to start is to read in a quiet place when your mind is fresh and the light is good. It's better to sit up straight than to slouch or lie down, and far better to be a little ill at ease than too comfortable. Using trial and error, you'll find what works best for you, and when you sit down to take the ACT, you'll know how to focus intently on any reading passage presented to you.

7. **Keeping a reading record.** *Do more than just read and forget.* To give reading a meaningful place in your life, you should probably do more than just pick books off the shelf at random, read them, and put them back. Start compiling a lifetime reading list by recording the names and authors of the books you read. A personal comment or a one-line summary next to each entry will refresh your memory of the book in future years. After spending hours in a book's company, give yourself a record of the experience.

For still richer personal remembrances, some people keep reading journals, a book of blank pages that they fill up with thoughts and ideas inspired by their reading. A reading journal is ordinarily a place to record and reflect on the experience of journeying through a book. Hence, the word—*journal.* Books often ignite imagination, provoke thought, and kindle memories.

Reading can be more of a pleasure, too, when you share your books with others. Some people derive great joy from talking about their reading. The give-and-take of ideas stimulates them. They learn not just about the books they've read but about themselves, too. When you and a friend have read the same book, you suddenly have more in common. You've shared the kind of experience that strengthens friendships. In short, reading expands you and your world as almost no other activity can.

8. **Selecting your reading.** *Read books of quality that you enjoy;* this is by far the best preparation for the ACT Reading Test. Cramming is no substitute for a years-long habit of good reading.

Following is a list of suggested books for high school students preparing to take the ACT. Titles on the list have been chosen for their quality and for their consistent ability to please readers. The majority of the listed books come from the fiction shelf, mainly because high school students generally prefer reading fiction. Yet, well-rounded readers need nonfiction, too—biography, accounts of true experience, history, works about culture, and books that explore important issues of our day. (Titles in **bold-face type** are available at most bookstores in the *Barron's Book Notes* versions.)

SUGGESTED BOOK LIST

Prose Fiction

James Agee, *A Death in the Family*
Sherwood Anderson, *Winesburg, Ohio*

Jane Austen, ***Pride and Prejudice***
Richard Bach, *Jonathan Livingston Seagull*

Charlotte Bronte, **Jane Eyre**
Emily Bronte, **Wuthering Heights**
Pearl Buck, **The Good Earth**
Willa Cather, **My Antonia**
Sandra Cisneros, *House on Mango Street*
Joseph Conrad, **Heart of Darkness; Lord Jim**
Stephen Crane, **The Red Badge of Courage**
Charles Dickens, **David Copperfield; A Tale of Two Cities; Great Expectations**
Theodore Dreiser, *An American Tragedy; Sister Carrie*
Louise Ehrlich, *Love Medicine*
George Eliot, **Silas Marner**
Ralph Ellison, **Invisible Man**
F. Scott Fitzgerald, **The Great Gatsby**
Gustave Flaubert, **Madame Bovary**
Arthur Golden, *Memoirs of a Geisha*
William Golding, **Lord of the Flies**
David Guterson, *Snow Falling on Cedars*
Thomas Hardy, **The Mayor of Casterbridge; Return of the Native; Tess of the d'Urbervilles**
Nathaniel Hawthorne, **The Scarlet Letter; House of the Seven Gables**
Joseph Heller, **Catch-22**
Ernest Hemingway, **The Old Man and the Sea; A Farewell to Arms; For Whom the Bell Tolls**
Herman Hesse, *Siddhartha; Demian*
Aldous Huxley, **Brave New World**
Henry James, **Turn of the Screw; Daisy Miller**
Ken Kesey, **One Flew Over the Cuckoo's Nest**
Barbara Kingsolver, *Animal Dreams, The Poisonwood Bible*
John Knowles, **A Separate Peace**
D. H. Lawrence, **Sons and Lovers**
Harper Lee, **To Kill a Mockingbird**
Sinclair Lewis, *Main Street; **Babbit***
Richard Llewellyn, *How Green Was My Valley*
W. Somerset Maugham, *Of Human Bondage*
Alice McDermott, *Charming Billy*
Herman Melville, **Moby Dick; Billy Budd**
Toni Morrison, *Beloved*
Faye Ng, *Bone*
George Orwell, *1984*
Alan Paton, **Cry, the Beloved Country**
Ayn Rand, *The Fountainhead*
O. E. Rølvaag, *Giants in the Earth*
Arundhati Roy, *The God of Small Things*
Louis Sachar, *Holes*
J. D. Salinger, **A Catcher in the Rye**
Upton Sinclair, **The Jungle**
John Steinbeck, **The Grapes of Wrath;** *East of Eden*
Bram Stoker, *Dracula*
William Styron, *The Confessions of Nat Turner*
Leo Tolstoy, **Anna Karenina;** *War and Peace*
Mark Twain, **Huckleberry Finn**
Kurt Vonnegut, Jr., *Slaughterhouse Five*
Alice Walker, *The Color Purple*
Robert Penn Warren, **All the King's Men**
Edith Wharton, **Ethan Frome;** *The Age of Innocence*
Richard Wright, **Native Son**

Humanities

Sally Barnes, *Terpsichore in Sneakers*

Aaron Copland, *What to Listen for in Music*
Marcia Davenport, *Mozart*
Billie Holiday, *Lady Sings the Blues*
Sidney Lumet, *Making Movies*
Norman Mailer, *Picasso*
Mary McCarthy, *The Stones of Florence*
John McPhee, *The Ransom of Russian Art*
Richard and Sally Price, *Enigma Variations*
Gladys Schmidt, *Rembrandt*
Marcia B. Siegal, *The Shapes of Change*
Piero Ventura, *Great Painters*
Simon Winchester, *The Professor and the Madman*

Social Sciences

Jane Addams, *Twenty Years at Hull House*
Mitch Albom, *Tuesdays with Morrie*
Frederick Lewis Allen, *Only Yesterday; Since Yesterday*
Bruno Bettelheim, *The Children of the Dream*
Daniel Boorstin, *The Americans*
Coraghessan Boyle, *The Tortilla Curtain*
Alan Brinkley, *Voices of Protest*
Tom Brokaw, *The Greatest Generation*
Dee Brown, *Bury My Heart at Wounded Knee*
Philip Caputo, *A Rumor of War*
Alistair Cooke, *Alistair Cooke's America*
Richard D'Ambrosio, *No Language but a Cry*
Jen Gish, *Mona*
Daniel Goleman, *Emotional Intelligence*
Arthur Haley, *The Autobiography of Malcolm X*
John F. Kennedy, *Profiles in Courage*
Maxine Hong Kingston, *The Woman Warrior*
Anthony Lewis, *Gideon's Trumpet*
Oscar Lewis, *La Vida; A Death in the Sanchez Family*
James McBride, *Color of Water*
Frank McCourt, *Angela's Ashes, 'Tis*
Milton Meltzer, *Brother, Can You Spare a Dime?*
Jessica Mitford, *Kind and Unusual Punishment*
Judith Moore, *Never Eat Your Heart Out*
Steven Phillips, *No Heroes, No Villains*
Christine Spaks, *The Elephant Man*
Studs Terkel, *Hard Times; Working*
Piri Thomas, *Down These Mean Streets*
Barbara Tuchman, *A Distant Mirror*
Barbara Wertheimer, *We Were There*

Natural Sciences

Joy Adamson, *Born Free*
Henry Beston, *The Outermost House*
Bill Bryson, *A Walk in the Woods*
Barry Commoner, *The Politics of Energy*
Gerald Durrell, *The Amateur Naturalist*
Loren Eiseley, *The Immense Journey*
Colin Fletcher, *The Man Who Walked Through Time*
Martin Gardner, *The Relativity Explosion*
Thomas Goldstein, *Dawn of Modern Science*
Jane Goodall, *In the Shadow of Man*
Stephen Jay Gould, *Ever Since Darwin*
Gail K. Haines, *Test-Tube Mysteries*
James Herriot, *All Creatures Great and Small*
Homer H. Hickam, *October Sky*
Margaret O. and Lawrence E. Hyde, *Cloning and the New Genetics*

Robert Jastrow, *Until the Sun Dies*
Sebastian Junger, *The Perfect Storm*
Gary Kinder, *Ship of Gold in the Deep Blue Sea*
Jon Krakauer, *Into Thin Air*
Erik Larson, *Isaac's Storm*
Aldo Leopold, *Sand County Almanac*
Konrad Lorenz, *On Aggression*
John McPhee, *The Curve of Blinding Energy; In Suspect Terrain*
Jonathan Miller, *The Body in Question*

Raymond A. Moody, *Life after Life*
Farley Mowat, *Never Cry Wolf*
Christopher Reeve, *Still Me*
David Ritchie, *The Ring of Fire*
Carl Sagan, *Cosmos; The Dragons of Eden*
Mary Lee Settle, *Water World*
Anne Simon, *The Thin Edge*
Dava Sobel, *Longitude*
John and Mildred Teal, *Life and Death of a Salt Marsh*
James Watson and Francis Crick, *The Double Helix*

TACTICS

You've probably observed that people cope with tests in a variety of ways. In fact, the manner in which you take a test is as personal and individual as your fingerprints.

Considering the variety of test-taking styles, it would take a very long list to describe every tactic that has helped other students taking the ACT Reading Test. What works for them may not work for you and vice versa. Nevertheless, some tactics help everyone, regardless of ability or test-taking style. Many of the following tactics can improve your score. Give them an honest chance to work for you.

1. **Pace yourself.** You have less than nine minutes per passage. If you spend five minutes reading a passage, you still have four minutes left to answer ten questions, or almost 25 seconds per question. These numbers may vary, depending on the level of difficulty of the passage or the questions.

2. **Understand the test directions.** Know what the directions say before you walk into the exam room. The directions will be similar to the following:
   This test consists of four passages, each followed by ten multiple-choice questions. Read each passage and then pick the best answer for each question. Fill in the spaces on your answer sheet that correspond to your choices. Refer to the passage as often as you wish while answering the questions.

3. **Decide on a reading technique.** On the ACT, different approaches to a reading passage carry different gains and losses.

OPTION	TECHNIQUE	GAINS/LOSSES
A	*Read the passage carefully from start to finish.* Don't try to remember every detail. As you read, ask yourself, "What is this passage really about?" You can usually get the general idea in two or three lines. When finished reading, state the author's main point. Even an incorrect statement gives you an idea to focus on as you work on the questions.	Takes longer at the start, but allows you to make up the time later.
B	*Skim the passage for its general idea.* Read faster than you normally would to figure out the type of passage it is: fiction, humanities, social science, or natural science. At the same time, try to sense what the author is saying. Read the passage just intently enough to get an impression of its content. Don't expect to keep details in mind. Refer to the passage as you answer the questions.	Saves time and keeps your mind free of needless details.
C	*Skim the passage to get its general meaning; then go back and read it more thoroughly.* Two readings, one fast and one slow, enable you to grasp the passage better than if you read it only once. During your second reading, confirm that your first impression was accurate. Proceed to the questions.	Requires the most time but offers you the firmest grip on the passage.

4. **Concentrate on paragraph openings and closings.** Since ACT passages are generally written in standard English prose, most of them are constructed according to a common pattern—that is, they consist of two or more paragraphs. Except for paragraphs in fictional passages, most have a topic sentence supported by specific detail. More often than not, the topic sentence is located near the beginning of the paragraph. Sometimes, too, the final sentence of the paragraph suggests, perhaps with a mere phrase or two, the main point of the paragraph.

Knowing how passages are constructed can speed up your reading and also guide your search for answers to the questions. When reading quickly for the gist of a passage, for instance, focus on paragraph openings and closings. Skip the material in between until you need the details to answer certain questions.

5. **Use paragraphs as clues to help you understand the passage.** Writers generally take pains to organize their material. They decide what goes first, second, third. Usually, the arrangement follows a logical order, although sometimes material is arranged to build suspense or to surprise the reader. Most often, though, paragraphs are used to build the main idea of a passage. Each paragraph in some way reinforces the author's point.

Sometimes, authors state their main point early in the passage. They use the remaining paragraphs to support what they said at the beginning. At other times, authors reverse the process, writing several paragraphs that lead inevitably to the main idea. Occasionally, a main idea shows up somewhere in the middle of a passage, and, at other times, it doesn't appear at all. Rather, it's implied by the contents of the whole passage. It's so apparent that to state it outright is unnecessary.

There's no need on the ACT to figure out the main point of each paragraph. The point of one paragraph in a difficult passage, though, may provide a clue to the meaning of the whole passage. Understanding the second paragraph, for example, may clarify the point of the first one, and the two together may reveal the intent of the entire passage.

6. **Decide whether to use an underlining technique.**

Option A. *Underline key ideas and phrases.* Since you have a pencil in your hand during the ACT, use it to highlight the important points of a reading passage. When you come to an idea that sounds important, quickly draw a line under it or put a checkmark next to it in the margin. Underlining may be better, because you'll be rereading the words as your pencil glides along. On the other hand, underlining is time-consuming. Whatever you do, though, use your pencil sparingly or you may end up with most of the passage underlined or checked.

Option B. *Don't underline anything.* The rationale here is that, without having read the passage at least once, you can't know what's important. Furthermore, underlining takes time and you may be wasting seconds drawing lines under material that won't help you answer the questions. The time you spend underlining might better be spent rereading the passage or studying the questions. Anyway, a 750-word passage won't contain so much material that you can't remember most of it when you start to look for answers to the questions.

Option C. *Underline answers only.* After you have read the questions and returned to the passage, use your pencil to identify tentative answers to the questions. Underline only a word or two, no more than is necessary to attract your attention when you look back to the passage for answers. Consider using checks or other marks; they take less time than underlining but serve the same purpose.

7. **Decide when to read the questions.**

Option A. *Read the questions before you read the passage.* Because it's almost impossible to remember ten, or even five or six, questions about material you haven't read, just review the questions in order to become acquainted with the kinds of information you are expected to draw out of the passage. Identify the questions as "MI" (main idea), "SD" (specific detail), "Interp" (interpretation of phrase or idea), and so on. (You can devise your own system.) When you know the questions beforehand, you can read a passage more purposefully. Instead of reading for a general impression, you can look for the main idea of the passage, seek out specific details, and locate the meaning of a phrase or idea. Exercising this option requires you to become familiar with the varieties of questions typically asked on the ACT, an effort that could save you precious time during the test itself.

Option B. *Read the questions after you read the passage.* With the passage fresh in your mind, you can probably answer two or three questions immediately. On other questions, you can eliminate one or two obviously wrong choices. Just "x" them and forget them. With a few questions and choices eliminated, direct your second reading of the passage to the remaining questions. You'll read still more purposefully if you note the question types beforehand, as suggested by Option A.

Option C. *Read the questions one by one, not as a group.* After reading the passage, start with the first question and answer it by referring to the passage. Then go on to the next question. This approach is slow but thorough. It's comfortable, too, since you needn't keep large amounts of information in mind all at once, just a question at a time. Don't be a slave to the order of the questions. If you can't answer a question, skip it for the time being and go on to the next one. Go back later if you have time. Whatever you do, don't even think of answering a question before reading the passage from start to finish. Misguided students first read a question, then start to read the passage in search of an answer. Before they know it, time runs out, and they're far from finishing.

8. **Suspend your prior knowledge.** Occasionally, a reading passage may deal with a subject you know about. Because all the questions are derived from the passage in front of you, all your answers should be, too. Cast aside your prior knowledge and read both passage and questions with an open mind.

9. **Identify each question by type (referring or reasoning).** With experience you can learn to spot question types quickly. Without getting bogged down in making small distinctions, label each question by its type. Usually the wording of a question will tell you whether you can find the answer by *referring* directly to the passage or by using your *reasoning* powers. Questions that ask what a passage *indicates,* as in "What does the second paragraph indicate about . . .?", are almost always referring questions. Other referring questions can often be recognized by their straightforward wording and by certain tag phrases such as
    "according to the passage, . . ."
    "the passage clearly indicates . . ."
    "the passage says . . ."
    The words used in reasoning questions vary according to the intent of the questions. Those that begin with something like "On the basis of information in the passage, which . . .?" are usually reasoning questions, which can also be identified by such tag phrases as
    "infer from the passage that . . ."
    "the passage implies that . . ."
    "the passage suggests that . . ."
    "probably means that . . ."
    "one can conclude that . . ."
    "the main idea . . ."
    "the main thought . . ."
    "the primary purpose . . ."
    With a little practice you can easily learn to identify referring and reasoning questions. Once you know how to distinguish between them, you can vary your approach to find the right answers. For example, when a question asks you to identify what the author of the passage *says,* you'll know instantly that you are dealing with a referring question and that you should search the passage for explicit material. In contrast, a question that asks about the main thought of a passage calls for a different approach, perhaps rereading the passage's opening and closing paragraphs and inferring the author's purpose.

Identifying your strengths and weaknesses will enable you to practice the skills needed to boost your score. If, for instance, you repeatedly stumble on questions that ask you to reason out the main idea of a passage, you may be reading the passages too slowly, paying too much attention to details to recognize the main flow of ideas. The problem can be remedied by consciously pressing yourself to read faster.

On the actual test, answer first the types of questions you rarely get wrong on ACT practice exercises, perhaps the main idea questions or those that ask about specific details. Then devote the bulk of your time to the types that have given you more trouble. The order in which you answer the questions is completely up to you. You alone know which question types you customarily handle with ease and which give you trouble.

10. **Answer general questions before detail questions.** General questions usually ask you to identify the author's point of view or the main idea of the passage. A reader with a good understanding of the whole passage can often answer general questions without rereading a word. That's not always so with detail questions. When you're asked for a specific fact or for an interpretation of a word or phrase, you may have to return to a particular place in the passage to find the answer. That takes time, and, since speed is important on the ACT, it makes sense to get the easier questions out of the way before tackling the more time-consuming ones.

General questions are thought to be harder than detail questions only because you need to understand the whole passage to answer them. But they're usually not any harder, and may often be easier. In either case, you'll rarely find general questions among the first five questions about a reading passage.

11. **Do the easy passages first.** Although the passages on the ACT are supposed to be arranged according to difficulty, with the easiest one first, don't count on it. After all, if you've always experienced success with natural science passages, and you have trouble with fiction, go first to the natural science passage, even if it's last on the test. In short, lead with your strength, whatever it may be. If you're equally good in everything, then stick with the order of the test.

12. **Stay alert for "switchbacks."** These are the words and phrases frequently used to alert you to shifts in thought. The most common switchback word is *but*. You may know *but* as a harmless conjunction, but it may turn into a trap for an unwary reader. (Notice how the second *but* in the preceding sentence is meant to shift your concept of the word—i.e., think of *but* not merely as a harmless conjunction, *but* think of it also as a trap!) If you ignore *but*, you miss half the author's point. Here's another example:

Candidates for public office don't need to be wealthy, *but* money helps.

Other switchback words and phrases that function like *but* include *although* ("*Although* candidates for public office don't need to be wealthy, money helps"), *however, nevertheless, on the other hand, even though, while, in spite of, despite, regardless of.*

In your normal reading, you may hardly notice switchback words. On the ACT, however, pay attention to them. Many questions are asked about sentences that contain switchbacks. The reason: a test must contain questions that trap careless readers. Therefore, don't rush past the switchbacks in your hurry to read the passages and find answers. In fact, you can improve your vigilance by scanning a few of the practice passages in this book with the sole purpose of finding switchbacks. Circle them. In no time you'll start to pick them up almost automatically.

Summary of Test-Taking Tactics

1. Pace yourself.

2. Understand the test directions.

3. Decide on a reading technique.
   Option A: Read the passage carefully from start to finish.
   Option B: Skim the passage for its general idea.
   Option C: Skim the passage to get its general meaning; then go back and read it more thoroughly.

4. Concentrate on paragraph openings and closings.

5. Use paragraphs as clues to help you understand the passage.

6. Decide whether to use an underlining technique.
    Option A: Underline key ideas and phrases.
    Option B: Don't underline anything.
    Option C: Underline answers only.

7. Decide when to read the questions.
    Option A: Read the questions before you read the passage.
    Option B: Read the questions after you read the passage.
    Option C: Read the questions one by one, not as a group.

8. Suspend your prior knowledge.

9. Identify each question by type.

10. Answer general questions before detail questions.

11. Do the easy passages first.

12. Stay alert for "switchbacks."

… and a thirteenth for good measure: *Practice, practice, practice!* Then decide: Which of these twelve tactics help you to do your best?

PROSE FICTION

Passages

One passage of prose fiction appears on the ACT. Before you read a word, you'll probably recognize its distinctive look: quotation marks, several short lines of text, frequently indented sentences. Even without dialogue, though, you'll know that it's fiction before you've read more than a few lines. It will be a piece of a story, perhaps describing a place, portraying a person, or showing characters in action.

Fiction comes in many forms and styles, from simple folk stories and fairy tales to confusing, nearly impenetrable novels and short stories. On the ACT the passage is straightforward, and you are asked to demonstrate that you can use clues found in the text to determine where and when the action takes place, to understand what is happening in the story, and to recognize the human emotions or conflicts that motivate the characters. In short, it's a test of your capacity to understand what the author of the passage intended to say to the reader.

Here, for example, is a prose passage consisting only of dialogue.* As you read it, identify the characters, the time and place, and the situation:

"I'd like you to do that assignment before you leave today."

"I can't. I have to go home. My mother wants me to shovel the walk."

"But I insist. You have to do it."

"I'm not going to."

"Listen, Charles, you were absent all last week with chicken pox. Now you have to make up the work. I've put the assignment on the board."

"No!"

"Yes."

"Make me. I dare you."

"Oh, Charles, dear, I can't make you. You know that, but I just want you to do well in my class. Don't you understand?"

"I don't care. Math is so stupid."

"Math isn't stupid."

"It is!"

---

*The passages used for illustration and practice exercises in this chapter may be shorter or longer than the 750 words typical of ACT passages. Accordingly, you should not be concerned with time when doing the practice exercises.

"Look, Charles, I can't stay here all day and argue. I have to eat. After lunch I'm going to call your mother and ask her if you can stay."

"Don't."

"Why not?"

"Just don't."

"But why?"

"Just don't call her. I'll stay, O.K."

"You mean you don't want to get into trouble?"

"She'll get mad and won't let me play."

"Play what?"

"With my friends."

"Why?"

"Just forget it, O.K.? I'll stay and do math."

"Good, Charles. I knew you'd see it my way. I'll see you at three o'clock."

Although the author doesn't tell you who is talking in the dialogue, it's pretty obvious after a line or two. Nor are you told the place, the time, the season, and the circumstances of the conversation, but you can deduce all those details by paying attention to the speakers' words. Likewise, you should be able to tell Charles's approximate age and whether the teacher is a man or a woman. You may also conclude that Charles is a stubborn little kid, but one who knows when he's beaten. Perhaps you've inferred, too, that the teacher has a mean streak, not because she forces Charles to stay after school, but because she insists on having the last word. She provokes Charles, trying to prove that she's the boss.

Similarly, in an ACT passage of prose fiction without dialogue, you are expected to use clues to assess the characters' personalities and feelings, details of setting, conflict, and mood, as well as the author's intent.

By carefully reading the following segment of a well-known short story, you'll see the wealth of information that can be crammed into just a few lines of narration.

As the men trooped heavily back into the front room, the two little windows presented views of a turmoiling sea of snow. The huge arms of the wind were making attempts—mighty, circular, futile—to embrace the flakes as they sped. A gate-post like a still man with a blanched face stood aghast amid this profligate fury. In a hearty voice Scully announced the presence of a blizzard. The guests of the blue hotel, lighting their pipes, assented with grunts of lazy masculine contentment. No island of the sea could be exempt in the degree of this little room with its humming stove. Johnnie, son of Scully, in a tone which defined his opinion of his ability as a card-player, challenged the old farmer of both grey and sandy whiskers to a game of High-Five. The farmer agreed with a contemptuous and bitter scoff. They sat close to the stove, and squared their knees under a wide board. The cowboy and the Easterner watched the game with interest. The Swede remained near the window, aloof, but with a countenance that showed signs of an inexplicable excitement.

Stephen Crane, *The Blue Hotel*

From this passage you should be able to draw some fairly accurate conclusions about the hotel and about the breed of men gathered there. Do you recognize that Johnnie is a braggart and that the farmer would like to prove that Johnnie is more hot air than substance? Do you realize that the other men, except for the Swede, are curious about the outcome of the card game? Do you also notice that these are tough, hard men, accustomed to being outdoors, but now caught inside a small, smoky room that contrasts sharply to the raging blizzard outside? Do you sense a tension in the room, suggested most forcefully by the contest between the two card players sitting with squared knees under a wide board and also somewhat by the Swede's face that showed signs of an "inexplicable excitement"?

Perhaps you didn't infer all that during your first reading of the passage. That's not surprising. The author is a nineteenth-century writer, and he used language and sentence structure more akin to his own time than to ours. Also, you may have been puzzled by some of the vocabulary—*turmoiling, blanched, aghast, profligate, countenance*—words you don't run into every day. Yet, those words are not out of reach. Their meanings can be figured out from context. The word *turmoiling,* for example, is practically defined for you in the next sentence: "mighty, circular," the furious motion of snowflakes in a storm.

During your second reading of the passage, ideas that you hadn't observed the first time may be revealed to you. Even if you find nothing new, however, remember that on the ACT you are not asked to be a literary analyst. You're given multiple-choice questions, and, although you may not have noticed every detail or sensed all shades of meaning as you read the passage, questions about the passage often illuminate what you failed to see on your own.

A typical prose fiction passage consists of both dialogue and narration. Besides questions about *setting, character, mood,* and *use of language,* you may also be asked to *specify the main point* of the passage, *make comparisons, draw inferences,* and *arrange events in the order in which they occurred.* Fiction passages on the ACT often come from the works of contemporary authors, as does the passage that follows.

> That evening, when his mother was sitting at her dressing table getting ready to go out, Tommy stood behind her and asked, with all the innocence and guile he could muster, which was quite a lot, "How old are you and Daddy, Mother?"
>
> "Twenty-two, darling, and Daddy's twenty-three," she replied, glancing at his face in her mirror as she brushed her hair.
>
> "When did you vote?" he asked.
>
> "Your father's right, you do ask a lot of questions." She was slightly exasperated. "Let me see, when was the last election . . .?"
>
> "I know you're not twenty-two," Tommy said, his voice level.
>
> "Now how do you know that?" his mother asked gaily, teasing him, rummaging in the drawer for her lipstick, which she always sucked into a little point like a pencil.
>
> "Because Mrs. Steer told me you're forty-three or forty-four, and I *know* she's right. You lied." The tears he could not shed in front of Mrs. Steer, lest she think him a still greater fool and a sissy besides, welled up in his eyes and trickled slowly down his cheeks. His sense of betrayal was dismaying and acute. It was almost as if he had learned that his mother was not really his mother, or his father his father, but that he was a foundling, taken before his memory awakened from the Evelyn MacCracken Children's Home, a graceless brick structure with a fire chute that sat by itself in the midst of a large and treeless lot on top of MacCracken Hill.
>
> "Oh, my baby," his mother said, when she looked up from her lipstick and saw his face in the mirror. "You mustn't be so sensitive. Don't cry. It was just a joke, a little white lie, not a real lie." She turned toward him. "It didn't mean anything—just a silly little teasing joke."
>
> "Wipe your eyes," she commanded, handing him a scrap of tissue, dismissing his tears, "and stop being silly about it. You mustn't be a baby." His mother was very matter-of-fact, but at the same time she hugged him, and gave him her amethyst to play with, and helped him pick the jewelry she would wear that night.

> William McPherson, *Testing the Current*

In this passage, you witness a conversation between Tommy and his mother, who, at the moment, is more interested in applying makeup than in talking with her small son. Facts in the passage reveal that Tommy is a worried child. He frets about being considered a sissy by Mrs. Steer, and he is pained by his mother's little white lie about her age. Questions on the ACT might ask you to make inferences about Tommy's as well as his mother's personality. Tommy's thoughts reveal his attitude toward both Mrs. Steer and his mother. What can you infer from the fact that he won't cry in front of Mrs. Steer, but that he readily sheds tears in his mother's presence? The ACT could also ask you to put into sequence a number of the events mentioned in the passage. Some events may occur at the time of the incident in the passage, such as Tommy's crying, but others, such as Tommy's conversation with Mrs. Steer, may have taken place earlier.

Sample Questions

The Prose Fiction passage on the ACT will be followed by six questions that require you to reason out the answers (reasoning questions) and by four questions that refer directly to information presented in the passage (referring questions).

Passages of prose fiction can be rich with subtle meanings and implications that lie below the surface of the story. Although your ability to recognize what is taking place in a story is crucial, your interpretation of events is even more important. Questions on the ACT test your ability to uncover levels of meaning, just as most college courses demand that you do more than remember facts. Depth of understanding counts heavily.

Because this type of question tests your reasoning ability, you won't find answers stated, or even paraphrased, in the passage. (In fact, you should always be suspicious of choices that have been lifted word for word out of the passage. Usually, they are traps for hasty readers.) Use whatever clues you can find in the passage to reason out the best answer. Frankly, there is no foolproof method for figuring out answers to reasoning questions. Consider every word as a potentially useful clue to answering the question correctly.

It may seem that the factual, or referring, questions are easier to answer than the reasoning questions. In general, that may be true, but not always. For instance, you can probably answer more easily the sample reasoning questions that follow this next excerpt than the referring questions. In this well-known Civil War tale, a Southerner, Peyton Farquhar, is about to be hanged as a spy. He stands on a railroad bridge with a noose around his neck.

> He closed his eyes in order to fix his last thoughts upon his wife and children. The water, touched to gold by the early sun, the brooding mists under the banks at some distance down the stream, the fort, the soldiers, the piece of drift—all had distracted him. And now he became conscious of a new disturbance. Striking through the thought of his dear ones was a sound which he could neither ignore nor understand, a sharp, distinct, metallic percussion like the stroke of a blacksmith's hammer upon the anvil; it had the same ringing quality. He wondered what it was, and whether immeasurably distant or near by—it seemed both. Its recurrence was regular, but as slow as the tolling of a death knell. He awaited each stroke with impatience and—he knew not why—apprehension. The intervals of silence grew progressively longer; the delays became maddening. With their greater infrequency the sounds increased in strength and sharpness. They hurt his ear like the thrust of a knife; he feared he would shriek. What he heard was the ticking of his watch.

Ambrose Bierce, *An Occurrence at Owl Creek Bridge*

Sample referring questions:

1. The passage indicates that, just before being put to death, Farquhar tries to think about
   A. the beauty of his surroundings.
   B. anything other than his impending doom.
   C. his family.
   D. why this is happening to him.

   To answer this and other referring questions, skim the passage in search of words that correspond to each choice. Sometimes a choice will repeat the words in the passage, but be wary of such duplication. The repetition may be a trap. More than likely, the choices will paraphrase or summarize ideas in the passage. Where you find a thought or idea that seems closely related to the choice, read it carefully to determine whether it's the answer you need.

   Choice **A** summarizes in a phrase all the beauty that Farquhar sees. If you read the second sentence to the end, however, you see that the beauty of nature distracts him from what he really wants to think about. **B** refers to an idea not mentioned in the passage. **C** paraphrases the contents of the first sentence. "Family" is clearly a synonym for "wife and children." Choice **C** is the correct answer. **D** refers to an idea not mentioned in the passage.

   Question 1 is a relatively easy referring question. Here is a more challenging one:

2. According to the passage, which emotion did Farquhar NOT experience during the moment before he was hanged?
   F. Frustration
   G. Impatience
   H. Fear
   J. Sorrow

   To find the best answer, you must search the entire passage for an example of each emotion that Farquhar feels. The one you *don't* find is the answer. Obviously, it's more of a challenge to find three wrong answers than to find a single correct one. As you did for question 1, skim the passage for words and ideas that correspond to each choice.

   Choice **F** names the emotion that Farquhar experiences as he tries in vain to shut out the pounding in his ears. **G** names Farquhar's emotion as he waits impatiently for each stroke. **H** names an emotion that Farquhar feels while resisting the urge to shriek out loud. **J** refers to an emotion *not* mentioned in the passage. Therefore, **J** is the correct answer.

Sample reasoning questions:

3. Based on information in the passage, Farquhar probably "feared he would shriek," because he doesn't want:
   A. his wife and children to hear his screams.
   B. the soldiers to know that he is scared of dying.
   C. to disturb the peacefulness of early morning.
   D. to lose control of himself.

   To answer this question, you must infer from whatever information is given about Farquhar and his situation a reason he might want to keep himself from shrieking. Consider the likelihood offered in each choice.

   Choice **A** could not be correct, because Farquhar's family is not at the scene. **B** implies that Farquhar is scared, but nothing in the passage suggests that he is afraid to die. **C** is unrelated to Farquhar's state of mind. **D** is correct. Farquhar, a spy, is portrayed as a highly rational person, one who masters his fears and emotions. It would be out of character, even moments before death, for him to lose his calm.

4. The ticking of the watch in Farquhar's ears signifies:
   F. that each second just before death grows increasingly important.
   G. that the pressure has made Farquhar crazy.
   H. the footsteps of the approaching executioner.
   J. the excited pounding of Farquhar's heart.

   To answer this reasoning question, you must interpret the beating sound inside Farquhar's head, using clues from the passage. Examine the possibilities of each choice:

   Choice **F** describes Farquhar's condition. Since he has just moments to live, each remaining second of life acquires importance. **F** is the correct answer. **G** raises a valid point. A man on the verge of execution might well lose his mind, but Farquhar shows no symptoms of insanity. **H** contradicts information in the last sentence of the passage, that the beating sound is the tick of Farquhar's watch. **J** may accurately describe Farquhar's physical state. His heart probably is racing, but we are told that the sound comes from the ticking of his watch.

   It often helps to be acquainted with referring and reasoning questions in order to decide quickly whether to skim the passage to find the answer or whether to think about more general meanings and implications. Real reading comprehension, however, lies not in identifying question types, but in your ability to answer questions as arranged on the ACT itself and based on a prose fiction passage of the standard 750-word length.

   Try the following passage for practice. Use the tactics for reading ACT passages suggested earlier in this chapter. Also, try out one of the suggested approaches to answering the questions. Compare your approach to the analysis following each question.

> One December evening on her return from class, Anna found a postcard
> from Warren in her mailbox. She pressed the button for the elevator and
> examined the picture on the card: it was of an orange magnified so many

times the skin looked like the surface of a warm and glossy planet, the
5 opposite of the violet winter outside. Until the elevator came, Anna
listened to the all-news radio station her landlady played day and night to
keep burglars away, then she tucked the postcard in her shoulder bag, went
into the elevator, and used the slow trip to the fourth floor to study the walls
for new drawings and mottoes.

10   Anna tried not to expect very much. She had established a routine and
she followed it: secretarial work at a midtown tax accounting firm, dance
class up the street from the office three evenings a week, a graduate class in
social work to see if that might be her career. But Anna couldn't help
imagining her life as an egg that was cracking very slowly—sooner or later
15 a creature would emerge from the shell. The coming change was now only
an inner conviction, a shape observed too closely to be discerned.

She had moved to the neighborhood less than a year before, and by
moving downtown, Anna felt that she'd changed countries. On her walk
home from the subway each night she checked the new landmarks: a
20 Korean discount store that hung its wares from the canopy in all weather; a
stone church that resembled a chess piece; the small corner store where she
bought milk or juice in small containers from the nearly blind owner. He
was afraid, he confided often in Anna, that an uptown gourmet takeout
chain would try to take over now that he was old.

25   She was lucky to have found the apartment, she knew, and at first it
seemed like a perfect place. Even the two little boys who lived next door
with their mother, who was divorced, seemed proof of Anna's new brand of
domesticity; in the Riverside Drive building where she'd lived with
Warren there were few children. But afternoons and evenings the boys
30 played a game of their own invention and until they went to sleep Anna had
to listen to the thud of a ball hitting the apartments' common wall, the
thunder of the chase.

Soon after she'd moved in Anna went next door and talked to their small,
sharp-faced mother, whose black eyes sparked for a fight and who had
35 introduced herself to Anna as Mrs. Morgan, not offering a first name, only
a title.

Anna said, "I hate to complain, but the noise the boys make playing
ball—"

She spoke softly and made self-deprecating gestures to downplay the
40 intent of her speech—a request that they stop the game forever. She was
surprised when Mrs. Morgan exploded at her. Everything was wrong, it
seemed: the way Anna left her umbrella outside her door and let a stream of
water trickle to Mrs. Morgan's welcome mat on rainy days; the noise late at
night, after the eleven o'clock news, of Chopin on Anna's stereo; that
45 Anna's phone had rung once thirty times on a night when Anna was out
of town.

In a flash of intuition, Anna guessed that Mrs. Morgan would have liked
to invoke the authority of the absent Mr. Morgan, as Anna would have liked
to call up a masculine party to settle the matter. But there were only the two
50 women in the hallway and the little boys caged in their room, thumping the
ball even then. Anna backed away from the small furious woman and
retreated into her apartment, locking the door behind her.

"Boys playing," she heard echoing in the hallway. "In this day and age
you complain about boys playing!"

55 Anna made a wish that Mrs. Morgan would soon marry a wealthy man and move elsewhere. If not, she thought, the boys would grow up and leave home, but what would become of Anna? Was she to remain silent through their childhood years of wall basketball and their adolescent wild music? Who had called her and rung thirty times and never bothered to call again?

Laura Furman, *Watch Time Fly*

1. Anna spends most of her days:
   A. in training for a full-time job.
   B. taking courses in a nearby university.
   C. working in an office.
   D. teaching dance at an uptown studio.

 The question asks you to pick out a specific detail about Anna. To find the answer, skim the passage in search of a word, phrase, or idea that refers to the question. In line 10, you find "established a routine," a phrase similar in meaning to "spends most of her days." The second paragraph, therefore, is the place to look for the answer.

 Choice **A** is not mentioned in the passage. **B** tells what Anna does on some evenings during the week. **C** describes Anna's job; she works as a secretary in a tax accounting firm. **C** is correct. **D** tells what Anna does three evenings a week.

2. When Anna meets Mrs. Morgan for the first time, she notices Mrs. Morgan's:
   F. age.
   G. domesticity.
   H. independence.
   J. aloofness.

 This question asks you to identify a specific detail. To answer, first pick out the key words in the question, probably "meets" and "first time." Skim the passage for a reference related to the key words. Line 33 begins with the words, "Soon after she'd moved in . . .," a phrase closely related to the key words. Reread this paragraph more slowly in search of the answer.

 Choice **F** is not mentioned in the passage. **G** is one of Mrs. Morgan's qualities, but Anna doesn't notice it at their first meeting. **H** is not mentioned in the passage. In fact, Anna observes later that Mrs. Morgan, being a single parent, is far from independent. **J** is an idea that fits Mrs. Morgan, who introduces herself without "offering a first name, only a title." **J** is correct.

3. According to the passage, Mrs. Morgan's major complaint is that Anna:
   A. stays out too late.
   B. makes too much noise.
   C. doesn't answer the telephone promptly.
   D. is unfriendly toward her two sons.

 The question's introductory phrase, "According to the passage," indicates that the answer will be a particular thought or idea specifically stated in the passage. Skim the passage in search of a word, thought, or idea that corresponds to the key word in the question, probably "complaint." Line 37, which begins with Anna stating, "I hate to complain, but . . .," is followed by a paragraph of complaints from Mrs. Morgan.

 Choice **A** is not mentioned in the passage. **B** refers to most of Mrs. Morgan's complaints about Anna. **B** is correct. **C** is included, because Mrs. Morgan complains about the ringing of Anna's telephone, but it is too specific to be the major complaint. **D** probably describes Anna's feelings, but it is not one of Mrs. Morgan's complaints.

4. Anna probably moved to a new neighborhood:
   F. to be closer to the university.
   G. to create a new life for herself.
   H. because she could not afford the rent in her old apartment.
   J. because the new neighborhood was a more interesting place to live.

 The word "probably" is a clue that you won't find the answer stated specifically in the passage. Instead, you need to draw a conclusion about Anna's motives, using whatever facts you know about her. In short, the answer is a judgment based on your reading of the facts.

Choice **F** seems like a possibility, but no facts in the passage indicate that this was one of Anna's concerns. **G** is supported by the facts that Anna has recently moved downtown, lives alone, and takes social work courses to see if that might be her career—all suggesting that she's trying to create a new life for herself. **G** is correct. **H** is a good reason to move, but it is not mentioned in the passage. **J** is true, but the passage does not suggest that as a reason for Anna's move.

5. At some time in the past Anna had:
   A. been a social worker.
   B. been living with Warren.
   C. moved to New York City.
   D. children of her own.
   The directness of this question indicates that you need to search for a specific detail in the passage about Anna's past. Since most of the passage is about Anna's present life, skim the passage to find references to her past, most of which appear in lines 25 to 36.

   Choice **A** could not be right, because the passage says Anna is taking a class in social work "to see if that might be her career." **B** is supported by lines 28-29, which says that Anna used to live with Warren. **B** is correct. **C** may be true, although the passage doesn't say whether Anna is a native New Yorker. **D** is a trap for overeager readers who see the word "children" and leap for this choice. Children had lived in the same Riverside Drive building as Anna, but they weren't hers.

6. Which of the following statements best explains why Mrs. Morgan explodes at Anna (lines 40-41)?
   F. Mrs. Morgan thinks Anna has no right to complain.
   G. Mrs. Morgan thinks that her two sons are angels.
   H. Mrs. Morgan thinks that playing ball gives her two sons their daily exercise.
   J. Mrs. Morgan resents Anna's lifestyle.
   This question asks you to interpret a character's actions. To answer it, go directly to the place in the passage where Mrs. Morgan's outburst occurs. Look for clues to her behavior in the material just before and just after she explodes. To Mrs. Morgan, Anna is a nuisance who does "everything" wrong.

   Choice **F** is a reasonable explanation for Mrs. Morgan's explosion. Being a neighbor with several annoying habits, Anna has no right to complain about the boys' ballplaying. **F** is correct. Neither **G** nor **H** is mentioned in the passage. **J** may be valid in terms of the entire passage, but Anna's lifestyle is not Mrs. Morgan's immediate concern when she explodes at Anna.

7. Anna guesses that Mrs. Morgan's hostility is caused by:
   A. her suspicion of strangers.
   B. the difficulty she's having with her two sons.
   C. the fact that Mr. Morgan is gone.
   D. Anna's thoughtlessness as a neighbor.
   This is a question that asks you to interpret a character's thoughts. To answer the question, reread lines 47–52, in which Anna has a flash of intuition about Mrs. Morgan. Anna thinks that she has suddenly discovered the secret of her neighbor's anger. Answer the question based on your understanding of Anna's sudden insight.

   Choice **A** could explain Mrs. Morgan's hostile behavior, but it is not implied by the passage. **B** could contribute to Mrs. Morgan's anger, but it is not suggested in the passage. **C** coincides with Anna's realization that Mrs. Morgan is bitter about being left by Mr. Morgan to raise two active little boys. **C** is correct. **D** sets off Mrs. Morgan's outburst but is not the basic cause of her hostility.

8. After the argument with Mrs. Morgan, Anna feels:
   F. hopeful that the boys will stop playing ball.
   G. determined not to let Mrs. Morgan bother her any more.
   H. regretful that she had not been firmer with Mrs. Morgan.
   J. trapped in the circumstances of her life.
   This question asks you to interpret a character's thoughts. To find the answer, reread the last paragraph, in which Anna yearns for relief from the oppression of Mrs. Morgan and her sons. How realistic is Anna's wish? What is implied by Anna's question about the mysterious phone call while she was away? Taken all together, what do

Anna's thoughts reveal about her state of mind?

Choice **F** is a part of Anna's fantasy, not a realistic hope for the future. **G** is not mentioned in the passage. **H** may describe Anna's feelings, but self-reproach is not mentioned. **J** describes Anna's state of mind. Her frustration comes not from the boys' basketball games but from uncertainty about whether she can ever change her life. **J** is correct.

9. Anna imagines her life as a cracking egg (second paragraph) because:
   A. she is finding out who she really is.
   B. she is a fragile person, easily broken.
   C. her life is coming apart.
   D. she has led a sheltered life until now.

This question asks you to see beyond the literal meaning of an idea to its implied or symbolic meaning. To find the answer, reread the segment of the passage where the symbol is located. The context may reveal the meaning. If not, expand your search for clues to the rest of the passage. In this instance, consider all you know about Anna's life. In what way does her life resemble a cracking egg?

Choice **A** alludes to lines 14 and 15, which say that "sooner or later a creature [Anna] would emerge from the shell." Anna is being reborn, but she has not yet discovered what she will be in her new life. **A** is correct. **B** seems like a good interpretation, because eggs are easily broken. The passage, however, portrays Anna as a fairly strong person, trying to make a fresh start in life. **C** seems like reasonable description of a cracked egg, but the passage shows Anna trying to put her life back together. **D** is unrelated to the image of a cracked egg.

10. The image in the passage that best represents the story's main idea is:
   F. the stone church that resembles a chess piece.
   G. a warm and glossy planet.
   H. the violet winter outside.
   J. the ringing phone that no one answers.

This question has two parts. First you must identify the main theme of the passage, then pick the image that symbolizes that theme. To identify the main theme, reread or skim the entire passage for a general impression. Think of why the author may have created this particular set of characters in this particular time and place. Why did the author choose to emphasize certain details while ignoring others? What are the major events in the passage? What is the point of each event? Come to some reasonable conclusion about what the author may have had in mind.

With your conclusion in mind, turn to the four choices. Which image comes closest to representing your idea of the passage's main point?

Choice **F** has little to do with the main point of the passage. **G** refers to the picture on Warren's postcard and seems to represent a mirror image of the world occupied by Anna and Mrs. Morgan. **H** suggests a cool, quiet place. But Mrs. Morgan's hot temper, the diversity in the neighborhood, and Anna's attempts to fill her days and nights with activity do not support the image. **J** suggests a desperate attempt by someone to make contact with another person. Anna's experience with Mrs. Morgan is a living example of difficult communication. Also, perhaps Anna and Warren split up because they didn't communicate. Notice that there's no mention of a message on the postcard that Warren sent to Anna. **J** is correct.

PRACTICE EXERCISES

While answering the ten questions about the following prose fiction passage, use the strategies you learned as you studied the sample questions in this chapter. Answers and explanations follow the questions.

> The doctor spent a long time with her in the bedroom, alone, sitting on the edge of the bed, asking questions. She stared at him most of the time with pallid, boring eyes. After a time he went downstairs and gave Mortimer a pipe of tobacco and walked about the yard, among the crying
> 5 geese, and talked to me.
> "All she can talk about is how she's been no good to me," Joe said. "How I'm not to go near her. How she hates herself. How she's been a failure all the time."

The doctor did not answer; the geese cried and squawked among the
10 barns.

"Neither one of us is sleeping well," Joe said. "I can't put up with it. I
can't stand it much longer."

"Was there something that began it?"

"The calf. We lost a calf about three weeks ago. She blamed herself for
15 that."

"Never thought of going away from here?" the doctor said.

"Away?"

"How long have you lived here?"

"Five and twenty years. Nearly six and twenty."

20 "I believe you might do well to move," the doctor said.

"Move? Where to? What for?"

"It might be that everything here has the same association. This is where
she wanted her children and this is where she never had them. She might
be happier if you moved away from here."

25 "She misses children. She'd have been all right with children," Joe
said.

"Think it over," the doctor said. "She needs a rest too. Get her to take it
a little easier. Get a girl to help in the kitchen and with the hens. It'll be
company for her. Perhaps she won't think of herself so much."

30 "All right. It upsets me to see her break her heart like that."

"I wish I were a farmer. If I were a farmer you know what I'd like to
do?" the doctor said. "Grow nothing but corn. That's the life. Give up
practically everything but corn. With the cows and stock and birds it's all
day every day. But with corn you go away and you come back and your
35 corn's still there. It's a wonderful thing, corn. That's what I'd like to do.
There's something marvelous about corn."

The following spring they moved to a farm some distance up the hill.
All their married lives they had lived on flat land, with no view except the
hedges of their own fields and a shining stretch of railway line. Now they
40 found themselves with land that ran away on a gentle slope, with a view
below it of an entire broad valley across which trains ran like smoking
toys.

The girl who answered their advertisement for help was short and dark,
with rather sleepy brown eyes, a thick bright complexion and rosy-
45 knuckled hands. She called at the house with her mother, who did most of
what talking there was.

"She's been a bit off colour. But she's better now. She wants to work in
the fresh air a bit. You want to work in the fresh air, don't you, Elsie?"

"Yes," Elsie said.

50 "She's very quiet, but she'll get used to you," her mother said. "She
don't say much, but she'll get used to you. She's not particular either.
You're not particular, are you, Elsie?"

"No," Elsie said.

"She's a good girl. She won't give no trouble," her mother said.

55 "How old is she?" Mortimer said.

"Eighteen," her mother said. "Eighteen and in her nineteen. She'll be
nineteen next birthday, won't you Elsie?"

"Yes," Elsie said.

The girl settled into the house and moved about it with unobtrusive
60 quietness. As she stood at the kitchen sink, staring down across the farm-
yard, at the greening hedgerows of hawthorn and the rising fields of corn,
she let her big-knuckled fingers wander dreamily over the wet surfaces of
the dishes as if she were a blind person trying to trace the pattern. Her
brown eyes travelled over the fields as if she were searching for some-
65 thing she had lost there.

Something about this lost and dreamy attitude gradually began to puzzle
Mrs. Mortimer. She saw in the staring brown eyes an expression that
reminded her of the glazed eyes of a calf.

"You won't get lonely up here, will you?" she said. "I don't want you
70 to get lonely."

"No," the girl said.

"You tell me if you get anyways lonely, won't you?"

"Yes."

"I want you to feel happy here," Mrs. Mortimer said. "I want you to
75 feel as if you was one of our own."

As the summer went on the presence of the girl seemed occasionally to
comfort Mrs. Mortimer. Sometimes she was a little more content; she did
not despise herself so much. During daytime at least she could look out
on new fields, over new distances, and almost persuade herself that what
80 she saw was a different sky. But at night, in darkness, the gnaw of self-
reproaches remained. She could not prevent the old cry from breaking
out: "Don't come near me. Not yet. Soon perhaps—but not yet."

Once or twice she even cried: "You could get someone else. I wouldn't
mind. I honestly wouldn't mind. It's hard for you. I know it is. I wouldn't
85 mind."

Sometimes Mortimer, distracted too, got up and walked about the yard
in summer darkness, smoking hard, staring at the summer stars.

1. The doctor visits Mrs. Mortimer because:
   A. her long-term depression has taken a turn for the worse.
   B. she is upset about the loss of a calf.
   C. she thought she might be pregnant.
   D. she is distraught about growing old.

2. Joe attributes his wife's condition to the fact that:
   F. she has low self-esteem.
   G. he has not been a success as a farmer.
   H. he and Mrs. Mortimer are childless.
   J. she works too hard tending the farm.

3. By describing her daughter as "a bit off colour," (line 47) Elsie's mother appar-
   ently means that Elsie:
   A. has been in some kind of trouble in the past.
   B. has been ill.
   C. has spent time in a mental institution.
   D. does not talk much.

4. The passage portrays Elsie as a person who
   F. aims to please her employers.
   G. is disconnected from the real world.
   H. wants to get ahead in life.
   J. is immature for her age.

5. The doctor tells Joe to do all of the following EXCEPT:
   A. plant corn.
   B. move to a new place.
   C. hire some help.
   D. convince Mrs. Mortimer not to work so hard.

6. According to the passage, Elsie's presence on the farm enables Mrs. Mortimer
   to:
   F. feel less lonely.
   G. spend less time washing the dishes.
   H. plant a garden.
   J. feel better about herself.

7. By comparing the Mortimers' new farm with their old one (lines 37–42) the
   author suggests that:
   A. the new farm must have been very expensive.
   B. the Mortimers' perspective on life is about to change for the better.
   C. Joe finally has a chance to plant a large field of corn.
   D. the couple will need help in maintaining the place.

8. Mrs. Mortimer probably finds comfort in Elsie's presence (lines 76–77)
   because:
   F. Elsie has eased the burden of household chores.
   G. the two women confide in each other.

H. Mrs. Mortimer feels less lonely than before.

J. Elsie reminds Mrs. Mortimer of the calf that died.

9. Overall, the Mortimers' relocation to a new farm:

    A. dramatically changed Mrs. Mortimer's life.

    B. made no significant difference in Mrs. Mortimer's life.

    C. allowed Mrs. Mortimer to pretend that Elsie was the daughter she never had.

    D. brought more honesty into the relationship between husband and wife.

10. Which of the following attitudes is NOT implied by Mrs. Mortimer's words to her husband (lines 83–85)?

    F. She feels unable to be intimate with her husband.

    G. She wants Mr. Mortimer to know that she loves him.

    H. She thinks that she doesn't deserve her husband's love.

    J. She knows that Mr. Mortimer and Elsie are having an affair.

ANSWERS AND EXPLANATIONS

1. **A** This answer is confirmed by Joe's comments to the doctor (lines 6–8). Joe says, "All she can talk about is how she's been no good to me. . . . she hates herself . . . she's been a failure all the time." B is Joe's explanation of what set off his wife's latest episode of depression. C and D are not mentioned in the passage.

2. **H** This answer is stated in line 25: "She misses children. She'd have been all right with children." F is true but is an effect rather than a cause of Mrs. Mortimer's condition. G is not discussed in the passage. J accurately describes Mrs. Mortimer but is not the cause of her condition.

3. **B** This remark by Elsie's mother is borne out by the next sentence: "But she's better now." Neither A nor C is implied by Elsie's behavior. D accurately describes Elsie: She speaks only in monosyllables, but to be "a bit off colour" suggests a more severe problem than speaking very little.

4. **G** Elsie hardly speaks, stares out the window, and has a "lost and dreamy attitude" (line 66). F and H are not implied by the passage. You may believe that Elsie does not act like an eighteen-year-old, but the author does not have that in mind in his portrayal of Elsie.

5. **A** The doctor does not advise Joe to plant corn. He only tells Joe what he (the doctor) would do if he owned a farm. On the other hand, he recommends moving to a new farm (line 20), hiring a girl (line 28), and persuading Mrs. Mortimer "to take it a little easier" (lines 27–28).

6. **J** The passage indicates that because of Elsie's presence, Mrs. Mortimer doesn't "despise herself so much" (line 78). F may be true, but the passage does not say so; G is probably true but is not stated, and H is neither stated nor implied in the passage.

7. **B** The descriptions of the two farms emphasize the terrain and the view. The old farm is flat and closed in by hedges, suggesting a prison-like existence; the new farm looks out from a hill onto a broad valley that seems to offer the Mortimers an opportunity to expand their lives. A, C, and D may be accurate inferences but are not implied by the descriptions of the farms.

8. **H** This is the best answer because the root of Mrs. Mortimer's problem seems to be her childlessness and isolation. Loneliness is on her mind; she even cautions Elsie about feeling lonely (lines 69–70). F is an inference that may be drawn from the passage, but overwork is not Mrs. Mortimer's main problem. G is not discussed in the passage. J is partly true, but the death of the calf is not Mrs. Mortimer's main problem.

9. **B** Based on the description of the Mortimers towards the end of the passage (lines 80–87), their lives have remained relatively unchanged despite the move to the new farm. A is inaccurate. Although C may be vaguely implied, it is not necessarily so; D is not mentioned in the passage.

10. **J** Nothing in the passage suggests that Joe and Elsie are lovers. Choices F, G, and H are all possible interpretations of Mrs. Mortimer's words.

HUMANITIES

Passages

The humanities passage on the ACT relates to such creative and cultural disciplines as history, art, music, architecture, theater, and dance. The passage may discuss Impressionist painting or the origins of jazz. It could be a portrait of Sir Laurence Olivier, an analysis of current Soviet literature, or a critique of modern dance—almost any sort of passage on a multitude of topics.

A passage about a cultural matter will sometimes consist only of *facts*. Consider this brief history of ballet costumes:

> Early in the history of ballet, dancers wore bulky but elaborate costumes on the stage. As dancers' technique improved, however, costumes were redesigned. They became lighter and revealed the movement and steps of the performers. By the start of the 18th century, ballet skirts had risen above the ankles, and heels had been removed from dancing slippers. Over time, as dancers developed spectacular movements and jumps, costumes continued to grow simpler, less cumbersome, and more revealing. Today, most ballet costumes weigh but a few ounces and cling tightly to the body of the dancers.

This passage is a factual chronology, sweeping across centuries in just a few sentences. As often as including a totally factual passage, the ACT will include a passage of interpretation dressed up as fact. A passage that after a quick reading may seem factual and objective may actually be full of opinions. Take this one, for instance, about Johann Strauss, the nineteenth-century composer known as the "Waltz King":

> Perhaps the Vienna that Johann Strauss immortalized in his waltzes never did exist, but the Viennese waltz as he perfected it became the symbol for millions at a time when the world was young and gay—a symbol of romance projected through the magic of three-four time.
>
> The great waltzes—Blue Danube, Wine, Women and Song, Artist's Life and the rest—are more than mere ballroom dances. They are an idealization of the spirit of the dance. Their flowing measures—by turn capricious, nostalgic, gay—capture the poetry of the waltz. . . .

> Joseph Machlis, *Johann Strauss*

Everyone who reads this excerpt may agree fully with the author's statements about Strauss's music. Yet, the content is mostly interpretive. The only hard fact in the text is that Strauss wrote waltzes entitled "Blue Danube," "Wine, Women and Song," and "Artist's Life." Frequently on the ACT you are asked to distinguish between fact and opinion.

If the ACT humanities passage is not about fine or performing arts, it may be about history. You may find a passage about the Middle Ages, World War II, or any other topic often taught in social studies classes. On the other hand, you may get a sample of cultural history, the history of architecture, for example. Or you might find a piece of literary history, something like the following passage about the origins of the modern novel.

> The telling of tales is one of the earliest forms of human pastime, and its origins are lost in the mists of antiquity. From the primitive form of the fable, or *example,* as it was sometimes called, designed to teach some principle, it grew and took on a multitude of expressions which reflected the taste of successive epochs. Before Cervantes's day there existed all the derivations of the epic, the novels of extraordinary adventures, the romances of chivalry, the pastoral novels, the earliest of the Moorish and picaresque novels, these latter both of Spanish invention. But the novel as we know it today came into being with *Don Quixote*. All these preceding forms meet and fuse in a new and glorious synthesis. Cervantes was so in advance of his day that, despite the instant popularity of *Don Quixote,* it had no immediate successors; and it was not until the nineteenth century, when the novel came to be the prevailing literary mode, that his invention was fully understood and

utilized. The realistic novel, what Thackeray called "the novel without a hero," dealing with ordinary people seen against their commonplace background, had its origins in Cervantes. And its finest cultivators, forerunners like Fielding, Stern, Smollett in the eighteenth century, Flaubert, Dickens, Dostoievsky, Pérez Galdós, our own Mark Twain, who was never without a copy of *Don Quixote* in his pocket, William Faulkner, who is quoted as saying that he has two passions, his daughter and *Don Quixote*—in short, all novelists deserving of the name have acquired the basic canons of their art directly or indirectly from Cervantes.

Harriet de Onis, Introduction to Miguel de Cervantes, *Six Exemplary Novels*

Even if you've never heard of Miguel de Cervantes, you ought to remember his name after reading this passage. He is an outstanding figure in the history of literature. The central idea of the passage is that Cervantes's *Don Quixote* is the father of all modern novels. If you missed that point, the introductory material in the passage may have misled you. The lengthy account of storytelling before *Don Quixote* takes up almost half the passage. But then the author states the main idea plainly: "… the novel as we know it today came into being with *Don Quixote*."

On the ACT, in addition to recognizing the basic intent of the passage, you should also expect to locate some of its secondary ideas. For example, the author in the preceding excerpt believes that literature reflects the values of the era in which it is written. Can you find in the passage where that idea is stated or implied? Another of the secondary ideas in that passage is that novelists influence each other's work. If you reread the passage now, you may well derive several more implications. Have you noticed that you're never told precisely why *Don Quixote* inspired Fielding, Flaubert, Faulkner, and the others? Perhaps that information is implied by the assertion that Cervantes fused several literary forms into a "glorious synthesis." Still another question to ponder is why *Don Quixote* was not fully appreciated until the nineteenth century.

Perhaps you've observed that the subject matter of the humanities doesn't always lend itself to exact answers. Unlike chemists or engineers, writers about art or literature must often rely on words rich in connotation but imprecise in meaning. Many humanities passages are filled with ambiguous language. Sometimes you encounter prose that can make you dizzy—this sentence, for example, from the pen of an art critic: "With regard to the apprehension articulated by the nouveau minimalists, I consider the yearning for a new kind of harmony and new esthetic clarity as the cornerstone on which modern art will achieve unexpected rationality."

At the same time, though, many writers in the humanities express themselves with absolute grace and clarity. They pride themselves in expressing hard-to-grasp ideas in lucid and intelligible writing. In the following passage, listening to music is compared to traveling on a train. The author renders a highly individual and largely emotional experience in understandable, visual terms. As you read this passage, notice that it contains virtually no facts. Based solely on the author's perceptions, it describes what generally happens when a person listens to music.

When we listen to a musical work we are somewhat in the position of the traveler in a train who watches the landscape speed by his window. He carries away only a general impression. With each additional trip through the same territory, the details emerge from the mass and engrave themselves upon his mind—a house here, a clump of trees there—until the terrain has become a clear and familiar pattern.

So too our first hearing of a work is apt to leave us at best with a hazy image. As we become familiar with the piece, we grow increasingly aware of what is in it. First to engage our attention, of course, is the melody. For melody is the most directly appealing element of music. The melody is, what we sing and hum and whistle, what we associate most with inspiration. "It is the melody which is the charm of music," said Haydn a century and a half ago, "and it is that which is most difficult to produce. The invention of a fine melody is a work of genius."

The melody is the musical line that guides our ear throughout the composition. It is the basic idea of the piece, the theme—in much the same way that war or passion is the theme of a novel. It will be stated either at the outset or fairly early in a composition. It may disappear from view for a time; but sooner or later it will return, either in its original guise or in some altered form. The melody is the thread upon which hangs the tale, to which everything in the work is related; the link that binds the musical action into a unity. As Aaron Copland puts it, "the melody is generally what the piece is about."

In painting, the line is set off against a background that gives us perspective—the illusion of depth. Similarly in music the melody line does not exist alone. We hear melody against a background of harmony that supports and shades it, lending it richness, color, weight. Harmony is the element of depth in music. The third dimension.

Joseph Machlis, How to Listen to Music

If you found this passage on the ACT, you'd probably need to know that the writer's intent is to analyze the experience of listening to music, that melody moves a listener in several different ways, and that harmony supports melody. Moreover, you might need to grasp several other ideas not explicitly stated but strongly suggested, such as the idea implied by the whole passage that composers follow a number of complex principles as they write a piece of music.

Sample Questions

Of the ten questions that follow the humanities passage on the ACT, seven will be reasoning questions and the remainder, referring questions.

After reading the following passage about the American poet Robert Frost, answer the sample questions.

Louis Untermeyer in his introduction to a book of Frost's poems wrote that the character as well as the career of Robert Frost gives the lie to the usual misconceptions of the poet. Frost has been no less the ordinary man for being an extraordinary creator. The creator, the artist, 5 the extraordinary man, is merely the ordinary man intensified; a person whose life is sometimes lifted to a high pitch of feeling and who has the gift of making others share his excitement.

There are curious contradictions in the life of Robert Frost. Though his ancestry was New England he was born in California; the most 10 American of poets, he was first recognized in England and not in the U.S.; not believing in competitions he never entered them, yet he won the Pulitzer Prize four times; the "rough conversational tones" of his blank verse are remarkable for their lyrical music. Though he has chosen one part of the country on which to focus his poetry, no poetry so 15 regional has ever been so universal.

Ruth Levin, Ordinary Heroes: The Story of Shaftsbury

Sample referring questions:

1. According to the passage, a distinctive quality of Frost's poetry is its:
   A. obvious symbolism.
   B. spirituality.
   C. unusual rhymes.
   D. association with one section of the country.

To answer this referring question, you must find words, phrases, and ideas in the passage that are similar in meaning to each of the choices. Skim the passage and notice that most of the first paragraph is about poets, while most of the second paragraph pertains to Frost's life and poetry. Therefore, look for the answer in the second paragraph.

Choice **A** refers to a quality not mentioned in the passage. **B** brings up an idea not discussed in the passage. **C** contradicts the passage, which states that Frost wrote blank verse, or poetry without rhyme. **D** paraphrases part of line 14. **D**, therefore, is correct.

2. According to the passage, Robert Frost could be considered "the most American of poets" for all of the following reasons EXCEPT that:

   F. his verses are often patriotic.

   G. his poetry often sounds like everyday American speech.

   H. his background is American.

   J. he focused his poetry on a specific section of America.

   To answer this question, you must reread the passage and locate references to the four choices. The one you *don't* find is the correct answer. This variation in ACT questions calls for close reading and takes longer than single-choice answers, especially when you have to find material scattered throughout a full-length passage. In this question, though, all the references to "the most American of poets" are concentrated in the second paragraph.

   Choice **F** refers to an idea *not* mentioned in the passage. **F** is correct. **G** is a reference to the "rough conversational tones" of Frost's poetry. **H** refers to the fact that his family came from New England. **J** alludes to the regionalism of Frost's poetry, mentioned in line 15 of the passage.

Sample reasoning questions:

3. The author of the passage apparently believes that Robert Frost's life was:

   A. typical of a poet's life.

   B. extraordinary.

   C. rather ordinary.

   D. no different from that of farmers in Vermont.

   Material that discusses the quality of Frost's life is found in lines 3–6. Look there to figure out which of the four choices most accurately describes the author's intent. Draw your conclusion only after you've carefully reread the entire paragraph and considered each choice separately.

   Choice **A** is contradicted by lines 2–3 of the paragraph. Frost's life "gives the lie" to stereotypical images of poets. **B** seems to correspond with the author's intent. Frost is called both "an extraordinary creator" and an "extraordinary man." **B** is correct. **C** seems like a possible answer, but since Frost is called an "ordinary man intensified," he must be considered extraordinary. **D** is not related to material in the passage.

4. The passage suggests that a successful poet must:

   F. be misunderstood by society.

   G. avoid acting like an ordinary man.

   H. endow ordinary matters with excitement.

   J. invent new forms and styles of expression.

   The correct answer to this reasoning question must be inferred from the first paragraph of the passage, where the author generalizes about successful poets.

   Choice **F** may accurately describe many poets, but it brings up an idea not discussed in the passage. **G** may describe the behavior of some poets, but it is a generalization outside the scope of the passage. **H** closely resembles the description of a creative artist found in lines 4–7. **H** is correct. **J** raises a matter not discussed in the passage.

Ten sample questions and answer explanations follow this approximately 750-word humanities passage. Compare your approach to the analysis following each question.

> American Pop art was created and developed in New York, but found rapid
> and early acceptance and a particular individual character on the West Coast,
> where activity was focused on the two centers of Los Angeles in the south and
> San Francisco in the north. Los Angeles emerged as the more important center,
> 5 and was the first to recognize the genius of Andy Warhol, giving him his first
> one-man show as a fully fledged Pop artist in 1962. The city of Los Angeles
> itself, perhaps the most extraordinary urban environment in the world, was an
> important influence on West Coast Pop, and it is also, of course, the home of
> Hollywood, itself an important influence on Pop art everywhere. Equally
> 10 significant are the various exotic subcultures that flourish in the area: those of
> the surfers, the hot-rodders, the drag-racers, the car customizers and the outlaw
> motor cycle clubs like Satan's Slaves and, most famous of all, Hell's Angels.
>
> Commemorated in the title of Tom Wolfe's essay *The Kandy Kolored
> Tangerine Flake Streamline Baby,* the amazing paint jobs and baroque body-

15 work created by the car customizers and the elaborate decorations of the California surfboards are examples of an industrial folk art of great impact and brilliance which has set the tone for much West Coast Pop art. So too are the bizarre drag-racing cars and hot rods, and so is the Hell's Angels' "chopped hog," a Harley-Davidson 74 which in the hands of the Angels is stripped down

20 and rebuilt to become virtually a mobile piece of sculpture. The Angels' uniform is also a rich item of folk art, particularly the sleeveless denim jacket bearing the "colors": a winged skull wearing a motor cycle helmet with the name Hell's Angels above with, below, the letters MC and the local chapter name, e.g. San Bernardino. These jackets may be further decorated with

25 chains, swastikas and other signs, slogans and emblems: such as the number 13 (indicating use of marijuana), the notorious red wings, or the Angels' motto "Born to lose."

The world of customizing and of the big bikes is strongly reflected in the work of one of the two major Los Angeles Pop artists. Billy Al Bengston has

30 worked since 1960 on a series of paintings of chevrons and motor-bike badges and parts treated as heraldic devices, the images placed centrally on the canvas and painted in glowing colors with immaculate precision and a high degree of finish. About 1962 his painting took on an even greater richness and gloss, when he began to use sprayed cellulose paint on hardboard and later actually on

35 sheets of metal, thus getting even closer to the technique and medium of his sources. Some of these metal sheet works are artfully crumpled, thus adding a suggestion of accident and death to the glamorous perfection of the painted emblem.

The other major Los Angeles Pop artist is Ed Ruscha (pronounced, the artist

40 insists, as Ruschay). He began using Pop imagery (packaging) in 1960 in paintings like *Box Smashed Flat,* where presentation of commercial imagery and what looks like Edwardian commercial lettering is still combined with a painterly style. But his painting quickly took on an almost inhuman exquisiteness, precision and perfection of finish, as in *Noise . . .* of 1963.

45 Like [Robert] Indiana, Ruscha is fascinated by words, and these have always formed the principal subject matter of his paintings and graphics. In some works the words appear in isolation floating against backgrounds of beautifully graded color that give a feeling of infinite colored space. Sometimes associated images are introduced, such as the cocktail olive in *Sin,* and sometimes the

50 word is given a specific context, as with the company names (e.g. "Standard") for which the architecture becomes a setting in Ruscha's garage paintings (*Standard Station, Amarillo, Texas*). One lithograph, where the word Hollywood streams unforgettably out of the sunset in the steep zooming perspective and giant lettering of wide-screen title sequences, exemplifies the manner in

55 which Ruscha depicts his words in such a way that their meaning is conveyed pictorially as well as verbally.

Garages in themselves are one of Ruscha's most important motifs after words. They first appear in his work in 1962, not in painting or graphic work, but in a book: *Twenty-six Gasoline Stations,* consisting of 26 absolutely

60 deadpan, factual, non-arty photographs of Western garages. The attitude behind these photographs comes very close to that of the New York Pop artists, and especially Warhol: the acceptance of aspects of the world which no one had considered in an art context before.

Simon Wilson, *Pop*

1. Based on the passage, it seems that California is uniquely qualified to host the Pop art movement because:
   A. California is the home of many unconventional people and trends.
   B. Andy Warhol lived there.
   C. New York art critics rejected certain styles of Pop art.
   D. as a big state, California has more open space for displaying Pop.

Concentrate your search for the answer on lines 3–27 of the passage, which describe California lifestyles and subcultures. Infer from the description why California was receptive to Pop art. Or, conversely, what is there about Pop art that appealed to people in California?

Choice **A** supports what line 10 implies, that the unconventional quality of California life has provided this unconventional art form a hospitable place to take root and grow. **A** is correct. **B** is wrong because, according to line 61, Andy Warhol was a New York Pop artist. **C** is not supported by the passage. **D** may be a valid observation, but it is not mentioned in the passage.

2. The term *folk art,* as used in the passage, can best be defined as:
   F. a form of primitive, crudely executed art.
   G. art that emphasizes bizarre and fantastic themes.
   H. art that is created by amateur artists and artisans.
   J. the design and decoration of everyday objects.

   To interpret the term, skim the passage to find where folk art is discussed. In line 16, the author calls surfboards, drag-racing cars, a Harley-Davidson, and Hell's Angels' uniforms examples of folk art. All are objects that are not commonly thought to be art. After being decorated and redesigned, however, they qualify as examples of folk art.

   Choice **F** is not a good one, because folk art is not necessarily primitive or crudely done. **G** is wrong, because folk art gets its identity not from its themes, but from the objects themselves. **H** is wrong, because some folk artists are professionals. **J** is implied by the second paragraph, which lists everyday objects as examples of folk art. **J** is correct.

3. All of the following are cited in the passage as examples of California folk art EXCEPT:
   A. the uniforms of the Hell's Angels.
   B. decorated surfboards.
   C. Ruscha's photographs of gasoline stations.
   D. hot rods with unusual and bizarre paint jobs.

   To answer this question, skim the passage for references to folk art. Look for the specific examples listed in the four choices. Before you decide on the correct answer, however, you must infer the author's definition of folk art from the examples given in lines 14–20. The choice that *doesn't* fit the definition is the answer to the question.

   Choices **A, B,** and **D** qualify as folk art. **C** does *not* fall into the category of folk art. **C** is correct.

4. West Coast Pop was influenced by all of the following EXCEPT:
   F. the surfboard subculture.
   G. the movie industry.
   H. motorcycle clubs.
   J. Los Angeles freeways.

   Skim the first half of the passage (lines 1 to 38), where influences on West Coast Pop are discussed. The influence *not* specifically stated is the answer to the question.

   Choices **F** and **H** are named as an influence in lines 15 to 20. **G** is named as an influence in lines 8–9. **J** is *not* mentioned in the passage. **J** is correct.

5. Based on information in the passage, whose creative work is least likely to be shown in a museum of Pop art?
   A. Robert Indiana
   B. Tom Wolfe
   C. Billy Al Bengston
   D. Andy Warhol

   To answer this question, find references in the passage to the work of each person. Which of them is not a Pop artist?

   Choice **A** is an artist whose work is discussed in lines 45–46. **B** is a writer, not a Pop artist, according to line 13. **B** is correct. **C** is "one of the two major Los Angeles Pop artists" (line 29). **D** is a major figure in Pop art, according to lines 5 and 6.

6. Which of the following statements about Pop art is supported by information in the passage?
   F. Pop is a form of artistic expression that flouts conventionality.
   G. Pop is an influential movement in the history of American art.
   H. Pop is a short-lived, but powerful, artistic fad.
   J. Pop is an eccentric movement that should not be taken seriously.

   This question asks you to draw a conclusion from information in the passage. Try to locate material in the passage that supports each choice.

   Choice **F** is an excellent one, because much of the passage discusses the odd creations of Pop artists. **F** is correct. Although **G** may be true at some time in the future, it is not now, however. Also, the passage does not mention Pop's influence on American art. **H** may be true, but the passage does not mention the duration of the Pop art movement. **J** expresses an opinion not in the passage.

7. Based on information in the passage, one might infer that the creations of both Bengston and Ruscha have been influenced by:
   A. life on and along the highways.
   B. the Los Angeles scene.
   C. the drug culture.
   D. Hollywood movies.

   To answer this question, reread the accounts of Bengston and Ruscha in lines 29 through 57. Then, reason out the best answer.

   Choice **A** is a good one, because car customizing and motorcycles are reflected in Bengston's work. Lines 51 and 57 indicate that Ruscha painted garages. Both artists apparently have been influenced by things of the highway. **A** is correct. **B** alludes to the fact that both artists come from Los Angeles, but the city has not been influential on their art. **C** is not mentioned as an influence on their art. **D** is not mentioned as a factor in their art.

8. The author implies that the freshest and most original works of Pop art are:
   F. Bengston's crumpled sheets of metal.
   G. Ruscha's photographs of garages.
   H. customized cars.
   J. paintings of boxes and packages.

   To answer this question, infer what the author thought about each of the works listed. Which opinion includes a description similar in meaning to the phrase "freshest and most original?"

   Choices **F** and **H** are not described as fresh and original. **G** is compared to Andy Warhol's works, which portray "aspects of the world which no one had considered in an art context before" (lines 62 and 63). Thus, Ruscha, like Warhol, is an original! **G** is correct. **J** is called many things but not fresh or original.

9. Based on the passage, the most important distinguishing feature of West Coast Pop is its:
   A. slick superficiality.
   B. derivation from local industrial folk art.
   C. wild colors and designs.
   D. use of symbolism.

   This question asks you to pick the single most important idea about West Coast Pop from a passage containing dozens of ideas on the topic. To find the answer, either skim or carefully read the whole passage. Focus on opening and closing paragraphs, paying particular attention to the first and last sentences of each. In one of those places, you'll often find the main idea or at least a clue that will lead you to the main idea. To answer this question, don't bother to look at the second half of the passage, which focuses narrowly on the work of individual artists. Main ideas show up more frequently in more general paragraphs. Another popular location for main ideas is the start of a passage's second paragraph. After writing an introductory paragraph, authors usually present their main ideas. If you can't find a main idea stated anywhere, you must infer it from your impression of the whole passage.

   Choices **A** and **D** are not mentioned as essential elements of West Coast Pop. **B** is stated outright in lines 14–17. **B** is correct. **C** is mentioned, but not sufficiently to be the main idea.

10. Which of the following statements about New York Pop is implied in the passage?
    F. Symbolism is an important ingredient of New York Pop art.
    G. New York Pop artists create more sensational works than West Coast Pop artists.
    H. New York Pop contains more humor than West Coast Pop.
    J. New York Pop art portrays fewer fantasy and dreamlike images than West Coast Pop.

To answer this question, look through the passage for references to New York Pop (line 61). Draw an inference based on information you find.

Choice **F** is not mentioned in the passage. **G** is wrong. All the evidence suggests the opposite. **H** is wrong. The passage suggests the opposite. **J** is supported by the final paragraph, which says that Ruscha's photos of 26 gas stations resemble New York Pop: "deadpan, factual, non-arty." New York Pop artists, it seems, are not given to dreamlike, fantastic subjects. **J** is correct.

PRACTICE EXERCISES

Try your hand at the following humanities passage and questions. Use question-answering tactics that you learned while working on the preceding sample questions. Answers and explanations follow the questions.

Historically the journey that jazz has taken can be traced with reasonable accuracy. That it ripened most fully in New Orleans seems beyond dispute although there are a few deviationists who support other theories of its origin. Around 1895 the almost legendary Buddy Bolden and Bunk
5 Johnson were blowing their cornets in the street and in the funeral parades which have always enlivened the flamboyant social life of that uncommonly vital city. At the same time, it must be remembered, Scott Joplin was producing ragtime on his piano at the Maple Leaf Club in Sedalia, Missouri; and in Memphis, W.C. Handy was evolving his own spectacu-
10 lar conception of the blues.

Exactly why jazz developed the way it did on the streets of New Orleans is difficult to determine even though a spate of explanations has poured forth from the scholars of the subject. Obviously the need for it there was coupled with the talent to produce it and a favorable audience to
15 receive it. During those early years the local urge for musical expression was so powerful that anything that could be twanged, strummed, beaten, blown, or stroked was likely to be exploited for its musical usefulness. For a long time the washboard was a highly respected percussion instrument, and the nimble, thimbled fingers of Baby Dodds showed sheer genius on
20 that workaday, washday utensil.

The story of the twenties in Chicago is almost too familiar to need repeating here. What seems pertinent is to observe that jazz gravitated toward a particular kind of environment in which its existence was not only possible but, seen in retrospect, probable. On the South Side of
25 Chicago during the twenties the New Orleans music continued an unbroken development.

The most sensationally successful of all jazz derivatives was swing, which thrived in the late thirties. Here was a music that could be danced to with zest and listened to with pleasure. (That it provided its younger
30 auditors with heroes such as Shaw, Sinatra, and Goodman is more of a sociological enigma than a musical phenomenon.) But swing lost its strength and vitality by allowing itself to become a captive of forces concerned only with how it could be sold; not how it could be enriched. Over and over it becomes apparent that jazz cannot be sold even when its
35 practitioners can be bought. Like a truth, it is a spiritual force, not a material commodity.

During the closing years of World War II, jazz, groping for a fresh expression, erupted into bop. Bop was a wildly introverted style developed out of a certain intellectualism and not a little neuroticism. By now
40 the younger men coming into jazz carried with them a GI subsidized education and they were breezily familiar with the atonalities of Schönberg, Bartók, Berg, and the contemporary schools of music. The challenge of riding out into the wide blue yonder on a twelve-tone row was more than they could resist. Some of them have never returned. Just
45 as the early men in New Orleans didn't know what the established range of their instruments was, so these new musicians struck out in directions which might have been untouched had they observed the academic dicta adhering even to so free a form as jazz.

The shelf on jazz in the music room of the New York Public Library
50 fairly bulges with volumes in French, German, and Italian. It seems strange to read in German a book called the *Jazzlexikon* in which you will find scholarly résumés of such eminent jazzmen as Dizzy Gillespie and Cozy Cole. And there are currently in the releases of several record companies examples of jazz as played in Denmark, Sweden, and
55 Australia. Obviously the form and style are no longer limited to our own country. And jazz, as a youthful form of art, is listened to as avidly in London as in Palo Alto or Ann Arbor.

Arnold Sungaard, "Jazz, Hot and Cold"

1. Based on the passage, one can infer that the origin of modern jazz is:
   A. traceable to the streets of New Orleans.
   B. too obscure to be precisely identified.
   C. the blues songs of the early twentieth century.
   D. the music of slaves in the South.

2. According to the passage, early jazz was primarily a form of:
   F. funeral music.
   G. piano music rearranged for other instruments.
   H. music arranged by bandleaders.
   J. songs performed by street musicians and vocalists.

3. The passage indicates that swing declined in popularity because:
   A. bop replaced it.
   B. swing is not a true derivative of jazz.
   C. swing became too commercialized.
   D. musical tastes changed as a result of World War II.

4. According to the passage, the appeal of swing music lies primarily in its:
   F. beautiful melodies.
   G. brassy sound.
   H. catchy lyrics.
   J. rhythms.

5. The author's main purpose in the passage is to:
   A. explain why jazz is played all over the world.
   B. trace the origins of jazz.
   C. show the influence of jazz on popular music.
   D. describe the main characteristics of jazz.

6. It can be inferred from the passage that New Orleans was a hospitable place for jazz to develop because of the city's:
   F. flamboyant social life.
   G. proximity to the Mississippi River.
   H. acceptance of Baby Dodds.
   J. musical tradition.

7. That the author finds it "strange" (line 51) to read foreign books about jazz and to hear recordings of jazz from abroad implies that:
   A. non-Americans lack the spirit and soul for jazz.
   B. jazz played abroad is an imitation of the real thing.
   C. future developments in jazz may come from unexpected places.
   D. jazz is a uniquely American art form.

8. All of the following descriptions of bop also apply to jazz EXCEPT:
   F. bop arose out of a need for a new form of music.
   G. bop was improvised and spontaneously performed.
   H. bop began as a reaction to existing schools of musical thought.
   J. bop was influenced by earlier forms of music.

9. By calling the rise of Shaw, Sinatra, and Goodman a "sociological enigma" (lines 30–31), the author implies that the three musicians:
   A. were not appreciated solely for their musical talent.
   B. do not seem like typical heroes for young people.
   C. took a long time to become popular.
   D. enjoyed enormous popularity in their day.

10. The author's assertion in lines 38 and 39 that bop "developed out of a certain intellectualism and not a little neuroticism" means that bop musicians:
    F. knew that jazz could benefit from musical techniques invented by classical composers.
    G. understood modern music and needed to experiment with newer musical techniques.
    H. made a thoughtful effort to push jazz to its limits.
    J. tried out new musical forms to show their dissatisfaction with the state of contemporary music.

ANSWERS AND EXPLANATIONS

1. **B** The correct choice, B, is suggested by the first paragraph, which cites several different theories about the origin of jazz. A is just one of the theories given in the first paragraph. C is not mentioned as an origin of jazz. D is not discussed in the passage.

2. **F** This correct answer is supported by line 5, which shows the link between early jazz and funeral parades in New Orleans. G suggests the music of Scott Joplin, but, in the early days of jazz, Joplin's music was performed only on the piano. H contrasts with the spontaneity associated with early jazz. J is not discussed in the passage.

3. **C** This answer is correct, because it affirms the statement in line 31 about swing's loss of strength and vitality. A is true, but, according to the passage, swing was already in decline when bop became popular. B contradicts information given in line 27 about swing music. D is not discussed in the passage.

4. **J** Rhythm gives swing its appeal, particularly to dancers. The passage states that swing "could be danced to with zest" (line 28). F is not a quality of swing music. G is a part of swing music's appeal, but not its most appealing quality. H is not a characteristic of swing music.

5. **C** This answer reveals the primary concern of most of the passage. A is discussed in lines 40–42, but it is too limited to be the passage's main purpose. B is discussed early in the passage, but is also too limited to be the main purpose of the passage. D is mentioned throughout the passage, but does not receive the emphasis it needs to be the main purpose.

6. **J** This correct choice is supported by the statement in line 13 that New Orleans had a need for jazz, the talent to produce it, and a favorable audience to receive it. F exemplified the lifestyle of New Orleans, but did not cause jazz to develop. G is not mentioned in the passage. H is an example of one musician, but it took more than one person to provide jazz with a home.

7. **D** This answer is suggested by the contents of the final paragraph. A contains

a criticism of foreign musicians that the passage does not imply. B is not implied by the passage. C may be a valid observation, but it is not implied in the passage.

8. H The correct choice, H, applies only to bop. F is common to both jazz and bop, according to lines 13 and 37. G is common to both jazz and bop, although jazz is probably freer than bop. J applies to jazz as well as to bop.

9. B This is a reference to the unusual excitement that these three unlikely heroes evoked among young fans in the late 30's and the 40's. A is not implied by the phrase or by the passage itself. C is not implied by the passage. D is true, but in the context of the passage the enigma refers more specifically to popularity among young people.

10. G Choice G is supported by the passage: Many bop composers were educated and could not resist "riding out . . . on a twelve-tone row." F implies that bop musicians wanted to make jazz better, but jazz did not need help, only "fresh expression." H may have been what some bop musicians had in mind, but the idea is not stated or implied in the passage. J is only half right. Bop musicians sought new forms, but they were not dissatisfied with the music of their day.

SOCIAL SCIENCES

Passages

The ACT reading comprehension test includes a passage from the social sciences. By definition, *social* sciences focus on people, usually people in groups. A social scientist may be interested in *anthropology,* the study of society's customs and values and the relationships of people to each other and their environment. *Economics,* or how people earn and spend money, is also a social science, as are *sociology,* the study of society's functions and institutions, and *political science,* the study of people's laws and governments. *Psychology* is also considered a social science, even though psychologists study individual behavior as well as the behavior of groups.

You can answer all the questions related to the ACT passage if you understand the main principles of writing followed by social scientists. More often than not, social scientists write to inform others about their observations, to report on their research, and to expound their theories. Their domain is reality, not the world of the imagination. Therefore, a passage from the pen of an economist writing informatively about inflation reads this way:

> Suppose workers' nominal wages are set by a long-term contract to increase with the average rate of inflation. On average, then, their real wages will be unchanged. But as inflation goes above and then below its average level, their real wages will go below and then above its anticipated average level. Because of the uncertainty as to what their actual real wages will be, workers who sign long-term contracts will demand extra compensation. Real wages will increase. The result will be higher real wages and a fall of employment. Some economists estimate that the increased fluctuations in the inflation rate our nation has experienced since 1979 have raised the real rate of interest by about one percentage point.

> Walter J. Wessels, *Economics*

This passage may seem hard to follow at first. Although it contains some specialized terms *(nominal wages, real wages, long-term contract, real rate of interest),* the terms aren't so technical that you can't figure them out. Be assured that the passage makes sense, even to readers not well-versed in economics. Economics is about causes and effects. When one value (wages, interest rate, employment, taxes, savings, etc.) changes, several other values also change. Some go up and some go down. To deal with an economics passage on the ACT, you don't need to know which causes will lead to which effects. All the information you need will be provided. Your job is to read the passage thoroughly and answer the questions.

Social scientists are concerned about problems ranging from drug addiction to depression, from child abuse to abortion. Social science literature is filled with books and articles about such crucial issues. The passage on the ACT may be an argument for or against a policy or issue. Yet, you can expect it to be relatively free of inflammatory language and controversial opinion. A passage about an issue that usually evokes strong feelings will be written objectively. Yet, some issues really don't have two sides. No one, for instance, favors AIDS or child abuse.

In the following passage, the author blames the growing problem of homelessness on recent changes in mental health policies. The author's position is not meant to provoke an argument, but it strongly expresses a point of view. You should read the passage as though it's fact, but be aware that it's mostly opinion. In any case, ACT questions about this passage would try to determine whether you understand the author's ideas, not whether you agree with them.

> The link between homelessness and mental illness is a topic of considerable interest and concern to designers of mental health policies and programs. The dramatic rise in the number of homeless people in this country has prompted wide speculation about causes. An emerging viewpoint is that mental health policies that severely underserve vulnerable people are a major cause of homelessness. Two policy areas, in particular, have been identified. First, the deinstitutionalization of mental hospitals, including the failure of aftercare and community support programs, frequently is linked to homelessness. Second, restrictive admission policies that function to keep all but the most disturbed people out of psychiatric hospitals are postulated to having affected the rising numbers of homeless people.
>
> Gerald J. Bean, Jr., Mary E. Stefl, and Stephen R. Howe,
> "Mental Health and Homelessness: Issues and Findings"

You may have observed this passage is impersonal, serious, authoritative. It doesn't explain. It expects you to understand complex ideas. Clearly, it's not meant for beginning readers. Some of the words may seem unusual. Unless you're accustomed to reading material from the social sciences, you've probably never before seen *underserve* and *deinstitutionalization*. These are samples of jargon, words used by professionals with a given specialty to speak to each other. It's "in" talk. Yet, it's not so far "in" that an outsider cannot grasp the meaning of the words.

Your reading in social studies classes has most likely given you a taste of historical writing like this:

> When the British government began to increase its military presence in the colonies in the mid-eighteenth century, Massachusetts responded by calling upon its citizens to arm themselves in defense. One colonial newspaper argued that it was impossible to complain that his act was illegal since they were "British subjects, to whom the privilege of possessing arms is expressly recognized by the Bill of Rights" while another argued that this "is a natural right which the people have reserved to themselves, confirmed by the Bill of Rights, to keep arms for their own defense." The newspaper cited Blackstone's commentaries on the laws of England, which had listed the "having and using arms for self preservation and defense" among the "absolute rights of individuals." The colonists felt they had an absolute right at common law to own firearms.
>
> Together with freedom of the press, the right to keep and bear arms became one of the individual rights most prized by the colonists. When British troops seized a militia arsenal in September, 1774, and incorrect rumors that colonists had been killed spread through Massachusetts, 60,000 citizens took up arms. A few months later, when Patrick Henry delivered his famed "Give me liberty or give me death" speech, he spoke in support of a proposition "that a well regulated militia, composed of gentlemen and freemen, is the natural strength and only security of a free government. . . ." Throughout the following revolution, formal and informal units of armed citizens obstructed British communication, cut off foraging parties and harassed the thinly stretched regular forces. When seven states adopted state "bills of rights" following

the Declaration of Independence, each of those bills of rights provided either for protection of the concept of militia or for an express right to keep and bear arms.

Report of the Senate Subcommittee on the Constitution,
"The Right to Keep and Bear Arms"

This passage probably has the familiar ring of a social studies textbook. Authors of textbooks usually cover historical periods and issues in fairly broad terms. They support generalizations with facts and with apt quotations and statistics. On the ACT, you should read the facts, of course, but more important is recognizing the function of those particular facts. In other words, if you know the general idea each fact is meant to support or illustrate, you probably understand the whole passage. For example, it may be interesting to read that 60,000 Massachusetts colonists reached for their guns in September 1774, but it's far more important to understand why the author included that information. In this instance, the author wanted to show that colonists believed in the fundamental right to protect themselves with firearms.

Do you also perceive that a point of view is expressed in the passage? By selecting certain words and details, the author reveals a bias in favor of the rights of U.S. citizens to keep and bear arms, a right that has grown out of a tradition begun centuries ago. Keep in mind that authors have feelings about their subjects. Total objectivity is an ideal rarely achieved. A passage may appear to present just the facts, but readers should stay alert for underlying feelings and opinions that come to the surface every so often.

Sample Questions

Seven of the ten questions that follow the Social Science passage on the ACT will ask you to reason out the answers. The remaining three questions ask you about material explicitly stated in the passage.

Answer the four sample questions following this passage about terrorism. Techniques for answering these questions are similar to those you used for the sample Prose Fiction and Humanities passages.

Democracies have always been subject to terrorist attacks. Our constitutional rights, the restrictions set on police power, and our citizens' enjoyment of due process of the law—the very qualities of our society that terrorists despise—are the same qualities that make us easy prey. Although our citizens view this as a
5 cruel irony, we have within our free society the tools with which not only to fight terrorists but to keep them at bay. We have superbly trained law enforcement people at every level of government, we have the use of court-authorized surveillance and search warrants, and we have a system of laws that allows us to fight terrorism as a crime instead of a political act, to put terrorists on trial in
10 our criminal courts, and to convict those found guilty.

Consequently, we never need cave in to terrorist demands. At times we may wish desperately to save the lives of hostages, but we can and should depend on the strength of our system to protect those lives. If we allow our feelings, as intense as they may be, to control our actions, society will lose its strongest
15 defense against terrorists. The demise of terrorism will be hastened when the freedom-loving countries send out a strong and clear message to the world's terrorists that terror, like other crimes, does not pay!

Sample referring questions:

1. According to the passage, U.S. citizens are popular targets for terrorists because they:
   A. usually don't carry firearms.
   B. represent everything that terrorists hate.
   C. are not accustomed to worrying about their personal safety.
   D. are rich and arrogant.

Before you skim the passage to find the location of the answer, identify what you will look for as your eyes move quickly through the text. Since the question asks why terrorists like to pick on Americans, keep the phrase "popular targets" in mind. Within a few seconds you may pick out "easy prey" (line 4), an idea that may well explain why Americans are "popular targets." Where you found "easy prey," then, is the section of the passage to reread in search of the correct answer.

Choice **A** may be true most of the time, but no such idea is stated in the passage. **B** reiterates a phrase in the passage, "qualities of our society that terrorists despise." Therefore, **B** is correct. **C** and **D** are not mentioned in the passage.

2. The author of the paragraph says that terrorists should be treated like any other law-breakers because:

   F. terrorists deserve punishments that fit their crimes.
   G. we should always act like humane people.
   H. the Constitution forbids cruel and unusual punishment.
   J. America has an effective criminal justice system.

    Before skimming the passage for the location of the answer, identify the key words in the question, most likely "treated" and "other lawbreakers." That part of the passage where you find such related phrases as "law enforcement," "system of laws," "on trial," and "criminal courts" (lines 6–10) is the section to reread.

    Choices **F** and **G** may state the author's beliefs, but neither idea is mentioned in the passage. **H** is a valid statement, but it is not mentioned in the passage. **J** restates the author's opinion. **J** is correct.

Sample reasoning questions:

3. The phrase *enjoyment of due process of the law* (second sentence) means that citizens:
   A. have a basic right to pursue pleasure and happiness.
   B. may protest against distasteful laws.
   C. are protected by the laws of our society.
   D. can sue the government to redress grievances.

    To figure out the answer, find the phrase in the passage and look for contextual clues. The phrase is included as one of three fundamental rights that belong to citizens in a democracy. "*Enjoyment*" is not used in its usual sense, but rather in the sense of *having* or *being in possession of.* Our citizens, the passage says, *have* or *possess* "due process of the law." Review each choice for the best definition.

    Choice **A** is the right of every citizen, but it is not the right of "due process." **B** is a right, but our right to protest is not the equivalent of "due process of the law." **C** is a fundamental right that lawbreaking terrorists naturally despise. **C** is the correct answer. **D** is the right of every citizen, but it is not on the same level of importance as the others mentioned in the passage.

4. Which of the following ideas most accurately states the main point of the passage?
   F. Terrorists feel a particular hatred for democratic countries.
   G. The U.S. criminal justice system is the best deterrent against terrorism.
   H. Countries must never give in to terrorist demands.
   J. Cooperation by the free countries of the world can stop terrorism.

    To answer main-idea questions, you need an overview of the whole passage. Each of the four possible answers may be inferred from the passage, but only one of them encompasses more of the passage than the others. Although counting the number of sentences devoted to a particular subject may reveal the main idea, just as often the main idea may be stated briefly or not at all. Therefore, rely on your sense of the entire passage to find the answer.

    Choice **F** is too insignificant to be the main idea. **G** summarizes much of the first paragraph. The idea is reiterated in a slightly different form in the second paragraph. **G** is the correct answer. **H** and **J** are too limited to be the main idea.

Here is a Social Science passage about cults in America, followed by ten sample questions for you to answer. Compare your approach to the analysis following each question.

       Putting today's cults in "proper perspective" is no easy task. The historical perspective reflects some consensus: most comments about the Peoples Temple seemed to agree, as William Pfaff said in *The New Yorker,* that "messianic cults commonly arise in periods of trouble or social crisis" and "among uprooted
5 people, among marginal people without an assured place in society, or among those whose accepted values or social assumptions have been broken down or undermined." Theodore Roszak, convinced that "cults and charismatic leaders are among the irrepressible constants of human society," concluded that "people surrender their freedom to totalitarian masters . . . [because] they are
10 morally desperate."

Harvard theologian Harvey Cox sees the appeal of the "new religions" as a reflection on established churches, which "have become more or less part of the furniture. They don't provide much of an alternative, as Jesus did or as St. Francis did." People who join the new groups, Cox said, "want a life with
15 [other] people which is not in competitive terms. There is a side to us that doesn't want to compete. They call each other brother and sister. They share things." Pollster George Gallup, speaking in 1977, noted that leaders of established churches "appear to have very little idea of the changing levels of religious involvement in this nation, let alone commitment." He cited a survey
20 showing that six million Americans were active in Transcendental Meditation, five million practiced yoga, three million were followers of the charismatic movement, three million were involved in mysticism and two million in Eastern religions.

The fact that so many Americans are involved in non-traditional forms of
25 spiritual search may well point to a common denominator, as Cox and Gallup suggest. But it doesn't help to explain how the Unification Church, for example, has succeeded in recruiting and converting perhaps 3,000 young people, generally with some college education and from middle- or upper-class backgrounds.

30 Ex-Moonies—many of whom have been "rescued" by their families and "deprogrammed"—seem agreed that their recruiters practiced a studied deception. The candidates were first invited to share a meal with a group of other young people, living together and engaged in some idealistic venture such as "New Education Development." Once inside, they were surrounded by their
35 new "friends," who employed "love-bombing" techniques to win their confidence. No mention of the Unification Church or the Rev. Moon was made at the outset; only as the recruits displayed their acceptance of their "new family" were they introduced to Moon's belief-system and its aims.

Margaret Thaler Singer, a University of California psychologist who has
40 worked with several hundred young cultists and ex-cultists, found that "the groups' recruitment and indoctrination procedures seemed to involve highly sophisticated techniques for inducing behavioral change." Many of those recruited, she learned, "joined these religious cults during periods of depression and confusion, when they had a sense that life was meaningless." Once
45 enlisted, they experienced indoctrination in these terms:

The cults these people belonged to maintain intense allegiance through the arguments of their ideology, and through social and psychological pressures and practices that, intentionally or not, amount to conditioning techniques that constrict attention, limit personal relationships, and
50 devalue reasoning. . . .

The exclusion of family and other outside contacts, rigid moral judgments of the unconverted outside world, and restriction of sexual behavior are all geared to increasing followers' commitments to the goals of the group and in some cases to its powerful leader.

55 Singer and others who have looked closely at today's cults do see a difference (from cults of the past) that is more than a distinction. It lies in the sophisticated use of a technology of persuasion that has emerged in the 20th century. The more general academic view is voiced by Cox, who sees no "discontinuity" between the persuasive techniques of the advertising world and those of the
60 "new religions." The TV child who overdoses on Sugar Pops is thus equated with the cultist "hooked" by a new messiah.

William A. Korns, "Cults in America and Public Policy"

1. According to the passage, the main difference between cults of the 20th century and cults of the past lies in their:
   A. attraction to depressed and confused people.
   B. size.
   C. use of technology.
   D. sophisticated recruitment techniques.
   To start answering this question about an idea explicitly stated in the passage, identify the key words in the question, probably "difference" and "20th century." Skim the passage in search of words that correspond to the key words. You'll find them in the last paragraph, which you should reread carefully.
   Choice **A** refers to people who have always been vulnerable to cultists. **B** is wrong, because the passage does not compare the size of past and present-day cults. **C** may trap an overeager reader who sees the word "technology" and opts for this choice. The entire phrase, "sophisticated use of a technology of persuasion," however, refers to psychology and propaganda, not to "technology" in the usual sense of the word. **D** refers to the idea that recruiters for modern cults use sophisticated techniques of persuasion. **D** is correct.

2. According to a survey cited in the passage, millions of Americans engage in spiritual activities which include all of the following EXCEPT:
   F. yoga.
   G. Zen Buddhism.
   H. Transcendental Meditation.
   J. mysticism.
   To answer this question, identify the key words in the question—most likely, "survey" and "spiritual activities." Skim the passage for words equivalent to the key words. At line 19 you find the word "survey." That's where to conduct your search.
   Choice **F** is named as one of America's popular spiritual activities. **G** is a spiritual activity, but it is *not* listed in the passage. Therefore, **G** is correct. **H** and **J** are both included in the list of spiritual activities.

3. The passage indicates that most ex-Moonies believe that:
   A. they had been tricked into joining the Moonies.
   B. their experience as Moonies was valuable to them.
   C. they made close friendships while they were Moonies.
   D. Moonies have destructive values and harmful motives.
   To answer this question, skim the passage for a reference to the key word, "ex-Moonies." Line 30 is the place to begin looking for the answer.
   Choice **A** coincides with the statement in the passage that "recruiters practiced a studied deception." **A** is correct. **B** is not mentioned in the passage. **C** is a trap for the unwary. Ex-Moonies report having made "friends," but the quotation marks suggest that cult members only posed as friends. **D** is vaguely implied throughout the passage but is never stated outright.

4. According to the passage, the Unification Church has appealed mostly to people:
   F. who live in affluent suburbs.
   G. with no particular religious affiliation.
   H. who are middle-aged and are looking for something new in life.
   J. with more than a high school education.
   To answer this question, identify the key words in the question. Skim the passage for references to the Unification Church and the type of people it attracts. You'll find this information in lines 26–29.
   Choice **F** may sound right, because middle- and upper-class people often live in affluent suburbs. But they live elsewhere, too, and the passage does not mention suburbs. **G** is not mentioned in the passage. **H** can trap a careless reader who sees "middle-class" instead of "middle-aged." **J** makes sense since college people have more than a high school education. **J** is correct.

5. The author's primary purpose in this passage is to:
   A. explain the role of cults in modern society.
   B. compare cults with religion.

C. explain why present-day cults have become popular.

D. prove that, historically, cults have filled a social need.

Approach this "main-idea" question as you have previous ones. Let your general impression of the passage guide you to the right answer.

Choice **A** could be an answer, but it is too broad for a passage of this length. **B** is not significantly discussed by the passage. **C** corresponds to the contents of much of the passage. **C** is correct. **D** is mentioned briefly in the passage, but it is too limited to be the main idea.

6. As described in the passage, the recruitment methods used by Moonies probably work best:

F. when everyone in a family participates.

G. with young, lonely people.

H. with people engaged in some idealistic venture.

J. when the work is done in secret.

This question asks you to reason inductively, to draw a general rule or principle out of a set of facts. Basically, inductive thinking works this way:

FACT 1: Sylvia went out without a coat when it was below zero.

FACT 2: Sylvia caught a cold.

General rule or principle to be drawn from these facts: Wear a coat when you go outside in below-zero weather, or you'll end up like Sylvia.

To answer question 6, use the facts in the passage to draw your conclusion about the Moonies' recruitment practices.

Choice **F** contradicts the passage, which says that families "rescue" their kids from the Moonies. **G** is supported by the passage, which says that Moonies share meals with young, lonely recruits, as well as feign friendship and promote idealistic causes for which to work. **G** is correct. **H** cannot be correct. People championing their own causes don't need additional causes promoted by the Moonies. **J** is irrelevant to the passage.

7. Based on information in the passage, cults are likely to form in a society with all of the following characteristics EXCEPT:

A. changing values and attitudes.

B. strong religious institutions.

C. a large population of mobile or uprooted people.

D. substantial inequality between the social classes.

To answer this question, identify the one choice that names a condition you probably *won't* find in a society where cults flourish. Suggestions for answering question 6 apply here, too. If you understood the passage when you first read it, you may even try to guess the right answer before rereading.

Choice **A** is wrong, because line 6 says that cults flourish where "accepted values or social assumptions have been broken down or undermined." **B** is a good choice, since the passage fails to mention the presence of strong religious institutions. **B** is correct. **C** is not a good choice. Line 4 states explicitly that cults arise "among uprooted people." **D** suggests a society in turmoil, a society that is likely to be receptive to the formation of cults.

8. Harvey Cox's assertion that established churches "have become more or less part of the furniture" (line 12) implies that:

F. organized churches make no room for young people to join.

G. the churches are too set in their ways.

H. religion is solidly entrenched in the American way of life.

J. America's religious institutions are obsolete.

Any time a question asks you for the implied or understood meaning of a quoted phrase or idea, go directly to the passage and read the quotation in its context. Look for clues just before and just after the quotation. If you fail to find a clue, determine, if possible whether the author is saying something generally favorable, generally unfavorable, or neutral. By doing so, you may be able to eliminate one or more choices.

Choice **F** is possible if you infer that established churches exclude young people on purpose. Neither Cox's statement nor the rest of the passage suggests that, however. **G** implies that churches fail to provide alternatives for people seeking to join new religious groups. **G** is correct. **H** is too broad. Cox makes no reference to the place of churches in American life. **J** is a possible answer if you ignore the millions of Americans who attend established churches. Cox's statement refers only to people in search of alternative religions.

9. By labeling cultists as "morally desperate" (line 10), Theodore Roszak means that people join cults because:

A. they don't know what's right and what's wrong.

B. they've sinned and they're sorry.

C. they'll do anything to change their lifestyles.

D. they are extremely depressed.

Because this question asks you for the implied meaning of a phrase, follow the suggestions for question 8 as you look for the answer.

Choice **A** is a possible answer. The word *"morally"* indicates an issue of right and wrong. Roszak also says "people surrender their freedom to totalitarian masters," an idea which suggests that cultists want to be told the right way and the wrong way to conduct their lives. **A** is correct. **B** is a poor choice. Morally desperate people are not necessarily remorseful. **C** suggests the desperation of cultists, but ignores the cause of their desperation. **D** may trap readers who confuse *morale* (i.e., one's mood and spirits) with *morals* (standards of right and wrong).

10. In the passage, which of the following is stated as a fact rather than an opinion?

F. "cults commonly arise in periods of trouble" (lines 3 and 4).

G. "cults . . . are among the irrepressible constants of human society" (lines 7 and 8).

H. leaders of established churches "appear to have very little idea of the changing levels of religious involvement in this nation" (lines 18 and 19).

J. Many . . . "joined these religious cults during periods of depression and confusion" (line 43).

Start to answer such "fact/opinion" questions by locating all the quotes in the passage and marking them with an asterisk (*). Then recall your grade-school definition of a "fact": *A piece of information that can be proved, indisputably and beyond question.* Any statement not a fact is an opinion.

Search each choice for words that convey an attitude or a belief. Look also for words with ambiguous definitions. For example, how long is a *long* time? What is ordinary about *ordinary* people? Where no such indefinite words appear, you'll probably find the answer.

If all the choices contain ambiguous or judgmental words, go back to the passage and examine the context of each choice. Look for an opinion that may have been expressed as part of a larger factual statement.

Choice **F** could be fact, but in context it expresses Pfaff's opinion. Notice that writers "seemed to agree" with Pfaff. A strictly factual statement would not be subject to the agreement of others. **G** is a statement of Roszak's belief. The word "irrepressible" is clearly judgmental. **H** expresses Gallup's opinion about the knowledge of church leaders. **J** is a statement presented in the passage as a research finding. That Singer drew such a conclusion is beyond dispute. Therefore, **J** is correct.

PRACTICE EXERCISES

Now that you've seen the tactics used to answer many Social Science questions, try your skills on the following passage. Answers and explanations follow the questions.

All energy which is not needed to maintain life can be considered as surplus energy. This is the source of all sexual activity; it is also the source of all productive and creative work. This surplus of energy shows itself in the mature person in generosity, the result of the strength and overflow which the individual can no longer use for further growth and which
5 therefore can be spent productively and creatively. The mature person is no longer primarily a receiver. He receives but also gives. His giving is not primarily subordinated to his expectation of return. It is giving for its own sake. Giving and producing as Dr. Leon Saul correctly emphasizes

10 in his book on maturity, are not felt by the mature person as an obligation and duty; he gives, produces and spends his energies with pleasure in the service of aims which lie outside of his own person. Just as for the growing child, receiving love and help are the main sources of pleasure, for the mature person pleasure consists primarily in spending his energies
15 productively for the sake of other persons and for outside aims. This generous outward directed attitude is what in ethics is called altruism. In the light of this view, altruism, the basis of Christian morality, has a biological foundation; it is a natural, healthy expression of the state of surplus characteristic for maturity.

20 You may have the impression that I am speaking of something unreal, of a blueprint instead of reality. But we must realize that things in nature never correspond to abstract ideals. The platonic ideal of maturity in its pure and complete form is never found in nature and is only approached by human beings to a greater or lesser degree. Every adult carries in
25 himself certain emotional remnants of childhood. Even the most perfect machine does not fulfill the ideal conditions of Carnot's famous heat machine which exists only on paper—an apparatus which works with the theoretically calculated maximum effectiveness in converting heat into useful mechanical energy. There is always attrition; a part of heat energy
30 is lost for productive uses. The same is true for the living organisms, which essentially is a complicated thermodynamic machine.

Whenever life becomes difficult, beyond the individual's capacity to deal with its pressing problems, there is a tendency to regress towards less mature attitudes, in which a person could still rely on the help of parents
35 and teachers. In our heart, deep down, we all regret being expelled from the garden of Eden by eating from the tree of knowledge—which symbolizes maturity. In critical life situations, most persons become insecure and may seek help even before they have exhausted all their own resources. Many occupations require so much responsibility that a
40 person's ability is taxed beyond his inner means. I could not use a better example than the occupation of the nurse. The nurse's function towards the patient in many respects resembles the maternal role because it is so one-sided in relation to giving and receiving. Like the child, the patient demands help and attention and gives little in return.

45 It must be realized that there is a proportion between receiving and giving which has limits for each individual and which cannot be transgressed without ill results. As soon as a person begins to feel that his work becomes a source of displeasure for him, this is the sign that the balance between giving and receiving is disturbed. The load must be reduced to
50 such an extent that the work becomes again a source of pleasure. It is therefore highly important that the occupational and the private life should be in a healthy compensatory relationship to each other. Many occupations in which a person assumes leadership and must take care of the dependent needs of others, involve an unusual amount of respon-
55 sibility. Even the most mature person has his own dependent needs, requires occasional help and advice from others.

Franz Alexander, "Emotional Maturity"

1. According to the passage, mature people can be identified by:
    A. their level of surplus energy.
    B. their desire to work in behalf of others.
    C. the types of jobs they seek.
    D. their ability to deal with problems.

2. All of the following consume surplus energy EXCEPT:
   F. physical exercise.
   G. eating.
   H. sexual activity.
   J. going to school.

3. According to lines 32–44, adults with particularly difficult problems will often:
   A. look to others for help.
   B. get depressed until the problems are solved.
   C. look inside themselves for sources of strength.
   D. seek inspiration from role models.

4. The primary point made by the author of the passage is that maturity is:
   F. almost always a function of a person's age.
   G. usually achieved through one's profession.
   H. based on how one spends time and energy.
   J. an attitude or a state of mind.

5. According to the passage, someone whose work demands too much giving over a period of time is likely to:
   A. have a nervous breakdown.
   B. forget how to relax.
   C. enjoy the work less.
   D. settle into a rut.

6. The word *compensatory,* as used in line 52, means:
   F. well-paying.
   G. balanced.
   H. pleasurable.
   J. natural.

7. The ideas of Dr. Leon Saul (lines 9 to 12) imply that:
   A. if you don't enjoy work, you are probably immature.
   B. enjoying schoolwork is a sign of maturity.
   C. it is natural for a mature person to work in behalf of others.
   D. if you make more money than you need, you are immature.

8. The author compares the garden of Eden (line 36) to:
   F. childhood.
   G. maturity.
   H. naiveté.
   J. insecurity.

9. Based on information in the passage, which of the following people has a job most likely to become a source of displeasure?
   A. A social worker
   B. A mail carrier
   C. A foreman on a factory assembly line
   D. A surgeon

10. The author refers to Carnot's heat machine (line 26) to illustrate the point that:
    F. mature people often work tirelessly—in effect, like machines.
    G. one's energies should be used productively.
    H. adults are guided by what they learned as children.
    J. a human being can come close to, but never attain, an ideal state.

ANSWERS AND EXPLANATIONS

1. B   This answer is stated in the first paragraph, which says that mature people derive pleasure from serving others. A is not specific enough. The passage indicates that a mature person uses surplus energy for productive and creative work. C and D are probably valid to a degree, but neither is discussed in the passage.

2. **G** Since G is necessary for maintaining life, and it does *not,* therefore, consume surplus energy, it is the correct answer. F *is* considered an outlet of surplus energy by the author of the passage. H is cited in line 2 as an outlet for surplus energy. J is not essential for maintaining life. Therefore, it consumes surplus energy.

3. **A** This choice describes what most people in critical life situations tend to do. B is not mentioned as a mature way to cope with problems. C is what some people do, but it's not discussed in the passage. D describes a way to cope with problems, but the passage doesn't mention it.

4. **H** This is a good choice, because it summarizes the point made by the author throughout the passage: Maturity is based on the time and energy devoted to serving causes beyond oneself. F does not coincide with the main point of the passage. G is valid to a certain extent, but it is not broad enough to be the main point of the entire passage. J is valid to a point, but the idea is not discussed sufficiently to be the main idea of the passage.

5. **C** This alternative is discussed in lines 47–50, which states that work can become a source of displeasure when it demands too much giving. A and B may be true in life, but neither is discussed in the passage. D may happen, but whether it is likely to occur is not mentioned in the passage.

6. **G** The correct answer, G, conveys the idea in the passage that a person needs a balance between giving and receiving in both work and private life. F is close to a common definition of the word. In the context of the passage, however, it is wrong. H may describe a "compensatory relationship," but it's not the definition of the word. J may be vaguely implied by the context, but it is not the definition of the word.

7. **C** This choice is suggested by the idea in the passage that a mature person regards work as something that is done for its own sake and for the rewards derived from serving others. A is not consistent with Saul's ideas. B and D are not implied by the passage.

8. **F** Childhood is the time of life before the loss of innocence, aptly symbolized by the garden of Eden. G is the time of life after the loss of innocence, symbolized in the passage by the tree of knowledge. H is similar in meaning to the innocence symbolized by the garden of Eden, but it has a different connotation. J is not relevant.

9. **A** A social worker is most likely to give to others while getting little in return. B is not the type of "giving" job the author of the passage had in mind. C is not considered a "giving" type of occupation. D serves people in need, but not in the same way as a nurse, the example of a "giving" occupation cited in lines 41–43.

10. **J** This answer restates the principle of Carnot's machine, an ideal device that exists only in theory. Similarly, the perfectly mature person is an ideal, not something that exists in reality. F, G, and H do not apply to the allusion to Carnot's heat machine.

NATURAL SCIENCES

Passages

Out of a flood of publications by biologists, ecologists, chemists, physicists, geologists, and other natural scientists, the ACT questioners pick one passage. It comes from a textbook or an article, a research or lab report—from almost any scientific writing. The only certainty is that it pertains to the natural world.

A passage of scientific writing can be a wide-ranging story about the world's endangered species. Or it can be an excerpt from a report on hypothermia, or the greenhouse effect, or volcanoes, or brain waves. Whatever the topic, the passage will probably contain many factual statements, along with statistics and other data, all intended to give an accurate account of reality. There is no science fiction on this part of the ACT.

Science writers usually adopt a serious tone. They write dispassionately, because personal feelings have little place in scientific reporting. In the following account of genetic research, for example, the author's sense of awe has been held in check:

Genetic diseases used to be considered quite rare. Today it is recognized that innumerable people suffer the consequences of disorders due wholly or in part to defective genes or chromosomes (the rod shaped packages of genetic material inside the nucleus of a cell).

Genetics is now progressing so rapidly, on so many fronts, that it is revolutionizing medical research. It is producing a new understanding of how cancer develops, for instance. It is helping researchers design more effective and less harmful drugs. It is providing precise information on who is most vulnerable to what kind of illness, and who would particularly avoid certain environmental agents. Perhaps most importantly, it is bringing new insights into the function of regulatory genes which affect all human growth and development, from birth to death.

As recently as 1956, however, scientists were uncertain about the correct number of chromosomes in a human cell. Mammalian genetics still depended primarily on the slow-paced method of mating two animals and studying their offspring. This approach worked quite well in mice. But since human beings have relatively few children, who take a long time to grow up and reproduce, the study of human genetics was particularly difficult. It remained largely an observational science, much as atomic physics was between the time of the Greeks and the 19th century. Early physicists had deduced the existence of atoms from the properties of matter, but they had no proof of it. Similarly, the geneticists deduced the existence of genes from the properties of organisms and their progeny, but could neither analyze nor manipulate the particles about which they built elaborate theories. Their experiments dealt with the entire animal, rather than with chromosomes or genes.

The idea that human traits are under the control of distinct factors (later called genes), half coming from the father and half from the mother, goes back to the early 1860's and the experiments of the Austrian monk Gregor Mendel with different types of pea plants. He showed that in some cases an inherited trait will be expressed because of the presence of a single "dominant" factor, while in other cases two "recessive" factors are required for a trait to be expressed.

Maya Pines, "The New Human Genetics: How Gene
Splicing Helps Researchers Fight Inherited Disease"

Have you noticed that the most important point in the passage is a giveaway? The author leads you directly to the main idea with "Perhaps most importantly, . . ." (second paragraph), an unmistakable clue that you're about to be told something vital.

If the preceding passage appeared on the ACT, in addition to identifying the main idea, you probably would need to understand why the author draws a parallel between the science of genetics and early work in atomic physics. Both sciences are "observational"—that is, primitive—and are built on theory, not proof. Moreover, you could be asked about the history of genetics and about the utility of genetic information. You may also be asked to recognize the problems of scientists doing genetic research on human subjects rather than working with plants and laboratory animals.

You may have learned about genetics in a high school biology class. If so, this passage probably told you nothing new. On the other hand, don't presume that what you studied in high school gives you easy access to a passage. You may know, for example, that one of the choices provided as a possible answer to a question may be excellent. If the passage doesn't support that choice, however, don't pick it. You're being tested only on the contents of the passage, not on what you may have learned about the subject elsewhere.

Another type of writing from the natural sciences is meant to alert readers to a problem. Few published works about the deteriorating environment, for example, are strictly informative. Lethal air and filthy water are not subjects to be unemotional about. Notice that the following passage, while informative, also holds a warning about contaminating one of the earth's major sources of clean water:

Most groundwater originates as precipitation, percolates into the soil much as water fills a sponge, and moves from place to place along fractures in rock, through sand and gravel, or through channels in formations such as cavernous limestone. Constantly encountering resistance from the surrounding material, groundwater moves in a manner considerably different from that of surface water. Varying with the type of formation, its flow ranges from a fraction of an inch to a few feet per day. These movement characteristics are important to an understanding of groundwater contamination, since concentrations of pollutants called plumes will also move very slowly, with little dilution or dispersion.

"Unconfined" aquifers are the most susceptible to contamination. These aquifers are not protected by an overlying layer of impermeable material and may occur fairly close to the land surface. The volume of water available in unconfined aquifers will fluctuate with usage and with seasonal replenishment or "recharging" of the source of precipitation.

In contrast to this type of aquifer is the "confined" aquifer which is bounded on top and below by layers of relatively impermeable material. Confined aquifers generally occur at greater depths and their impermeable layers may offer a certain measure of protection from contamination. Some confined aquifers have no recharge zone at all and must be recognized as a finite resource which cannot be replenished.

Concern, Inc. *Groundwater*

Unlike the author who wrote about genetics, this one doesn't hand you the main point of the passage. Rather, the idea that groundwater must be understood in order to keep it pure is dispersed throughout the discussion. In addition to being aware of the writer's point of view about groundwater, you may be required to know the differences between confined and unconfined aquifers, to have a general idea of how water moves underground, and to recognize how aquifers become polluted.

The passage contains some specialized language. The word *aquifer* is used several times, so often in fact, that it's hard not to know what it means by the end of the passage. The word *plumes* appears in the first paragraph, but the writer defines it. *Percolates* is also defined. *Impermeable,* while not a technical word, can give you trouble. Since *impermeable* material is contrasted with spongy material, the meaning becomes apparent.

Required reading in most school science courses is often far more exacting than the science passage on the ACT. While taking chemistry or earth science in school, you are immersed in the subject, and your teachers and texts take you deep into its contents. The natural science passage on the ACT, on the other hand, is accessible to the general reader. The two samples of science writing you've seen so far offer no insurmountable challenges to an alert college-bound student. But you must also be ready for more difficult reading, a passage taken from the literature of scientific research, for example. Researchers often fill their reports with the technical terms of their disciplines. Don't get stuck on these specialized words and phrases. Your aim is to discover the general message of the passage. No passage on the ACT will be beyond reach.

The following passage reports on the cytoskeleton of cells—that is, on the internal structure that keeps a cell from collapsing or changing its shape.

Many cells in a multicellular organism must combine the seemingly contradictory traits of stability and mobility. With few exceptions, multicellular organisms begin to develop when a motile sperm meets an egg. Many cell divisions occur, and then cells migrate to their final positions. During life, individual cells divide frequently, and certain specialized cells move through the body to accomplish various tasks. In addition, every cell must have a mechanism for moving materials within itself. Balancing the need for movement is the requirement for cell stability. A cell must maintain its shape against the pressure of surrounding cells. Keeping a cell firm while enabling it to move are the twin roles played by the cytoskeleton.

For a long time, microscopists believed that the cytoplasm surrounding the cell's organelles was completely unstructured. But as scientists began to use newer and gentler fixitives to prepare cells for electron microscopy, a lacy network of fibers was revealed. These structures crisscross the cell like girders and it was hypothesized (and later shown experimentally) that, like an animal's bony skeleton, these structures play a role in giving the cell its shape. For this reason, they are known collectively as the cytoskeleton.

There are three main kinds of cytoskeletal fibers—microfilaments, microtubules, and intermediate filaments—which are distinguishable both by their structure and by their protein composition. All three support and stiffen the cell. In addition to their structural roles, microtubules and microfilaments are essential for a variety of dynamic whole-cell activities, including division, contraction, and crawling, as well as for the movement of vesicles within the cell.

"The Cytoskeleton, the Cell's Physical Props"

The passage contains some technical concepts and language from the field of microbiology, but don't let the terminology discourage you. On the ACT you will not be asked details that involve knowledge of highly specialized language, so if you've never even heard of cytoskeletons, microtubules, and vesicles, it's still possible to make sense of the passage.

Sample Questions

Six reasoning questions and four referring questions follow the Natural Science passage on the ACT. Answer the two samples of each after you read this passage on whales.

No animal in prehistoric or historic times has ever exceeded the whale, in either size or strength, which explains perhaps its survival from ancient times. Few people have any idea of the relative size of the whale compared with other animals. A large specimen weighs about ninety tons, or thirty times as much as
5 an elephant, which beside a whale appears about as large as a dog compared to an elephant. It is equivalent in bulk to one hundred oxen, and outweighs a village of one thousand people. If cut into steaks and eaten, as in Japan, it would supply a meal to an army of one hundred and twenty thousand men.

Whales have often exceeded one hundred feet in length, and George Brown
10 Goode, in his report on the United States Fisheries, mentions a finback having been killed that was one hundred and twenty feet long. A whale's head is sometimes thirty-five feet in circumference, weighs thirty tons, and has jaws twenty feet long, which open thirty feet wide to a mouth that is as large as a room twenty feet long, fifteen feet high, nine feet wide at the bottom, and two
15 feet wide at the top. A score of Jonahs standing upright would not have been unduly crowded in such a chamber.

The heart of a whale is the size of a hogshead. The main blood artery is a foot in diameter, and ten to fifteen gallons of blood pour out at every pulsation. The tongue of a right whale is equal in weight to ten oxen, while the eye of all whales
20 is hardly as large as a cow's, and is placed so far back that it has in direction but a limited range of vision. The ear is so small that it is difficult to insert a knitting needle, and the brain is only about ten inches square. The head, or "case" contains about five hundred barrels, of ten gallons each, of the richest kind of oil, called spermaceti.

Whale Fishery of New England

Sample referring questions:

1. According to the passage, whales, in addition to being unusually large creatures, are also distinctively:
   A. fast swimmers.
   B. powerful.
   C. adaptable to their environment.
   D. intelligent.

As suggested for previous referring questions, skim the passage for thoughts and ideas that refer specifically to each choice.

Choice **A** is not mentioned in the passage. **B** corresponds to information about the strength of whales in the first sentence of the passage. **B** is correct. **C** is not discussed in the passage. **D** contradicts the information in line 22 about the very small size of a whale's brain.

2. According to the passage, all parts of a whale are physically huge EXCEPT its:
   F. heart.
   G. mouth.
   H. eyes.
   J. tongue.

   To answer this question, find a reference to each body part of the whale. If the passage doesn't mention that part or if it fails to say how big it is, you have probably found the answer.

   Choice **F** is described in line 17. The heart is the "size of a hogshead." If you don't know the dimension of a hogshead, you can infer it from the next sentence, which tells you about the one-foot diameter of a whale's main artery. **G** is described in line 13. The mouth is the size of a large room. **H** is discussed in lines 19 and 20. The whale's eye is "hardly as large as a cow's." **H** is the correct answer. **J** is described in lines 18 and 19. The tongue of a right whale weighs as much as ten oxen.

Sample reasoning questions:

3. Based on information in the passage, it is not uncommon for whales to grow as long as:
   A. 35 feet.
   B. 100 feet.
   C. 120 feet.
   D. 185 feet

   Answer this question as you did previous reasoning questions. From information in the passage, draw a reasonable conclusion about the usual size of whales.

   Choice **A** is smaller than any whale mentioned in the passage. **B** is a reasonable answer based on the fact that whales "have often exceeded one hundred feet in length (line 9). **B** is correct. **C** describes the size of a whale cited as an exceptionally long one. **D** is larger than any whale mentioned in the passage.

4. The passage suggests that people have used whales in all of the following ways EXCEPT:
   F. as a source of oil.
   G. for sport fishing.
   H. as food.
   J. as a subject for stories.

   Notice that the question uses the word "suggests." That means you probably won't find specific material in the passage about people's use of whales. Look for implications. The correct answer will be the implication that is *not* in the passage.

   Choice **F** refers to material at the end of the passage. People use the "richest kind of oil, called spermaceti." **G** is *not* in the passage. **G** is the correct answer. **H** refers to a statement in line 7 that whalesteak is eaten in Japan. **J** alludes to the biblical story of Jonah and the whale, mentioned in line 15.

Here is a Natural Science passage about hibernation. After you have read it, answer the ten sample questions. Compare your approach to the analysis following each question.

> Have you ever wondered what it is that tells groundhogs when to begin hibernating in winter and when to awaken in spring? Biologists have, for if they could tap that enzyme, chemical, gene or whatever, they might be able to apply it to other species, including man.
>
> 5   Hibernation, unlike sleep, is a process in which all unnecessary bodily functions are discontinued, for example, growth. The animal's body temperature remains about 1° above the temperature of its environment. During this period, animals appear to be immune to disease and if subjected to a lethal dose of radiation, the animal will not die until the hibernation period is over. (As a
> 10 point of interest, bears do not hibernate, they only sleep more deeply in winter.)

Early in this century, Dr. Max Rubner proposed that aging was a result of the amount of energy expended in tissues. "Rubner found that the total lifetime energy expenditure per gram of tissue during the adult stage is roughly constant for several species of domestic animals. 'The higher the metabolism, the

15 shorter the life span and vice versa.'"

In this vein, scientists found that the storage of body fat was vital to a hibernating animal's survival: it loses 20–40 percent of its body weight while dormant. The body fat involved here is called "brown fat" and differs structurally from normal, white fat cells which gives it a greater heat producing

20 potential. A low temperature signals the brown fat to increase in temperature, which warms the animal's blood and spreads the warmth to other parts of the body. Newborn human babies have an unusually high percentage of brown fat which diminishes as they grow older. Adults do have some brown fat, and those with underproductive thyroid glands have more than normal:

25   Rats subjected to cold temperatures show an increased ratio of brown
    fat to white fat. It seems reasonable to expect that cold acclimation in
    man, through a carefully controlled program of cyclic hypothermia . . .,
    will increase brown fat deposits. After these deposits reach a certain body
    level, they might perform the same regulatory functions in human

30   hibernation that brown fat performs in natural hibernators.

About ten years after Rubner's experiments, Drs. Jacques Loeb and John Northrop discovered that reduced temperatures extended the life span of fruit flies. In applying this to animals, however, those that were not natural hibernators or who had not been prepared for hibernation, developed ventricu-

35 lar fibrillations (where the heart muscle quivers and stops pumping blood). When a person "freezes to death" this is the cause, not ice crystals forming in the veins.

The process involved in artificially cooling an animal's body temperature is called induced hypothermia. Research in this field led space biologist Dale L.

40 Carpenter (McDonnell Douglas—Long Beach) to determine that both hibernating and non-hibernating animals have the same basic temperature control and he believes that "were a non-hibernating mammal to be artificially biochemically prepared with proper enzymes and energy producing chemicals, it could hibernate." He found that if an animal was cooled just until its heart began

45 quivering and then rewarmed, it could survive. If cooled a second time, a slightly lower temperature could be achieved before ventricular fibrillations occurred, and so on. Each exposure to the cold seemed to condition the heart to accept lower temperatures. This is cyclic hypothermia.

Even with this kind of progress, however, the search goes on for the chemical

50 or enzyme that triggers the hibernation process, that tells the animals it is winter or spring. Scientists hope to gain some insight into this mystery from human infants, who besides having more brown fat than adults, seem less susceptible to ventricular fibrillations. They have different forms of hemoglobin and myoglobin in their tissues which are more efficient in attracting and releasing

55 oxygen. This may hold the clue.

If hibernation could be induced in humans, this could solve the problem of interstellar travel. One would not have to worry about travelling near the speed of light, for the crew would not age as fast and would have more time to reach their destination. Maxwell Hunter suggests that this "biological time dilation"

60 be applied not only to the crews, but to those that remain on Earth.

    We are thus faced with the prospect of a whole society dilated in time.
    This would form the basis for a Galactic Club which was based on travel
    rather than communication. . . .

65 We are not talking about timefaring in the classic science fiction sense where people are able to go both backward and forward in time at will . . . We are postulating, rather, dilating the time experienced by people in one direction in the future . . . which would permit a society to expand throughout the galaxy. If, when one went to bed at night, he actually went into hibernation during which many months passed, it would not seem 70 any different to him than a standard eight-hour sleep . . . When a ship returned home, its crew would be greeted by friends, business colleagues, etc. who had aged no more than the crew.

Report of the Committee on Science and Technology,
"The Possibility of Intelligent Life in the Universe"

1. By pointing out that freezing to death is not caused by ice crystals in the veins (line 36), the author of the passage implies that:
   A. the research findings of Drs. Loeb and Northrop are questionable.
   B. death by freezing results from several complex causes.
   C. readers should not believe the old wives' tale about ice crystals in the veins.
   D. freezing is different from ordinary frostbite.

   To infer what the author had in mind, look to the passage for clues. The author used quotation marks for the phrase "freezes to death," an indication that it shouldn't be taken literally. In effect, the author is saying that the phrase is imprecise, that death is not caused by the actual freezing of blood or by the freezing of any other part of the body.

   Choice **A** is irrelvant. **B** may sound right, but notice the ambiguous word "several." The passage states the death is caused by ventricular fibrillation, which is a single cause, not "several" causes. **C** implies that many people believe that "freezing to death" occurs when ice crystals form in the veins. Here, the author is setting the record straight. **C** is correct. **D** is a poor choice. The passage does not mention frostbite.

2. A conclusion that may be drawn from research described in the passage is that:
   F. in severe cold a human infant is likely to survive longer than an adult.
   G. a person with many brown fat cells will live longer than someone with many white fat cells.
   H. animals living in cold places live longer than animals in warm places.
   J. metabolic rates in animals remain constant throughout life.

   To answer a question using inductive reasoning, you need to think logically and to find the evidence in the passage for drawing a valid conclusion. Guard against overgeneralization. A conclusion may sound right, but if you can't find material in the passage to back it up, consider it wrong! Similarly, on its face a conclusion may seem invalid, but if it can be supported with facts in the passage, you have to consider it correct.

   Question writers take great pains to avoid arguments over answers to test questions. In their phrasing of questions and answers they often include such hedging words as *may, often, almost, mostly, usually, generally, rarely, sometimes*—words that forestall controversy.

   In answering ACT questions, be wary of conclusions stated as absolutes. They are *often* invalid precisely because they leave no room for exceptions. On the other hand, correct answers will *often* contain a hedging word that renders the statement valid.

   Choice **F** seems to correspond with the statement that newborn human babies have an "unusually high percentage of brown fat which diminishes as they grow older" (lines 22 and 23). Since brown fat, according to the passage, serves as a warming agent, it stands to reason that a baby can tolerate severe cold longer than an adult. Notice also that this choice contains the hedging phrase "is likely." **F** is correct. **G** implies that the focus of the passage is longevity rather than hibernation. Since longevity is not the real issue in the passage, however, this is not a good choice. **H** is wrong, because the passage does not discuss animals living in warm places. Notice also that this choice is stated as an absolute, which makes it immediately suspect. **J** is wrong. Since the passage alludes to metabolism in "the adult stage" of life, you may assume that other stages are characterized by different rates of metabolism.

3. Based on information in the passage, all of the following are valid conclusions EXCEPT:
   A. human beings may some day have the ability to hibernate.
   B. long-term space exploration will be given a big boost when the process of hibernation is fully understood.
   C. it remains unclear why certain creatures have the capacity to hibernate.
   D. by means of hibernation the life span of human beings can be extended indefinitely.

   To find the answer, identify the one conclusion that *cannot* legitimately be drawn from the facts in the passage. The discussion after question 2 may give you some hints on how to think out the answer.

   Choice **A** is valid. It is the premise in the passage on which the discussion of interstellar travel is based. **B** is valid. The last part of the passage points out that long-term space travel depends on learning the secrets of hibernation. **C** is valid. Much of the passage is about past and present efforts to understand hibernation. **D** is *not* valid. Although aging slows down during hibernation, it doesn't stop altogether. Hibernation may lengthen life but not extend it indefinitely. **D** is correct.

4. As used in the passage, the meaning of *metabolism* is the:
   F. rate at which food is digested.
   G. speed at which an organism uses up energy.
   H. rate at which blood replenishes its supply of oxygen.
   J. rate at which the bodily functions of a hibernating animal slow down.

   Even if you know the word, don't depend on your prior knowledge of what it means. Because "metabolism" is a common word, it's likely that the question is asking for an uncommon definition. Don't be fooled into choosing the most popular definition. Determine the meaning of the word only from the way it is used on the passage.

   Choice **F** corresponds to the everyday definition of metabolism. The passage, however, does not link metabolism to the digestion of food. **G** resembles the explanation of metabolism given in the passage: "energy expenditure per gram of tissue." **G** is correct. **H** is discussed in the passage but not in connection with metabolism. **J** has nothing to do with metabolism.

5. As used in the passage, the word *dilated* (line 61) means all of the following EXCEPT:
   A. causing years to seem like no more than a moment.
   B. programming space travelers to hibernate during stellar voyages.
   C. having the earth's people hibernate for the same span of time as stellar travelers.
   D. assuring that people remain young by means of hibernation.

   The word "dilated" is not unusual, but the idea of a "dilated" society (line 61) is. The word may be defined right in the text or implied by the general meaning of the passage. You'll see the consequences of "dilating" a society by rereading lines 56 through 72.

   Choice **A** is a consequence of a dilated society. **B** is a feature of a dilated society. **C** describes what happens in a dilated society. Space travelers return to friends, business colleagues, etc., who had aged no more than they had during flights to the stars. **D** is *not* a consequence of a dilated society. Therefore, **D** is correct.

6. Based on information in the passage, in which of the following ways are animals in deep sleep similar to animals in hibernation?
   F. Body temperature
   G. Resistance to disease
   H. Slowing down of bodily functions
   J. Rate of growth

   To answer this comparison question, draw your inference out of the parts of the passage where you find references to hibernation and sleep.

   Choice **F** is wrong. Only hibernating animals experience changes in body temperature as the environment warms and cools (lines 5–7). **G** is wrong. Line 8 says that hibernating animals appear to have a natural immunity to disease. Sleep, on the other hand, is no defense against disease. **H** is supported by lines 5–9. The bodily functions of all animals, whether in hibernation (like the groundhog) or in deep sleep (like the bear), slow down during extended periods of rest. **H** is correct. **J** is wrong. Growth continues during sleep, but during hibernation, according to line 6, it stops.

7. Hibernating animals differ from nonhibernating animals in all of the following ways EXCEPT in the:

A. number of brown fat cells.

B. presence of a certain enzyme in the body.

C. tolerance to extremely cold temperatures.

D. metabolic rate.

Because characteristics of hibernating animals are discussed throughout the passage, deal with the choices one at a time.

Choice **A** is wrong. Lines 16–18 indicate that hibernating animals have a higher percentage of brown fat cells than other animals. **B** is wrong. Lines 3 and 50 refer to scientists' quest to find the enzyme that sets off hibernation. Presumably, nonhibernating animals lack such an enzyme. **C** is wrong. Experiments described in lines 31 to 35 found that natural hibernators withstand cold temperatures more readily than nonhibernators. **D** is a good choice, because the passage discusses metabolism as a function of the life span of *all* animals, hibernators and nonhibernators alike. **D** is correct.

8. Based on the passage, which of the following procedures holds the greatest promise for inducing human hibernation?

F. Promoting the growth of brown fat cells in the body

G. Changing the activity of the thyroid gland

H. Conditioning the heart to adapt to lower temperatures

J. Increasing the amount of oxygen in body tissue

Solving a problem from facts is not far different from drawing a conclusion, but, to answer this question, use deductive, instead of inductive, reasoning—that is, consider a number of pieces of information to determine the only reasonable solution to the problem. For example:

FACT 1: Arthur lies dead on the floor with a bullet hole in his chest.

FACT 2: Harold stands over Arthur with a smoking gun in his hand.

PROBLEM: Figure out who killed Arthur.

You can assume that the ACT will present problems somewhat harder to solve than Arthur's murder. The point is to use every available scrap of evidence to solve the problem.

Choice **F** is discussed in lines 16–30. At one time, brown fat cells seemed like a key to human hibernation, but years of research have been unsuccessful. **G** is discussed in line 24. People with underproductive thyroids have a more than normal amount of brown fat cells. To induce the formation of more brown fat cells by slowing the thyroid, however, is hazardous to health. **H** is fully discussed in the passage, but in spite of some progress, the search for a better answer goes on. **J** is discussed in line 55, which says this procedure "may hold the clue." **J** is correct.

9. Based on information in the passage, scientists can predict which of two kittens from the same litter is likely to live longer by:

A. studying the brown fat cell/white fat cell ratio in each kitten.

B. analyzing the kittens' enzyme secretions.

C. measuring the kittens' metabolic rates.

D. comparing the amounts of hemoglobin and myoglobin in each kitten's blood.

To answer this question, search the passage for references to longevity. Since life span is discussed in the second paragraph, focus your attention there.

Choice **A** is wrong, because the passage discusses brown and white fat cells with regard to heat production in the body, not to life span. **B** is wrong. According to the passage, enzymes are thought to bring about hibernation and have nothing to do with length of life. **C** coincides with Rubner's finding that the "higher the metabolism, the shorter the life span and vice versa" (lines 14 and 15). **C** is correct. **D** is wrong, because the composition of blood, while important to hibernation, has nothing to do with longevity.

10. In which of the following sequences (from earliest to latest) were these discoveries made?

I. In extreme cold, nonhibernating animals develop ventricular fibrillations.

II. The heart can be conditioned to adapt to low temperatures.

III. An organism's energy expenditure is related to its life span.

IV. Fruit flies live longer when their body temperature is lowered.

F. I, III, IV, II
G. III, II, IV, I
H. III, IV, I, II
J. IV, I, III, II

Sequence questions such as this consume a good deal of time on the ACT. Consider saving them for last. By then you'll know how much test time remains, and you won't neglect other, less time-consuming questions.

First skim the passage to locate the four sequenced items. Mark them I, II, III, and IV. Begin by finding either the first or the last item in the sequence. Nonfiction passages often cue the reader with such words and phrases as *first, to begin, initially, in the first place, to start, early on, finally, in conclusion, last, in the end, most recently.* Intermediate steps are often cued with *then, next, also, soon after, in the meantime, secondly, in addition,* and many other similar transitional words.

Once you've identified either the first or last item, go directly to the question choices and start eliminating those that can't be right. If you know the first item in a sequence, start looking for the last item, and vice versa. Once you've located both the first and the last items, you may have the answer. If you haven't, of course, you'll also need to identify either the second or third item.

Choice **F** is wrong. The paragraph in which ventricular fibrillations (lines 34 and 35) are discussed, begins with the phrase "About ten years after Rubner's experiments, . . ." Discover number I, therefore, could not have occurred first. **G** seems like a possibility. According to line 12, discovery number III was made by Rubner early in this century. Therefore, the proper sequence must begin with III. The last number in this choice refers to a discovery made ten years after Rubner's. Since more recent discoveries are discussed later in the passage, discovery I cannot be last in the sequence. **H** is a possibility. Aside from choice **G,** it is the only one that starts with discovery number III. Indeed, this sequence corresponds with the order of discoveries described in the passage. **H** is correct. **J** is wrong, because it begins with discovery number IV, which took place after Rubner's work.

PRACTICE EXERCISES

In this practice exercise you will have a chance to demonstrate your mastery of the tactics for answering questions about Natural Science reading passages. Answers and explanations follow the questions.

The history of science is composed of three periods: antiquity; classical science, starting with the Renaissance; and modern science, which started at the turn of this century.

What characterizes the *science of antiquity* is the naive faith in the
5 perfection of our senses and reasoning. What man sees is the ultimate reality. Everybody, being by necessity the center of his universe, knew there was no doubt that ours is a flat earth and man is the center, as expressed in the *cosmology* of Ptolemy. If we touch something, we find it either hard or soft, wet or dry, cold or warm; so these qualities had to be
10 the ultimate building stones of the universe, as taught by Aristotle. There is an "up" and "down," an absolute space, as expressed in Euclidean geometry. Human reasoning was thought to lead to more reliable results than crude trial and experiment, as reflected by the *dictum* of Aristotle that a big stone falls faster than a small one. What is remarkable about this
15 statement is not that it is wrong, but that it never occurred to Aristotle to try it. He probably would have regarded such a proposal as an insult.

Two thousand years later, in that great awakening of the Western mind called the Renaissance, something new must have happened to the human mind. A boisterous young man, Galileo by name, went up a leaning tower
20 with two stones, one big and one small, and dropped them simultaneously, having asked his companions to observe which of the two arrived first on the pavement below. They arrived simultaneously. This same man doubted the perfection of his senses, built a telescope to

improve the range of his eyes, and thus discovered the rings of Saturn and
25 the satellites of Jupiter. This was a dramatic discovery because nobody
had seen these before. So it now seemed scarcely credible that the whole
universe could have been created solely for man's pleasure or temptation.

Galileo was but one of the first swallows of an approaching spring.
Somewhat earlier, Copernicus had already concluded that it was not
30 absolutely necessary to suppose that the sun rotates around the earth; it
could be the other way around. Johannes Kepler replaced simple observation and reasoning with careful measurement. Somewhat later, Antony
van Leeuwenhoek, a greengrocer at Delft, in Holland, improved the
range of his senses by building a microscope. With it he discovered a
35 new world of living creatures too small to be seen by the naked eye. Thus
began the science which I will call "classical," which reached its peak
with Sir Isaac Newton, who, with the concept of gravitation, made a
coherent system of the universe.

This *classical science* replaced divine whims by natural laws, cor-
40 rected many previous errors, and extended man's world into both the
bigger and smaller dimensions, but it introduced nothing new that man
could not "understand." By the word "understand" we simply mean that
we can correlate the *phenomenon* in question with some earlier experience of ours. If I tell you that it is gravitation which holds our globe to the
45 sun, you will say "I understand," though nobody knows what gravitation
is. All the same, you "understand" because you know that it is gravitation
which makes apples fall, and you all have seen apples fall before.

For several centuries, this classical science had little influence on
everyday life or human relations and was merely the intellectual play-
50 ground of the selected few who wanted to look deeper into Nature's
cooking pot.

Around the turn of this century (1896), two mysterious discoveries
signified the arrival of a new period, the period of *modern science*. The
one was that of Wilhelm Röntgen, who discovered new rays which could
55 penetrate through solid matter. The other was the discovery of radioactivity by Antoine Henri Becquerel, a discovery which shook the solid
foundation of our universe, built of indestructible matter.

Albert Szent-Györgyi, "Horizons of Life Sciences," in *Ideas in Science*,
ed. Oscar H. Fidell, Washington Square Press, (N.Y., 1966), pp. 167–9.

1. Based on information in the passage, all of the following sciences were prac-
    ticed in antiquity EXCEPT:
    A. medicine.
    B. physics.
    C. astronomy.
    D. mathematics.

2. According to the passage, scientists of ancient times believed that:
    F. the gods had created the universe for the happiness of man.
    G. man's intuition led to an understanding of the physical principles that gov-
       erned the universe.
    H. rational thought could unlock all the secrets of science.
    J. answers to the mystery of life were found within each person.

3. The author of the passage implies that scientists of antiquity were:
    A. well-meaning.
    B. lazy.
    C. short-sighted.
    D. proud of their achievements.

4. Ptolemy was known for his "cosmology," a term that may best be compared to modern-day:
   F. geography.
   G. astrology.
   H. geology.
   J. astronomy.

5. Galileo's astronomical discoveries led to the belief that:
   A. the earth was not the center of the universe.
   B. extraterrestrial life could exist somewhere in the universe.
   C. the universe was not created for the benefit of mankind.
   D. the universe was much larger than anyone had imagined.

6. Based on information in the passage, Galileo's greatest achievement was to:
   F. correct Aristotle's mistakes.
   G. initiate a new age of science.
   H. invent the telescope.
   J. make science more understandable to the general public.

7. All of the following occurred during the age of classical science EXCEPT:
   A. universal scientific rules began to be recognized.
   B. technological inventions extended man's horizons.
   C. the law of gravity was finally explained and understood.
   D. reason became less important than measurement and observation.

8. The passage implies that science had virtually no effect on the daily life of most people until the:
   F. Renaissance.
   G. work of Sir Isaac Newton.
   H. twentieth century.
   J. discoveries of Wilhelm Röntgen.

9. The word "understand" appears in quotation marks (line 42) to suggest that:
   A. gravity cannot be understood; the best we can do is observe its effect.
   B. it signifies the mastery of highly specialized scientific knowledge.
   C. the author is being sarcastic, since it takes years of study to understand gravity.
   D. you have to take gravity on faith; there is no rational explanation for it.

10. The modern age of science seems to have come about when:
    F. scientists began to discover mysterious phenomena that could not be understood by ordinary people.
    G. the nature of matter began to be understood.
    H. X-rays were invented.
    J. the effects of radiation began to be explored.

ANSWERS AND EXPLANATIONS

1. A Medicine is the only science not mentioned in the passage. Lines 8–10 indicate that Aristotle practiced physics (Answer B), Ptolemy was an astronomer (C), and Euclid worked in mathematics (D).

2. H This answer is supported by the ideas expressed in the second paragraph, which says that the application of human reasoning was the preferred method of scientific research during the age of antiquity. G is wrong because the passage does not refer to intuition. F is partly true, but the passage doesn't discuss the creator of the universe. J is not mentioned in the passage.

3. C This response is suggested by the description of the ancients' disregard of scientific experimentation. Choice A is not at issue in the passage. B is an incorrect inference. D is not discussed.

4. J Ptolemy's concern was the shape and place of the earth in the universe; hence, he was an astronomer. F relates to the arrangement of the earth's features. G examines the placement of the stars, and H is the study of the composition and internal structure of the earth.

5. C   This answer is stated in lines 26 and 27. As a result of Galileo's work, it became clear that the universe had not, after all, been created solely for man's pleasure. Choice A refers to the work of Copernicus. Neither B nor D is discussed in the passage.

6. G   This answer is strongly suggested by lines 17–19. F, H, and J refer to Galileo's work, but they are not considered his *greatest* achievements.

7. C   This is the best answer because, according to lines 45–46, gravity cannot really be understood. Choice A is discussed in lines 37–38. B refers to the invention of both the telescope and the microscope. D refers to methods of research conducted by Keppler.

8. H   Lines 48–53 state that until the age of modern science, only an elite group of intellectuals were interested in scientific study.

9. A   In lines 49 to 53 the law of gravity is described as an acknowledged but inexplicable force in the universe.

10. G   The passage refers to scientists who began to understand the nature of solid matter. F seems to refer to supernatural events not discussed in the passage. H and J are valid, but neither marks the birth of the modern age of science.

SAMPLE READING TEST

Now that you are acquainted with the various types of reading passages and questions on the ACT, see whether you can apply what you have learned. This exercise consists of four passages, each accompanied by ten questions. Because the passages in this Sample Test vary in length from those on the ACT Reading Test, you may wish to allow yourself about forty-five minutes, rather than the thirty-five minutes allotted on the ACT, to complete the exercise. Don't let yourself be distracted by the time limit, however. For the moment, devote yourself to recalling and using the test-taking tactics suggested throughout this chapter.

DIRECTIONS: This test consist of four passages, each followed by ten multiple-choice questions. Read each passage and then pick the best answer for each question. Refer to the passage as often as you wish while answering the questions.

Passage I

SOCIAL SCIENCE: This passage is adapted from an article titled "Freedom of Inquiry Is for Hopeful People" by Gerald W. Johnson. The passage discusses the relationship between a government and its people.

When Jefferson listed "the pursuit of happiness" as one of the rights that government cannot justly take from any man, except as punishment for crime, he stepped into a dark and mysterious corner of the realm of ideas. Nobody denies the truth of what he said; but the reason for that is that nobody knows exactly what it means.

The word *happiness* cannot be defined precisely because it means different things to different people, or to the same people at different times or in different circumstances. The word "pursuit" is almost as vague. Together, they express an idea that a man cannot always comprehend as it applies to himself, and that he can rarely, if ever, comprehend as it applies to anyone else.

The only interpretation of this phrase that is not open to some fatal objection seems to be this: the right to the pursuit of happiness is the right to be let alone.

Instantly, this raises the question, how is government going to govern if it lets people alone? The function of government is not to let people alone, but to interfere with them. Government is instituted to protect certain inalienable rights, among them life, liberty, and the pursuit of happiness; therefore its business, its reason for being, is to interfere with those who would infringe these rights, and not merely to interfere, but to prevent their doing what they would like to do. These people may be wrong, but they are nevertheless people, and they do not like it when government stops them from doing as they please.

There is no logical answer to this. The only answer is an illogical one—considered what would happen if government were abolished altogether. In that case, the right to the pursuit of happiness would not be respected at all. The strongest would impose his will on all others, and there would be no liberty except the liberty of the strongest. This is anarchy; and it was the secret fear of some founders of the republic that democracy must inevitably degenerate into anarchy.

Furthermore, there are some men—never a majority, but a definite number, and important out of all proportion to their number—for whom the pursuit of happiness consists in finding out what is true. They are critics of everything; and among other things they are critics of government, which lays upon the American government the duty of protecting those who attack it. This is the basis of the maxim beloved of early liberals, "That government is best that governs least." It means that government should interfere with the individual only as far as is absolutely necessary to protect the general welfare.

Two factors work constantly against this ideal—one is human nature, the other is the passage of time. Any group of men given a chance to wield power—and a government is just that—will try to extend that power. This is the first factor. As more people are crowded together in the same area, more activity by government is required to maintain order. This is the second factor. Neither can be eliminated. Each is capable of becoming a threat to all liberty. Since some extension of governmental power is necessary as the population grows, it is easy for governors to convince themselves that any extension of their power is justifiable. This tendency must be held within bounds by steady counterpressure from people who know their rights and mean to maintain them.

1. According to the passage, the phrase "pursuit of happiness" is difficult to define because:
   A. no one knows exactly what Jefferson had in mind.
   B. each generation views happiness differently.
   C. the words have different meanings to different people.
   D. the meaning of the phrase has changed since Jefferson wrote it.

2. The author believes that a widely acceptable definition of "pursuit of happiness" is the right of people:
   F. to do whatever they please provided they don't interfere with the rights of others.
   G. to be free of interference by the government.
   H. to be free of all laws that restrict their pleasure.
   J. to seek happiness in whatever way they want.

3. During the early days of the country, liberals believed that government:
   A. should base its decisions on what is best for the greatest number of people.
   B. should be as inconspicuous as possible in people's lives.
   C. is the servant of the people.
   D. has the right to protect itself from criticism.

4. The last paragraph in the passage implies that governments must be carefully monitored because:
   F. they tend to expand their power as time goes on.
   G. over time, an entrenched bureaucracy is certain to develop.
   H. as government grows, it inevitably starts to limit the people's freedoms.
   J. big organizations are susceptible to corruption.

5. The main purpose of the passage is to:
   A. define the term, "pursuit of happiness."
   B. alert readers to the dangers of big government.
   C. argue that democracy is a difficult form of government to maintain.
   D. clarify the relationship between the government and the people.

6. Based on information in lines 29–34, which of the following is NOT likely to occur if government were to be abolished?

F. Anarchy would spread.
G. The weak would fall prey to the strong.
H. The right to pursue happiness would no longer be respected.
J. Society would become more alert to the dangers of dictatorship.

7. Some of America's founding fathers feared the emergence of anarchy in the United States because:
   A. too much influence was given to the people.
   B. the government didn't claim enough power to prevent it.
   C. many colonists were almost fanatic in their desire for basic liberties.
   D. Jefferson's ideals were too abstract and lofty to be used as a solid defense against it.

8. According to the passage, some citizens have interpreted "the pursuit of happiness" to mean:
   F. the right to state their opinions in a free press.
   G. being confident that the government will always tell the truth.
   H. the freedom to express their views about anything at all.
   J. having the government help people who need it the most.

9. Which of the following does the author of the passage believe to be the basic purpose of government?
   A. To protect the rights of the individual.
   B. To provide for the general welfare of the population.
   C. To allow people to express themselves freely.
   D. To permit people to pursue happiness in whatever manner they choose.

10. The passage suggests that an educated citizenry is important because:
    F. intelligent and well-educated people are needed to run the country.
    G. people need to know their rights in order to maintain them.
    H. educated people will put up with less interference by the government.
    J. it takes a well-informed people to choose its government's leaders wisely.

Passage II

NATURAL SCIENCE: From a U.S. Department of the Interior publication on underground water, this passage describes the aquifer, the area beneath the earth's surface where water flows.

The word *aquifer* comes from two Latin words: *aqua,* or water, and *ferre,* to bring. The aquifer may be a layer of gravel or sand, a layer of sandstone or of cavernous limestone, or even a large body of nonlayered rock that has
5 sizable openings.

An aquifer may be only a few feet thick, or tens or hundreds of feet. It may be just below the surface, or hundreds of feet below. It may underlie a few acres or many square miles. The Dakota Sandstone in the West
10 carries water over great distances, across several states. Many aquifers, however, are only local in extent. Underneath the water-bearing rocks everywhere, at some depth, are rocks that are watertight. This depth may be a few hundred feet, or tens of thousands of feet.

5 The amount of water that a given rock can contain depends on its porosity—the spaces between the grains or the cracks that can fill with water. If the grains are all about the same size, or well-sorted, as the geologists say, the spaces between them account for a large proportion of the 20 whole volume. This is true of gravel and sand. However, if the grains are poorly sorted, that is, not all the same size, the spaces between the larger grains will fill with small grains instead of water. Poorly sorted rocks do not hold as much water as well-sorted rocks.

25 If water is to move through the rock, the pores must be connected. If the rock has a great many connected pore spaces, of which a large part are sizable, the rock is permeable. Large amounts of water are available to a well from saturated permeable rocks. But if the pores or cracks 0 are small, poorly connected, or nearly lacking, the aquifer can yield only a small amount of water to a well. The porosity of different kinds of rocks varies widely. In some the porosity is less than 1 percent; in others, mostly unconsolidated rock such as sand and gravel, it may be as 5 high as 30 to 40 percent.

A rock that will be a good source of water must contain either many pore spaces, or many cracks, or both. A compact rock such as granite, almost without pore spaces, may be permeable if it contains enough sizable fractures. 0 Nearly all consolidated rock formations are broken by cracks, called *joints*. The joints are caused by the same kinds of stresses in the earth's crust that cause earthquakes. At first they are just hairline cracks, but they tend to open through the day-to-day action of rain, sun, and frost. The 5 ice crystals formed by water that freezes in rock crevices will cause the rocks to split open. Heating by the sun and cooling at night cause expansion and contraction that produce the same result. Water will enter the joints and gradually dissolve away the rock, enlarging the opening.

If the joints intersect each other, water can move from one to another, much as it flows through the water pipes in a municipal water system. Granite and slate are less porous than sandstone. When water circulates in them, it does so through joint cracks. The water yield of wells drilled in these rocks depends on how many joints are intersected by the well, and how wide they are.

Water will move faster in certain kinds of rocks. A clayey silt having only very tiny pores will not carry water very readily, but a coarse gravel will carry water freely and rapidly. Some rocks, like limestone, are cavernous; they contain hollowed-out openings. Gravel also has numerous open spaces. Water may travel through it at rates of tens or hundreds of feet per day. In silt or fine sand it may move only inches a day. Flow of streams is measured in feet per second; movement of ground water is usually measured in feet per year.

There is no strict correlation between the water-bearing capacity of rocks and the depth at which they are found. A dense granite may be found at the surface, as 70 in New England, while a porous sandstone may lie several thousand feet down, as in the Great Plains. However, on average, porosity and permeability grow less as depth increases. Rocks that yield fresh water have been found at depths of more than 6,000 feet (and salty water has come 75 from oil wells at depths of more than 20,000 feet), but most wells drilled deeper than 2,000 feet find little water. The pores and cracks in the rocks at great depths are closed up because of the weight of overlying rocks.

Helene L. Baldwin and C.L. McGuiness,
A Primer on Ground Water

11. The passage suggests that most aquifers consist of:
   A. rocks only.
   B. sand and rocks in equal amounts.
   C. sand only.
   D. more rocks than sand.

12. Which of the following determines the porosity of rock?
   F. the temperature of the water
   G. the overall dimensions of the rock
   H. the similarity of the grains that make up the rock
   J. the length of hairline cracks on the rock's surface

13. Which of the following most accurately describes a rock that is *permeable?*
   A. It is likely to be more narrow than wide.
   B. It is generally a few feet thick.
   C. It contains more cracks than pores.
   D. It contains numerous connected pores.

14. All of the following may help to turn watertight rocks into water-bearing rocks EXCEPT:
   F. the sun's heat.
   G. sub-freezing temperatures.
   H. the flow of water.
   J. veins of soft material in the rock.

15. By comparing joints in rock to pipes in a municipal water system (lines 51–52), the author stresses the point that:
   A. water flows through joints at a steady rate.
   B. joints must connect to each other like water pipes.
   C. joints are essential to an aquifer as a water system is essential to a municipality.
   D. a municipal water system is always underground.

16. In which type of rock are productive aquifers most likely to be found?
   F. granite
   G. a blend of slate and granite
   H. limestone
   J. sandstone

17. An aquifer consisting of nonporous consolidated rock formations is a good source of water when:
   A. it contains many wide joints.
   B. an earthquake occurs.
   C. water alternatively freezes and melts.
   D. many hairline cracks run across its surface.

18. An aquifer consisting of gravel will be a better source of water than an aquifer consisting of clay because:
   F. gravel has more well-sorted grains than clay.
   G. clay is more porous than gravel.
   H. gravel pores tend to fill up with sand.
   J. the grains in clay are larger than the grains in gravel.

19. An aquifer is not likely to be found a great distance below the earth's crust because:
   A. water flows very slowly at great depths.
   B. oil far belowground pushes the water toward the surface.
   C. compressed rocks are not porous.
   D. the action of rain, sun, and frost have no effect on rocks far below the surface.

20. Overall, the passage implies that the most promising place to drill a well is:
   F. in a limestone or gravel aquifer less than 2,000 feet underground.
   G. in the Dakota Sandstone aquifer.
   H. in New England granite that is close to the surface.
   J. in a large-jointed slate aquifer more than 2,000 feet below the earth's surface.

Passage III

PROSE FICTION: This passage is from "An Old Oregonian in the Snow," a short story by Joachim Miller. The passage describes Joe Meek, a legendary character in the Old West.

I was once, when riding express, "snowed under" with a famous old pioneer in the great cañon that splits Camas Prairie in two and breaks the monotony of its vast levels.

A wild unpeopled and unknown land it was then, but it
5   has since been made immortal by the unavailing battles of Chief Joseph for the graves of his fathers.

Joe Meek! The many books about him tell you he was a savage, buckskinned delegate to Congress from the unorganized territory of Oregon, who lived with the
10 Indians. These statements are almost all untrue. His was a plain, pastoral nature, and he shunned strife and notoriety. He had none of Kit Carson's dash about him, none of Davy Crockett's daring, nor had he Fremont's culture and capacity for putting himself well before the world; he
15 ranked all these men both in the priority and peril of his enterprises.

Indeed, before the chiefest of them was really heard of he had called the people of the far Northwest together under the great pines by the sounding Oregon,* and made
20 solemn protest against the pretensions of England to that region. These settlers sent this man over the plains alone, a journey of more than half a year, to beg the President that they might be made or remain a portion of the United States while most of the now famous mountaineers were
25 yet at their mother's knee. I know of no figure in our history that approaches his in grandeur except that of President Houston, of the Lone Star Republic. And yet you search in vain for his name among those who sat in our Capitol in those early days. Some say he arrived at Wash-
30 ington when Congress was not in session, and so did not present his credentials. Others say that he lost his papers

on the way in one of his perilous passages of a stream. And then again I am told that he never had any credentials to present; that the territory had no official existence at
35 that time, and as Congress had not then become as adept in coining States and Territories, the pioneers of the Oregon River gave him no authority to appear in Congress, but that his mission was entirely with the President.

But the spectacle of this man setting out in mid-winter
40 to ride alone over an untracked distance of three thousand miles, the loyalty of this people, their peril from savages, as well as the cupidity of Great Britain, I count one of the finest on the page of pioneer history.

I suspect that his mission was fruitful of little, for he
45 was, as new people came pouring in, quietly relegated to the background, and never afterward came conspicuously forward, save as an occasional leader in the wars against the Indians. But the undertaking and the accomplishment of this terrible journey alone ought to keep his memory
50 green forever. And, indeed, had fate placed him in any other spot than isolated Oregon, he surely now would not be so nearly forgotten.

When gold was discovered in Idaho—or Ida*h*ho, an Indian word meaning, in a broad sense, mountain of
55 light—Joe Meek, now an old man, could not resist the temptation to leave his home in the woods of Oregon and again brave the plains.

But he was no longer in any great sense a conspicuous figure. He, so far from being a leader, was even laughed
60 at by his own people, the Oregonians, the new, young people who had journeyed into the country after his work had been done—the old story of the ingratitude of republics. And if he was laughed at by the long-haired, lank and blanketed Oregonian, he was despised by the quick,
65 trim, sharp and energetic Californian who had now overrun Oregon on his way to the new Eldorado.

I wonder if the world would believe the half that could be written of the coarseness, the lawlessness of these un-organized armies that surged up and down the Pacific
70 coast in search of gold a quarter of a century ago? I know of nothing like these invasions in history since the days of the Goths and Vandals.

Two wild and strong streams of humanity, one from Oregon and the other from California, had glowed inhar-
75 moniously, tumultuously, together on and there, down in the deep cañon that cleft the wide and wintry valley through the middle, this stream of life stopped, as a river that is frozen.

A hundred men, trying to escape the "blizzard," tum-
80 bled headlong into the cañon together, and took shelter there as best they could beside the great basalt that had tumbled from the high, steep cliffs of the cañon. They crept under the crags, anywhere to escape the bitter cold.

And how the Californian did despise the Oregonian!
85 He named him the "webfoot" because his feet were moc-casined and he came from the land of clouds and rain. The bitter enmity and bad blood of Germany and France were here displayed in epitome and in the worst form. A wonder, indeed, if there would not be some sort of
90 tragedy played here before the storm was over.

Joachim Miller, "An Old Oregonian in the Snow"

*Early name for the Columbia River

21. When the narrator of the passage meets Joe Meek, Joe:
   A. has news to deliver from Washington, D.C.
   B. is past his prime.
   C. is on a mission to see the President of the United States.
   D. is about to get into another fight.

22. The narrator meets Joe Meek in person during:
   F. a rodeo.
   G. the Gold Rush.
   H. an Indian war.
   J. a battle between Californians and Oregonians.

23. Joe Meek travels to Washington, D.C. in order to:
   A. represent the people of Oregon in Congress.
   B. seek government aid in fighting Chief Joseph.
   C. prevent Oregon from being annexed by Great Britain.
   D. demonstrate his courage and daring nature.

24. According to the passage, Joe Meek is a forgotten hero because:
   F. he grew old and senile before his time.
   G. he was too eccentric to become a classical American hero.
   H. his mission to Washington failed.
   J. the Oregon territory was too remote to produce enduring heroes.

25. The cañon referred to in the passage (lines 2, 80):
   A. marks the boundary between California and Oregon.
   B. contained a wooden shelter to protect the trav-elers.
   C. divides a huge, flat valley.
   D. was shaped by the Oregon (now the Columbia) River.

26. Many rumors persist about Joe Meek, but the one certainty is that:
   F. he lost his papers enroute from Oregon to Washington, D.C.
   G. he once lived with the Indians.
   H. he traveled across the continent by himself.
   J. he met the President of the United States.

27. The narrator believes that Joe Meek deserves greater recognition for his exploits because Joe:
   A. undertook important and dangerous missions.
   B. outlived other heroes like John Fremont and Kit Carson.
   C. was more daring than Davy Crockett.
   D. set a standard for heroism that others followed.

28. After he returned from Washington, Joe Meek did all of the following EXCEPT:
   F. fight Indians.
   G. search for gold.
   H. settle in the woods.
   J. run for public office.

29. In the passage, the traditional antipathy between Californians and Oregonians is exemplified by their:
   A. behavior during the Idaho gold rush.
   B. attitude toward Joe Meek.
   C. ability to deal with cold and snow.
   D. disrespect for the law.

30. According to the passage, many people of Oregon failed to appreciate Joe Meek's work in their behalf because:
   F. he refused to take credit for his success.
   G. so many rumors circulated about Joe that they didn't know what to believe.
   H. his work didn't affect them directly.
   J. it wasn't fashionable to honor such men.

Passage IV

HUMANITIES: This passage, from Wesley Barnes' *The Philosophy and Literature of Existentialism,* describes the thoughts of the French philosopher and writer André Gide.

In considering André Gide, novelist (1869–1951), we have a French Protestant in conflict with his desire to taste the more lively aspects of life. His revolt took the course of freedom from parental and other social ties, sexual
5 unconventionality, a frank and nonhypocritical way of meeting experience, and a private and bizarre morality. Gide, mellowing somewhat, would never accept orthodox religion. He had much of the Renaissance spirit within him. With a will as strong as Luther's, with an influence
10 on him from the Bible as strong as any early Puritan's, Gide also brought a pagan spirit worthy of a Herrick or Donne in their earlier days. However, Gide went well beyond their pagan spirit to out-devil the devil. Compared to the indictments which sent Socrates to his death as a
15 corrupter of youth, Socrates' alleged offenses must be considered tepid indeed when put next to the incitements and corruptions Gide offered to youth in his long life.

Gide encouraged the revolt against rational and literary values. Not only did he encourage the revolt against, but
20 also urged the negation of that traditional world of values prior to 1916. He supported Dada. (Dadaism was a revolt in poetry and painting formulated during World War I. Its theses were that all social conventions must go; the individual could do no wrong if he did not write tradi-
25 tionally; one must behave outrageously in public. Complete anarchy must reign. The movement finally collapsed from its own excesses in 1926. The existential qualities come from an overturning of all traditionals in the name of the freedom of the individual spirit.) Gide's article—
30 "Dada"—encouraged the movement's supporters to refuse to be confined and to abolish every tie to the past.

Gide's support of Dadaism, his theories, and his own personal life, aided the existential trend through breaking down conventions and traditions in the myths. One effec-
35 tive way to break down absolutes is to give their original meanings a new twist. The French dramatists (Cocteau, Anouilh, and Giraudoux), with Gide a leader, sneered at old meanings, but gave the myths more humanity, if more profanity. In an excellent account in *The Classical Tradi-
40 tion,* Gilbert Highet traces the reinterpretation of the myths. Gide's *Oedipus* indicates one coming from nowhere, one with no traditions, one with no past history, one with no outside support, and therefore, one in a magnificent position. We are close to the existentialist
45 here. In the epic and traditional sense, the hero stood with the basic essentials of his society.

Gide was as effective as Ibsen in striking at the Victorian inhibitions: in those Victorian prohibitions were supports for traditional conduct, particularly in the social
50 life of the family. There is vitality in Gide, as opposed to the more philosophic nature of Nietzsche. Part of the violent irresponsibility of Gide came from his problem

with love. The existentialist is not eager and not able to find a way to involve himself in love with someone else.
55 The relationship must be one he can enter, but one he can leave with no possibility that he will start out as subject and end as object. Gide, religious in nature, and equally irreligious, did much to aid Sartre in abolishing God. His use of the myth was such as to take away dignity and any
60 touch of the sacred. However, Gide's work with the myth was not as disastrous as his view of Christianity in literature. He stated, and with undeniable force, that for a Christian to be a tragic figure is nearly impossible. If a person repents with any degree of sincerity, the soul is
65 saved. In theory, if a person can escape the temporal law, he could commit any number of serious offenses and have his soul saved if he repented.

Wesley Barnes, *The Philosophy and Literature of Existentialism*

31. According to the passage, the Dada movement faded away because:
   A. it was too outrageous.
   B. it was corrupt.
   C. Gide and others became disillusioned with it.
   D. World War I began.

32. According to the passage, Gide was deeply influenced by:
   F. Socrates.
   G. the Bible.
   H. the thinkers of the Renaissance.
   J. Hendrick Ibsen.

33. Based on information in the passage, Gide had the LEAST in common with:
   A. Donne.
   B. Cocteau.
   C. Nietzsche.
   D. Sartre.

34. The use of the word *disastrous* in line 61 suggests that, in the author's view, Gide:
   F. ruined the stories of classical mythology.
   G. was an atheist.
   H. didn't understand Christianity.
   J. distorted Christian doctrine.

35. According to the passage (lines 11 and 13), Gide went well beyond Herrick and Donne to "out-devil the devil." This means that, compared to Herrick and Donne, Gide:
   A. had more radical religious views.
   B. had a more intense fear of the devil.
   C. had a more evil influence on his readers.
   D. was more fascinated by devil-worship.

36. Based on information in the passage, which of the following statements is most clearly an opinion rather than a fact about Gide?
   F. Gide influenced the beliefs of others.
   G. Gide lived an unconventional life.
   H. Gide rejected orthodox Christianity.
   J. Gide was a leader among French writers of his time.

37. The main purpose of the passage is to explain Gide's:
- **A.** values and philosophy.
- **B.** lifestyle.
- **C.** literary output.
- **D.** place in cultural history.

38. Based on the material in lines 21–29, Dadaists probably believe all of the following EXCEPT:
- **F.** it is acceptable for a man to wear lipstick.
- **G.** the family is an obsolete institution.
- **H.** war is the natural condition of humankind.
- **J.** originality is what gives art its value.

39. Based on ideas in lines 53–57, one might infer that existentialists:
- **A.** have the ability to control their emotions.
- **B.** love only themselves and other existentialists.
- **C.** do not care about earthly matters.
- **D.** do not value enduring relationships with other people.

40. *Oedipus* is cited in the passage (line 41) to illustrate Gide's:
- **F.** religious background.
- **G.** concern for humanity.
- **H.** spiritualism.
- **J.** rejection of classical literature.

ANSWER KEY

1.	C	6.	J	11.	D	16.	H	21.	B	26.	H	31.	A	36.	G
2	G	7.	A	12.	H	17.	A	22.	G	27.	A	32.	G	37.	A
3.	B	8.	H	13.	D	18.	F	23.	C	28.	J	33.	C	38.	H
4.	F	9.	A	14.	J	19.	C	24.	J	29.	A	34.	J	39.	D
5.	D	10.	G	15.	B	20.	F	25.	C	30.	H	35.	A	40.	G

ANSWER EXPLANATIONS

1. C This answer is found in lines 7–10, which states that the meaning of "happiness" varies from person to person. Choice A is incorrect because Jefferson's intent is not critical to defining the term. B and D are wrong because neither is mentioned in the passage.

2. G A paraphrase of this answer is found in lines 15–16. None of the other answers is mentioned in the passage.

3. B The answer corresponds to material in lines 44–45, which alludes to one of the beloved maxims of early liberals: "That government is best which governs least." Choice A, C, and D express beliefs that may be liberal, but the passage does not discuss them.

4. F Lines 49–51 imply this answer in the discussion of human nature and time—two factors that cause government to change. G may be true but it's irrelevant, H is a questionable assertion, and J may be true but not germane to the passage.

5. D This is the best choice because most of the passage directly or indirectly pertains to the rights of the people and their government. The passage discusses choice A, B, and C, but only as ancillary matters.

6. J This is the only event that is not mentioned in lines 29–34. Therefore J is the correct answer.

7. A Lines 32–34 argue that when excessive power is granted to the people, the strong could impose their will on the weak, resulting in anarchy. B is a reasonable answer but not as clearly related to the text of the passage. C is not discussed in the passage. D, although mentioned in the passage, is not related to anarchy.

8. H In lines 41–43, the author refers (somewhat humorously) to people who derive happiness from criticizing everything, including government. G is discussed in the passage, but only as a goal of a free society, not as a practice that creates happiness. F and J are not mentioned in the passage.

9. A Lines 23–25 state that the government's main business is to prevent infringement on the people's rights. B, C, and D certainly are worthy goals, but are not the government's primary concern.

10. G This idea is strongly suggested in the last sentence of the passage. Citizens must know their rights in order to maintain them. F, H, and J, although valid observations, are not discussed in the passage.

11. D The opening paragraph of the passage says what aquifers are made of. Although sand is listed, most of the items on the list are rocks.

12. H The discussion of porosity (lines 15–24) says that spaces hold more water when grains are all about the same size. F and G are not mentioned as factors in determining porosity. J cannot be a factor because water cannot pass through a surface crack.

13. D The permeability of rocks is discussed in lines 25–35. According to lines 26–28, the most important factor in permeability is the number of "connected pore spaces." A is not mentioned in the passage. B is wrong because the thickness of an aquifer is not related to permeability. C is also incorrect because the relative merits of cracks and pores are not discussed here.

14. J In lines 40–49 all the choices except J are mentioned as contributors to the creation of joints. Therefore, J is the correct answer.

15. B The analogy is made to show that joints intersect each other (line 50), like pipes in a municipal water system. A, C, and D are matters not discussed in the passage.

16. H The passage describes limestone as "cavernous" (line 60), that is, full of large holes. F and G are named as the least porous rocks. J holds more water than slate and granite, according to lines 52–53, but not as much as limestone.

17. A Lines 40–41 indicate that wide joints often make consolidated rocks permeable. B is not a good answer because lines 41–42 say that joints are caused by "the kinds of stresses" that cause earthquakes, not by earthquakes themselves. C alone will not cause consolidated rock to become a good source of water. D is only the first step in making nonporous consolidated rock permeable.

18. F Lines 15–20 indicate that rocks with well-sorted grains hold more water than rocks with poorly sorted grains. Gravel is cited as an example of rock with well-sorted grains. G is contradicted by line 58, which says that clay will not carry water very readily. H is not correct because the passage says small grains tend to fill up rock with only poorly sorted grains. J is not a proper conclusion to be drawn from information in the passage.

19. C According to lines 76–78, water-bearing rocks are rare at great depths because of the "weight of overlying rocks." A and B are not discussed in the passage. D is an accurate statement but does not explain why aquifers rarely occur far below the surface of the earth.

20. F Aquifers of limestone and gravel are identified in the passage as the most permeable rocks. The passage also says that little water is found farther below ground than 2,000 feet. G is cited in the passage as an example of an aquifer that is far-reaching, not one that is especially productive. H is mentioned in the passage but not in the context of a promising site to drill wells. J is not mentioned in the passage.

21. B Joe Meek is a "famous old pioneer" (line 2) when the narrator meets him. The events named by choices A, C, and D took place long ago, when Joe was a young man.

22. G The blizzard that drove the two men together occurred during the Idaho gold rush (lines 53–59). Choice F is not mentioned in the passage. H took place long before. With regard to J, Californians and Oregonians never actually engaged in a specific battle; theirs was a long-standing conflict.

23. C Lines 20–21 indicate that Joe was sent to "protest against the pretensions of England." Choice A is incorrect because Joe's congressional service is more myth than fact. B is not mentioned in the passage. Although D is true, it was not the main purpose of Joe's trip.

24. J The narrator says that Joe might have been a famous hero had he been from "any other spot than isolated Oregon" (lines 50–51). Choice F is not discussed in the passage. G may be true but is not discussed. H contradicts information in the passage.

25. C The first paragraph of the passage sets the scene in a vast prairie divided by the canyon. Choice A is not mentioned in the passage. B is invalid; the people camped under crags to get away from the cold. Choice D is mentioned in the passage but in a different context.

26. H The narrator says that Joe's solo journey across the continent was his most memorable achievement. The other choices refer to events that may or may not have actually occurred.

27. A Line 16 says that the "priority and peril" of Joe's enterprises were greater than those of more famous figures in the history of the West. B is incorrect; the passage does not discuss the longevity of heroes. Choice C is contradicted by lines 12–14, and D is incorrect because Joe is an obscure pioneer hero, the opposite of a standard bearer.

28. J Nothing in the passage suggests that Joe had ambitions for elective office. However, lines 47–48 say that Joe was an "occasional leader in the wars against the Indians." Later, when gold was discovered in Idaho, he left his home in the woods (lines 53–57) to join the rush.

29. A The last paragraph of the passage is the narrator's comment on the hostilities between the two groups while caught in the snowstorm during the gold rush. With regard to B, C, and D, the choices list characteristics that Oregonians and Californians had in common.

30. H According to lines 44–47, the "new people" of Oregon took no interest in the work that Joe did for Oregon before they got there. Choice F may be valid, but Joe's modesty is not discussed in the passage. Choice G is true, but unrelated to the question of why Joe received no appreciation. J is not mentioned in the passage.

31. A This choice is supported by line 27, which says that Dadaism "collapsed from its own excesses in 1926." B is an opinion held by many critics, but it does not explain Dada's demise. C contradicts information in the passage. D is irrelevant to the decline of Dada.

32. G The correct answer, G, is supported by line 10, which states that the Bible strongly influenced Gide. F is compared to Gide in line 15, but is not considered an influence on him. H is not mentioned in the passage. J is compared to Gide in line 47, but is not considered an influence on him.

33. C Nietzsche was more philosophical than Gide, according to the fourth paragraph. A has a "pagan spirit" similar to Gide's, according to line 11. B is a dramatist who shared Gide's views, according to line 36. D had religious views similar to Gide's, according to line 58.

34. J This answer is implied by the explanation of Gide's deviant views on traditional Christian doctrine. F and G are not mentioned in the passage. H is probably not valid. Gide merely disregarded traditional Christian doctrine.

35. A This choice correctly suggests that Gide's views on religion were more extreme than Herrick's and Donne's. B is not supported by the passage.

C may be the author's opinion but is irrelevant to the question. D is not mentioned in the passage.

36. G This statement expresses an opinion about Gide's lifestyle, which may have been conventional for an artist at the time but unconventional from a traditionalist's point of view. F is a fact supported by evidence throughout the passage. H is a fact supported by statements in lines 7–8 and 57–58. J is a fact supported by the line 37.

37. A This correct answer captures the essence of the passage, which focuses on the beliefs and attitudes reflected in Gide's writing. B is implied by the passage but is not its main point. C is mentioned in the passage but not sufficiently enough to be the main purpose. D is too broad.

38. H This answer is correct, because it is *not* mentioned in the passage. F and G can be inferred from the Dadaists' rejection of all social conventions. J is implied throughout lines 18–31.

39. D The correct choice, D, supports the idea that existentialists need to enter and leave relationships without emotional attachments. Choice A contradicts Gide's views on Victorian inhibitions. B and C are not supported by the passage.

40. G This answer describes Gide's reinterpretation of *Oedipus,* which presents the hero as a more down-to-earth character, one who "stood with the basic essentials of his society." F is unrelated to Gide's *Oedipus.* H contradicts Gide's basically materialistic value structure. J is not supported by the passage.

4 Science Reasoning Review and Practice

THE SCIENCE REASONING TEST

Be prepared for a science test that is probably different from any you have ever taken. It will draw on your general background in science, but will not ask you to make use of your knowledge of scientific facts. Everything you need to know in order to answer the questions will be given to you. This is a test of science reasoning, not knowledge of subject matter.

All questions are multiple choice. Your choice of answer will be in the form of key letters (either A-B-C-D or F-G-H-J in alternate questions). There are 40 questions altogether, and you have 35 minutes in which to answer them by filling in the appropriate spaces on the answer sheet.

The questions are in seven groups, each group containing five or six questions. Each group starts with a passage of information in the form of graphs, diagrams, paragraphs, or tables. The questions in each group can be answered from the information in the passage.

Testing Reasoning Skills

In the Science Reasoning Test, there are three distinctly different kinds of passages, each testing a different kind of reasoning skill.
- Data Representation. Two or three of the seven passages will present you with some sort of graph or chart. The questions that follow will ask you to interpret the information given and to draw conclusions from it.
- Research Summaries. Three or four passages will each present you with a description of a scientific experiment and the results of the investigation. You will be asked to evaluate the experimental method, to interpret the results, and to appreciate some of the implications of the experimental findings.
- Conflicting Viewpoints. One passage will give you two paragraphs to read. The paragraphs will deal with some controversial scientific question. The scientists who wrote the paragraphs disagree with each other. You will be asked to evaluate the arguments of each, identify the points of disagreement, and recognize the evidence that each scientist cites in favor of his viewpoint. You will not be asked to decide who is right.

Cognitive Levels

Within each group of questions, the level of difficulty is graded. The first questions in the group are the easiest; as you go further into the group, the questions will call for deeper levels of understanding. Three cognitive levels are tested in each group:
- Understanding. These questions, about two in each group, test only your ability to know what the passage is saying. If it is a graph, do you know what the variables are and what values of them are presented? If it is an experiment, can you identify the nature of the experimental problem and the kind of data that were taken? If it is a controversy, do you know what are the points at issue?
- Analysis. About three questions will ask you to find the deeper meanings in the passage. If it is a graph, can you tell how the variables relate to each other and what is implied by the relationship? If it is an experiment, were controls adequate, and what conclusions logically flow from the data? If it is a controversy, how well do the arguments flow from the facts presented by each scientist?
- Generalization. What further study might be suggested by the graph, experiment, or controversy? How do the results impact society at large? What does the study imply for systems that were not part of the study itself?

Your Science Background

Exposure to science in the course of your life helps to provide skills that enhance your chances of making a good grade on the ACT Science Reasoning Test. You might wish to try to evaluate your background. "Yes" answers to the questions that follow are indications of life experiences that contribute to your background in science:

- Have you taken science courses? Any secondary school courses in science can add to your understanding. Most schools require some science, but often there are additional, optional courses as well. Did you take any?
- Did you do much laboratory work? Investigation is the heartbeat of science, and a science course that includes extensive hands-on experience is of greatest value.
- Was your laboratory experience open-ended? School science experiments are often cookbook type, with detailed instructions given and a predetermined answer expected. While these have some value they are not as useful as experiments that allow some individual initiative.
- Have you ever undertaken an experiment of your own? This is the ultimate exposure to the process of science, where you have to define a problem, plan procedures, take measurements, and reach a conclusion based on your findings.
- Do you have a hobby that impinges on some area of science, such as automobile mechanics, gardening, fly fishing, bird watching, telescope making, or rocketry? If so, do you study the principles involved?
- Do you read about science? Newspapers and magazines provide plenty of opportunity to keep up on the latest developments in all fields of science. For you, the value of these articles is that they provide insight into the process that produces advancement in science.
- Are you naturally skeptical, so that you look at advertising claims or stories of new or unusual phenomena or processes and try to judge their validity by examining the evidence on which they are based? Have you learned to distrust anecdotal evidence and to understand the need for controlled experiments?
- Do you tend to distrust claims of paranormal phenomena, such as telepathy, astrology, channeling, spiritualism, palmistry, encounters with aliens from space, and clairvoyance?
- Do you have a good science vocabulary? You might try to evaluate this by looking at the glossary beginning on page 352 to see how many of the terms you recognize.

While all these elements of background may enhance your chances of a good score, any student who can read carefully and reason logically can do well on this test.

Improving Your Prospects

The best preparation for the Science Reasoning Test is to do as many comparable tests as you can. The science part of this book will give you carefully analyzed samples of the three kinds of questions, as well as three complete tests to work on.

There is something else you can do that will help. Read about science—not textbooks, but newspaper and magazine articles about new developments. Magazines such as *Science Digest* and *Discover* are excellent sources. Some newspapers have superb science coverage; when you read the daily paper, pay particular attention to articles about new developments in science. The *Los Angeles Times* and *The New York Times* (Tuesday's edition) have extensive specialty coverage of science. For detailed study, select articles that deal with advances in fundamental science, rather than material about new kinds of technology.

In reading such articles, use the same kind of technique that is recommended in taking the ACT. First, read the whole article as quickly as you can, without stopping to understand all the details. Then look at it again and highlight the information that is most crucial to understanding the whole article. In particular, look for the kind of information that is relevant to the three kinds of questions in the Science Reasoning Test:

- Data Presentation: If there are diagrams or graphs, study them to make sure you know exactly what variables are represented, what values of the variables are given, how these values were obtained, and how they relate to each other.
- Research Summaries: If experimental results are quoted, see what experiments were done and what was found. How were measurements made? Were there adequate controls? How does the conclusion follow from the results of the experiment?
- Conflicting Viewpoints: A good journalist always tries to present all sides of an issue, and many new discoveries contradict canonical ideas. If scientists disagree with the con-

clusions reached in the article, what is the nature of the disagreement and what is the evidence that each side brings to uphold its viewpoint?

Finally, always look for suggestions in the article of questions left unanswered, additional data needed, the impact of the new discovery on the future progress in science, and the impact of the discovery on society at large.

TACTICS

There is a special skill to taking a multiple-choice test. In some cases, there is even a danger of getting the "wrong" answer by knowing too much. This is because it may be possible to read into the question some subtle idea that did not occur to the person who wrote the question. Good item-writers try to avoid this pitfall, but they do make mistakes. In this test, the candidate who gets the right answer is not necessarily the one who knows most about the subject. It is the one who understands the passage thoroughly and *bases the choice of answer strictly on the contents of the passage.* Extraneous information can lead you to confusion and misinterpretation of the question.

A multiple-choice test is highly structured and formalized. To do well in such a test, you must be thoroughly familiar with the mechanics of the test. This is one reason why you should take the Model Examinations in this book under precisely the same conditions that you will meet in the testing room. Time yourself; take no more than 35 minutes for the whole test. Do not use a calculator, nor any writing instrument other than a soft lead pencil with an eraser on it.

There is always some anxiety in a testing situation, but you can reduce it by being familiar with the forms of the test in advance. If the test looks familiar, you will not waste time figuring out how to go about answering questions. When you go into the testing room, for example, you should expect to find that in some questions the choices are labelled **A, B, C,** and **D,** while in others your choices will be **F, G, H,** and **J.** You should know what the answer sheet will look like, and that you must mark it with a soft lead pencil. And you must expect to find a group of five to seven questions relating to each passage. With all these mechanical details out of the way, you can go into the testing room ready to work. You should also know that there are certain tactics that will enable you to demonstrate your ability to the best advantage.

- *Start by scanning the passage.* Read the passage or look at the data presentation quickly, just to get a rough idea of what it is all about. This should take no more than 20 seconds. Do not stop to study in detail any part that you do not understand. With this background, you are ready to move into a more careful study of the passage.

- *Read the passage again.* Now you can take as much as a minute or even more to understand the passage thoroughly. Feel free to mark up the test booklet with notes. Underline key words.

- *Answer the first question in the group.* In most tests, it is a good policy to skip questions you cannot answer immediately, but there is an exception in this test. The first question in each group will probably be a simple test of understanding. If you cannot answer it, you may well get the others wrong also. If necessary, go back to the passage to find the answer. If you cannot answer the first question, skip the whole passage and come back to it later.

- *Skip the hard questions.* After you have answered the first question, do not initially spend more than 30 seconds or so on any question. If you have time at the end, you can come back and reread the questions you could not get the first time around.

- *Read all the choices.* If you think you have found the right answer at once, do not stop reading. You may discover that there is some idea that has not appeared in the one you think is right. Think of the process as one of eliminating the incorrect answers, rather than selecting the right one. You may find that you can throw out three of the four choices quite easily.

- *If the answers are numerical, estimate.* Calculation takes time, and you should avoid it whenever possible. You can usually eliminate three obviously wrong choices quite easily. For example, suppose a graph shows that an object has traveled 32 meters in seven seconds, and you are asked to find its speed. You are given these choices:
  - **A.** 220 m/s
  - **B.** 40 m/s
  - **C.** 4.6 m/s
  - **D.** 1.4 m/s

You know that 32 divided by 7 will be a little over 4, so you can pick out **C** as the answer without doing the calculation.

- *Pace yourself.* With 35 minutes to answer the questions for seven passages, you have just five minutes for each passage. If you find yourself spending more than that on one passage, skip it and come back to it later. On average, you should spend about two minutes reading each passage and 30 seconds answering each question.
- *Answer every question.* When you have finished doing the easy questions, go back and try again on some that you skipped. If you have only 30 seconds left at the end, turn to the answer sheet, find those questions you have not answered, and mark them at random. However, be careful not to give more than one answer to any question. There is no penalty for guessing, but an item will be marked wrong if you have given two answers.

WORDS YOU SHOULD KNOW

Although the Science Reasoning Test will not call on you for any extensive knowledge of the sciences, it will use many words of the common scientific vocabulary. Study the terms listed below, and if any of them are unfamiliar, learn what they mean.

absolute zero the lowest possible temperature, about $-273°C$.

acid a substance that forms hydronium ions (H_3O^+) in water; having a pH less than 7.

acid rain rain made acid by absorbing sulfur and nitrogen oxides from polluted air.

adrenalin a hormone of the adrenal gland, secreted in times of emergency.

air mass a large body of air characterized by certain values of temperature and humidity.

algae simple, green organisms with cell walls, but without the complex structure of plants.

alkali a strongly basic hydroxide.

alloy a substance composed of two or more metals.

alternating current an electric current that reverses direction periodically.

amino acid organic chemicals with an acid group ($-COOH$) at one end and an amino group ($-NH_2$) at the other; the constituent molecules of proteins.

anemia substandard concentration of red blood cells.

antibody a blood protein that protects the body from foreign chemicals or microorganisms.

aorta the largest artery, carrying blood out of the left ventricle.

artery a muscular-walled blood vessel that distributes blood to the body tissues.

atmosphere the layer of air surrounding the earth.

atom the smallest part of an element.

bacteria the smallest and simplest one-celled organisms, having neither nucleus nor other organelles.

barometer an instrument for measuring atmospheric pressure.

bedrock the solid rock underlying the loose material at the earth's surface.

boiling point the temperature at which, at any given pressure, the liquid and gas phases of a substance are in equilibrium.

calorie a quantity of heat energy, equal to 4.185 joules. The Large Calorie of the nutritionist is a kilocalorie, equal to 1000 calories.

capillary 1. a thin tube into which water can rise by adhesion to the surface. 2. a tiny blood vessel connecting an artery to a vein and providing interchange of materials between blood and tissue.

carbohydrate a substance such as sugar and starch, whose molecules are composed of atoms of carbon, hydrogen, and oxygen with two parts hydrogen to one oxygen.

catalyst a substance that increases the rate of a chemical reaction without being used up in the reaction.

chemical formula conventional representation of the atomic composition of a compound.

chemical reaction a process in which the molecular or ionic composition of one or more substances is altered.

chemical symbol the one- or two-letter code for an element.

chlorophyll the green substance in the cells of plants and algae that catalyzes photosynthesis.

chromosomes the thread-like structures in nuclei (and in bacteria) that carry the genes.

circuit a set of electric conductors, connected in such a way as to form a complete path between the poles of the source of electric energy.

colon the large intestine.

combustion a chemical process, usually an oxidation, that produces heat and light.

compound a substance of definite chemical composition, consisting either of positive and negative ions in definite ratios or of molecules composed of definite kinds and numbers of atoms.

concentration the amount of a substance contained in a given volume of a solution or other mixture.

conductor a material through which heat or electric current may pass.

convection the distribution of heat due to the rising of warmer fluids over colder ones.

crystal a solid having plane faces because its molecules or ions are arranged in linear arrays.

density the amount of mass (or other property) per unit volume of a substance.

diaphragm 1. the vibrating element of a microphone or loudspeaker. 2. the transverse muscle layer that separates the abdomen from the chest cavity in mammals. 3. a contraceptive device that functions by covering the entrance to the uterus.

diffusion 1. the spontaneous spreading of a liquid or gas due to the intrinsic motion of its molecules. 2. the scattering of light, as by reflection from a rough surface.

digestion the process of enzymatic breakdown of large organic molecules into smaller, soluble ones.

dilute solution a solution in which the solute has a low concentration.

DNA deoxyribose nucleic acid, the substance of the genes.

ductless gland an endocrine organ.

ecology the study of the relationships between organisms and with their inorganic environment.

electric charge the property of particles (such as electrons and protons) by which they exert forces on each other without respect to their mass.

electric current a flow of electric charge, typically carried by electrons through a metal or by ions through a solution or a plasma.

electromagnetic waves disturbances in electric and magnetic fields propagating through space, including light, infrared and ultraviolet radiation, radio waves, X-rays, etc.

electron a particle found in all atoms having a small mass and a single unit of negative electric charge.

electrostatic force the force particles exert on each other because of their electric charge.

element a substance consisting of only one species of atom, so that it cannot be decomposed by chemical means.

embryo an organism in the earliest stages of its development.

endocrine organ a gland that secretes hormones into the blood.

energy a physical quantity having the dimension of work and measured in joules, whose total quantity remains constant through all interactions and transformations.

enzyme a substance, usually a protein, produced by living cells and acting as a catalyst.

epicenter the point on the earth's surface directly above the geological shift that causes an earthquake.

erosion the movement of rock, sand, etc., due to natural forces.

esophagus the tube that carries food from the mouth to the stomach; gullet.

evaporation conversion of a liquid into the gaseous phase by escape of molecules from the surface.

evolution the process by which species undergo drastic changes over long periods of time.

excretion the disposal of metabolic wastes from the body, as by urination.

fault a crack in the earth's crust, along which crustal movement takes place.

fermentation an enzyme-controlled reaction that takes place in the absence of oxygen, such as the conversion of sugar to alcohol by the action of yeast.

fertilization 1. the process of applying nutrients to the soil to stimulate plant growth. 2. the union of a sperm and an egg cell to form a zygote.

fission 1. reproduction of a one-celled organism by splitting into two equal parts. 2. splitting of an atomic nucleus into approximately equal parts, with the release of energy.

flood plain the flat region around an old river, which becomes covered with water at times of high runoff.

food chain an array of organisms in which each serves as food for the one above.

fossil the preserved remains of a long-extinct organism.

frequency the number of cycles completed in a unit time in any cyclic phenomenon, such as a vibration.

front the boundary between two air masses.

fusion 1. the melting of a solid. 2. a nuclear reaction in which two small nuclei combine to form a larger one, accompanied by the release of energy. 3. the union of isogametes of one-celled organisms.

galaxy an agglomeration of many millions of stars.

gamete a sex cell, such as egg or sperm.

gas a substance, usually of very low density, that has no surfaces of its own but will spread to fill its container.

gene the particle that carries hereditary information from one generation to another and controls the production of proteins in a living cell.

genetics the study of biological inheritance.

glacier a large mass of ice moving down a valley or across a continent.

glucose the simple sugar ($C_6H_{12}O_6$) that forms the fundamental energy supply of all nucleated organisms.

gravity the mass-dependent force by which any two objects in the universe attract each other.

greenhouse effect the warming of the earth resulting from atmospheric gases trapping heat that reradiates from the earth's surface.

habitat the part of an ecosystem that is occupied by a given organism.

heat energy that passes from one system to another because of a difference in temperature.

helix a spiral shaped like a spring, characteristic of the DNA molecule.

herbivore an animal that eats plants only.

hormone a substance secreted into the blood by an endocrine gland that controls chemical processes in other parts of the body.

humidity the amount of water vapor in the air.

igneous rock rock formed by the hardening of liquid rock emerging from deep within the earth, either to the surface or within the crust.

inertia the property of objects to remain in a state of rest or uniform motion in a straight line unless acted on by an outside force.

infrared rays electromagnetic waves of wavelength longer than those of visible light, but shorter than microwaves.

insulator a substance that blocks the passage of heat or electric current.

insulin a hormone, produced in the pancreas, that controls the metabolism of glucose.

ion an atom or group of atoms that has acquired either a positive charge by losing one or more electrons, or a negative charge by gaining electrons.

isobar a line on a weather map connecting points of equal barometric pressure.

isotope a variety of an element distinguished by its atomic mass number, but having the same atomic number as all other isotopes of the element.

jet stream a rapidly flowing mass of air high in the atmosphere.

Kelvin scale the SI temperature scale, which has its zero at the absolute zero of temperature.

kinetic energy the energy of an object as measured by its mass and velocity.

latent heat the heat added or removed from a substance that produces a change of phase with no change in temperature.

latitude the distance north or south of the equator, measured in degrees.

light year the distance light travels in a year.

liquid a substance that takes the shape of its container, up to a definite upper surface.

liter a unit of volume equal to 1000 cubic centimeters.

longitude the distance east or west of the prime meridian, measured in degrees.

lunar eclipse condition in which the earth comes between the sun and the moon so that the moon is in the earth's shadow.

magnet a device made of a ferromagnetic material, such as steel, which can exert forces on other such materials.

magnetism the excess force (above the electrostatic force) exerted on each other by charges in motion.

mass the quantity of substance in an object, measured either by its acceleration when a force is applied or by its gravitational attraction to other objects.

melting the change of matter from solid to liquid.

melting point the temperature at which the solid and liquid phases of a substance can exist in equilibrium.

menstruation the monthly process by which the lining of the uterus sloughs off, accompanied by bleeding through the vagina.

mineral an earth substance with specified chemical constitution.

molecule a particle consisting of one or more atoms bound together, and comprising the smallest quantity of a non-ionic substance.

muscle an organ that produces motion of body parts or change in shape of organs by contracting.

natural selection the tendency of individuals or species best adapted to a particular environment to leave larger numbers of offspring.

nerve an organ that controls body functions by carrying electrochemical impulses.

neuron a nerve cell.

neutron a neutral particle that is part of the nuclei of atoms, with mass slightly larger than that of a proton.

nitrogen a gaseous element, atomic number 7, that makes up 79 percent of the atmosphere and is an important constituent of many organic compounds.

nucleus 1. the massive, charged center of an atom, composed of protons and neutrons. 2. a structure in a cell, surrounded by a membrane and containing the chromosomes. 3. a particle of dust in the atmosphere around which water condenses, forming a raindrop.

organic compound a molecular chemical compound based on carbon.

osmosis the diffusion of water through a membrane.

outcrop a part of the bedrock protruding through overlying sediments.

ovary 1. in animals, an organ that produces egg cells. 2. the part of the stigma of a flower that contains the ovules.

parasite an organism that is nourished by invading or attaching itself to and feeding on another organism.

pH a method of expressing the acidity or alkalinity of a solution, based on the concentration of hydrogen ions.

photosynthesis the process by which green plants and algae, in the presence of sunlight, convert carbon dioxide and water into glucose, giving off oxygen as a waste.

placenta the organ of a mammalian embryo (and a few other kinds of embryos) by which the embryo is attached to the uterus.

plasma 1. the liquid part of the blood. 2. a highly ionized gas.

pollution the accumulation of unsightly, unhealthy, and other undesirable materials in the environment.

potential difference in an electric field, the change in potential energy of an electric charge in moving from one position to another.

precipitation 1. the condensation of atmospheric water into rain, snow, sleet, etc. 2. the process by which a substance in solution solidifies.

pressure force per unit of area.

prime meridian the arbitrary zero of longitude, passing through Greenwich, England.

protein one of the characteristic substances of living things, whose molecules are composed of many amino acid units.

proton the massive particles, having a single unit of positive charge, that compose the charged part of a nucleus.

radioactivity the spontaneous breakdown of unstable atomic nuclei, with the release of energetic rays and particles.

reflex a simple, automatic response to a stimulus.

relative humidity the amount of water vapor in the atmosphere, expressed as a percent of the maximum value at a given temperature.

respiration 1. the passage of air in and out of the lungs. 2. the process by which oxygen passes through membranes into the blood, as in lungs, gills, or wet skin. 3. the process by which cells derive energy from the oxidation of glucose.

sedimentary rock rock formed by the consolidation of sediments such as sand or mud, or by precipitation from solution.

seismograph an instrument for studying earthquakes by analyzing the waves they produce in the earth's crust.

semen the body secretion that carries sperms out.

solar eclipse condition in which the moon comes between the earth and the sun, blocking out the sun.

sound wave a disturbance in air or other substance that is propagated as a vibration.

sperm a male gamete, typically self-propelled.

spinal cord the mass of nerve tissue in vertebrates that runs from the brain through the bones of the spinal column.

starch the complex carbohydrate that is the main form of energy storage in plants.

symbiosis the condition in which two organisms live intimately together for mutual benefit.

temperature the average random kinetic energy of the molecules of a substance, which determines whether it will gain or lose heat to other objects.

testis an organ that produces sperms.

thermometer a device for measuring temperature.

toxin a poisonous substance produced by bacteria.

ultraviolet radiation electromagnetic waves with wavelength shorter than visible light and longer than X-rays.

umbilical cord the organ of a mammalian embryo that connects the embryo to the placenta.

uterus the organ of female mammals in which the embryo grows.

vaccine a material used to induce immunity to a specific disease.

vapor the gaseous phase of a substance that exists as a liquid under ordinary conditions.

vein 1. a thin-walled, valved blood vessel carrying blood toward the heart. 2. the branching supporting structures of a leaf or an insect wing. 3. a thin layer of a mineral filling a crack in the bedrock.

vertebrae the bones that are arrayed linearly to form the back-bone of vertebrates.

virus a submicroscopic particle that can become self-reproducing inside a living cell.

volt the unit of measure of electric potential difference, which provides the condition for the flow of an electric current.

weight the gravitational force that the earth or other astronomical object exerts on an object near its surface.

X-ray electromagnetic radiation of wavelength shorter than ultraviolet.

zygote a cell formed by the fusion of two gametes.

DATA REPRESENTATION QUESTIONS

Every experiment and many kinds of theoretical studies present results in some kind of numerical matrix. This can be a data table, the familiar line graph, a bar graph, or any other kind that the author can think up. Three of the passages in the Science Reasoning Test will be some kind of data presentation, and about 15 of the questions will ask you to interpret those passages. You may find that the passage presents you with data in a form that you have never seen before.

Here is a sample Data Representation passage that illustrates the kind of question that might be asked at each of the three cognitive levels:

Two species of the microorganism *Paramecium* are grown in cultures, and the population density is measured daily. The upper graph shows the results if the two species are raised in separate cultures. The lower graph shows the results if the two species are grown together in a single culture.

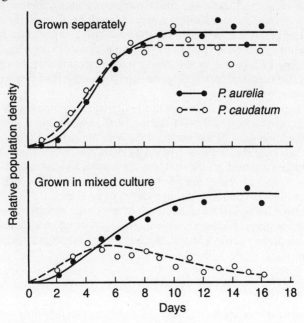

1. When the two species are grown together,
   A. both species reach maximum population density in 18 days.
   B. both species stop reproducing after 12 days.
   C. populations of both species grow fastest after 4 days.
   D. both species reproduce fastest after 2 days.

This question is at the *understanding* level of cognition. Both **B** and **D** are wrong because the graphs do not indicate rate of reproduction; the population density depends on other factors in addition to reproduction rate. **A** is wrong because the graph levels off at a maximum at 10 days, not 18. The slope of the graph indicates the rate of increase of the population density, and is greatest just after 4 days; the answer is **C**.

2. When the two species are cultured together,
    F. *P. aurelia* is unaffected, but it inhibits the population of *P. caudatum.*
    G. *P. aurelia* reproduces more rapidly than *P. caudatum.*
    H. it takes about a week for the populations to begin to interfere with each other.
    J. each species inhibits the population growth of the other.

This is an *analysis* question. **G** is wrong because other factors than reproduction rate may affect the population size. **F** is wrong because the population of *P. aurelia* grows more slowly in the presence of *P. caudata* than without it. **H** is wrong because the growth of the *P. caudatum* population starts to diminish in less than 5 days. The answer is **J**.

3. Comparison of the two graphs seems to imply that
    A. the two species of *Paramecium* are competing for the same resources.
    B. no two microorganisms can live successfully in the same culture.
    C. *P. caudatum* could not survive in the wild.
    D. *P. aurelia* is a more common species than *P. caudatum.*

This question calls on you to decide what general conclusion can reasonably be reached from the information given. **B** is wrong because the experiment deals with only two organisms, and says nothing about any other combinations. **C** and **D** are both wrong because conditions in the wild are nothing at all like those in a culture dish. It seems reasonable that *P. caudatum* is losing out in competition with *P. aurelia;* the answer is **A**.

Most of the Data Presentation passages will give you numerical data. There are certain techniques to follow in answering questions based on this kind of passage. Start by asking yourself certain questions about the chart, graph, or table.

What are the variables? In a data chart, the names of the variables will usually appear at the tops of the columns. If there are more than two columns, there may be more than two variables. In a graph, the names of the variables will be given at the side and bottom of the graph. A line graph may contain more than one curve, representing different experiments or different experimental conditions that are additional variables. In this case, the separate curves may be labelled, or the curves may be distinguished from each other in some way and a key supplied. In any case, be sure you understand just what variable distinguishes one curve from another.

What are the units of measure? These will usually be given along with the name of the variable. In a data chart, they will be at the top of the column. In a graph, they will be stated at the bottom and sides of the graph, along with the name of the variable.

What are the values of the variables? In a data chart, the values are entries in the table. In a graph, the values are read off the scales at the bottom and sides of the graph.

Are there any trends? Check to see whether there is an obvious consistent increase or decrease of any values as you move through the chart or graph.

Are there any correlations? If there are trends in any of the variables, how do they relate to trends in other variables? As one variable increases, does another increase or decrease?

These questions are not always applicable, but if they are, it will help you try to find answers to them.

Sample Passages

While any scientist can invent methods of data representation to suit his particular needs, certain kinds are in common use. Here are some examples of forms of numerical data representation that might be encountered.

Data tables. This is the most direct way of presenting data. It is nothing more than a list of the values of the variables. Example: The table below gives the elemental composition of the earth's crust, in two forms:

**Composition of the Earth's Surface: Atoms of Each Element
in a Sample of 10,000 Atoms, and Percent by Weight**

Element	Symbol	No. of Atoms	Percent by Weight
Oxygen	O	5330	49.5
Silicon	Si	1590	25.7
Hydrogen	H	1510	0.9
Aluminum	Al	480	7.5
Sodium	Na	180	2.6
Iron	Fe	150	4.7
Calcium	Ca	150	3.4
Magnesium	Mg	140	1.9
Potassium	K	100	2.4
All others	—	370	1.4
Total		10,000	100.0

Variables? There are three: the name of the element and two numerical variables (the number of atoms of each kind and the relative weight of each). The second column is not an additional variable; it is simply another way of specifying the values of the variable in Column 1.

Units? This question does not apply to Columns 1 and 2, since the entries in these columns are not measurements. In this table, the units are named in the title of the chart and in the head of each column. In Column 3 the unit is the number of atoms in a sample of 10,000. In Column 4 it is percent by weight, and it does not involve the total number of atoms in the sample.

Values? These are the numbers in the column. In Column 3, for example, we learn that out of every 10,000 atoms, 5,330 are oxygen. Column 4 tells us that these oxygen atoms constitute 49.5 percent of the weight of the sample.

Trends? There are none. Do not be misled by the fact that the numbers in Column 3 are decreasing. This is only because the person who made the chart elected to list the elements in order of decreasing frequency. There can be no trends because the entries in Column 1 are not numerical.

Correlations? Columns 3 and 4 both show decreasing values going down the column. This only indicates that the element with fewer atoms contributes less to the weight of the sample. The interesting fact here is that there are deviations from the strict order. Hydrogen, for example, is the third most common element, but its weight is less than any of the others. This should tell you that each hydrogen atom weighs far less than any other atom in the group.

Line Graphs. This is the most usual way of representing a function of two variables. In pure mathematics, the variables are x and y, but in scientific applications, they are usually measured quantities of some sort. If there are more than two variables, the graph may contain several curves. The example shown represents the rate at which gases are exchanged in the lungs and skin of a frog, per unit of body weight, as a function of temperature.

Variables? There are no less than four in this graph, two of them numerical: temperature, exchange rate, kind of gas, and body organ. Exchange rate and temperature are measured quantities and form the axes of the graph. The other variables are distinguished by labels on the curves.

Units? This question applies only to the numerical variables that form the function. Temperature is in degrees Celsius and exchange rate is in milliliters of gas per kilogram of body weight per hour.

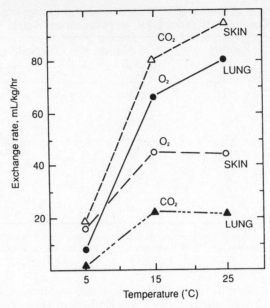

Values? These are represented by the coordinates of points on the graph. Looking at the curve for "CO_2 lung," for example, the point at 15°C is at the level of about 21 mL/kg/hr on the ordinate. On this graph, it is interesting to note that each curve has been drawn from only 3 data points.

Trends? Surely, all values of the exchange rate increase with temperature, except that two of them drop off slightly at temperatures above 15°C.

Correlations? At all levels, "O_2 skin" and "CO_2 lung" move the same way, as do "CO_2 skin" and "O_2 lung."

Isolines. These are lines used to represent the values in a scalar field, which is a region in which some variable takes on different values at every point. The most familiar example, perhaps, is the isobars of a weather map. These lines are drawn such that any given line passes through points of equal barometric pressure. The pressure at any point on the map can be found by interpolating between the isobars. Other examples:

- *Isotherms,* drawn through points of equal temperature on a weather map.
- *Contour lines,* drawn through points of equal elevation on a contour map.
- *Isobaths,* drawn through points of equal water depth on navigation charts.
- *Isogones,* drawn through points of equal magnetic deviation on geologic charts.
- Other lines, not dignified by special names, may be drawn through points of equal light intensity in a room, equal electric potential in an engineering chart, equal gene frequency in a population, etc.

In the example below, the isotherms are drawn through points of equal oceanic surface temperature.

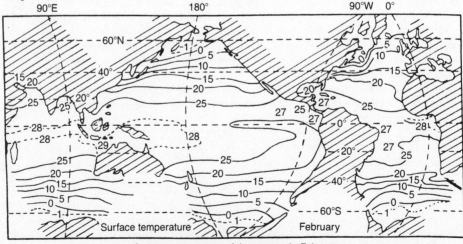

Surface temperature of the oceans in February

Variables? Latitude, longitude, and temperature.

Units? Degrees north or south of the equator for latitude, degrees east or west of the prime meridian for longitude, degrees Celsius for temperature.

Values? These must be found by interpolation between the three kinds of lines. For example, what is the average February surface temperature of the ocean at latitude 20° N, longitude 150° W? First, find 20° N, which is halfway between the equator and the 40° N latitude line. Next, move horizontally along this latitude, left of the 180° longitude line to a position ⅓ of the way to the 90° longitude line. That point is between the 20°C and the 25°C isotherms, a little closer to the latter. The temperature is therefore 23°C.

Trends? Only a rough correlation; the temperature decreases with higher latitudes, both north and south.

Bar Graphs. A bar graph is used to show the distribution of some variable when there is no functional relationship with another variable. If several variables are involved, more than one graph is needed. In the bar graphs shown below, a comparison is made between the skull lengths of European moles before and after the severe winter of 1946-7.

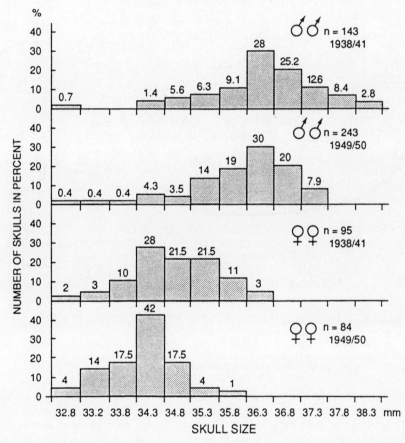

Variables? In each graph, there are two numerical variables: along the abscissa, skull length (within 0.25 mm); on the ordinate, percent of the total number of moles that fall in each range. The four graphs give data for four groups: males and females before and after the hard winter. The additional information given is the actual number of moles in each of the four groups.

Units? For skull size, millimeters; for the length of each bar, percent of the total.

Values? These are read from the ordinate scale, for each size category. In this example, the value of the ordinate is also written in, so that it is unnecessary to read it off the scale. In the top graph (143 males, measured from 1938 to 1941) the bar for the skull length 35.8 mm extends to just under 10% on the ordinate scale; the actual value is given as 9.1%.

Trends? In each of these graphs there is a typical normal distribution, with the largest number of individuals falling near the middle of the distribution and successively smaller numbers on both sides of the center. It is also clear that in both groups, females have smaller skulls than males.

Correlations? At all times, the females' skulls are smaller. Also, the skull lengths were considerably smaller after the hard winter.

Samples of Qualitative Data Representation

The examples above give the most widely used methods of representing measurement data. Many others are in use, and any scientist can invent one as he feels the need for it. In addition to these, there are many kinds of diagrammatic representations, that may not involve measurement at all. These will be used to show the relationships between phenomena or parts of a system. While it is impossible to describe all of them, here are some that are in wide use.

Flow diagrams. Diagrams like the one below are used to show that some substance or quantity undergoes changes as it passes from system to system. The sample below has no numbers, but other diagrams of this sort will indicate the amount or percent of the quantity passing from system to system. Such diagrams have been used to illustrate the energy cycle in the biosphere, the usage of energy in the economy, the passage of water through the earth, the changes in rocks, and so on. The usual questions about the variables do not apply unless there are actual numbers on the chart.

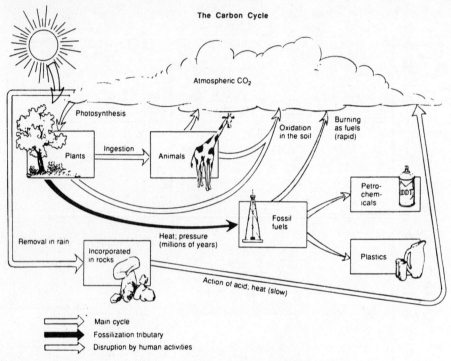

Reprinted with the permission of Macmillan Publishing Company from *Chemistry for Changing Times* by John W. Hill. Copyright © 1988 by Macmillan Publishing Company.

Each arrow in the diagram represents a passage of carbon from one system to another. The three arrows from the box labelled *plants,* for example, show that the carbon in the tissues of plants can be eaten by animals, passed off into the atmosphere as carbon dioxide, or converted into fossil fuels. If numbers or percents were given, you might be asked what fraction of the total goes into each of these pathways.

Geologic diagrams. Properties of the earth's crust are typically represented as cross-section diagrams, showing the relationships of the different layers of rock. The sample below shows underlying igneous bedrock, with a layer of limestone above it, and topped by a layer of shale.

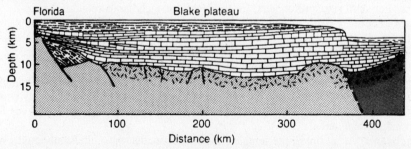

From **Physical Geology** by Edgar W. Spencer. © 1983 by Addison-Wesley Publishing Company. Reprinted by permission of the publisher.

The rather flat upper surface of the igneous base rock indicates that it must have been eroded flat at some time in the past. The overlying limestone layer could only have been deposited in salt water, so the bedrock must have sunk beneath the ocean. The shale layer, coming on top of the limestone, was deposited later, and may indicate an uplift of the adjacent land mass from which the sediments came.

If you are presented with such a diagram, you will be given a key to identify the various kinds of rocks.

Family Trees. A passage consisting of a family tree may give rise to questions in the field of genetics. The example below is typical.

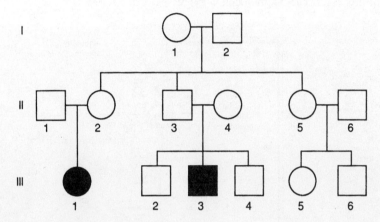

From **Problem Solving in Biology, 3rd edition** by Eugene W. Kaplan. © 1983 by Macmillan Publishing Company. Reprinted by permission of the publisher.

In such a diagram, circles represent females and squares, males. A hereditary trait that appears is shown (in this case) by black. In Generation I, 1 and 2 are parents of II-2, II-3 and II-5. The gene is clearly recessive, since it is expressed in the offspring of parents who do not show the trait. Therefore, III-1 and III-3 must be homozygous for the gene. Since each of them must get the gene from both parents, II-1, II-2, II-3 and II-4 must be heterozygous. Either I-1 or I-2 must also be heterozygous, since they gave rise to a heterozygous daughter and son. Any of the others could also be heterozygous, but there is not enough information to tell which.

Evolutionary trees. A diagram like the one below is often used to express the evolutionary relationships between different groups of organisms.

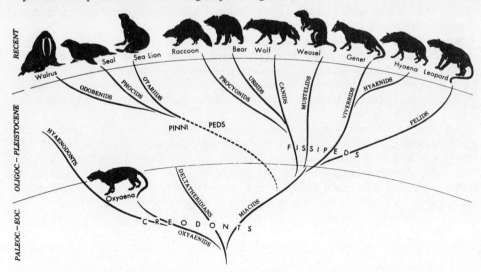

From **Evolution of the Vertebrates,** 2nd edition, Colbert, (ISBN 0471-16466-6). Reprinted by permission of Wiley-Liss, Inc., a subsidiary of John Wiley & Sons, Inc.

In this diagram, living forms are arrayed across the top. The rest of the diagram represents forms that lived in the past. Geologic periods for these life forms are named on the left. Each branching point in such a diagram represents a common ancestor. The diagram shows, for example, that the seals and the walruses had a common ancestor in the Oligo-Pleistocene era. This common ancestor branched from the line leading to the sea lions at an earlier time. This is expressed in the statement that the seals are more closely related to the walrus than to the sea lions. Dotted lines indicate more than usual uncertainty about relationships.

Process Diagrams. Diagrams are used to describe a connected series of chemical or other kinds of processes. The diagram below expresses such a series.

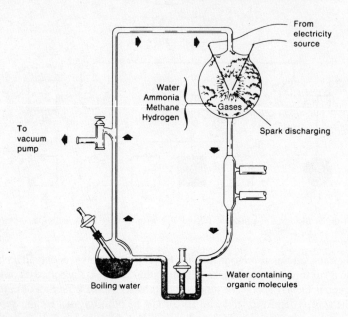

Arrows indicate the sequence of processes. In this case, there is no arrow pointing to an entry into the system, so it must be a closed system. The diagram does not specify whether the vacuum pump is there merely to maintain vacuum, or to drain off any gases that are formed. What it does show is that anything produced by the spark operating on a mixture of gases is drained off into boiling water, where it might be dissolved.

Others. There is no way to prepare for every kind of data presentation that you might encounter, because authors make them up as needed. Consider the diagram below, for example. The author has elected to represent the earth's history as a clock instead of as a linear sequence. The idea, apparently, was to make the time relationships more comprehensible, ignoring the contradiction that a clock repeats itself but the earth's history does not.

The origin of the earth is at 12 o'clock. Time goes clockwise from there, until present time is reached at 12 o'clock. There is a time scale representing billions of years; each billion-year interval is divided into quarters. The information presented is the time of origin of each major group of organisms. The line marked eucaryotic organisms, for example, is shown as possibly starting at 1.9 billion years (dotted line), probably by 1.3 billion years, and certainly by .9 billion years, where the solid line begins.

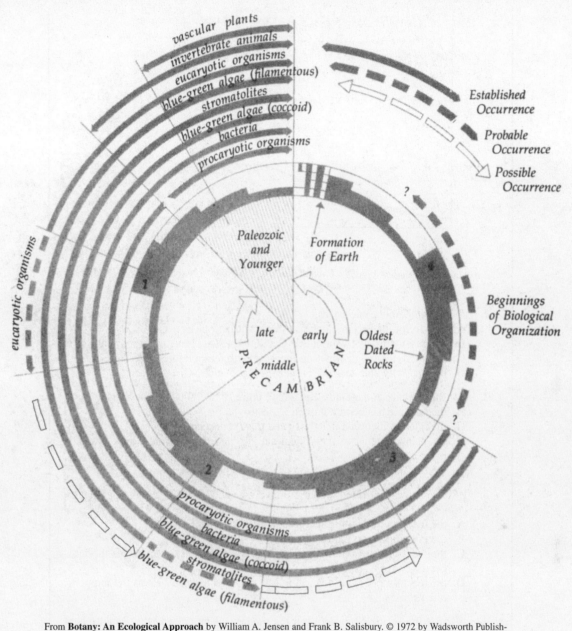

Established Occurrence

Probable Occurrence

Possible Occurrence

Beginnings of Biological Organization

vascular plants
invertebrate animals
eucaryotic organisms
blue-green algae (filamentous)
stromatolites
blue-green algae (coccoid)
bacteria
procaryotic organisms

eucaryotic organisms

Paleozoic and Younger

Formation of Earth

late
early
Oldest Dated Rocks
P.RE.CAM.BRIAN
middle

procaryotic organisms
bacteria
blue-green algae (coccoid)
stromatolites
blue-green algae (filamentous)

From **Botany: An Ecological Approach** by William A. Jensen and Frank B. Salisbury. © 1972 by Wadsworth Publishing Company, Inc. Reprinted by permission of the publisher.

Try these passages for practice. Since they are data representation questions, you must be able to answer certain questions, if they apply. What are the variables? What are the units of measure? How are values read from the data? Are there trends? Are there correlations?

PRACTICE EXERCISES: DATA REPRESENTATION QUESTIONS

Passage 1

In the diagram that follows, Curve I shows how the theoretical activity of an enzyme varies with temperature. Curve II shows the theoretical rate at which the enzyme is destroyed as the temperature rises. Curve III is the net reaction rate of the enzyme, Curve I minus Curve II. The dotted lines represent measured reaction rates for two other enzymes.

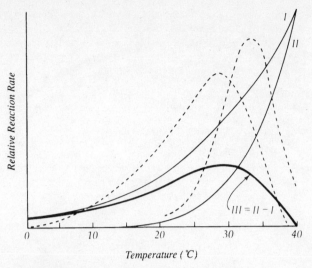

Temperature (°C)

From **Botany: An Ecological Approach** by William A. Jensen and Frank B. Salisbury. © 1972 by Wadsworth Publishing Company, Inc. Reprinted by permission of the publisher.

1. As the temperature increases,
   A. activity of an enzyme increases and destruction decreases.
   B. activity increases to about 30° C and decreases above that temperature.
   C. both activity and destruction increase with temperature.
   D. both activity and destruction decrease above 30° C.

2. For the enzyme in the study, the temperature of 30° C is a point at which:
   F. the enzyme has been completely destroyed.
   G. the rates of theoretical activity and destruction are equal.
   H. the balance between theoretical activity and destruction results in maximum activity.
   J. there is negligible destruction of the enzyme.

3. If the enzyme-controlled preparation were heated to 45° C and then gradually cooled,
   A. the reaction rate would increase and peak at 30° C.
   B. there would be no reaction at all.
   C. the reaction rate would start out high and gradually drop off as the temperature drops.
   D. the reaction rate would start out low and steadily increase as the temperature drops.

4. What is the relationship between the theoretical model and the actual measured values for real enzymes?
   F. Real enzymes agree exactly with the theoretical model.
   G. The information given does not provide an answer to the question.
   H. Real enzymes incorporate the same processes as the theoretical model, but with different constants.
   J. Real enzymes do not follow the theoretical model at all.

5. What step should be taken to determine the optimum temperature of an industrial process that uses an enzyme-controlled reaction?
   A. Control the temperature at 30° C.
   B. Experimentally determine the temperature at which the reaction rate is greatest.
   C. Find the highest theoretical activity rate of the enzyme.
   D. Find the best compromise between high reaction rate and minimum destruction of the enzyme.

ANSWERS AND EXPLANATIONS

The independent variable in this graph is temperature, and the dependent variables are different for each curve. For Curve I, it is the theoretical enzyme activity; for Curve II it is the rate of destruction of the enzyme; for the others, it is the net reaction rate. Temperature is in °C, but no units are given for the dependent variables; only relative rates are indicated. The value of temperature is read off the scale. The trends in both Curve I and Curve II show a definite increase with temperature, but in Curve II the increase starts out slow and then rises steeply. The dotted curves plot the behavior of two real enzymes. Now let's look at the answers.

1. **C** This is an *understanding* question, requiring you just to read the graph. Curve I is activity and Curve II is destruction, and both increase with temperature.

2. **H** This is an *analysis* question. Ability to read the graph is not enough; you have to figure out what it is saying. The enzyme has been partially, but not completely, destroyed since activity is still going on. The two rates are not equal, since at that temperature the value for theoretical activity is considerably greater than for destruction. The net reaction rate curve peaks at 30°C, so the activity is maximum at that temperature.

3. **B** Again, you must *analyze* the meaning of the graphs. Curve II shows complete destruction of the enzyme at 40° C, and cooling the reaction mixture down will not bring the enzyme back to life.

4. **H** *Analysis* again. The curves for the real enzymes show precisely the same pattern as the theoretical curve, so J is wrong. F is wrong because the peaks of activity are not at the same temperature as in the theoretical model. Since the pattern is the same, it is reasonable to assume that the same processes are at work, but with different constants.

5. **D** Now you have to *generalize* the meaning of the curves to a broader context. Choice A is wrong because every enzyme has different constants. It might seem that B is right, but at the maximum reaction rate temperature, the enzyme is being destroyed at a considerable rate, and would have to be replaced in the reaction vessel. C is wrong because theoretical activity is highest where the enzyme is completely destroyed. The engineer in charge would have to make a compromise between a good reaction rate and the need to replace the enzyme.

Passage 2

The graphs below show the variation of salt concentration (salinity), temperature, and oxygen concentration at various depths in the Bering Sea. (Note: 0/00 means parts per thousand.)

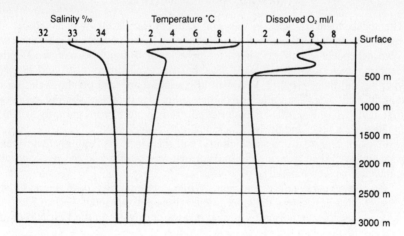

Reprinted with permission from Pickard, *Descriptive Physical Oceanography,* © 1963 by Pergamon Press PLC.

1. According to the graphs, how does salinity vary with depth?
   A. Salt concentration is greatest at or near the surface.
   B. Salt concentration increases uniformly with depth.
   C. Salt concentration is lowest near the surface, and changes only slightly below 1000 m.
   D. Salt concentration is twice as great near the bottom as at the surface.

2. If a diver were rising from a depth of 3000 m, what changes would be registered for most of the trip?
   F. The water would be getting warmer, saltier, and richer in oxygen.
   G. The water would be getting colder, less salty, and richer in oxygen.
   H. The water would be getting colder, less salty, and poorer in oxygen.
   J. The water would be getting warmer, less salty, and poorer in oxygen.

3. Which of the following hypotheses would account for some of the information in the graphs?
   A. Oxygen enters the water through the surface from the air, but little is carried to great depths.
   B. Higher temperatures allow more salt to be held in solution.
   C. Direct heating of the water by the sun has very little effect on the ocean.
   D. Large amounts of salt in solution prevent oxygen from dissolving.

4. A certain kind of fish thrives best at a temperature of 3° C, but needs over 34.2 parts per thousand of salt in its water. According to the graphs, under what conditions would it be most likely to survive?
   F. It would have to live within 100 m of the surface.
   G. It would have to tolerate low oxygen concentration.
   H. Its favored habitat would be below 2000 m.
   J. If the oxygen concentration were high enough, it could thrive in any part of the sea.

5. From these graphs, what general statement could be made about one or more variables in all parts of the ocean?
   A. Salinity and oxygen concentration always increase at depths below 1000 m.
   B. Temperature always drops sharply with depth for the first 100 m.
   C. Salinity is always higher at lower temperatures.
   D. None of these, unless more information is available.

6. If 5 kilograms of sea water were taken from the surface and then allowed to evaporate, how much salt would be left?
   F. 16.5 grams
   G. 33 grams
   H. 165 grams
   J. 330 grams

ANSWERS AND EXPLANATIONS

The independent variable in this graph, depth, is placed on the vertical axis instead of its more usual position on the abscissa. There are three graphs, each with its own dependent variable: salinity, temperature, and dissolved oxygen. Depth is measured in meters, salinity in parts per thousand, temperature in °C, and dissolved oxygen in milliliters per liter. Values of all variables are read off the scales on top and at the right side. The trends are complex. Salinity increases sharply with depth at first, and then only a little at greater depth. Temperature drops abruptly to 100 m, then increases a little, and decreases gradually to greater depths. Oxygen concentration drops, increases, drops substantially, and then increases slightly with greater depths. Below 500 m, there are definite correlations: salinity and oxygen concentration increase while temperature decreases.

1. C An *understanding* question. While concentration does increase with depth, it surely does not double; it goes from about 32.9 to 34.4. The increase is not uniform; it increases drastically in the first 500 m, and then only a little from there on down.

2. J Again, a simple test of your *understanding* of the graph. Starting at the bottom and going up, the graphs move to the left (lower) for salinity and oxygen, and to the right (higher) for temperature.

3. A Now you are required to *analyze* the meanings in the graph. In the first 500 m of the water, the oxygen level drops from 6.3 to 1.4 mL/L, so it surely seems that the oxygen enters from the air and little of it penetrates deeply. B is wrong because below 500 m, temperature drops and salin-

ity actually rises. C is wrong because the water is warmest at the surface, where the sun strikes it. D is wrong because both salt concentration and dissolved oxygen increase together below 500 m.

4. **G** This is a *generalization* question, requiring you to take several factors into account. Let's eliminate the wrong answers. J is wrong because the fish has to have certain temperatures regardless of the oxygen supply. H is wrong because the temperature is too low below 2000 m. F is wrong because the salinity is too low in the first 100 m. The salinity and temperature are about right at about 500 m but the oxygen concentration is lowest there.

5. **D** This question is a warning not to *generalize* from insufficient data. The graphs were made from data taken in the Bering Sea, and there is no particular reason to believe that the same patterns are universal.

6. **H** *Analysis.* Salinity at the surface is about 33 parts per thousand, or 33 grams per kilogram. In 5 kg of sea water, there would be 5×33 g of salt. You should be able to select the right answer without bothering to do the arithmetic.

Passage 3

Female lizards of a certain species can exhibit either male-like or female-like behavior. The chart shows kind of behavior, hormone levels, and size of a developing ovum.

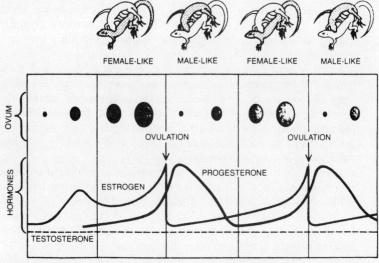

1. What event marks the change from female-like to male-like behavior?
   A. Minimum progesterone level
   B. Sudden increase in estrogen level
   C. Ovulation
   D. Growth of the ovum

2. Which of the following would explain the pattern of hormone production by the ovary?
   F. As the ovum grows, the ovary produces more progesterone.
   G. Progesterone and estrogen production both decrease as the ovum grows.
   H. Progesterone production is stimulated by the concentration of estrogen in the blood.
   J. At the time of ovulation, hormone production by the ovary switches from estrogen to progesterone.

3. Which of the following statements best accounts for the development of either male-like or female-like behavior?
   A. High estrogen levels produce male-like behavior.
   B. High progesterone levels produce male-like behavior.

    C. Low estrogen levels produce female-like behavior.
    D. High progesterone levels produce female-like behavior.

4. Which of the following changes might be the cause of the growth of the ovum?
    F. Increase in estrogen level
    G. Male-like behavior
    H. Increase in progesterone level
    J. Female-like behavior

5. There are no males in this species, and all eggs develop without fertilization. What might be a reasonable hypothesis to explain the existence of male-like behavior?
    A. The species has evolved from one in which male courtship behavior stimulates females to ovulate.
    B. At certain stages, the production of the male hormone testosterone induces male-like behavior.
    C. In all male lizards, high progesterone levels induce courtship behavior.
    D. Female-like behavior in male lizards of other species induces females to ovulate.

ANSWERS AND EXPLANATIONS

1. **C** The behavior is female-like in the second phase, and male-like in the third. Therefore, the transformation occurs at the end of the second phase, where the word OVULATION appears on the chart. Choice A is wrong because at the time of transformation, progesterone level is increasing. B is wrong because at that moment, estrogen level drops sharply. D is wrong because the ovum is growing steadily long before the transformation.

2. **J** Ovulation is marked by a sudden drop in estrogen level and a rapid increase in progesterone, so it seems as though the ovary is switching from one to the other. F is wrong because progesterone actually drops almost to zero during the middle phase of ovum growth. G is wrong because progesterone level first drops and then rises during ovum growth. H is wrong because progesterone level decreases drastically while estrogen level is increasing.

3. **B** The conversion to male-like behavior coincides with a rapid increase in progesterone level. Choice A is wrong because estrogen level drops suddenly when the change to male-like behavior occurs. C is wrong because the change to female-like behavior occurs while the estrogen level is increasing. D is wrong because the change to female-like behavior occurs when progesterone level is very low.

4. **F** Estrogen level is increasing all the while the ovum is growing. G is wrong because the ovum grows rapidly while the behavior is female-like. H is wrong because the ovum starts its growth when there is no progesterone. J is wrong because there is substantial ovum growth during the male-like phase.

5. **A** It is clear that the female-like lizard ovulates when stimulated by a male-like partner, at the end of phase 2. B is wrong because the chart shows that there is no substantial testosterone production at any stage. C is wrong because there is no evidence that male lizards have any progesterone at all. D is wrong because there is no evidence that any male lizards exhibit female-like behavior.

Passage 4

The table below gives the amounts and sources of the various kinds of air pollutants produced in the United States during the year 1977, in millions of metric tons.

Source	Particulates	Oxides of sulfur	Oxides of nitrogen	Organic vapors	Carbon monoxide
Transportation	1.1	0.8	9.2	11.5	85.7
Electric utilities	3.4	17.6	7.1	0.1	0.3
Industries	6.6	7.4	5.7	11.4	8.9
Solid waste	0.4	0	0.1	0.7	2.6
Fires	0.7	0	0.1	4.5	4.9
Buildings	0.2	1.6	0.9	0.1	0.3

1. How much carbon monoxide is added to the air of the United States during an average month?
   A. 103 million metric tons
   B. 85.7 million metric tons
   C. 8.6 million metric tons
   D. 5.1 million metric tons

2. Acid rain is produced by the chemical combination of rain water with sulfur and nitrogen oxides in the air. Which of the following would be most effective in reducing the amount of acid rain?
   F. Insulation of buildings to reduce the amount of fuel used.
   G. Cleaning of stack gases produced in manufacturing.
   H. Better control of forest fires.
   J. Cleaning of stack gases produced in electric power plants.

3. Which of the following pollution control practices would have no effect on the problem of acid rain?
   A. Improved antipollution devices in cars.
   B. Reduction in the burning of tropical forests.
   C. Use of low-sulfur coal in electric power plants.
   D. Conversion of home heating from coal to nitrogen-free natural gas.

4. Which of the following possible improvements in technology would reduce air pollution and, at the same time, improve the efficiency of the use of fuel?
   F. Filtering the particulates out of the waste gases produced by industrial processes.
   G. Recovering the sulfur from the smoke stacks of electric utilities for use in making sulfuric acid.
   H. Recovering the organic vapors from industrial processes for use in making commercial solvents.
   J. Returning the carbon monoxide produced by automobile engines into the cylinders to be burned as fuel.

5. Which of the following technological innovations would probably NOT be a practical way to reduce air pollution?
   A. Converting industries to reliance on electricity rather than on coal or oil fired furnaces.
   B. A program to improve the insulation of buildings.
   C. Providing all new automobiles with afterburners to convert organic vapors to carbon dioxide and water.
   D. Light-rail transport systems that would greatly reduce the automobile traffic in cities.

ANSWERS AND EXPLANATIONS

1. **C** This is simply a matter of reading the question carefully. Obtain the total carbon monoxide for the year by adding figures in the last column. To get the monthly average, divide by 12.

2. **J** The amount of sulfur and nitrogen oxides produced by electric power plants is far greater than that produced by all other sources combined. This is surely the best place to attack the problem.

3. **B** Since fires produce no oxides of sulfur, and very little of nitrogen, controlling forest fires would not do anything to reduce the amount of acid rain.

4. **J** While all four of the choices would help to reduce the amount of pollution in the air, and G and H would also produce useful byproducts, the question specifically asks for a method of improving fuel economy. Only burning of carbon monoxide as fuel meets this criterion.

5. **A** Since electric power plants produce more pollutants than anything else, conversion of industries to electricity would not do any good. Improving insulation would reduce the need to burn fuel in buildings; afterburners would keep organic pollutants out of the air; light-rail transport would cut down on the number of automobiles.

RESEARCH SUMMARIES QUESTIONS

The passage for these questions consists of a description of two or more experiments, followed by a statement of the results of the experiments. Your task is to answer five or six questions based on the results. You will succeed if you know what to look for. For purposes of discussing tactics, one experiment will be exemplified.

Here is a sample of a typical Research Summaries passage, along with a typical question at each of the three cognitive levels:

A series of experiments was done to test the hypothesis that air pollution affects fertility.

Experiment 1

Four groups of female mice, with 40 mice in each group, were mated and then exposed to different diets and concentrations of carbon monoxide in the air. The two diets tested were high protein (16%) and low protein (8%). Air was either free of carbon monoxide or contaminated with 65 parts per million of carbon monoxide. This is a pollution level that can be found in cities with heavy traffic. The number of females who became pregnant was then recorded:

High protein, clean air:	38
High protein, polluted air:	36
Low protein, clean air:	19
Low protein, polluted air:	9

Experiment 2

The experiment was repeated, this time using ozone instead of carbon monoxide as the pollutant:

High protein, clean air:	35
High protein, polluted air:	22
Low protein, clean air:	20
Low protein, polluted air:	21

1. Since the problem deals with the effects of polluted air, why were groups of mice exposed to clean air?
   A. to keep a healthy strain of mice going
   B. so that they could be compared with mice exposed to polluted air
   C. so that the effects of protein in the diet could be evaluated
   D. to compare the effects of ozone and carbon monoxide

This is an *understanding* level question. It asks you to apply your knowledge of the meaning of a control. Unless there was a group given clean air, there is no way of telling whether the pollutants really make a difference in the fertility of the mice. The answer is **B.**

2. Which of the following conclusions is justified by the data?
  A. Carbon monoxide pollution by itself reduces the fertility of mice.
  B. A high protein diet promotes good health in mice.
  C. Proteins protect the fertility of mice against the damage caused by carbon monoxide.
  D. Air pollutants reduce the fertility of mice fed on a low protein diet.

This is an *analysis* question. You must study the data and find in it an implication that supports one of the offered answers. **A** is probably not a good answer because there is very little difference between the mice in good air and air polluted with carbon monoxide. (You must be prepared to make judgment calls in deciding between two answers.) **B** is wrong because nothing in the experiment deals with the general health of the mice. **D** is wrong because there is no justification for extending the results from the carbon monoxide experiment to pollutants in general; indeed, ozone seems to make very little difference, if the protein level is low. The answer is **C**; fertility is little affected by carbon monoxide if there is plenty of protein, but mice produce very few offspring in air polluted with carbon monoxide if the protein level in the diet is low.

3. Which of the following would be an appropriate response to the results of this experiment?
  A. Start a program to inform women who want to become pregnant that they should move to regions with lower air pollution.
  B. Do a similar experiment on women, to see if their ability to become pregnant is affected by air pollutants.
  C. Start a massive campaign to reduce air pollution, particularly in cities.
  D. Start a research program to find out more about how air pollutants affect the fertility rate in animals.

This *generalization* question requires you to apply the results of the experiment in a broader area. **A** is wrong because mice are not women; there is no evidence that women would react the same way. **B** is wrong; it is good theoretical science, but where would you find women who would volunteer for the experiment? **C** is wrong; while reducing air pollution would probably be a good idea, this experiment does not provide enough evidence to justify such a massive program. **D** is a good idea; with more data in hand, it might be possible to get a better idea of how women might be affected.

Tactics

It is worthwhile to approach the Research Summaries questions in a systematic way. Here are some hints as to the best way to attack these questions, along with a sample passage to show you how these hints apply.

Understand the problem. Each description of an experiment starts with a statement of what the experiment is designed to find out. Read this statement carefully; do not go any further until you are quite sure that you understand exactly what the experimental problem is.

Here is a sample of such a problem statement:

A horticulturist investigated the effects of using a high-nitrogen fertilizer on the growth of privet plants.

Understand the design. Next, study the description of the experimental method. It may be accompanied by a diagram. Try to relate the design of the experiment to the problem that the experiment is designed to solve.

For the sample problem we are considering, the experimental design is as follows:

Fifty 1-year-old privet plants were divided into 10 lots of 5 plants each. All were watered every third day with equal amounts of water. In 9 of the lots, different amounts of high-nitrogen fertilizer were added to the water once every 2 weeks for a year. The heights of the plants were measured at the end of the year.

Identify the variables. Research problems can fall into two general categories. In some problems, the investigator studies some aspect of the natural world, often making measurements of some kind. By comparing measurements, the scientist hopes to come to some understanding of the nature of the process under study. Generally, there will be two or more variables, and what is being sought is a relationship between the variables. If the research problem you are given is of this kind, your first job is to identify the variables.

The second category of research is the experiment. Here, the investigator plays a more active part, varying some condition to see what will happen. The independent variable is the quantity that the experimenter adjusts or controls in some way. Presumably, this will make something else change. The something else is the dependent variable. Just as in the other kind of problem, you must first be sure that you understand what the variables are.

In the sample we are using, the independent variable is the amount of fertilizer, and the dependent variable is the heights of the plants at the end of the year.

Identify the controls. In an experiment, and sometimes in a strictly observational problem, there is always the danger that some unsuspected variable is affecting the outcome. The experimenter must make sure that whatever outcome is observed is due to changes in the independent variable, not in something else. The way to be sure is to include controls in the experiment. Controls are precautions taken to eliminate all variables except the independent variable.

In our sample experiment, all plants must have identical soil, air, light, and so on. All the plants must be genetically identical. Further, to make sure that the minimum amount of fertilizer has an effect, a special control sample must be included. This is a group of plants that are given no fertilizer. Unless this control group turns out to be different from the experimental groups, there is no way to be sure that the minimum amount of fertilizer is affecting the growth of the plants.

Study the results. The outcome of the experiment may be presented in words, in a diagram, or (most often) in the form of a data table. In such a table, the independent variable appears on the left, and the dependent variable on the right.

For our experiment, a table of experimental results might look like this:

Fertilizer concentration (g/L)	Average height of plant (cm)
0	22.2
5	25.3
10	29.0
15	28.7
20	29.2
25	29.0
30	28.6
35	20.9
40	16.3
45	13.0

An important control in this experiment is the first data point, when no fertilizer was used. Without this, there would be no way to tell whether 5 g/L of fertilizer had any effect at all.

What trend do you notice in these data? You should see that the fertilizer helps, but that over a wide range the amount is not important. There is no significant difference in plant height between 10 g/L and 30 g/L. However, it is also clear that, if too much fertilizer is used, growth is retarded.

Look for flaws in the experiment. Are the controls adequate? Is the conclusion justified by the data? Are the experimental errors so great as to invalidate the results?

In the sample experiment, for example, the experimenter did not specify that all the plants be genetically identical. Another flaw is the failure to describe exactly how the height of the plants was measured.

Once you thoroughly understand the nature of the experiment and the meaning of the results, you should be able to deal with the multiple-choice questions based on the experiment.

Sample Questions

There will be six or seven Research Summaries questions based on a single passage. Look at the following questions, based on the sample experiment described above. Note the reasoning on which your choice of answer might be based.

1. What is the most efficient rate for a commercial grower to apply fertilizer to the privet plants?
   A. 5 g/L   C. 20 g/L
   B. 10 g/L   D. 40 g/L
   The answer is B. Higher concentrations cost more, but will not produce any further improvement. Furthermore, too much will actually do damage.

2. If a horticulturist is growing chrysanthemums to produce flowers, how would she know how much fertilizer to use?
   F. Perform an identical experiment with chyrsanthemums.
   G. Use 10 g/L of fertilizer.
   H. Perform a similar experiment with chrysanthemums, but use a different dependent variable.
   J. Grow the plants in sunlight because it is known that sunlight stimulates the formation of flowers.
   The answer is H. The best fertilizer for privet may not be best for chrysanthemums, so G is wrong. The experiment described deals only with growth, not flower formation, so F is wrong. J tells the horticulturist nothing about how much fertilizer is best. She needs a similar experiment, but with flower formation as the dependent variable.

3. In order for the results of this experiment to be meaningful, which of the following would NOT have to be the same for all the experiment samples?
   A. The soil in which the specimens were planted.
   B. The amount of time it took for the plants to flower.
   C. The particular variety of privet used.
   D. The number of hours of daylight to which the plants were exposed.
   The answer is B, since the experimental design proposes only to evaluate rate of growth, not flowering. If none of the other variables were controlled, the experimenter could never be sure whether the differences in growth were due to the fertilizer, or to the soil, the plant variety, or the exposure to daylight.

4. What part of the experimental design was included for the purpose of determining the smallest concentration of fertilizer that has any effect on growth?
   F. Giving one group water only
   G. Using an interval of 5 g/L between fertilizer concentrations
   H. Including a 10-g/L sample
   J. Using plants from a single genetic stock
   The answer is F. This is an important control. Unless there is a different outcome between no fertilizer and 5 g/L, there is no evidence that the 5 g/L of fertilizer did anything.

5. Which of the following situations would NOT invalidate the results of the experiment?
   A. Accidental destruction of the sample given 20 g/L of fertilizer
   B. The discovery that half of the plants had been potted in a different soil
   C. The discovery that the water used already contained substantial amounts of nitrogen
   D. The discovery that some of the plants had been taken from a different variety of privet
   The answer is A; results of the experiment are quite clear even without this sample. B and D are wrong because a different soil or a different variety might cause differences in the outcome. C is wrong because the nitrogen in the water has not been taken into account in the effort to find the optimum amount.

6. Which of the following hypotheses is suggested by the data?
   F. High concentrations of fertilizer damage the roots of plants.
   G. Privet plants cannot grow unless there is nitrogen in the soil.
   H. If all other conditions are equal, the amount of fertilizer used does not affect plant growth.
   J. Any addition of fertilizer to the soil slows photosynthesis.

The answer is F. G is wrong because we have no idea whether there was any nitrogen in the soil of the control, where the plants did grow. H is wrong because the experiment did not test a variety of conditions. J is wrong because we would expect slowing down of photosynthesis to retard growth, while the experiment shows that moderate amounts of fertilizer increase growth. F is right because it offers a reasonable explanation for the growth retardation produced by 35 g/L of fertilizer.

PRACTICE EXERCISES: RESEARCH SUMMARIES QUESTIONS

The Research Summaries questions in the test are likely to be more complex than the example given above. Try the following questions.

Passage 1

A physicist is investigating the effect that different conditions have on the force of friction. The material used is an ordinary brick, with a mass of 1.8 kg. It is pulled across the surface of a wooden table. Friction is measured by pulling the brick with a string attached to a spring scale, calibrated in newtons (N). When the brick is pulled at constant speed, the reading on the scale is equal to the force of friction between the brick and the table top.

Experiment 1

The brick is placed on the table in three different positions. First, it is allowed to rest on its broad face (area = 180 cm^2), then on its side (area = 130 cm^2), and finally on its end (area = 56 cm^2).

Table 1

Area (cm^2)	Friction (N)
180	7.1
130	7.3
56	7.2

Experiment 2

A wooden block of mass 0.6 kg is made to the same dimensions as the brick, and the experiment is repeated.

Table 2

Area (cm^2)	Friction (N)
180	1.2
130	1.1
56	1.2

Experiment 3

This time, the wooden block is loaded by adding 1.2 kg of extra mass on top of it, to give it the same weight as the brick.

Table 3

Area (cm²)	Friction (N)
180	3.5
130	3.6
56	3.7

1. From Experiment 1, it would be reasonable to hypothesize that:
   A. the surface area of contact does not affect the amount of friction.
   B. friction is large in a brick-to-wood contact.
   C. the amount of friction depends on the way the weight of the object is distributed.
   D. heavy objects have more friction than light ones.

2. Which combination of experiments shows that the amount of friction depends on the weight of the object?
   F. Experiment 1 and Experiment 2
   G. Experiment 1 and Experiment 3
   H. Experiment 2 and Experiment 3
   J. Experiment 1, Experiment 2, and Experiment 3

3. In doing Experiment 3, what was the purpose of adding enough weight to the wooden block to make its weight equal to that of the brick?
   A. To test the hypothesis that adding weight increases friction
   B. To find the relationship between surface area of contact and friction
   C. To find out whether the density of the material influences the amount of friction
   D. To control other factors and test the effect of the nature of the materials in contact

4. The experimenter repeated the experiment with the unloaded wooden block mounted on three tiny wooden points, which were the only contact with the table top. If the results of all these experiments hold good for extreme values of the experimental variables, about how much would the friction be?
   F. About 0.4 N
   G. Substantially less than 1.2 N
   H. About 1.2 N
   J. Substantially more than 1.2 N

5. Common experience indicates that it is much harder to slide some boxes across a floor than others. Which of the following reasons why this is true is demonstrated in these experiments?
   A. Friction is greater if there is more surface in contact.
   B. A heavy box will have more friction against the floor than a light one.
   C. Objects of irregular shape have more friction because they dig into the floor.
   D. The amount of friction depends on how the weight of the object is distributed.

6. The results of these experiments suggest that, if three bricks were piled up and pulled along as before, the amount of friction would be about:
   F. 3.6 N.
   G. 7.2 N.
   H. 14.4 N.
   J. 22.6 N.

ANSWERS AND EXPLANATIONS

1. **A** In spite of the fact that one surface is almost three times as great as another, there is no substantial difference in the amount of friction. The small differences are surely due to experimental variation. This is obvious when it is noted that the value obtained for the 130-cm^2 surface is a little larger than that for the 180-cm^2 surface. B is wrong because there is no comparison with other readings to decide what constitutes large friction. C is wrong because the experiment did not vary weight distribution. D is wrong because the same object was used throughout.

2. **H** In these two experiments, both the surface area of contact and the kind of materials in contact are the same, and the only difference is in the weight. The other three choices all include Experiment 1, in which a different kind of material is in contact with the surface, and this might be the reason for the difference in results.

3. **D** With the weight added, all other variables are controlled and the only difference between the brick and the wooden block, as far as contact with the table top is concerned, is in the nature of the material. The other choices are wrong because the experiment makes no comparison of different weights, surface areas, or densities.

4. **H** The data indicate that friction does not depend on surface area of contact. This is tested to extreme limits by repeating the experiment with a very small surface area. If the relationships hold up for extreme values, the friction should be the same for a very small area as for a large one.

5. **B** Comparing Experiment 2 with Experiment 3 shows that, even if the materials and the surface area in contact are the same, friction is greater when the weight of the object is greater. There is no evidence in these experiments that shape or weight distribution affects friction. Choice A is wrong because the experiments do not show any difference due to surface area.

6. **J** Experiments 2 and 3 show that, when the effective weight of the wooden block is increased by raising the mass from 0.6 kg to 1.8 kg, the friction triples. This suggests that friction is proportional to the weight of the object. Since three bricks weigh three times as much as one, the friction with three bricks ought to be three times as great as with a single brick.

Passage 2

A geologist is investigating the factors that affect the speed of flow of the water in a river. He measures the speeds at various points at the surface: center and edge of a straight part of a river, and the inside and outside of a curved section. He also measures the speed at the bottom of a straight section. This is done in the spring and again in summer:

Location in river	Speed, m/s summer, 1.2 m deep	Speed, m/s spring, 4.1 m deep
Bottom, center of straight part	1.6	1.8
Surface, center of straight part	4.2	11.9
Surface, edge of straight part	2.8	6.0
Surface, outer edge of curve	5.0	13.5
Surface, inner edge of curve	0.7	1.4

1. In what part of the river does the amount of water in the river have the LEAST effect on the speed of the water?
   A. The edge of a straight section
   B. The bottom
   C. The surface
   D. The outer edge of a curved section

2. What significant question CANNOT be answered from the data taken in this research program?
   F. In what part of the river are the banks eroded most rapidly?
   G. How does the curvature of the river affect the speed at the bottom?
   H. How does the depth of the river affect the speed of flow?
   J. What happens to the surface speed of the water as it moves into a curved section of the river?

3. Comparison of the surface speeds in either summer or spring would seem to imply that:
   A. the water is shallow in the inside of a curved section.
   B. most of the water is flowing in the straight part of the river.
   C. there is more water in straight sections of the river than in curved sections.
   D. the deepest water is in the center of the straight sections.

4. Which of the following environmental hazards would a plant have to tolerate in order to thrive in the outer edge of a curved part of the river?
   F. Periods of near-stagnant water
   G. Drastic changes in water depth and speed
   H. Changes in water temperature between spring and summer
   J. Abrasion by sediments held in suspension

5. In traveling on a river, which tactic is likely to be most efficient?
   A. In curved sections, travel upstream in the middle and downstream at the edges.
   B. In straight sections, keep as close to the edge as possible.
   C. In curved sections, use the outer parts of the curves downstream and the inner parts upstream.
   D. In straight sections, always use the middle of the river.

6. According to the data, a straight river differs in several ways from one with many curves. One difference is that in a straight river:
   F. the speed of the water would not vary much throughout the year.
   G. the amount of water flowing would be greater.
   H. the water would be flowing more slowly along the bottom than at the surface.
   J. the various speeds would not change much as the investigator moved upstream.

ANSWERS AND EXPLANATIONS

1. B   When the data for spring and summer are compared, it is clear that the speed along the bottom does not change much.

2. G   No measurements were taken of the speed at the bottom of curved sections of the river. Erosion of the banks would be greatest where the speed is highest; there is a consistent correlation showing that the speed of flow is fastest where the river is deepest; when the water enters a curve, it speeds up on the outer sections and slows down on the inside of the curve.

3. A   Every comparison shows that deeper water flows faster; it is faster in spring than in summer and at the center of the river than at the edges. It is reasonable to suppose that the slow water on the inside of curves flows over a shallow depth.

4. G   At the outer edge, the water is much deeper and faster-flowing in spring than in summer. The other choices are wrong because the data do not indicate periods of stagnant water, and present no evidence about water temperature or sediments.

5. C   You want the fastest water on the way downstream, and the slowest water on the way upstream. Choice A is wrong because upstream travel can find slower water in the inner edge, and downstream travel can find faster water at the outer edge. B is wrong because this is a poor tactic on the way downstream, where the faster water is available in the middle of the river. Conversely, D fails to take advantage of the slower water at the edges when traveling upstream.

6. J   In a curved river, the faster water is constantly swinging from side to side, always hitting the outside of the curves; in a straight river, there is nothing happening that will make one side different from the other. F is wrong because the speed varies according to the amount of water, whether the river is straight or curved. G is wrong because nothing in the data indicates such a difference. H is wrong because it is true for all rivers, straight or curved.

Passage 3

A bacteriologist cultures a blood specimen and finds that it produces two kinds of bacterial colonies. One kind of bacteria, designated *R*, grows in red colonies; the other, called *Y*, produces yellow colonies. To study the metabolism of these bacteria, she performs the following experiments:

Experiment 1

R is cultured on three different media. It grows well on a medium containing glucose only. It grows poorly on a medium containing amino acids only. It grows well on a medium containing both glucose and amino acids.

Experiment 2

Y is cultured on the same three media. It grows poorly on the glucose medium, and not at all on the amino acid medium. On the medium containing both nutrients, it grows vigorously.

Experiment 3

R and *Y* are grown together on the three different media. On the glucose medium, only *R* grows. On the amino acid medium, *R* grows poorly and *Y* not at all. On the medium containing both nutrients, only *Y* grows.

1. Which statement is true about the nutritional requirements of the *R* bacteria?
    A. They need both glucose and amino acids in order to grow vigorously.
    B. They can survive and prosper on glucose alone.
    C. Amino acids tend to retard their growth.
    D. They cannot grow without glucose.

2. Which statement is true about the nutritional requirements of the *Y* bacteria?
    F. They cannot survive without both glucose and amino acids.
    G. They can survive without glucose, but must have amino acids.
    H. They can survive without amino acids, but must have glucose.
    J. If they have glucose, the presence of amino acids is irrelevant.

3. Which hypothesis best explains the results obtained when both bacteria are grown together on a glucose-only medium?
    A. The *Y* bacteria do not survive because they need amino acids.
    B. The *Y* bacteria produce some substance that promotes the growth of *R* bacteria.
    C. The *R* bacteria grow vigorously and win out in competition with the *Y* bacteria.
    D. The *R* bacteria promote the growth of the *Y* bacteria.

4. Under what circumstances do the *Y* bacteria produce a substance that prevents the growth of the *R* bacteria?
   F. When there is an adequate supply of glucose
   G. When the *R* bacteria are weakened because of a shortage of amino acids
   H. When the *Y* bacteria have a plentiful supply of amino acids
   J. When the *Y* bacteria have both glucose and amino acids available

5. In another experiment, both kinds of bacteria were cultured on a medium containing glucose, amino acids, and ethyl alcohol. The *R* bacteria grew, but the *Y* bacteria did not. Which of the following hypotheses could NOT explain these results?
   A. Ethyl alcohol is poisonous to *Y* bacteria, but not to *R* bacteria.
   B. In the presence of ethyl alcohol, *R* bacteria produce a substance that is poisonous to *Y* bacteria.
   C. Ethyl alcohol is necessary for the growth of *R* bacteria, but not *Y* bacteria.
   D. Ethyl alcohol prevents *Y* bacteria from making use of amino acids.

6. What steps might an experimenter take to see whether any practical outcome might be realized from these experiments?
   F. Test the *Y* bacteria to see whether they can inhibit the growth of many other kinds of bacteria.
   G. Test the *Y* bacteria to see whether they can grow on a different combination of amino acids.
   H. Test the *R* bacteria to see whether an increased concentration of amino acids will enhance their growth.
   J. Test the *R* bacteria to see whether they can grow on other sugars besides glucose.

ANSWERS AND EXPLANATIONS

1. B   Experiment 1 showed that they grow well on glucose alone. Choice A is wrong because there is nothing in the results to indicate that amino acids improved their growth. C is wrong because they did well when amino acids were added to the glucose; with amino acids alone, they did poorly because they had no glucose. D is wrong because they survived, although weakly, on amino acids alone.

2. H   The *Y* bacteria grew, weakly, on a medium with glucose but no amino acids. That is why F and G are wrong. J is wrong because they did much better when amino acids were added.

3. A   Experiment 2 showed that the *Y* bacteria cannot survive without amino acids. The presence of the *R* bacteria is irrelevant.

4. J   When both nutrients are available, the *R* bacteria are completely eliminated by the presence of the *Y* bacteria. F and G are wrong because, with glucose along, it is the *R* bacteria that win out. H is wrong because the *Y* bacteria need glucose as well as amino acids to grow well.

5. C   Nothing in the experimental results tells whether the *R* bacteria could grow without ethyl alcohol. Choices A, B, and D would all provide adequate explanations for the lack of *R* bacteria.

6. F   The discovery that the *Y* bacteria could eliminate many kinds of bacteria might well lead to the discovery of a new antibiotic. All the other choices might be of interest, but do not seem to point in the direction of anything useful.

Passage 4

A chemist is testing the effectiveness of various materials in absorbing the particles produced by a radioactive source.

Several metals are to be tested to determine their effectiveness in blocking the passage of the particles emitted by a radioactive substance. A Geiger counter counts these particles, finding first that the counter, placed anywhere, records a normal background that averages 22 randomly spaced counts per minute. When a radioactive source is placed nearby, the count becomes, on average, 178 counts per minute. Various thicknesses of three different metals, each with a different density, are placed between the source and the counter. The counter now records the rate at which particles pass through the metal to the counter.

Counts per minute on Geiger counter

Thickness of metal (mm)	Aluminum: 2.8 g/cm³	Tin: 5.6 g/cm³	Lead: 11.2 g/cm³
0	178	178	177
1	155	131	84
2	135	98	47
3	118	76	32
4	103	59	26
5	91	48	24
6	81	40	23
7	72	35	22
8	65	31	22
9	59	28	23
10	53	26	22

1. To find the actual numbers of particles that pass through the various metals, all of the numbers of counts in the table must be changed. How?
   A. Add 22 to each reading to account for the background radiation.
   B. Subtract 22 from each reading to account for the background radiation.
   C. Add 178 to each reading to account for the stream of particles when it is unimpeded by metal sheets.
   D. Subtract each reading from 178 to account for the stream of particles when it is unimpeded by metal sheets.

2. The first sheet of aluminum removes 23 particles from the stream, but the tenth sheet removes only 6 particles. Why is there such a difference?
   F. The tenth sheet is probably thinner than the first sheet.
   G. The number of particles entering the tenth sheet is far less than the number entering the first sheet.
   H. The energy of the particles may be weakened by their passage through the first 9 sheets.
   J. Many of the particles scatter out of the tenth sheet instead of going straight through it.

3. Why is the zero reading for lead less than the zero reading for aluminum and tin?
   A. Lead has a much higher density than either aluminum or tin.
   B. Background radiation is less for lead than for either aluminum or tin.
   C. Aluminum and tin emit radiation, while lead does not.
   D. Emission of particles is randomly distributed, so there will always be some variation in the number of clicks.

4. What hypothesis might be suggested to account for the fact that 2 mm of aluminum has nearly the same stopping power as 1 mm of tin?
   F. Stopping power is proportional to density.
   G. The similarities in values might be pure coincidence.
   H. The crystal structure of aluminum is less compact than the crystal structure of tin.
   J. A given mass of any two metals has approximately the same stopping power.

5. According to the results of this experiment, what steps might be taken to shield a piece of apparatus so as to keep out essentially all radioactive particles, including the normal background?
   A. None; some will always get through.
   B. Surround it with a shield of any metal 20 mm thick.
   C. Surround it with a shield of tin 16 mm thick.
   D. Surround it with a shield of lead 3 mm thick.

6. Suppose a fourth experiment were done using sheets of osmium, which has a density of 22 g/cm³. About how many counts would the Geiger counter register if the stream of particles went through 2 such sheets?
   F. 25
   G. 48
   H. 66
   J. 82

ANSWERS AND EXPLANATIONS

1. **B** Every count number in the chart includes 22 counts of background radiation. This must be subtracted to find the actual number of counts due to the radioactive sample.

2. **G** Each sheet removes a certain fraction of all the particles that enter it. The number entering the first sheet is 156 (= 178 – 22), and the number leaving is 133. The 23 that have been removed are 15% of the number that enter. The 6 removed by the last sheet are approximately 15% of the 37 that enter. F is wrong because all the sheets are specified to be 1 mm thick. H and J are wrong because no evidence is presented concerning the energy of the particles, or of scattering.

3. **D** It is stated that emission of particles is random, and the numbers are only averages. There is bound to be some variation in the counts during one-minute intervals. All the other choices are wrong because the zero readings are taken without the metals in place, so they can have no effect on the reading.

4. **F** Since tin has twice the density of aluminum, and also twice the stopping power, it is reasonable to suggest that stopping power is proportional to density. G is wrong because the same relationship can be found for other values of aluminum and tin, and for tin and lead. H is wrong because no evidence of crystal structure is given. J is wrong because it is only the thickness of the metal that counts, and mass would depend on the size of the plates as well.

5. **C** The figures suggest that 16 mm of tin would have the same stopping power as 8 mm of lead. The 22 counts entering when the stream of particles is blocked by 8 mm of lead is all background; none of the particles are getting through. Choice A is wrong because it is clear that 7 mm of lead completely blocks the particles, allowing the Geiger counter to register only the background. B is wrong because there is no reason to believe that 20 mm of aluminum would work; in fact, it would not. D is wrong because 3 mm of lead shows a count that is still above the background.

6. **F** Since osmium has twice the density of lead, we would expect that the count with 2 mm of osmium would be about the same as the count with 4 mm of lead. This is the pattern throughout.

CONFLICTING VIEWPOINTS QUESTIONS

Scientific information is never complete. While ideas and theories are developing, scientists will continue to disagree with each other. It is these disagreements that provide the spur for research. Experiments and other forms of investigation are specifically designed to resolve points at issue. It is through this dialogue of scientists with each other and with nature that consensus is eventually reached.

In the Conflicting Viewpoints questions, you will be given short paragraphs representing the ideas of two scientists. They will disagree with each other. Your job is to analyze the arguments and information in the two paragraphs. You will be asked to identify the nature of the disagreement, to tell why each of the scientists has arrived at the opinion expressed, and to identify forms of evidence that might resolve the conflict.

In this type of question, you will not be asked to decide which of the two scientists is correct. You will be required to identify points of agreement and disagreement. You may be asked to identify kinds of evidence that would tend to support or to deny either of the two viewpoints.

Here is a sample Conflicting Viewpoints passage, with a sample of possible questions at each of the three cognitive levels.

Two scientists disagree on the causes of the long-term trend of a warmer earth.

Scientist A:

There has been a steady increase in the average temperature of the earth for the last 150 years. Since 1861, the average temperature, all over the world, has gone up one degree Fahrenheit. This may not seem like much, but if the trend continues, the result will be disastrous. The polar ice caps would melt, flooding all coastal areas and reducing the total land area of the earth by 30 percent. All climatic zones would change; farmland would turn to desert and forest would turn into prairie. This change in global climate is caused by the accumulation of certain gases in the atmosphere. Due to our massive burning of coal, oil and gas, the carbon dioxide level in the atmosphere has more than doubled. Carbon dioxide is like a blanket around the earth, preventing the radiation of heat out into space. Unless drastic steps are taken to reduce the buildup of carbon dioxide, the world as we know it will disappear. Industry must learn to function without releasing this and other greenhouse gases into the air.

Scientist B:

Before placing an enormously expensive burden on industry, we must be sure of our ground. While the greenhouse effect may well be a part of the reason for the warming of the earth, it cannot be the whole story. Most of the temperature increase occurred before 1940, but most of the carbon dioxide increase has happened since then. Something else is contributing to the warming of the earth. The temperature of the earth depends strongly on the level of sunspot activity on the sun. The sun heats up during high sunspot years. The "little ice age" of 1640 to 1720, when the average temperature was two degrees lower, was a period of low sunspot activity. Solar activity goes through cycles. When activity is high, increased levels of ultraviolet radiation deplete the ozone layer of the upper atmosphere and the increased flow of charged particles from the sun affects the formation of clouds. All of these effects have complex and poorly understood effects on the earth's climate, and could easily result in long-range and cyclic climate changes.

1. The two scientists agree that
   F. sunspot activity affects the climate of the earth.
   G. there is a long-range trend to a warmer earth.
   H. the major cause of warming is carbon dioxide.
   J. something must be done to avert a catastrophe.

This is an *understanding* question. **F** is wrong because Scientist A does not address the question of sunspot activity at all. **H** is wrong because Scientist B thinks that sunspot activity may play the major role. **J** is wrong because Scientist B's theory precludes the possibility of ameliorative action. The answer is **G**; both agree that the earth has gotten warmer.

2. In responding to Scientist B, Scientist A might reply that
   A. the measured value of the increase in sunspot activity is far too small to account for the observed warming.
   B. it is widely known that it is the carbon dioxide in the atmosphere that produces the warming.
   C. the flow of charged particles from the sun actually decreases during periods of high sunspot activity.
   D. it is possible to cut down on the atmospheric carbon dioxide by promoting the growth of plants.

To answer this *analysis* question, you have to eliminate proffered answers that do not deal with issues discussed by either scientist, such as **D**. Appeals to authority, like **B**, are not acceptable scientific debate. **C** is an insult to scientist A, who surely knows the properties of an easily measurable phenomenon. The answer is **A**, because there is a strong element of judgment in making this decision, particularly since Scientist B admits that the phenomena are not well understood.

3. What course of action might be suggested by Scientist B and opposed by Scientist A?
   F. Convene a committee of industry and government leaders to determine what steps can be taken to reduce carbon dioxide emission.
   G. Start a long-range research project to explore the possibility of neutralizing the flow of charged particles from the sun.
   H. Investigate the possibility that other greenhouse gases such as methane have an important effect on warming.
   J. Start a long-range research project to evaluate the relative importance of carbon dioxide and sunspot activity.

Now you must look for an appropriate *generalization*. **F** is wrong because Scientist B does not believe that carbon dioxide is at the heart of the problem. **G** is wrong; Scientist B has not committed himself to the idea that charged particles are the major culprit. **H** is wrong; neither scientist has suggested that other gases are involved. **J** is right; Scientist B feels that more information is needed, but Scientist A might object to a long-range project because the problem of carbon dioxide is too urgent.

Tactics

In approaching a question of this type, start by reading it quickly. This may be enough for you to apply the first important tactic: *Identify the basic disagreement.* Consider, for example, this passage:

What effect does crash dieting have on long-term loss of weight? Two scientists present opposing views.

Scientist 1

People who repeatedly gain and lose weight acquire a permanent, long-term change in their metabolism. Their metabolism slows down, so that they use less food energy than others. The result is that the excess energy in their food becomes stored as fat. This means that crash dieting is self-defeating. Experiments on rats have shown that alternating underfeeding with overfeeding results in a lower metabolic rate. The lower rate enabled the rats to gain weight more easily, with less food than they would ordinarily need. Further, a study of high school wrestlers found that some of them lost and regained weight as much as 10 times during the wrestling season. In the off-season, they were no fatter than those whose weight did not vary, but their metabolic rate was substantially lower. The implication is that people who crash-diet and then regain weight are likely to experience more and more difficulty in losing it.

Scientist 2

There is no real evidence that repeated gain and loss of weight makes it more difficult to lose. The studies on rats are suggestive, but there is no reason to believe that they have any implication for obese human beings. The study involving high school wrestlers was severely flawed. The wrestlers in the study were all in summer camp, after the end of the wrestling season. The dieters may have been artificially holding their weight down by careful control of their diets, and this is known to lower the metabolism. There is no evidence that this lowered metabolism made it more difficult to lose weight. There is another study, in which the subjects were not rats or wrestlers, but obese people who had lost weight and then gained it back. When they regained weight, their metabolism was just the same as it was before they dieted. Furthermore, there was no difference in their ability to lose weight again.

You can analyze this passage, and any other like it, by asking yourself a series of questions about it. Only after you have answered them in your own mind are you in a position to look at the questions you will have to answer.

What is the basic question at issue? Does repeated gain and loss of weight make it more difficult to lose?

What is the position of each of the scientists on the question? Scientist 1 says yes; Scientist 2 says no.

What evidence does Scientist 1 bring to justify his position? Two studies: one on rats and one on high school wrestlers.

What evidence does Scientist 2 bring to support his position? A study of obese people.

What flaws does Scientist 2 find in the position of Scientist 1? The experiments were done on rats and high school athletes, not on obese people. There was inadequate control because the diets of the high school wrestlers in summer camp were not monitored. No connection was made between lowered metabolism and difficulty in losing weight.

What flaws does Scientist 1 find in the position of Scientist 2? In this particular passage, Scientist 1 does not rebut Scientist 2. You may find that this is often the case.

Sample Questions

Here are some multiple-choice questions that might be asked about this passage:

1. The position taken by Scientist 1 involves the hypothesis that:
   A. a lower metabolic rate makes it more difficult to lose weight.
   B. the metabolism of a rat is exactly like that of a human being.
   C. high school wrestlers generally have a weight problem.
   D. large amounts of food do not necessarily contain large amounts of energy.

   The answer is A. In both of the experiments cited by Scientist 1, the only outcome found was lower metabolism, and he assumed that this resulted in more difficulty in losing weight. B is wrong because exact similarity in all respects is not needed; a rough resemblance is enough to suggest a relationship. C is wrong because there is no implication that any of the results are relevant to high school wrestlers generally. D is wrong because neither scientist addressed the question of the energy content of different foods.

2. Scientist 2 could claim that the study he cites is more meaningful because:
   F. it was done with a higher degree of accuracy.
   G. it had better controls.
   H. it was done with the subjects to which the problem applies.
   J. it did not use metabolism as a measure of weight loss.

   The answer is H. Weight loss is a problem for obese people, not high school athletes or rats. F and G are wrong because Scientist 2 said nothing about either accuracy or controls. J is wrong because Scientist 1 used metabolism as a measure of *ability* to lose weight, not as a measure of weight loss.

3. What is a point on which both scientists agree implicitly?
   A. Repeated gain and loss of weight is undesirable.
   B. Science must be concerned with finding ways to help people control their weight.
   C. Ways should be found to help people to lower their metabolism.
   D. Experiments with rats are of no use in making decisions about people.

   The answer is B. Both scientists are discussing the theory behind the problems of helping people to lose weight; they disagree on the means. Choice A is wrong because Scientist 2 could find no evidence for this statement. C is wrong because Scientist 2 claims there is no proof that a lower metabolism makes it more difficult to lose weight. D is wrong; Scientist 1 quoted experiments with rats, and even Scientist 2 conceded that they may have some value.

4. What serious flaw did Scientist 2 find in one of the experiments cited by Scientist 1?
   F. The rats were not given the same diet as the wrestlers.
   G. There was inadequate control of the diet of the wrestlers.
   H. The wrestlers were not tested during the wrestling season.
   J. The metabolism of the rats was not tested before the experiment.

   The answer is G. Apparently, there was some suspicion that the wrestlers who dieted were still dieting in camp. F is wrong because no experiment was made, or could be made, comparing the reaction of the rats with that of the wrestlers. H is wrong because the experiment specifically called for measuring metabolism after the period of varying weight. J is wrong because Scientist 2 did not bring this question up. He had no reason to suspect Scientist 1 of complete incompetence.

5. When other studies of this problem are made, which of the following outcomes would tend to strengthen the position of Scientist 1?

   A. The discovery that monkeys fed an inadequate diet develop unusually low metabolism.

   B. An experiment showing that rats with artificially lowered metabolism eat less than other rats.

   C. A study showing that obese people eat more than thin people.

   D. A study of people with unusually low metabolism, showing that they can maintain body weight with smaller amounts of food.

   The answer is D. Scientist 2 had cast doubt on the proposition that a lower metabolism indicates the need for smaller amounts of food. A is wrong because neither scientist raised the question of adequacy of diet. B is wrong because this experiment does not address the question of the relationship between amount of food consumed and weight gain. C is wrong because it says nothing about the problem of alternate weight gain and loss.

6. Which of the following questions about proper diet would be answered, at least in part, by the resolution of this disagreement?

   F. Is it better to lose weight, at the risk of regaining it, or just to stay obese?

   G. Is it important to control the amount of fat in the diet?

   H. In dieting to lose weight, is it important to be under the care of a doctor?

   J. Are overweight persons at an exceptionally great risk of still further increase in weight as they grow older?

   The answer is F. If Scientist 1 is right, repeated loss and regain of weight predisposes to still greater weight gain. The study says nothing about the amount of fat in the diet (G), the need for a doctor's supervision (H), or aging (J).

PRACTICE EXERCISES: CONFLICTING VIEWPOINTS QUESTIONS
Passage 1

Frogs all over the world are in trouble. Populations are diminishing or disappearing, and many frogs are being born with deformities such as extra legs or limbs missing completely. Scientists are trying to find out why this is happening.

Scientist 1

Frogs are a sentinel species, like the canary that tells miners when their air is poisoned. The death and deformity of so many frogs is telling us that our environment is polluted.

A likely cause of the damage to frogs is that the growing tadpoles are being subjected to unusually high levels of ultraviolet radiation. Air pollution has significantly damaged the ozone layer of the atmosphere, allowing more of the damaging ultraviolet rays to reach the earth. In one experiment, when salamander eggs were subjected to normal levels of ultraviolet radiation, 85 percent died before hatching. It seems likely that this radiation is also damaging frogs.

Chemical pollution is another suspect. One pond in Minnesota was found to produce many deformed frogs. When frog embryos were laboratory-raised in water taken from that pond, three quarters of them grew with developmental deformities. One possible cause is Methoprene in the water, a chemical that is widely used to control mosquitoes and fleas. Methoprene mimics a hormone that controls certain developmental processes in the growing embryo, and could seriously interfere with the process of organ formation.

Other hormone mimics are also suspected. Several kinds are produced in the chemical decay of certain plastics and pesticides. Studies are continuing in efforts to find out just what chemicals are involved.

Meanwhile, we must surely take note of the fact that these deformed and dying frogs are giving us the message that pollutants produced by human activity are placing our worldwide biological system in jeopardy.

Scientist 2

There are serious flaws in the experiments that have attributed the frog crisis to pollution. The ultraviolet experiment was done with salamanders, not frogs. Frogs are different; they have an enzyme that repairs the damage caused by ultraviolet radiation. Methoprene is not a serious candidate, since it can do its damage only in concentrations hundreds of times greater than has ever been found in a pond. Further, it has been shown that the areas where there is Methoprene in the water and those with high concentrations of deformed frogs do not match. No study has yet been able to tie in any specific chemical pollutant to a pond that produces deformed frogs.

It is probable that there is more than one frog problem. A dead embryo is not the same as a frog with a missing arm or with too many legs. A missing arm or leg might be the work of a heron or predatory fish that made a grab for the frog and managed to get only part of it. This surely happens, but no one knows how frequently; no studies have been done. Also, the frequency of unfavorable mutant genes in frog populations has not been evaluated.

While there may be many reasons why frogs are deformed, only one reason has been thoroughly substantiated. The main, and perhaps the only, thing that makes a frog grow extra hind legs, is a parasitic worm, a type of trematode. These worms lay their eggs in tadpoles. The eggs hatch out into little larvae that form hard cysts in the body of the tadpole. For various reasons, the favorite place for these cysts to form is in the region where the hind legs are forming. Field studies on five different species of frogs in different parts of the country have found trematode parasites at the bases of the limbs of deformed frogs.

While the case for pollutants has not been ruled out, parasitism is the only cause of developmental anomalies for which the detailed mechanism of the process is known. It is quite possible that parasites are responsible for other kinds of malformations.

1. The two scientists agree that:
   A. pollution is the main cause of abnormal development in frogs.
   B. there is a worldwide epidemic of death and malformation in frogs.
   C. the main cause of developmental anomaly is ultraviolet radiation.
   D. trematode parasitism causes a frog to form extra legs.

2. Scientist 2 challenges the evidence for Methoprene as a cause because:
   F. the required dosages are not found in nature.
   G. Methoprene has been shown to be safe.
   H. the necessary experiments were done on salamanders, not frogs.
   J. it has been shown that the cause of the deformities is parasites.

3. According to Scientist 2, an important fact that Scientist 1 has overlooked is that:
   A. it has been shown that ultraviolet radiation has no effect on salamanders.
   B. wherever frogs are becoming deformed, there are parasites in the water.
   C. there has been no increase in the amount of ultraviolet radiation reaching the earth as the ozone layer becomes depleted.
   D. there is no correlation between the occurrence of deformed frogs and the presence of Methoprene in the water.

4. The position taken by Scientist 1 would be greatly strengthened by the discovery that:
   F. there are no parasites in certain ponds that produce deformed frogs.
   G. deformed frogs are not found in certain parts of the world.
   H. there is a common polluting chemical that causes deformation of frog embryos.
   J. parasites can be found in frogs that have not become deformed.

5. A serious limitation of the position of Scientist 2 is that:
   A. it accounts for only one kind of damage to frogs.
   B. it fails to explore the details of the process by which the damage is produced.

C. it relies on the artificial introduction of a plastic bead into the developing embryo.

D. it overlooks the possibility that there may be many causes of deformity.

6. What is a likely response that Scientist 1 might make to the statement of Scientist 2?

F. Scientist 2 is wrong because it is known that the developmental errors in frogs are the result of environmental pollution.

G. Scientist 2 is damaging the international effort to deal with chemical pollution of the environment.

H. Even if Scientist 2 is right, the world must still deal with the problem of chemical pollution.

J. In the face of a worldwide pollution problem, it is a waste of time and money to investigate frog parasites.

ANSWERS AND EXPLANATIONS

1. **B** Both scientists are addressing the problem of the epidemic of deformed embryos in frogs. Scientist 2 challenges the evidence showing that ultraviolet radiation and chemical pollution are the cause, so A and C are wrong. D is wrong because Scientist 1 does not discuss the parasite problem.

2. **F** Scientist 2 points out that it would take an enormous dose of Methoprene to produce the observed deformities. There is no evidence as to the safety of Methoprene, so G is wrong. H is wrong; that evidence applies to the ultraviolet problem, not Methoprene. Scientist 2 agrees that there may be many causes in addition to parasites, so J is wrong.

3. **D** Scientist 2 points out that there is no match between deformed frogs and Methoprene. A is wrong because the effect of ultraviolet radiation on salamanders is not an issue. Scientist 1 does not address the problem of parasites, or of the level of ultraviolet radiation, so B and C are wrong.

4. **H** Scientist 1's main thesis is that deformation is caused by environmental pollution, so the discovery of a pollutant that can be shown to cause deformation would greatly strengthen his position. F and J are wrong because Scientist 1 does not challenge the idea that some parasites may cause deformation in some frogs but not others. G is wrong because geographic data of this kind would not support the position of Scientist 1 unless correlation with pollution could be shown.

5. **A** The trematode hypothesis accounts only for extra limbs, but not for missing limbs or early death. B is wrong because Scientist 2 specifically states the mechanism that interferes with development has been found. C is wrong; the plastic bead actually reinforces the idea that the extra legs are the result of mechanical interference with development. D is wrong because Scientist 2 specifically makes the point that many other causes may be involved.

6. **H** Scientist 1 sees the frog problem as only a part of the pollution of the earth. F is wrong because Scientist 2 has taken no position on pollution. G is wrong because Scientist 2 has said nothing to disparage the idea that pollution may be at fault. J is wrong; any scientist knows that many investigations are important even though they have no immediate application.

Passage 2

What is causing the loss of trees in the Appalachians? Two differing opinions are presented below.

Scientist 1

The forests of the high Appalachian Mountains are being destroyed. Millions of dead spruce and fir trees cover the peaks of the mountains, from Maine to Georgia. The new growth is low shrubbery, like blackberries, instead of trees. These forests are dying because of a combination of air pollution and unusual weather patterns. Recent years have shown a substantial increase in the concentration of ozone and of nitrogen and sulfur oxides in the air. The oxides come from the burning of fossil fuels. Rain, snow, and fog in the mountains pick up these oxides and turn acid. Ozone is produced by the action of ultraviolet light on hydrocarbons in the air, which are found in automobile exhaust and wastes from certain industrial processes. This pollution has been going on for decades, and the effect is cumulative. The last straw was added by the unusually high temperatures and drought of recent years. Unless serious steps are taken to reduce air pollution, there is a distinct danger that we will lose all our forests.

Scientist 2

There is no substantial evidence that air pollution is the culprit in the Appalachians. Trees in the high mountains are living precariously at best and are easily destroyed. The hot, dry summers and cold winters of recent years could easily account for the damage. Also, the spruce budworm and other insect pests are now unusually abundant and have done a great deal of damage to the trees. There have been other instances of massive die-off of trees at high elevations in years past, when the air was purer. If the chief source of damage were air pollution, we would expect that the damage would be worse at lower elevations, where the factories and automobiles that produce pollution are concentrated. Yet there is little evidence of damage to the commercial forests at lower elevations. This does not mean that we should ignore air pollution; it is clearly a threat, and we must learn more about it and develop ways to control it.

1. According to Scientist 2, what would be expected to happen to the forest in future years?
   A. Return of a permanent, self-sustaining forest in the high Appalachians
   B. Permanent conversion of the high mountains to low-growing shrubbery instead of trees
   C. Development of timber-producing commercial forest in the high mountains
   D. Regeneration of the forest, which will again be killed off from time to time

2. Without challenging any facts, what might Scientist 1 say to counter Scientist 2's argument about the effect of insect pests?
   F. Insects do not really do much damage.
   G. The insects have been able to proliferate so well because pollution has weakened the trees.
   H. Insect populations are being well controlled by birds.
   J. Insects are actually helpful because they cross-pollinate the trees.

3. What further development would weaken the case made by Scientist 2?
   A. Destruction of the blackberry bushes that are replacing the forests
   B. Evidence of damage to commercial forests at lower elevations
   C. Insect infestations of low-level forests
   D. Evidence that the mountain-top forests are showing signs of healthy regeneration

4. What is the opinion of Scientist 2 with respect to the problem of the effect of polluted air on the high forests?
   F. Polluted air does not damage forests, and no action is needed.
   G. The evidence is inadequate to prove that the damage in the high Appalachians is due to polluted air, but the problem needs to be studied further.
   H. Polluted air damages trees and may soon present a problem to commercial forests at lower levels.
   J. There is no substantial pollution in the air at high elevations, so it is not damaging the trees.

5. Suppose there were to appear a healthy new crop of spruce and fir trees on the mountain tops. Which of the following studies would NOT contribute to a resolution of the difference of opinion between the two scientists?
   A. A study to determine whether there has been any change in the ozone levels in the air
   B. A study of weather patterns over the preceding few years
   C. A study of changes in automobile exhausts due to new antipollution devices in cars
   D. A study of the conditions under which spruce seeds survive in the soil

6. What is a point on which both scientists agree?
   F. The air is being polluted by waste products of industry and transportation.
   G. The spruce budworm is a major cause of the destruction of forests.
   H. Stressful weather conditions alone can account for the destruction of the Appalachian forests.
   J. Low-elevation commercial forests are in imminent danger of destruction by polluted air.

7. To refute Scientist 2's opinion, Scientist 1 might:
   A. show that there is extensive damage to trees wherever in the world the air pollution levels are high.
   B. show that healthy spruce forests recover easily from damage by the spruce budworm.
   C. claim that spruce trees thrive at lower elevations, but are poorly adapted to the extremes of mountaintop weather.
   D. show that, because of atmospheric circulation patterns, the air at high elevations is not heavily polluted.

ANSWERS AND EXPLANATIONS

1. **D** Scientist 2 believes that from time to time unusual weather conditions kill off the high forest, even if there is no air pollution. Choice A is wrong because Scientist 2 does not believe that the forest can ever be permanent. B is wrong because he thinks that the forest can regenerate itself after it has been destroyed. C is wrong because he has never made any such suggestion.

2. **G** Scientist 1 believes that pollution has damaged the trees, and might well suggest that this damage makes them subject to attack by insects. The other answers are wrong because they ignore the observable facts that the insects are rife and harmful.

3. **B** One of the points that Scientist 2 makes is that pollution at low levels does not seem to be damaging the forests there. Choice A and C are irrelevant. D is wrong because regeneration of the high forest would support Scientist 2's contention that forest destruction occurs naturally from time to time.

4. **G** Scientist 2 makes no claim that polluted air is innocent; but only that the evidence for its guilt is not conclusive. That is why F and H are wrong. He makes no claim that mountain air is unpolluted, so J is wrong.

5. **D** Choice A and C are wrong because, if such studies showed a substantial decrease in pollution, Scientist 1's claim that pollution destroys the forest would be upheld. B is wrong because a correlation of weather patterns with forest regeneration would tend to support Scientist 2.

6. **F** Both scientists recognize the existence of pollution, and both see that it is a problem. G is wrong because Scientist 1 might well think that the insects can damage only unhealthy trees. H is wrong because Scientist 1 thinks that the main cause of damage is pollution, and the weather is just a contributing factor. J is wrong because Scientist 2 has not found any damage to low-elevation trees, although he might agree that this could be a long-range problem.

7. A   This would strongly reinforce Scientist 1's opinion that the major cause of damage to trees is air pollution. B is wrong because Scientist 2 believes that forest destruction and recovery are common events. C is wrong because Scientist 2 thinks that mountaintop trees may be destroyed by extremes of weather alone. D is wrong because any such demonstration would undermine Scientist 1's claim that air pollution is the chief culprit.

Passage 3

Two scientists disagree on the advisability of adding a substance called MMT to gasoline.

Scientist 1

The benefits of MMT in motor fuel have been shown by extensive tests on a variety of engines. MMT improves the octane rating and fuel efficiency of gasoline, so that motorists get more miles for their gallons. This alone would reduce the amount of tailpipe pollution by decreasing the total amount of gasoline burned. There is an even greater environmental benefit to the use of MMT. MMT in the gasoline reduces the amount of sulfur and nitrogen oxides in the exhaust gases. Critics have suggested that the high manganese content of MMT poses a danger, but this is no problem. Manganese is a necessary nutrient in small quantities, and even large quantities are not dangerous. Experiments on monkeys have shown that even large amounts of manganese are quickly detoxified and excreted by the liver. In any event, the amount of manganese in MMT is extremely small, compared with what we get from air, food, and water. Subway riders get a lot more manganese in the air than they could ever get from automobile exhaust; the steel rails of the subways are 12 percent manganese, and the constant friction with the wheels continually releases some into the air. The use of MMT has been studied, from every aspect, more than any other fuel additive, and there is no danger of making the kind of mistakes that led to adding lead to gasoline. The people who are opposed to the use of MMT are prejudiced by the experience with lead, and really should take another look at MMT; they will discover that it is an entirely different material.

Scientist 2

Manganese in the air is a real threat that must not be ignored. We must not repeat the tragic error made when we introduced lead into gasoline. While it is true that manganese in the blood is rapidly detoxified, manganese in the air is a different problem. Inhaled manganese does not go through the blood to the liver; it travels from the nose directly into the brain, via the olfactory nerve. Studies with various animals have shown that manganese in the brain causes neurological disorders much like Parkinson's disease. While airborne manganese has not been shown to pose any danger in the short range, adding MMT to gasoline would expose us to a new toxic pollutant that we would be breathing daily for life. There have been no long-range studies to determine what levels of manganese in the air are safe for human beings over long time periods. It took many years of experience to demonstrate that lead in gasoline produces neurological damage in children. We have no idea what damage manganese can do to children and fetuses. Until such information is available, it is dangerous and foolhardy to introduce another pollutant into the air we breathe. Incidentally, the savings to motorists are illusory; manganese deposits on the spark plugs, hoses, and ignition control devices in a car, and would cost motorists more in repairs than they would save in gasoline mileage.

1.   The two scientists agree that:
   A. MMT improves the mileage performance of gasoline.
   B. motorists who use gasoline containing MMT would save money in the long run.
   C. MMT would reduce the danger due to breathing polluted air.
   D. MMT does not pose risks similar to those of lead in gasoline.

2. Scientist 2 claims that the chief fault of Scientist 1's position is that it:
   F. claims that MMT provides considerable benefits in reducing air pollution.
   G. exaggerates the financial benefits of the new additive.
   H. neglects to take into account possible long-range effects.
   J. denies that MMT in the gasoline would add manganese to the air.

3. Scientist 1 feels that the concerns of Scientist 2 are unwarranted because:
   A. manganese in the body is rapidly detoxified by the liver.
   B. the amount of manganese that MMT would add to the air is negligible compared with what is already there.
   C. there is no evidence that inhaled manganese can get to the brain.
   D. manganese is a mineral that is a usual and necessary component of the diet.

4. New experiments could discredit the position of Scientist 2 if they showed that:
   F. inhaled manganese enters the body only into the bloodstream and not the nerves.
   G. the ability of the liver to detoxify manganese has been grossly exaggerated.
   H. air ordinarily contains negligible amounts of manganese.
   J. even large amounts of manganese in the blood do not do any damage to the musculature or the endocrine system.

5. Past experience with lead added to gasoline enters into this dispute because:
   A. the two scientists do not agree that lead in gasoline poses threat of harm.
   B. the physiological effects of manganese are similar to those of lead.
   C. Scientist 1 feels that past experience with lead has clouded the whole MMT issue.
   D. lead and manganese are both known to travel to the brain through the olfactory nerve.

6. There is no way to design an experiment to settle this disagreement promptly because:
   F. there is no way to find out for certain whether manganese actually enters the brain by way of the olfactory nerve.
   G. manganese is always present in the food and in the blood.
   H. there are many different pollutants in the air that would confuse the whole issue.
   J. Scientist 2 claims only that the effects, if any, would be found only after many years of exposure.

ANSWERS AND EXPLANATIONS

1. A   Scientist 2 does not challenge the contention of Scientist 1 that the additive improves mileage. B is wrong because Scientist 2 claims that the cost of repairs will wipe out the saving. C is wrong because Scientist 2 is concerned about the possible long-range damage due to breathing manganese. D is wrong because Scientist 2 compares the danger from manganese with the problems that came from lead.

2. H   Scientist 2 is concerned that nothing is known about the long-range effect of breathing manganese. F is wrong because Scientist 2 does not deny that the additive would significantly reduce the tailpipe emission of oxides. G is wrong because this is only a minor point, not the main thrust of the conflicting opinion. J is wrong because Scientist 1 admits that manganese would be added to the air, claiming only that the amount is negligible compared with what is already there.

3. B   Scientist 1 notes that there already is far more manganese in the air than would be added by the use of MMT. A is wrong because this is never questioned; it is manganese in the brain, not the blood, that is the danger. C is wrong because Scientist 1 never questioned this statement by Scientist 2. The use of manganese in the diet is not an issue with either scientist.

4. F   Scientist 2 is chiefly concerned with the possibility that manganese can pass through the olfactory nerve to the brain. G is wrong because Scientist 2's argument concerns only the manganese that travels directly to the brain. H is wrong because the amount of manganese normally in the air has no bearing on the discussion. Since only the effect of the manganese on the brain is at issue, J is wrong.

5. C   Scientist 1 suggests that Scientist 2 is influenced by the discovery that long-term exposure to lead is harmful. A is wrong because both scientists implicitly acknowledge that lead is harmful. B and D are wrong because there is nothing in either statement comparing the two elements.

6. J   The disagreement centers on long-range effects, which could be found only by extensive studies over many years. There is no reason to doubt that experiments could detect the passage of manganese through nerves, so F is wrong. G is wrong because manganese in the food and blood is not an issue. H is wrong because it is possible to design controls for other variables.

Passage 4

Could life have originated as a result of the chemical processes taking place at hot volcanic vents in the ocean floor? Two scientists present conflicting views.

Scientist 1

Large quantities of ocean water are heated in the crust, and emerge from volcanic vents at pressures of 200 atmospheres or more, and temperatures above 300°C. Conditions at these vents are ideal for the chemical processes that led to the earliest forms of life. The water is rich in the simple compounds that go into the formation of the organic materials of life: hydrogen, nitrogen, hydrogen sulfide, carbon monoxide, carbon dioxide, and methane. Many metallic ions are also present, and they are effective catalysts. In the deep ocean, the chemical synthesis processes would be protected from the destructive effects of ultraviolet light from the sun, and from the impact of meteorites. The heat of the vents would supply the energy needed to combine these simple molecules into the amino acids, sugars, and nucleotides that make up the basic chemistry of all life. Experiments have shown that in the presence of metallic catalysts at high temperature carbon monoxide, ammonia, and hydrogen will combine to form a great variety of amino acids and the nitrogenous bases that are a component of nucleic acids. The earliest life forms still exist at these vents; bacteria taken from them survive and prosper in cultures kept at high temperature and pressure.

Scientist 2

Although the chemical processes cited by Scientist 1 do in fact occur, the efficiency of these processes is far too low to account for the accumulation of large quantities of amino acids, sugars, and nitrogenous bases. It is true that a hot water solution of ammonia and methane produces various amino acids, but the amount formed is extremely tiny. Large amounts of organic materials have been produced from a mixture of ammonia, carbon monoxide, and hydrogen, but this was done in the gaseous phase. There is no evidence that it could happen in water solution. Furthermore, tests of these organic materials show that, even if they could be formed, they are very unstable at high temperatures. High pressure offers some protection, but they still disintegrate in less than half an hour. Sugars disintegrate even faster. Even if amino acids could be formed and would remain stable, they could not combine to form proteins. This is a hydrolysis process, in which a water molecule is removed when a peptide bond is formed. Experimentally, this does not work in a dilute solution where there is plenty of water. Thus, the experimental evidence shows clearly that the chemical processes leading to the earliest life could not take place at volcanic vents in the ocean floor.

1. The two scientists would disagree in their reactions to which one of the following statements?
   A. Life probably originated by a series of chemical processes that produce ever more complex molecules.
   B. Amino acids can be formed under appropriate conditions by combination of ammonia, carbon dioxide, and hydrogen.
   C. At very high pressures, amino acids are stable when the temperature rises above 300°C.
   D. Ultraviolet rays would tend to disrupt the chemical processes that lead to life.

2. Which of the following discoveries would substantially weaken the case made by Scientist 1?
   F. The experiments that purported to show that some bacteria can survive at temperatures above 120°C were invalid.
   G. Ultraviolet light is not harmful to certain bacteria if they are grown at high pressure.
   H. With the proper catalyst, synthesis of amino acids from ammonia, carbon monoxide, and hydrogen can take place in water solution.
   J. In some of the ocean floor vents, the temperature of the water is as low as 95°C.

3. Scientist 2 claims that amino acids formed in the vents could not contribute to the formation of life because they are unstable at high temperatures. What argument might Scientist 1 make to rebut this?
   A. The experiments were done in a laboratory setting, not in the ocean.
   B. Bacteria in the water might have assimilated the amino acids as fast as they were formed.
   C. Life might have originated without previous formation of amino acids.
   D. The half-hour survival of the amino acids gives them enough time to rise into cooler water.

4. Scientist 1 notes that concentrated, complex organic mixtures are found in the sedimentary deposits near the vents. How might Scientist 2 refute the claim that this shows that organic synthesis takes place in the vents?
   F. Show that these deposits result from decay of dead organisms that live near the vents
   G. Show that such deposits occur sporadically at a few vents, not at all of them
   H. Demonstrate that the deposits contain many kinds of organic and inorganic substances, not just those that go into the formation of life
   J. Prove that it is theoretically impossible for organic materials to survive in the chemical environment of the sediments

5. What experiment might Scientist 1 attempt to perform that would greatly strengthen her case?
   A. Find a way to make amino acids in a dilute solution combine into large protein molecules
   B. Create a living cell by combining simple chemicals under conditions of high temperature and pressure
   C. Produce amino acids from a mixture of various gases, such as ammonia and methane
   D. Produce a variety of bacteria that can exist by metabolizing carbon monoxide, methane, and ammonia

6. Underlying the arguments of Scientist 2 is the assumption that:
   F. there are many hot volcanic vents on the ocean floor.
   G. the chemical processes that lead up to life require various metallic ions to serve as catalysts.
   H. the early stages in the development of life require large quantities of stable amino acids.
   J. it is impossible to find a series of chemical processes that could result in the formation of a living cell.

7. Both scientists agree that, in the search for the origin of life, a feature of the early earth that must be found is:
   A. a region free of ultraviolet light and meteors.
   B. a set of circumstances in which simple chemicals can combine to form stable amino acids.
   C. a region where there is a gaseous mixture of ammonia, methane, and other chemicals.
   D. a part of the ocean in which there is a plentiful supply of sugar and oxygen.

ANSWERS AND EXPLANATIONS

1. **C** An important part of Scientist 2's argument is based on experiments showing that amino acids decay quickly at high temperatures. Choice A is wrong because both scientists are looking for conditions in which this may occur. B is wrong because both agree that this occurs under certain conditions. D is wrong because Scientist 2 did not address this question; she would probably agree.

2. **F** If these experiments are invalid (as has, in fact, been shown), Scientist 1 has no evidence that life can exist at such high temperatures. G is wrong because the disruptive effect of ultraviolet light is not a fundamental part of Scientist 1's argument. H is wrong because such a discovery would greatly strengthen the case for the origin of life in the ocean waters. J is completely irrelevant; the disagreement deals only with the hot water vents.

3. **D** Scientist 1 could propose that the newly formed amino acids can survive indefinitely once they get into cool water. Choice A is wrong because the survival of the amino acids at high temperature does not depend on where the experiment is done. B is wrong; the discussion concerns the origin of life, and there could be no bacteria before life originated. Since both scientists agree that amino acids are a necessary step in the origin of life, C is wrong.

4. **F** The discovery that the organic matter came from living things would completely destroy this argument as a point in favor of Scientist 1. Since no one has claimed that life must originate at *all* vents, G is wrong. H is wrong because the existence of uninvolved kinds of molecules is irrelevant. The organic deposits do exist, and any theory to the contrary must be in error, so J is wrong.

5. **A** If this can be done, it would surely refute one of the objections made by Scientist 2. B is not a feasible experiment. C is wrong because this has already been done. D is wrong because the existence of bacteria implies that life has already originated.

6. **H** Two of Scientist 1's objections are that, under the conditions at the vents, amino acids are (1) scarce and (2) unstable. F is irrelevant. Scientist 2 did not go into the question of catalysts, so G is wrong. J is wrong because Scientist 2 is questioning only the mechanism for the origin of life proposed by Scientist 1, and does not dispute that it could occur in some other place.

7. **B** This agrees with the general understanding that life originated by a series of chemical processes that produced ever more complex combinations. Choice A is wrong because Scientist 2 did not go into this problem. C is wrong because no one has suggested that the steps in chemical synthesis can occur only in the gas phase. No one has suggested that sugar is needed, and all would agree that oxygen would poison the process; therefore D is wrong.

Passage 5

Is Yucca Mountain in Nevada a suitable place to establish a storage facility for high-level nuclear wastes?

Scientist 1

Yucca Mountain is a most unsuitable place to build a long-term storage facility for high-level nuclear waste. What is needed is a secure place, far from any population center, that can be relied on to remain dry for at least 10,000 years. The plan calls for storage of the waste in 115 miles of underground tunnels. It is true that Yucca Mountain is in a remote desert area and the water table is now quite low. However, the rock is full of cracks and faults, a sure sign that there has been a great deal of seismic activity in the area. Many of these cracks are filled with a form of calcite called travertine, which is formed only by deposition from hot springs. This proves that there must have been a lot of water in these rocks at one time. This water could only have risen up from below. The water table must have risen, due either to a change in climate or to a change in the geological structure of the underlying rock. If the water table could rise once, it could do so again. A new fault, produced by an earthquake, could flood the tunnels with water from sources deep in the rock. The thousands of tons of radioactive wastes will be stored in canisters, which will be very hot all the time. If the storage facility is flooded, it will suddenly be filled with an enormous amount of steam, which could blow the top off the mountain and spread radioactive material over much of the country. The effects would be much worse than an attack by nuclear bombs.

Scientist 2

The Yucca Mountain area is completely dry and has never had a high water table. At present the water table is more than 500 meters down, far below the proposed depth of the storage tunnels. The calcite deposits are not travertine, which is produced only in hot springs. The deposits are produced by evaporation of rain water. In much of the Nevada desert, rocks rich in calcite are ground down into fine powder due to the action of blowing sand. This powder is raised into the air by wind and then picked up by raindrops. The Yucca Mountain area once had a somewhat wetter climate, and calcite-laden rain deposited the calcite on the ground. When the water seeped into cracks and evaporated, it left deposits of calcite behind. A trench cut into the rock to trace a calcite vein discovered that the vein became narrower as it was traced downward. This showed that it arose from water coming from above, not from below. It is true that some travertine deposits from ground water have been found in the area, but they are all far too deep to be of concern for the project.

1. Both scientists agree that:
   A. Yucca Mountain has always been dry.
   B. travertine is produced only by hot springs.
   C. a deposit of calcite proves the presence of hot springs.
   D. the water table at Yucca Mountain will probably rise much higher some time in the future.

2. Scientist 2 believes that:
   F. there is no evidence for past seismic activity in the Yucca Mountain region.
   G. water in the tunnels would not be a source of any danger.
   H. radioactive materials in the tunnels would present an environmental hazard.
   J. there is no reason to fear that ground water will rise into the tunnels.

3. Scientist 1, but not Scientist 2, believes that:
   A. an earthquake could flood the tunnels.
   B. no calcite is deposited in cracks from rainwater.
   C. there is no evidence that the climate was wetter in the past.
   D. high-level radioactive materials are dangerous.

4. Which of the following would be evidence supporting the position of Scientist 1?

F. The discovery of substantial amounts of calcite dissolved in rainwater.

G. Veins of a calcite mineral that become considerably larger as they go deeper into the crust below the storage chamber.

H. Analysis of plant remains showing that the climate was considerably wetter in the past.

J. Chemical analysis showing that there are large amounts of impurities in the calcite.

5. People living in the region of Yucca Mountain might be biased in favor of the position of Scientist 2 because the proposed storage facility:

A. might be a source of radioactive contamination of the air.

B. would employ many local people.

C. would make a large area of the desert unavailable for recreational use.

D. would make an important contribution to the solution of the problem of disposal of radioactive waste.

ANSWERS AND EXPLANATIONS

1. B   Both agree that wherever there is travertine, there must have been hot springs. Scientist 1 calls the observed deposits travertine, while Scientist 2 thinks they are a different form of calcite. Choice A is wrong because Scientist 1 believes that the calcite deposits came from ground water. C is wrong because neither scientist denies that another form of calcite can be deposited from rain water. Scientist 2 sees no reason to think that the water table in Yucca Mountain has ever been much higher than it is now, so D is wrong.

2. J   Scientist 2 agrees that flooding the tunnels would be disastrous, so G is wrong; he sees no geological evidence to suggest that the water table has ever risen to the level of the tunnels. He has not questioned the evidence of past seismic activity, and has not raised the question of environmental pollution.

3. A   Scientist 1 presents evidence that there have been many earthquakes in the past, and that they have resulted in a rise in the water table. She does not question the presence of calcite deposited from rainwater, or that the climate used to be wetter. Both scientists agree that radioactive materials are dangerous and must be stored in safety.

4. G   Veins of calcite that are much bigger at lower depths could only be the result of deposition from water rising from the water table. None of the other choices bear on the question of whether the calcite deposits arise from below.

5. B   If Scientist 2 is right, the facility would be built in Yucca Mountain, and there would be jobs for local people. Choices A and C argue against the construction of the facility, and would tend to promote bias in favor of Scientist 1. D does not tend to favor Yucca Mountain over any other location.

SAMPLE SCIENCE REASONING TEST

Now that you have had practice on all three kinds of questions, here is a complete test, much like the one you will have to take. In trying it out, it is important that you time yourself. Allow only 35 minutes to complete the whole test. Remember these rules:

For each passage, study it carefully and answer the first question.

For the other questions, skip any that you cannot answer within a half minute or so.

When you have finished all those questions, go back and work on the ones you skipped. If you are not sure of an answer, make your best guess.

If you still have any unanswered questions and there is only a minute left, enter answers at random.

Look at your clock and start NOW. Good luck!

> DIRECTIONS: This test consists of several distinct passages. Each passage is followed by a number of multiple-choice questions based on the passage. Study the passage, and then select the best answer to each question. You are allowed to reread the passage.

Passage I

The graph below indicates the numbers of three different kinds of rare plants that were found in a grassy plot over a period of years.

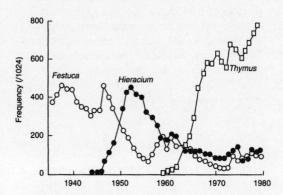

1. Which plants were present in approximately equal numbers in 1950?
   A. *Festuca* and *Thymus*
   B. *Festuca* and *Hieracium*
   C. *Hieracium* and *Thymus*
   D. *Hieracium, Festuca,* and *Thymus*

2. Which of the following statements correctly describes the situation in 1963?
   F. The densities of both *Festuca* and *Hieracium* were rapidly decreasing.
   G. The density of *Thymus* was much greater than that of either of the other two plants.
   H. All three plants had equal and unchanging densities.
   J. All three plants had equal densities, but one was increasing.

3. What was happening to the density of *Hieracium* in 1950?
   A. It was increasing at the rate of 20 units per year.
   B. It was increasing at the rate of 75 units per year.
   C. It did not change at all during that year.
   D. It was increasing at some undetermined rate.

4. Suppose a fourth species were introduced and found conditions there favorable for its growth. Based on experience with the species already there, what pattern might be expected for its density in the next ten years?
   F. It could not survive in competition with those already there.
   G. Its density might be expected to increase slightly for a couple of years and then level off.
   H. It might be expected to remain at low density for a few years and then increase rapidly.
   J. Its density might be expected to increase for a few years and then decrease rapidly.

5. Which of the following is NOT a possible explanation for the changes that took place after 1950?
   A. There was a period of drought.
   B. *Festuca* and *Hieracium* were unable to thrive in competition with *Thymus*.
   C. A newly arrived insect pest fed on some plants, but not others.
   D. A great increase in the shrubbery in the plot made the whole area more shady.

From *Plant Ecology,* Michael J. Crawley, editor. Blackwell Scientific Publications, 1986.

Passage II

Three experiments are done to test the relative survivability of different mutant strains of fruit fly (*Drosophila*) when different strains are grown together.

Experiment 1

Three pure-bred strains of *Drosophila* are used: wild type, white-eye, and yellow-body. Fifty fertilized eggs of each strain are placed, separately, into standard culture bottles. They go through larval stages, and then form pupae. The adults that hatch out of the pupa cases are counted:

     wild type: 42   white-eye: 36   yellow-body: 25

Experiment 2

Pairs of strains are grown together, with their larvae in the same culture bottle. Fifty eggs of each strain are placed in the bottle, and the number of adults of each kind that hatch out of the pupa cases are counted:

    Trial 1: wild type, 43   white-eye, 16
    Trial 2: wild type, 38   yellow-body, 22
    Trial 3: white-eye, 18   yellow-body, 27

Experiment 3

Fifty eggs of each of the three strains are placed in the same culture bottle, with the following numbers of adults produced:

     wild type: 33   white-eye: 8   yellow-body: 20

6. In Experiment 2 what was the purpose of growing two different strains of larvae in the same bottle?
   - F. To find out how competition between strains affects survivability
   - G. To test the effect of crowding of larvae in the culture bottles
   - H. To determine the results of crossing two different strains
   - J. To see whether the white-eye or yellow-body character can be transferred from one larva to another

7. What important variable was controlled by Experiment 1?
   - A. Availability of food supply
   - B. Survivability of each strain in the absence of competition
   - C. Number of eggs to be used in the experiment
   - D. Transformation of larvae to the pupa stage

8. Comparison of the results shows that competition:
   - F. increases the survivability of the wild type.
   - G. is most detrimental to the yellow-body.
   - H. is most favorable to the yellow-body.
   - J. is most detrimental to the white-eye.

9. What design factor in the experiments was crucial in establishing the existence of competition between strains?
   - A. Keeping all culture bottles under the same conditions.
   - B. Supplying only enough food for about 60 larvae
   - C. Testing strains in advance to be sure they were pure-bred
   - D. Using no more than 3 different strains

10. What do these results imply about the structure of natural populations?
    - F. About one fourth of all flies in nature are expected to be yellow-bodied.
    - G. One reason why the wild type is most common in nature is that its larvae survive best in competition.
    - H. There will be no white-eyed flies in natural populations.
    - J. In the course of time, white-eyed and yellow-bodied flies will completely disappear in nature.

11. The evidence seems to show that yellow-bodied flies do not suffer in competition with the wild type. Why, then, are there so few yellow-bodied flies in nature?
    - A. The evidence is misleading because the total number of flies in the experiment is so small.
    - B. White-eyed flies promote the survivability of the yellow-bodied, and they are rare in nature.
    - C. Under natural conditions, many factors other than competition determine survivability.
    - D. When yellow-bodied flies mate with wild type, their offspring are wild type.

Passage III

Experiments were done to find out how long it takes for the immune system to come into operation.

Experiment 1

Nonvirulent bacteria were injected into a nonimmune rabbit, and the numbers of bacteria were assayed for three days, at ten-hour intervals.

Experiment 2

Virulent bacteria were injected into a nonimmune rabbit, and bacteria levels were assayed.

Experiment 3

Another rabbit was immunized against the bacteria, and then injected with bacteria. The same assay was done.

The graph below shows the results of these experiments.

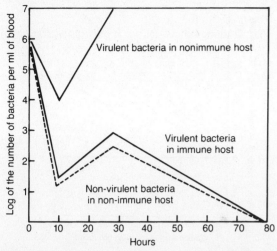

From Stanier/Doudoroff/Adelberg. *The Microbial World,* 2e © 1963, p. 601. Reprinted by permission of Prentice Hall, Inc. Englewood Cliffs, New Jersey.

12. In what way was the change in concentration of virulent bacteria in a nonimmune host different from the others?
    F. It increased after the first 10 hours.
    G. It did not decrease after the period of increase.
    H. It increased steadily throughout the entire period.
    J. It decreased more rapidly at first.

13. What inference can be drawn from the graphs?
    A. Virulent bacteria always cause the death of any host.
    B. Nonvirulent bacteria can be as dangerous as virulent bacteria.
    C. The immune system offers no protection against virulent bacteria.
    D. The immune system makes virulent bacteria no worse than nonvirulent bacteria.

14. What inference can be drawn from the data for the first 10 hours?
    F. The body of the host is able to promote an attack against all bacteria.
    G. In that period, the immune system cannot distinguish virulent from nonvirulent bacteria.
    H. In that period, immunity offers no protection against virulent bacteria.
    J. Virulent bacteria will kill a nonimmune host.

15. During what period does the immune system provide protection?
    A. The first 10 hours only
    B. 10 hours to 30 hours
    C. 10 hours to 80 hours
    D. Throughout the whole 80 hours

16. Which of the following hypotheses might emerge from the graphs?
    F. Nonimmune animals have no protection against invading bacteria.

    G. There are two different mechanisms of immunity, one of which is lacking in nonimmune animals.
    H. The immune system of an immune host cannot control the concentration of nonvirulent bacteria.
    J. Virulent bacteria cause the host animal to develop immunity.

Passage IV

To find out how the current through various materials is controlled, a physicist applies various potential differences to three different objects and measures the current produced in each case.

Experiment 1: 10 meters of #30 copper wire

Potential difference (volts)	Current (milliamperes)
0	0
0.2	60
0.4	120
0.6	180
0.8	240
1.0	300

Experiment 2: 10 meters of #30 aluminum wire

Potential difference (volts)	Current (milliamperes)
0	0
0.2	40
0.4	80
0.6	120
0.8	160
1.0	200

Experiment 3: OC26 transistor

Potential difference (volts)	Current (milliamperes)
0	0
0.2	5
0.4	15
0.6	60
0.8	115
1.0	190

17. What scales on the voltmeter and ammeter would be most appropriate in making these measurements?
    A. 0-20 V, 0-20 A
    B. 0-5 V, 0-5 A
    C. 0-1 V, 0-10 A
    D. 0-1 V, 0-0.5 A

18. Why were wires of identical dimensions used in Experiments 1 and 2?
    F. To increase the variety of readings of the current
    G. To determine how the material of which the wire is made affects the current
    H. To determine how the dimensions of the wire affect the current
    J. To compare the properties of a wire with those of a transistor

19. Which readings serve as controls on the proper adjustment of the meters?
    A. The readings on the transistor
    B. All the zero readings
    C. All the readings at 1.0 volt
    D. The readings on the copper wire

20. When a 10-volt potential difference is applied to the aluminum wire, the ammeter records 1100 milliamperes. This indicates that:
    F. the proportionality between potential difference and current does not hold for large values.
    G. there is no usable rule relating potential difference to current.
    H. large potential differences reduce the current in the wire.
    J. aluminum wire reacts differently from copper wire.

21. Resistance is defined as the ratio of potential difference to current. Which of the following statements holds true over the range of values in the experiments?
    A. All three objects have the same resistance.
    B. The objects have different resistances, but the resistance is constant for each.
    C. None of the objects has constant resistance.
    D. The wires, but not the transistor, have constant resistance.

22. On the basis of these experiments, what hypothesis might be proposed?
    F. Transistors respond to applied potential differences in the same way as metal wires.
    G. In any circuit, a transistor will have more current than a wire.
    H. Transistors are too unreliable to be used in most electronic circuits.
    J. Transistors and wires can be used for different purposes in electronic circuits.

Passage V

The following graph shows the carbon dioxide uptake per minute in a leaf of a soybean plant, at various concentrations of oxygen and carbon dioxide in the air (ppm = parts per million; μg = microgram). Plants use carbon dioxide in photosynthesis, but they also use oxygen and make carbon dioxide in respiration.

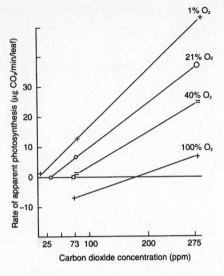

23. In a normal atmosphere, 21% oxygen and 200 ppm carbon dioxide, how much CO_2 does a leaf take up in an hour?
    A. $24 \, \mu g$
    B. $600 \, \mu g$
    C. $1440 \, \mu g$
    D. $4200 \, \mu g$

24. The rate of uptake of carbon dioxide increases as
    F. carbon dioxide concentration increases and oxygen concentration decreases.
    G. oxygen concentration increases and carbon dioxide concentration decreases.
    H. both oxygen and carbon dioxide concentrations increase.
    J. both oxygen and carbon dioxide concentrations decrease.

25. It is reasonable to conclude that
    A. the leaves need a certain minimum level of oxygen concentration in order to take up carbon dioxide.
    B. high concentrations of carbon dioxide have a tendency to inhibit photosynthesis.
    C. if the CO_2 concentration is high enough, uptake with 40% oxygen in the air can always be as great as it is with 21% oxygen.
    D. leaves will take up carbon dioxide only if there is a certain minimum concentration of CO_2 in the air.

26. Which of the following is NOT a reasonable supposition from the data?
    F. The leaf produces more carbon dioxide than it uses in photosynthesis only if the oxygen concentration is 100%.
    G. High levels of oxygen in the air inhibit photosynthesis.
    H. Respiration, producing carbon dioxide, is much greater at higher levels of oxygen concentration.
    J. The rate of photosynthesis is greater at higher levels of CO_2 concentration.

27. Measurements have shown that, due to the growth of industry, the concentration of CO_2 in the atmosphere has increased in the past century. How do forests influence this situation?
    A. They mitigate the problem by increasing their uptake of CO_2.
    B. They aggravate the problem by increasing their use of oxygen.
    C. They aggravate the problem by increasing their growth rate.
    D. They have no effect because respiration rate increases as fast as photosynthesis.

Passage VI

A chemist performs a series of experiments to determine the relative chemical activities of three metals. Metal A is considered more active than metal B if metal A will replace metal B in a solution. Metal B will plate out on metal A.

Experiment 1

A piece of steel wool is placed into a solution of copper sulfate. Copper sulfate is blue because of the copper ions in it. The result of the experiment is that metallic copper forms on the steel wool and the blue solution turns colorless.

Experiment 2

A bundle of fine copper wire is placed into a solution of iron(II) sulfate, which is colorless. No change is observed.

Experiment 3

A fine spray of metallic mercury is inserted into a solution of copper sulfate. No change is observed.

Experiment 4

A bundle of fine copper wire is inserted into a solution of mercuric sulfate, which is colorless. The wire acquires a coating of the silvery color of mercury, and the solution acquires a bluish tint.

28. The results of Experiments 1 and 2 indicate that:
    F. copper is more active than iron.
    G. relative activity depends on how the experiment is done.
    H. iron is more active than copper.
    J. the two metals are probably equally active.

29. In Experiment 4, why did the solution become bluish?
    A. Some of the copper of the wire went into solution.
    B. Removal of the mercury revealed the true color of the solution.
    C. The silvery color of the deposited mercury reflects light and has a bluish cast.
    D. Some of the mercury in the solution changes to copper, which gives the solution a bluish color.

30. Why was there no reaction in Experiment 2?
    F. Copper is not soluble in water.
    G. The metal in the solution is the more active of the two.
    H. Metallic iron and metallic copper cannot mix.
    J. The iron sulfate solution was already saturated.

31. What would probably happen if steel wool were placed into a solution of mercuric sulfate?
    A. It is impossible to predict the result without experiment.
    B. Mercury would plate out on the steel wool.
    C. Nothing would happen.
    D. The solution would turn bluish.

32. Suppose fibers of metal X were placed into separate solutions of mercuric, copper, and iron sulfates. Copper and mercury deposit on the metal, but iron does not. Which of the following represents the order of activity of the four metals, from highest to lowest?
    F. Metal X, mercury, copper, iron
    G. Mercury, copper, metal X, iron
    H. Copper, mercury, iron, metal X
    J. Iron, metal X, copper, mercury

33. An investigator hypothesizes that the relative activity of any metal depends only on the structure of its own atoms. Which of the following observations would support this view?
    A. In their reactions with sulfates, all the metals can be arranged in a linear sequence according to their activities.
    B. In any kind of reaction, there will always be some metals that are more active than others.
    C. If one metal is more active than another, it will be more active in any chemical reaction, not just with sulfates.
    D. In any reaction, it is always possible to compare two metals and find out which is more active.

Passage VII

Will future human evolution increase the number of twins in the population? Two scientists present opposing views.

Scientist 1

It is an established principle, the rule of Darwinian fitness, that natural selection favors the individuals who leave the largest number of viable and fertile offspring. It is also known that there is a genetic tendency that causes some women to produce more than one ovum at a time. These women will bear twins more often than other women. Since they have more offspring than other women, selection will favor them and the frequency of twin births will increase with time. This did not happen in the past because the conditions of life were so different. A woman in a hunter-gatherer society had to spend much of her time collecting plant food, while carrying her baby with her. She also had to be ready to run or otherwise protect herself from wild animals. Her chance of survival, avoiding both starvation and predation, was much worse if she was carrying two babies instead of only one. Thus, the genes that promote twinning carried an enormous liability, which more than offset the selective advantage of having twins. Under modern conditions, however, these negative features disappear and a woman who bears twins is likely to leave more offspring than one who does not. The frequency of the gene that promotes the release of more than one ovum at a time will increase in the population.

Scientist 2

You cannot think of evolutionary change in terms of a single feature. When many factors affect an outcome, it is necessary to consider how they interact to produce an optimum condition. Twins are often born prematurely, and their average birth weight is only 5.5 pounds. Single babies, on the average, come into the world weighing 7.5 pounds. Premature birth and low birth weight result in many kinds of medical problems. Twins' prospects for survival to a normal, healthy reproductive age are less than those for singly born babies. An evolutionary tendency to overcome this deficiency would call for mothers to produce twins weighing in at 7.5 pounds each. This would be an enormous strain on the mother, since she would have to gain more weight during pregnancy. The only way to neutralize this liability would be for women to be much bigger, weighing more than 200 pounds. This would, however, introduce another liability: strains on the skeleton and musculature. Evolution would have to produce a complete redesign of the body. The gain in selective value produced by twinning would be far outweighed by these disadvantages. Modern civilization has not changed the fact that single births are optimum for human women.

34. What is the basic question on which the two scientists disagree?
- **F.** Is human evolution a continuing, ongoing process?
- **G.** Do human twins start life at a disadvantage?
- **H.** Does natural selection favor genes that produce twins?
- **J.** Is the tendency to produce twins hereditary?

35. To refute Scientist 2's argument, Scientist 1 might point out that:
- **A.** modern medical science has greatly improved the survival rate of infants with low birth weights.
- **B.** many twins result from the division of a single fertilized egg, and this is not genetically controlled.
- **C.** evolutionary change is extremely slow, and there is no evidence that the human species has changed much in the last 100,000 years.
- **D.** large women have twins as frequently as small women do.

36. The arguments of both Scientist 1 and Scientist 2 would be invalidated if new evidence indicated that:
- **F.** the rate of twin births has not changed in the past century.
- **G.** genetics really makes very little difference in whether or not a woman produces twins.
- **H.** women in hunter-gatherer societies have twins more often than women in civilization.
- **J.** the genetic tendency to produce twins passes to women from their fathers, not their mothers.

37. What piece of statistical evidence would greatly strengthen Scientist 2's position?
- **A.** Twins born at 5.5 pounds have a poorer survival rate than babies born singly at 5.5 pounds.
- **B.** Twins born at 7 pounds have the same survival rate as babies born singly at 7 pounds.
- **C.** Twins born to large women have a better survival rate than twins born to small women.
- **D.** Twins born to small women have a better survival rate than twins born to large women.

38. Underlying the arguments of both scientists is the assumption that:
- **F.** production of twins is a desirable prospect for the human species.
- **G.** women who bear twins are healthier, on the average, than women who do not.
- **H.** the genetic composition of the father is irrelevant to the probability of a woman's bearing twins.
- **J.** natural selection acts on human beings in the same way as on other animals.

39. Which of the arguments of Scientist 1 was not refuted by Scientist 2?
- **A.** Modern medicine has no effect on the rate at which twins are born.
- **B.** In primitive conditions, natural selection will favor single births.
- **C.** Survival rate is a basic biological factor that is not influenced by external conditions.
- **D.** Large women are inherently capable of producing twins with large birth weights.

40. Scientist 2 claims that Scientist 1 has overlooked an important general principle of biological science. What is it?
- **F.** All biological factors interact with each other, and selective value depends on the optimal combination of values of many factors.
- **G.** Genetic factors influence all aspects of development, and must be considered in any long-term prediction.
- **H.** Genetic factors cannot be considered alone, but must be analyzed in terms of their interaction with external conditions.
- **J.** Evolution is the result of natural selection acting on the genetic composition of individuals.

ANSWER KEY

1.	B	6.	F	11.	C	16.	G	21.	D	26.	F	31.	B	36.	G
2	J	7.	B	12.	G	17.	D	22.	J	27.	A	32.	J	37.	C
3.	B	8.	J	13.	D	18.	G	23.	C	28.	H	33.	C	38.	J
4.	H	9.	B	14.	F	19.	B	24.	F	29.	A	34.	H	39.	B
5.	B	10.	G	15.	D	20.	F	25.	D	30.	G	35.	A	40.	F

Analysis Chart

Kind of Question	Skill Level			Possible Score	Your Score
	Understanding	**Analysis**	**Generalization**		
Data Representation	1, 2, 23, 24	3, 4, 25	5, 26, 27	10	
Research Summaries	6, 7, 12, 17, 18, 19, 28, 29, 30	8, 9, 13, 14, 15, 20, 31	10, 11, 16, 21, 22, 32, 33	23	
Conflicting Viewpoints	34, 38, 39	35, 36, 37	40	7	

Total   40   _____

Percent Correct: _____

ANSWERS AND EXPLANATIONS

1. B The curves for *Festuca* and *Hieracium* cross in 1950, indicating that the density of both plants was the same. *Thymus* did not appear at all until 1960.

2. J Since the three graphs all cross at this time, all three plants had equal densities; *Thymus* was increasing rapidly. The density of *Hieracium* had dropped, but remained nearly steady from 1963 to 1973. *Festuca* was dropping slowly.

3. B The density increased from nearly 0 in 1946 to 450 in 1952, an increase of 450 units in six years. This rate of 75 units per year remained steady for the entire six-year period.

4. H Both *Hieracium* and *Thymus* were newly introduced and followed the same pattern: low density for three or four years and then rapid increase for the next six years. This is the only evidence available.

5. B *Festuca* began its decline in 1947 and *Hieracium* in 1952, but *Thymus* did not appear until 1959. *Thymus* might well be more tolerant of dry weather, shade, and that particular bug than the other two species.

6. F With two different strains in competition, one or the other might prove to be better adapted. G is wrong because crowding could be tested, without introducing a different variable, by simply using more eggs of either strain. H is wrong because there is no mating in the larval stage. J is wrong because the experimental design does not allow for the testing of any such transfer, which is most unlikely in any event.

7. B If the effect of competition is to be established, it is important to know how well each strain survives when there is no competition. None of the other choices represents a variable in the experiment.

8. J The number of white-eyed adults that hatch is drastically less than the control number (Experiment 1) whenever one of the other strains is present.

9. B Note that in Experiments 2 and 3 only about 60 larvae produced adults, even though there were 100 or 150 eggs. If there were no restriction on the food supply, it is possible that all the eggs could survive in the same numbers as in Experiment 1.

10. G Whenever other strains are present with the wild type, it is the others that suffer, while the wild type maintains its predominance. F is wrong because there is no reason to believe that the numbers of eggs laid in nature are like those in the bottle. H and J are wrong because competition does not completely eliminate the white-eyed and yellow-bodied forms.

11. C Do not confuse a culture bottle with nature. There is no evidence to support any of the other choices.

12. G All concentrations increased after the first 10 hours, so F is wrong. H is wrong because none of them increased steadily. J is wrong because the decrease for virulent bacteria in a nonimmune host is actually slower than the others at first.

13. D The graphs show clearly that, if the host is immunized to the bacteria, the concentration follows the same pattern as for nonvirulent bacteria. Choice A is wrong because the graph does not show death. B is wrong because the graph says nothing about how dangerous the bacteria are. C is surely wrong; the immune organism has converted the increase of concentration to a decrease.

14. F The graph shows that all concentrations, even for the virulent bacteria, decrease in the first 10 hours. G is wrong because even in the first 10 hours the concentration of virulent bacteria is greater if the host is not immune. H is wrong; the immune system has managed to reduce the concentration. J is wrong; no data for death are given.

15. D At all times, the concentration is less in the immune than in the nonimmune host.

16. G During the first 10 hours, there is an immune mechanism that is acting on all the bacteria; at 16 hours, the immune host has another mechanism. F and H are wrong because the concentration of virulent bacteria drops in the first 10 hours, even in the nonimmune host. Since there is no information about the way immunity develops, J is wrong.

17. D For best precision, you want the smallest scale that will incorporate the largest reading. The largest potential difference reading is 1 V, so a 1-volt scale will do very well. The largest current reading is 300 mA, or 0.3 A.

18. G The dimensions are being controlled to eliminate them from consideration, so H is wrong. The only uncontrolled variable is the substance of the wire.

19. B The meter must be zeroed; that is, it must be adjusted to make sure that it reads zero when there is no current or potential difference.

20. F For all the readings in the table, the ratio between potential difference and current is constant at 200 mA/V. The ratio for the 10-V setting, however, is only 110 mA/V. G is wrong because there is surely a usable rule below 1 V, and further investigation might turn up a usable rule at higher potentials. H is wrong; the large potential difference increased the current; it was just not as much as might have been expected. J is wrong because there is no evidence about the behavior of copper wire at higher potential differences.

21. D Checking the ratios at the smallest and largest values gives these results: copper wire, $0.20/60 = 0.0033$ and $1.00/300 = 0.0033$; aluminum wire, $0.20/40 = 0.0050$ and $1.0/200 = 0.0050$; transistor, $0.2/5 = 0.040$ and $1/190 = 0.0053$. The ratios are constant for the wires, but not for the transistor.

22. J Since transistors and wires have different but reliable properties, they can be used for different purposes. F is wrong because the ratio of potential difference to current (for small currents) is constant for the wires, but not for the transistor. G is wrong because no information is given about the circuits. H is wrong because Experiment 3 gives no information about the reliability of transistors.

23. C On the graph marked 21% oxygen, the point at about 200 ppm CO_2 corresponds to about 24 μg CO_2 per minute. Multiplying by 60 gives the amount take up in an hour.

24. F All of the graphs show rising values toward the right, where the CO_2 concentration is rising. Comparing the graphs with each other shows that the highest values of uptake occur with the upper graphs, where O_2 concentration is smallest.

25. D All four graphs reach zero uptake at some minimum value of CO_2 concentration. A is wrong because there is no evidence dealing with a complete absence of oxygen. B is wrong because all graphs show that the rate increases as CO_2 concentration goes up. C is wrong because there is no reason to believe that this relationship goes up indefinitely.

26. F The data point at 100% O_2, 75 ppm CO_2, is the only one showing a negative value of uptake, indicating that production of CO_2 is greater than the amount used in photosynthesis. However, F is not a reasonable assumption because there is no reason to believe that this would not be true for concentrations of O_2 between 40% and

100%. G is probably true because uptake drops when O_2 concentration goes up. H seems to be true; at high O_2 concentration, production of CO_2 exceeds usage. J is certainly true; at every level uptake increases with CO_2 concentration.

27. A The data in the graph show that at any oxygen concentration, plants will take up more CO_2 as the amount in the air rises. If they grow more, they take up still more.

28. H Copper has come out of solution in the form of copper metal. The loss of copper changes the color of the solution. Iron must have replaced copper in the solution, so iron is more active. This follows from the definition of a more active metal, given in the first paragraph of the passage.

29. A The blue color indicates the presence of copper in solution. B is wrong because we have no reason to believe there is any such thing as the "true color" of the solution. C is wrong because we have no indication that the mercury coating is bluish. D is wrong because mercury cannot change into copper.

30. G Since iron is more active than copper, copper cannot replace iron in the solution. F is wrong; in the blue solution, copper is dissolved. Nothing in the experiment points to either H or J.

31. B Since iron is more active than copper (Experiment 1) and copper is more active than mercury (Experiment 4), it is reasonable to assume that iron is more active than mercury. Therefore, iron will replace mercury in solution, and the mercury will deposit on the steel wool.

32. J We already know from the experiments that iron is more active than copper, and copper than mercury. Since metal X replaces copper and mercury from solution, it must be more active than either of them. It does not, however, replace iron.

33. C The atomic structure of a metal atom is the same as it enters into any reaction. If atomic structure is what determines activity, then the relative activities of two metals do not depend on what the specific chemical reaction is. Choice A is wrong because a ranking with sulfates does not prove that the ranking would hold in other reac-

tions. B and D prove only that there are different levels of activity in different reactions.

34. H Both scientists agree that evolution continues and might involve changes in the frequency of genes producing twins, so F and J are wrong. Scientist 1 does not challenge the statement that twins have lower survival rates, so G is wrong. The only point at issue is whether the result of selection will be a higher frequency of twinning.

35. A Scientist 2 argues that twinning has a negative selective value because twins are born small, but gains in medical science might nullify this disadvantage. None of the other choices is germane.

36. G Both Scientist 1 and Scientist 2 assume that the tendency to produce twins is hereditary; they disagree only on how this will change the evolutionary trend. F is wrong because both would agree that a century is too short a time to show any effect. H is wrong because neither scientist makes any such claim. J is wrong because it would make no difference in the survival value of the gene.

37. C Scientist 2 claims that large, healthy twins could be produced only by larger women, and statistics to this effect would support his case. B is wrong because this point is not at issue.

38. J Both scientists base their arguments on natural selection of the most favorable combination of traits; they disagree on what that combination might be. F is wrong because neither scientist makes any value judgment. G is wrong because neither scientist makes any such claim. H is wrong because the arguments of neither scientist require any such assumption.

39. B This claim is made by Scientist 1, and not addressed by Scientist 2. The others are wrong because Scientist 1 does not make any such claims.

40. F This is the core of Scientist 2's rebuttal; Scientist 1 has not considered all the genetic interactions involved. G is wrong because both scientists agree that genetic factors are central to the issue. H is wrong because both scientists considered external conditions; they disagreed on which ones were important. J is wrong because they agreed on this point.

PART FOUR

Model Examinations

Model Examination A

The purpose of Model Examination A is to help you evaluate your progress in preparing for the actual ACT. Take the examination under simulated testing conditions and within the time limits stated at the beginning of each test. Try to apply the test-taking tactics recommended in this book. Detach the Answer Sheet and mark your answers on it.

After you finish the examination, check your answers against the Answer Keys and fill in the Analysis Charts. Rate your total scores by using the Performance Evaluation Chart on page 8. Read all of the Answer Explanations.

The Analysis Charts will indicate where you need further review. Go back to Part Three to reinforce specific areas. Then try Model Examination B to evaluate your progress.

Directions: Mark one answer only for each question. Make the mark dark. Erase completely
ny mark made in error. (Additional or stray marks will be counted as mistakes.)

TEST 1

	10 Ⓕ Ⓖ Ⓗ Ⓙ	20 Ⓕ Ⓖ Ⓗ Ⓙ	30 Ⓕ Ⓖ Ⓗ Ⓙ	40 Ⓕ Ⓖ Ⓗ Ⓙ	50 Ⓕ Ⓖ Ⓗ Ⓙ	60 Ⓕ Ⓖ Ⓗ Ⓙ	70 Ⓕ Ⓖ Ⓗ Ⓙ
1 Ⓐ Ⓑ Ⓒ Ⓓ	11 Ⓐ Ⓑ Ⓒ Ⓓ	21 Ⓐ Ⓑ Ⓒ Ⓓ	31 Ⓐ Ⓑ Ⓒ Ⓓ	41 Ⓐ Ⓑ Ⓒ Ⓓ	51 Ⓐ Ⓑ Ⓒ Ⓓ	61 Ⓐ Ⓑ Ⓒ Ⓓ	71 Ⓐ Ⓑ Ⓒ Ⓓ
2 Ⓕ Ⓖ Ⓗ Ⓙ	12 Ⓕ Ⓖ Ⓗ Ⓙ	22 Ⓕ Ⓖ Ⓗ Ⓙ	32 Ⓕ Ⓖ Ⓗ Ⓙ	42 Ⓕ Ⓖ Ⓗ Ⓙ	52 Ⓕ Ⓖ Ⓗ Ⓙ	62 Ⓕ Ⓖ Ⓗ Ⓙ	72 Ⓕ Ⓖ Ⓗ Ⓙ
3 Ⓐ Ⓑ Ⓒ Ⓓ	13 Ⓐ Ⓑ Ⓒ Ⓓ	23 Ⓐ Ⓑ Ⓒ Ⓓ	33 Ⓐ Ⓑ Ⓒ Ⓓ	43 Ⓐ Ⓑ Ⓒ Ⓓ	53 Ⓐ Ⓑ Ⓒ Ⓓ	63 Ⓐ Ⓑ Ⓒ Ⓓ	73 Ⓐ Ⓑ Ⓒ Ⓓ
4 Ⓕ Ⓖ Ⓗ Ⓙ	14 Ⓕ Ⓖ Ⓗ Ⓙ	24 Ⓕ Ⓖ Ⓗ Ⓙ	34 Ⓕ Ⓖ Ⓗ Ⓙ	44 Ⓕ Ⓖ Ⓗ Ⓙ	54 Ⓕ Ⓖ Ⓗ Ⓙ	64 Ⓕ Ⓖ Ⓗ Ⓙ	74 Ⓕ Ⓖ Ⓗ Ⓙ
5 Ⓐ Ⓑ Ⓒ Ⓓ	15 Ⓐ Ⓑ Ⓒ Ⓓ	25 Ⓐ Ⓑ Ⓒ Ⓓ	35 Ⓐ Ⓑ Ⓒ Ⓓ	45 Ⓐ Ⓑ Ⓒ Ⓓ	55 Ⓐ Ⓑ Ⓒ Ⓓ	65 Ⓐ Ⓑ Ⓒ Ⓓ	75 Ⓐ Ⓑ Ⓒ Ⓓ
6 Ⓕ Ⓖ Ⓗ Ⓙ	16 Ⓕ Ⓖ Ⓗ Ⓙ	26 Ⓕ Ⓖ Ⓗ Ⓙ	36 Ⓕ Ⓖ Ⓗ Ⓙ	46 Ⓕ Ⓖ Ⓗ Ⓙ	56 Ⓕ Ⓖ Ⓗ Ⓙ	66 Ⓕ Ⓖ Ⓗ Ⓙ	
7 Ⓐ Ⓑ Ⓒ Ⓓ	17 Ⓐ Ⓑ Ⓒ Ⓓ	27 Ⓐ Ⓑ Ⓒ Ⓓ	37 Ⓐ Ⓑ Ⓒ Ⓓ	47 Ⓐ Ⓑ Ⓒ Ⓓ	57 Ⓐ Ⓑ Ⓒ Ⓓ	67 Ⓐ Ⓑ Ⓒ Ⓓ	
8 Ⓕ Ⓖ Ⓗ Ⓙ	18 Ⓕ Ⓖ Ⓗ Ⓙ	28 Ⓕ Ⓖ Ⓗ Ⓙ	38 Ⓕ Ⓖ Ⓗ Ⓙ	48 Ⓕ Ⓖ Ⓗ Ⓙ	58 Ⓕ Ⓖ Ⓗ Ⓙ	68 Ⓕ Ⓖ Ⓗ Ⓙ	
9 Ⓐ Ⓑ Ⓒ Ⓓ	19 Ⓐ Ⓑ Ⓒ Ⓓ	29 Ⓐ Ⓑ Ⓒ Ⓓ	39 Ⓐ Ⓑ Ⓒ Ⓓ	49 Ⓐ Ⓑ Ⓒ Ⓓ	59 Ⓐ Ⓑ Ⓒ Ⓓ	69 Ⓐ Ⓑ Ⓒ Ⓓ	

TEST 2

	8 Ⓕ Ⓖ Ⓗ Ⓙ Ⓚ	16 Ⓕ Ⓖ Ⓗ Ⓙ Ⓚ	24 Ⓕ Ⓖ Ⓗ Ⓙ Ⓚ	32 Ⓕ Ⓖ Ⓗ Ⓙ Ⓚ	40 Ⓕ Ⓖ Ⓗ Ⓙ Ⓚ	48 Ⓕ Ⓖ Ⓗ Ⓙ Ⓚ	56 Ⓕ Ⓖ Ⓗ Ⓙ Ⓚ
1 Ⓐ Ⓑ Ⓒ Ⓓ Ⓔ	9 Ⓐ Ⓑ Ⓒ Ⓓ Ⓔ	17 Ⓐ Ⓑ Ⓒ Ⓓ Ⓔ	25 Ⓐ Ⓑ Ⓒ Ⓓ Ⓔ	33 Ⓐ Ⓑ Ⓒ Ⓓ Ⓔ	41 Ⓐ Ⓑ Ⓒ Ⓓ Ⓔ	49 Ⓐ Ⓑ Ⓒ Ⓓ Ⓔ	57 Ⓐ Ⓑ Ⓒ Ⓓ Ⓔ
2 Ⓕ Ⓖ Ⓗ Ⓙ Ⓚ	10 Ⓕ Ⓖ Ⓗ Ⓙ Ⓚ	18 Ⓕ Ⓖ Ⓗ Ⓙ Ⓚ	26 Ⓕ Ⓖ Ⓗ Ⓙ Ⓚ	34 Ⓕ Ⓖ Ⓗ Ⓙ Ⓚ	42 Ⓕ Ⓖ Ⓗ Ⓙ Ⓚ	50 Ⓕ Ⓖ Ⓗ Ⓙ Ⓚ	58 Ⓕ Ⓖ Ⓗ Ⓙ Ⓚ
3 Ⓐ Ⓑ Ⓒ Ⓓ Ⓔ	11 Ⓐ Ⓑ Ⓒ Ⓓ Ⓔ	19 Ⓐ Ⓑ Ⓒ Ⓓ Ⓔ	27 Ⓐ Ⓑ Ⓒ Ⓓ Ⓔ	35 Ⓐ Ⓑ Ⓒ Ⓓ Ⓔ	43 Ⓐ Ⓑ Ⓒ Ⓓ Ⓔ	51 Ⓐ Ⓑ Ⓒ Ⓓ Ⓔ	59 Ⓐ Ⓑ Ⓒ Ⓓ Ⓔ
4 Ⓕ Ⓖ Ⓗ Ⓙ Ⓚ	12 Ⓕ Ⓖ Ⓗ Ⓙ Ⓚ	20 Ⓕ Ⓖ Ⓗ Ⓙ Ⓚ	28 Ⓕ Ⓖ Ⓗ Ⓙ Ⓚ	36 Ⓕ Ⓖ Ⓗ Ⓙ Ⓚ	44 Ⓕ Ⓖ Ⓗ Ⓙ Ⓚ	52 Ⓕ Ⓖ Ⓗ Ⓙ Ⓚ	60 Ⓕ Ⓖ Ⓗ Ⓙ Ⓚ
5 Ⓐ Ⓑ Ⓒ Ⓓ Ⓔ	13 Ⓐ Ⓑ Ⓒ Ⓓ Ⓔ	21 Ⓐ Ⓑ Ⓒ Ⓓ Ⓔ	29 Ⓐ Ⓑ Ⓒ Ⓓ Ⓔ	37 Ⓐ Ⓑ Ⓒ Ⓓ Ⓔ	45 Ⓐ Ⓑ Ⓒ Ⓓ Ⓔ	53 Ⓐ Ⓑ Ⓒ Ⓓ Ⓔ	
6 Ⓕ Ⓖ Ⓗ Ⓙ Ⓚ	14 Ⓕ Ⓖ Ⓗ Ⓙ Ⓚ	22 Ⓕ Ⓖ Ⓗ Ⓙ Ⓚ	30 Ⓕ Ⓖ Ⓗ Ⓙ Ⓚ	38 Ⓕ Ⓖ Ⓗ Ⓙ Ⓚ	46 Ⓕ Ⓖ Ⓗ Ⓙ Ⓚ	54 Ⓕ Ⓖ Ⓗ Ⓙ Ⓚ	
7 Ⓐ Ⓑ Ⓒ Ⓓ Ⓔ	15 Ⓐ Ⓑ Ⓒ Ⓓ Ⓔ	23 Ⓐ Ⓑ Ⓒ Ⓓ Ⓔ	31 Ⓐ Ⓑ Ⓒ Ⓓ Ⓔ	39 Ⓐ Ⓑ Ⓒ Ⓓ Ⓔ	47 Ⓐ Ⓑ Ⓒ Ⓓ Ⓔ	55 Ⓐ Ⓑ Ⓒ Ⓓ Ⓔ	

TEST 3

	6 Ⓕ Ⓖ Ⓗ Ⓙ	12 Ⓕ Ⓖ Ⓗ Ⓙ	18 Ⓕ Ⓖ Ⓗ Ⓙ	24 Ⓕ Ⓖ Ⓗ Ⓙ	30 Ⓕ Ⓖ Ⓗ Ⓙ	36 Ⓕ Ⓖ Ⓗ Ⓙ
1 Ⓐ Ⓑ Ⓒ Ⓓ	7 Ⓐ Ⓑ Ⓒ Ⓓ	13 Ⓐ Ⓑ Ⓒ Ⓓ	19 Ⓐ Ⓑ Ⓒ Ⓓ	25 Ⓐ Ⓑ Ⓒ Ⓓ	31 Ⓐ Ⓑ Ⓒ Ⓓ	37 Ⓐ Ⓑ Ⓒ Ⓓ
2 Ⓕ Ⓖ Ⓗ Ⓙ	8 Ⓕ Ⓖ Ⓗ Ⓙ	14 Ⓕ Ⓖ Ⓗ Ⓙ	20 Ⓕ Ⓖ Ⓗ Ⓙ	26 Ⓕ Ⓖ Ⓗ Ⓙ	32 Ⓕ Ⓖ Ⓗ Ⓙ	38 Ⓕ Ⓖ Ⓗ Ⓙ
3 Ⓐ Ⓑ Ⓒ Ⓓ	9 Ⓐ Ⓑ Ⓒ Ⓓ	15 Ⓐ Ⓑ Ⓒ Ⓓ	21 Ⓐ Ⓑ Ⓒ Ⓓ	27 Ⓐ Ⓑ Ⓒ Ⓓ	33 Ⓐ Ⓑ Ⓒ Ⓓ	39 Ⓐ Ⓑ Ⓒ Ⓓ
4 Ⓕ Ⓖ Ⓗ Ⓙ	10 Ⓕ Ⓖ Ⓗ Ⓙ	16 Ⓕ Ⓖ Ⓗ Ⓙ	22 Ⓕ Ⓖ Ⓗ Ⓙ	28 Ⓕ Ⓖ Ⓗ Ⓙ	34 Ⓕ Ⓖ Ⓗ Ⓙ	40 Ⓕ Ⓖ Ⓗ Ⓙ
5 Ⓐ Ⓑ Ⓒ Ⓓ	11 Ⓐ Ⓑ Ⓒ Ⓓ	17 Ⓐ Ⓑ Ⓒ Ⓓ	23 Ⓐ Ⓑ Ⓒ Ⓓ	29 Ⓐ Ⓑ Ⓒ Ⓓ	35 Ⓐ Ⓑ Ⓒ Ⓓ	

TEST 4

	6 Ⓕ Ⓖ Ⓗ Ⓙ	12 Ⓕ Ⓖ Ⓗ Ⓙ	18 Ⓕ Ⓖ Ⓗ Ⓙ	24 Ⓕ Ⓖ Ⓗ Ⓙ	30 Ⓕ Ⓖ Ⓗ Ⓙ	36 Ⓕ Ⓖ Ⓗ Ⓙ
1 Ⓐ Ⓑ Ⓒ Ⓓ	7 Ⓐ Ⓑ Ⓒ Ⓓ	13 Ⓐ Ⓑ Ⓒ Ⓓ	19 Ⓐ Ⓑ Ⓒ Ⓓ	25 Ⓐ Ⓑ Ⓒ Ⓓ	31 Ⓐ Ⓑ Ⓒ Ⓓ	37 Ⓐ Ⓑ Ⓒ Ⓓ
2 Ⓕ Ⓖ Ⓗ Ⓙ	8 Ⓕ Ⓖ Ⓗ Ⓙ	14 Ⓕ Ⓖ Ⓗ Ⓙ	20 Ⓕ Ⓖ Ⓗ Ⓙ	26 Ⓕ Ⓖ Ⓗ Ⓙ	32 Ⓕ Ⓖ Ⓗ Ⓙ	38 Ⓕ Ⓖ Ⓗ Ⓙ
3 Ⓐ Ⓑ Ⓒ Ⓓ	9 Ⓐ Ⓑ Ⓒ Ⓓ	15 Ⓐ Ⓑ Ⓒ Ⓓ	21 Ⓐ Ⓑ Ⓒ Ⓓ	27 Ⓐ Ⓑ Ⓒ Ⓓ	33 Ⓐ Ⓑ Ⓒ Ⓓ	39 Ⓐ Ⓑ Ⓒ Ⓓ
4 Ⓕ Ⓖ Ⓗ Ⓙ	10 Ⓕ Ⓖ Ⓗ Ⓙ	16 Ⓕ Ⓖ Ⓗ Ⓙ	22 Ⓕ Ⓖ Ⓗ Ⓙ	28 Ⓕ Ⓖ Ⓗ Ⓙ	34 Ⓕ Ⓖ Ⓗ Ⓙ	40 Ⓕ Ⓖ Ⓗ Ⓙ
5 Ⓐ Ⓑ Ⓒ Ⓓ	11 Ⓐ Ⓑ Ⓒ Ⓓ	17 Ⓐ Ⓑ Ⓒ Ⓓ	23 Ⓐ Ⓑ Ⓒ Ⓓ	29 Ⓐ Ⓑ Ⓒ Ⓓ	35 Ⓐ Ⓑ Ⓒ Ⓓ	

1   1 1 1 1 1 1 1 1 1 1   1

EXAMINATION A
Model English Test
45 Minutes—75 Questions

DIRECTIONS: The following test consists of 75 under-lined words and phrases in context, or general questions about the passages. Most of the underlined sections contain errors and inappropriate expressions. You are asked to compare each with the four alternatives in the answer column. If you consider the original version best, choose letter **A** or **F:** NO CHANGE. For each question, blacken on the answer sheet the letter of the alternative you think best. Read each passage through before answering the questions based on it.

Passage I

(1)

Americans are living longer. The number of citizens sixty years or older totaled more than forty million in 1999, and one out of every nine Americans were sixty-five or older. Because advances in medical science and a more healthful lifestyle have lengthened the life spans of we Americans, more and more of us

are finding that the time comes when we either no longer want to—or can— live on our own.

(2)

Unfortunately, in the past the words *retirement home* often brought to mind images of impersonal, lonely places. [4] However, conditions in retirement homes can vary, some homes earning awards for excellence in nursing care, and others earning citations for

1. A. NO CHANGE
   B. is
   C. have been
   D. was

2. F. NO CHANGE
   G. we, Americans,
   H. us Americans
   J. us, Americans,

3. A. NO CHANGE
   B. to or can live
   C. to, or can live
   D. to, or can, live

4. This idea (of "impersonal, lonely places") could best be illustrated in this passage by employing which of the following writing strategies?
   F. Explaining a process
   G. Persuasion
   H. Defining
   J. Description

GO ON TO THE NEXT PAGE.

1   1 1 1 1 1 1 1 1 1   1

negligence. [5] Regulations regarding nursing homes are

becoming <u>stricter than a research clinic,</u> and it is possi-
        ₆

ble to find retirement conditions that are positive and

comfortable. [7]

(3)

But at the same time, the sad fact remains that,

although most nursing homes are now licensed by the

state, <u>unclean and unhealthy conditions can still be</u>
       ₈

<u>found.</u> Even if the homes follow the licensing
₈

procedures perfectly, the law does not guarantee a

<u>warm friendly</u> staff or atmosphere. [10]
₉

(4)

When looking at nursing homes, <u>qualities should</u>
                                 ₁₁

<u>be placed</u> in priority order. Family members should
₁₁

remember, as they look, that attitude toward patients—

5. Which of the following writing strategies would permit the writer to present details about both housing extremes?
   A. Classifying and dividing
   B. Narration
   C. Comparison and contrast
   D. Persuasion

6. F. NO CHANGE
   G. stricter
   H. stricter than clinics
   J. stricter than they once were

7. Suppose that at this point in the passage the writer wanted to add more information about the impact of government regulations on retirement home conditions. Which of the following additions would be most relevant to the passage as a whole?
   A. A description and brief history of the agencies regulating nursing homes
   B. A bibliography of government reports and summaries published by regulating agencies
   C. A separate paragraph summarizing briefly the recent activity and success of regulating agencies
   D. Inclusion of a typical case report on an existing nursing institution

8. F. NO CHANGE
   G. one can still find unclean and unhealthy conditions.
   H. conditions can be found of uncleanliness and unhealthiness.
   J. many of them are unclean and unhealthy.

9. A. NO CHANGE
   B. warm - friendly
   C. warm: friendly
   D. warm, friendly

10. The writer could most effectively strengthen this paragraph by adding:
    F. a list of retirement homes found to be substandard in cleanliness.
    G. an anecdote about a woman who has lived in a home for 20 years.
    H. details and examples that typify unclean and unhealthy conditions.
    J. details of the licensing procedure that homes are required to complete.

11. A. NO CHANGE
    B. interested parties should place qualities
    C. qualities are certainly to be placed
    D. the patient should place qualities

GO ON TO THE NEXT PAGE.

1   1   1   1   1   1   1   1   1   1   1

the morale and personal contact—can be just as impor-

tant as new buildings, which, if they do not contain

human warmth, can be little better than prisons.

(5)

For these reasons, it <u>behooves us</u> to take the time
₁₂

to carefully check out the nursing homes the family is

considering. If members of the family cannot carry out

all of the necessary steps, they should have a friend or

relative help with the evaluation.

12. F. NO CHANGE
   G. best suits us
   H. is very important
   J. is not a bad idea

(6)

Not everyone who is in a nursing home requires

the 24-hour skilled care offered there. Many residents

are in homes because they can no longer care for them-

selves at home, and have nowhere else to go. However,

alternatives to nursing homes do exist for people who

need less care. [13]

13. Which of the following means of discussing alternatives to 24-hour skilled nursing care would be
most compatible with the methods employed so far
in this passage?
   A. Detailed interviews with nursing home inmates
who have experienced both forms of care
   B. Insertion of medical records of patients who
have been moved from occasional care to 24-
hour care
   C. A short paragraph mentioning several alternatives to 24-hour care
   D. Inclusion of a personal diary written by an elderly patient who made the change to permanent care

(7)

Home care <u>services, which</u> allow a patient to stay
₁₄

in a familiar environment rather than being placed in a

nursing home, are an option if the elderly person needs

only limited help, since home care causes far less dis-

ruption to normal life. Such services are provided by a

variety of public, voluntary, and private agencies. [15]

14. F. NO CHANGE
   G. services which
   H. services that
   J. services

15. Choose the sequence of paragraph numbers that
make the structure of the passage most logical.
   A. NO CHANGE
   B. 7, 2, 3, 1, 5, 4, 6
   C. 1, 2, 3, 5, 4, 6, 7
   D. 1, 2, 7, 3, 4, 5, 6

GO ON TO THE NEXT PAGE.

1 1 1 1 1 1 1 1 1 1 1 1

Passage II

Cultural activities form the loom on which the talents, skills, and dreams of individuals <u>can sprout</u> into
₁₆

something colorful and <u>distinctive—a play, pageant,</u> art
₁₇
center, music festival, museum, library, garden, park—

to enrich community life. [18]

Cultural activities are central to Rural Areas Development, a nationwide effort by rural people and those

in public service and private endeavors who work with

<u>it</u> to enrich the quality of life. [20]
₁₉

What may not be recognized by area leaders whose

primary interest is in economic development <u>is when</u>
₂₁
cultural activities can be part of the steam that supplies

the drive.

The first heritage festival of Lawrence County in

Arkansas illustrates how a cultural activity may emerge

from a ferment of economic development and, in turn,

engender still newer ideas for <u>farther</u> social and
₂₂
economic gain, as well as other cultural activities.

Lawrence County, a mainly rural area in northeastern

Arkansas, had a population of 17,000 in <u>nineteen-sixty.</u>
₂₃
Its eastern half is fertile. The Black River runs beneath

the delta, planted to rice, soybeans, and cotton, and the

hills, where the farms are in livestock and poultry.

16. F. NO CHANGE
    G. can be woven
    H. can be sprouted
    J. can swell

17. A. NO CHANGE
    B. distinctive, a play, a pageant
    C. distinctive. A play, a pageant
    D. distinctive; a play, a pageant

18. Which of the following terms needs to be more carefully defined if the first paragraph is to carry substantial meaning?
    F. Pageant
    G. Cultural activities
    H. Loom
    J. Music festival

19. A. NO CHANGE
    B. they
    C. him
    D. them

20. Which of the following suggestions would improve the beginning of this passage?
    F. NO CHANGE
    G. OMIT the second paragraph.
    H. Combine the first and second paragraphs.
    J. Move the second paragraph to the end of the passage.

21. A. NO CHANGE
    B. is that
    C. is because
    D. is for

22. F. NO CHANGE
    G. even farther
    H. further
    J. furthermore

23. A. NO CHANGE
    B. nineteen-sixty A.D.
    C. 1960
    D. nineteen hundred and sixty

GO ON TO THE NEXT PAGE.

1 **1** **1** **1** **1** **1** **1** **1** **1** **1** **1**

Family-type farms employ a third of the work force. [25]
 24

Farmers nevertheless made up the largest occupa-
 26
tional group in the Lawrence County Development

Council when it was organized in 1962. Seventeen

members of the Council were farmers—nine in general
 27
farming, six livestock and poultry producers, one a
 27
dairyman, another a ricegrower. Also on the Council
 27
were an industrial worker, two bankers, and several

local businessmen and homemakers.

Addressing itself to the economic advancement of
 28
the county, the Council spent its first two years of
 28
existence. It supported a one-mill tax to guarantee con-
 28
struction of an industrial building in Walnut Ridge, the

county seat and the largest town. It was instrumental in

getting a comprehensive manpower inventory and eco-

nomic base study of the area it arranged for workshops
 29
in farm management. It helped leaders of Imboden to

24. F. NO CHANGE
   G. Family type farms
   H. Family type-farms
   J. Family, type farms

25. This paragraph contains a major organizational
problem. Which of the following critical statements
best describes this problem?
   A. The paragraph does not contain enough specific details to support the main point.
   B. The first sentence of the paragraph presents an
idea that is not developed in the body of the
paragraph.
   C. No beginning thesis or topic is presented.
   D. There are many ideas in the paragraph, none of
them developed.

26. F. NO CHANGE
   G. on the contrary
   H. however
   J. thus

27. A. NO CHANGE
   B. —nine in general farming, six in livestock and
poultry production, one in dairy production,
another in rice farming.
   C. —nine are general farmers, six as livestock
and poultry producers, one a dairyman, another
a ricegrower.
   D. —nine as general farmers, six livestock and
poultry producers, one a dairyman, another a
ricegrower.

28. F. NO CHANGE
   G. During its first two years, the Council
addressed the economic advancement of the
county.
   H. Addressing itself to the economic advancement
of the county, the Council spent its first two
years of existence.
   J. The Council spent its first two years of existence while addressing itself to the economic
advancement of the county.

29. A. NO CHANGE
   B. area, it
   C. area. It
   D. area but it

GO ON TO THE NEXT PAGE.

initiate a housing project for twenty elderly persons. [30]

30. Which of the following is a major flaw in the structure and sense of this passage?
    F. It omits all mention of children; children are certainly an important part of rural America.
    G. It fails to mention public works projects.
    H. The whole point of the passage is that cultural activities can "supply the drive" for social and economic development, but the passage does not address that issue at all.
    J. The passage does not list enough accomplishments of the Lawrence County Development Council.

Passage III

Of all the musical instruments produced by human skill, the three <u>of which are the most distinguished</u> are
₃₁
the violin, the piano, and the pipe organ. Of these, the violin still remains the instrument of the virtuoso. No method <u>to play it</u> has yet been <u>discovered</u> except by the
₃₂   ₃₃
slow and tedious process of learning it. It is the

instrument of the <u>accomplish</u> musician. [35]
₃₄

On the other hand, self-playing devices have been employed successfully with both the piano and the organ—but with this difference. Piano music derives

some of its <u>essentialness</u> from the personality of the
₃₆
player. The touch of human fingers has never been exactly reproduced by mechanical devices. In some

31. A. NO CHANGE
    B. that are most distinguished
    C. of those that are distinguished
    D. most distinguished

32. F. NO CHANGE
    G. playing at
    H. in playing it
    J. of playing it

33. A. NO CHANGE
    B. invented
    C. divined
    D. developed

34. F. NO CHANGE
    G. accomplishing
    H. accomplished
    J. more accomplished

35. Which of the following writing strategies would permit the writer to present details about all three types of instruments?
    A. Classifying and dividing
    B. Narration
    C. Comparison and contrast
    D. Persuasion

36. F. NO CHANGE
    G. pith
    H. quality
    J. life-blood

GO ON TO THE NEXT PAGE.

1   1 1 1 1 1 1 1 1 1   1

compositions, however, the mechanical piano player

approaches the pianist, although not by any means
         37

in all. [38]

The pipe organ consequently is made for auto-
                    39
mated playing. There is virtually nothing the organist

can do with his or her hands or feet that cannot be

duplicated by mechanical devices. When an organ man-

ual is touched, the resulting tone is the exact same,
                                        40

whether the touch be hard or soft, slow or quick. The
                 41   42
tone continues at the same volume until the key is

released. Brilliancy, variety, and other qualities are

obtained by other sets of pipes, and these pipes are

brought into play by pulling out stops. Such stops can

be pulled by mechanical means just as effectively as by

human fingers. If the organ music is correctly cut in the

music roll, with all the stops, couplers, and swells

operated at the proper places, the most acutest ear
                                    43
cannot distinguish between the human organist and

37. A. NO CHANGE
   B. approaches the sound of the pianist
   C. comes close to the piano
   D. typifies the piano

38. The writer could most effectively strengthen the passage at this point by adding:
   F. documentation and detail to support opinions delivered as facts.
   G. a review of all the orchestral instruments, including their musical ranges.
   H. a discussion of the great violin makers of the past.
   J. a detailed description of organ structure and mechanism.

39. A. NO CHANGE
   B. on the contrary
   C. to be sure
   D. similarly

40. F. NO CHANGE
   G. exact identical
   H. same
   J. equal

41. A. NO CHANGE
   B. is
   C. was
   D. has been

42. F. NO CHANGE
   G. soft, slow, or quick.
   H. soft: slow or quick.
   J. soft slow or quick.

43. A. NO CHANGE
   B. the acute ear
   C. the more acute ear
   D. the most acute ear

GO ON TO THE NEXT PAGE.

the organist who is mechanical. [45]
44

44. **F.** NO CHANGE
    G. the organist, who is mechanical.
    H. the mechanical organist.
    J. the organist who is a nonhuman.

45. The main purpose of this passage is to provide:
    A. a discussion of the virtues of the mechanical organ.
    B. a history of music.
    C. a comparison of the violin, piano, and organ.
    D. a general discussion of mechanized musical instruments.

Passage IV

Until his death, Charles Darwin complained that even many of his scientific critics failed to grasp the meaning of his theory of selection; it is not unlikely
46
that if he were still alive the complaint would be

repeated. [47] Even where full comprehension of his theory of the causes of organic evolution has been reached, precise determination of the degree of its

46. **F.** NO CHANGE
    G. it is not likely
    H. it is likely
    J. it is probable

47. When a passage mentions that a famous figure *complained* about a fact or situation, how might the reader be given greater understanding of the personality and character of that subject?
    A. By inclusion of a description of the occurrence
    B. By quoted examples of what he or she actually said
    C. By references to how other persons present at the time reported the conversation
    D. By a speculative commentary on what he or she meant

adequacy—for adequate in great measure it surely is—
48
has not yet been attained. The generalization that underlies it is so broad, the facts by which it must be verified or limited are always, it seems, accumulating,
49
and the problems interrelated with it are so intricate, that finality with regard to it must be indefinitely postponed. That must be left for the biology of the future.
50

48. **F.** NO CHANGE
    G. adequacy; for
    H. adequacy, for
    J. adequacy for

49. **A.** NO CHANGE
    B. are so always accumulating
    C. are so constantly accumulating
    D. are accumulating

50. **F.** NO CHANGE
    G. This
    H. Those
    J. That judgment

Moreover, there need be little hesitation in express-
51
ing an estimate of the great naturalist and his

51. **A.** NO CHANGE
    B. In addition
    C. In other words,
    D. However,

GO ON TO THE NEXT PAGE.

1   1   1   1   1   1   1   1   1   1   1   1

thought. They are obviously among the greatest intellectual forces of the early twentieth century, as they were of the nineteenth. Notwithstanding certain limitations, which Darwin himself unduly <u>emphasizes</u>, he was one of the greatest of men intellectually, and, without qualification, one of the most attractive of personalities; <u>this</u> must always remain true, whatever may be the ultimate verdict of science in regard to details of his hypotheses. Persons thus grandly molded have nothing to fear from the perspective of time. <u>He was one cool cucumber at one of history's junctures.</u>

Darwin insisted that the principle of natural selection is only one of the causes of evolution of species, "the main but not the exclusive means of <u>modification," and</u> he was also profoundly aware of the evolutionary importance of the underlying

problems of variability, heredity, and <u>isolating</u> that

<u>has occupied</u> so absorbingly the attention of the post-Darwinians. Naturalists, almost without exception, no longer doubt that natural selection, as expounded by him, is a cause of the evolution of species, and a most important one, and <u>stood</u> as a general law that explains

the causation of organic evolution. <u>This view will be supported by the biology of the future, if Darwin's place</u> in the history of science cannot be far

below that of Newton. [60]

52. **F.** NO CHANGE
    G. emphasize
    H. emphasized
    J. had emphasized

53. **A.** NO CHANGE
    B. this assessment
    C. this alone
    D. this quality

54. **F.** NO CHANGE
    G. He has been one cool cucumber at one of history's junctures.
    H. He is one cool cucumber at one of history's junctures.
    J. OMIT this sentence.

55. **A.** NO CHANGE
    B. modification" and
    C. modification." And
    D. modification;" and

56. **F.** NO CHANGE
    G. isolatability
    H. isolation
    J. isolate

57. **A.** NO CHANGE
    B. had occupied
    C. has been occupied
    D. have occupied

58. **F.** NO CHANGE
    G. has stood
    H. stands
    J. will have stood

59. **A.** NO CHANGE
    B. If this view is supported by the biology of the future, Darwin's place
    C. This view will be supported by the biology of the future, although Darwin's place
    D. Nevertheless, this view is supported by the biology of the future, when Darwin's place

60. Readers are likely to regard the passage as best described by which of the following terms?
    F. Biographical   **H.** Laudatory
    G. Confessional   **J.** Inspirational

GO ON TO THE NEXT PAGE.

1   1 1 1 1 1 1 1 1 1   1

Passage V

Almost everywhere spread through the British Isles
<u>spread through</u>
61

are to be found antiquities. These are carefully marked

on governmental, and many private maps
<u>governmental, and many private</u>
62

and historians describe them in publicly available
<u>and historians describe them</u>
63

guides. Governmental agencies, the National Trust,

and private landlords are most accommodating in

permitting visits to these unattended sites, most of
<u>most of</u>
64

which are unsupervised yet immaculate. ☐65
<u>which are unsupervised yet immaculate.</u>
64

With interesting exceptions, the rock graphics of

the British Isles are a collection of pits, rings, and

grooves, as well as carefully-carved symbols of
<u>carefully-carved</u>
66

Neolithic power (axheads, fertility symbols, etc.) and

roughly sculpted monoliths. The pit, ring, and groove

sites usually are found on horizontal surfaces, because
<u>because</u>
67

many power symbols are found on vertical surfaces of

menhirs (upright monoliths) lintels, and the walls of
<u>monoliths</u>)
68

constructions. In the more than five hundred megalithic
<u>five hundred</u>
69

stone constructions, many have a number of menhirs

whose natural shape has been abetted by human enter-

prise into a variety of shapes. Stonehenge is the

61. A. NO CHANGE
   B. widely dispersed through
   C. throughout
   D. all over, in nook and crook

62. F. NO CHANGE
   G. governmental; and many private
   H. governmental—and many private
   J. governmental and many private

63. A. NO CHANGE
   B. and described
   C. and describing
   D. and descriptively

64. F. NO CHANGE
   G. most of which are unsupervised although immaculate.
   H. most of which are immaculate.
   J. most of which are unsupervised.

65. Suppose this passage were written for an audience that was unfamiliar with antiquities and British history. The writer could most effectively strengthen the passage by:
   A. including a brief summary of the biographies of British monarchs.
   B. describing with detail and illustration just what an *antiquity* is.
   C. supplying a current map of England.
   D. defining in great detail the term *National Trust.*

66. F. NO CHANGE
   G. carefully, carved
   H. carefully carved
   J. carefully and carved

67. A. NO CHANGE
   B. while
   C. although
   D. yet

68. F. NO CHANGE
   G. monoliths),
   H. monoliths,)
   J. monoliths,

69. A. NO CHANGE
   B. 500
   C. 5 hundred
   D. five-hundred

GO ON TO THE NEXT PAGE.

1   1   1   1   1   1   1   1   1   1   1

incorporating universal structure <u>by which</u> one can dis-
70
cern many of the features found elsewhere. In Scotland

<u>are found</u> a special series of menhirs that depict sym-
71
bols, both pre-Christian and Christian, as well as human

figures, angels, and scenes. [72]

    Surely one of the earliest stones to be erected is the

one near present-day Edinburgh in an area that came

under Britannic control by A.D. 480. [73] Christianity

came to this region between the fifth and the seventh

centuries: St. Ninian founded the Candida Case

monastery near Whithorn on the Solway in A.D.

379–398; St. Oran established holy places in Iona,

Mull, and Tiree before A.D. 548. [74] The form of Chris-

tianity was the monastic and hermitic type traditionally

called Celtic, which demanded poverty and obedience

from its clergy, who were all monks. [75]

70. F. NO CHANGE
    G. with which
    H. for which
    J. in which

71. A. NO CHANGE
    B. was found
    C. has always been found
    D. is found

72. Readers are likely to regard the passage as best
    described by which of the following terms?
    F. Fictional
    G. Scholarly
    H. Dramatic
    J. Persuasive

73. How can this paragraph be changed so that it will
    be more meaningful and understandable to a young
    reader?
    A. Include a chart of rock types, listing origins,
        scientific names, and descriptions.
    B. Provide a detailed description of many Euro-
        pean prehistoric stoneworks.
    C. Describe more fully the one stone mentioned
        in the first sentence.
    D. Add a comparison of Easter Island monoliths
        with the Stonehenge monuments.

74. Look over the structure of this paragraph as it has
    unfolded so far. With which one of the following
    characterizations do you agree?
    F. It is surely and soundly organized, consisting
        of a general statement at the beginning that is
        supported throughout.
    G. It is not organized very well. It begins with a
        statement about monastic orders, but does not
        develop that idea.
    H. It is not organized very well. It begins with a
        statement about a stone, but then switches to
        the history of Christianity in the region.
    J. It is not organized very well. It begins with a
        brief history of Britannic rule, and then seems
        to shift to a history of Pict temples.

75. This paragraph would be strengthened by:
    A. supplying more details about the Christian
        leaders.
    B. beginning the paragraph with a general state-
        ment that encompasses the details presented in
        the body.
    C. including a short lesson on rock formation.
    D. defining the hermitic form of Christianity.

END OF TEST 1
STOP! DO NOT TURN THE PAGE UNTIL TOLD TO DO SO.

2   2   2   2   2   2   2   2   2   2   2

Model Mathematics Test
60 Minutes—60 Questions

DIRECTIONS: After solving each problem, darken the appropriate space on the answer sheet. Do not spend too much time on any one problem. Make a note of the ones that seem difficult, and return to them when you finish the others. Assume that the word *line* means "straight line," that geometric figures are not necessarily drawn to scale, and that all geometric figures lie in a plane.

---

1. Which of the following statements about the subsets of real numbers is false?

   A. Every whole number is an integer.
   B. Some rational numbers are integers.
   C. 0 is a nonnegative real number.
   D. 3.14 is an irrational number.
   E. Some integers are negative.

2. Jane's score on her first test was 72%. On her second test she received a score of 81%. What percent increase did she have?

   F. 9%
   G. $11\frac{1}{9}\%$
   H. 12.5%
   J. $88\frac{8}{9}\%$
   K. 112.5%

3. $4^2 - 3 - 5 \cdot 8 - 2[(-3) - (-7)] = ?$
   A. 192
   B. -7
   C. -43
   D. -33
   E. -35

4. Five boxes, each one $2\frac{3}{8}$ feet high, are stacked in a room with a 12-foot ceiling. How much space is there between the top box and the ceiling?
   F. 2 feet
   G. 1 foot
   H. 2 inches
   J. 1 inch
   K. None of these

5. Which of the following inequalities corresponds to the graph?

   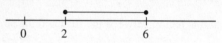

   A. $x \le 6$
   B. $x \ge 2$
   C. $|x - 2| \le 6$
   D. $|x - 4| \le 2$
   E. $|x - 6| = 2$

6. What is the lowest common denominator of the fractions $\frac{5}{4x^2y}$, $\frac{7}{6xy^2}$, and $\frac{-4}{15xy}$?
   F. xy
   G. $30xy$
   H. $60xy$
   J. $360x^2y^2$
   K. $60x^2y^2$

7. What is the complete factorization of the polynomial $4x^3 - 24x^2 + 36x$?
   A. $4x(x - 3)^2$
   B. $x(2x - 6)^2$
   C. $x(4x - 12)(x - 3)$
   D. $x(4x^2 - 24x + 36)$
   E. $4x(x^2 - 6x + 9)$

8. Which of the following numbers is composite?
   F. 1
   G. 43
   H. $\frac{2}{3}$
   J. 57
   K. 83

9. If $a = -3$ and $b = 4$, then $ab^2 - (a - b) = ?$
   A. 151
   B. 55
   C. -49
   D. -47
   E. -41

GO ON TO THE NEXT PAGE.

2 **2** **2** **2** **2** **2** **2** **2** **2** **2** **2**

10. Which of the following is an inscribed angle in the diagram?

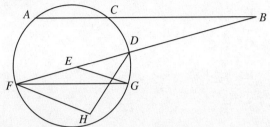

   F. $\angle ABF$
   G. $\angle DFG$
   H. $\angle FEG$
   J. $\angle DEG$
   K. $\angle FHD$

11. Jon starts out on a trip at 40 mph. If $\frac{1}{2}$ hour later

Joel starts out on the same route at 50 mph, which equation may be used to determine how long it will take Joel to overtake Jon?

   A. $40\left(x + \frac{1}{2}\right) = 50x$

   B. $40x + \frac{1}{2} = 50x$

   C. $40x = 50\left(x + \frac{1}{2}\right)$

   D. $4(x + 30) = 50x$

   E. $40x = 50x + 30$

12. If lines l, m, and n are parallel, and $AB = 2$, $AC = 8$, and $EF = 5$, what is the length of $\overline{DE}$?

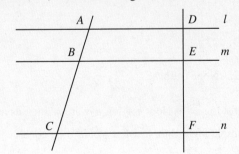

   F. 15

   G. $3\frac{1}{5}$

   H. $1\frac{2}{3}$

   J. $1\frac{1}{5}$

   K. $\frac{3}{5}$

13. $5\frac{1}{8} - 3\frac{5}{6} = ?$

   A. $1\frac{7}{24}$

   B. $2\frac{17}{24}$

   C. $1\frac{1}{2}$

   D. $1\frac{1}{8}$

   E. $1\frac{7}{24}$

14. In the diagram, the right angles are marked and $AB = BC = CD = DE = EF = 1$. What is the length of $\overline{AF}$?

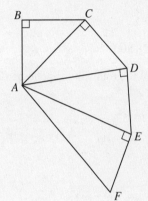

   F. 2
   G. 3
   H. 5
   J. $\sqrt{5}$
   K. $\sqrt{6}$

15. What is the common decimal numeral for one hundred six and twenty-eight ten thousandths?
   A. 106.00028
   B. 106.0028
   C. 106.028
   D. 106.28
   E. 106,280,000

16. What is the solution set for $3 - (x - 5)$
$= 2x - 3(4 - x)$?

   F. $\left\{-\frac{3}{2}\right\}$

   G. $\left\{\frac{3}{10}\right\}$

   H. $\left\{\frac{10}{3}\right\}$

   J. $\emptyset$

   K. $\{5\}$

GO ON TO THE NEXT PAGE.

17. Which of the following is an arithmetic sequence?
 A. $\frac{1}{2}, \frac{1}{4}, \frac{1}{6}, \frac{1}{8}, \ldots$
 B. 2, 4, 8, 16, ...
 C. 2, 5, 10, 17, ...
 D. 5, 11, 17, 23, ...
 E. −1, 3, −9, 27, ...

18. What is the value of i^{53}?
 F. 1
 G. i
 H. −1
 J. $-i$
 K. 0

19. How many 4-person committees can be selected from a group of 10 people?
 A. 1
 B. 40
 C. 210
 D. 5040
 E. 3,628,800

20. Which of the following trigonometric equations is false for all x?
 F. $\sin x = \frac{2}{\sqrt{5}}$
 G. $\tan x = -100$
 H. $\sec x = \frac{\sqrt{3}}{4}$
 J. $\cos^2 x + \sin^2 x = 1$
 K. $\cos x = -0.1439$

21. In the diagram, two chords of the circle intersect at point E. If $AE = 3$, $DE = 5$, and $CE = 2$, what is the length of $\overline{BE}$?

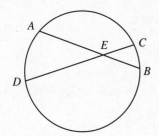

 A. $1\frac{1}{5}$
 B. $3\frac{1}{3}$
 C. 4
 D. $7\frac{1}{2}$
 E. $8\frac{1}{3}$

22. What is the probability of drawing a heart from a well-shuffled standard deck of playing cards?
 F. $\frac{1}{4}$
 G. $\frac{1}{52}$
 H. $\frac{1}{13}$
 J. $\frac{4}{13}$
 K. 1

23. Which expression is equal to $x - [3x - (1 - 2x)]$ when completely simplified?
 A. $-3x^2 + 2x - 1$
 B. $-4x + 1$
 C. 1
 D. −1
 E. $-4x - 1$

24. If $f(x) = 2x - 5$ and $g(x) = 1 + x^2$, then what is equal to $f(g(3))$?
 F. $2\sqrt{2} - 5$
 G. 2
 H. 10
 J. 15
 K. 16

25. If the length of a rectangle is 1 foot less than twice its width and its perimeter is 34 feet, what is the length of the rectangle in feet?
 A. 6
 B. 11
 C. $11\frac{2}{3}$
 D. $22\frac{1}{3}$
 E. None of these

26. If $2 \log_3 x - \frac{1}{2} \log_3 y + \log_3 z$ were written as a single logarithm, to what would it be equal?
 F. $\log_3 \frac{x^2 z}{\sqrt{y}}$
 G. $\log_3 \frac{x^2}{z\sqrt{y}}$
 H. $\log_3 \frac{xz}{y}$
 J. $\log_3 \frac{4xz}{y}$
 K. $\log_3 (x^2 - \frac{y}{2} + z)$

GO ON TO THE NEXT PAGE.

2 **2** **2** **2** **2** **2** **2** **2** **2** **2** **2**

27. Which expression would be appropriate to complete the following equation in order for the equation to illustrate the commutative property of addition: $5(3 + 0) = ?$
    A. $5(3)$
    B. $(3 + 0)5$
    C. $5(0 + 3)$
    D. $5(3) + 5(0)$
    E. $5(3) + 0$

28. In a class of 27 students, $\frac{2}{3}$ are male. Five-sixths of the males in the class received a grade of C. How many male students received a grade of C?
    F. 6
    G. 12
    H. 15
    J. 18
    K. 24

29. Which equation corresponds to the graph?

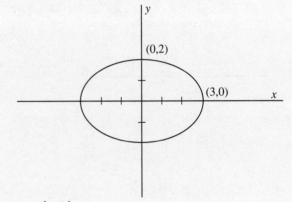

    A. $\frac{x^2}{9} + \frac{y^2}{4} = 1$

    B. $\frac{x^2}{9} - \frac{y^2}{4} = 1$

    C. $\frac{x^2}{3} + \frac{y^2}{2} = 1$

    D. $\frac{y^2}{4} - \frac{x^2}{9} = 1$

    E. $(x - 3)^2 + (y - 2)^2 = 0$

30. Which of the following is a quadratic equation in one variable?
    F. $5(x + 3) + 4 = 2x - 7$
    G. $5x(x + 3) + 4 = 2x - 7$
    H. $5x(x^2 + 3) + 4 = 2x - 7$
    J. $y = 3x^2 + 5x - 7$
    K. None of these

31. What is the solution set of $\sqrt{x + 1} = x - 1$?
    A. $\{0, 1\}$
    B. $\{3\}$
    C. $\{0\}$
    D. $\{0, 3\}$
    E. $\{-1, 1\}$

32. Which expression is equivalent to $\sqrt[3]{-12a^4b^2} \cdot \sqrt[3]{-6a^2b^2}$ in simplest radical form?
    F. $\sqrt[3]{72a^6b^4}$
    G. $-2a^2b \sqrt[3]{9b}$
    H. $2a^2b \sqrt[3]{9b}$
    J. $a^2b \sqrt[3]{72b}$
    K. $2 \sqrt[3]{9a^6b^4}$

33. Given m $\angle ABD = 62°$ and m $\angle BDC = 28°$, what is the measure of $\angle ADB$?

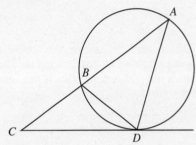

    A. $90°$
    B. $100°$
    C. $118°$
    D. $152°$
    E. $180°$

34. What is the solution set of the following system of equations?

$$2x - 5y = 13$$
$$3x + 2y = -19$$

    F. $\left\{\left(\frac{4}{19}, \frac{4}{19}\right)\right\}$
    G. $\{(-3, -1)\}$
    H. $\{(4, -1)\}$
    J. $\{(-1, -3)\}$
    K. None of these

35. What base eight numeral corresponds to $90_{(ten)}$?
    A. $882_{(eight)}$
    B. $102_{(eight)}$
    C. $110_{(eight)}$
    D. $132_{(eight)}$
    E. $112_{(eight)}$

GO ON TO THE NEXT PAGE.

36. If the measure of arc $ADC = 200°$ and $\overline{AB}$ and $\overline{BC}$ are tangent to circle O, what is the measure of $\angle OCA$?

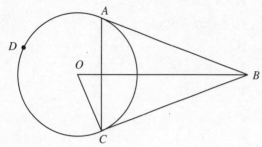

   F.   40°
   G.   20°
   H.   10°
   J.   8°
   K.   5°

37. Suppose that a circular region (radius 2 cm) is cut from a square with sides 9 cm, leaving the shaded region shown in the diagram. What is the area of the shaded region?

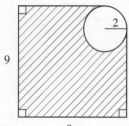

   A. $81 - 4\pi$
   B. $77 - 3\pi$
   C. $78 - 4\pi$
   D. $80 - 4\pi$
   E. $81 - 3\pi$

38. Which statement is always true concerning an obtuse angle?
   F.   It measures less than 90°.
   G.   It measures greater than 180°.
   H.   It is the supplement of another obtuse angle.
   J.   There can be only one in a triangle.
   K.   There cannot be one in a quadrilateral.

39. What is the simplified form of the complex fraction

$$\frac{\dfrac{x}{y} - \dfrac{y}{x}}{\dfrac{1}{x} - \dfrac{1}{y}} ?$$

   A. $x + y$
   B. $x - y$
   C. $-x - y$
   D. $\dfrac{x^2 - y^2}{y - x}$
   E. $\dfrac{x^2 - y^2}{x - y}$

40. Which of the following statements is false?
   F.   All isoceles triangles are similar.
   G.   If two lines are cut by a transversal, the alternate interior angles are equal.
   H.   All circles are congruent.
   J.   The angles of a triangle are supplementary.
   K.   All four of the above are false.

41. Which of the following is the graph of the solution set of the inequality $|x - 3| > 2$?

   A.
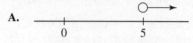

   B.

   C.

   D.

   E.

42. If $\overline{AC} \perp \overline{BD}$, $DE = 2$, $BE = 1$, $EC = \frac{1}{2}$, what is the length of $\overline{AB}$?

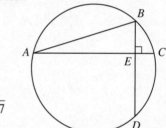

   F. $\sqrt{17}$
   G.   4
   H. $\sqrt{5}$
   J.   3
   K.   2

43. In the diagram, lines m and n in a plane are cut by transversal l. Which statement would allow the conclusion that $m \parallel n$?

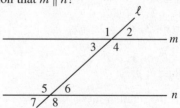

   A. $m \angle 1 = m \angle 4$
   B. $\angle 3$ and $\angle 4$ are supplementary
   C. $m \angle 3 = m \angle 8$
   D. $m \angle 3 = m \angle 6$
   E. $\angle 1$ and $\angle 6$ are complementary

GO ON TO THE NEXT PAGE.

2 **2 2 2 2 2 2 2 2 2 2**

44. How many terms does the complete expansion of $(x + 2y)^9$ have?
F. 8
G. 9
H. 10
J. 18
K. 81

45. Which of the following is NOT a rational number?
A. 0.5
B. $0.\overline{5}$
C. $\sqrt{48}$
D. $\sqrt{49}$
E. 15%

46. What is the period of the following function:
$y = 2 \tan (3x - \frac{\pi}{2})$?
F. 1
G. π
H. $\frac{\pi}{3}$
J. $\frac{\pi}{2}$
K. $\frac{2\pi}{3}$

47. In a windstorm a tower was bent at a point one fourth of the distance from the bottom. If the top of the tower now rests at a point 60 feet from the base, how tall, in feet, was the tower?
A. 100
B. 80
C. $60\sqrt{2}$
D. $60\sqrt{3}$
E. $240\sqrt{2}$

48. Which of the following is NOT the equation of a conic section?
F. $2x^2 + 5y^2 - 2x + 7y - 8 = 0$
G. $y = 3x^2 + 7x - 3$
H. $y = 2^x + 5$
J. $\frac{x^2}{9} - \frac{(y-3)^2}{16} = 1$
K. $(x - 2)^2 + (y + 3)^2 = 25$

49. If $\cos \theta = \frac{-1}{2}$ and θ is in quadrant III, what is the value of $\sin 2\theta$?
A. $\frac{1}{2}$
B. $\frac{-1}{2}$
C. $\frac{\sqrt{3}}{2}$
D. $\frac{-\sqrt{3}}{2}$
E. -1

50. Given quadrilateral *ABCD*, which statement would allow the conclusion that *ABCD* is a parallelogram?

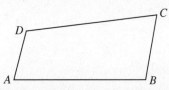

F. $m \angle A = m \angle C$
G. $AD = BC$
H. $m \angle A + m \angle D = 180°$
J. $\overline{AD} \parallel \overline{BC}$
K. None of these

51. What is the standard form of the equation of the line perpendicular to the graph of $2x + 3y = 7$ at point (2, 1)?
A. $x = 2$
B. $2x - 3y = 1$
C. $3x - 2y = 4$
D. $3x + 2y = 8$
E. $y = 1$

52. Which of the following is NOT a real number?
F. $\frac{0}{5}$
G. $3 - 9$
H. $\sqrt{25}$
J. $-\sqrt{7}$
K. $\sqrt{-4}$

53. What is the degree of the polynomial $2^2x^2yz - 2^3x^3yz - 3$?
A. 0
B. 4
C. 5
D. 6
E. 8

54. Tangent line $\overleftrightarrow{AD}$ and chord $\overline{AC}$ intersect at point *A*. If the measure of arc *ABC* = 220°, what is the measure of $\angle CAD$?

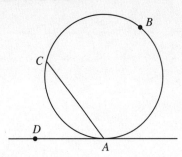

F. 220°
G. 110°
H. 140°
J. 70°
K. 35°

GO ON TO THE NEXT PAGE.

2   2 2 2 2 2 2 2 2 2   2

55. Which of the following is NOT equal to the others?
   A. 0.015
   B. 1.5×10^{-2}
   C. 1.5%
   D. $\dfrac{3}{200}$
   E. (0.3)(0.005)

56. What is the simplified form of $\dfrac{6}{4 - \sqrt{2}}$?

   F. $12 + 3\sqrt{2}$

   G. $\dfrac{3\sqrt{2}}{2\sqrt{2} - 1}$

   H. $\dfrac{4 + \sqrt{2}}{3}$

   J. $\dfrac{12 + 3\sqrt{2}}{7}$

   K. $\dfrac{24 + 6\sqrt{2}}{14}$

57. Which of the following is equivalent to $|x - 5| > 2$?
   A. $x > 7$
   B. $x + 5 > 2$
   C. $x < 3$
   D. $x > 7$ or $x < 3$
   E. $x < -3$

58. In r ABC ($\angle C$ is the right angle), $\overline{CD}$ is drawn perpendicular to $\overline{AB}$ If $AD = 3$ and $BD = 12$, what is the length of $\overline{DC}$?

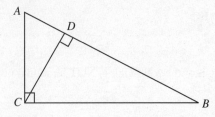

   F. 6
   G. $3\sqrt{5}$
   H. $7\dfrac{1}{2}$
   J. 9
   K. $4\dfrac{1}{2}$

59. Which of the following expressions is NOT equal to cos (–512°) ?
   A. cos 208°
   B. –cos 28°
   C. sin (–62°)
   D. sin 152°
   E. cos 152°

60. The gravitational attraction between two bodies varies inversely as the square of the distance between them. If the force of attraction is 64 pounds when the distance between the bodies is 9 feet, what is the force, in pounds, when they are 24 feet apart?
   F. 5184
   G. 729
   H. 216
   J. 24
   K. 9

END OF TEST 2
STOP! DO NOT TURN THE PAGE UNTIL TOLD TO DO SO.

3 3 3 3 3 3 3 3 3 3 **3**

Model Reading Test

35 Minutes—40 Questions

DIRECTIONS: This test consists of four passages, each followed by ten multiple-choice questions. Read each passage and then pick the best answer for each question. Fill in the spaces on your answer sheet that correspond to your choices. Refer to the passage as often as you wish while answering the questions.

Passage I

HUMANITIES: This passage is from Theodore Gracyk's *Rhythm and Noise: An Aesthetics of Rock*. In this excerpt the author explains the complications of defining musical genres such as rock, pop, and rock and roll.

The distinction between rock and rock 'n' roll was firmly established among rock fans, musicians, and critics by 1967 and was taken for granted in early issues of *Rolling Stone*. Rock is generally understood as popular
5 music closest to, but superseding, rock and roll; it is sometimes contrasted with "pop," which is regarded as more commercial in its aims. Jon Landau reflects common wisdom when he says that "The Beatles, the Stones and Dylan were the first inductees to rock's (as opposed
10 to rock and roll's) pantheon."

Yet critical efforts to delineate rock as a distinct musical genre have been few and have tended to emphasize its cultural impact. Just as Duke Ellington disdained the label "jazz" (he preferred the more inclusive phrase
15 "Negro music"), critic Robert Christgau proposes "semi-popular music" as a better phrase than "rock." It acknowledges that genuine mass popularity, measured by record sales, often eludes influential and critically acclaimed musicians. In 1973, Christgau proposed that
20 rock was "all music derived primarily from the energy and influence of the Beatles—and maybe Bob Dylan, and maybe you should stick pretensions in there someplace." But "influence" covers a multitude of sins. It may seem that their status as songwriters is foremost, but their po-
25 sition as *recording* artists has equal relevance to their status as founders of rock.

Bob Dylan's supposedly commercial sellout of 1965, when he began recording and then playing concerts with an amplified band, is a key event in the break from rock
30 and roll. His self-titled debut album (recorded in 1961) features only two original compositions; the other eleven are blues and traditional folk tunes. Dylan was marketed as a "folk" musician, and subsequently as a protest singer. Critics and fans recognized that the folk and blues

35 traditions predated rock and roll and so regarded them as purer and less commercial than rock and roll. (Muddy Waters, master of the electrified Chicago blues, was also marketed as a folk musician at this time; witness albums with such titles as *Folk Singer* and *The Real Folk Blues*.)
40 The audience for this music typically disdained rock and roll and regarded Dylan's decision to electrify as an abandonment of "genuine" music. So they seem at a loss to comprehend the *aesthetic* motivation for his change of direction. At his second electric concert, at Forest Hills,
45 one fan taunted him with the shouted question, "Where's Ringo?" In the same vein, a reviewer remarked that fans who came for "protest songs … got the Beatles, instead." The Beatles still represented rock and roll, although not for very much longer. Dylan represented something else,
50 supposedly more artistic even if *musically* simpler. "Folk records" were not perceived as commercial and mass-marketed popular music. The irony here is that Dylan was aggressively marketed by Columbia Records, and "Blowin' in the Wind" had been a major hit for Peter,
55 Paul and Mary in 1963.

It is difficult, today, to grasp the anger that was directed against Dylan. His concerts throughout 1965 and 1966 were a nightly repeat of the turmoil that had greeted Stravinsky's *Le Sacre du Printemps* in 1913. Many crit-
60 ics began talking about a "new" and "old" Dylan, as though discussing two different people. One letter to *Sing Out!* took the form of an obituary: "His last illness, which may be termed an acute case of avarice, severely affected Mr. Dylan's sense of values, ultimately causing his un-
65 timely death." And there is that sublime moment, preserved on the so-called Royal Albert Hall bootleg, when someone screams "Judas!" and Dylan drawls "I don't believe you. You're a liar!" before launching a majestic version of his current hit, "Like a Rolling Stone." In
70 retrospect, it seems that popular-music audiences were not yet prepared for the possibility of artists who were stylistically adept and willing to abandon genres as frequently as a snake sheds its skin. In short, while Dylan's songs were acknowledged to be lyrically complex and
75 challenging, the audience was not prepared for any *musical* challenge or surprise. Hence, their sense of betrayal and ensuing anger.

Theodore Gracyk, Rhythm and Noise: An Aesthetics of Rock

GO ON TO THE NEXT PAGE.

1. The author alludes to "Blowin' in the Wind" (line 54) as an example of:
   A. a folk song that became popular.
   B. a protest song.
   C. one of Dylan's greatest hits.
   D. a song that Dylan wrote.

2. According to the passage, Bob Dylan disappointed many of his fans and followers by:
   F. performing music written by people other than himself.
   G. spending more time making records than playing in live concerts.
   H. turning his back on rock music.
   J. switching from folk guitar to electric guitar.

3. The author of the passage attributes Bob Dylan's "sellout" (line 27) to Dylan's
   A. boredom with the same old music year after year.
   B. desire to be different from other recording stars.
   C. wish to make more money in record sales.
   D. attempt to make a comeback after a long time out of the limelight.

4. The term "genuine" music (line 42) refers to:
   F. Duke Ellington's style of music.
   G. music in the folk and blues traditions.
   H. the kind of music played by Muddy Waters.
   J. early Beatles' music.

5. The author refers to Stravinsky's *Le Sacre du Printemps* (line 59) in order to illustrate that:
   A. Bob Dylan often spoke insultingly to his audience.
   B. Stravinsky was a musical rebel.
   C. the piece marked a turning point away from traditional music.
   D. the audience was upset.

6. Duke Ellington said that he played "Negro music" rather than "jazz" (lines 14–15) because:
   F. jazz was too narrow a term.
   G. he knew that white people played jazz, but they wouldn't play "Negro music."
   H. Ellington, a Harlem musician, did not want to be associated with New Orleans jazz.
   J. jazz reminded Ellington of the time his people were slaves.

7. The passage says that the Beatles and Bob Dylan are esteemed figures in the rock music world for all of the following reasons EXCEPT:
   A. they were the first to be installed in rock music's Hall of Fame.
   B. they composed and performed songs that they had written themselves.
   C. they made a huge number of recordings.
   D. they are considered to be among the founders of the entire rock movement.

8. Based on information in the passage, the historical relation between rock music and rock and roll is:
   F. rock music grew out of the rock-and-roll tradition.
   G. rock and roll developed from rock music.
   H. the two types of music grew up independent of each other.
   J. rock music and rock and roll were considered identical until 1967.

9. According to the passage, the term "rock" music is hard to define because:
   A. rock music keeps changing over time.
   B. rock music in its purest form is no longer being written or recorded.
   C. critics and musicians have never agreed on its meaning.
   D. rock music is too diverse.

10. Robert Christgau proposes that a better name for rock music is "semi-popular music" (lines 15–16) because:
    F. not all of the best rock music becomes popular with the public.
    G. rock music is usually not as popular as rock and roll.
    H. rock is mostly second-rate music that tries to imitate the Beatles and Bob Dylan.
    J. today's rock music is rarely as popular as the Beatles and Bob Dylan in their prime.

GO ON TO THE NEXT PAGE.

3 3 3 3 3 3 3 3 3 3 3

Passage II

PROSE FICTION: This passage is taken from the novel *Too Late the Phalarope* by the South African author Alan Paton. In this scene, one character tries to help another overcome a bout of anger and depression.

Yes, I thought to myself, it's in the kitchen that the work is done. My brother must have known it, but he never thought one would be touched by a word of thanks. I felt suddenly tired and old, and pitied myself, and re-
5 membered my lip and that no man had ever wanted me. I do not dwell on these things in my thoughts, you must not think it. I count my blessings, as they say. For the Lord gave me a good home, and a little money of my own, and a brother that for all his ways was an upright man, and
10 just; and a sister-in-law for whom I would any time die. For she gave me her children to be as my own, especially the one, and knew I loved him perhaps beyond all wis- dom, and never denied me. But one does not always count one's blessings; strange it is that one should go from the
15 sweet mood to the black in one brief moment. I went to the pantry and sat down, and stared at the floor.

—Tante, what's wrong?

I started at his voice, for I did not hear him come, but it was too late to put on another face. He came and stood by
20 me, and lifted my rough hands, and turned them upwards and looked at them, and moved his thumbs over them with gentleness.

—What's wrong, he said.

But I would not look at him. He held my hands more
25 tightly, but kept moving his thumbs over their roughness. Then he said, in a voice that meant he would not be silent, I asked you what was wrong.

I pulled my hands away from him.

—Ag, I said, I'm angry that I was born.

30 But he did not comfort or chide me, or tell me not to be a fool, or say come back to the party, or say anything at all. He stood there, not saying anything, not touching me, and I knew that I had put the black mood into him also, and for shame I could not look at him.

35 Then he said, it's I that should be angry I was born.

But I said to him, not looking at him, what do you mean?

But he did not answer me. I got to my feet and took him by the arms, but he looked over me, and I was not
40 tall enough to see his eyes.

—Tell me, I said urgently, tell me.

—Ag, it's nothing, he said, it comes and it goes.

I tried to go back so that I could see his face, but he held me and would not let me, as though it were impor-
50 tant I should not see it until he had time to recover, for he had opened the door of his soul and now repented it. And so strange was this for him, who was himself so strong and sure, and not a man for holding people unless he were in command of himself and them, that I knew it was
55 true that he had opened the door, and that I had forced myself into it, and that he was forcing me out, so that he could shut it again. So I lost my sense, being myself tired and in the black mood, and forgot the bitter lessons that he himself had taught me in the past; and I was *vasber-*
60 *ade,* that is I mean determined, to find out what was wrong. So I went to the pantry door and shut it, and knew the moment I had done it that I had not shut myself in but had shut myself out. He might have said to me Tante, that's enough, or he might have said, must I teach you
65 again, but he did not say that, seeing me standing at the door, and knowing I was already humbled and defeated.

—Tante, he said gently, I told you it comes and goes. What about some coffee?

Alan Paton, *Too Late the Phalarope*

11. The events in the passage take place:
    A. during a party.
    B. at a funeral.
    C. while dinner is being prepared in the kitchen.
    D. after dinner.

12. What is the relationship of the two characters in the passage?
    F. She is the man's sister-in-law.
    G. She is the man's sister.
    H. She is the man's aunt.
    J. They are friends, but not related.

13. The speaker in the passage has gone into the pantry:
    A. to prepare some food for her family.
    B. to look for something she had lost.
    C. because she is hungry.
    D. because she needs to be alone with her thoughts.

14. The speaker's black mood has been brought on by:
    F. her age.
    G. an insulting remark.
    H. self-pity.
    J. loss of love.

GO ON TO THE NEXT PAGE.

15. The speaker feels shame (line 34) in front of the man because:
    A. he has caught her crying.
    B. she has revealed a deep, personal secret.
    C. she realizes that he is in greater despair than she is.
    D. she has infected him with her black mood.

16. The speaker wants to look into the man's eyes (line 40) in order to:
    F. understand his anger.
    G. see if he is telling the truth.
    H. see if he is crying.
    J. let him see that she understands him.

17. The man prevents the speaker in the passage from looking into his face by:
    A. turning around.
    B. holding her close to him.
    C. diverting his eyes.
    D. covering his face.

18. Tante shuts the pantry door because:
    F. she wants to have an uninterrupted talk with him.
    G. noise from the next room is distracting.
    H. they shouldn't be seen together.
    J. the man refuses to speak unless the door is closed.

19. The last line of the passage—"What about some coffee?"—implies all of the following EXCEPT:
    A. The man wants to change the subject.
    B. After an emotional experience, Tante needs something to perk her up.
    C. He's not willing to reveal anything more about his dark mood.
    D. He doesn't want Tante to worry about him.

20. The narrator's overall description of her encounter with the man suggests that:
    F. the two have had similar encounters before.
    G. she often pries into other people's affairs.
    H. the man ordinarily keeps his feelings to himself.
    J. there is a basic lack of trust between the two of them.

GO ON TO THE NEXT PAGE.

3 **3 3 3 3 3 3 3 3 3 3**

Passage III

SOCIAL SCIENCE: This passage is from a monograph titled "When School's Out and Nobody's Home" by Peter Coolsen et al. The passage discusses studies of children's reactions to coming home to an empty house after school.

How do children feel when they come home from school to an empty house or apartment? Do they feel lonely, deserted, resentful, and angry? Or do they feel proud, trusted, responsible, independent, and grown up? 5 Or doesn't it matter very much one way or the other?

One of the most revealing portraits, albeit unscientific, came about as an accidental outcome of a survey by *Sprint,* a language arts magazine published for fourth- to sixth-grade children by Scholastic, Inc. Readers were 10 invited to respond in writing to this theme: "Think of a situation that is scary to you. How do you handle your fear?" The editors got an overwhelming response— probably more than 7,000 letters all told, and 5,000 of them dealt with the <u>fear of being home alone</u>, mostly after 15 school while parents were working.

There are other studies, carefully constructed, that bear out the findings suggested in the responses to *Sprint.* Long and Long report that many children in self-care fear <u>attack from intruders</u> and <u>from other children</u>, particularly 20 siblings. Zill's national survey of children is consistent with these findings. Some 32% of the males and 41% of the females reported that they worried when they had to stay at home without an adult; 20% of both boys and girls admitted <u>being afraid to go outside to play</u>. Rodman and 25 his colleagues, however, report no significant difference between children in self-care and children under the care of adults in a study conducted in a medium-sized city. Rodman contends that studies reporting more fear among children in self-care lack appropriate comparison groups 30 and are subject to interviewer bias. Long and Long respond that their studies have probed more deeply, and that they have done a better job of establishing a relationship with children in which they can express their fear. Another explanation for the discrepancies is that the level 35 of fear for children in self-care varies from setting to setting, being greatest for children in urban apartments (the focus of the Longs' research) and least for children whose homes are in safer small towns, rural areas, or close-knit neighborhoods.

40 Steinberg studied 865 children in grades five, six, eight, and nine in a small midwestern city. He classified their after-school experience on a continuum from "home with parent, other adult, or older sibling" to "unsupervised, hanging out." He found that the less directly 45 supervised the children, the more likely they were to be susceptible to peer pressure (to conform to peer influence rather than make decisions for themselves). What is more,

parents who use an "authoritative" approach rather than "authoritarian" or "permissive" ones have children who 50 are less susceptible to peer influence. *Authoritative* here means parents who ask children for their opinions but maintain ultimate control.

Analyses of the calls children in self-care make to telephone support services provide additional clues to the 55 child's experience. In State College, Pennsylvania, "PhoneFriend" provides a case in point. Of the 1,370 calls received during the first year of operation, 60% were classified as "just want to talk" or "bored," while 19% were classified as "lonely" and 15% as "scared," "wor-60 ried," or "sad or crying." Relatively few dealt with practical emergencies such as cuts and scrapes (4%) or home maintenance problems (3%). (The system allowed multiple classification of each call, which is why those numbers add up to more than 100%.) Who did the calling? 65 Children seven or younger made up 33% of the calls; another 33% were from eight- to nine-year-olds; 17% from ten- to eleven-year-olds; and 17% from children twelve and older. Most (82%) of the PhoneFriend volunteer responses were "affective," i.e., listening and re-70 flecting feelings. Clearly one of the significant issues facing children in self-care is morale and peace of mind.

Peter Coolsen, Michelle Seligson, and James Garbarino, "When School's Out and Nobody's Home"

21. As used in the passage, the term *self-care* pertains to children who:
  A. function well without adult supervision.
  B. participate in experiments of independent living.
  C. return to empty apartments and houses after school.
  D. are legally "neglected" and no longer live with their parents.

22. Steinberg (line 40) found that children often left on their own:
  F. frequently make friends with older people.
  G. rapidly develop independence and self-sufficiency.
  H. spend an excessive amount of time "hanging out."
  J. are more than likely to be followers instead of leaders.

23. An analysis of calls to "PhoneFriend" shows that children phoned for all of the following reasons EXCEPT:
  A. a practical joke or prank.
  B. a feeling of isolation.
  C. boredom.
  D. an emergency situation.

GO ON TO THE NEXT PAGE.

3 3 3 3 3 3 3 3 3 3 3

24. Studies of children's feelings about self-care take into account all of the following factors EXCEPT:
    F. the number of children in the family.
    G. age.
    H. where the children live.
    J. sex.

25. The research studies described in the passage indicate that the GREATEST need of children in self-care is:
    A. help in keeping unwanted intruders away from their homes.
    B. safe places to play.
    C. training in how to deal with emergencies.
    D. help in coping with their fears.

26. On the basis of the passage, which group of words most accurately describes how children feel about self-care?
    F. Disinterested, apathetic, unconcerned
    G. Embittered, resentful, upset
    H. Content, resigned, stoic
    J. Uncertain, fearful, sad

27. The passage states that peer influence is strongest on children whose parents:
    A. are permissive.
    B. fail to communicate with their children.
    C. are strict.
    D. involve them in family decisions.

28. Based on the passage, research findings about self-care are often contradictory for all of the following reasons EXCEPT that:
    F. some researchers use better methods than others.
    G. children are often unreliable sources of information.
    H. some researchers are better able to elicit valid information from children.
    J. researchers often study groups of children with different socioeconomic backgrounds.

29. The author of the passage believes that the findings of the *Sprint* survey (line 8):
    A. should not be taken seriously.
    B. are interesting but not conclusive.
    C. contain information about children's fears too important to ignore.
    D. are enlightening but cannot be supported by evidence from more scientific studies.

30. Which of the following statements would NOT be a valid conclusion to draw from the *Sprint* survey (line 8)?
    F. Children 9 to 11 years old often feel fearful and insecure.
    G. The parents of many fourth, fifth, and sixth graders work outside the home.
    H. Being left home alone is a cause of anxiety among children from 9 to 11 years old.
    J. Children in grades 4 to 6 enjoy writing letters about what scares them.

Passage IV

NATURAL SCIENCE: This passage, from a publication titled "The Health Effects of Caffeine," discusses the complexities of governing the use of caffeine in food and beverages.

The use of beverages that contain caffeine has been debated for centuries. In almost every part of the world where coffee and tea have been available, religious or government leaders have tried to ban or restrict its use. All
5 such attempts, until the present time, lacked scientific credibility.

New studies linking caffeine use to central nervous system problems and birth defects in test animals have prompted scientists and policy makers in the U.S. to
10 reconsider caffeine's regulatory status. This is a complex task, however, because caffeine is regulated under three different sections of the Federal Food, Drug, and Cosmetic Act. It is a natural ingredient in coffee and tea, a food additive in soft drinks, and an added ingredient in over-
15 the-counter drugs.

Foods containing any poisonous or hazardous substance are defined as adulterated and prohibited by the Food and Drug Act. However, foods which naturally contain harmful substances may be permitted if the
20 amount of the substance does not ordinarily injure health. Thus, foods containing caffeine, like coffee and tea, are approved despite caffeine's adverse health effects at high dose levels.

As a food additive, caffeine is regulated as a "gener-
25 ally recognized as safe" (GRAS) substance. Because of this regulatory status, food processors are not required to prove caffeine's safety before adding it to their products. Instead, caffeine's long and widespread history of use is considered sufficient proof of safety. The Food and Drug
30 Administration (FDA) has published rules which limit the amount of caffeine that can be added to foods.

Caffeine is also an ingredient in many over-the-counter drug preparations. The Food and Drug Act specifies that all drug ingredients must be safe and effective for
35 their intended use. Caffeine is an effective stimulant which is why it is added to pain relievers and cold remedies.

GO ON TO THE NEXT PAGE.

3   **3 3 3 3 3 3 3 3 3 3**

When used as directed in these medicines, caffeine is safe and presents no health hazards to the vast majority of consumers.

40   In 1978, a committee of the Federation of American Societies for Experimental Biology reviewed all the scientific evidence on caffeine. Based on caffeine's stimulant properties, this advisory group recommended to the FDA that caffeine be removed from the so-called GRAS list of
45 food chemicals. As a result of this and petitions from other groups, the FDA proposed new regulations for caffeine use in 1980. If these proposals are adopted, caffeine will be removed from the GRAS list. The FDA will also amend the current rule which governs the mandatory use of
50 caffeine in certain soft drinks.

      Removing caffeine from the GRAS list would have little immediate impact on consumers. This action would require food processors to gather additional scientific evidence to prove caffeine is safe. During the time needed
55 to conduct proper studies, caffeine would still be available for use. However, if food processors fail to provide this required information, or find additional evidence that caffeine is harmful, the FDA could take action to ban the use of caffeine as a food additive.

60   Current regulations state that caffeine must be an ingredient in "cola" and "pepper" flavored soft drinks. About 10 percent of the caffeine in these products is obtained naturally from cola nuts, the chief flavoring agent. The remaining 90 percent is added caffeine.

65   Current rules do not require added caffeine other than that naturally present in cola nuts. Added caffeine is an optional ingredient which must be listed on the product label. The caffeine derived from cola nuts does not have to be listed among the product ingredients.

70   Under the new FDA proposal, both natural and added caffeine would become optional ingredients in cola and pepper soft drinks. Thus, manufacturers could make an essentially caffeine-free product by decaffeinating cola nuts and avoiding added caffeine. The new proposal
75 would also require that any caffeine, whether added or natural, be listed on the ingredient label.

      These proposed regulations would not affect the use of caffeine in non-cola soft drinks or in over-the-counter drugs.

American Council on Science and Health,
"The Health Effects of Caffeine"

31. Based on information in the passage, the Food and Drug Administration:
  A. plans to amend the rules governing the use of caffeine in food products.

  B. forces soft-drink manufacturers to keep caffeine in colas and pepper-flavored drinks to a minimum.
  C. makes laws that must be followed by food manufacturers.
  D. pays more attention to caffeine in food products than to caffeine in over-the-counter drugs.

32. Despite its apparent hazards, caffeine has not been banned from food products because:
  F. it has a long and honorable history of use.
  G. consumers can avoid caffeine by reading ingredient labels.
  H. small quantities have never been proved harmful.
  J. food manufacturers claim that the caffeine controversy has been exaggerated.

33. According to the passage, which of the following is most likely to occur if caffeine is taken off the GRAS list?
  A. All soft drinks will be caffeine-free.
  B. Manufacturers will stop adding caffeine to food products.
  C. All food products containing caffeine will be labeled with a warning to consumers.
  D. Manufacturers of food products will be required to prove that caffeine is harmless.

34. "Generally recognized as safe" (lines 24–25) is:
  F. a description of caffeine used by manufacturers of food products.
  G. an official government designation applied to any number of food products.
  H. a phrase called "misleading" by the Federation of American Societies for Experimental Biology.
  J. the FDA's stamp of approval that appears on pain relievers and cold remedies containing caffeine.

35. As used in line 17, the word *adulterated* means:
  A. prohibited.
  B. unlawful.
  C. lethal.
  D. dangerous.

36. Based on the passage, when changes are planned in federal food and drug laws, the government must consider the interests of all of the following groups EXCEPT:
  F. pharmacists who dispense over-the-counter drugs.
  G. manufacturers of food products.
  H. consumer groups.
  J. scientists and other researchers.

GO ON TO THE NEXT PAGE.

3   3   3   3   3   3   3   3   3   3   3

37. Manufacturers of soft drinks add caffeine to their products because:
    A. caffeine makes drinks more flavorful.
    B. consumers enjoy the lift they get from caffeine.
    C. caffeine helps to keep the drink from spoiling.
    D. it is one of the least expensive food additives.

38. According to the passage, past attempts to ban drinks containing caffeine have failed because:
    F. people refused to change their habits.
    G. the tea, coffee, and soft drink industries were too strong.
    H. opponents of caffeine lacked scientific data to back up their objections.
    J. lawmakers could not agree on how to enforce anti-caffeine regulations.

39. Which of the following properties of caffeine is not indicated by information in the passage?
    A. It is addictive.
    B. It has been shown to be hazardous to laboratory animals.
    C. It is found in nature.
    D. It makes sick people feel better.

40. The author of the passage seems primarily concerned with:
    F. procedures for amending the Federal Food, Drug, and Cosmetic Act.
    G. the future of caffeine in foods.
    H. warning readers about the hazards of caffeine.
    J. the need for more scientific investigation of the effects of caffeine.

END OF TEST 3
STOP! DO NOT TURN THE PAGE UNTIL TOLD TO DO SO.

4   4 4 4 4 4 4 4 4 4 4   4

Test 4: Science Reasoning
35 Minutes—40 Questions

DIRECTIONS: This test consists of several distinct passages. Each passage is followed by a number of multiple-choice questions based on the passage. Study the passage, and then select the best answer to each question. You are allowed to reread the passage. Record your answer by blackening the appropriate space on the answer sheet.

Passage I

The charts below show the composition of the average American diet as it exists (solid) and as recommended by the National Research Council (cross-hatched). The kilocalorie is a measure of the energy content of food.

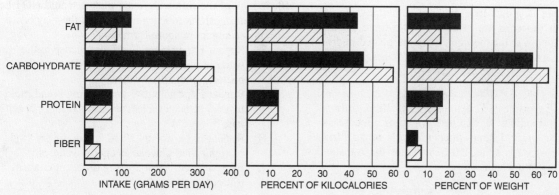

1. If the recommendations of the National Research Council were followed, people would eat:
   A. more protein and less fiber.
   B. more protein and less fat.
   C. more carbohydrate and less fat.
   D. more fiber and less protein.

2. Comparison of the charts shows that:
   F. most of our food energy comes from proteins.
   G. we now get much more of our energy from carbohydrates than from fats.
   H. we cannot increase our energy intake by eating more fiber.
   J. the quantities of fats and carbohydrates in our present diet are approximately equal.

3. According to these recommendations, what comment can be made about the present American diet?
   A. It is overloaded with carbohydrates.
   B. It has too much fiber.
   C. It does not have enough fat.
   D. It contains the proper amounts of proteins.

4. If the recommendations for a changed diet were followed, our diet would have about:
   F. four times as much carbohydrate as fat.
   G. two and a half times as much carbohydrate as fat.
   H. equal amounts of carbohydrate and fat.
   J. nearly twice as much carbohydrate as fat.

5. Comparison of the percent by weight of the different nutrients in the diet and the percent of energy each supplies shows that:
   A. 1 gram of fat supplies more energy than 1 gram of carbohydrate.
   B. 1 gram of carbohydrate supplies more energy than 1 gram of protein.
   C. 1 gram of protein supplies about three times as much energy as 1 gram of fiber.
   D. 1 gram of carbohydrate supplies more energy than 1 gram of fat.

GO ON TO THE NEXT PAGE.

4 4 4 4 4 4 4 4 4 4 4

Passage II

A bacteriologist is investigating the use of glucose by a type of bacterium as a source of energy in spore formation.

Experiment 1

The bacteria are grown in a nutrient solution containing a supply of glucose. When the glucose has been largely depleted, the contents of each cell shrink away from the cell wall and form a spore, which is highly resistant to environmental damage of all kinds.

Experiment 2

A culture of the bacteria is grown in a medium containing little glucose. The bacteria use the glucose as they grow, but do not form spores when the glucose has been depleted.

Experiment 3

A culture is grown in a medium containing ample glucose, but the cells are removed while there is still plenty of glucose in the medium. They are placed in distilled water, and form spores in about 13 hours.

Experiment 4

As in Experiment 3, cells are transferred from a glucose-rich medium to distilled water. If glucose is added to the water 5 hours later, the cells never form spores. If glucose is added 10 hours after the transfer, spores form 3 hours later.

6. Comparison of Experiments 1 and 2 shows that:
   F. glucose is necessary for the bacteria to grow.
   G. the process of spore formation needs a good supply of glucose.
   H. bacteria can protect themselves against unfavorable conditions by forming spores.
   J. spore formation is inhibited by large concentrations of glucose.

7. A reasonable hypothesis from Experiment 3 is that:
   A. distilled water promotes the formation of spores.
   B. distilled water retards the formation of spores, but does not prevent it.

C. bacterial cells store enough glucose to form spores.
D. bacterial cells are able to form spores without any source of glucose.

8. Experiment 1 indicates that spore formation is stimulated by deprivation of glucose. Considering the results of Experiment 4, how long must this deprivation continue?
   F. Less than 5 hours
   G. Somewhere between 5 and 10 hours
   H. More than 10 hours
   J. At least 13 hours

9. In Experiment 4, adding glucose to the distilled water after 10 hours:
   A. causes spores to form 3 hours later.
   B. delays the formation of spores for 3 hours.
   C. speeds up the formation of spores by 5 hours.
   D. has no effect at all on the formation of spores.

10. Which of the following experiments would NOT be useful in efforts to learn more about the way bacteria use sugars in spore formation?
   F. Repeat Experiment 4 adding glucose to the water at various times after transferring the bacteria to distilled water.
   G. Repeat Experiments 3 and 4 using bread molds instead of bacteria as the spore-forming organism.
   H. Repeat Experiments 1 and 2 using other kinds of sugar than glucose as energy sources.
   J. Repeat Experiment 2 using different concentrations of glucose.

11. According to these experiments, what condition must be met in order for this type of bacterium to form spores?
   A. A good supply of glucose in the medium, followed by a period in which there is little glucose
   B. A steady supply of glucose in high concentration
   C. A prolonged period of glucose deprivation
   D. A sudden increase in the concentration of glucose in the medium

GO ON TO THE NEXT PAGE.

Passage III

The graph below represents the number of boys born per thousand girls in the United States for a period of years ($\male$ = males; $\female$ = females).

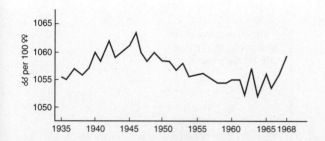

The following graph represents the sex ratio at birth as a function of the ages of the parents. (Sex ratio is the fraction of all newborn babies that are male.)

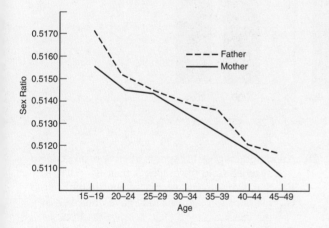

12. The sex ratio in 1946 was:
  F. 1063/2063
  G. 1063/2000
  H. 1063/2
  J. 1063/1052

13. Which general statement is true?
  A. There has been a steady decline in the proportion of male births.
  B. At all times, more boys than girls are born.
  C. The total number of male births decreases with the age of the parents.
  D. Younger parents have more children than older ones.

14. A couple in their early twenties decide that they would like to have a girl. Would it be a good idea for them to wait five years?
  F. No. The probability of having a boy goes up substantially in those years.
  G. Yes. The probability of having a girl goes up substantially during those years.
  H. No. The increased probability of having a girl is too small to make much difference.
  J. Yes. The probability of having a boy goes down substantially during those years.

15. The sex ratio increased during the war years 1940 to 1946, and started to rise again during the Vietnam War in 1967. This increase has been noticed during war years in other countries and during other wars. A possible explanation is that:
  A. many men are killed in wars, so the number of male babies increases to compensate.
  B. as younger men die in the war, more babies are fathered by older men.
  C. prolonged periods of sexual abstinence favor the production of the kinds of sperm that produce male babies.
  D. this may be merely a statistical accident with no real significance.

16. Is it the age of the mother or of the father that is most significant in determining the sex ratio?
  F. The father, since the line for the father lies always above the line for the mother.
  G. The mother, since the line for the mother lies always below that for the father.
  H. They affect the result equally, since both follow the same pattern of decrease with age.
  J. It is impossible to tell from the graphs because people generally tend to marry spouses of about their own age.

GO ON TO THE NEXT PAGE.

4 4 4 4 4 4 4 4 4 4 4 4

Passage IV

The chart below gives the number of diagnosed cases of diabetes in the United States from the years 1958 to 1995, and projections for total cases in 2000 and 2025.

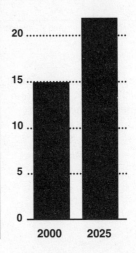

The Diabetes Explosion

Diabetes has skyrocketed in the United States. Below, diagnosed cases over the past four decades

Total projected cases, including those that are undiagnosed

DATA NOT AVAILABLE

Source: National Institute of Health

The New York Times, September 7, 1999.

---

17. Between 1960 and 1980, the number of diagnosed cases of diabetes in the United States increased by:
   A. 1 million.
   B. 2 million.
   C. 4 million.
   D. 6 million.

18. The biggest annual increase in the number of diagnosed cases occurred in:
   F. 1995.
   G. 1991.
   H. 1986.
   J. 1973.

19. It is projected that the number of undiagnosed cases in the year 2000 will be about:
   A. 15 million.
   B. 13 million.
   C. 10 million.
   D. 5 million.

20. An important possible source of error in any conclusion reached from the graphs is that:
   F. data from several years are unavailable.
   G. methods of diagnosis may have improved over the years.
   H. some years show very little increase, while in others, the increase is large.
   J. there is no clue as to the reason for the increase.

21. One assumption made in preparing this chart is that:
   A. there is some increasing factor in the American lifestyle that promotes the development of diabetes.
   B. the trend to increase the incidence of diabetes in the American population will continue for some years.
   C. the health of Americans is increasingly at risk from diabetes.
   D. undiagnosed cases of diabetes are on the increase.

GO ON TO THE NEXT PAGE.

4 4 4 4 4 4 4 4 4 4 4 **4**

Passage V

The ideal gas law is a rule for determining approximately the relationship between volume, pressure, and temperature of a gas. Experiments were done to determine how closely real gases obey this law. These are the gases that were tested, with their respective molecular weights:

Gas	Formula	Molecular weight
helium	He	4
nitrogen	N_2	28
carbon dioxide	CO_2	44
xenon	Xe	54
sulfur dioxide	SO_2	64

Experiment 1

A 1-liter steel cylinder is equipped with a pressure gauge and a thermometer. The cylinder is filled with various gases, in turn, at a temperature of 200 K (–73.2°C). The gases are heated and the pressure is measured at various temperatures. The chart below shows the pressure as calculated from the ideal gas law, and the actual pressures measured at various temperatures.

Temperature (kelvins)	Pressure (atmospheres)					
	Ideal	He	N_2	CO_2	Xe	SO_2
200	1.00	1.00	1.00	1.00	1.00	1.00
500	2.50	2.50	2.51	2.52	2.52	2.54
800	4.00	4.00	4.02	4.04	4.05	4.08
1100	5.50	5.50	5.53	5.56	5.57	5.62
1400	7.00	7.00	7.03	7.07	7.09	7.16
1700	8.50	8.50	8.54	8.59	8.62	8.70
2000	10.00	10.00	10.05	10.11	10.14	10.24

Experiment 2

The same gases are inserted, in turn, into a 1-liter cylinder fitted with a piston that can be pushed in to decrease the volume of the gas, thus increasing the pressure. The cylinder is kept in a water bath that keeps the temperature constant. The pressure is measured at various volumes. As before, the value calculated from the ideal gas law is also listed in the table.

Volume (cm^3)	Pressure (atmospheres)					
	Ideal	He	N_2	CO_2	Xe	SO_2
1000	1.00	1.00	1.00	1.00	1.00	1.00
500	2.00	2.00	2.12	1.98	1.97	1.96
250	4.00	4.02	4.25	3.93	3.85	3.82
100	10.00	10.12	12.32	9.01	8.86	8.55
50	20.00	20.52	34.93	15.87	15.28	13.87

22. If a quantity of gas is heated at constant volume, what might result from using the ideal gas law to predict the pressure?
   F. An incorrect and useless prediction.
   G. A small overestimation.
   H. A small underestimation.
   J. A minor and unpredictable error.

23. Of the gases measured, which behaves LEAST like an ideal gas?
   A. Helium, always
   B. Nitrogen, always
   C. Sulfur dioxide always
   D. It depends on the nature of the experiment

24. What is the most probable explanation of the fact that no deviation from the ideal gas pressure was found when the volume of helium was reduced from 1000 cm^3 to 500 cm^3?
   F. Helium maintains its pressure until its volume is reduced more substantially.
   G. There was an unpredicted drop in the temperature during the experiment.
   H. Measurements were made only to the nearest hundredth of an atmosphere.
   J. Helium is an ideal gas at moderate pressures.

25. As the volume is decreased at constant temperature, what would result from using the ideal gas law to predict the pressure?
   A. Constant minor overestimation.
   B. Either overestimation or underestimation depending on the gas being studied.
   C. Constant underestimation.
   D. Unpredictably, either overestimation or underestimation.

26. Why does the first row of the data for both experiments show a value of 1.00 atmosphere regardless of which gas was used?
   F. Every experiment was started arbitrarily at ordinary atmospheric pressure.
   G. At low pressure, all gases obey the ideal gas law.
   H. Deviations from the ideal gas law are very small at low pressure, and were not detected.
   J. This is pure coincidence; that value might be different if other gases were tried.

GO ON TO THE NEXT PAGE.

27. Which of the following hypotheses is suggested by the data?
  A. The ideal gas law gives the most accurate predictions at high temperatures and pressures.
  B. The ideal gas law always gives a good approximation of pressure.
  C. As a gas is compressed at constant temperature, its pressure is inversely proportional to its volume.
  D. At constant volume, gases with the smallest molecules obey the ideal gas law most closely.

Passage VI

If the highest possible pile is made of a quantity of loose material, the sides of the pile form an angle with the horizontal called the *angle of repose*. This is the largest angle at which the material can remain without having some of it slide down.

The angles of repose of various materials were measured with the apparatus shown in the sketch below. The material, such as sand, is placed in a hopper and then allowed to flow through an opening until it piles up below. The angle of the side of the pile is then measured.

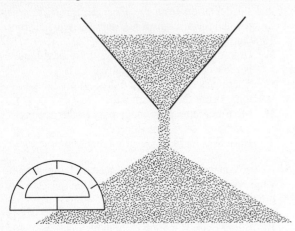

Experiment 1

Smooth, dry, quartz sand, of water-abraded, rounded grains, is sieved and sorted according to size. Each size, separately, is fed into the hopper, and the angle of repose is measured for each.

Grain size (mm)	Angle of repose (degrees)
0.1	18
0.5	20
1.0	23
1.5	25
2.0	28
2.5	30

Experiment 2

Crushed marble, made of dry, sharp-angled fragments of many sizes, is sieved and sorted by size. Each size is then fed separately into the hopper.

Grain size (mm)	Angle of repose (degrees)
1.0	28
1.5	30
2.0	33
2.5	35
3.0	36
3.5	37
4.0	37

Experiment 3

Using the same method, the angles of repose of various other kinds of materials are measured:

Substance	Angle of repose
Crushed marble, unsorted, mixed 1.0–4.0 mm	37
Crushed marble, 3.0 mm, mixed 3 parts to 1 part water	12
Water-abraded sand, 3.0 mm, mixed 3 parts to 1 part water	12
Garden soil, dry	27
Garden soil, slightly moist	46
Garden soil, saturated with water	14

28. The angle of repose depends on:
  F. the size of the particles only.
  G. the particle shape and water content of the material only.
  H. the particle size and shape and the water content of the material.
  J. the particle size and water content of the material only.

GO ON TO THE NEXT PAGE.

4 4 4 4 4 4 4 4 4 4 4 4 **4**

29. The experimenter compares the results of Experiments 1 and 2, and concludes that the angle of repose is larger for sharp-angled than for rounded particles. This conclusion might be challenged because:
   - A. there was no control of the chemical composition of the material.
   - B. no experiments were done with rounded particles larger than 2.5 mm.
   - C. no experiments were done with angled particles smaller than 1.0 mm.
   - D. all angles of repose were measured as accurate to only the nearest whole degree.

30. What is a reasonable hypothesis based on the trials in Experiment 3?
   - F. Wet sand will pile up in taller piles than an equal quantity of dry sand.
   - G. As a pile of water-saturated garden soil dries out, it will slump to form a lower, wider pile.
   - H. Natural abrasion of sand, mixed with water, causes its angle of repose to decrease.
   - J. In a dry sample of mixed sizes, the angle of repose depends on the size of the largest fragments in the mixture.

31. In hilly or mountainous regions, landslides occur during the rainy season. According to the results of these experiments, why is this so?
   - A. Water flowing downhill carries soil along with it.

   - B. When materials are mixed with water, the angle of repose becomes smaller.
   - C. Water abrades the soil particles and makes them smooth and round.
   - D. The slope of the hillsides is less than the angle of repose in the dry season.

32. The results of Experiment 2 suggest a relationship between angle of repose and particle size of angled fragments. What additional kind of material might be used to test this hypothesis?
   - F. Crushed feldspar, sorted at 3.0 mm
   - G. Marble particles 3.0 mm wide, abraded to produce rounding
   - H. Sharp-angled marble fragments 5.0 mm wide
   - J. Rounded marble particles 3.0 mm wide

33. A company in the business of supplying building and paving materials keeps various kinds of sand and gravel piled up in storage. For equal amounts of material, which of the following materials would use the largest amount of land space?
   - A. Beach sand, consisting of rounded grains
   - B. Builders' sand, consisting of sharp-angled grains
   - C. Crushed stone, consisting of sharp-angled particles
   - D. River gravel, consisting of well-rounded particles

Passage VII

People, especially women, tend to lose bone density as they get older, a condition called osteoporosis. Bones weaken and break easily. Two scientists disagree on whether drinking milk is a good way to help avoid the condition.

Scientist 1

For years, nutritionists have been saying that older people, especially women, should drink milk as a protection against osteoporosis. The theory is that milk is a rich source of calcium, which is a crucial element in the building of bones. However, there is reason to doubt that adding milk to the diet is of any value. In many countries, such as China, the dietary intake of dairy products is very small, yet the Chinese have lower rates of osteoporosis than countries where the diet is rich in calcium. Additional evidence comes from a 12-year study of 78,000 nurses, which suggests that milk is of no value. This study found that those who drank two or more glasses of milk a day actually had a slightly increased rate of bone fractures. The reason seems to be that milk is a high-protein food, and other studies have shown that high levels of protein in the diet make the blood more

acid, which tends to remove calcium from the bones. Calcium is only one factor in maintaining bone health; bone building depends not only on calcium in the diet, but also phosphorus, magnesium, zinc, and vitamin D, which are not present in milk. You can get these, and all the calcium you need, from green vegetables, nuts, and beans. Milk is high in fat, and even without milk, there is too much fat in the American diet. A good diet, and avoidance of smoking and excess alcohol consumption provide the best protection. It also helps to have the right genes, but there is nothing you can do about that. What you can do, most of all, is exercise. Muscles exerting forces on the bones stimulate the strengthening of the bones, and this is the most important element in any program to avoid osteoporosis.

Scientist 2

A good supply of calcium in the diet is important not only to maintain strong bones, but also for proper functioning of muscles and nerves. Milk is rich in calcium, and should be used by people growing older. The statistics for Chinese women are misleading; these are mostly rural women, whose high level of physical activity keeps

GO ON TO THE NEXT PAGE.

4 4 4 4 4 4 4 4 4 4 **4**

their muscles and bones healthy. The nurses' study had a basic flaw; its data are questionable because they are based only on what the nurses said. This kind of study is never as valuable as one in which the variables are controlled by the experimenter. In a well-controlled study of 1800 elderly French women, it was shown that those who took calcium supplements had 30 percent fewer hip fractures than those who took placebos. Dozens of other well-designed studies have shown the same relationship. Exercise is vital, but one study showed that it is of no value unless the subject gets at least 1100 milligrams of calcium a day. A pint of milk supplies half of that. Anyone can avoid taking in excess fat with the milk by drinking fat-free milk. While vegetables in the diet are important sources of other vitamins and minerals, it is difficult to get enough calcium and vitamin D from vegetables. Vitamin D is needed for the body to incorporate calcium into the bones, and all our milk now contains added vitamin D. The effect of dietary protein on bone density is still an open question, raised chiefly by ideologically committed vegetarians. In any event, even a pint of milk a day supplies only a small part of the usual intake of proteins. There is still no reason to challenge the time-honored recommendation of nutritionists that older people should drink more milk.

34. The two scientists agree that:
   F. protein is an important component of a healthy diet.
   G. milk contains an element important for maintaining bone density.
   H. older women should take artificial calcium supplements.
   J. vegetables are a good source of the minerals needed for good bones.

35. The chief point of contention between the two scientists is whether:
   A. vitamin D is important for maintaining bone health.
   B. proteins promote osteoporosis.
   C. milk contains a good amount of calcium.
   D. the benefits of milk outweigh its disadvantages.

36. Scientist 2 questions the value of the study of drinking milk in the nurse group because:
   F. nurses are a special group with unique dietary habits.

   G. the data on which the conclusion is based are unreliable.
   H. no attention was paid to the kind of milk that the nurses drank.
   J. no attempt was made to evaluate the level of physical activity of the subjects.

37. Scientist 2 questions the importance of the observations about Chinese women because:
   A. there is an uncontrolled variable in the study.
   B. the sample was too small to be meaningful.
   C. it was not possible to get accurate data.
   D. there was no control group.

38. Scientist 2 expresses doubts about the relationship between osteoporosis and proteins in the diet because it seems that:
   F. the studies done to test the hypothesis were not adequately controlled.
   G. the nutritionists who foster the idea that proteins promote osteoporosis are not unbiased.
   H. no rigid tests were done to find out whether proteins make the blood more acid.
   J. it is well known that proteins are a vital part of any balanced diet.

39. Both scientists would probably agree that one action older women should take to deal with the osteoporosis problem is to:
   A. eat less high-protein food.
   B. take calcium supplements.
   C. drink only low-fat milk.
   D. get regular bone-density examinations.

40. Scientist 1 could question the position of Scientist 2 if:
   F. Scientist 2 has a history of support for vegetarianism.
   G. the studies quoted by Scientist 2 were funded by the Dairy Institute.
   H. new controlled studies showed that an excess of calcium in the diet leads to heart problems.
   J. the National Institutes of Health issued a strong warning against having too much fat in the diet.

END OF TEST 4
STOP! DO NOT RETURN TO ANY OTHER TEST.

ANSWER KEYS AND ANALYSIS CHARTS

MODEL ENGLISH TEST

1.	D	16.	G	31.	D	46.	F	61.	C
2.	H	17.	A	32.	J	47.	B	62.	J
3.	A	18.	G	33.	D	48.	F	63.	B
4.	J	19.	D	34.	H	49.	C	64.	H
5.	C	20.	H	35.	A	50.	J	65.	B
6.	J	21.	B	36.	H	51.	D	66.	H
7.	C	22.	H	37.	B	52.	H	67.	B
8.	J	23.	C	38.	F	53.	B	68.	G
9.	D	24.	F	39.	B	54.	J	69.	A
10.	H	25.	B	40.	H	55.	A	70.	J
11.	B	26.	J	41.	A	56.	H	71.	D
12.	H	27.	B	42.	F	57.	D	72.	G
13.	C	28.	G	43.	D	58.	H	73.	C
14.	F	29.	C	44.	H	59.	B	74.	H
15.	C	30.	H	45.	A	60.	H	75.	B

Analysis Chart

Skills	Questions	Possible Score	Your Score
Usage/Mechanics			
Punctuation	3, 9, 14, 17, 24, 48, 55, 62, 66, 68	10	
Basic Grammar and Usage	1, 2, 6, 19, 21, 23, 34, 50, 53, 69, 70, 71	12	
Sentence Structure	8, 11, 26, 29, 31, 39, 41, 43, 44, 49, 51, 52, 56, 57, 58, 59, 63, 67	18	
Rhetorical Skills			
Strategy	4, 5, 10, 13, 18, 30, 35, 38, 47, 65, 72, 73	12	
Organization	7, 15, 20, 25, 27, 28, 42, 45, 64, 74, 75	11	
Style	12, 16, 22, 32, 33, 36, 37, 40, 46, 54, 60, 61	12	

Total: 75   _____

Percent Correct: _____

MODEL MATHEMATICS TEST

1.	D	13.	A	25.	B	37.	B	49.	C
2.	H	14.	J	26.	F	38.	J	50.	K
3.	E	15.	B	27.	C	39.	C	51.	C
4.	K	16.	H	28.	H	40.	K	52.	K
5.	D	17.	D	29.	A	41.	D	53.	C
6.	K	18.	G	30.	G	42.	F	54.	J
7.	A	19.	C	31.	B	43.	D	55.	E
8.	J	20.	H	32.	H	44.	H	56.	J
9.	E	21.	B	33.	A	45.	C	57.	D
10.	G	22.	F	34.	K	46.	H	58.	F
11.	A	23.	B	35.	D	47.	C	59.	D
12.	H	24.	J	36.	H	48.	H	60.	K

Analysis Chart

Content Area	Skill Level			Possible Score	Your Score
	Basic Skills	**Application**	**Analysis**		
Pre-Algebra Algebra	1, 8, 15, 27, 45, 52, 53, 55	2, 3, 6, 9, 13, 16, 23, 31, 34, 35, 37, 39	4, 11, 25, 28	24	
Intermediate Algebra Coordinate Geometry	17, 29, 30, 44, 48, 51, 56	5, 7, 22, 24, 26, 32, 57	18, 19, 41, 47, 60	19	
Geometry	10, 38, 40, 43, 50	12, 14, 21, 33, 36, 42, 54, 58		13	
Trigonometry	20, 46	49, 59		4	

Total: 60 _____

Percent Correct: _____

MODEL READING TEST

1.	A	11.	A	21.	C	31.	C
2.	J	12.	H	22.	J	32.	H
3.	C	13.	D	23.	A	33.	D
4.	G	14.	H	24.	F	34.	G
5.	D	15.	D	25.	D	35.	D
6.	F	16.	F	26.	J	36.	F
7.	A	17.	B	27.	A	37.	A
8.	G	18.	F	28.	F	38.	H
9.	D	19.	B	29.	B	39.	A
10.	F	20.	H	30.	J	40.	G

Analysis Chart

Passage Type	Referring	Reasoning	Possible Score	Your Score
Prose Fiction	11, 14, 15, 17	12, 13, 16, 18, 19, 20	10	
Humanities	3, 4, 7	1, 2, 5, 6, 8, 9, 10	10	
Social Sciences	22, 24, 27	21, 23, 25, 26, 28, 29, 30	10	
Natural Sciences	32, 33, 38, 39	31, 34, 35, 36, 37, 40	10	

Total: 40 _____

Percent Correct: _____

MODEL SCIENCE REASONING TEST

1.	C	11.	A	21.	B	31.	B
2.	H	12.	F	22.	H	32.	H
3.	D	13.	B	23.	D	33.	A
4.	F	14.	H	24.	H	34.	G
5.	A	15.	C	25.	B	35.	D
6.	G	16.	J	26.	F	36.	G
7.	C	17.	C	27.	D	37.	A
8.	G	18.	G	28.	H	38.	G
9.	D	19.	D	29.	A	39.	D
10.	G	20.	G	30.	J	40.	G

Analysis Chart

Kind of Question	Skill Level			Possible Score	Your Score
	Understanding	Analysis	Generalization		
Data Representation	1, 12, 13, 17, 18	2, 3, 16, 19, 20	4, 5, 14, 15, 21	15	
Research Summaries	6, 22, 23, 26, 28	7, 8, 9, 24, 25, 29	10, 11, 27, 30, 31, 32, 33	18	
Conflicting Viewpoints	34, 35, 36	37, 39	38, 40	7	

Total: 40 _____

Percent Correct: _____

Answer Explanations: ENGLISH TEST

1. **D** The singular subject *one* requires a singular verb, so A and C are wrong. Choice B is incorrect because both the verb *totaled* in the same sentence and the verb in question refer to the year 1999, which is in the past.

2. **H** An objective-case pronoun is required after the preposition *of;* hence choices F and G are wrong. The comma in G and J is unnecessary.

3. **A** The dash is appropriately employed here to dramatize the pathos of *or can.*

4. **J** The first sentence of the paragraph mentions *images,* and therefore calls for description.

5. **C** To present an orderly and economical review of both nursing home extremes, with details characteristic of each type, the best choice of those given is the comparison/contrast strategy.

6. **J** The adverbial clause *than they once were* helps maintain the sequence of tenses in this paragraph.

7. **C** This passage is characterized by quick summaries and sparse detail. It would not be consistent with the rest of the passage to include detailed material.

8. **J** The clause *many of them are unclean and unhealthy* is the best choice because the pronoun *them* refers to the existing *nursing homes;* the other choices introduce a new subject.

9. **D** Parallel adjectives occurring before a noun must be separated by commas.

10. **H** The paragraph is about conditions within nursing homes; the other options touch on related but basically irrelevant subject matter.

11. **B** If the noun *qualities* is used as the subject (A and C), the introductory phrase becomes a dangling participle. *Interested parties* is a better choice of subject than *the patient* (D) because, as the passage makes clear, choosing a home is usually a family undertaking.

12. **H** The phrase *behooves us* (F) is archaic; *best suits us* (G) and *is not a bad idea* (J) depart from the serious tone of the passage.

Answer Explanations: ENGLISH TEST *(continued)*

13. C This article is almost journalistic in style, given to quick summary and unembellished detail. Only a sparse summary paragraph would be appropriate in this context.

14. F The relative pronoun *which,* preceded by a comma, is needed to introduce a nonrestrictive clause.

15. C Paragraph 5 begins with the phrase *For these reasons.* With a quick scanning of the passage, it is clear that the reasons referred to are given at the end of paragraph 3, and that paragraph 5 should follow.

16. G The metaphor in this sentence is that of a loom; the verb *can be woven* maintains the metaphor.

17. A The dash correctly sets off examples.

18. G The term *cultural activities* is the focus of this passage, and yet it is not clearly defined.

19. D The antecedent of the pronoun in question is *rural people.*

20. H Paragraphs 1 and 2 both deal with the concept *cultural activities* and belong together.

21. B The word *that* is needed before the last clause to make it a noun clause. The conjunction *when* (A), *because* (C), or *for* (D) cannot introduce a clause used as a predicate nominative.

22. H *Farther* is used to refer to a measurable distance or space. *Further* means "greater in measure, time, and degree."

23. C Use digits for dates; years are almost never spelled out.

24. F Hyphenate a compound adjective that precedes the noun it modifies.

25. B The first sentence suggests that a heritage festival may begin economic development, but the paragraph as it stands does not pick up that idea.

26. J The preceding sentence makes the point that farms in this area employ a third of the work force. Here the conjunction should be *thus* for that reason. The other options suggest contrast, which is meaningless at this point.

27. B The repetition of the preposition *in* and the noun *farming* or *production* results in parallelism.

28. G The three awkward options employ the phrase *spent its years of existence* in various versions, all of them unnatural sounding. The correct choice is a strong, clear statement.

29. C The pattern in this paragraph has been to give each accomplishment of the Council its own sentence. Also, choices A and B are run-on sentences.

30. H The paragraph does describe economic development, but does not explain how cultural activities "supplied the drive" for such development.

31. D All choices but *most distinguished* are either awkward or unnecessarily wordy.

32. J The most familiar idiom using these words is *method of playing.*

33. D Fine shades of meaning separate these words, but the only sound one to use here is *developed.*

34. H The participle *accomplished* modifies *musician* and is the most sensible choice. *More accomplished* compares *two* musicians.

35. A Classifying and dividing is the strategy that permits a writer full scope in exploring three or more subjects in one passage.

36. H The only meaningful choice is *quality.*

37. B Only the correct phrase conveys meaning that relates to the point being made in the paragraph—the difference in sound between the human and the mechanical piano player.

38. F The statements listing the three most distinguished musical instruments and comparing a player piano with a concert pianist are very opinionated; the passage would be more substantial if some hard data accompanied the opinions.

39. B The statement about the organ is in contrast to those made about other instruments, so a transitional word that indicates contrast is required.

40. H The other options are either redundant (F and G) or inferior (J).

41. A The word *whether* signals the need for the subjunctive mood at this point.

42. F Two characteristics are being considered in the sentence; *pressure* ("hard or soft") and *speed* ("slow or quick"), so each pair should remain intact, the pairs separated by a comma.

43. D *Most acutest* (A) is a double superlative, *more acute* (C) incorrectly suggests that there are only two listeners, and *acute* (B) lacks the force of the superlative and is therefore misleading.

44. H All the other options are awkward and wordy, and are not parallel to *the human organist.*

Answer Explanations: ENGLISH TEST *(continued)*

45. A The point of the passage is to persuade potential buyers to consider an organ.

46. F This phrase, not a common one in popular English, is appropriate to the deliberate, reflective tone of this passage.

47. B Quoted material, when available, is one of the most effective means of representing a person's thought and personality.

48. F The dash is appropriately used here to punctuate a parenthetical aside.

49. C This sentence consists of three clauses ending with predicate adjectives—*broad, (constantly) accumulating,* and *intricate*—each adjective (or adverb) modified by the adverb *so.* The only choice that maintains this parallel structure is C.

50. J The pronoun *that* does not have a clear antecedent here, so a noun should be supplied.

51. D This sentence is in contrast to the ideas expressed in the preceding paragraph.

52. H The past tense is appropriate here. The historical present is usually reserved for discussions of what a writer says or thinks in a particular work of literature.

53. B The pronoun *this* almost never is adequate by itself; a noun is required here for clarity.

54. J This sentence is incompatible in style and content with the rest of the passage.

55. A Coordinate sentences, that is, two independent clauses joined by a coordinate conjunction, must be separated by a comma.

56. H Three parallel prepositional phrases modify the noun *problems* in this sentence: problems *of variability, (of) heredity,* and *(of) isolation.* The object of the preposition is always a noun.

57. D The pronoun *that* refers to the plural *problems,* and the verb must agree. The tense must be the present perfect (*have occupied*) since the reference is to the immediate past.

58. H The present tense is required because natural selection still stands as a general law today.

59. B The statement regarding Darwin's place in history *depends upon* how his theories are regarded in the future—thus the need for the *if* clause at the beginning of the sentence.

60. H If nothing else, this passage praises Darwin.

61. C The use of *throughout* is clear and direct; the other options are awkward or wordy.

62. J There is no need for any punctuation between the parallel adjectives *governmental* and *(many) private.*

63. B The verb *described* completes the parallel pair of passive verbs *are ... marked* and *(are) described.*

64. H The word *unattended* in the preceding clause renders the word *unsupervised* redundant.

65. B An understanding of the word *antiquities* is essential to an understanding of the passage.

66. H Word combinations containing an *-ly* word should not be hyphenated. The adverb *carefully* modifies the adjective *carved,* and there should be no hyphen between them.

67. B Instead of a subordinating conjunction indicating *cause,* what is required here is a conjunction signaling *contrast* (*vertical* versus *horizontal*).

68. G The comma separating items in a series must come after the parenthesis.

69. A Spell out an occasional number that can be expressed in one or two words; with the exception of numbers from twenty-one through ninety-nine, which are always hyphenated, compound numbers are not hyphenated.

70. J *In which* is the only prepositional phrase that draws focus to the structure itself.

71. D The subject of this sentence is the singular *series.*

72. G This passage has all the characteristics of a scholarly paper, including assumption of some sophistication on the part of the reader, close attention to detail, and esoteric language.

73. C The paragraph begins with a bare statement about a significant prehistoric stone, one of the earliest erected. A younger reader would require more detail to understand the significance of such early monoliths.

74. H This paragraph seems to have two main ideas needing development: the stone first mentioned, and the development of Christianity in the region. With two main ideas, the structure is deeply flawed.

75. B The paragraph needs either to be restructured or to be introduced by a general statement that could accommodate both of the ideas present in the paragraph.

Answer Explanations: MATHEMATICS TEST

1. D Although 3.14 is frequently used as an approximate for π, it is rational since it represents $3\frac{14}{100}$ or $\frac{314}{100}$.

2. H Jane's score increased 9 percentage points. The question is "9 is what percent of 72?" $A = 9$, P is unknown, and $B = 72$.

$$\frac{P}{100} = \frac{9}{72}\left(=\frac{1}{8}\right)$$
$$8P = 100$$
$$P = 12.5$$

3. E $4^2 - 3 - 5 \cdot 8 - 2[(-3) - (-7)]$
$= 4^2 - 3 - 5 \cdot 8 - 2[(-3) + 7]$
$= 4^2 - 3 - 5 \cdot 8 - 2[4] = 16 - 3 -$
$5 \cdot 8 - 2[4]$
$= 16 - 3 - 40 - 8 = 13 - 40 - 8 =$
$-27 - 8$
$= -35$

4. K The space at the top is found by multiplying 5 times $2\frac{3}{8}$ and then subtracting the product from 12.

$$12 - 5\,(2\tfrac{3}{8}) = 12 - 5\left(\frac{19}{8}\right)$$
$$= 12 - \left(\frac{95}{8}\right)$$
$$= 12 - 11\frac{7}{8} = \frac{1}{8}$$

(This means $\frac{1}{8}$ of a foot.)

$\frac{1}{8}$ (12 inches) $= 1\frac{1}{2}$ inches

5. D The inequality $|x - 4| \le 2$ is easily translated to
$$-2 \le x - 4 \le 2$$
$$2 \le x \le 6$$
The solution set of this inequality is the set of numbers between 2 and 6 inclusive. These are the numbers shown on the graph.

6. K The lowest common denominator is the least common multiple of the denominators.
$4x^2y = 2 \cdot 2x^2y$,
$6xy^2 = 2 \cdot 3xy^2$,
$15xy = 3 \cdot 5xy$
   To find the lowest common denominator, use each factor the greatest number of times it appears in any of the factorizations.

$$\text{LCD} = 2 \cdot 2 \cdot 3 \cdot 5x^2y^2 = 60x^2y^2$$

7. A The greatest common factor must be factored out first.
$4x^3 - 24x^2 + 36x$
$= 4x(x^2 - 6x + 9)$
(a perfect square trinomial)
$= 4x(x - 3)^2$

8. J Composite numbers are whole numbers, greater than 1, that are not prime. The numbers 1 and $\frac{2}{3}$ are not greater than 1, and 43 and 83 are prime, but $57 = (3)(19)$.

9. E $ab^2 - (a - b)$ $= (-3)4^2 - [(-3) - 4]$
$= (-3)4^2 - [(-3) + (-4)]$
$= (-3)4^2 - (-7)$
$= (-3)\,16 - (-7)$
$= -48 - (-7)$
$= -48 + 7 = -41$

10. G Among the choices only $\angle DFG$ has its vertex on the circle.

11. A

	$D =$	$r \cdot$	t
Jon	$40\left(x + \frac{1}{2}\right)$	40	$x + \frac{1}{2}$
Joel	$50x$	50	x

The distances are equal, so the equation is
$$40\left(x + \frac{1}{2}\right) = 50x$$

12. H Three or more parallel lines cut transversals in the same proportion, so
$$\frac{AB}{BC} = \frac{DE}{EF}$$
$$\frac{2}{6} = \frac{DE}{5} \qquad (BC = AC - AB)$$
$$6(DE) = 10$$
$$DE = \frac{5}{3} = 1\frac{2}{3}$$

13. A
$5\frac{1}{8}$ $5\frac{3}{24}$ The LCD is 24.

$-3\frac{5}{6}$ $-3\frac{20}{24}$

$4\frac{27}{24}$ Borrow $\frac{24}{24}$ from the 5

$-3\frac{20}{24}$ and add to $\frac{3}{24}$.

$1\frac{7}{24}$

14. J Use the Pythagorean Theorem to first find the length of $\overline{AC}$.
$$(AC)^2 = 1^2 + 1^2$$
$$AC = \sqrt{2}$$
   Then $\overline{AC}$ is a leg of $\triangle ACD$. Another application of the Pythagorean Theorem yields
$$(AC)^2 + (CD)^2 = (AD)^2$$
$$(\sqrt{2})^2 + 1^2 = (AD)^2$$
$$2 + 1 = (AD)^2$$
$$AD = \sqrt{3}$$
Repeating this process two more times gives $AF = \sqrt{5}$.

Answer Explanations: MATHEMATICS TEST *(continued)*

15. B The last digit must be in the ten thousandths position.

16. H $3 - (x - 5) = 2x - 3(4 - x)$
$3 - x + 5 = 2x - 12 + 3x$
$8 - x = 5x - 12$
$8 = 6x - 12$
$20 = 6x$
$x = \dfrac{20}{6} = \dfrac{10}{3}$

17. D An arithmetic sequence is one whose successive terms differ by a constant. Only in D is there a constant difference between terms.

18. G If the exponent on i is a multiple of 4, the result is 1. But if there is a remainder when the exponent is divided by 4, then it has the following values:

rem	i^n
1	i
2	-1
3	$-i$
0	1

$53 \div 4 = 13$ rem 1, so $i^{53} = i$.

19. C This is a combination problem. The number of combinations of n things taken r at a time is given by the formula:

$$_nC_r = \frac{n!}{(n-r)!\,r!}$$

The number of 4-person committees is

$$_{10}C_4 = \frac{10!}{(10-4)!\,4!}$$

$$= \frac{10!}{6!\,4!}$$

$$= \frac{10 \cdot 9 \cdot 8 \cdot 7 \cdot 6!}{6! \cdot 4 \cdot 3 \cdot 2 \cdot 1}$$

$$= \frac{10 \cdot 3 \cdot 7}{1} = 210$$

20. H Since $\dfrac{\sqrt{3}}{4} < 1$ and the range of the secant function is $\{x \mid x > 1 \text{ or } x < -1\}$, there are no angles for which $\sec x = \dfrac{\sqrt{3}}{4}$.

21. B If two chords intersect in a circle, the product of the segments of one chord equals the product of the lengths of the segments of the other.
$3x = (5)(2)$
$\quad = 10$
$x = 3\frac{1}{3}$

22. F The sample space consists of all 52 cards in the deck. The event "drawing a heart" can be satisfied by any one of the 13 hearts.
$$P(\text{Heart}) = \frac{13}{52} = \frac{1}{4}.$$

23. B $x - [3x - (1 - 2x)] = x - [3x - 1 + 2x]$
$\qquad\qquad\qquad\qquad = x - 3x + 1 - 2x$
$\qquad\qquad\qquad\qquad = -4x + 1$

24. J If $g(x) = 1 + x^2$, then
$g(3) = 1 + 3^2 = 1 + 9 = 10$. So
$f(g(3)) = f(10) = 2(10) - 5 = 20 - 5 = 15$

25. B Let x = width of the rectangle.
Then $2x - 1$ = length.
  The perimeter of a rectangle is found by the formula $P = 2w + 2L$. The equation is

$34 = 2x + 2(2x - 1)$
$34 = 2x + 4x - 2$
$34 = 6x - 2$
$36 = 6x$
$x = 6$

But $x = 6$ is the width. The question is "What is the length?"
$2x - 1 = 2(6) - 1 = 12 - 1 = 11$

26. F $2 \log_3 x - \dfrac{1}{2} \log_3 y + \log_3 z$
$= \log_3 x^2 - \log_3 \sqrt{y} + \log_3 z$
$= \log_3 \dfrac{x^2 z}{\sqrt{y}}$

27. C By the commutative property of addition
$$5(3 + 0) = 5(0 + 3)$$

28. H The number of male students receiving a grade of C is $\dfrac{5}{6}$ of $\dfrac{2}{3}$ of 27.
$\dfrac{5}{6} \cdot \dfrac{2}{3} \cdot 27 = \dfrac{5}{6} \cdot 18$
$\qquad\qquad = 15$

29. A An equation of an ellipse with center at the origin, x-intercepts 3 and -3, and y-intercepts 2 and -2 is
$$\frac{x^2}{9} + \frac{y^2}{4} = 1$$

30. G The equation $5x(x + 3) + 4 = 2x - 7$ is equivalent to $5x^2 + 13x + 11 = 0$. This is a quadratic equation in one variable.

31. B Square both sides of the radical equation.
$(\sqrt{x + 1})^2 = (x - 1)^2$
$\qquad x + 1 = x^2 - 2x + 1$
$\qquad x^2 - 3x = 0$

Answer Explanations: MATHEMATICS TEST *(continued)*

$$x(x - 3) = 0$$
$$x = 0 \quad x - 3 = 0$$
$$x = 3$$

Both potential solutions must be checked in the original equation.

Check 0: $\sqrt{0 + 1} \overset{?}{=} 0 - 1$
$$1 \ne -1$$
0 is not in the solution set.

Check 3: $\sqrt{3 + 1} \overset{?}{=} 3 - 1$
$$\sqrt{4} \overset{?}{=} 2$$
$$2 = 2 \quad \text{The solution set is } \{3\}.$$

32. H $\sqrt[3]{-12a^4b^2} \ \sqrt[3]{-6a^2b^2} = \sqrt[3]{72a^6b^4}$

Now separate the radicand into cube and noncube factors.
$$= \sqrt[3]{8a^6b^3 \cdot 9b}$$
$$= 2a^2b \sqrt[3]{9b}$$

33. A If m $\angle ABD = 62°$, then the measure of arc $AD = 124°$. If m $\angle BDC = 28°$, then the measure of arc $BD = 56°$. So the measure of arc $ADB = (56 + 124)° = 180°$, and the measure of an angle inscribed in a semicircle = $90°$.

34. K Multiply the top equation by 2 and the bottom equation by 5.
$$2(2x - 5y) = 13$$
$$5(3x + 2y) = -19$$
This gives
$$4x - 10y = 26$$
$$\underline{15x + 10y = -95}$$
$$19x = -69$$
$$x = \frac{-69}{19}$$
None of the choices has this value for x.

35. D $90 \div 8 = 11$ remainder $\underline{2}$
$11 \div 8 = \underline{1}$ remainder $\underline{3}$
The last quotient and the remainders in reverse order give the digits in the proper order. The answer is D.

36. H The measure of
$$\angle ABC = \frac{1}{2}(200 - 160)° = 20°.$$
$\triangle ABC$ is an isosceles triangle, so $\angle ACB = 80°$. Since a radius is perpendicular to a tangent at the point of tangency, $\angle OCA = (90 - 80)°$.

37. B In reality the shaded portion represents the big square minus $\frac{3}{4}$ of the circle minus a small 2×2 square.

$$9^2 - \frac{3}{4}(\pi 2^2) - 2^2 = 81 - 3\pi - 4$$
$$= 77 - 3\pi$$

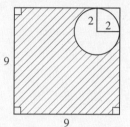

38. J There can be only one obtuse angle in a triangle.

39. C Multiply the numerator and denominator by xy:

$$\frac{xy\left(\frac{x}{y} - \frac{y}{x}\right)}{xy\left(\frac{1}{x} - \frac{1}{y}\right)} = \frac{x^2 - y^2}{y - x}$$
$$= \frac{(x - y)(x + y)}{y - x}$$
$$= -(x + y) \text{ because } y - x$$
and $x - y$ are opposites.

40. K All four statements are false.

41. D $|x - 3| > 2$ is equivalent to
$$x - 3 > 2 \text{ or } x - 3 < -2$$
$$x > 5 \text{ or } x < 1$$

42. F First find AE.
$$(BE)(ED) = (AE)(EC)$$
$$(1)(2) = AE\left(\frac{1}{2}\right)$$
$$AE = 4$$
Then use the Pythagorean Theorem.
$$4^2 + 1^2 = (AB)^2$$
$$16 + 1 = (AB)^2$$
$$AB = \sqrt{17}$$

43. D If two lines are cut by a transversal in such a way that a pair of alternate interior angles are equal, the lines are parallel.

44. H The binomial expansion of $(a + b)^n$ has $n + 1$ terms.

45. C The only one of these numbers that cannot be written as a fraction is $\sqrt{48}$. Note that $0.\overline{5} = 0.5555 \ldots$ is a nonterminating repeating decimal, which is rational.

46. H The period of the function $y = a \tan b(x - c)$ is $\frac{\pi}{|b|}$. So the period of the given function is $\frac{\pi}{3}$ since this function can be rewritten as $y = 2 \tan 3(x - \frac{\pi}{6})$.

Answer Explanations: MATHEMATICS TEST *(continued)*

47. C Let x = height of the tower. Then the distance from the ground to the bend is $\frac{x}{4}$, and the slanted part is $\frac{3x}{4}$. Use the Pythagorean

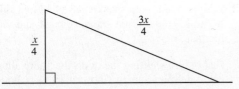

Theorem:
$$\left(\frac{x}{4}\right)^2 + 60^2 = \left(\frac{3x}{4}\right)^2$$
$$\frac{x^2}{16} + 60^2 = \frac{9x^2}{16}$$
$$\frac{8x^2}{16} = \frac{x^2}{2} = 60^2$$
$$x^2 = 2(60^2)$$
$$x = 60\sqrt{2}$$

48. H Exponential functions do not represent conic sections.

49. C If $\cos\theta = \frac{-1}{2}$ and θ is in quadrant III, then
$$\sin\theta = -\sqrt{1 - \cos^2\theta}$$
$$= -\sqrt{1 - \left(\frac{-1}{2}\right)^2} = -\sqrt{1 - \frac{1}{4}}$$
$$= -\sqrt{\frac{3}{4}} = -\frac{\sqrt{3}}{2}$$
$$\sin 20 = 2\sin\theta\cos\theta$$
$$= 2\left(\frac{-\sqrt{3}}{2}\right)\left(\frac{-1}{2}\right)$$
$$= \frac{\sqrt{3}}{2}$$

50. K None of these choices is enough to prove that *ABCD* is a parallelogram.

51. C The slope of the given line can be found from the slope-intercept form:
$$y = \frac{-2}{3}x + \frac{7}{3}$$

Since the slope is $\frac{-2}{3}$, the slope of the line perpendicular to it is $\frac{3}{2}$. Using the point-slope form of the equation of the line, we have
$$y - 1 = \frac{3}{2}(x - 2)$$
$$2y - 2 = 3x - 6$$
$$3x - 2y = 4$$

52. K Square roots of negative numbers are imaginary.

53. C Degree concerns itself only with the exponents on the *variables*. The degree of a polynomial is the greatest of the degrees of its terms. The degree of the first term is 4; of the second term, 5; and of the third, 0.

54. J The measure of arc $AC = (360 - 220)° = 140°$. The angle formed by a chord and a tangent line is measured by half of the intercepted arc. The measure of $\angle CAD = 70°$.

55. E 0.015
$$1.5 \times 10^{-2} = 0.015$$
$$1.5\% = 0.015$$
$$\frac{3}{200} = 0.015$$
$$(0.3)(0.005) = 0.0015$$

56. J Multiply the numerator and denominator by the conjugate of the denominator.
$$\frac{6(4 + \sqrt{2})}{(4 - \sqrt{2})(4 + \sqrt{2})} = \frac{6(4 + \sqrt{2})}{16 - 2} = \frac{6(4 + \sqrt{2})}{14}$$
$$= \frac{3(4 + \sqrt{2})}{7} = \frac{12 + 3\sqrt{2}}{7}$$

57. D $|x - 5| > 2$ is equivalent to
$$x - 5 > 2 \quad \text{or} \quad x - 5 < -2$$
$$x > 7 \quad \text{or} \quad x < 3$$

58. F The altitude to the hypotenuse of a right triangle is the mean proportional between the two segments of the hypotenuse.
$$\frac{AD}{DC} = \frac{DC}{BD}$$
$$\frac{3}{DC} = \frac{DC}{12}$$
$$(DC)^2 = 36$$
$$DC = 6$$

59. D $\cos(-512°) = \cos(208°)$
Add $2(360°)$ to the angle. The reference angle is $(208 - 108)°$. Cofunctions of complementary angles are equal. $-62°$ is in Quadrant IV, where the sine is negative.

60. K
$$g = \frac{k}{d^2}$$
$$64 = \frac{k}{9^2}$$
$$k = 64(81)$$
$$g = \frac{64(81)}{24^2}$$
$$= \frac{8 \cdot 8(9 \cdot 9)}{(8 \cdot 3)(8 \cdot 3)}$$
$$= 9 \qquad \text{This can be obtained easily by canceling.}$$

Answer Explanations: READING TEST

1. **A** Because folk-type songs rarely became commercial successes, the author cites "Blowin' in the Wind" as an exception to the rule.

2. **J** In lines 39–40, the author says that Dylan's "decision to electrify" upset Dylan's audience.

3. **C** By using the word *commercial* to describe the sellout, the author suggests that Dylan's change was not an artistic, but a financial, decision.

4. **G** In lines 33–35, the passage says that because "the folk and blues tradition predated rock and roll, it was purer," or more genuine, than rock and roll.

5. **D** The reference is to show how angry Dylan's audience had become when he changed his style of music in the mid-1960s.

6. **F** Ellington preferred "the more inclusive phrase "Negro music,'" indicating that jazz was only one type of music that he performed.

7. **A** Lines 22–25 indicate ways in which the Beatles and Dylan have influenced rock music. Their membership in the Hall of Fame is not mentioned.

8. **G** The first paragraph states that rock supersedes rock and roll; that is, it is the larger musical form from which rock and roll emerged.

9. **D** The passage states that rock music, although generally regarded as "popular" music, consists of many different forms.

10. **F** In lines 17–19, the passage explains Christgau's view that "genuine mass popularity, as measured by record sales, often eludes influential and critically acclaimed musicians."

11. **A** In line 31 the speaker refers to a party in progress.

12. **H** In line 17, the man calls the woman "Tante," a common name for an aunt. Also in the first paragraph, she mentions one of her brother's children whom she loved "perhaps beyond all wisdom" (line 12). The man may very well be that person, her nephew.

13. **D** The speaker's behavior suggests that, in her sudden black mood, she escaped to the pantry to be alone: "I went to the pantry and sat down, and stared at the floor" (lines 15–16).

14. **H** Lines 3–5 indicate that she pities herself after she remembers her lip (presumably deformed in some way) and that no man had ever wanted her. Once the black mood overcomes her, she feels "suddenly tired and old."

15. **D** Her shame results from putting the black mood into him also (line 33).

16. **F** Attempting to draw out an explanation of his anger, she tries to make eye contact with him.

17. **B** In lines 43–44, the speaker says that he held on to her to keep her from standing back and viewing his face.

18. **F** Just before shutting the door, the Tante alludes to her determination to find out what is bothering the man. Closing the door is a sign of her resolve to get to the bottom of his dark mood.

19. **B** The man's question suggests that the episode is over and that he no longer wishes to discuss it. It also indicates that his dark mood is over. As he says, "it comes and goes" (line 62).

20. **H** According to lines 45–49, it was "strange" for this man to open his soul to others. Having done it briefly, he now regrets it.

21. **C** The author's concern is children returning to empty homes after school.

22. **J** The passage states explicitly (lines 44–47) that children with little supervision are highly susceptible to peer pressure.

23. **A** The telephone calls cited in lines 57–62 were serious ones. The children needed to talk with someone; they never called just for fun.

24. **F** The number of children in the family is not mentioned in the passage.

25. **D** All the problems are mentioned in the passage, but the subject of children's fears (lines 14–24, 59–60, and 71) receives the most attention.

26. **J** The passage emphasizes that many children are unhappy and scared when they have to take care of themselves.

27. **A** Steinberg's study (line 49) shows that children of permissive parents are most apt to be influenced by peers.

28. **F** Researchers challenge each other's findings for many different reasons, but not by criticizing their colleagues' methods.

29. **B** The author thinks the findings were revealing but in need of support from research conducted more scientifically.

30. **J** Although 7000 children wrote letters, the paragraph does not indicate that they enjoyed writing them.

Answer Explanations: READING TEST *(continued)*

31. C The FDA's legal powers are implied throughout the passage.

32. H According to lines 18–23, caffeine in small amounts poses no threat to health. Adverse effects come only from high doses.

33. D Lines 52–54 state that this action "would require food processors to gather additional scientific evidence to prove caffeine is safe."

34. G The GRAS designation comes from the Federal Food, Drug, and Cosmetic Act, which regulates the ingredients of all processed foods.

35. D *Adulterated* usually means impure. Here, however, the word means excessively impure, or dangerous.

36. F The concerns and interests of pharmacists are not mentioned in the passage.

37. A Caffeine comes from cola nuts, a flavoring agent.

38. H Lines 4–6 say that previous attempts to ban or restrict the use of beverages containing caffeine "lacked scientific credibility."

39. A The addictive quality of caffeine is not stated anywhere in the passage.

40. G The passage concentrates on what will happen if regulations governing the use of caffeine are changed.

Answer Explanations: SCIENCE REASONING TEST

1. C The intake chart shows that the recommended carbohydrate is more than the carbohydrate consumed, and the recommended fat is less than the fat consumed. The other choices are wrong because there is no recommendation for a change in the protein.

2. H The energy chart shows that fiber supplies no energy at all. F is wrong because the energy chart shows much less energy from protein than from carbohydrates or fats. Since the chart shows about equal amounts of energy now obtained from fats and carbohydrates, G is wrong. J deals with quantity, not energy, and the intake chart shows that the quantity of carbohydrates is far greater than the amount of fat.

3. D The two bars match perfectly for protein intake. A is wrong because the bar for recommended carbohydrate is longer than that for actual intake. Similarly, more, not less, fiber is recommended, so B is wrong. C is wrong because the recommended diet is reduced in fat.

4. F The bars for recommended intake show about 80 g of fat and 330 g of carbohydrate.

5. A When the values for present diet are used, fats are about 23% of our diet by weight, and supply 43% of our energy; carbohydrates constitute 58% of our food, but give us only 45% of our energy. B is wrong because the ratio of percent by weight to energy for carbohydrates (58%/45%) is about the same as the ratio for proteins (16%/13%). C is wrong because fiber supplies no energy at all, and 3 times 0 is 0. D is the opposite of A.

6. G In Experiment 2, where there was little glucose, the bacteria were unable to form spores. F is wrong because no data about growth were presented. H is wrong because Experiments 1 and 2 have nothing to do with the usefulness of spores. J is wrong because Experiment 1 shows that glucose actually promotes spore formation.

7. C Since Experiment 1 shows that glucose is needed, and there is none in distilled water, it is quite likely that the bacterial cells stored glucose when it was available. A and D are wrong because Experiment 1 shows that the bacteria need glucose to form spores. B is wrong because we have no data indicating how long it took to form spores when there is plenty of glucose.

8. G Experiment 4 shows that if glucose is added in less than 5 hours spore formation is prevented, but if it is added after 10 hours spores form anyway.

9. D In Experiment 3, spores formed 13 hours after the cells were put into distilled water; in Experiment 4, the same thing happened, even though glucose was added after 10 hours.

10. G Bread mold spores are entirely different from bacterial spores, and there is no reason to believe that any similarity exists in the way they are formed.

11. A In both Experiment 1 and Experiment 3, spores were formed when a period of growth in an ample supply of glucose was followed by glucose deprivation. B is wrong because no spores are

Answer Explanations: SCIENCE REASONING TEST (continued)

formed as long as there is plenty of glucose in the medium. Experiment 2 shows that no spores can be formed unless there is first an ample supply of glucose, so C is wrong. There is no evidence anywhere to support D.

12. F Adding male births (1063) and female births (1000) gives a total of 2063; males are 1063 of this total.

13. B Although the sex ratio went down, it then went up, and was always more than 0.5, which would indicate equal numbers of boys and girls. No information was given about total numbers.

14. H While parents are in their twenties, the sex ratio decreases by only about 1 or 2 parts per thousand, not enough to take into account.

15. C A is wrong because it is not an explanation, since it fails to suggest a mechanism by which the result is brought about. B is wrong because the second graph indicates that older men produce a smaller fraction of boys, not a larger one. D is wrong; you are told that this effect has been noticed in many wars and many countries, so it is unlikely that this result is coincidental. By elimination, C is the only feasible answer of those offered.

16. J Since spouses are generally only a little different in age, there is no way that the graphs can distinguish the effect of the mother's age from that of the father's.

17. C In 1960 it was about 1.5 million; in 1980, about 4.5 million.

18. G The difference between the 1990 bar and the 1991 bar is more than one million, larger than any of the other yearly jumps. The 1973 bar is longer than the 1968 bar by the same amount, but the intervening years are missing.

19. D If the present trend continues for another 5 years, the number of diagnosed cases will be about 10 million in the year 2000. Since the total for that year is expected to be 15 million, 5 million will be undiagnosed.

20. G It is possible that part, or even all, of the increase is simply because more cases are being found. F is wrong; the steady increase is apparent even without those years. H is wrong because the minor fluctuations do not negate the overall trend. J is wrong because the only function of the graph is to show the trend, without ascribing any cause.

21. B The chart predicts 22 million cases by 2025,

more than double the rate of 1995. A is wrong because the chart makes no statement as to the cause of the increase. C is a valid conclusion from the chart, not an assumption. D is wrong because there is nothing in the yearly data that gives any indication of the number of undiagnosed cases.

22. H The actual pressures are always a little higher than those predicted by the ideal gas law; using this law will give an underestimation, so G is wrong. F is wrong because the error is small and the value calculated would be good enough for many purposes. J is wrong because the error is not unpredictable once the special properties of each gas are known.

23. D Nitrogen deviates most from ideal values in the pressure-volume experiment, but sulfur dioxide deviates most in the temperature-volume experiment. In all cases, helium behaves most like an ideal gas.

24. H It is probable that the pressure rose to, say, 2.001 atmospheres, which would not have been detected at the level of accuracy to which the experiment was done. F is wrong because the pressure actually doubled when the volume dropped to half. Don't insult the experimenter by answering G. It is never safe to conclude that additional accuracy would not reveal something different, so J is wrong.

25. B At all volumes, helium and nitrogen had higher pressures than predicted; and carbon dioxide, xenon, and sulfur dioxide had lower pressures. The result can be predicted once you know which gas is being studied.

26. F You have to start the experiment with some gas in the cylinder, and the experimenter decides how much and at what pressure and temperature. Why bother to use anything but what is already there?

27. D The pressure-temperature chart shows no detectable deviation for the smallest molecules (helium) and successively more for each of the larger molecules. Deviations from the ideal gas law get larger, not smaller, as the pressure goes up. C expresses the ideal gas law; the whole burden of this experiment is to test deviations from this law.

28. H Experiments 1 and 2 show that the angle of repose increases with grain size. Comparison of these two experiments shows that sharp-angled fragments have a larger angle of repose than rounded ones. The soil samples of Experiment 3 show that water content is also involved.

Answer Explanations: SCIENCE REASONING TEST *(continued)*

29. A The two experimental materials differ in both shape and composition of the particles, and no effort was made to distinguish between these two possible causes of the difference found. B and C are wrong because the evidence from particles from 1.0 to 2.5 mm, in both experiments, provides a clear contrast. D is wrong because the differences are of several degrees and are consistent, so accuracy of 1 degree is sufficient to produce an answer.

30. J The angle of repose for the mixed sample of crushed marble is the same as for the largest size of the screened samples. F is wrong because the angle of repose is smaller for wet than for dry sand, so the pile of wet sand will be lower than the pile of dry. G is wrong because the angle of repose is smaller for the saturated soil; the pile becomes more stable as it dries out. H is wrong because two of the results in Experiment 3 show no difference between rounded and sharp-angled fragments, as long as both are very wet.

31. B The soil is piled up, possibly to its angle of repose when dry. When it gets wet, the angle of repose decreases, so the angle of the hill is larger than the new angle of repose. A is wrong because the experiments do not deal with the effects of running water. C is wrong because the particles are not abraded as they rest during the dry season. D is surely true, but it says nothing about the effect of rain.

32. H The hypothesis must be that the angle of repose does not increase for particles beyond 3.5 mm, and this can be tested by trying larger particles.

33. A The experiments show that small, rounded particles have the smallest angle of repose. They will form lower, flatter piles and thus will spread out more on the ground.

34. G Both stress the importance of dietary calcium for the prevention of osteoporosis. F is wrong because neither scientist raises the question of the importance of protein. Scientist 1 thinks vegetables are an adequate source of calcium and supplements are unnecessary; Scientist 2 doubts that vegetables are an adequate source.

35. D Scientist 2 believes that milk is by far the best dietary source of bone-building calcium, and casts doubt on its supposed disadvantage. Both agree that vitamin D is important and that there is a great deal of calcium in milk. Scientist 2 is not convinced that proteins are harmful.

36. G Scientist 2 points out that the only source of data is the statements of the nurses themselves as to how much milk they drink, and there were no independent assessments. While the other choices might be legitimate objections to the study, they were not made by the scientist.

37. A The variable is the level of physical activity, which is known to promote good bones and might be the reason for the difference. Accuracy of the data and size of the sample were not in question. The control is provided by the known data for women in other parts of the world.

38. G Scientist 2 notes that those who think proteins are bad for us are vegetarians, committed to a meat-free diet for other reasons. He did not question the validity of the physiological data, although he might well have done so. All agree that proteins are vital in the diet, and this does not affect the issue.

39. D A is wrong because Scientist 2 has doubts about the protein relationship. B is wrong because Scientist 1 thinks we get all the calcium we need from vegetables. C is wrong because Scientist 1 thinks it is the proteins in milk that must be avoided. Anyone would agree that D is a good idea; a checkup could make it possible to deal with the problem early.

40. G The studies support the use of milk, and surely the Dairy Institute is not an unbiased source of information. F is wrong because it is Scientist 1, not Scientist 2, who may have a bias in favor of vegetarianism. H is wrong; it might be expected that appropriate levels of dietary calcium could be established. J is wrong because Scientist 2 specifically recommends fat-free milk.

Model Examination B

The purpose of Model Examination B is to help you evaluate your progress in preparing for the actual ACT. Take the examination under simulated testing conditions and within the time limits stated at the beginning of each test. Try to apply the test-taking tactics recommended in this book. Detach the answer sheet and mark your answers on it.

After you finish the examination, check your answers against the Answer Keys and fill in the Analysis Charts. Rate your total scores by using the Performance Evaluation Chart on page 8. Read all of the Answer Explanations.

The Analysis Charts will indicate where you need further review. Compare your results with those of Model Examination A, then go back to Part Three to reinforce specific areas. Then try Model Examination C to evaluate your progress.

Directions: Mark one answer only for each question. Make the mark dark. Erase completely any mark made in error. (Additional or stray marks will be counted as mistakes.)

TEST 1

	10 Ⓕ Ⓖ Ⓗ Ⓙ	20 Ⓕ Ⓖ Ⓗ Ⓙ	30 Ⓕ Ⓖ Ⓗ Ⓙ	40 Ⓕ Ⓖ Ⓗ Ⓙ	50 Ⓕ Ⓖ Ⓗ Ⓙ	60 Ⓕ Ⓖ Ⓗ Ⓙ	70 Ⓕ Ⓖ Ⓗ Ⓙ
1 Ⓐ Ⓑ Ⓒ Ⓓ	11 Ⓐ Ⓑ Ⓒ Ⓓ	21 Ⓐ Ⓑ Ⓒ Ⓓ	31 Ⓐ Ⓑ Ⓒ Ⓓ	41 Ⓐ Ⓑ Ⓒ Ⓓ	51 Ⓐ Ⓑ Ⓒ Ⓓ	61 Ⓐ Ⓑ Ⓒ Ⓓ	71 Ⓐ Ⓑ Ⓒ Ⓓ
2 Ⓕ Ⓖ Ⓗ Ⓙ	12 Ⓕ Ⓖ Ⓗ Ⓙ	22 Ⓕ Ⓖ Ⓗ Ⓙ	32 Ⓕ Ⓖ Ⓗ Ⓙ	42 Ⓕ Ⓖ Ⓗ Ⓙ	52 Ⓕ Ⓖ Ⓗ Ⓙ	62 Ⓕ Ⓖ Ⓗ Ⓙ	72 Ⓕ Ⓖ Ⓗ Ⓙ
3 Ⓐ Ⓑ Ⓒ Ⓓ	13 Ⓐ Ⓑ Ⓒ Ⓓ	23 Ⓐ Ⓑ Ⓒ Ⓓ	33 Ⓐ Ⓑ Ⓒ Ⓓ	43 Ⓐ Ⓑ Ⓒ Ⓓ	53 Ⓐ Ⓑ Ⓒ Ⓓ	63 Ⓐ Ⓑ Ⓒ Ⓓ	73 Ⓐ Ⓑ Ⓒ Ⓓ
4 Ⓕ Ⓖ Ⓗ Ⓙ	14 Ⓕ Ⓖ Ⓗ Ⓙ	24 Ⓕ Ⓖ Ⓗ Ⓙ	34 Ⓕ Ⓖ Ⓗ Ⓙ	44 Ⓕ Ⓖ Ⓗ Ⓙ	54 Ⓕ Ⓖ Ⓗ Ⓙ	64 Ⓕ Ⓖ Ⓗ Ⓙ	74 Ⓕ Ⓖ Ⓗ Ⓙ
5 Ⓐ Ⓑ Ⓒ Ⓓ	15 Ⓐ Ⓑ Ⓒ Ⓓ	25 Ⓐ Ⓑ Ⓒ Ⓓ	35 Ⓐ Ⓑ Ⓒ Ⓓ	45 Ⓐ Ⓑ Ⓒ Ⓓ	55 Ⓐ Ⓑ Ⓒ Ⓓ	65 Ⓐ Ⓑ Ⓒ Ⓓ	75 Ⓐ Ⓑ Ⓒ Ⓓ
6 Ⓕ Ⓖ Ⓗ Ⓙ	16 Ⓕ Ⓖ Ⓗ Ⓙ	26 Ⓕ Ⓖ Ⓗ Ⓙ	36 Ⓕ Ⓖ Ⓗ Ⓙ	46 Ⓕ Ⓖ Ⓗ Ⓙ	56 Ⓕ Ⓖ Ⓗ Ⓙ	66 Ⓕ Ⓖ Ⓗ Ⓙ	
7 Ⓐ Ⓑ Ⓒ Ⓓ	17 Ⓐ Ⓑ Ⓒ Ⓓ	27 Ⓐ Ⓑ Ⓒ Ⓓ	37 Ⓐ Ⓑ Ⓒ Ⓓ	47 Ⓐ Ⓑ Ⓒ Ⓓ	57 Ⓐ Ⓑ Ⓒ Ⓓ	67 Ⓐ Ⓑ Ⓒ Ⓓ	
8 Ⓕ Ⓖ Ⓗ Ⓙ	18 Ⓕ Ⓖ Ⓗ Ⓙ	28 Ⓕ Ⓖ Ⓗ Ⓙ	38 Ⓕ Ⓖ Ⓗ Ⓙ	48 Ⓕ Ⓖ Ⓗ Ⓙ	58 Ⓕ Ⓖ Ⓗ Ⓙ	68 Ⓕ Ⓖ Ⓗ Ⓙ	
9 Ⓐ Ⓑ Ⓒ Ⓓ	19 Ⓐ Ⓑ Ⓒ Ⓓ	29 Ⓐ Ⓑ Ⓒ Ⓓ	39 Ⓐ Ⓑ Ⓒ Ⓓ	49 Ⓐ Ⓑ Ⓒ Ⓓ	59 Ⓐ Ⓑ Ⓒ Ⓓ	69 Ⓐ Ⓑ Ⓒ Ⓓ	

TEST 2

	8 Ⓕ Ⓖ Ⓗ Ⓙ Ⓚ	16 Ⓕ Ⓖ Ⓗ Ⓙ Ⓚ	24 Ⓕ Ⓖ Ⓗ Ⓙ Ⓚ	32 Ⓕ Ⓖ Ⓗ Ⓙ Ⓚ	40 Ⓕ Ⓖ Ⓗ Ⓙ Ⓚ	48 Ⓕ Ⓖ Ⓗ Ⓙ Ⓚ	56 Ⓕ Ⓖ Ⓗ Ⓙ Ⓚ
1 Ⓐ Ⓑ Ⓒ Ⓓ Ⓔ	9 Ⓐ Ⓑ Ⓒ Ⓓ Ⓔ	17 Ⓐ Ⓑ Ⓒ Ⓓ Ⓔ	25 Ⓐ Ⓑ Ⓒ Ⓓ Ⓔ	33 Ⓐ Ⓑ Ⓒ Ⓓ Ⓔ	41 Ⓐ Ⓑ Ⓒ Ⓓ Ⓔ	49 Ⓐ Ⓑ Ⓒ Ⓓ Ⓔ	57 Ⓐ Ⓑ Ⓒ Ⓓ Ⓔ
2 Ⓕ Ⓖ Ⓗ Ⓙ Ⓚ	10 Ⓕ Ⓖ Ⓗ Ⓙ Ⓚ	18 Ⓕ Ⓖ Ⓗ Ⓙ Ⓚ	26 Ⓕ Ⓖ Ⓗ Ⓙ Ⓚ	34 Ⓕ Ⓖ Ⓗ Ⓙ Ⓚ	42 Ⓕ Ⓖ Ⓗ Ⓙ Ⓚ	50 Ⓕ Ⓖ Ⓗ Ⓙ Ⓚ	58 Ⓕ Ⓖ Ⓗ Ⓙ Ⓚ
3 Ⓐ Ⓑ Ⓒ Ⓓ Ⓔ	11 Ⓐ Ⓑ Ⓒ Ⓓ Ⓔ	19 Ⓐ Ⓑ Ⓒ Ⓓ Ⓔ	27 Ⓐ Ⓑ Ⓒ Ⓓ Ⓔ	35 Ⓐ Ⓑ Ⓒ Ⓓ Ⓔ	43 Ⓐ Ⓑ Ⓒ Ⓓ Ⓔ	51 Ⓐ Ⓑ Ⓒ Ⓓ Ⓔ	59 Ⓐ Ⓑ Ⓒ Ⓓ Ⓔ
4 Ⓕ Ⓖ Ⓗ Ⓙ Ⓚ	12 Ⓕ Ⓖ Ⓗ Ⓙ Ⓚ	20 Ⓕ Ⓖ Ⓗ Ⓙ Ⓚ	28 Ⓕ Ⓖ Ⓗ Ⓙ Ⓚ	36 Ⓕ Ⓖ Ⓗ Ⓙ Ⓚ	44 Ⓕ Ⓖ Ⓗ Ⓙ Ⓚ	52 Ⓕ Ⓖ Ⓗ Ⓙ Ⓚ	60 Ⓕ Ⓖ Ⓗ Ⓙ Ⓚ
5 Ⓐ Ⓑ Ⓒ Ⓓ Ⓔ	13 Ⓐ Ⓑ Ⓒ Ⓓ Ⓔ	21 Ⓐ Ⓑ Ⓒ Ⓓ Ⓔ	29 Ⓐ Ⓑ Ⓒ Ⓓ Ⓔ	37 Ⓐ Ⓑ Ⓒ Ⓓ Ⓔ	45 Ⓐ Ⓑ Ⓒ Ⓓ Ⓔ	53 Ⓐ Ⓑ Ⓒ Ⓓ Ⓔ	
6 Ⓕ Ⓖ Ⓗ Ⓙ Ⓚ	14 Ⓕ Ⓖ Ⓗ Ⓙ Ⓚ	22 Ⓕ Ⓖ Ⓗ Ⓙ Ⓚ	30 Ⓕ Ⓖ Ⓗ Ⓙ Ⓚ	38 Ⓕ Ⓖ Ⓗ Ⓙ Ⓚ	46 Ⓕ Ⓖ Ⓗ Ⓙ Ⓚ	54 Ⓕ Ⓖ Ⓗ Ⓙ Ⓚ	
7 Ⓐ Ⓑ Ⓒ Ⓓ Ⓔ	15 Ⓐ Ⓑ Ⓒ Ⓓ Ⓔ	23 Ⓐ Ⓑ Ⓒ Ⓓ Ⓔ	31 Ⓐ Ⓑ Ⓒ Ⓓ Ⓔ	39 Ⓐ Ⓑ Ⓒ Ⓓ Ⓔ	47 Ⓐ Ⓑ Ⓒ Ⓓ Ⓔ	55 Ⓐ Ⓑ Ⓒ Ⓓ Ⓔ	

TEST 3

	6 Ⓕ Ⓖ Ⓗ Ⓙ	12 Ⓕ Ⓖ Ⓗ Ⓙ	18 Ⓕ Ⓖ Ⓗ Ⓙ	24 Ⓕ Ⓖ Ⓗ Ⓙ	30 Ⓕ Ⓖ Ⓗ Ⓙ	36 Ⓕ Ⓖ Ⓗ Ⓙ
1 Ⓐ Ⓑ Ⓒ Ⓓ	7 Ⓐ Ⓑ Ⓒ Ⓓ	13 Ⓐ Ⓑ Ⓒ Ⓓ	19 Ⓐ Ⓑ Ⓒ Ⓓ	25 Ⓐ Ⓑ Ⓒ Ⓓ	31 Ⓐ Ⓑ Ⓒ Ⓓ	37 Ⓐ Ⓑ Ⓒ Ⓓ
2 Ⓕ Ⓖ Ⓗ Ⓙ	8 Ⓕ Ⓖ Ⓗ Ⓙ	14 Ⓕ Ⓖ Ⓗ Ⓙ	20 Ⓕ Ⓖ Ⓗ Ⓙ	26 Ⓕ Ⓖ Ⓗ Ⓙ	32 Ⓕ Ⓖ Ⓗ Ⓙ	38 Ⓕ Ⓖ Ⓗ Ⓙ
3 Ⓐ Ⓑ Ⓒ Ⓓ	9 Ⓐ Ⓑ Ⓒ Ⓓ	15 Ⓐ Ⓑ Ⓒ Ⓓ	21 Ⓐ Ⓑ Ⓒ Ⓓ	27 Ⓐ Ⓑ Ⓒ Ⓓ	33 Ⓐ Ⓑ Ⓒ Ⓓ	39 Ⓐ Ⓑ Ⓒ Ⓓ
4 Ⓕ Ⓖ Ⓗ Ⓙ	10 Ⓕ Ⓖ Ⓗ Ⓙ	16 Ⓕ Ⓖ Ⓗ Ⓙ	22 Ⓕ Ⓖ Ⓗ Ⓙ	28 Ⓕ Ⓖ Ⓗ Ⓙ	34 Ⓕ Ⓖ Ⓗ Ⓙ	40 Ⓕ Ⓖ Ⓗ Ⓙ
5 Ⓐ Ⓑ Ⓒ Ⓓ	11 Ⓐ Ⓑ Ⓒ Ⓓ	17 Ⓐ Ⓑ Ⓒ Ⓓ	23 Ⓐ Ⓑ Ⓒ Ⓓ	29 Ⓐ Ⓑ Ⓒ Ⓓ	35 Ⓐ Ⓑ Ⓒ Ⓓ	

TEST 4

	6 Ⓕ Ⓖ Ⓗ Ⓙ	12 Ⓕ Ⓖ Ⓗ Ⓙ	18 Ⓕ Ⓖ Ⓗ Ⓙ	24 Ⓕ Ⓖ Ⓗ Ⓙ	30 Ⓕ Ⓖ Ⓗ Ⓙ	36 Ⓕ Ⓖ Ⓗ Ⓙ
1 Ⓐ Ⓑ Ⓒ Ⓓ	7 Ⓐ Ⓑ Ⓒ Ⓓ	13 Ⓐ Ⓑ Ⓒ Ⓓ	19 Ⓐ Ⓑ Ⓒ Ⓓ	25 Ⓐ Ⓑ Ⓒ Ⓓ	31 Ⓐ Ⓑ Ⓒ Ⓓ	37 Ⓐ Ⓑ Ⓒ Ⓓ
2 Ⓕ Ⓖ Ⓗ Ⓙ	8 Ⓕ Ⓖ Ⓗ Ⓙ	14 Ⓕ Ⓖ Ⓗ Ⓙ	20 Ⓕ Ⓖ Ⓗ Ⓙ	26 Ⓕ Ⓖ Ⓗ Ⓙ	32 Ⓕ Ⓖ Ⓗ Ⓙ	38 Ⓕ Ⓖ Ⓗ Ⓙ
3 Ⓐ Ⓑ Ⓒ Ⓓ	9 Ⓐ Ⓑ Ⓒ Ⓓ	15 Ⓐ Ⓑ Ⓒ Ⓓ	21 Ⓐ Ⓑ Ⓒ Ⓓ	27 Ⓐ Ⓑ Ⓒ Ⓓ	33 Ⓐ Ⓑ Ⓒ Ⓓ	39 Ⓐ Ⓑ Ⓒ Ⓓ
4 Ⓕ Ⓖ Ⓗ Ⓙ	10 Ⓕ Ⓖ Ⓗ Ⓙ	16 Ⓕ Ⓖ Ⓗ Ⓙ	22 Ⓕ Ⓖ Ⓗ Ⓙ	28 Ⓕ Ⓖ Ⓗ Ⓙ	34 Ⓕ Ⓖ Ⓗ Ⓙ	40 Ⓕ Ⓖ Ⓗ Ⓙ
5 Ⓐ Ⓑ Ⓒ Ⓓ	11 Ⓐ Ⓑ Ⓒ Ⓓ	17 Ⓐ Ⓑ Ⓒ Ⓓ	23 Ⓐ Ⓑ Ⓒ Ⓓ	29 Ⓐ Ⓑ Ⓒ Ⓓ	35 Ⓐ Ⓑ Ⓒ Ⓓ	

1 1 1 1 1 1 1 1 1 1 1 1

EXAMINATION B
Model English Test
45 Minutes—75 Questions

DIRECTIONS: The following test consists of 75 under-lined words and phrases in context, or general questions about the passages. Most of the underlined sections contain errors and inappropriate expressions. You are asked to compare each with the four alternatives in the answer column. If you consider the original version best, choose letter A or F: NO CHANGE. For each question, blacken on the answer sheet the letter of the alternative you think best. Read each passage through before answering the questions based on it.

Passage I

(1)

Abraham Lincoln has been quoted as advising a new lawyer, "Young man, it's more important to know what cases not to take than it is to know the law." New attorneys soon learn to recognize what cases will probably be unprofitable, or they quickly end up looking for new jobs <u>in the newspaper because of lack of funds.</u> $\boxed{2}$
₁

(2)

During the initial interview with the client, the lawyer discovers whether or not a case is meritorious. Examples of cases without merit include an argument with neighbors over a pesky dog or an accident that results from the victim's own negligence, such as some-one falling in a local supermarket because <u>they were</u>
₃

<u>drunk.</u> This <u>questionable and dubious</u> type of case can
₃   ₄
be easily seen as lacking merit, because each of the ele-ments of a tort (a civil wrongdoing) was not present, and thus no law was broken. <u>We must all try to behave</u>
₅
<u>as adults as we wend our way through this troubled</u>
₅
<u>interval.</u>
₅

1. A. NO CHANGE
   B. because of lack of funds.
   C. in the newspaper.
   D. OMIT the underlined portion.

2. Is the quotation from Abraham Lincoln an appro-priate way to begin this passage?
   F. Yes, because quotations are always better than straight prose as attention-getters.
   G. No, because it misleads the reader, suggesting that Lincoln is the topic of the passage.
   H. No, because it is too short a quotation to add any meaning.
   J. Yes, because Abraham Lincoln is an authority figure, often quoted because of the truth and simplicity of his statements.

3. A. NO CHANGE
   B. he or she was drunk.
   C. they had been drinking.
   D. they were considerably under the influence.

4. F. NO CHANGE
   G. OMIT the underlined portion.
   H. questionable
   J. dubious

5. A. NO CHANGE
   B. We must all try to be mature.
   C. We must all do our best.
   D. OMIT the underlined portion.

GO ON TO THE NEXT PAGE.

1   1 1 1 1 1 1 1 1 1   1

(3)

Finally, there is the type of case in which the prospective client has been represented in the matter by another attorney. Accepting such a case can be risky, <u>although</u> multiple lawyers are evidence of a worthless
₆

6. F. NO CHANGE
G. when
H. because
J. similarly

<u>case an</u> uncooperative client, or a client who does not
₇

7. A. NO CHANGE
B. case. An
C. case, an
D. case: an

pay his or her bill. Even if the reason for the <u>client's</u>
₈

8. F. NO CHANGE
G. clients
H. client
J. clients'

changing attorneys is a good <u>one—let's say</u> a personal-
₉
ity clash between the client and the prior attorney—it makes the new lawyer's task of reaching a fair settlement with the other party strategically difficult.

9. A. NO CHANGE
B. one, let's say
C. one (let's say
D. one let's say

(4)

There are some cases that seem to have merit but are economically unfeasible for a new attorney to handle. Such cases are easy to spot once a <u>full, adequate</u>
₁₀
<u>enough disclosure</u> of the facts has been obtained from
₁₀
the client during the initial interview. One type of unprofitable case is the "hurt feelings" case stemming from an incident where the defendant has <u>been guilty of</u>
₁₁
<u>caddish behavior—but what young man in springtime</u>
₁₁
<u>has been able to resist the pull of the heart?—but</u>
₁₁
where the victim cannot prove he or she has been specifically damaged, or where damages are nominal. For instance, in an action for slander, not only is it difficult to prove <u>slander but also</u> the monetary damage to
₁₂
the victim resulting from the slanderous action may be small or even nonexistent. In these kinds of cases, a

10. F. NO CHANGE
G. full, adequate disclosure
H. full, adequate, complete disclosure
J. full disclosure

11. A. NO CHANGE
B. been guilty of caddish behavior—but sometimes that happens to young people—
C. been guilty of wrongful behavior,
D. OMIT the underlined portion.

12. F. NO CHANGE
G. slander, but also
H. slander. But also
J. slander; but also

GO ON TO THE NEXT PAGE.

1   1 1 1 1 1 1 1 1 1 1   1

prospective client may be so righteously angered as to

say that he or she does not care about the money, that it

is the principle that matters, that may be true for the
13

prospective client, but the attorney cannot pay his sec-

retary's salary, his office rent, or his malpractice insur-

ance premium will not be reduced with a client's
14

"prinicple." 15

13. **A.** NO CHANGE
    B. matters that
    C. matters. That
    D. matters: that

14. **F.** NO CHANGE
    G. premium reduction
    H. premium reduced
    J. premium

15. Choose the sequence of paragraph numbers that
    makes the structure of the passage most logical.
    A. NO CHANGE
    B. 1, 4, 2, 3
    C. 1, 3, 2, 4
    D. 1, 2, 4, 3

Passage II

(1)

Of all the many differences between people, there

is one that goes more deeper than any other or than all
16

combined, and that is whether the person are parents or
17

not. Variations in cultural background, religion,
17

politics, or education do not come close to parent

versus nonparent differences. 18

(2)

Conversely, few if any knickknacks remain whole in

a home with small children, the only plants left are those
19

hanging, brown and wilted, from a very high ceiling.

Instead, toys strewn carelessly about the various living
20

areas. The somewhat disheveled rooms usually look
21

slightly askew, since little ones delight in moving furni-

ture around and are especially prone to do so unless a
22

16. **F.** NO CHANGE
    G. deeper
    H. deep
    J. deepest

17. **A.** NO CHANGE
    B. is a parent or not.
    C. is parents or not.
    D. are a parent or not.

18. This passage was probably written for readers who:
    F. are experts in child development.
    G. are expecting a child.
    H. are general readers.
    J. are childless.

19. **A.** NO CHANGE
    B. children the only
    C. children: the only
    D. children. The

20. **F.** NO CHANGE
    G. toys strew
    H. toys were strewn
    J. toys are strewn

21. **A.** NO CHANGE
    B. disheveled rooms
    C. rooms
    D. somewhat, disheveled rooms

22. **F.** NO CHANGE
    G. after
    H. as
    J. when

GO ON TO THE NEXT PAGE.

1   1 1 1 1 1 1 1 1 1   1

guest or two <u>are expected</u>. Walls are usually smudged
with the prints of tiny hands and feet (yes, feet—don't
ask me how) and decorated with children's artwork,
which also adorns the refrigerator, kitchen cabinets,
message center, and any other available blank space. To
a parent, there is no such thing as a sparkling clean mirror or window. <u>A handy way to clean windows</u>
<u>and mirrors is by using crushed newsprint.</u> Children
simply cannot keep from touching—with their hands,
noses, mouths, whatever—clean mirrors and windows.
It has something to do with marking one's territory, I
believe. [25]

(3)

The very way a house is decorated proclaims the
owner's status. My childless friends have plants, expensive accessories, and elegant knickknacks placed strategically about their <u>finely-furnished</u> homes. Framed
prints hang on their spotlessly white walls, while their
mirrors and windows sparkle. [27]

(4)

Another <u>distinguishing</u> great difference between
people without children and people with them is their
attitude toward life. Before my daughter came along
five years ago, I was a competent legal secretary, a
faithful wife, and a person who enjoyed a quiet lifestyle
interspersed with an occasional party or outing. I was
<u>well-adjusted but ill-prepared</u> for chaotic living, and, I
see now, quite naive. [30]

23. **A.** NO CHANGE
    B. are expecting.
    C. is expected.
    D. will be expected.

24. **F.** NO CHANGE
    G. OMIT the underlined portion.
    H. Clean windows with newsprint.
    J. A handy way to clean windows is with newsprint.

25. Which of the phrases below demonstrates the intent of the writer to be whimsical and humorous?
    A. toys strewn carelessly
    B. marking one's territory
    C. sparkling clean mirror
    D. available blank space

26. **F.** NO CHANGE
    G. finely furnished
    H. finely, furnished
    J. furnished

27. Examination of paragraphs 2 and 3 reveals that the author of this passage wants to emphasize:
    A. fine art in American homes.
    B. styles and decor in contemporary homes.
    C. the impact of children on a home.
    D. indoor plant styles in contemporary American homes.

28. **F.** NO CHANGE
    G. OMIT this word
    H. discriminating
    J. differentiating

29. **A.** NO CHANGE
    B. well adjusted but ill-prepared
    C. well adjusted but ill prepared
    D. well-adjusted but ill prepared

30. Choose the sequence of paragraph numbers that makes the structure of the passage most logical.
    F. NO CHANGE
    G. 1, 3, 2, 4
    H. 1, 3, 4, 2
    J. 1, 4, 2, 3

GO ON TO THE NEXT PAGE.

1 1 1 1 1 1 1 1 1 1 1 1 1

Passage III

(1)

The very idea of a community among nations are
unique. From the city-states of ancient Greece to the
modern nations of our era, communities have to join
forces to defend their individual interests. Economic,
political, and military conditions have imposed their
own imperatives, requiring shifting alliances and coali-
tions of expedience. But the contemporary community
of nations—a free association based on shared principles and an increasingly shared way of life; emerged
only with the evolution of the democratic idea. Just as a

free people argue the issues and choose their own government, so do free nations choose their friends and
allies. We are joined not just by common interests but
also by ideals of freedom and justice that transcends the

dictates of necessity. 36

(2)

Our community and our heritage has enemies. Over
the past two centuries, as separate entities or in concert,
free peoples have defended themselves against marauders
and tyrants, against militarists and imperialists, against
Nazis and the Leninist totalitarians of our time. We have
seen our heritage shaking to its roots. The graves of Nor-
mandy and the death camps of the Third Reich bears permanent witness to the vulnerability of all we cherish.

31. **A.** NO CHANGE
    B. had been
    C. is
    D. were

32. **F.** NO CHANGE
    G. had
    H. will have had
    J. have had

33. **A.** NO CHANGE
    B. life—emerged
    C. life: emerged
    D. life, emerged

34. **F.** NO CHANGE
    G. its
    H. his or her
    J. our

35. **A.** NO CHANGE
    B. transcending
    C. transcended
    D. transcend

36. Is the reference to ancient Greece in the second
    sentence appropriate in this passage?
    F. No, because there is no connection between
    two eras thousands of years apart.
    G. Yes, because ancient Greece is a model for
    democratic societies.
    H. No, because the United States does not have
    city-states.
    J. Yes, because this is one of the earliest histori-
    cal instances of communities joining forces for
    the common good.

37. **A.** NO CHANGE
    B. have
    C. had
    D. will have had

38. **F.** NO CHANGE
    G. shaken
    H. shook
    J. shaked

39. **A.** NO CHANGE
    B. bear
    C. bore
    D. borne

GO ON TO THE NEXT PAGE.

1   1 1 1 1 1 1 1 1 1 1   1

(3)

In the last forty years, we have seen other evidence of the determination of our adversaries. We saw it in the Berlin Wall, built <u>defensive</u> as a symbol of the fear
our civilization and its values evoke in a totalitarian world. During the Cold War, the Soviets, of course, had their values as well. They valued a regime that imposed an unchallenged order in <u>their</u> own sphere and

fomented instability and division elsewhere. ☐42

(4)

This community has long been a minority of humanity. <u>In our own time, however, we have seen our numbers increase.</u> In recent decades we have been joined by like-minded nations around the Pacific Basin; by the struggling young democracies of Latin America; and, of course, by Israel, whose very existence is a constant reminder of the sacrifices and struggles that may be required if civilization is to be secured. Together, we stand for something that no other alliance in history has <u>represented; the</u> advancement of the rights of the individual, and the conviction that governments founded on these rights are, in Lincoln's words, "the last best hope of men on earth." ☐45

40. **F.** NO CHANGE
G. in a defensive way
H. defensive and antagonistic
J. defensively

41. **A.** NO CHANGE
B. its
C. there
D. they're

42. Is the reference to the Berlin Wall meaningful at this place in the passage?
F. No, because it virtually changes the subject.
G. No, because the Berlin Wall was an inanimate object, and the passage is about people.
H. Yes, because the Berlin Wall was created after World War II.
J. Yes, because it is a specific example of the determination mentioned in the first sentence of the paragraph.

43. How do you regard the supporting material that follows this statement?
A. It is ineffective; it does not support the initial statement at all.
B. It is effective because it lists countries that have made human rights a paramount concern.
C. It is ineffective because it does not list numbers or demonstrate with charts.
D. It is effective because it ends with a quotation from Lincoln.

44. **F.** NO CHANGE
G. represented, the
H. represented: the
J. represented. The

45. Choose the sequence of paragraph numbers that makes the structure of the passage most logical.
A. NO CHANGE
B. 1, 4, 2, 3
C. 1, 3, 2, 4
D. 1, 4, 3, 2

Passage IV

(1)

My Antonia depicts life on the Nebraska prairie during the early 1900s, mirroring Willa Cather's own experiences as a girl living on the "Great Divide," as

GO ON TO THE NEXT PAGE.

1 1 1 1 1 1 1 1 1 1 1 1

that part of Nebraska <u>had been called.</u> The protagonist
₄₆

of the novel, <u>Antonia Shimerda</u> was modeled on Annie
₄₇

Sadilek, an <u>actual living</u> Bohemian girl hired by one of
₄₈

Willa Cather's neighbors in the town of Red Cloud. 49

(2)

A close friend of Willa Cather, the author of *My Antonia,* has written, "Willa forever preferred rural life, although she was never quite so inartistic as to announce that 'the country is preferable to the <u>city'."</u>
₅₀
Certainly, *My Antonia,* Willa Cather's third prairie novel, is a joyous song of praise for "the virtues of a settled agricultural existence" as opposed to life in the cities. Her belief that the ideal civilization is to be found in the country, <u>albeit</u> a country tempered with
₅₁
such desirable urban qualities as cultural refinement and order, is developed by the use of <u>multi-level</u>
₅₂
contrasts and comparisons, both obvious and symbolic. 53 54

46. F. NO CHANGE
   G. was called
   H. is called
   J. called

47. A. NO CHANGE
   B. , Antonia Shimerda,
   C. Antonia Shimerda
   D. Antonia Shimerda,

48. F. NO CHANGE
   G. actual, living
   H. living
   J. actual

49. This paragraph serves as a summary of the novel being discussed in this passage. How might it be strengthened?
   A. NO CHANGE
   B. It should describe the Great Plains setting more fully.
   C. It should give us the entire plot of the story, not part of it.
   D. It should supply more details regarding the family background of the Shimerdas.

50. F. NO CHANGE
   G. city' ".
   H. city.' "
   J. city."

51. A. NO CHANGE
   B. nevertheless
   C. and
   D. yet

52. F. NO CHANGE
   G. multi level
   H. multilevel
   J. many level

53. This paragraph begins with a quotation from a close friend of Willa Cather. Is the use of the quotation relevant to the passage?
   A. No, it is irrelevant and has no bearing on the passage or paragraph.
   B. No, it is misleading, dealing with Willa Cather's life, rather than the substance of the passage.
   C. Yes, it is a valuable insight from a reliable source; in addition, it is relevant to the paragraph and passage.
   D. Yes, it is a humorous touch that does no harm.

54. This passage was probably written for readers who:
   F. are beginning readers in a youngsters' educational program.
   G. are practiced readers who enjoy novels about small-town America and its people.
   H. are Midwesterners who want to learn more about their heritage.
   J. are authors themselves.

GO ON TO THE NEXT PAGE.

(3)

A richly creative novel, *My Antonia* has been analyzed through a number of critical approaches. John H. Randall's criticism <u>dealt</u> with broad thematic questions regarding Cather's arguments for certain values and ideas, such as the urban versus the bucolic life, using the mythic or archetypal school of criticism to explain many of the symbols <u>employed</u> by the author to show her beliefs. James E. Miller explains the symbolism of the three different cycles used by Cather in the novel: the seasons of the year, the phases of Antonia's life, and, most important to this essay, <u>the people move westward in cycles</u> to America's frontiers. Wallace Stegner, a novelist in his own right, wrote an essay

about *My Antonia*. <u>In which</u> he used archetypal criticism in relation to Antonia's identification with the land, and the psychological approach to show how Cather's life and character were crucial to the novel's central theme of country versus city values. 59 60

55. A. NO CHANGE
B. had dealt
C. deals
D. has been dealing

56. F. NO CHANGE
G. being employed
H. employing
J. employ

57. A. NO CHANGE
B. the people moved westward in cycles
C. the cycles in the movement of people westward
D. the people were frequently moving westward in cycles

58. F. NO CHANGE
G. *My Antonia* in which
H. *My Antonia;* in which
J. *My Antonia*—in which

59. This paragraph begins with the general statement: "… *My Antonia* has been analyzed through a number of critical approaches." In what ways does the rest of the paragraph support or fail to support this statement?
A. It supplies the names of several critical approaches and defines them in detail.
B. It avoids the mention of critical approaches, but names three critics and discusses their ideas.
C. It names three critics, but says little about critical approaches.
D. It names three critics and their specific critical approaches to the novel, identifying the critical schools employed by two of them.

60. Choose the sequence of paragraph numbers that makes the structure of the passage most logical.
F. NO CHANGE
G. 1, 3, 2
H. 3, 2, 1
J. 3, 1, 2

GO ON TO THE NEXT PAGE.

1 1 1 1 1 1 1 1 1 1 1 1

Passage V

(1)

It is impossible to adhere rigidly to a particular

global vision without accepting the fact that, in prac-

tice, a certain number of contradictions and inconsisten-

cies will always arise in the process of translating

philosophy into <u>concrete and tangible</u> action. The fact

61

that a nation possesses <u>a notion of its clear</u> international

62

priorities, however, serves to minimize the chances that

its policies will merely drift in the tide of global events or

become deadlocked by their mutual incompatibility. [63]

(2)

<u>By leading</u> the more complex international decision-

64

making structure of the new millennium, the United States

will have to recognize and accept that our major interna-

tional <u>cronies</u> will occasionally have priorities and interests

65

that differ from our own. <u>This</u> is inherently a healthy

66

sign of the pluralistic nature of modern international

<u>politics, we</u> need not be reluctant about working for the

67

advancement of our own interests, but we should not

despair when we sometimes fail to achieve all that we

desire. In practical terms, however, our prospects for

success can be increased <u>though</u> we are sensitive to the

68

61. A. NO CHANGE
 B. concrete, tangible, and material
 C. concrete
 D. concrete and palpable

62. F. NO CHANGE
 G. a notion clear of its
 H. a notion
 J. a clear notion of its

63. The writer could most effectively strengthen the
 passage at this point by adding which of the following?
 A. A list of countries that comprise the international population
 B. A clearer introductory statement concerning
 what is meant by "translating philosophy into
 concrete action"
 C. A list of "global events"
 D. A list of "contradictions and inconsistencies"

64. F. NO CHANGE
 G. Leading
 H. In order to lead
 J. Although leading

65. A. NO CHANGE
 B. partners
 C. buddies
 D. pals

66. F. NO CHANGE
 G. These priorities
 H. This priority
 J. This independence

67. A. NO CHANGE
 B. politics we
 C. politics. We
 D. politics yet we

68. F. NO CHANGE
 G. if
 H. but
 J. unless

GO ON TO THE NEXT PAGE.

particular constraints and policy goals that influence the
actions of other <u>nations, states, and governments.</u> ☐70
₆₉

(3)

At the outset, we need to recognize that the solutions to the major foreign policy issues of the future
will largely be determined on the basis of collective
leadership. <u>The United States will no longer be able</u>
₇₁
<u>simply to undertake unilateral action to resolve specific</u>
₇₁
<u>international situations.</u> We have now grown beyond
₇₁
the era in which the global power of the United States
was absolute and <u>unchallenged, and</u> it would be danger-
₇₂
ous and futile to attempt a restoration of the post-World
War II balance of forces. <u>The overwhelming truth is</u>
₇₃
<u>that human beings have created destructive weaponry</u>
₇₃
<u>they are no longer able to control.</u> Instead we must
₇₃
move toward an appreciation of the central role that the
United States will continue to play in reconciling competing international interests. ☐74 ☐75

69. A. NO CHANGE
    B. nations and governments.
    C. nations.
    D. nations, states, governments, provinces, and
        entities.

70. Readers are likely to regard the passage thus far as
    best described by which of the following terms?
    F. Conciliatory
    G. Hostile
    H. Apologetic
    J. Confessional

71. This sentence alone indicates that the intention of
    the author is to be:
    A. descriptive.
    B. persuasive.
    C. poetic.
    D. sentimental.

72. F. NO CHANGE
    G. unchallenged and
    H. unchallenged. And
    J. unchallenged: and

73. A. NO CHANGE
    B. Human beings have created destructive
        weaponry.
    C. OMIT the underlined portion.
    D. Human beings have created destructive
        weaponry they cannot control.

74. The word *instead* at the beginning of the last sen-
    tence serves as a transition between which of the
    following stances?
    F. From unchallenged global power to peace-
        maker
    G. From peacemaker to warrior
    H. From unchallenged global power to warrior
    J. From hostility to aggressiveness

75. Choose the sequence of paragraph numbers that
    makes the structure of the essay most logical.
    A. NO CHANGE
    B. 3, 1, 2
    C. 3, 2, 1
    D. 1, 3, 2

END OF TEST 1
STOP! DO NOT TURN THE PAGE UNTIL TOLD TO DO SO.

2   2 2 2 2 2 2 2 2 2   **2**

Model Mathematics Test

60 Minutes—60 Questions

DIRECTIONS: After solving each problem, darken the appropriate space on the answer sheet. Do not spend too much time on any one problem. Make a note of the ones that seem difficult, and return to them when you finish the others. Assume that the word *line* means "straight line," that geometric figures are not necessarily drawn to scale, and that all geometric figures lie in a plane.

---

1. The following expression $\dfrac{a}{b} - \dfrac{c}{d} = ?$

   A. $\dfrac{a-b}{cd}$

   B. $\dfrac{a}{d} - \dfrac{c}{b}$

   C. $\dfrac{ad-bc}{bd}$

   D. $\dfrac{a-c}{bd}$

   E. $\dfrac{a-d}{bc}$

2. If $x \neq 0$, which of the following is equal to $\dfrac{2x^4 + x^3}{x^6}$?

   F. $\dfrac{3}{x^3}$

   G. $\dfrac{x+1}{x^2}$

   H. $2x^2 + x^3$

   J. $\dfrac{2x+1}{x^3}$

   K. $\dfrac{2x+1}{x}$

3. A certain city has 1600 public telephones. Three-fourths of the phones have dials. If one-third of the dial phones are replaced by push-button phones, how many dial phones remain?
   A. 800
   B. 750
   C. 700
   D. 600
   E. 400

4. If x and y are both positive integers, which of the following is NOT necessarily an integer?
   F. $x+y$ J. x^y
   G. $x-y$
   H. xy K. $\dfrac{x}{y}$

5. If a negative number is subtracted from a positive number, which of the following will always be the result?
   A. Zero
   B. A positive number
   C. A negative number
   D. A number having the sign of the number with the larger absolute value
   E. A number having the sign of the number with the smaller absolute value

6. What is the solution set of the equation $\dfrac{5}{4x-3} = 5$?
   F. $\{7\}$
   G. $\{4\}$
   H. $\{2\}$
   J. $\{1.5\}$
   K. $\{1\}$

7. If t represents the tens digit of a two-digit number, and u represents the units digit, which of the following expressions represents the number?
   A. $t+u$
   B. $10t+u$
   C. $10u+t$
   D. $10(t+u)$
   E. tu

8. What is the simplified form of the product of the two polynomials $(x-1)(x^2+x+1)$?
   F. x^3+1
   G. x^3-1
   H. x^3-x-1
   J. x^3+x^2+x
   K. x^3+2x^2+2x+1

9. The number $3_{(five)}$ (written in base five) is equivalent to what symbol in base two?
   A. 3
   B. 11
   C. 101
   D. 100
   E. 111

GO ON TO THE NEXT PAGE.

10. Which of the following numbers is equal to the others?

F. 2.5%

G. $\frac{1}{40}$

H. $2.5(10^{-2})$

J. $\frac{75}{30}$

K. 0.025

11. If apples are 35 cents or 3 for $1.00, how much is saved on each apple by buying them 3 at a time?

A. 5 cents

B. $1.05

C. $\frac{3}{5}$ cents

D. $1\frac{2}{3}$ cents

E. $11\frac{2}{3}$ cents

12. If Joan can run 1 mile in a minutes, how much of a mile has she run after b minutes if she runs at a constant rate?

F. $\frac{a}{b}$

G. $\frac{b}{a}$

H. $\frac{1}{ab}$

J. ab

K. $\frac{a+b}{a}$

13. Which of the following is NOT a real number?

A. $\sqrt[5]{0}$

B. 5^0

C. 0^5

D. $0 \cdot 5$

E. $\frac{5}{0}$

14. $3\frac{3}{5} \times 4\frac{1}{6} = ?$

F. 15

G. $7\frac{23}{30}$

H. $\frac{108}{125}$

J. $\frac{17}{30}$

K. $\frac{1}{15}$

15. Yvette has 5 more nickels than dimes. If the value of her money is $1.30, how many coins of each kind does she have?

A. 12 dimes and 7 nickels

B. 5 dimes and 16 nickels

C. 5 dimes and 10 nickels

D. 7 dimes and 12 nickels

E. 3 dimes and 20 nickels

16. What is the tenth term of the arithmetic sequence 3, 8, 13, . . . ?

F. 18

G. 43

H. 48

J. 53

K. None of these

17. What is the solution set of the equation $0.2(100 - x) + 0.05x = 0.1(100)$?

A. $\left\{-33\frac{1}{3}\right\}$

B. $\{10\}$

C. $\{40\}$

D. $\left\{66\frac{2}{3}\right\}$

E. $\left\{95\frac{95}{399}\right\}$

18. Which of the following statements if false?

F. A regular triangle is equilateral.

G. A regular quadrilateral is a square.

H. An interior angle of a regular pentagon has a measure of 108°.

J. A regular polygon of seven sides does not exist.

K. All of these statements are true.

19. What is the simplest form of the radical $\sqrt[3]{54x^4y^6}$?

A. $3xy^2 \sqrt[3]{2x}$

B. $3x^2y^3 \sqrt[3]{6}$

C. $3y^3 \sqrt[3]{2x^4}$

D. $3x^2 \sqrt[3]{6y^6}$

E. $3xy^2 \sqrt[3]{6x}$

20. Which of the following is NOT an equation of a conic section?

F. $y = 5x^2 - 3x + 2$

G. $x^2 + y^2 - 5x + 2y - 7 = 0$

H. $2x^2 - 5y^2 = 7$

J. $y = x^3$

K. $\frac{(x+2)^2}{25} + \frac{(y-3)^2}{16} = 1$

21. What is the degree of $-5x^2y + 3xy^3 + 2xy + 6$?

A. 9

B. 5

C. 4

D. 3

E. 2

GO ON TO THE NEXT PAGE.

2   2 2 2 2 2 2 2 2 2   2

22. What is the solution set of the following system of equations?

$$2x - y = 5$$
$$x + y = 1$$

F. $\{(2,1)\}$
G. $\{2\}$
H. $\{(3, 1)\}$
J. $\{(4, -3)\}$
K. $\{(2, -1)\}$

23. A number from the set $\{1, 2, 3, ..., 20\}$ is selected at random. What is the probability that the number is even and less than 10?

A. $\frac{1}{2}$
B. $\frac{9}{20}$
C. $\frac{1}{5}$
D. $\frac{9}{40}$
E. $\frac{1}{4}$

24. If $x \neq 0$ and $y \neq 0$, what is the simplified form of the complex fraction $\dfrac{x + y}{\dfrac{1}{x} + \dfrac{1}{y}}$?

F. $\dfrac{x + y}{xy}$
G. $\dfrac{xy}{x + y}$
H. $(x + y)^2$
J. $2 + \dfrac{x}{y} + \dfrac{y}{x}$
K. xy

25. If m $\angle ABC = 70°$, then m $\angle ADC = ?$

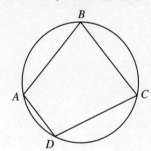

A. $35°$
B. $70°$
C. $90°$
D. $110°$
E. $140°$

26. If $a > b$, then $|a - b| + |b - a|$ is equal to what expression?

F. 0

G. $2a$
H. $2b$
J. $2a + 2b$
K. $2a - 2b$

27. What is the value of -3^{-2}?

A. 6
B. 9
C. -9
D. $\dfrac{-1}{9}$
E. $\dfrac{1}{9}$

28. What is the center of the ellipse with the equation $x^2 + 4y^2 - 4x + 24y + 36 = 0$?

F. $(2, 1)$
G. $(1, 2)$
H. $(2, -3)$
J. $(-2, 3)$
K. $(1, 4)$

29. Nick can do a certain job in 2 hours less time than it takes Bonnie to do the same job. If they can complete the job together in 7 hours, what equation could be used to determine how long it would take Bonnie to do the job alone?

A. $7(x - 2) = 7x$
B. $\dfrac{7}{x - 2} = \dfrac{7}{x}$
C. $7(x - 2) + 7x = 1$
D. $\dfrac{7}{x - 2} + \dfrac{7}{x} = 1$
E. None of these

30. Which of the following is the graph of a one-to-one function?

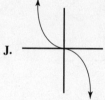

F.

J.

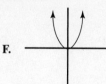

G.

K.

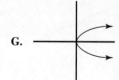

H.

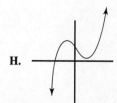

GO ON TO THE NEXT PAGE.

2   **2** **2** **2** **2** **2** **2** **2** **2** **2**   **2**

31. Which of the following numbers could NOT be the base of an exponential function?

   A. $\dfrac{1}{2}$

   B. 1

   C. 2

   D. 3

   E. $\sqrt{5}$

32. What is the simplified form of the expression $(5x - 3y^2)^2$?

   F. $25x^2 + 9y^4$

   G. $25x^2 - 9y^4$

   H. $25x^2 - 30xy + 9y^2$

   J. $25x^2 - 15xy^2 + 9y^4$

   K. $25x^2 - 30xy^2 + 9y^4$

33. What is the reciprocal of i?

   A. 1

   B. -1

   C. i.

   D. $-i$

   E. None of these

34. What is the simplified form of the expression $\dfrac{a^{-3}bc^2}{a^{-4}b^2c^{-3}}$? (Assume that the variables are not equal to zero. Write without negative exponents.)

   F. $\dfrac{c^5}{a^7b}$

   G. $\dfrac{ac^5}{b}$

   H. $\dfrac{a^7c^5}{b}$

   J. $\dfrac{c}{ab}$

   K. $\dfrac{a^7}{bc^5}$

35. In right triangle ABC, m $\angle A = 30°$, m $\angle B = 60°$, and $AC = 6$. What is the length of $\overline{AB}$?

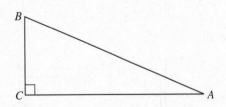

   A. $3\sqrt{2}$

   B. $6\sqrt{3}$

   C. $4\sqrt{2}$

   D. $3\sqrt{3}$

   E. $4\sqrt{3}$

36. Which of the following is identically equal to sin $2A$?

   F. $1 - \cos^2 2A$ J. $2 \sin A$

   G. $2 \sin A \cos A$ K. None of these

   H. $\dfrac{1}{\sec 2a}$

37. What is the solution set of $3x^2 - 4x - 6 = 0$?

   A. $\left\{\dfrac{-2}{3}, 3\right\}$

   B. $\left\{\dfrac{2 + 2\sqrt{22}}{3}, \dfrac{2 - 2\sqrt{22}}{3}\right\}$

   C. $\left\{\dfrac{4 + \sqrt{22}}{3}, \dfrac{4 - \sqrt{22}}{3}\right\}$

   D. $\left\{\dfrac{4 + i\sqrt{66}}{6}, \dfrac{4 - i\sqrt{66}}{6}\right\}$

   E. $\left\{\dfrac{2 + \sqrt{22}}{3}, \dfrac{2 - \sqrt{22}}{3}\right\}$

38. What is the simplified form of the radial expression $3\sqrt{3} - \sqrt{48} + 3\sqrt{\dfrac{1}{3}}$?

   F. 0

   G. $\sqrt{3}$

   H. $4\sqrt{3} - 2\sqrt{12}$

   J. $3\sqrt{3} - 2\sqrt{12} + \sqrt{3}$

   K. It is already in simplest form.

39. Which of the following equations does NOT define a function?

   A. $y = x + 2$

   B. $x = y + 2$

   C. $y = 2^x$

   D. $y = x^2$

   E. $x = y^2$

40. If tangent $\overline{CD}$ is 6 cm long and $BC = 4$, what is the length of $\overline{AB}$?

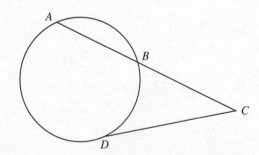

   F. $2\dfrac{2}{3}$

   G. 3

   H. 4

   J. 5

   K. 6

GO ON TO THE NEXT PAGE.

41. Diane averages 12 miles per hour riding her bike to work. Averaging 36 miles per hour on the way home by car takes her $\frac{1}{2}$ hour less time. What equation could be used to determine how far she travels to work?

A. $12x + 36x = 30$

B. $\frac{x}{12} = \frac{x}{36} + \frac{1}{2}$

C. $\frac{x}{12} + \frac{x}{36} = 30$

D. $\frac{x}{36} = \frac{x}{12} - \frac{1}{2}$

E. $\frac{36}{x} = \frac{12}{x} + \frac{1}{2}$

42. What are the coordinates of the midpoint of a segment with endpoints $A(3, 7)$ and $B(-5, -6)$?

F. $(0, 0)$

G. $\left(1, \frac{-1}{2}\right)$

H. $\left(-1, \frac{1}{2}\right)$

J. $(-2, 1)$

K. $(8, 13)$

43. What is the solution set of the radical equation $\sqrt{2x - 3} = -5$?

A. $\{-1\}$ **D.** $\{14\}$

B. $\{4\}$ **E.** $\varnothing$

C. $\{7\}$

44. Which of the following statements is false?

F. Every whole number is an integer.

G. Some rational numbers are natural numbers.

H. The set of integers is a subset of the set of real numbers.

J. $\sqrt{49}$ is a rational number.

K. None of these statements is false.

45. If an equilateral triangle is inscribed in a circle of radius 8 cm, what is the perimeter of the triangle?

A. $24\sqrt{3}$ **D.** 12

B. $8\sqrt{3}$ **E.** 24

C. $4\sqrt{3}$

46. What is the domain of the function

$f(x) = \dfrac{x + 3}{x^2 - 2x - 3}$?

F. All real numbers

G. $\{x \mid x$ is a real number and $x \neq -3\}$

H. $\{x \mid x$ is a real number and $x \neq 3$ and $x \neq -1\}$

J. $\{x \mid x$ is a real number and $x \neq 3$, $x \neq -1$, and $x \neq -3\}$

K. $\{x \mid x \neq 0\}$

47. Circles A and B are tangent to each other. $\overline{CD}$ is a common tangent to the two circles. If the radius of circle A is 5 and the radius of circle B is 3, what is the length of $\overline{CD}$?

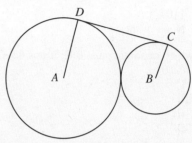

A. 4

B. 8

C. $\sqrt{34}$

D. $2\sqrt{15}$

E. $2\sqrt{17}$

48. If $\overline{AD}$ is a diameter and m $\angle C = 125°$, what is the measure of $\angle A$?

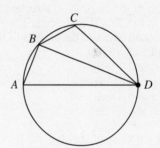

F. $35°$

G. $55°$

H. $62.5°$

J. $90°$

K. $125°$

49. If $AC = 8$ and $BD = 6$, then what is the length of $\overline{BC}$?

A. 1

B. 5

C. $7\frac{1}{2}$

D. 15

E. There is not enough information.

50. If $A(-3, 4)$ lies on the terminal side of angle θ, what is the value of $\sec \theta$?

F. $\frac{-3}{5}$ **J.** $\frac{-4}{3}$

G. $\frac{4}{5}$ **K.** $\frac{5}{4}$

H. $\frac{-5}{3}$

GO ON TO THE NEXT PAGE.

51. What is the value of $\sum\limits_{k=1}^{5} 2k^2$?
   A. 2
   B. 50
   C. 52
   D. 110
   E. None of these

52. In which quadrant must θ lie if $\cos\theta > 0$ and $\cot\theta < 0$?
   F. I
   G. II
   H. III
   J. IV
   K. No such angle exists.

53. Let A and B be any two sets. Which of the following statements is always true?
   A. $(A \cup B) \subseteq A$
   B. $(A \cap B) \subseteq B$
   C. $(A \cup B) \subseteq (A \cap B)$
   D. $B \subseteq (A \cap B)$
   E. $(A \cup B) = (A \cap B)$

54. The length of the diagonal of a rectanglar piece of wood is $\sqrt{145}$ feet. If one side is 1 foot longer than the other, what are the lengths of the sides?
   F. 8 feet and −9 feet
   G. 8 feet and 9 feet
   H. 12 feet and 13 feet
   J. 5 feet and 6 feet
   K. 2 feet and 36 feet

55. Which is the value of $\sin\left(\cos^{-1}\frac{2}{3}\right)$?
   A. $\dfrac{2}{3}$
   B. $\dfrac{\sqrt{5}}{3}$
   C. $\dfrac{-\sqrt{5}}{3}$
   D. $\dfrac{\pm\sqrt{5}}{3}$
   E. $\dfrac{\sqrt{13}}{3}$

56. Jon scored 75, 84, and 80 on his first three tests. What score must he get on his fourth test so that his average will be at least 80?
   F. 81
   G. Greater than 81
   H. Less than 81
   J. Greater than or equal to 81
   K. Less than or equal to 81

57. What is the measure of an exterior angle of a regular octagon?
   A. 45°
   B. 60°
   C. 72°
   D. 120°
   E. 135°

58. If the lengths of the diagonals of a rhombus are 6 and 8 meters, what is the perimeter, in meters, of the rhombus?

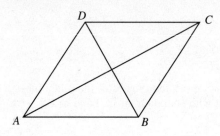

   F. 5
   G. 14
   H. 20
   J. 28
   K. 40

59. Which of the following statements is true?
   A. Complements of complementary angles are equal.
   B. A line segment has only one bisector.
   C. A line perpendicular to a segment also bisects the segment.
   D. An isosceles triangle may also be scalene.
   E. None of these statements is true.

60. In $\triangle ABC$, $\overline{AB} \perp \overline{BC}$ and $\overline{BD} \perp \overline{AC}$. If $BD = 4$ and $AC = 10$, what is the length of $\overline{AD}$ (the shorter portion of the hypotenuse)?

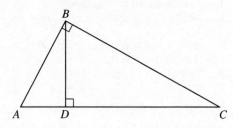

   F. 2
   G. 3
   H. 4
   J. 6
   K. 8

END OF TEST 2
STOP! DO NOT TURN THE PAGE UNTIL TOLD TO DO SO.

Model Reading Test

35 Minutes—40 Questions

DIRECTIONS: This test consists of four passages, each followed by ten multiple-choice questions. Read each passage and then pick the best answer for each question. Fill in the spaces on your answer sheet that correspond to your choices. Refer to the passage as often as you wish while answering the questions.

Passage I

SOCIAL SCIENCE: This passage is from a governmental report on domestic violence titled "Characteristics of the Abusive Situation." It discusses several problems faced by abused and battered spouses.

Abusive husbands systematically isolate their wives from family and friends. Even women who seek legal, medical or emotional help view themselves as unable to succeed against their all-powerful husbands who, they
5 fear, will "pay witnesses to lie in court," "kill my family if I testify," "get custody of the children," and "refuse to give me a divorce." Physical and emotional abuse of women is an exercise of power and control in which the weight of society has been traditionally on the side of the
10 oppressor. Thus, battered women who feel powerless to alter their circumstances are reacting realistically to what they have experienced. They are trapped, and their descriptions of the responses of police, prosecutors and judges are not paranoid delusions.

15 Many victims have been beaten repeatedly and their attackers have not been apprehended and punished. Assault is a crime. Legally it makes no difference if the victim and her attacker are strangers or are married to each other. Yet police officers often refuse to arrest husbands
20 (or live-in companions) who beat their wives. Police, prosecutors, judges and society in general share the prejudice that women provoke men by constant nagging, overspending or questioning their virility. Verbal provocation, even assuming it exists, however, is not justification
25 for violence.

The absence of negative sanctions gives the abusive family member license to continue his threats and violence. The lack of societal restraints on the husband's violence, the emphasis on defendant's rights in the courts,
30 the long court delays, the opportunity for intimidation, the husband's promises of reform and the woman's fear of economic privation contribute to the drop out rate of 50 percent by battered-wife complainants in the criminal courts and in the Family Court.

35 Civil actions for support, separation or divorce are also subject to delays which make it virtually impossible to get emergency relief. Judges frequently refuse to "throw a man out of his home," so it is the woman and children who must leave. Crowded court calendars make
40 the legal process work in favor of the person who controls the family income and assets. Getting temporary alimony or maintenance and child support can take months, sometimes as long as a divorce itself. Unless there is a refuge for battered women, the abused wife may be forced to live
45 with her husband during a divorce action.

Equitable distribution of property may also be problematic for the financially dependent spouse because the litigation to define, evaluate and divide the property can continue for years and is very costly. The ultimate irony is
50 that, even when the battered wife gets an award for alimony and child support, the amount of support is usually inadequate for her to maintain herself and the children. Moreover, often it is not paid at all.

Because the separated or divorced wife cannot rely on
55 payment of court-ordered support, many battered wives stay with their husbands. Professor Richard J. Gelles, a sociologist who studied battered wives, found that the wives who hold a job are better able to obtain assistance and leave the abusive situation . . . Viewing the difficult
60 situation in which legal, economic and social realities place the battered woman, one should ask: where does this woman get the stamina to survive the attacks and the courage to leave? Part of the work of the helping professionals is to convince the battered woman that she must
65 use the enormous strength she has for self-preservation, not just for self-sacrifice.

The legal system requires that an injured adult initiate and follow through with the steps necessary to obtain protection, child custody, financial support, divorce or
70 money damages. Usually the injured person bears the expense of engaging an attorney to represent her in a civil case. The legal process is complex and confusing so that referral to a sympathetic and competent lawyer is important. Other helping professionals must understand the laws con-

GO ON TO THE NEXT PAGE.

75 cerning family violence if they are to provide effective support. Accompanying a client to court helps develop a first-hand sense of the obstacles that the client faces.

80 The victim of domestic violence is in the best position to decide if legal action will be the most effective way to stop the violence or psychological abuse. Her decision on this matter must be respected. If just moving away (and getting a divorce if necessary) will work, then there is no reason to get entangled in a complicated legal process in which control is given to an unknown judge. But there are

85 situations in which police assistance and court protection are essential.

Governor's Commission on Domestic Violence,
"Characteristics of the Abusive Situation"

1. According to the passage, the main reason that abused women often feel helpless is that:
   A. they don't know where to turn for help.
   B. society customarily takes the man's side.
   C. they can't afford to seek assistance.
   D. witnesses to incidents of abuse are hard to find.

2. One can infer that, in general, law enforcement officials think that incidents of wife abuse:
   F. should be settled within the family, if possible.
   G. are less serious than conflicts between strangers.
   H. should be blamed equally on the husband and the wife.
   J. have often been provoked by the wife.

3. The clause "their descriptions . . . are not paranoid delusions . . ." in lines 12–14 implies that battered women:
   A. often cannot separate fantasy from reality.
   B. tend to exaggerate incidents of abuse.
   C. feel maltreated by those from whom they seek help.
   D. frequently need psychological help.

4. The passage indicates that half the lawsuits brought against abusive husbands remain incomplete because of all the following reasons EXCEPT that the:
   F. husband and wife are reconciled.
   G. wife feels threatened by loss of financial support.
   H. courts take too long to hear cases.
   J. husband pledges to stop abusing his wife.

5. The passage suggests that, in an emergency, an abused wife should:
   A. call a neighbor.
   B. immediately report her husband to the police.
   C. try to go to a shelter for battered women.
   D. contact a social worker.

6. Which of the following statements most accurately summarizes the author's view on how to solve the problems of abused wives?
   F. Change the legal system to give abused wives special consideration.
   G. Help abused women overcome feelings of hopelessness.
   H. Strictly enforce the laws governing alimony payments.
   J. Educate society about the problems of abused wives.

7. A primary purpose of the passage is to:
   A. argue for new laws to protect abused women.
   B. convince readers that abusive behavior is never justified.
   C. point out the injustices faced by abused women.
   D. advise abused women of their rights.

8. The passage implies that the severest hardships of abused women pertain to:
   F. fears of bodily harm.
   G. lack of financial support.
   H. psychological trauma.
   J. the well-being of their children.

9. According to the passage, an abused wife may invoke all of the following legal remedies EXCEPT:
   A. filing for an official separation from her husband.
   B. maintaining custody of the children.
   C. forcing the husband to continue financial support.
   D. requiring the husband to pay her attorney's fees.

10. The passage suggests that, to stop domestic violence, an abused woman should turn to the courts only when:
    F. there is no alternative.
    G. she suffers psychological trauma.
    H. her husband would be charged with criminal behavior.
    J. she can get help from an understanding lawyer.

GO ON TO THE NEXT PAGE.

Passage II

NATURAL SCIENCE: This passage is from a government health report on the symptoms, causes, and treatment of Alzheimer's disease.

Microscopic brain tissue changes have been described in Alzheimer's disease since Aloise Alzheimer first reported them in 1906. These are the plaques and tangles—senile or neuritic plaques (degenerating nerve cells
5 combined with a form of protein called amyloid) and neurofibrillary tangles (nerve cell malformations). The brains of Alzheimer's disease patients of all ages reveal these findings in autopsy examination.

Computer-Assisted Tomography (CAT scan) changes
10 become more evident as the disease progresses—not necessarily early on. Thus an Alzheimer's CAT scan performed in the first stages of the disease cannot in itself be used to make a definitive diagnosis of Alzheimer's disease; its value is in helping to establish whether certain disorders
15 (some reversible) that mimic Alzheimer's disease are present. Later on, CAT scans often reveal changes characteristic of Alzheimer's disease, namely an atrophied (shrunken) brain with widened sulci (tissue indentations) and enlarged cerebral ventricles (fluid chambers). . . .

20 As research on Alzheimer's disease progresses, scientists are describing other abnormal anatomical and chemical changes associated with the disease. These include nerve cell degeneration in the brain's nucleus basalis of Meynert and reduced levels of the neurotransmitter ace-
25 tylcholine in the brains of Alzheimer's disease victims. But from a practical standpoint, the "classical" plaque and tangle changes seen at autopsy typically suffice for a diagnosis of Alzheimer's disease based on brain tissue changes. In fact, it is only through the study of brain tissue
30 from a person who was thought to have Alzheimer's disease that definitive diagnosis of the disorder can be made.

The "clinical" features of Alzheimer's disease, as opposed to the "tissue" changes, are threefold:
1. Dementia—significant loss of intellectual abilities such
35 as memory capacity, severe enough to interfere with social or occupational functioning;
2. Insidious onset of symptoms—subtly progressive and irreversible course with documented deterioration over time;
40 3. Exclusion of all other specific causes of dementia by history, physical examination, laboratory tests, psychometric, and other studies.

Based on these criteria, the clinical diagnosis of Alzheimer's disease has been referred to as "Alzheimer's
45 diagnosis by exclusion," and one that can only be made in the face of clinical deterioration over time. There is no specific clinical test or finding that is unique to Alzheimer's disease. Hence, all disorders that can bring on similar symptoms must be systematically excluded or "ruled out." This
50 explains why diagnostic workups of individuals where the

question of Alzheimer's disease has been raised can be so frustrating to patient and family alike; they are not told that Alzheimer's disease has been specifically diagnosed, but that other possible diagnoses have been dismissed, leav-
55 ing Alzheimer's disease as the likely diagnosis by the process of elimination.

Scientists hope to develop one day a specific test for Alzheimer's disease, based on a specific laboratory or genetic finding ("marker"). Some think that the results from
60 genetic research may lead to a diagnostic marker for certain persons evaluated for Alzheimer's disease. For example, recent research has discovered a protein, called "Alzheimer's disease-associated protein," in the autopsied brains of Alzheimer's patients. The protein is mainly con-
65 centrated in the cortex covering the front and side sections of the brain, regions involved in memory function. If researchers can perfect a test to detect the protein in the cerebrospinal fluid, it may be possible to use this method of diagnosis on living patients. Many scientists are working
70 at developing other tests or procedures that may someday identify living persons with the disorder, perhaps even early in its course before behavioral changes become evident. Still, a specific diagnostic marker for Alzheimer's disease is not yet available.

75 Meanwhile, Alzheimer's disease is the most overdiagnosed and misdiagnosed disorder of mental functioning in older adults. Part of the problem, already alluded to, is that many other disorders show symptoms that resemble those of Alzheimer's disease. The crucial difference, though, is that
80 many of these disorders—unlike Alzheimer's disease—may be stopped, reversed, or cured with appropriate treatment. But first they must be identified, not dismissed as Alzheimer's disease or senility.

U.S. Department of Health and Human Services,
Useful Information on Alzheimer's Disease

11. According to the passage, Alzheimer's disease:
  A. is most likely to strike during old age.
  B. was unknown before 1906.
  C. is hereditary.
  D. is more common in women than in men.

12. Which of the following is NOT a symptom of Alzheimer's disease?
  F. Loss of memory.
  G. Gradual deterioration of social skills.
  H. Increasingly severe headaches.
  J. Declining ability to figure out solutions to everyday problems.

13. The passage says that the most telling indication of Alzheimer's disease is:
  A. a shrunken brain.
  B. fluid in the brain.
  C. degeneration of nerve cells.
  D. discoloration of brain tissue.

GO ON TO THE NEXT PAGE.

3 3 3 3 3 3 3 3 3 3 3

14. The passage implies that the key to accurate diagnosis of Alzheimer's disease lies in:
    F. more advanced technology.
    G. greater understanding of diseases similar to Alzheimer's.
    H. more thorough study of the chemistry of the brain.
    J. genetic research.

15. A scientist preparing to work with Alzheimer's disease would probably be well advised to study:
    A. anatomy.
    B. organic chemistry.
    C. psychology.
    D. nutrition.

16. The passage suggests that Alzheimer's disease is "over-diagnosed and misdiagnosed" (lines 75–76) because:
    F. medical research on Alzheimer's disease is still in its infancy.
    G. its symptoms are like those of several other diseases.
    H. inflated statistics will increase funds allocated to Alzheimer's research.
    J. the symptoms of Alzheimer's disease vary from person to person.

17. The passage suggests that one important reason for diagnosing Alzheimer's disease in living people is:
    A. that physicians will then know how to handle Alzheimer's patients.
    B. to improve the treatment of victims of similar, but reversible, diseases.

C. to reduce the death rate of Alzheimer's patients.
D. to emotionally prepare patients and their families for the onset of the disease.

18. The author of the passage apparently believes that the most frustrating aspect of Alzheimer's disease for patients and their families is:
    F. not knowing for sure that the patient has been properly diagnosed.
    G. that Alzheimer's symptoms differ according to the individual.
    H. that no one can predict how long before a patient is totally disabled by the disease.
    J. that few Alzheimer's patients recover from the disease.

19. According to the passage, computers:
    A. have limited value in diagnosing Alzheimer's disease.
    B. are essential to physicians working with Alzheimer's patients.
    C. help doctors make definitive diagnoses of Alzheimer's disease.
    D. are useful in tracing the progress of Alzheimer's disease in individual patients.

20. Based on the passage, it is safe to assume that:
    F. Alzheimer's disease will never be cured.
    G. a vaccine may one day prevent Alzheimer's disease.
    H. current research is focusing on diagnosis of Alzheimer's disease.
    J. Alzheimer's disease is becoming more prevalent in our society.

Passage III

PROSE FICTION: This passage is an excerpt from "The Egg," a short story by Sherwood Anderson. In it the narrator recounts his family's vain attempt to run a successful chicken farm.

My father was, I am sure, intended by nature to be a cheerful, kindly man. Until he was thirty-four years old he worked as a farm hand for a man named Thomas Butterworth whose place lay near the town of Bidwell,
5 Ohio. He had then a horse of his own and on Saturday evenings drove into town to spend a few hours in social intercourse with other farm hands. . . . At ten o'clock Father drove home along a lonely country road, made his horse comfortable for the night and himself went to bed,
10 quite happy in his position in life. He had at that time no notion of trying to rise in the world.

It was in the spring of his thirty-fifth year that Father married my mother, then a country schoolteacher, and in the following spring I came wriggling and crying into the
15 world. Something happened to the two people. They became ambitious. The American passion for getting up in the world took possession of them.

It may have been that Mother was responsible. Being a schoolteacher she had no doubt read books and maga-
20 zines. She had, I presume, read of how Garfield, Lincoln and other Americans rose from poverty to fame and greatness and as I lay beside her—in the days of her lying-in—she may have dreamed that I would some day rule men and cities. At any rate, she induced Father to give up
25 his place as a farm hand, sell his horse and embark on an independent enterprise of his own. . . .

The first venture into which the two people went turned out badly. They rented ten acres of poor stony land on Grigg's Road, eight miles from Bidwell, and launched
30 into chicken raising. I grew into boyhood on the place and got my first impressions of life there. From the beginning they were impressions of disaster and if, in my turn, I am a

GO ON TO THE NEXT PAGE.

3 3 3 3 3 3 3 3 3 3 **3**

gloomy man inclined to see the darker side of life, I
attribute it to the fact that what should have been for me
35 the happy joyous days of childhood were spent on a
chicken farm.

One unversed in such matters can have no notion of
the many and tragic things that can happen to a chicken. It
is born out of an egg, lives for a few weeks as a tiny fluffy
40 thing such as you will see pictured on Easter cards, then
becomes hideously naked, eats quantities of corn and
meal bought by the sweat of your father's brow, gets
diseases called pip, cholera and other names, stands
looking with stupid eyes at the sun, becomes sick and dies.
45 A few hens and now and then a rooster, intended to serve
God's mysterious ends, struggle through to maturity. The
hens lay eggs out of which come other chickens and the
dreadful cycle is thus made complete. It is all unbelieva-
bly complex. Most philosophers must have been raised on
50 chicken farms. One hopes for so much from a chicken and
is so dreadfully disillusioned. Small chickens just setting
out on the journey of life, look so bright and alert and they
are in fact so dreadfully stupid. They are so much like
people they mix one up in one's judgments of life. If
55 disease does not kill them they wait until your expectations are thoroughly aroused and then walk under the
wheels of a wagon. . . . In later life I have seen how a
literature has been built up on the subject of fortunes to be
made out of the raising of chickens. . . . Do not be led astray
60 by it. It was not written for you. Go hunt for gold on the
frozen hills of Alaska, put your faith in the honesty of a
politician, believe if you will that the world is daily
growing better and that good will triumph over evil, but
do not read and believe the literature that is written
65 concerning the hen. . . .

I, however, digress. My tale does not primarily
concern itself with the hen. If correctly told it will center
on the egg. For ten years my father and mother struggled
to make our chicken farm pay and then they gave up that
70 struggle and began another. They moved into the town of
Bidwell, Ohio, and embarked in the restaurant business.
After ten years of worry, . . .we threw all aside and packing
our belongings on a wagon drove down Grigg's Road
toward Bidwell, a tiny caravan of hope looking for a new
75 place from which to start on our upward journey through
life.

Sherwood Anderson, "The Egg"

21. The narrator of the story views life pessimistically
    because:
    A. he grew up on a chicken farm.
    B. his parents never succeeded at anything they
       did.
    C. his life has been all work and no play.
    D. he and his family were always in debt.

22. The books and magazines mentioned in lines
    20–21:
    F. aided Mother in her work as a schoolteacher.
    G. indicate that Mother was well-educated.
    H. gave Mother ideas about how one ought to
       conduct one's life.
    J. were given to Mother in the hospital.

23. When he abandoned chicken farming, Father was
    about:
    A. 35 years old.
    B. 40 years old.
    C. 45 years old.
    D. 50 years old.

24. Which of these changes did NOT take place after
    Father got married?
    F. Father gave up his job at Butterworth's.
    G. Father became an ambitious person.
    H. Father stopped his Saturday-night socializing
       with the boys.
    J. Father wanted to stop working on a farm.

25. According to the narrator, in which way do chick-
    ens resemble human beings?
    A. Chickens, like people, appear to be brighter
       than they really are.
    B. Chickens, like children, are expensive to bring
       up.
    C. Chickens, as well as humans, are dirty, dis-
       eased, and smelly.
    D. Tragedies befall both chickens and humans.

26. According to the narrator, one of the few pleasures
    in raising chickens is that:
    F. you have the chance to witness the life cycle.
    G. the creatures are cute when they are chicks.
    H. if you are lucky, you can become rich.
    J. you'll never run out of eggs.

27. The narrator's opinion of books and articles written
    about chicken farming is that they are:
    A. all a pack of lies.
    B. not written for anyone who is serious about
       raising chickens.
    C. likely to make readers overly ambitious.
    D. meant only for people with nothing to lose.

28. Mother's ambition for her family's success led to
    all EXCEPT which of the following consequences?
    F. Father's cheerful and kindly disposition was
       changed.
    G. Mother and Father became poverty-stricken.
    H. Mother and Father were forced to work very
       hard.
    J. Mother and Father thought that they were fail-
       ures.

GO ON TO THE NEXT PAGE.

3 3 3 3 3 3 3 3 3 3 3

29. Which pair of adjectives most accurately convey the narrator's feelings about his childhood?
    A. resentful/bitter
    B. detached/unemotional
    C. satirical/humorous
    D. sentimental/sad

30. "Most philosophers must have been raised on chicken farms" (fifth paragraph) means that chicken farming:
    F. gives you a philosophical outlook on life.
    G. exposes you to profound issues like good and evil, life and death.
    H. allows you time to think.
    J. is so complex that only a philosopher can comprehend it.

Passage IV

HUMANITIES: This passage is excerpted from a history of classical music from the 18th century to the present. It discusses the types of drama that developed into opera as we know it today.

In antiquity the drama grew out of the "mysteries," the religious representations connected with temple worship. In the Middle Ages we witness a similar transition. By elaborating the religious ceremonies on feast days, the church
5 gradually instituted a sort of sacred spectacle which proved a powerful attraction for the populace. From the 12th century onward we can observe this practice. It began with miracle plays, with dramatized episodes from the lives of the saints. First performed within the church itself, these plays were later
10 relegated to the square in front of the church. They had achieved the desired effect. More than that, they were attracting throngs too large even for the vast nave of the cathedral. The demand for them continued. But under the blue dome of the sky, with the cathedral portico for a proscenium, the character and
15 the technique of these plays had to meet new conditions.

The removal from the hallowed interior of the church and the atmosphere of myrrh and incense to the open, and the more pungent aroma of the street, resulted in imparting a brisker air and a coarser flavor to the play. One of the favorite devices in
20 building the stage for these "sacred representations" was to divide the structure into three sections: a middle or main section represented the earthly plane upon which were enacted the principal incidents of the story; rising above it was an upper section representing the heavenly abode or paradise; for reasons
25 of symmetry as much as of theological doctrine, a lower section depicted the regions of hell. If Heaven and Paradise were peopled with actors in the guise of saints and angels, Hell had to have its lost souls and its devil. We may be sure that his part was not always a grateful one, and that upon many an occasion
30 he was vigorously and indignantly hissed off the stage by the righteous spectators. Therefore we can only sympathize with the poor fellow if he tried to win favor with the public by fair means or foul. To render himself *dramatis persona grata* he resorted to the ingenious device of being funny. Now, a funny
35 devil was perfectly harmless and not at all objectionable. In fact, he soon had the public on his side. He became "the hit of the show." The comic element made inroads. The grotesque and obscene little sculptures in which the cathedral masons gave vent to their spirit of hilarity and irreverence, had their
40 echo on the stage in farcical antics and profane language. The church did not find it easy to lay the ghost it had called up. By 1548 the mystery plays had degenerated to such an extent that the "Brotherhood of the Passion," which long enjoyed a sort of monopoly in the giving of these performances, was ordered to
45 stop them. If the spectacles ceased to be given as sacred performances, they continued in a different guise as secular entertainments. Carnival mummery and the *Commedia del arte* became national institutions. Theatrical performances found their strongholds at the courts of kings and princes. For the
50 celebration of royal birthdays, nuptials, state visits—or on any plausible pretext—they were the ideal form of diversion, because they were the most lavish and the most picturesque. They pressed into service *all* the arts; they offered an opportunity for fantastic illumination, reckless pomp, and the
55 glorifying of lovely women. . . .

The whole period of the Italian Renaissance is dominated by the love of display, of military and civic processions—called *trionfi*—which were the joy of the rabble. The nobility had its private high days and high
60 nights. Royalty indulged in whole weeks of revelries. The inventiveness of court poet, court painter, and court musician could not work fast enough to produce ever new and startling surprises. The poet earned his wages by more or less delicate flattery of his employer, to which end
65 he found mythological allegory most conveniently at hand. He turned Jupiter and Mars, Venus and Diana into complimentary disguises too easily pierced. Personal and political allusions stuck out everywhere in his poem. He was gone allegory-mad. There was nothing to stop him.
70 The general culture, the wide acquaintance with the classic writers enabled everybody in the audience to penetrate the symbolism of character and actions. So when in 1513, as Vasari reports, a poet in Florence decided to present the spectacle of a young boy, naked but gilt from head to
75 foot, there was probably not a person in the crowd who did not instantly recognize in the little fellow a personification of "the golden age."

Carl Engel, "The Beginnings of Opera"

31. According to the passage, theater originated in:
    A. the ceremonies of ancient cultures.
    B. Medieval traditions.
    C. 12th-century church services.
    D. street theater of the Renaissance.

GO ON TO THE NEXT PAGE.

32. Based on the passage, the term "miracle plays" (lines 7–8) may best be described as:
- **F.** rites performed on religious occasions.
- **G.** colorful spectacles that attracted worshipers to church.
- **H.** recreations of significant moments in the lives of saints.
- **J.** exposés showing how saints performed miracles.

33. Moving the performances of religious plays from inside the church to out-of-doors resulted in all of the following EXCEPT:
- **A.** larger audiences.
- **B.** a change in the solemn character of the plays.
- **C.** widespread use of everyday language.
- **D.** greater realism in the stories.

34. Religious dramas were often performed on a three-part set in order to:
- **F.** remind the audience of the Christian trinity.
- **G.** accommodate playwrights whose works contained three acts or scenes.
- **H.** add variety to the performance.
- **J.** approximate Hell, Heaven, and earth.

35. Over time, religious plays lost their sacred qualities for all of the following reasons EXCEPT:
- **A.** plays were removed from the inside of the church to the town square.
- **B.** actors often portrayed the devil as a likeable character.
- **C.** some of the plays may have contained earthy language.
- **D.** the church started to lose its influence in the lives of the people.

36. The attitude of the church toward the changes taking place in the theater during the Renaissance can best be described as:

- **F.** satisfaction.
- **G.** regret.
- **H.** pride.
- **J.** indifference.

37. For the nobility and upper classes, the spectacle of the theater represented a:
- **A.** way to show off their wealth and power.
- **B.** form of entertainment.
- **C.** means of religious observance.
- **D.** reaction to the authority of the church.

38. Poets enjoyed a heyday during the Renaissance partly because:
- **F.** aristocratic patrons of the arts paid well to be favorably portrayed in verse.
- **G.** the old classic poets and playwrights were brought back into vogue.
- **H.** so-called *trifoni* (line 58) required vast quantities of music, art, and, of course, poetry.
- **J.** it became the rage to glorify beautiful women in poetry.

39. The "Brotherhood of the Passion" (line 43) was ordered to cease performing mystery plays by:
- **A.** the rabble.
- **B.** a group of authoritarian noblemen.
- **C.** leaders of the *Commedia del arte*.
- **D.** the church.

40. The report (lines 72–77) that "not a person in the crowd" failed to recognize the "personification of 'the golden age'" can best be explained by:
- **F.** the popularity of Vasari, the widely read author of the early 1500s.
- **G.** the widespread appreciation and understanding of classical allusions.
- **H.** the spectacle of a naked boy covered with gold paint in the streets of Florence.
- **J.** the common practice of associating *gold* with "the golden age."

END OF TEST 3
STOP! DO NOT TURN THE PAGE UNTIL TOLD TO DO SO.

Model Science Reasoning Test

35 Minutes—40 Questions

DIRECTIONS: This test consists of several distinct passages. Each passage is followed by a number of multiple-choice questions based on the passage. Study the passage, and then select the best answer to each question. You are allowed to reread the passage. Record your answer by blackening the appropriate space on the answer sheet.

Passage I

The diagram below summarizes the chemical processes that produce acid rain.

NO is nitric oxide.
NO_2 is nitrogen dioxide.
SO_2 is sulfur dioxide.
SO_3 is sulfur trioxide.
CO is carbon monoxide.
CO_2 is carbon dioxide.

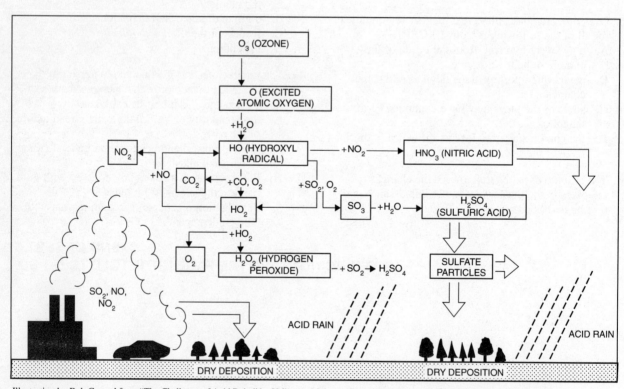

Illustration by Bob Conrad from "The Challenge of Acid Rain," by Volker A. Mohnen. Copyright © August 1988 by *Scientific American, Inc.* All rights reserved.

GO ON TO THE NEXT PAGE.

4 4 4 4 4 4 4 4 4 4 4 **4**

1. What is in smokestack gases and automobile exhaust that ultimately produces acid rain?
    A. Ozone
    B. Carbon dioxide
    C. Oxides of sulfur and nitrogen
    D. Nitric and sulfuric acids

2. Acid rain forms as a result of the reaction of hydrogen peroxide with:
    F. sulfur dioxide.
    G. water.
    H. nitrogen dioxide.
    J. sulfuric acid.

3. Carbon monoxide is removed from the air when it reacts with:
    A. nitric oxide to form nitric acid.
    B. sulfur dioxide to form sulfuric acid.

C. oxygen to form water.
D. oxygen to form carbon dioxide.

4. What gas combines directly with atmospheric water to form a polluting acid?
    F. Nitrogen dioxide
    G. Sulfur trioxide
    H. Sulfur dioxide
    J. Ozone

5. What substance that makes an important contribution to acid rain does not originate in the oxides of the exhaust gases?
    A. Sulfuric acid
    B. Ozone
    C. Nitrogen dioxide
    D. Sulfur trioxide

Passage II

In the sterilizing process, instruments and cultures are exposed to high temperatures for a definite length of time. The diagram below displays the combinations of temperature and time required to kill various kinds of microorganisms. The six graph areas represent the living stages of bacteria, yeasts, and molds, and the spore stages of these kinds of organisms.

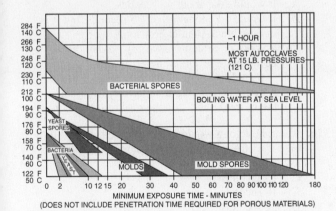

MINIMUM EXPOSURE TIME - MINUTES
(DOES NOT INCLUDE PENETRATION TIME REQUIRED FOR POROUS MATERIALS)

6. The kind of microorganism that is most difficult to kill is:
    F. mold spores.
    G. bacterial spores.
    H. yeasts.
    J. yeast spores.

7. If a laboratory technician keeps instruments in boiling water for 3 hours, the result of the procedure is to kill:
    A. mold spores

B. bacterial spores.
C. all spores.
D. all organisms.

8. What procedure could be used to kill off mold spores in a culture, but leave the yeast spores still viable?
    F. Hold the culture at 80°C for 20 minutes.
    G. Keep the culture at 90°C for 8 minutes and then at 85°C for another 5 minutes.
    H. Keep the culture at 70°C for 10 minutes.
    J. No combination of time and temperature can do this.

9. The chart suggests that, by controlling time and temperature, a technician might be able to:
    A. kill off bacterial spores while leaving live bacteria viable.
    B. kill all bacterial spores without destroying all the mold spores.
    C. kill off certain kinds of bacterial spores and leave other kinds still viable.
    D. destroy all living bacteria without killing off the living yeasts.

10. What general biological rule might be suggested by the contents of this graph?
    F. Microorganisms form spores to enable them to survive all kinds of unfavorable conditions.
    G. Molds are more sensitive than bacteria to temperature.
    H. Spore formation in microorganisms is a mechanism that protects the species against high temperatures.
    J. Spores are a vital mechanism for the reproduction of certain microorganisms.

GO ON TO THE NEXT PAGE.

4 4 4 4 4 4 4 4 4 4 4

Passage III

Experiments are done to study some of the factors that determine the rate of a reaction. When sulfuric acid acts on potassium iodate, elemental iodine is released. Iodine signals its presence by turning starch blue.

Experiment 1

A test solution is made of sulfuric acid and soluble starch in water. If potassium iodate is added, iodine accumulates at some definite rate. When the iodine reaches a certain concentration, the solution suddenly turns blue. Various concentrations of potassium iodate solution are used, and the time required for the mixture to turn blue is measured.

Potassium iodate concentration (%)	Time (seconds)
10	18
9	20
8	22
7	24
6	26
5	29
4	32

Experiment 2

To determine the effect of temperature on reaction rate, a 5% solution of potassium iodate is added to the test solution at various temperatures.

Temperature (° C)	Time (seconds)
5	36
15	31
25	27
35	24
45	22

11. Starch was added to the solution because:
    A. it speeds the reaction that produces iodine.
    B. it provides a test for the presence of elemental iodine.

C. it slows down the reaction so that the time becomes easily measurable.
D. it prevents the sulfuric acid from destroying the potassium iodate.

12. Experiment 1 shows that:
    F. elemental iodine turns starch blue.
    G. at higher iodate concentration, iodine is liberated more quickly.
    H. the rate of the reaction depends on the concentration of sulfuric acid used.
    J. the release of elemental iodine occurs suddenly.

13. Experiment 2 is an example of a general rule that:
    A. higher concentrations speed reactions.
    B. higher concentrations slow down reactions.
    C. higher temperatures speed reactions.
    D. higher temperatures slow down reactions.

14. Experiment 1 was done at a temperature of about:
    F. 10° C
    G. 20° C
    H. 30° C
    J. 40° C

15. By studying the results of this experiment, what can be concluded as to the time the reaction would take at a temperature of – 15° C?
    A. It would take about 48 seconds.
    B. It would take longer than 36 seconds, but it is impossible to predict how long.
    C. It is not possible to make any prediction because the results of the experiment are too scattered.
    D. It might take a long time, or the whole thing might freeze and stop the reaction.

16. About how long would it take for the starch to turn blue if a 10% solution of potassium iodate was used at 45° C?
    F. 15 seconds
    G. 18 seconds
    H. 22 seconds
    J. 29 seconds

GO ON TO THE NEXT PAGE.

4 4 4 4 4 4 4 4 4 4 4 **4**

Passage IV

The graphs below represent the percentages of fat and of water in the human body, by age and sex.

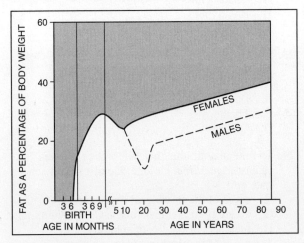
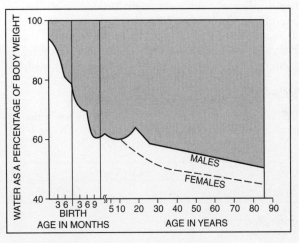

17. During the adolescent years, the most notable change is:
  A. a decrease in fat percentage for boys.
  B. an increase in fat percentage for girls.
  C. a decrease in water percentage for boys.
  D. an increase in water percentage for girls.

18. The percent of fat in the body increases most rapidly during:
  F. middle age.
  G. adolescence.
  H. babyhood.
  J. the prenatal period.

19. At age 60, the amount of water in the body of a 150-pound man is:
  A. the same as that in a 150-pound woman.
  B. twice as much as that in a 150-pound woman.
  C. about the same as that in a 140-pound woman.
  D. about the same as that in a 160-pound woman.

20. The percentage of body weight made up of both water and fat is:
  F. greater for females after adolescence.
  G. greater for males after adolescence.
  H. approximately the same for both sexes after adolescence only.
  J. approximately the same for both sexes at all ages after birth.

21. What hypothesis about the role of sex hormones during adolescence might be advanced from the graphs?
  A. Both male and female sex hormones cause an increase in the percent of fat in the body.
  B. Male hormones cause a reduction in the percent of fat and an increase in the percent of water.
  C. Female hormones have a much greater influence than male hormones on the percent of water.
  D. Male hormones cause the growth of male secondary sex characteristics.

GO ON TO THE NEXT PAGE.

4 4 4 4 4 4 4 4 4 4   **4**

Passage V

Seeds are tested for their ability to produce substances that kill microorganisms. Each seed is placed on cultures of two bacteria (*Staphylococcus* and *Escherichia*) and two molds. Seeds are classified on a scale of 0 (no effect) to 5 (strong effect), according to the amount of microorganism-free space that develops around the seed.

Experiment 1

Seeds of two members of the Lily family are tested against four different microorganisms:

Microorganism	Lily Family	
	Garlic	Daylily
Staphylococcus	4	0
Escherichia	5	4
Bread mold	2	2
Penicillium mold	3	0

Experiment 2

The same experiment is repeated using seeds of two members of the Composite family:

Microorganism	Composite Family	
	Dandelion	Thistle
Staphylococcus	5	5
Escherichia	4	5
Bread mold	4	3
Penicillium mold	2	2

Experiment 3

The experiment is then done with two members of the Legume family:

Microorganism	Legume Family	
	Soybean	Alfalfa
Staphylococcus	0	0
Escherichia	4	2
Bread mold	2	3
Penicillium mold	3	4

22. Which of the microorganisms is most susceptible to attacks by the chemicals produced by seeds?
    F. *Staphylococcus*
    G. *Escherichia*
    H. Bread mold
    J. *Penicillium* mold

23. Of the following, which kind of seed is more effective against molds than against bacteria?
    A. Alfalfa
    B. Daylily
    C. Thistle
    D. Garlic

24. To find an antibiotic that will protect oranges against *Penicillium* mold, a scientist would concentrate on:
    F. seeds of the thistle and its close relatives.
    G. a variety of members of the Composite family.
    H. members of the Legume family.
    J. seeds of the daylily and its relatives.

25. What conclusion can be reached about bread mold?
    A. It can survive by attacking seeds.
    B. It is highly resistant to chemical poisoning.
    C. It cannot be destroyed by seeds of the Composite family.
    D. It is moderately susceptible to attack by many kinds of seeds.

26. What hint might a scientist trying to find an antibiotic to control *Staphylococcus* infections get from these experiments?
    F. Looking for seeds that produce such an antibiotic would be a waste of effort.
    G. It would be inadvisable to concentrate on seeds of the Legume family.
    H. It would be wise to concentrate on *Penicillium* mold and its close relatives.
    J. The scientist should not waste time trying the bread mold and its close relatives.

27. Which of the following ecological hypotheses is supported by the evidence of these experiments?
    A. Molds are better able to survive than bacteria wherever the two kinds of microorganisms compete.
    B. The Legume family produces valuable fodder crops because its seeds have a high survival rate.
    C. The bacteria *Escherichia* and *Staphylococcus* may be highly damaging to leguminous crops.
    D. The Composite family has so many successful sturdy weeds because its seeds destroy microorganisms.

GO ON TO THE NEXT PAGE.

4   4 4 4 4 4 4 4 4 4 4   4

Passage VI

Experiments are done to test the optical properties of lenses immersed in media having different indices of refraction.

Experiment 1

A lens made of flint glass, index of refraction 1.720, is tested. A beam of parallel light rays is sent into the lens, and the distance from the lens to the point of convergence of the beam is measured. This is the focal length of the lens. This focal length is measured with the lens immersed in media of various indices of refraction.

Medium	Index of refraction	Focal length (cm)
Air	1.00	8
Folinol	1.24	13
Water	1.33	20
11% Sugar solution	1.50	39
Carbon disulfide	1.62	95
Methylene iodide	1.74	*

*Rays do not converge at all.

Experiment 2

Another lens is tested. It is made of the same kind of glass as in Experiment 1, but this lens is thicker, more strongly curved.

Medium	Index of refraction	Focal length (cm)
Air	1.00	5
Folinol	1.24	8
Water	1.33	12
11% Sugar solution	1.50	24
Carbon disulfide	1.62	60
Methylene iodide	1.74	*

Experiment 3

A lens made of a new plastic is then tested. This lens is identical in size and shape to the glass lens in Experiment 2.

Medium	Index of refraction	Focal length (cm)
Air	1.00	13
Folinol	1.24	34
Water	1.33	360
11% Sugar solution	1.50	*
Carbon disulfide	1.62	*
Methylene iodide	1.74	*

28. The index of refraction column is the same in all three experiments because:
   F. all three lenses have the same basic properties.
   G. the same liquids are used in all three experiments.
   H. the temperatures at which the experiments are performed are carefully controlled.
   J. the color of the light source is not allowed to change from one experiment to another.

29. As the index of refraction of the medium increases, what happens to the rays of light emerging from the lens?
   A. They converge more strongly in all cases.
   B. They converge more strongly on leaving the glass lenses, but not the plastic lens.
   C. They converge less strongly in all cases.
   D. They converge less strongly on leaving the plastic lens, but not the glass lens.

30. Making a lens thicker and more strongly curved:
   F. shortens the focal length.
   G. increases the focal length.
   H. increases the index of refraction.
   J. decreases the index of refraction.

31. A reasonable hypothesis that can be derived from Experiments 1 and 2 is that:
   A. a lens will not focus light if its index of refraction is lower than that of the medium it is in.
   B. methylene iodide tends to spread light out so that it does not come to a focus.
   C. the focal length of a lens depends entirely on the index of refraction of the medium it is in.
   D. the thicker a lens, the less the convergence it produces on the light that passes through it.

32. Measurements of the kind made in these experiments would NOT be useful in efforts to find:
   F. the index of refraction of a liquid.
   G. the way a prism in a fluid would bend light rays.
   H. the concentration of a sugar solution.
   J. the chemical composition of an unknown liquid.

33. The index of refraction of the plastic lens in Experiment 3 must be:
   A. less than 1.33.
   B. between 1.33 and 1.50.
   C. more than 1.33.
   D. more than 1.50.

GO ON TO THE NEXT PAGE.

4 4 4 4 4 4 4 4 4 4 4

Passage VII

Two scientists disagree on the question of the origin of petroleum.

Scientist 1

There have been many theories suggesting a non-organic origin of petroleum, but none of them have been successful. It is now accepted almost universally by geologists that petroleum comes from the decay of living things. Petroleum formation occurs in enclosed oceanic basins, such as the Black Sea. There must be an extremely large and continuous supply of marine organisms, adding their corpses to an accumulation at the bottom of the sea. They are quickly buried in sediment, so quickly that they do not have time to decay. In the enclosed basin, there is little circulation, so there is no supply of fresh, oxygenated water. In the absence of oxygen, there is little decay. The organic matter of the corpses degenerates into hydrocarbons, which accumulate as oil and gas. Since oil is lighter than water, it rises. As the deposits are covered with more sediments, the oil and gas rise into them and accumulate there. Petroleum geologists know that oil is often found in salt domes, formed by the evaporation of seawater.

Scientist 2

The current theory about the origin of petroleum postulates a very unlikely combination of circumstances. It needs an enclosed basin, exceptionally rich in marine life, with sediments pouring rapidly into it from the surrounding countryside. Although this combination might occur occasionally, it is too rare to account for the enormous earth areas underlain by petroleum. In my opinion, oil has been present deep in the earth since its origin. Meteorites, comets, and satellites are rich in hydrocarbons. The earth formed by agglomeration of these kinds of objects. After the earth formed, the hydrocarbons seeped upward, accumulating in porous sedimentary rocks. However, oil and gas are sometimes found seeping out of igneous rocks, which have no fossils at all, if these rocks have been thoroughly fractured by deep earthquakes. Oil wells now drill down to only about 15,000 feet. A recent explorational drilling found an oily sludge at 20,000 feet. If we could get to 30,000 feet, we would find an enormous pool of oil underlying the whole crust of the earth.

34. Both scientists agree that petroleum:
   F. forms at the bottom of the sea.
   G. seeps upward into sedimentary rocks.
   H. is present in great quantities below 30,000 feet.
   J. has always been present on earth.

35. Which of the following discoveries would greatly weaken the argument of Scientist 2?
   A. A vast oil deposit is found in sedimentary strata 20,000 feet deep.

B. A meteorite is analyzed and found to contain few hydrocarbons.
C. The sludge discovered at 20,000 feet turns out to be contamination from drilling oil.
D. A large accumulation of oil is found in highly fractured igneous rock.

36. According to Scientist 2, what strategy would be most likely to increase world supplies of petroleum?
   F. Drill wells to greater depths.
   G. Inccrease exploration of offshore sedimentary strata.
   H. Drill wells in igneous rocks.
   J. Develop techniques of extraction from meteorites.

37. Exploration of the Persian Gulf reveals that it is an enclosed body of water rich in marine life. According to the hypothesis of Scientist 1, what additional condition would be necessary in order for petroleum deposits to develop?
   A. Vertical circulation to carry oxygen downward
   B. High concentration of salt in the water
   C. An accumulation of meteorites
   D. Rapid deposition of sediments

38. Scientist 2 considers that oil seepage from igneous rocks is damaging to Scientist 1's theory because igneous rocks:
   F. are easily fractured by earthquakes.
   G. never contain fossils.
   H. are always located deep in the crust.
   J. contain many meteorites.

39. What evidence given by Scientist 1 was not refuted by Scientist 2?
   A. There have been many theories of a nonorganic origin of petroleum, and all of them have failed.
   B. Petroleum is very often found associated with salt domes.
   C. All petroleum deposits are in porous sedimentary rock.
   D. Meterorites come to earth in the ocean just as often as on land.

40. The chief objection that Scientist 2 has to the theory of Scientist 1 is that it:
   F. postulates the formation of petroleum in a highly unusual set of conditions.
   G. cannot account for the accumulation of petroleum in sedimentary rocks.
   H. arbitrarily rejects the theory of nonorganic origin.
   J. places a limit on the amount of petroleum that can be extracted from the earth.

END OF TEST 4
STOP! DO NOT TURN THE PAGE UNTIL TOLD TO DO SO.

ANSWER KEYS AND ANALYSIS CHARTS

MODEL ENGLISH TEST

1.	D	16.	G	31.	C	46.	H	61.	C
2.	J	17.	B	32.	J	47.	B	62.	J
3.	B	18.	H	33.	B	48.	J	63.	B
4.	G	19.	D	34.	F	49.	C	64.	H
5.	D	20.	J	35.	D	50.	H	65.	B
6.	H	21.	C	36.	J	51.	A	66.	J
7.	C	22.	J	37.	B	52.	H	67.	C
8.	F	23.	A	38.	G	53.	C	68.	G
9.	A	24.	G	39.	B	54.	G	69.	C
10.	J	25.	B	40.	J	55.	C	70.	F
11.	C	26.	G	41.	B	56.	F	71.	B
12.	G	27.	C	42.	J	57.	C	72.	F
13.	C	28.	G	43.	B	58.	G	73.	C
14.	J	29.	C	44.	H	59.	D	74.	F
15.	D	30.	G	45.	B	60.	G	75.	D

Analysis Chart

Skills	Questions	Possible Score	Your Score
Usage/Mechanics			
Punctuation	7, 9, 12, 26, 29, 33, 44, 47, 50, 72	10	
Basic Grammar and Usage	3, 8, 23, 31, 34, 35, 37, 38, 39, 40, 41, 66	12	
Sentence Structure	6, 13, 14, 16, 17, 19, 20, 22, 32, 46, 55, 56, 57, 58, 62, 64, 67, 68	18	
Rhetorical Skills			
Strategy	2, 18, 25, 27, 36, 42, 43, 49, 53, 54, 70, 71	12	
Organization	5, 15, 24, 30, 45, 59, 60, 63, 73, 74, 75	11	
Style	1, 4, 10, 11, 21, 28, 48, 51, 52, 61, 65, 69	12	

Total: 75 _____

Percent Correct: _____

MODEL MATHEMATICS TEST

1.	C	13.	E	25.	D	37.	E	49.	E
2.	J	14.	F	26.	K	38.	F	50.	H
3.	A	15.	D	27.	D	39.	E	51.	D
4.	K	16.	H	28.	H	40.	J	52.	J
5.	B	17.	D	29.	D	41.	D	53.	B
6.	K	18.	J	30.	J	42.	H	54.	G
7.	B	19.	A	31.	B	43.	E	55.	B
8.	G	20.	J	32.	K	44.	K	56.	J
9.	B	21.	C	33.	D	45.	A	57.	A
10.	J	22.	K	34.	G	46.	H	58.	H
11.	D	23.	C	35.	E	47.	D	59.	E
12.	G	24.	K	36.	G	48.	G	60.	F

Analysis Chart

Content Area	Skill Level			Possible Score	Your Score
	Basic Skills	**Application**	**Analysis**		
Pre-Algebra Algebra	1, 4, 5, 9, 10, 14, 21, 44	2, 6, 7, 17, 22, 24, 27, 32, 34, 37, 38, 43	3, 11, 12, 15	24	
Intermediate Algebra Coordinate Geometry	13, 20, 30, 31, 39, 46, 53	8, 16, 19, 23, 26, 28, 33	29, 41, 54, 56	18	
Geometry	18, 35, 42, 49, 51, 57, 59	25, 40, 45, 47, 48, 58, 60		14	
Trigonometry	36, 50	52, 55		4	

Total: 60 _____

Percent Correct: _____

MODEL READING TEST

1.	B	11.	A	21.	A	31.	A
2.	J	12.	H	22.	H	32.	H
3.	C	13.	C	23.	C	33.	D
4.	F	14.	J	24.	J	34.	J
5.	C	15.	B	25.	A	35.	D
6.	G	16.	G	26.	G	36.	G
7.	C	17.	B	27.	C	37.	B
8.	G	18.	F	28.	J	38.	F
9.	D	19.	A	29.	C	39.	D
10.	F	20.	H	30.	F	40.	G

Analysis Chart

Passage Type	Referring	Reasoning	Possible Score	Your Score
Prose Fiction	21, 22, 24, 26	23, 25, 27, 28, 29, 30	10	
Humanities	31, 33, 34	32, 35, 36, 37, 38, 39, 40	10	
Social Sciences	1, 4, 9	2, 3, 5, 6, 7, 8, 10	10	
Natural Sciences	11, 12, 13, 19	14, 15, 16, 17, 18, 20	10	

Total: 40 _____

Percent Correct: _____

MODEL SCIENCE REASONING TEST

1.	C	11.	B	21.	B	31.	A
2.	F	12.	G	22.	G	32.	J
3.	D	13.	C	23.	A	33.	B
4.	G	14.	G	24.	H	34.	G
5.	B	15.	D	25.	D	35.	C
6.	G	16.	F	26.	G	36.	F
7.	D	17.	A	27.	D	37.	D
8.	J	18.	J	28.	G	38.	G
9.	C	19.	D	29.	C	39.	B
10.	H	20.	J	30.	F	40.	F

Analysis Chart

Kind of Question	Skill Level			Possible Score	Your Score
	Understanding	Analysis	Generalization		
Data Representation	1, 2, 3, 6, 17, 18	4, 7, 8, 9, 19, 20	5, 10, 21	15	
Research Summaries	11, 12, 22, 23, 28, 29	14, 24, 25, 30, 31, 33	13, 15, 16, 26, 27, 32	18	
Conflicting Viewpoints	34, 35, 38	36, 37, 39	40	7	

Total: 40 _____
Percent Correct: _____

1. D All meanings carried by the underlined portion are implicit in the words preceding

Answer Explanations: ENGLISH TEST

it. The entire portion is redundant.

2. J The quotation is pertinent, short, and authoritative. As such, it is a sound way to begin the passage.

3. B The antecedent of the pronoun in question is the singular *someone.*

4. G The phrase *lacking merit* at the end of the clause is adequate characterization of the type of case under discussion.

5. D As idealistic as the thought is, it is off the topic and has no place in this passage.

6. H The logic of this sentence requires that a transitional word indicating *cause* be employed in this spot.

7. C Three or more items in a series must be set off by commas.

8. F The phrase *changing attorneys* is a gerund phrase, that is, a *noun* phrase. Since it is an activity of the noun *client,* that noun requires the pos-

sessive apostrophe and final *s.*

9. A Dashes are appropriate marks to set off a parenthetical phrase, especially if one intends to emphasize the phrase.

10. J All other options are wordy or redundant.

11. C Colloquial and whimsical language is not in keeping with the matter-of-fact tone of the passage.

12. G Coordinate clauses must be separated by a comma.

13. C A new sentence begins at this point.

14. J At this spot a third noun—namely, *premium*—should parallel the objects *salary* and *rent.*

15. D Paragraph 3 begins with a clear signal that it should follow paragraph 4 rather than precede it, specifically the word *Finally.*

16. G The adverb *more* and the comparative adverb ending *-er* are equivalent, and cannot be used

Answer Explanations: ENGLISH TEST *(continued)*

together. The result is a double comparison.

17. B The subject of this clause is the singular *person*.

18. H There is no suggestion or clue to suggest that the passage is intended for any one group.

19. D As it stands, the text contains a comma splice at this point; of the options, only the period break is correct.

20. J The present-tense, passive-voice verb is appropriate because the focus is on the toys, and the passage is written in the present tense. As it stands, this is a sentence fragment.

21. C The fact that the sentence later mentions that the rooms are "slightly askew" is reason enough to avoid the modifiers of the word *rooms*.

22. J The logic of this sentence requires that a conjunction indicating time be used at this transition; *when* is the only choice that makes sense.

23. A The verb agrees with the nearer subject (two) and is in the present tense.

24. G As interesting as the information may be, this sentence is wholly off the topic, and must be removed.

25. B The notion of children marking their territory with smudges and smears is humorous and whimsical. The other options do not suggest humor.

26. G A compound adjective preceding the noun it modifies is hyphenated, but the two words before *homes* do not comprise a compound adjective; one, *finely*, is an adverb modifying the adjective *furnished*.

27. C The enormous difference in the size of these paragraphs, as well as the amount of data they contain, shows the writer's bias.

28. G The noun *difference* clearly indicates that two kinds of people are being compared; *distinguishing* is not needed.

29. C A compound adjective that *precedes* the noun is hyphenated; one that *follows* the noun usually is not.

30. G The word *Conversely* is a clue that paragraph 2 must occur after paragraph 3; the words *another great difference* at the outset of paragraph 4 place it after paragraph 2.

31. C The subject of the sentence is the singular noun *idea*. The prepositional phrase *of a community*

among nations is a modifier of that noun. When the entire passage is read, it becomes apparent that the present tense is correct.

32. J The only tense that conveys past action over a span of time to the present is the present perfect tense of the verb, that is, *have had*.

33. B The parenthetical phrase *a free association based on shared principles and an increasingly shared way of life* has been set off by dashes rather than by brackets, an option generally chosen by writers to emphasize a phrase. There must be a dash at the end as well as the beginning of the phrase.

34. F When a collective noun such as *people* clearly refers to individual members of a group, it takes a plural pronoun. Here the plural verbs *argue* and *choose* indicate reference to individuals.

35. D The subject of the verb is the plural noun *ideals*. The prepositional phrase *of freedom* is a modifier of that noun.

36. J The writer is attempting to establish a precedent for nations to join forces; reference to the cooperation of Greek city-states is logical and meaningful.

37. B When a sentence has two or more subjects joined by *and*, the verb almost always is in the plural form. The present tense is correct.

38. G Here the past participle of the verb *to shake* acts as an adjective modifying the noun *heritage*.

39. B The subjects of this verb are the plural nouns *graves* and *camps*, not the noun *Reich*, which is part of a prepositional phrase modifying the noun *camps*.

40. J An adverb is needed to modify the participle *built*.

41. B The antecedent of the pronoun is the singular noun *regime*, not the pronoun *they*.

42. J The Berlin Wall is a very direct example of the evidence mentioned in the paragraph's first sentence, and the reference is therefore meaningful.

43. B The statement is followed by a list that supports the assertion that the number of "like-minded nations" is increasing.

44. H A colon is often used to introduce an appositive more dramatically or emphatically at the end of a sentence. A comma would be ineffective here.

45. B The first paragraph introduces the notion of

"a community among nations." Perusal of the passage quickly reveals that paragraph 4 begins with the words *This community* and belongs in position 2. Paragraphs 2 and 3 follow with appropriate clues at the beginning of each *(Our community* and *other evidence)* that point to the preceding paragraph.

46. H This verb must be in the present tense to express what is still true.

47. B The name *Antonia Shimerda* is in apposition with *protagonist* and is properly set off with two commas.

48. J The adjective *actual* is the only choice that indicates what is intended, that the girl was a genuine Bohemian girl. The other choices are either redundant or misleading.

49. C This "summary" is inconclusive; it should include more information about the story.

50. H Commas and periods are *always* placed *inside* quotation marks, even when there are single and double quotation marks because the sentence contains a quote within a quote.

51. A The word *albeit* means literally "although it be," a meaning that is required for the sense of the clause to remain intact, and that is not repeated in the other options.

52. H The prefix *multi* is most often incorporated with another word as a unit.

53. C Since the paragraph deals with Cather's preference in the novel to the country over the city, and since the entire passage is about the novel *My Antonia,* the quotation is clearly meaningful.

54. G This passage describes the pastoral life of a young girl in rural America in the early 1900s. It goes on to describe the novel as "a song of praise for agricultural existence as opposed to life in the cities."

55. C The passage is written in the present tense, and employs the historical present whenever necessary.

56. F *Employed* in this sentence is a participle modifying the noun *symbols.*

57. C To be parallel with the phrases naming the first two cycles, this one must begin with the noun *cycle,* rather than a clause describing it.

58. G No comma is needed. Choice F results in a sentence fragment beginning with *In which,* and neither the semicolon (H) nor the dash (J) is

appropriate.

59. D The body of the paragraph does a comprehensive job of developing the beginning generalization.

60. G Paragraph 1 begins with broad, general statements about the novel, and prepares the reader for the critical commentary that comes with the next paragraph, paragraph 3. Paragraph 2 is the summary paragraph that effectively ends this passage.

61. C The word *concrete* is clear; added words with the same meaning are unproductive and uneconomical.

62. J The adjective *clear* is meant to modify the noun *notion* and so must be placed before it. When *clear* is placed in other positions, it modifies other nouns and creates confusion.

63. B The introductory paragraph of this passage might well have spelled out the meaning of *translating philosophy into concrete action,* rather than leaving the expression in its somewhat unclear form.

64. H In its original form, this sentence creates an error in *predication,* that is, an error in which the beginning of the sentence is not consistent with the end.

65. B The other choices are colloquial and inconsistent with the rather formal and businesslike tone of the passage.

66. J The pronoun *this* almost never is adequate by itself; it must be followed by a noun for clarity of meaning.

67. C Any mark of punctuation weaker than a period or semicolon creates a run-on sentence. Two completely independent clauses are joined here.

68. G The logic of the sentence requires a conjunction signaling *condition,* such as *if,* in this spot. Conjunctions signaling other logical shifts, like *contrast* (F or H) or *restriction* (J) render the sentence meaningless.

69. C There is no point in repeating the meaning of a word redundantly. The word *nation* is clear; neither its meaning nor the meaning of the sentence is enriched or clarified by the addition of synonyms.

70. F The passage is clearly an attempt to demonstrate a peaceful foreign policy to the world.

71. B The attempt in this sentence and throughout the passage is to persuade more conservative Ameri-

Answer Explanations: ENGLISH TEST *(continued)*

cans that we cannot be what we were after World War II.

72. F Coordinate clauses, that is, independent clauses joined together by a coordinating conjunction (*and, but, for, or, yet*), are separated by a comma.

73. C As truthful as the statement may be, and as related to world politics, it has nothing to do with the point of the passage and must be removed.

74. F The passage progresses from the statement that *We have now grown beyond the era* (of unchallenged power) to the recognition that *we must move toward appreciation* (of our role as conciliators).

75. D The clue at the beginning of paragraph 3, *At the outset,* indicates the placement of the paragraph just after the introduction. The beginning of paragraph 2 is meaningful only if one has read paragraph 3.

Answer Explanations: MATHEMATICS TEST

1. C $\dfrac{a}{b} - \dfrac{c}{d} = \dfrac{ad}{bd} - \dfrac{bc}{bd}$

$= \dfrac{ad - bc}{bd}$

2. J First factor the numerator. $\dfrac{2x^4 + x^3}{x^6}$

$= \dfrac{x^3(2x + 1)}{x^6}$ Cancel x^3. $= \dfrac{2x + 1}{x^3}$

3. A $\dfrac{3}{4}(1600) = 1200$ phones have dials.

$\dfrac{1}{3}(1200) = 400$ dial phones are replaced by push-button phones.

$1200 - 400 = 800$ dial phones remain.

4. K $\dfrac{x}{y}$ is not necessarily an integer.

5. B For example: $5 - (-7) = 12$, which is positive.

6. K Multiply both sides by $4x - 3$.

($\dfrac{3}{4}$ is a restricted value.)

$\dfrac{5}{4x - 3}(4x - 3) = 5(4x - 3)$

$5 = 5(4x - 3) = 20x - 15$

$20 = 20x$

$x = 1$

7. B. Ten times the tens digit plus the unit digit: $10t + u$.

8. G Multiply each term of the first polynomial times each term of the second polynominal.

$(x - 1)(x^2 + x + 1)$

$= x^3 + x^2 + x - x^2 - x - 1$

$= x^3 - 1$

9. B Divide 3 by 2. The quotient is 1 and the remainder is 1. The base two numeral is $11_{(two)} = 1(2) + 1$.

10. J $\quad 2.5 = 0.025$

$\dfrac{1}{40} = 0.025$

$2.5(10^{-2}) = 0.025$

$\dfrac{75}{30} = 2.5$

11. D Each apple costs $\dfrac{100}{3} = 33\dfrac{1}{3}$ in the 3 for $1.00 deal. The difference between 35 cents and $33\dfrac{1}{3}$ is $1\dfrac{2}{3}$ cents.

12. G In 1 minute Joan can run $\dfrac{1}{a}$ part of a mile.

After b minutes, she has run $b\dfrac{1}{a} = \dfrac{b}{a}$.

13. E Division by 0 is never allowed.

14. F $3\dfrac{3}{5} \cdot 4\dfrac{1}{6} \quad = \dfrac{18}{5} \cdot \dfrac{25}{6}$

$= \dfrac{3}{1} \cdot \dfrac{5}{1}$ Cancel.

$= 15$

15. D Write two equations with two variables, n and d.

$n = d + 5$

$5n + 10d = 130$ Then substitute for n.

$5(d + 5) + 10d = 130$

$5d + 25 + 10d = 130$

$15d + 25 = 130$

$15d = 105$

$d = 7$

Then $n = 12$.

Answer Explanations: MATHEMATICS TEST *(continued)*

16. H In an arithmetic sequence, the nth term is given by
$$a_n = a_1 + (n-1)d$$

in which a_1 is the first term, n is the number of the term, and d is the common difference between terms. In the given sequence the tenth term is sought and the common difference is 5.
$$a_{10} = 3 + (10-1)5 = 3 + 45 = 48$$

17. D First multiply by 100 to get rid of the decimals.
$$100[0.2(100-x) + 0.05x] = 100[0.1(100)]$$
$$20(100-x) + 5x = 10(100)$$
$$2000 - 20x + 5x = 1000$$
$$-15x = -1000$$
$$x = 66\tfrac{2}{3}$$

18. J There certainly is a regular polygon of seven sides.

19. A $\sqrt[3]{54x^4y^6} = \sqrt[3]{27x^3y^6 \cdot 2x}$ Separate the radicand into cube and noncube parts.
$$= 3xy^2\sqrt[3]{2x}$$

20. J Conic sections are second-degree (or less) curves only. The equation $y = x^3$ is not of degree 2.

21. C The degree of a polynomial is the greatest of the degree of its terms. The degrees of the terms of the given polynominal are 3, 4, 2, and 0. The greatest degree is 4.

22. K Add the two equations.
$$\begin{aligned} 2x - y &= 5 \\ x + y &= 1 \\ \hline 3x &= 6 \\ x &= 2 \end{aligned}$$
Substitute $x = 2$ into either equation (say the second one).
$$2 + y = 1$$
$$y = -1$$

23. C The numbers 2, 4, 6, and 8 satisfy the conditions of being even and less than 10. $P(A) = \dfrac{4}{20} = \dfrac{1}{5}$.

24. K Multiply the numerator and denominator by the LCD, which is xy.
$$\dfrac{xy(x+y)}{xy\left(\dfrac{1}{x} + \dfrac{1}{y}\right)} = \dfrac{xy(x+y)}{y+x}$$
$$= xy$$

25. D Inscribed angle ABC intercepts are arc that is twice the measure of the angle, so arc ADC measures $140°$ and the measure of arc ABC is $(360 - 140)° = 220°$. The measure of inscribed angle ADC is half the measure of its intercepted arc: $110°$. (Opposite angles of an inscribed quadrilateral are supplementary.)

26. K Since $a > b$, then $a - b > 0$ and $b - a < 0$. The absolute value of a positive number is equal to that number, but the absolute value of a negative number is the opposite of the number.
$$|a - b| = a - b \text{ and } |b - a|$$
$$= -(b - a) = a - b.$$
$$|a - b| + |b - a| = (a - b) + (a - b)$$
$$= 2a - 2b.$$

27. D The expression -3^{-2} is properly read as "the opposite of 3 to the -2 power." Follow the rules for the order of operations:
$$-3^{-2} = -(3^{-2}) = -\left(\frac{1}{3^2}\right) = -\left(\frac{1}{9}\right)$$

28. H To put this equation into standard form, complete the square in both variables.
$$\begin{aligned} (x^2 - 4x\ \ ) + 4(y^2 + 6y\ \ ) &= -36 \\ (x^2 - 4x + 4) + (y^2 + 6y + 9) &= -36 + 4 + 36 \\ (x-2)^2 + 4(y+3)^2 &= 4 \\ \frac{(x-2)^2}{4} + \frac{(y+3)^2}{1} &= 1 \end{aligned}$$
The center is $(2, -3)$.

29. D This is a work-type word problem, for which the formula $w = rt$ applies. Let Bonnie's time to complete the job be x hours, then Nick's time is $x - 2$ hours. Her rate of work is $\dfrac{1}{x}$ part of the job per hour. His rate is $\dfrac{1}{x-2}$.

	w	$=$	r	t
Nick	$\dfrac{7}{x-2}$		$\dfrac{1}{x-2}$	7
Bonnie	$\dfrac{7}{x}$		$\dfrac{1}{x}$	7

The sum of the work column is equal to 1 (one completed job). The equation is
$$\frac{7}{x-2} + \frac{7}{x} = 1.$$

30. J A function is one-to-one if all of the ordered pairs in the function not only have different first components but also have different second components. This means that the graph must pass both the vertical line test and the horizontal line test. If a vertical line crosses the graph once at most, then it is a function. If a horizontal line crosses the graph once at most, then the function is one-to-one (and thus it has an inverse). Only J satisfies both tests.

31. B An exponential function is any function of the type:
$$f(x) = a^x, \text{ for } a > 0, a \neq 1.$$

Answer Explanations: MATHEMATICS TEST *(continued)*

32. K $(5x - 3y^2)^2 = 25x^2 - 30xy^2 + 9y^4$.

33. D The reciprocal of i is $\frac{1}{i}$. Multiply both numerator and denominator by the conjugate of the denominator, $-i$: $\frac{-i(1)}{-i(i)}$.

$$\frac{-i}{1} = -i$$

34. G $\dfrac{a^{-3}bc^2}{a^{-4}b^2c^{-3}} = a^{-3-(-4)}b^{1-2}c^{2-(-3)}$

$$= a^1 b^{-1} c^5$$

$$= \frac{ac^5}{b}$$

35. E The length of the longer leg of a 30-60-90 triangle is equal to $\sqrt{3}$ times the length of the shorter leg, and the length of the hypotenuse is twice the length of the shorter leg. The length of the longer leg is given, so to find the length of the shorter leg divide by $\sqrt{3}$.

$$BC = \frac{6}{\sqrt{3}} = 2\sqrt{3}$$

Therefore $AB = 2(2\sqrt{3}) = 4\sqrt{3}$

36. G The identity is $\sin 2A = 2 \sin A \cos A$.

37. E Use the quadratic formula:

$$x = \frac{-b \pm \sqrt{b_2 - 4ac}}{2a}$$

Here

$$x = \frac{4 \pm \sqrt{16 - (-72)}}{6}$$

$$= \frac{4 \pm \sqrt{88}}{6} = \frac{4 \pm 2\sqrt{22}}{6} = \frac{2 \pm \sqrt{22}}{3}$$

38. F $3\sqrt{3} - \sqrt{48} + 3\sqrt{\frac{1}{3}} = 3\sqrt{3} - 4\sqrt{3} + \sqrt{3} = 0$

39. E The two ordered pairs (4, 2) and (4, –2) both satisfy the equation $x = y^2$, and so it does not define a function.

40. J The length of a tangent is the mean proportional between the length of a secant from a common external point and the length of the secant's external segment.

$$\frac{x + 4}{6} = \frac{6}{4}$$
$$4x + 16 = 36$$
$$4x = 20$$
$$x = 5$$

41. D This is a uniform motion-type word problem, for which the formula $d = rt$ applies.

	D	=	r	t
Bike	x		12	$\frac{x}{12}$
Car	x		36	$\frac{x}{36}$

This time for the car trip is $\frac{1}{2}$ hour less than the time for the bike trip. The equation is:

$$\frac{x}{36} = \frac{x}{12} = \frac{1}{2}$$

42. H The midpoint formula is

$$\left(\frac{x_1 + x_2}{2}, \frac{y_1 + y_2}{2} \right)$$

Here

$$\left(\frac{3 + (-5)}{2}, \frac{7 + (-6)}{2} \right) = \left(-1, \frac{1}{2} \right)$$

43. E A square root radical by definition is positive. The solution set is empty.

44. K All these statements are true.

45. A The diagram shows a 30-60-90 triangle with the hypotenuse equal in length to the radius of the circle, the length of the shorter leg half the length of the hypotenuse, and the length of the longer leg $\sqrt{3}$ times the length of the shorter leg. The perimeter of the triangle is equal to 6 times the length of the longer leg of the triangle.

$$6(4\sqrt{3}) = 24\sqrt{3}$$

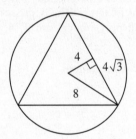

46. H The domain contains all real numbers except those for which the denominator is zero. Set the denominator equal to zero and solve.

$$x^2 - 2x - 3 = 0$$
$$(x - 3)(x + 1) = 0$$
$$x - 3 = 0 \qquad x + 1 = 0$$
$$x = 3 \qquad x = -1$$

47. D Draw the line of centers and a line parallel to $\overline{CD}$ through B ($\overline{BE} \parallel \overline{CD}$). The length of $\overline{AB}$ is the sum of the lengths of the radii of the circles. A radius of a circle is perpendicular to a tangent at the point of tangency. Therefore $BCDE$ is a rectangle.

$BC = 3$, so $DE = 3$.
$AD = 5$, so $AE = 2$.

Apply the Pythagorean Theorem to right triangle ABE.

$$(BE)^2 + 2^2 = 8^2$$
$$(BE)^2 + 4 = 64$$
$$(BE)^2 = 60$$
$$BE = \sqrt{60} = 2\sqrt{15}$$

Answer Explanations: MATHEMATICS TEST *(continued)*

And $BE = CD = 2\sqrt{15}$.

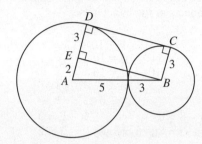

48. G The measure of inscribed angle C is half the measure of its intercepted arc BAD.

$$m \angle C = \frac{1}{2}(180 + m \text{ arc } AB)$$

$$125 = \frac{1}{2}(180 + m \text{ arc } AB).$$

$$250 = 180 + m \text{ arc } AB$$

$$m \text{ arc } AB = 70$$

Therefore arc $BCD = 180 - 70 = 110$. The measure of inscribed angle A is half the measure of its intercepted arc.

$$M \angle A = \frac{1}{2}(110) = 55.$$

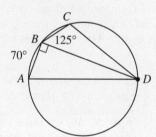

49. E There is not enough information to answer this question uniquely.

50. H The distance from the origin to A is

$$r = \sqrt{(-3)^2 + 4^2} = 5.$$

The definition of sec θ is $\frac{r}{x}$, so

$$\sec \theta = \frac{5}{-3}$$

51. D $\displaystyle\sum_{k=1}^{5} \quad 2k^2 = 2 \cdot 1^2 + 2 \cdot 2^2 + 2 \cdot 3^2$
$$+ 2 \cdot 4^2 + 2 \cdot 5^2$$
$$= 2 + 8 + 18 + 32 + 50 = 110$$

52. J Cosine is positive in quadrants I and IV; cotangent is negative in quadrants II and IV. There is an angle in quandrant IV that satisfies the given conditions.

53. B A Venn diagram will help clarify these statements. The statement in B, $(A \cap B) \subseteq B$, is true. Every element in the intersection of sets A and B is contained in B.

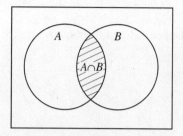

54. G Let one side be x; then the other side is $x + 1$. Use the Pythagorean Theorem:
$$x^2 + (x + 1)^2 = (\sqrt{145})^2$$
$$x^2 + x^2 + 2x + 1 = 145$$
$$2x^2 + 2x - 144 = 0$$
$$x^2 + x - 72 = 0$$
$$(x + 9)(x - 8) = 0$$
$$x + 9 = 0 \qquad x - 8 = 0$$
$$x = -9 \text{ (extraneous)} \qquad x = 8$$
Then $x + 1 = 8 + 1 = 9$.

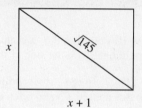

55. B Think of $\cos^{-1} \frac{2}{3}$ as an angle, θ. Then the question asks for sin θ, where θ is the angle whose cosine is $\frac{2}{3}$. This angle is in quadrant I.

$$\sin \theta = +\sqrt{1 - \cos^2 \theta}$$

$$= \sqrt{1 - \left(\frac{2}{3}\right)^2} = \sqrt{1 - \frac{4}{9}}$$

$$= \sqrt{\frac{5}{9}} = \frac{\sqrt{5}}{3}$$

56. J Let x be the score on the fourth test. Then
$$\frac{75 + 84 + 80 + x}{4} \geq 80$$
$$239 + x \geq 320$$
$$x \geq 81$$

57. A The sum of the exterior angles of any polygon is $360°$. In a regular polygon the angles have the same measure, so one exterior angle of a regular octagon is $\frac{360°}{8} = 45°$.

Answer Explanations: MATHEMATICS TEST *(continued)*

58. H The diagonals of a rhombus are perpendicular bisectors of each other. Therefore in right triangle *ABE*, *AE* = 4 and *BE* = 3. Use the Pythagorean Theorem.
$$(AB)^2 = 4^2 + 3^2 = 16 + 9 = 25$$
$$AB = 5$$
The perimeter of the rhombus is 4(5) = 20.

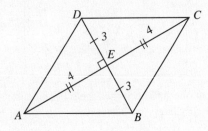

59. E All these statements are false.

60. F The length of the altitude of a right triangle is the mean proportional between the lengths of the two segments of the hypotenuse.
$$\frac{x}{4} = \frac{4}{10 - x}$$
$$x(10 - x) = 16$$
$$10x - x^2 = 16$$
$$0 = x^2 - 10x + 16$$
$$(x - 8)(x - 2) = 0$$
$$x - 8 = 0 \qquad x - 2 = 0$$
$$x = 8(\text{extraneous}) \qquad x = 2$$

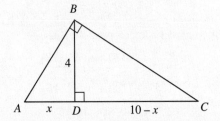

Answer Explanations: READING TEST

1. B Lines 9–10 state that the "weight of society has been traditionally on the side of the oppressor."

2. J Lines 20–23 suggest that police and others believe that abused women often provoke violent behavior in men.

3. C The clause implies that police, prosecutors, and judges sometimes contribute to the victim's feelings of helplessness.

4. F Reconciliation is not mentioned among the reasons listed in the third paragraph.

5. C Line 44 suggests that, if possible, the wife should seek refuge in a shelter for battered women.

6. G Lines 74–77 state that battered women need help to use the enormous strength they have for self-preservation.

7. C Most of the passage deals with the problems confronting abused women.

8. G The passage emphasizes financial hardships faced by abused women.

9. D This is not indicated by the passage.

10. F Lines 81–86 imply that the court should be used only as a last resort.

11. A Although line 7 says that Alzheimer's patients may be "of all ages," lines 75–77 indicate that the disease is most common among the elderly.

12. H Lines 34–39 mention loss of memory, deterioration of social skills, and the overall decrease of mental functioning. Only headaches are not mentioned.

13. C Lines 5–7 discuss the changes in nerve cells that are a clear-cut indication of Alzheimer's disease.

14. J According to lines 57–59, scientists are hopeful that genetic research will lead to foolproof diagnosis of Alzheimer's disease.

15. B Based on the account of current research on Alzheimer's (lines 61–69), scientists are studying proteins and other organic compounds found in the human body. Therefore, researchers must know organic chemistry.

16. G As explained in lines 78–79, "many other disorders show symptoms that resemble those of Alzheimer's disease."

17. B Because Alzheimer's is incurable, a means to identify it would allow physicians to provide proper treatment to patients with similar, but curable, diseases.

18. F Alzheimer's disease is diagnosed by the process of elimination (lines 43–45), but a positive identification of the disease cannot be made except by autopsy after the patient has died.

19. A Based on the second paragraph of the passage, computers are somewhat useful in diagnosing

Answer Explanations: READING TEST *(continued)*

Alzheimer's disease but cannot provide definitive diagnoses.

20. H The whole passage discusses the current state of research on diagnosing Alzheimer's disease.

21. A In lines 31–36, the narrator attributes his gloomy nature to a childhood spent on a chicken farm.

22. H In lines 18–26, the narrator presumes that Mother's reading was responsible for her ambition.

23. C Father married at 34 (in "his thirty-fifth year") and a year later launched a ten-year period as a chicken farmer.

24. J Father continued to work on a farm. After marriage, however, he owned it.

25. A The narrator comments in line 53 that chickens look so bright and alert, but are so stupid—much like people.

26. G In lines 39–40, the narrator describes a chick as "a tiny fluffy thing such as you will see pictured on Easter cards."

27. C Literature on the subject, according to lines 58–60, leads unsuspecting people astray by holding out unrealistic prospects of making a fortune by raising chickens.

28. J Mother and Father never believed they were failures. In spite of setbacks, according to lines 72–76, they continued on their "upward journey through life."

29. C The narrator gently pokes fun at life on the chicken farm of his youth.

30. F In the narrator's view (line 50), chicken farmers must be calm and hopeful (i.e., *philosophical* by nature) or they couldn't continue their work.

31. A The first lines of the passage indicate that drama grew out of religious worship in *antiquity* (i.e., ancient cultures).

32. H Line 8 of the passage says that miracle plays are "dramatized episodes from the lives of the saints."

33. D Changes that occurred when the plays moved into the square are alluded to in lines 10–19 of the passage. No mention is made of greater realism.

34. J According to lines 19–26, stages were built in three parts: a middle section representing the earthly plane, and two other sections representing Heaven and Hell.

35. D Moving the plays outdoors reduced the sacred qualities of the plays (lines 16–19). Actors playing the devil tried to win the public's favor (lines 31–33). The "brisker air and coarser flavor" (lines 18–19) suggest down-to-earth words and use of "profane language" (line 40). Only the declining influence of the church is not mentioned in the passage.

36. G Lines 40–45 suggest that the church had regrets about the hilarity and irreverence that had crept into the formerly sacred plays.

37. B According to lines 48–51, theatrical performances were "the ideal form of diversion" in the courts of kings and princes.

38. F The passage describes how court poets earned their wages—by "more or less delicate flattery" of their employers (lines 63–64).

39. D The church was dismayed about how the mystery plays had degenerated (line 42). Therefore, it put a stop to performances by the "Brotherhood of the Passion."

40. G Because the people were well acquainted with the classics, they would immediately grasp the poet's allusion to the golden age.

Answer Explanations: SCIENCE REASONING TEST

1. **C** The sketches of smokestacks and an automobile at the lower left of the diagram show that NO, NO_2, and SO_2 are in the exhausts. A is wrong because ozone comes from other sources, not the exhausts. B is wrong because it is not shown as a source of strong acids. D is wrong because nitric and sulfuric acids are not in the exhaust, but were formed in the atmosphere.

2. **F** This reaction is shown at the bottom center of the diagram, where H_2O_2 reacts with SO_2 to form H_2SO_4.

3. **D** This is the reaction just below the center of the diagram.

4. **G** The reaction is at the right center, where SO_3 is shown to combine with H_2O to from H_2SO_4. F is wrong because nitrogen dioxide combines with the hydroxyl radical, not with water. H is wrong because sulfur dioxide reacts with hydrogen peroxide, not with water, to form sulphuric acid. Ozone (J) does not react with water anywhere.

5. **B** Ozone is shown as coming from other sources, not directly from the exhaust gasses.

6. **G** All organisms except bacterial spores can be killed at temperatures below 100°C.

7. **D** This combination of temperature and time will kill bacterial spores; everything else will also be killed, since all other kinds of microorganisms will die at substantially lower temperatures.

8. **J** The chart shows that at every temperature, a longer time of sterilization is needed to kill mold spores than yeast spores.

9. **C** The destruction of bacterial spores is spread out, at 100°C, from 3 minutes to 3 hours, indicating that different kinds of bacterial spores will be killed at different exposure times. Killing bacterial spores also kills everything else, and yeasts are killed more quickly than bacteria.

10. **H** In every case, the spore stage is more resistant to destruction by heat than the living stage. No information is presented concerning other environmental hazards. In the living form, molds are more resistant than bacteria.

11. **B** The passage informs us that starch turns blue in the presence of elemental iodine, and the gist of the experiments is the determination of the liberation of iodine from the iodate.

12. **G** Looking down the data columns, you can see that, as the concentration of iodate gets smaller, the time delay increases. F is wrong because this

is part of the design of the experiment, not a hypothesis to be tested. H is wrong because the concentration of sulfuric acid is kept constant throughout. J is wrong because the passage says that the concentration of iodine increases gradually until it gets strong enough to turn the starch blue.

13. **C** Experiment 2 shows that, as the temperature increases, the time for the reaction decreases. A and B are wrong because the iodate concentration was not changed in Experiment 2.

14. **G** The iodate concentration in Experiment 2 was 5%. In Experiment 1 the time delay at 5% concentration was 29 seconds. Experiment 2 shows that this delay, with 5% iodate, occurs at a temperature between 15°C and 25°C.

15. **D** The temperature given is well below the freezing point of water, and if the whole setup freezes, the whole reaction might stop. All the other answers neglect this probability.

16. **F** Experiment 2 shows that the time for a 5% solution at 45°C is 22 seconds, and we would have to expect that it would be less for a 10% solution. The time would also have to be less than 18 seconds, because that was the time (Experiment 1) for 10% solution at 20°C.

17. **A** The graph for fat content in males (dashed line) shows a strong dip in the years 10 through 20.

18. **J** The rate of increase is represented by the steepness of the graph. The graph for fat content rises very sharply in the last 3 months before birth.

19. **D** The water content of a man is about 7% more than that of a woman of equal weight, so a woman would have to be approximately 7% heavier than a man to have the same amount of water. B is wrong because the graph does not have a zero for water content, and the value for a man only looks like (but is not actually) twice as much as for a woman.

20. **J** The graphs show that after birth, whenever the fat content is low, the water content is high, and the rule also applies to the sex difference. Thus, the sum of water and fat percentages differs very little at any age.

21. **B** In adolescence, when sex hormone activity is beginning very strongly, the fat content of boys drops and the water content increases. A is wrong because this sex-hormone effect is not seen in girls. C is wrong because at adolescence there is a marked change in the water content of boys, but only a gradual drop in girls.

Answer Explanations: SCIENCE REASONING TEST *(continued)*

22. G The ratings for attack against *Escherichia* are greater in four of the six trials than for any of the other microorganisms.

23. A Ratings for alfalfa seeds against molds are 4 and 2, but only 1 and 0 against bacteria. None of the others shows this kind of difference.

24. H The strongest attack on *Pennicillium* was made by seeds of the legumes, soybean and alfalfa.

25. D All six seeds attacked the bread mold, at the 2 level or higher. A is wrong because the experiment does not address this question. B is wrong because all 6 of the test seeds had some effect on the bread mold. C is wrong because both the dandelion and the thistle seeds had some effect.

26. G Neither of the legumes had any effect on *Staphylococcus,* so this family is not the place to look. F is wrong because some of the other seeds do attack *Staphylococcus.* H and J are wrong because this experiment gives no information about one microorganism attacking another.

27. D The dandelion and the thistle seeds attacked all microorganisms, mostly at high levels. A is wrong because the experiment gives no information about microorganisms competing with each other. B is wrong because the two legumes do not show a significantly higher ability to attack than any others. C is wrong because the experiment does not deal with the question of damage to crops.

28. G The index of refraction of each liquid is a property of the liquid used. F is wrong because the index of refraction of the liquid has nothing to do with the lens. H and J are wrong because the experimental design says nothing about temperature or color of light.

29. C All three data tables show an increase in focal length as the index of refraction of the medium increases. This means that the rays converge further from the lens.

30. F Comparing the results of Experiments 1 and 2 shows that the focal length of the thicker lens was always less than that of the thinner one, given the same medium.

31. A The index of refraction of the glass is 1.720, which is less than the index for methylene iodide, the only medium in which the light does not focus. B is wrong because the only information given about methylene iodide is its index of refraction. C is wrong because the properties of the glass surely matter, and Experiment 2 shows that the thickness of the lens is also involved. D is wrong; the thicker lens converges the light better, forming a shorter focal length.

32. J There is no reason to believe that knowledge of index of refraction would lead to knowledge of chemical composition. F is wrong because there is a clear correlation between focal length of the lens and the index of refraction of the liquid. G is wrong because knowledge of the behavior of light passing through a lens can be used in determining how it would act in passing through a prism. H is wrong because index of refraction could depend on the concentration of a sugar solution; in fact, it is so used.

33. B The experiment shows that the rays will converge only if the index of refraction of the lens is greater than that of the medium. Thus, the index of refraction of the lens must be greater than 1.33. If it were greater than 1.50, however, there would be convergence when the lens is in the 11% sugar solution, so it must be between 1.33 and 1.50.

34. G This is the only way to account for the accumulation of oil in porous sedimentary layers. F is wrong because Scientist 2 thinks that petroleum forms deep under the earth's crust. H is wrong because Scientist 1 does not believe this. J is wrong because Scientist 1 thinks oil has formed from marine organisms, which have not always been there.

35. C One of Scientist 2's most important items of evidence is the oil found in igneous rock at great depth. A would tend to strengthen Scientist 2's case. B is wrong because one meteorite would not mean anything, in view of the fact that many of them do contain hydrocarbons. D would greatly strengthen Scientist 2's theory because Scientist 1 cannot account for oil in igneous rocks.

36. F Scientist 2 believes there are vast deposits of petroleum deep in the earth's crust, left there by meteors. G is a strategy that Scientist 1 might suggest, but has nothing to do with Scientist 2's theory. H is wrong because, according to Scientist 2, the oil concentrates in sedimentary rocks. J is wrong because Scientist 2 has not suggested that the oil is still in meteorites.

37. D The marine-life corpses must be covered quickly to prevent oxidative decay. A would increase decay, not prevent it. B is irrelevant. Scientist 1's theory does not involve meteorites, so C is wrong.

38. G According to the theory of Scientist 1, oil forms from dead bodies, so it should form in sedimentary rocks, which contain lots of fossils.

39. B The fact that oil is found in association with salt seems to imply that oil has its origin in the bottom of the sea. A is wrong because this is a mere appeal to authority, not to evidence. C is wrong because both scientists agree that oil seeps upward into porous sedimentary rocks. D is wrong because Scientist 2's theory postulates that the hydrocarbons came to earth long before there were any oceans.

40. F Scientist 2 claims that the particular combination of circumstances suggested by Scientist 1 is so rare that it could not account for all the oil there is. G is wrong because Scientist 1's theory does account for accumulation in sedimentary rocks. H is wrong because Scientist 1 used evidence, not arbitrary authority, in his arguments. J is wrong because the potential usefulness of either theory has nothing to do with its validity.

Model Examination C

The purpose of Model Examination C is to help you evaluate your progress in preparing for the actual ACT. Take the examination under simulated testing conditions and within the time limits stated at the beginning of each test. Try to apply the test-taking tactics recommended in this book. Detach the answer sheet and mark your answers on it.

After you finish the examination, check your answers against the Answer Keys and fill in the Analysis Charts. Rate your total scores by using the Performance Evaluation Chart on page 8. Read all of the Answer Explanations.

Since this is the last model examination in this book, the Analysis Charts should indicate that you are ready to take the ACT. If, however, you still have weak areas, review those topics and retake the model examinations.

Directions: Mark one answer only for each question. Make the mark dark. Erase completely any mark made in error. (Additional or stray marks will be counted as mistakes.)

TEST 1

	10 Ⓕ Ⓖ Ⓗ Ⓙ	20 Ⓕ Ⓖ Ⓗ Ⓙ	30 Ⓕ Ⓖ Ⓗ Ⓙ	40 Ⓕ Ⓖ Ⓗ Ⓙ	50 Ⓕ Ⓖ Ⓗ Ⓙ	60 Ⓕ Ⓖ Ⓗ Ⓙ	70 Ⓕ Ⓖ Ⓗ Ⓙ
1 Ⓐ Ⓑ Ⓒ Ⓓ	11 Ⓐ Ⓑ Ⓒ Ⓓ	21 Ⓐ Ⓑ Ⓒ Ⓓ	31 Ⓐ Ⓑ Ⓒ Ⓓ	41 Ⓐ Ⓑ Ⓒ Ⓓ	51 Ⓐ Ⓑ Ⓒ Ⓓ	61 Ⓐ Ⓑ Ⓒ Ⓓ	71 Ⓐ Ⓑ Ⓒ Ⓓ
2 Ⓕ Ⓖ Ⓗ Ⓙ	12 Ⓕ Ⓖ Ⓗ Ⓙ	22 Ⓕ Ⓖ Ⓗ Ⓙ	32 Ⓕ Ⓖ Ⓗ Ⓙ	42 Ⓕ Ⓖ Ⓗ Ⓙ	52 Ⓕ Ⓖ Ⓗ Ⓙ	62 Ⓕ Ⓖ Ⓗ Ⓙ	72 Ⓕ Ⓖ Ⓗ Ⓙ
3 Ⓐ Ⓑ Ⓒ Ⓓ	13 Ⓐ Ⓑ Ⓒ Ⓓ	23 Ⓐ Ⓑ Ⓒ Ⓓ	33 Ⓐ Ⓑ Ⓒ Ⓓ	43 Ⓐ Ⓑ Ⓒ Ⓓ	53 Ⓐ Ⓑ Ⓒ Ⓓ	63 Ⓐ Ⓑ Ⓒ Ⓓ	73 Ⓐ Ⓑ Ⓒ Ⓓ
4 Ⓕ Ⓖ Ⓗ Ⓙ	14 Ⓕ Ⓖ Ⓗ Ⓙ	24 Ⓕ Ⓖ Ⓗ Ⓙ	34 Ⓕ Ⓖ Ⓗ Ⓙ	44 Ⓕ Ⓖ Ⓗ Ⓙ	54 Ⓕ Ⓖ Ⓗ Ⓙ	64 Ⓕ Ⓖ Ⓗ Ⓙ	74 Ⓕ Ⓖ Ⓗ Ⓙ
5 Ⓐ Ⓑ Ⓒ Ⓓ	15 Ⓐ Ⓑ Ⓒ Ⓓ	25 Ⓐ Ⓑ Ⓒ Ⓓ	35 Ⓐ Ⓑ Ⓒ Ⓓ	45 Ⓐ Ⓑ Ⓒ Ⓓ	55 Ⓐ Ⓑ Ⓒ Ⓓ	65 Ⓐ Ⓑ Ⓒ Ⓓ	75 Ⓐ Ⓑ Ⓒ Ⓓ
6 Ⓕ Ⓖ Ⓗ Ⓙ	16 Ⓕ Ⓖ Ⓗ Ⓙ	26 Ⓕ Ⓖ Ⓗ Ⓙ	36 Ⓕ Ⓖ Ⓗ Ⓙ	46 Ⓕ Ⓖ Ⓗ Ⓙ	56 Ⓕ Ⓖ Ⓗ Ⓙ	66 Ⓕ Ⓖ Ⓗ Ⓙ	
7 Ⓐ Ⓑ Ⓒ Ⓓ	17 Ⓐ Ⓑ Ⓒ Ⓓ	27 Ⓐ Ⓑ Ⓒ Ⓓ	37 Ⓐ Ⓑ Ⓒ Ⓓ	47 Ⓐ Ⓑ Ⓒ Ⓓ	57 Ⓐ Ⓑ Ⓒ Ⓓ	67 Ⓐ Ⓑ Ⓒ Ⓓ	
8 Ⓕ Ⓖ Ⓗ Ⓙ	18 Ⓕ Ⓖ Ⓗ Ⓙ	28 Ⓕ Ⓖ Ⓗ Ⓙ	38 Ⓕ Ⓖ Ⓗ Ⓙ	48 Ⓕ Ⓖ Ⓗ Ⓙ	58 Ⓕ Ⓖ Ⓗ Ⓙ	68 Ⓕ Ⓖ Ⓗ Ⓙ	
9 Ⓐ Ⓑ Ⓒ Ⓓ	19 Ⓐ Ⓑ Ⓒ Ⓓ	29 Ⓐ Ⓑ Ⓒ Ⓓ	39 Ⓐ Ⓑ Ⓒ Ⓓ	49 Ⓐ Ⓑ Ⓒ Ⓓ	59 Ⓐ Ⓑ Ⓒ Ⓓ	69 Ⓐ Ⓑ Ⓒ Ⓓ	

TEST 2

	8 Ⓕ Ⓖ Ⓗ Ⓙ Ⓚ	16 Ⓕ Ⓖ Ⓗ Ⓙ Ⓚ	24 Ⓕ Ⓖ Ⓗ Ⓙ Ⓚ	32 Ⓕ Ⓖ Ⓗ Ⓙ Ⓚ	40 Ⓕ Ⓖ Ⓗ Ⓙ Ⓚ	48 Ⓕ Ⓖ Ⓗ Ⓙ Ⓚ	56 Ⓕ Ⓖ Ⓗ Ⓙ Ⓚ
1 Ⓐ Ⓑ Ⓒ Ⓓ Ⓔ	9 Ⓐ Ⓑ Ⓒ Ⓓ Ⓔ	17 Ⓐ Ⓑ Ⓒ Ⓓ Ⓔ	25 Ⓐ Ⓑ Ⓒ Ⓓ Ⓔ	33 Ⓐ Ⓑ Ⓒ Ⓓ Ⓔ	41 Ⓐ Ⓑ Ⓒ Ⓓ Ⓔ	49 Ⓐ Ⓑ Ⓒ Ⓓ Ⓔ	57 Ⓐ Ⓑ Ⓒ Ⓓ Ⓔ
2 Ⓕ Ⓖ Ⓗ Ⓙ Ⓚ	10 Ⓕ Ⓖ Ⓗ Ⓙ Ⓚ	18 Ⓕ Ⓖ Ⓗ Ⓙ Ⓚ	26 Ⓕ Ⓖ Ⓗ Ⓙ Ⓚ	34 Ⓕ Ⓖ Ⓗ Ⓙ Ⓚ	42 Ⓕ Ⓖ Ⓗ Ⓙ Ⓚ	50 Ⓕ Ⓖ Ⓗ Ⓙ Ⓚ	58 Ⓕ Ⓖ Ⓗ Ⓙ Ⓚ
3 Ⓐ Ⓑ Ⓒ Ⓓ Ⓔ	11 Ⓐ Ⓑ Ⓒ Ⓓ Ⓔ	19 Ⓐ Ⓑ Ⓒ Ⓓ Ⓔ	27 Ⓐ Ⓑ Ⓒ Ⓓ Ⓔ	35 Ⓐ Ⓑ Ⓒ Ⓓ Ⓔ	43 Ⓐ Ⓑ Ⓒ Ⓓ Ⓔ	51 Ⓐ Ⓑ Ⓒ Ⓓ Ⓔ	59 Ⓐ Ⓑ Ⓒ Ⓓ Ⓔ
4 Ⓕ Ⓖ Ⓗ Ⓙ Ⓚ	12 Ⓕ Ⓖ Ⓗ Ⓙ Ⓚ	20 Ⓕ Ⓖ Ⓗ Ⓙ Ⓚ	28 Ⓕ Ⓖ Ⓗ Ⓙ Ⓚ	36 Ⓕ Ⓖ Ⓗ Ⓙ Ⓚ	44 Ⓕ Ⓖ Ⓗ Ⓙ Ⓚ	52 Ⓕ Ⓖ Ⓗ Ⓙ Ⓚ	60 Ⓕ Ⓖ Ⓗ Ⓙ Ⓚ
5 Ⓐ Ⓑ Ⓒ Ⓓ Ⓔ	13 Ⓐ Ⓑ Ⓒ Ⓓ Ⓔ	21 Ⓐ Ⓑ Ⓒ Ⓓ Ⓔ	29 Ⓐ Ⓑ Ⓒ Ⓓ Ⓔ	37 Ⓐ Ⓑ Ⓒ Ⓓ Ⓔ	45 Ⓐ Ⓑ Ⓒ Ⓓ Ⓔ	53 Ⓐ Ⓑ Ⓒ Ⓓ Ⓔ	
6 Ⓕ Ⓖ Ⓗ Ⓙ Ⓚ	14 Ⓕ Ⓖ Ⓗ Ⓙ Ⓚ	22 Ⓕ Ⓖ Ⓗ Ⓙ Ⓚ	30 Ⓕ Ⓖ Ⓗ Ⓙ Ⓚ	38 Ⓕ Ⓖ Ⓗ Ⓙ Ⓚ	46 Ⓕ Ⓖ Ⓗ Ⓙ Ⓚ	54 Ⓕ Ⓖ Ⓗ Ⓙ Ⓚ	
7 Ⓐ Ⓑ Ⓒ Ⓓ Ⓔ	15 Ⓐ Ⓑ Ⓒ Ⓓ Ⓔ	23 Ⓐ Ⓑ Ⓒ Ⓓ Ⓔ	31 Ⓐ Ⓑ Ⓒ Ⓓ Ⓔ	39 Ⓐ Ⓑ Ⓒ Ⓓ Ⓔ	47 Ⓐ Ⓑ Ⓒ Ⓓ Ⓔ	55 Ⓐ Ⓑ Ⓒ Ⓓ Ⓔ	

TEST 3

	6 Ⓕ Ⓖ Ⓗ Ⓙ	12 Ⓕ Ⓖ Ⓗ Ⓙ	18 Ⓕ Ⓖ Ⓗ Ⓙ	24 Ⓕ Ⓖ Ⓗ Ⓙ	30 Ⓕ Ⓖ Ⓗ Ⓙ	36 Ⓕ Ⓖ Ⓗ Ⓙ
1 Ⓐ Ⓑ Ⓒ Ⓓ	7 Ⓐ Ⓑ Ⓒ Ⓓ	13 Ⓐ Ⓑ Ⓒ Ⓓ	19 Ⓐ Ⓑ Ⓒ Ⓓ	25 Ⓐ Ⓑ Ⓒ Ⓓ	31 Ⓐ Ⓑ Ⓒ Ⓓ	37 Ⓐ Ⓑ Ⓒ Ⓓ
2 Ⓕ Ⓖ Ⓗ Ⓙ	8 Ⓕ Ⓖ Ⓗ Ⓙ	14 Ⓕ Ⓖ Ⓗ Ⓙ	20 Ⓕ Ⓖ Ⓗ Ⓙ	26 Ⓕ Ⓖ Ⓗ Ⓙ	32 Ⓕ Ⓖ Ⓗ Ⓙ	38 Ⓕ Ⓖ Ⓗ Ⓙ
3 Ⓐ Ⓑ Ⓒ Ⓓ	9 Ⓐ Ⓑ Ⓒ Ⓓ	15 Ⓐ Ⓑ Ⓒ Ⓓ	21 Ⓐ Ⓑ Ⓒ Ⓓ	27 Ⓐ Ⓑ Ⓒ Ⓓ	33 Ⓐ Ⓑ Ⓒ Ⓓ	39 Ⓐ Ⓑ Ⓒ Ⓓ
4 Ⓕ Ⓖ Ⓗ Ⓙ	10 Ⓕ Ⓖ Ⓗ Ⓙ	16 Ⓕ Ⓖ Ⓗ Ⓙ	22 Ⓕ Ⓖ Ⓗ Ⓙ	28 Ⓕ Ⓖ Ⓗ Ⓙ	34 Ⓕ Ⓖ Ⓗ Ⓙ	40 Ⓕ Ⓖ Ⓗ Ⓙ
5 Ⓐ Ⓑ Ⓒ Ⓓ	11 Ⓐ Ⓑ Ⓒ Ⓓ	17 Ⓐ Ⓑ Ⓒ Ⓓ	23 Ⓐ Ⓑ Ⓒ Ⓓ	29 Ⓐ Ⓑ Ⓒ Ⓓ	35 Ⓐ Ⓑ Ⓒ Ⓓ	

TEST 4

	6 Ⓕ Ⓖ Ⓗ Ⓙ	12 Ⓕ Ⓖ Ⓗ Ⓙ	18 Ⓕ Ⓖ Ⓗ Ⓙ	24 Ⓕ Ⓖ Ⓗ Ⓙ	30 Ⓕ Ⓖ Ⓗ Ⓙ	36 Ⓕ Ⓖ Ⓗ Ⓙ
1 Ⓐ Ⓑ Ⓒ Ⓓ	7 Ⓐ Ⓑ Ⓒ Ⓓ	13 Ⓐ Ⓑ Ⓒ Ⓓ	19 Ⓐ Ⓑ Ⓒ Ⓓ	25 Ⓐ Ⓑ Ⓒ Ⓓ	31 Ⓐ Ⓑ Ⓒ Ⓓ	37 Ⓐ Ⓑ Ⓒ Ⓓ
2 Ⓕ Ⓖ Ⓗ Ⓙ	8 Ⓕ Ⓖ Ⓗ Ⓙ	14 Ⓕ Ⓖ Ⓗ Ⓙ	20 Ⓕ Ⓖ Ⓗ Ⓙ	26 Ⓕ Ⓖ Ⓗ Ⓙ	32 Ⓕ Ⓖ Ⓗ Ⓙ	38 Ⓕ Ⓖ Ⓗ Ⓙ
3 Ⓐ Ⓑ Ⓒ Ⓓ	9 Ⓐ Ⓑ Ⓒ Ⓓ	15 Ⓐ Ⓑ Ⓒ Ⓓ	21 Ⓐ Ⓑ Ⓒ Ⓓ	27 Ⓐ Ⓑ Ⓒ Ⓓ	33 Ⓐ Ⓑ Ⓒ Ⓓ	39 Ⓐ Ⓑ Ⓒ Ⓓ
4 Ⓕ Ⓖ Ⓗ Ⓙ	10 Ⓕ Ⓖ Ⓗ Ⓙ	16 Ⓕ Ⓖ Ⓗ Ⓙ	22 Ⓕ Ⓖ Ⓗ Ⓙ	28 Ⓕ Ⓖ Ⓗ Ⓙ	34 Ⓕ Ⓖ Ⓗ Ⓙ	40 Ⓕ Ⓖ Ⓗ Ⓙ
5 Ⓐ Ⓑ Ⓒ Ⓓ	11 Ⓐ Ⓑ Ⓒ Ⓓ	17 Ⓐ Ⓑ Ⓒ Ⓓ	23 Ⓐ Ⓑ Ⓒ Ⓓ	29 Ⓐ Ⓑ Ⓒ Ⓓ	35 Ⓐ Ⓑ Ⓒ Ⓓ	

1 **1** **1** **1** **1** **1** **1** **1** **1** **1** **1** **1**

EXAMINATION C
Model English Test
45 Minutes—75 Questions

DIRECTIONS: The following test consists of 75 under-lined words and phrases in context, or general questions about the passages. Most of the underlined sections contain errors and inappropriate expressions. You are asked to compare each with the four alternatives in the answer column. If you consider the original version best, choose letter A or F: NO CHANGE. For each question, blacken on the answer sheet the letter of the alternative you think best. Read each passage through before answering the questions based on it.

Passage I

(1)

The knowledge, attitudes, and skill that children acquire concerning money come from a variety of sources. The most important is the family.

(2)

What a child learns at home is reinforced, weak-ened, or otherwise modified by the influence of his or her <u>friends adults</u> outside the home, and pressures in the
¹
social world at large. ☐2

1. **A.** NO CHANGE
   B. friends—adults
   C. friends: adults
   D. friends, adults

2. Suppose that at this point in the passage the writer wanted to add more information about pressures in the social world of a child. Which of the following additions would be most relevant to the passage as a whole?
   F. A brief classification of the social strata that may be part of children's lives.
   G. A scientifically accurate definition of *social pressure.*
   H. A simple anecdote about the way a child was influenced by the spending behavior of his or her peers.
   J. A case history of a mentally disturbed teenager with a history of antisocial behavior.

GO ON TO THE NEXT PAGE.

1 1 1 1 1 1 1 1 1 1 1

(3)

There are several important principles involved with sound money management <u>and that</u> children need
3
to learn. The most important is to spend wisely in such a way as to get full enjoyment and satisfaction. Another is to save for future purchases. Still another is <u>understanding</u> credit and how to use it well. Finally,
4
children need to have experience in earning money for

their own use. ⬚5

3. A. NO CHANGE
B. and which
C. and whom
D. that

4. F. NO CHANGE
G. comprehending
H. to understand
J. earning

5. This paragraph is organized according to which of the following schemes?
A. A series of comparison/contrast sentences.
B. "Nested" classifications, with several subdivisions of each topic.
C. A general statement followed by specific examples.
D. A narrative, with one event after another.

(4)

In other words, <u>he needs</u> to learn that money is
6
valuable as a tool in reaching goals rather than as a goal in itself. The implication for parents is that they need to resist the temptation to regard money only as a restricting, rather than also as a facilitating, element in their lives. <u>Being as how</u> adults overemphasize the impor-
7
tance of money, they should not be surprised when children also do so.

6. F. NO CHANGE
G. he or she needs
H. one needs
J. they need

7. A. NO CHANGE
B. If
C. Although
D. Thus,

(5)

These pressures are strong. Children themselves have become important consumers, having control over more money at earlier ages than ever before. A rise in family incomes, as well as an increase in the number of working adults, <u>have meant</u> that more parents can give
8
children more money for their own use. Business is

8. F. NO CHANGE
G. has meant
H. will have meant
J. meant

GO ON TO THE NEXT PAGE.

1 1 1 1 1 1 1 1 1 1 1

fully aware <u>of this</u>. Modern advertising regards
₉

children and teenagers as <u>awesome</u> targets. <u>The cost of</u>
₁₀   ₁₁
<u>clothes is rising at a truly alarming rate.</u> All of these
₁₁
factors emphasize the need to teach children how to

manage money.

(6)

On the other hand, <u>unless</u> adults in the company of
₁₂
children can enjoy some of the many fine things in the

world that require no expenditure of money and can

consistently meet children's needs for affection and

<u>companionship, they</u> are well on the way toward teach-
₁₃
ing these children the proper place that material posses-

sions <u>and worldly goods</u> should have in their lives. $\boxed{15}$
₁₄

9. **A.** NO CHANGE
   B. that
   C. that children are more mature
   D. that cash is more available

10. **F.** NO CHANGE
    G. massive
    H. major
    J. herculean

11. **A.** NO CHANGE
    B. The cost of children's clothes has remained stable.
    C. OMIT the underlined portion.
    D. The cost of clothes is just one of the factors that have contributed to inflation.

12. **F.** NO CHANGE
    G. until
    H. when
    J. although

13. **A.** NO CHANGE
    B. companionship they
    C. companionship: they
    D. companionship. They

14. **F.** NO CHANGE
    G. OMIT the underlined portion.
    H. and, thus, more worldly goods
    J. and goods

15. Choose the sequence of paragraph numbers that makes the structure of the passage most logical.
    A. NO CHANGE
    B. 1, 2, 6, 4, 3, 5
    C. 1, 2, 5, 3, 4, 6
    D. 1, 5, 6, 3, 4, 2

GO ON TO THE NEXT PAGE.

1   1 1 1 1 1 1 1 1 1   1

Passage II

(1)

Feet and shoes travel many miles. An average, healthy 7-year-old boy may take 30,000 steps every day, an accumulation that adds up to 10 miles per day and more than 300 miles a month. His mother, on a busy shopping day, may walk 10 miles. A police officer, in common with all of his or her fellow officers, walk
   16
about 15 miles on the beat.

(2)

The foot is a complicated structure of twenty-six small bones linked by many joints, attached to each other and to the leg bone by numerous ligaments, moved by muscles and tendons, nourished by blood vessels, controlled by nerves, and a covering of skin
   17
protects it. In a newborn infant, some of the bones are
   17
merely bone-shaped pieces of cartilage, a gristle-like substance. As a child grows, however, real bone
   18
appears within, and gradually spreads throughout the cartilage form. The heel, the largest bone, is not completed until the age of about 20 years. 19

(3)

During all this walking, feet carry the weight of the body, and provide the means to propel a person when
   20
he or she walks, climbs, and jumps. As a person steps out, the body weight travels down through the heel, along

16. F. NO CHANGE
   G. walked
   H. walks
   J. was walking

17. A. NO CHANGE
   B. and a covering of skin has protected it.
   C. and being covered by a covering of skin.
   D. and protected by a covering of skin.

18. F. NO CHANGE
   G. grows, however. Real
   H. grows, however real
   J. grows however, real

19. Suppose that at this point in the passage the writer wanted to add more information about foot anatomy. Which of the following additions would be most relevant to the passage as a whole?
   A. A discussion of common foot ailments and their treatment.
   B. An account of foot operations on some well-known athletes.
   C. More specific details about the muscles that control the feet, the bone tissue, the nerves and tendons.
   D. A brief account of some famous myths involving the feet, such as the one about Achilles.

20. F. NO CHANGE
   G. body. And provide
   H. body and provide
   J. body, and, provide

GO ON TO THE NEXT PAGE.

1 1 1 1 1 1 1 1 1 1 1 1

the outside of the foot to the ball, across the heads of

the long bones to the first metatarsal, and to the big toe.

The big toe launches the walking motion. One after the
                                          ―――――――――
                                                21

other, each foot in turn bears the total weight of the
―――――
  21

body. If your feet ache, try massaging them for 20
          ――――――――――――――――――――――――
                                        22

minutes. You will be amazed at the results. 23
―――――――――――――――――――――――――――――――
              22

(4)

Because a 7-year-old boy weighs 55 pounds, he
―――――――
   24

puts more than 800 tons of weight on his shoes every

day (55 pounds times 30,000 steps), or about 24 tons a

month. But a boy does more than walk. He jumps,

kicks, and often has waded through puddles. His shoes
          ――――――――――――――
                25

lead a rough life. Estimates of the active life of a

pair of shoes ranges from 20 days to 7 or 9 months; the
              ――――――
                26

average is about 10 weeks. In fact, no single component

or characteristic determine the life of a shoe. Fit is most
                   ―――――――――
                        27

important, and usually only the wearer can tell

21. A. NO CHANGE
   B. OMIT the underlined portion.
   C. One after the other—
   D. One after the other:

22. F. NO CHANGE
   G. If your feet ache, massage them!
   H. OMIT the underlined portion.
   J. If your feet ache, try massaging them, and you will be amazed at the results.

23. Is the description of the physical functioning of the foot appropriate in the passage?
   A. Yes, because the passage is actually about sports medicine.
   B. Yes, because the passage is about the stresses on the foot and footwear that are brought about by walking.
   C. No, there is no relevance to the rest of the passage.
   D. No, because it is already well understood that the foot exerts pressure.

24. F. NO CHANGE
   G. If
   H. Being that
   J. Since

25. A. NO CHANGE
   B. wades
   C. waded
   D. will have waded

26. F. NO CHANGE
   G. would range
   H. range
   J. has ranged

27. A. NO CHANGE
   B. determines
   C. will determine
   D. is determining

GO ON TO THE NEXT PAGE.

1   1 1 1 1 1 1 1 1 1   1

whether a shoe fits. Price alone certainly does not guar-

antee a good fit! [29] [30]
        28

28. **F.** NO CHANGE
    G. fit."
    H. fit?
    J. fit.

29. Are the statistics in the first sentence of the para-
    graph appropriate and meaningful?
    A. Yes, because the passage is about the stresses
        to the feet brought about by walking, jumping,
        and other physical activities.
    B. Yes, because the figures help us understand
        that everything has a physical consequence.
    C. No, because the passage is basically about the
        anatomy of feet.
    D. No, because the physical activity of a 7-year-
        old boy is irrelevant to the discussion.

30. Choose the sequence of paragraph numbers that
    makes the structure of the passage most logical.
    F. NO CHANGE
    G. 1, 2, 4, 3
    H. 1, 4, 2, 3
    J. 1, 3, 2, 4

Passage III

(1)

A park in the old part of Philadelphia not only is

preeminent among the sites associated with the signers

of the Declaration of Independence, but also notably

commemorates other major aspects of the nation's
    31
founding and initial growth and many momentous

national events. These include meetings of the First and

Second Continental Congresses, the Declaration was
                        32   33
adopted and signed, which marked the creation of the
    33
United States; and the labors of the Constitutional

Convention of 1787, which perpetuated it. [34]

31. **A.** NO CHANGE
    B. commemorate
    C. will commemorate
    D. has commemorated

32. **F.** NO CHANGE
    G. Congresses—
    H. Congresses;
    J. Congresses

33. **A.** NO CHANGE
    B. The Declaration was adopted and signed.
    C. the Declaration, adopted and signed,
    D. the adoption and signing of the Declaration,

34. Is the reference to the park a meaningful way to
    begin this passage?
    F. No, because the passage is not about recre-
        ational sites, but about the significance of
        Independence Hall.

GO ON TO THE NEXT PAGE.

G. No, because everything it signifies is covered elsewhere in the passage.

H. Yes, because the general reference to scenery is a good way to begin any discussion.

J. Yes, because the park is the site of fundamental historical events described in the passage.

(2)

Independence Hall was originally the statehouse
$\underline{\hspace{4cm}}$
35
for the province of Pennsylvania. In 1729 the provincial
$\underline{\hspace{4cm}}$
35
assembly set aside funds for the building, designed by

lawyer Andrew Hamilton. Three years later, construc-

tion began under the supervision and overview of mas-
$\underline{\hspace{4cm}}$
36
ter carpenter Edmund Wooley. In 1736 the assembly

moved into the statehouse, which was not fully com-

pleted until 1756. Thomas Jefferson was in France at
$\underline{\hspace{4cm}}$
37
the time. As American opposition to British colonial
$\underline{\hspace{2cm}}$
37
policies mounted, Philadelphia became a center of

organized protest. To decide on a unified course of

action, in 1774 the First Continental Congress met in

newly finished Carpenters' Hall, whose erection the

Carpenters' Company of Philadelphia had begun four
$\underline{\hspace{3cm}}$
38
years earlier. In 1775 the Second Continental Congress,

taking over the east room of the ground floor of the

statehouse from the Pennsylvania assembly, moved

from protest to resistance; Congress had created an
$\underline{\hspace{3cm}}$
39
army and appointed George Washington as commander

in chief. Thus, the final break with the Crown had not
$\underline{\hspace{1cm}}$
40

35. Does the first sentence of the paragraph provide a general basis for the specific supporting details that follow?

A. Yes, the sentence is a classic topic sentence followed by supporting details about the province of Pennsylvania.

B. Yes, the sentence suggests a plan, and the rest of the paragraph spells out the plan.

C. No, the sentence refers to a building that is mentioned again in the paragraph, but it does not adequately prepare the reader for the historical narrative that comprises the main part of the paragraph.

D. No, the sentence does not relate to any supporting material.

36. F. NO CHANGE
G. supervision
H. supervision as well as overview
J. supervision, and overview,

37. A. NO CHANGE
B. Thomas Jefferson had been in France at the time.
C. OMIT the underlined portion.
D. Thomas Jefferson would be in France at the time.

38. F. NO CHANGE
G. began
H. had began
J. has begun

39. A. NO CHANGE
B. will have created
C. has created
D. created

40. F. NO CHANGE
G. Finally,
H. Nevertheless,
J. In addition,

GO ON TO THE NEXT PAGE.

1 1 1 1 1 1 1 1 1 1 1

come; not until a year later would independence

<u>have been declared.</u> [42]
41

(3)

On July 2, 1776, Congress passed Richard Henry

Lee's resolution of June 7 recommending independ-

ence. <u>The delegates, then turning their attention to</u>
43

<u>Thomas Jefferson's draft of the Declaration, which had</u>
43

<u>been submitted on June 28.</u> After modification, it was
43

adopted on July 4. Four days later, in Independence

Square, the document was first read publicly to the citi-

zens of Philadelphia. In a formal ceremony on August

2, about fifty of the fifty-six signers affixed their signa-

tures to the <u>Declaration, the</u> others apparently did so
44

later. [45]

41. **A.** NO CHANGE
   B. be declared.
   C. declare itself.
   D. been declared.

42. This paragraph is organized according to which of the following schemes?
   F. A series of chronological references to Independence Hall, each at an important historical juncture.
   G. A general statement about Independence Hall, followed by specific information about the structure.
   H. A series of statements comparing and contrasting Independence Hall with other structures.
   J. A series of arguments about the historical importance of Independence Hall, followed by answers.

43. **A.** NO CHANGE
   B. Then turning the delegates' attention to Thomas Jefferson's draft of the Declaration, which had been submitted on June 28.
   C. The delegates then turned their attention to Thomas Jefferson's draft of the Declaration. Which had been submitted on June 28.
   D. The delegates then turned their attention to Thomas Jefferson's draft of the Declaration, which had been submitted on June 28.

44. **F.** NO CHANGE
   G. Declaration the
   H. Declaration—the
   J. Declaration; the

45. Choose the sequence of paragraph numbers that makes the structure of the passage most logical.
   A. NO CHANGE
   B. 2, 1, 3
   C. 1, 3, 2
   D. 2, 3, 1

GO ON TO THE NEXT PAGE.

1   1 1 1 1 1 1 1 1 1   1

Passage IV

(1)

The greatest problem with the abortion issue is that it is far more complex than it first appears. It is a moral issue because it involves what both sides admit is a decision to begin or terminate a life; it is a political issue because many laws encourage or discourage the practice of abortion; finally, social concerns are addressed, because all human beings are affected by the number of people born into the world.

(2)

One of the central issues of the new millennium is abortion. On one side of the question is the pro-lifers, a minority who believe that abortion is the taking of a life and that the government must protect the rights of all its citizens, including the right of an unborn infant to live. On the other side are the pro-choice advocates, comprising a majority of Americans who believe that abortion should be legal under certain circumstances, (particularly those involving the health of the mother) Researchers and pollsters have been surprised at the strength of these convictions and at the extent to which most people have pondered their beliefs.

(3)

However, the majority group that believes in some form of abortion is also willing to describe the medical

46. **F.** NO CHANGE
    G. abortion finally,
    H. abortion: finally,
    J. abortion, finally,

47. **A.** NO CHANGE
    B. social concerns have been addressed,
    C. it is of social concern,
    D. it is a social issue

48. **F.** NO CHANGE
    G. have been
    H. will be
    J. are

49. **A.** NO CHANGE
    B. Americans (who
    C. Americans, who
    D. Americans. Who

50. **F.** NO CHANGE
    G. circumstances, particularly those involving the health of the mother.
    H. circumstances (particularly those, involving the health of the mother).
    J. circumstances particularly those involving the health of the mother.

51. **A.** NO CHANGE
    B. Because
    C. For example,
    D. Although

52. **F.** NO CHANGE
    G. believe
    H. believed
    J. is believing

GO ON TO THE NEXT PAGE.

1   1 1 1 1 1 1 1 1   1

process as <u>when a life ends.</u> A woman's decision to
₅₃
abort her pregnancy can be viewed, according to more

than half of all the pro-choice people polled, as a choice

between two evils and a conscious acceptance of guilt

in the necessary termination of life. 54

(4)

The pro-lifer or anti-abortionist tends to be on the

right side of the political spectrum, sometimes believ-

ing that social programs are inherently <u>no good</u> and
₅₅

<u>impeding</u> human progress because they tend to discour-
₅₆
age initiative. Using the rule of common good, pro-

lifers ask what decision made by a woman contemplat-

ing abortion would bring about the greatest number of

positive consequences <u>that are beneficial</u> for all con-
₅₇
cerned—one of those concerned, of course, being the

unborn fetus. <u>A baby's fine features, such as eyelashes</u>
₅₈
<u>and fingernails, are fully developed by the age of ten</u>
₅₈
<u>weeks.</u> 59 60
₅₈

53. **A.** NO CHANGE
    B. where a life ends
    C. when you end a life.
    D. the end of a life.

54. Suppose that at this point in the passage the writer
    wanted to add more information about the abortion
    issue. Which of the following additions would be
    most relevant to the passage as a whole?
    F. A brief summary of views on the issue held by
    significant religious and political leaders.
    G. A list of hospitals that perform abortions.
    H. An expose of unlicensed or substandard abor-
    tion clinics.
    J. A case history of an abortion.

55. **A.** NO CHANGE
    B. ill advised
    C. bad news
    D. forbidden

56. **F.** NO CHANGE
    G. impeded
    H. impede
    J. impedes

57. **A.** NO CHANGE
    B. beneficial
    C. also beneficial
    D. OMIT the underlined portion.

58. **F.** NO CHANGE
    G. OMIT the underlined portion.
    H. A baby's fine features, for example, eyelashes
    and fingernails, are fully developed by the age
    of ten weeks.
    J. A baby's fine features, such as eyelashes and
    fingernails, being fully developed by the age of
    ten weeks.

59. For the most part, this passage is written according
    to which of the following strategies?
    A. Comparison/contrast
    B. Argument
    C. Description
    D. Narration

60. Choose the sequence of paragraph numbers that
    makes the structure of the passage most logical.
    F. NO CHANGE
    G. 1, 4, 3, 2
    H. 2, 3, 4, 1
    J. 2, 1, 3, 4

GO ON TO THE NEXT PAGE.

Passage V

(1)

The California Constitution requires that the Governor submit a budget with an explanation to both houses of the Legislature before January 11 of each year. The explanation must contain a complete spending plan, as well as an itemized statement of all expenditures provided by law or proposed by the Governor, and the proposed budget must be compared with last year's. After the Governor has submitted the budget, an appropriation bill, known as the Budget Bill, which reflects the proposed budget, is introduced into each house of the Legislature and referred to the Assembly Ways and Means Committee and the Senate Finance Committee, respectively. The Constitution requires that the Legislature pass the Budget Bill by midnight, June 15. Until the Budget Bill will have been enacted, neither house can send to the Governor any other appropriation bill, other than emergency measures. 63

(2)

Being a budget approaching 20 billion dollars, the five months allowed by the Constitution for all the item disagreements, resolutions, lobbying by special interest groups, and "dealing" by the legislatures on behalf of their constituents is hardly enough time. Yet, if the budget is not passed, the state of California literally ceases to function. All state employees are asked to stay

61. A. NO CHANGE
  B. and it must be compared with last year's budget.
  C. together with a comparison of the proposed budget with last year's.
  D. and it should contain a comparison of last year's and this year's budget.

62. F. NO CHANGE
  G. has been enacted,
  H. would have been enacted,
  J. was enacted,

63. Which of the following statements is best supported by the details supplied in this paragraph?
  A. The California Legislature and the Governor are in contention.
  B. The California Constitution punishes lawmakers who violate its rules.
  C. The California Constitution places a high priority on timely passage of the state budget.
  D. The California budget process is hopelessly politicized.

64. F. NO CHANGE
  G. Due to its being
  H. Being as how it is
  J. For

GO ON TO THE NEXT PAGE.

1   1 1 1 1 1 1 1 1 1   1

home. Traffic on the freeways is measurably
<u>reduced.</u> All state government offices and agencies

<u>close and even</u> the Legislature with its heavy responsi-

bilities has to operate with a skeleton staff. <u>When</u> an
absolute halt in services and business is so disruptive,

<u>and due to the very fact that</u> no other appropriation bill
can be sent to the Governor until the budget is passed,
both the Assembly and the Senate usually stay in session <u>continuously</u> until the impasse, whatever its genesis, is solved. It is not surprising, under such conditions,
that the Legislature and the Governor seem to find
solutions rather quickly to disputes and stalemates that
<u>have been festering</u> for months. 71

(3)

The orderly operation of the Government of
California depends on the state budget, a document
controlling expenditures that are larger than those of

<u>any American governmental jurisdiction</u> with the
exception of the city of New York and the U.S. Govern-

ment. Each year, the process of creating <u>the many parts
of the budget</u> begins in January with the Governor's

---

65. A. NO CHANGE
  B. Traffic, because it is on the freeway, is measur-
      ably reduced.
  C. OMIT the underlined portion.
  D. Traffic is reduced, especially on the freeways.

66. F. NO CHANGE
  G. close. And even
  H. close: Even
  J. close, and even

67. A. NO CHANGE
  B. If
  C. Because
  D. Until

68. F. NO CHANGE
  G. unless
  H. although
  J. because

69. A. NO CHANGE
  B. continually
  C. interminably
  D. repeatedly

70. F. NO CHANGE
  G. have been solved
  H. have been unresolved
  J. have been unknown

71. This passage was probably written for readers who:
  A. are tax accountants seeking to learn more
      about their vocation.
  B. are taxpayers and voters interested in how a
      state government works.
  C. enjoy scientific and quantitative facts.
  D. enjoy works of inspiration and solace.

72. F. NO CHANGE
  G. any other American governmental jurisdiction
  H. any, American governmental jurisdiction
  J. any American, governmental jurisdiction

73. A. NO CHANGE
  B. so many part of the budget
  C. a budget
  D. the workings of the budget

GO ON TO THE NEXT PAGE.

1   1 1 1 1 1 1 1 1 1   1

message to the Legislature. ☐74 ☐75

74. This paragraph emphasizes the importance of:
    F. the Government of California.
    G. the size of the budget.
    H. the budget.
    J. the Governor's message to the Legislature.

75. Choose the sequence of paragraph numbers that
    makes the structure of the essay most logical.
    A. NO CHANGE
    B. 3, 2, 1
    C. 3, 1, 2
    D. 2, 3, 1

**END OF TEST 1
STOP! DO NOT TURN THE PAGE UNTIL TOLD TO DO SO.**

2 **2** 2 **2** 2 **2** 2 **2** 2 **2** **2**

Model Mathematics Test

60 Minutes—60 Questions

DIRECTIONS: After solving each problem, darken the appropriate space on the answer sheet. Do not spend too much time on any one problem. Make a note of the ones that seem difficult, and return to them when you finish the others. Assume that the word *line* means "straight line," that geometric figures are not necessarily drawn to scale, and that all geometric figures in a place.

---

1. Which of the following is a monomial?
   A. $\sqrt{2x}$
   B. $\dfrac{2}{x}$
   C. $\dfrac{x}{2}$
   D. $x + 2$
   E. 2^x

2. Lisa's salary was raised 8%. If she now receives $5.67 per hour, what was her hourly salary before her increase?
   F. $0.45
   G. $5.22
   H. $5.25
   J. $5.30
   K. $6.12

3. The expression $5 + 2 \cdot 3^2 = ?$
   A. 441
   B. 121
   C. 63
   D. 41
   E. 23

4. What is the complete factorization of the polynomial $81x^2 - 36y^2$?
   F. $(9x - 6y)(9x + 6y)$
   G. $9(3x - 2y)^2$
   H. $9(3x - 2y)(3x + 2y)$
   J. $3(9x - 6y)(3x + 2y)$
   K. None of these

5. Which of the following numbers is NOT irrational?
   A. π
   B. $\sqrt{7}$
   C. $\sqrt{49}$
   D. 7.313113111311113 . . .
   E. $\sqrt{7} - \sqrt{3}$

6. What is the simplified form of the algebraic fraction $\dfrac{(x - y)^2}{y^2 - x^2}$?
   F. 1

7. Which of the following is a geometric sequence?
   A. 1, 3, 5, 7, . . .
   B. 1, 2, 4, 8, . . .
   C. $1, \dfrac{1}{2}, \dfrac{1}{3}, \dfrac{1}{4}, \dots$
   D. 1, 4, 9, 16, . . .
   E. 1, 4, 13, 40, . . .

8. Which is the solution set of the equation $4x - 2[3x - (x + 4)] = 5 - 2(x + 1)$?
   F. $\left\{\dfrac{-5}{2}\right\}$
   G. $\left\{\dfrac{5}{3}\right\}$
   H. $\left\{\dfrac{-11}{7}\right\}$
   J. $\{-2\}$
   K. $\emptyset$

9. If $\overline{AB}$ is a diameter, $\overline{BC}$ is a tangent, and m $\angle ABD = 25°$, what is the measure of $\angle BCD$?

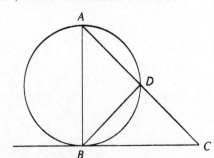

   G. -1
   H. $2xy$
   J. $\dfrac{y - x}{y + x}$
   K. $\dfrac{x - y}{x + y}$

   A. $90°$
   B. $65°$
   C. $32\frac{1}{2}°$
   D. $25°$
   E. $12\frac{1}{2}°$

GO ON TO THE NEXT PAGE.

2   **2** **2** **2** **2** **2** **2** **2** **2** **2**   **2**

10. Which of the following numbers is smallest?
    F. 7.2%
    G. $7.2 (10^{-2})$
    H. $\frac{72}{100}$
    J. (0.08)9
    K. (0.08)(0.09)

11. What is the value of the expression $xy^2(x - y)$ if $x = -3$ and $y = 2$?
    A. -180
    B. -60
    C. -12
    D. 12
    E. 60

12. If it takes 4 gallons of lemonade for a party of 20 children, how many gallons should one have on hand for a party of 30 children?
    F. 5
    G. 6
    H. 6.5
    J. 7.5
    K. 8

13. Which expression would be appropriate to complete the following equation in order for the equation to illustrate the associative property of addition: $3 + (-2 + 0) = ?$
    A. 1
    B. $3 + [0 + (-2)]$
    C. $[3 + (-2)] + 0$
    D. $3 + (-2)$
    E. $(-2 + 0) + 3$

14. Which of the following is a pure imaginary number?
    F. $\sqrt{-9}$
    G. $-\sqrt{9}$
    H. $5 + 2i$
    J. -1
    K. i^2

15. $7\frac{1}{4} - 2\frac{5}{6} = ?$
    A. $4\frac{5}{12}$
    B. $4\frac{1}{2}$
    C. $5\frac{7}{12}$
    D. $10\frac{1}{12}$
    E. None of these

16. Stan can do a certain job in 4 hours. If Fred can do the same job in 5 hours, which of the following equations could be used to determine how long it would take them to do the job if they worked together?
    F. $\frac{x}{4} + \frac{x}{5} = 1$
    G. $4x + 5x = 1$
    H. $\frac{x}{4} = \frac{x}{5}$
    J. $\frac{4}{x} + \frac{5}{x} = 1$
    K. None of these

17. Which of the following numbers is NOT composite?
    A. 1
    B. 28
    C. 51
    D. 93
    E. 143

18. Which of the following is equivalent to $|x + 3| \geq 2$?
    F. $x \geq -1$
    G. $x \leq -5$
    H. $x \geq -5$
    J. $x \geq -1$ or $x \leq -5$
    K. $-5 \leq x \leq -1$

19. What is the solution set of the equation $\frac{2x - 1}{3} + \frac{x + 2}{4} = \frac{1}{6}$?
    A. $\{0\}$
    B. $\left\{\frac{1}{11}\right\}$
    C. $\left\{\frac{-1}{11}\right\}$
    D. $\left\{\frac{-3}{11}\right\}$
    E. $\left\{\frac{4}{11}\right\}$

20. If $\overline{CE}$ is a tangent, $\overline{CD}$ is a radius and m $\angle ECB = 48°$, what is the measure of $\angle BAC$?

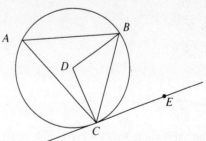

    F. 24°
    G. 42°
    H. 48°
    J. 84°
    K. 96°

GO ON TO THE NEXT PAGE.

2 **2** **2** **2** **2** **2** **2** **2** **2** **2** **2**

21. What is the degree of the expression
$(3x^2 + 5x - 3)^3 + 5$?
A. 2
B. 3
C. 4
D. 5
E. 6

22. What is the simplified form of the expression
$(2x - 3y)^2$?
F. $4x^2 + 9y^2$
G. $4x^2 - 9y^2$
H. $4x^2 - 6xy + 9y^2$
J. $4x^2 - 12xy + 9y^2$
K. $4x^2 + 12xy + 9y^2$

23. Which of the following ordered pairs corresponds
to a point in quadrant IV?
A. $(2, 0)$
B. $(0, -4)$
C. $(-2, 3)$
D. $(-1, -4)$
E. $(2, -8)$

24. What base ten numeral corresponds to $110110_{(two)}$?
F. 27
G. 54
H. 63
J. 108
K. 55,055

25. What is the product of the roots of the equation
$5x^2 - 8x + 7 = 0$?
A. $\dfrac{-7}{5}$
B. $\dfrac{7}{5}$
C. $\dfrac{8}{5}$
D. 7
E. 8

26. What is the value of $8^{-(2/3)}$?
F. 16
G. $\dfrac{-16}{3}$
H. 4
J. $\dfrac{1}{4}$
K. $\dfrac{-1}{4}$

27. The expression $3(10^5) + 2(10^3) + 4(10^2) + 7(10^1)$ is
the expanded form for what number?
A. 3,247
B. 30,247
C. 32,470
D. 302,470
E. 324,700

28. What is the lowest common denominator of the
fractions $\dfrac{2}{5a^2b^3}$, $\dfrac{7}{20ab^4}$, $\dfrac{8}{15a^3b^2}$?
F. $5ab^2$
G. $5a^3b^4$
H. $60ab^2$
J. $60a^3b^4$
K. $1500a^6b^9$

29. What is the average (mean) of the numbers 3, 4, 4,
5, 5, 5, 7, 8, 8, 9?
A. 5
6. 6
C. 5.8
D. 10
E. 58

30. Sue is paid \$200 per week plus 7% of her total
sales, t, for the week. Which of the following equa-
tions could she use to determine her salary, S, for a
particular week?
F. $S = 0.07(200 + t)$
G. $S = 0.07(200) + t$
H. $S = 200 + 0.07t$
J. $S = 1.07(200 + t)$
K. $S = 200t^{0.07}$

31. What is the simplified form of the complex fraction
$$\dfrac{\dfrac{1}{x} - \dfrac{1}{3}}{\dfrac{1}{x^2} - \dfrac{1}{9}}$$
A. 3
B. $\dfrac{1}{x + 3}$
C. $\dfrac{3 - x}{3x}$
D. $\dfrac{3x}{3 + x}$
E. $\dfrac{9x - 3x^2}{9 - x^2}$

32. Which of the following are the coordinates of the
vertex of the parabola whose equation is
$y = -2(x + 6)^2 - 9$?
F. $(2, -9)$
G. $(6, 9)$
H. $(-6, 9)$
J. $(6, -9)$
K. $(-6, -9)$

33. Which is the solution set of the equation
$\dfrac{x^2 + 9}{x^2 - 9} - \dfrac{3}{x + 3} = \dfrac{-x}{3 - x}$?
A. $\varnothing$
B. $\{0\}$
C. $\left\{\dfrac{1}{3}\right\}$
D. $\{2\}$
E. $\{3\}$

GO ON TO THE NEXT PAGE.

2 **2** **2** **2** **2** **2** **2** **2** **2** **2** **2**

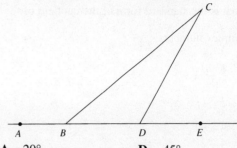

34. Which of the following is equal to $\frac{2.4(10^{-4})}{6(10^{-2})}$?
    F. $0.4(10^{-6})$
    G. $4(10^{-1})$
    H. $4(10^{-2})$
    J. $4(10^{3})$
    K. $4(10^{-3})$

35. What is the slope of the line that passes through the points with coordinates $(-5, 8)$ and $(-5, -3)$?
    A. -11
    B. 5
    C. 0
    D. $\frac{-1}{2}$
    E. The line has no slope.

36. The Smith family has 100 gallons of heating fuel on January 1. During January the Smiths use 20% of their fuel, and in February they use 25% of the remaining fuel. How many gallons of fuel are left on March 1?
    F. 40
    G. 45
    H. 50
    J. 55
    K. 60

37. If lines, l, m, and n are parallel, $\overline{AE} \perp l$, $AC = 10$, $CD = 14$, and $AF = 6$, what is the length of $\overline{DG}$?

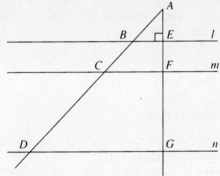

    A. 11.2
    B. 16
    C. 19.2
    D. $23\frac{1}{3}$
    E. 24

38. Which of the following is always true of an acute angle?
    F. Its measure is greater than 90°.
    G. It is the supplement of another acute angle.
    H. It cannot be equal to its own complement.
    J. Every quadrilateral must have at least one.
    K. All of these statements are false.

39. A triangle is drawn with one side on line $\overline{AE}$. If m $\angle ABC = 140°$ and m $\angle CDE = 60°$, what is the measure of $\angle BCD$?

    A. $20°$ D. $45°$
    B. $30°$ E. $50°$
    C. $40°$

40. A car radiator holds 12 liters. How much pure antifreeze, in liters, must be added to a mixture that is 4% antifreeze to make enough of a 20% mixture to fill the radiator?
    F. 0.48
    G. 2
    H. 2.4
    J. 2.88
    K. 3

41. In right triangle ABC, m $\angle C = 90°$, $AC = 2$, and $AB = 5$. What is the value of sin A?
    A. $\frac{2}{5}$
    B. $\frac{5}{2}$
    C. $\frac{\sqrt{21}}{.2}$
    D. $\frac{\sqrt{21}}{5}$
    E. $\frac{5}{\sqrt{21}}$

42. Which equation corresponds to the graph?

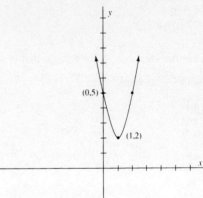

    F. $y = 7(x - 1)^2 - 2$
    G. $y = 3(x - 1)^2 + 2$
    H. $y = 7(x + 1)^2 - 2$
    J. $(x - 1)^2 + (y - 2)^2 = 1$
    K. None of these

GO ON TO THE NEXT PAGE.

2 2 2 2 2 2 2 2 2 2 2

43. What is the standard form of the quotient of the complex numbers $\dfrac{3-2i}{2+i}$?

A. $2-i$

B. $\dfrac{8-7i}{3}$

C. $\dfrac{4}{5}-\dfrac{7}{5}i$

D. $3+2i$

E. $4-2i$

44. In how many ways can six different books be arranged on a shelf?

F. 6

G. 30

H. 36

J. 64

K. 720

45. What is the value of $\log_2 \dfrac{1}{8}$?

A. $\dfrac{1}{3}$

B. $\dfrac{-1}{3}$

C. $\dfrac{1}{4}$

D. -3

E. 3

46. The ratio of the ares of two similar triangles is 9 to 16. What is the ratio of the lengths of the corresponding altitudes of these triangles?

F. 1 to 7

G. 3 to 4

H. 9 to 16

J. 4.5 to 8

K. 27 to 64

47. What is the smallest positive angle that is coterminal with $\dfrac{75\pi}{4}$ radians?

A. $120°$

B. $\dfrac{\pi}{4}$

C. $\dfrac{-\pi}{4}$

D. $\dfrac{3\pi}{4}$

E. $\dfrac{11\pi}{4}$

48. If $AE = 6$, $AB = 1\dfrac{2}{3}$, $BC = 1\dfrac{1}{4}$, and $DE = 1\dfrac{1}{12}$, what is the length of $\overline{CD}$?

F. $1\dfrac{1}{2}$

G. 2

H. $2\dfrac{2}{3}$

J. 4

K. $4\dfrac{11}{12}$

49. If the height, h, of a thrown object above the ground at any time, t, in seconds is given by the equation $h = -16t^2 + 64t$, in how many seconds will the object reach its maximum height?

A. 8

B. 4

C. 3

D. 2

E. 1

50. What is equal to the product $\sqrt{54x^4y^5} \cdot \sqrt{2x^2y^4}$ of radicals in simplest radical form? (Assume that x and y are nonnegative.)

F. $6x^3y^4 \sqrt{3y}$

G. $3x^3y^2 \sqrt{12y^5}$

H. $6x^3 \sqrt{3y^9}$

J. $2y^3 \sqrt{27x^6}$

K. None of these

51. Which of the following statements is always true regarding a parallelogram?

A. The diagonals are perpendicular to each other.

B. The sum of the angles is $180°$.

C. Opposite sides are both parallel and congruent.

D. There cannot be a right angle in any parallelogram.

E. Consecutive angles are complementary.

52. A square and a semicircular region have the same perimeter. If the length of the radius of the semicircular region is 8, what is the length of a side of the square?

F. 8π

G. 8

H. 2π

J. $\dfrac{8}{\pi}$

K. $4+2\pi$

GO ON TO THE NEXT PAGE.

2 **2** **2** **2** **2** **2** **2** **2** **2** **2** **2**

53. Which of the following is a pair of vertical angles?

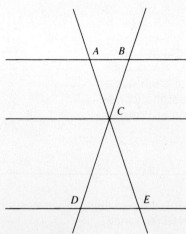

   A. ∠BAC, ∠CED
   B. ∠ACD, ∠ACB
   C. ∠CDE, ∠CED
   D. ∠ACB, ∠DCE
   E. ∠ACE, ∠BCD

54. Line $\overline{AD}$ is parallel to line $\overline{CE}$. If $AB = 4$, $BC = 9$, and $CE = 5$, what is the length of $\overline{AD}$?

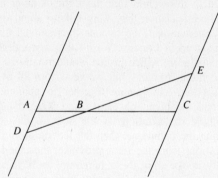

   F. 1
   G. 2
   H. $2\frac{2}{9}$
   J. $7\frac{1}{5}$
   K. $11\frac{1}{4}$

55. A kite is flying at the end of a taut string that is 50 feet long. The string makes an angle of 25° with the horizontal, and the person flying the kite holds the string 5 feet off the ground. How high is the kite from the ground?
   A. $5 + 50 \sin 25°$
   B. $5 + 50 \cos 25°$
   C. $5 + 50 \tan 25°$
   D. $5 + \dfrac{50}{\sin 25°}$
   E. $5 + \dfrac{\sin 25°}{50}$

56. Two chords, $\overline{AB}$ and $\overline{CD}$, intersect at E. If $AB = 8$, $CE = 2$, and $DE = 8$, what is the length of $\overline{AE}$?

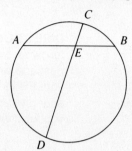

   F. 2
   G. 3
   H. 4
   J. 5
   K. 6

57. What is the maximum number of common tangents that can be drawn to any two circles?
   A. 1
   B. 2
   C. 3
   D. 4
   E. 5

58. Which of the following statements is true about polygons?
   F. All triangles are convex.
   G. All rectangles are quadrilaterals.
   H. The sum of the angles of a pentagon is 540°.
   J. A square is a rhombus.
   K. All these statements are true.

59. If $AB = BC$ and m $\angle ABC = 24°$, what is the measure of $\angle BDC$?

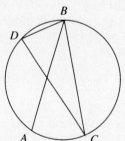

   A. 24°
   B. 48°
   C. 72°
   D. 78°
   E. 90°

60. What is the period of the function $y = -3 \sin (4x + \pi)$?
   F. 3
   G. 4
   H. $\dfrac{\pi}{4}$
   J. $\dfrac{\pi}{2}$
   K. $\dfrac{\pi}{3}$

END OF TEST 2
STOP! DO NOT TURN THE PAGE UNTIL TOLD TO DO SO.

3 3 3 3 3 3 3 3 3 3   3

Model Reading Test

35 Minutes—40 Questions

DIRECTIONS: This test consists of four passages, each followed by ten multiple-choice questions. Read each passage and then pick the best answer for each question. Fill in the spaces on your answer sheet that correspond to your choices. Refer to the passage as often as you wish while answering the questions.

Passage I

PROSE FICTION: This passage is an excerpt from *Germinal,* a novel written by Emile Zola. The novel takes place in a mining region of France where considerable conflict arises between the miners and their bosses.

Every night at about nine o'clock, when the bar would empty out, Etienne stayed on to talk to Souvarine. He would drink his beer in small sips, while the engineman would smoke one cigarette after another, his thin fingers
5 discolored by the tobacco. His veiled, mystic's eyes would dreamily follow the smoke; his unoccupied left hand would nervously move in the air. He usually ended up by putting a tame rabbit—a large female one, always swollen with pregnancy and allowed the freedom of the
10 house—on his lap. The rabbit, whom he had named "Poland," had grown to love him, and she would come to sniff his trousers, sit up, and scratch with her paws until he would pick her up, like a child. Then, huddled against him her ears flat back, she would close her eyes while he
15 endlessly stroked the gray silk of her fur with an unconscious, caressing gesture, finding tranquility in the soft and living warmth.

"You know, I've gotten a letter from Pluchart," Etienne said one evening.

20 There was no one else in the place but Rasseneur. The last customer had left, returning to the sleeping village.

"Well!" exclaimed the landlord, standing in front of his two roomers. "Pluchart! What's he up to?"

For two months Etienne had been carrying on a steady
25 correspondence with the Lille mechanic, whom he had decided to tell about his job at Montsou and who was now indoctrinating him, jumping at his chance to use Etienne to propagandize among the miners.

"What he's up to is that association, which is going very
30 well … It seems people from all over are joining up."

"And what do *you* think of their association?" Rasseneur asked Souvarine.

The latter, gently scratching Poland's head, blew out a jet of smoke and murmured quietly:

35 "More foolishness."

But Etienne became excited. The initial illusions of his ignorance and his natural predisposition to rebelliousness both acted to throw him into the fight of labor against capital. The association they were talking about was the
40 Workers' International, the famous International that had just been set up in London. Wasn't that a wonderful effort, a campaign in which justice would finally be victorious? No more frontiers, but workers from all over the world rising up and joining together to guarantee the
45 workingman the bread he earns. And what a magnificently simple organization: at the bottom, the section, representing the commune; then the federation, grouping all the sections from the same province; then the nation; and finally, above all of these, humanity itself, incarnated
50 in a general council in which each nation was represented by a corresponding secretary. Within six months they would conquer the earth and lay down the law to the bosses if they fail to fall into line!

"Just foolishness!" repeated Souvarine. "Your Karl
55 Marx is still at the stage of wanting to let natural laws operate. No politics and no conspiracies, isn't that right? Everything done in the open, and higher salaries the only aim … Well, don't talk to me about your evolution! Burn the cities, mow down the nations, wipe everything out—
60 and when there's nothing left of this rotten world, maybe a better one will grow in its place."

Etienne began to laugh. He did not always understand what his friend was talking about, and this theory of destruction seemed only a pose to him. Rasseneur, more
65 practical-minded, and with the common sense of a well-established man, did not even bother to get angry. He was interested only in precise information.

GO ON TO THE NEXT PAGE.

3 3 3 3 3 3 3 3 3 3 3 **3**

"Then you're going to try to set up a section in Montsou?"

70   That was what Pluchart, who was secretary of the Federation of the Nord, wanted, and he kept emphasizing the help the International would be able to give the miners if they ever went on strike. Actually, Etienne did think a strike was imminent: the business of the timbering would

75   end badly; it would take only one more unreasonable demand on the part of the Company to bring all the mines into a state of rebellion.

"The trouble is the dues," said Rasseneur judiciously. "Fifty centimes a year for the general fund and two francs

80   for the section doesn't seem like much, but I'll bet lots of men will refuse to give it."

"Especially," Etienne added, "since we would first have to set up an emergency fund, which could be turned into a strike fund if necessary … Still, now's the time to

85   think of these things. I'm ready, if the others are."

Emile Zola, *Germinal*

1. The first paragraph of the passage portrays Souvarine as someone who is:
   A. tense.
   B. intellectual.
   C. arrogant.
   D. soft-spoken.

2. Which of the following statements most accurately describes the relation of the characters in the passage?
   F. Etienne and Souvarine work together digging coal in the Montsou mine.
   G. Souvarine is Etienne's supervisor on the job.
   H. Rasseneur employs both Etienne and Souvarine.
   J. Etienne and Souvarine are Rasseneur's tenants.

3. Souvarine's attitude toward the Workers' International can best be described as:
   A. skeptical.
   B. supportive.
   C. indifferent.
   D. enthusiastic.

4. The letters that Pluchart, the Lille [a city in France] mechanic, sends to Etienne are meant to do all of the following EXCEPT:
   F. seek Etienne's help in the national union movement.
   G. educate Etienne about the international labor movement.
   H. stir up dissatisfaction among the miners.
   J. elicit information from Etienne about conditions at Montsou.

5. Etienne's enthusiasm for the Workers' International seems to stem mainly from his:
   A. Marxist background.
   B. natural tendency to be a troublemaker.
   C. long-time commitment to justice.
   D. quest for power.

6. Etienne laughs (line 62) because:
   F. he wants to annoy Souvarine.
   G. Souvarine has said something very funny.
   H. he thinks Souvarine himself is not being serious.
   J. he wants to show that he is not afraid of Souvarine.

7. Rasseneur is doubtful that a strike will occur because:
   A. the mine owners will comply with the workers' demands.
   B. the workers are afraid to lose their jobs.
   C. the authorities at Montsou will forbid it.
   D. the workers won't pay the fee required to join the union.

8. For Etienne, Pluchart's most persuasive argument in favor of a strike is that:
   F. the Workers' International will give aid to the striking workers.
   G. it will allow the Workers' International to declare victory over the corrupt bosses.
   H. it will lead to better hours and working conditions.
   J. the strike is likely to end within half a year.

9. Rasseneur is probably inquisitive about Etienne's plans for a strike because:
   A. he supports the workers.
   B. if a strike occurs, his business will be affected.
   C. he is a former miner himself.
   D. he plans to report Etienne to the owners of the mine.

10. Which of the following most accurately describes where each character in the passage stands on issues of social and political change?

    I = most radical
    II = moderately radical
    III = least radical

    F. I - Souvarine; II - Etienne; III - Rasseneur
    G. I - Rasseneur; II - Etienne; III - Souvarine
    H. I - Souvarine; II - Rasseneur; III - Etienne
    J. I - Etienne; II - Souvarine; III - Rasseneur

GO ON TO THE NEXT PAGE.

3 3 3 3 3 3 3 3 3 3 **3**

Passage II

HUMANITIES: This passage, from Gabriele Sterner's *Art Nouveau: An Art of Transition from Individual to Mass Society,* describes the unusual designs of the Spanish architect Antonio Gaudí.

Antonio Gaudí's strangely expressionistic architecture represented an attack against all previously known principles of construction. Straight lines were denied and hidden. The natural function of balances and supports was
5 concealed from the beholder. Instead of the old rules, imagination held sway; everything was permitted and nothing impossible. Just as Gallé reacted in a typically French way to the new style, Gaudí was honored almost as a saint; this can be explained by the situation that prevailed in
10 Catalonia at the time. The Catalonian *Renaiça* demanded political autonomy, since it was here alone in Spain that industrial progress was taking place. In addition, the province of Catalonia was the homeland of a prosperous middle class oriented toward international relations of all kinds.
15 Gaudí's style affirmed this new patriotic independence, and his personality was a reflection of the political sensibility of the region. Gaudí was also deeply religious in the sense of Spanish Catholicism; he was steeped in mystical ideas, which he sought to capture and express in his build-
20 ings. His world of forms included all types of animals and plants. Although abstract design was foreign to Gaudí, his art was informed with social ideas and had a broad social basis. For example, he built housing projects under the auspices of the Societat Obrera Mataronese, a cooperative
25 workers' association.

The most unique feature of Spanish art as opposed to that of northern countries is its Moorish influence. Since Arab art and architecture are characterized by an absence of human representations, artists were forced to turn to
30 ornamentation as the only permissible form of decoration and to perfect it. Europe and Africa unite with Spain, where incredible works have been produced over the course of centuries. The history of Spanish art is filled with paradoxes. Spanish Gothic, for example, is a true hybrid in
35 which mystical and spiritualized forms stand in dialectical opposition to the dynamism of a purely decorative urge. One sees walls covered with a dense tangle of branches in which pointed Gothic arches and the leaves of cruciferous plants become lost. Although a kind of textile pattern
40 emerges, it is one in which the weave can be neither discerned nor unraveled. . . .

This is the tradition in which Antonio Gaudí found himself. His early works include palaces and villas; however, Gaudí's late years were dedicated exclusively to the
45 construction of the otherworldly *Sagrada Familia* (Temple of the Poor), a church that was built through collections and endowments alone. Gaudí's bold solutions are combined with a great luxury of forms and wealth of materials. A tremendous variety of costly elements were
50 incorporated into Gaudí's works. Architecture was regarded as sculpture; façades were kneaded, as it were, until the eye of the beholder could no longer identify the individual elements. The ornamentation works its way from inside out and from the ground floor to the spires. Gaudí's
55 preference for plantlike ornamentation was pushed to its extreme. The churning dynamism of the entire structure captivates the viewer even if the forms are so exalted as to leave him breathless and confused.

Gaudí's architecture is characterized by experiments
60 with colored segments. He often clothed apparently independent architectural elements in colorful ceramic tiles which, in turn, seem to produce the effect of independent added decoration. The suggestion of straight lines is avoided. The tiles consist of interlocking fragments; this
65 arrangement has the effect of exaggerating the artist's attack upon traditional architecture. On the other hand, the asymmetrical tendency and amorphousness of Gaudí's designs are concealed by some added labile element. Everything is in motion. No other artist of the art nouveau
70 period matched this Catalonian individualist in eliciting highly picturesque critical comparisons: "flamboyant extravagance," architecture "like the curved back of a salamanderlike saurian," "labyrinth," "dune formations," "dried foam on the beach," "hollow dream constructions,"
75 "elongated beehives," "gigantic plant stalks" . . .

Gabriele Sterner, *Art Nouveau: An Art of Transition from Individual to Mass Society*

11. Based on information in the passage, Gaudí achieved recognition primarily for:
    A. founding a school of Spanish architecture.
    B. pioneering new architectural forms.
    C. helping to solve social problems through his architecture.
    D. designing churches.

12. A building designed by Gaudí would probably:
    F. have a symmetrical and balanced look.
    G. be uniform in color.
    H. have sharp angles and lots of glass.
    J. look like a piece of clay sculpture.

13. According to the passage, Gaudí was part of which artistic movement?
    A. Abstract Expressionism
    B. Neo-Moorish
    C. Art Nouveau
    D. Catalonian Spanish

14. Most often Gaudí decorated his buildings with:
    F. designs based on nature.
    G. abstract designs.
    H. bold murals depicting social problems.
    J. textiles.

GO ON TO THE NEXT PAGE.

15. According to the passage, Gaudí designed all of the following types of structures EXCEPT:
  A. public libraries.
  B. villas for wealthy patrons.
  C. houses for working people.
  D. places of worship.

16. A conclusion to be drawn from the discussion of Spanish Gothic architecture (lines 33–41) is that pure Gothic architecture:
  F. should not be altered or tampered with.
  G. originated in Spain.
  H. often represents biblical scenes.
  J. conveys a sense of mysticism and spiritualism.

17. Gaudí owes some of his achievement as an architect to which of the following?
  I. He lived in Catalonia.
  II. He was a devout Catholic.
  III. Architectural critics such as Gallé supported his work.
  A. I only
  B. II only
  C. I and II
  D. I and III

18. Based on the contents of the passage, which of the following statements is probably NOT an accurate conclusion to draw about Gaudí's work?
  F. Most of Gaudí's buildings are different from each other.
  G. A Gaudí building costs more to build than an ordinary building.
  H. Gaudí's buildings are best suited for warm climates.
  J. Gaudí's buildings probably don't appeal to everyone.

19. According to the passage, the influence of Moorish art has been felt:
  A. throughout the world.
  B. in Europe and Africa.
  C. primarily in Spain.
  D. primarily in prosperous countries.

20. The statement that Gaudí's structures leave the viewer "breathless and confused" (line 58) suggests that:
  F. some of Gaudí's work needs to be improved.
  G. Gaudí's work is surprising and exciting.
  H. few people understand Gaudí's architecture.
  J. viewing a Gaudí building is usually an unpleasant experience.

Passage III

NATURAL SCIENCE: This passage is from *The Sea Around Us* by Rachel Carson. In this excerpt Carson writes about undersea life in the very deepest parts of the ocean.

In their world of darkness, it would seem likely that some of the animals might have become blind, as has happened to some cave fauna. So, indeed, many of them have, compensating for the lack of eyes with marvelously
5 developed feelers and long, slender fins and processes with which they grope their way, like so many blind men with canes, their whole knowledge of friends, enemies, or food coming to them through the sense of touch.

The last traces of plant life are left behind in the thin
10 upper layer of water, for no plant can live below about 600 feet even in very clear water, and few find enough sunlight for their food-manufacturing activities below 200 feet. Since no animal can make its own food, the creatures of the deeper waters live a strange, almost parasitic existence
15 of utter dependence on the upper layers. These hungry carnivores prey fiercely and relentlessly upon each other, yet the whole community is ultimately dependent upon the slow rain of descending food particles from above. The components of this never-ending rain are the dead and
20 dying plants and animals from the surface, or from one of the intermediate layers. For each of the horizontal zones or communities of the sea that lie, in tier after tier, between the surface and the sea bottom, the food supply is different and in general poorer than for the layer above. There is a
25 hint of the fierce and uncompromising competition for food in the saber-toothed jaws of some of the small, dragonlike fishes of the deeper waters, in the immense mouths and in the elastic and distensible bodies that make it possible for a fish to swallow another several times its
30 size, enjoying swift repletion after a long fast.

Pressure, darkness, and—we should have added only a few years ago—silence, are the conditions of life in the deep sea. But we know now that the conception of the sea as a silent place is wholly false. Wide experience with
35 hydrophones and other listening devices for the detection of submarines has proved that, around the shore lines of much of the world, there is the extraordinary uproar produced by fishes, shrimps, porpoises and probably other forms not yet identified. There has been little
40 investigation as yet of sound in the deep, offshore areas, but when the crew of the *Atlantis* lowered a hydrophone into deep water off Bermuda, they recorded strange mewing sounds, shrieks, and ghostly moans, the sources of which have not been traced. But fish of shallower zones
45 have been captured and confined in aquaria, where their voices have been recorded for comparison with sounds heard at sea, and in many cases satisfactory identification can be made.

GO ON TO THE NEXT PAGE.

During the Second World War the hydrophone network set up by the United States Navy to protect the entrance to Chesapeake Bay was temporarily made useless when, in the spring of 1942, the speakers at the surface began to give forth, every evening, a sound described as being like "a pneumatic drill tearing up pavement." The extraneous noises that came over the hydrophones completely masked the sounds of the passage of ships. Eventually it was discovered that the sounds were the voices of fish known as croakers, which in the spring move into Chesapeake Bay from their offshore wintering grounds. As soon as the noise had been identified and analyzed, it was possible to screen it out with an electric filter, so that once more only the sounds of ships came through the speakers.

Rachel Carson, *The Sea Around Us*

21. According to the passage the layer of the ocean where food for animal life is most plentiful is:
    A. the bottom.
    B. an area below 600 feet deep.
    C. the area between 200 and 600 feet in depth.
    D. the uppermost layers of water.

22. Based on information in the passage, which of the following criteria is NOT likely to be used as a measure of underwater depth?
    F. Noise level recorded by undersea microphones
    G. Pressure per square inch
    H. Amount of light
    J. Amount of plant life

23. The passage indicates that many underwater animals cannot see because:
    A. the lack of light has gradually eliminated their capacity to see.
    B. they use sound waves instead of light to navigate in the darkness.
    C. they have learned to survive without seeing their enemies or their prey.
    D. their sense of touch has eliminated their need to see.

24. According to the passage, which of the following is NOT a use for a hydrophone?
    F. To listen to the sound of undersea fauna
    G. To search for unknown species of fish and other creatures
    H. To monitor the passing of surface vessels
    J. To detect submerged submarines

25. Animals that live near the bottom of the sea are most likely to be carnivorous because:
    A. they have developed sharp teeth and strong jaws with which to kill their prey.
    B. plants that grow far below the surface are not edible.

C. animals cannot make their own food, so they eat each other.
D. most surface vegetation is eaten before it sinks to the bottom of the sea.

26. The passage indicates that fish living far under water sometimes do not eat for extended periods of time because:
    F. food is scarce at certain times of the year.
    G. fish in the deepest parts of the ocean digest their food very slowly.
    H. weaker fish must compete for food with stronger fish.
    J. one large meal satisfies most fish for a long time.

27. Which of the following statements about the state of oceanographic research does the passage most clearly support?
    A. Undersea research is still incomplete.
    B. Technology used in undersea studies is still in a very primitive stage of development.
    C. More undersea research is conducted near shore than in mid-ocean.
    D. Military researchers have made several momentous discoveries about undersea life.

28. The phrase "enjoying swift repletion," as used in line 30, probably means that the fish:
    F. are in a state of being sated (i.e., filled to capacity).
    G. seem to enjoy eating after a long fast.
    H. digest their prey very quickly.
    J. continue to hunt for food even after devouring their prey.

29. By using the phrase "saber-toothed" to characterize some of the fishes that live in the deepest waters, the author is suggesting that the fishes:
    A. are still at an early stage of evolution.
    B. appear frightening to behold.
    C. are ferocious food-gatherers.
    D. are soon likely to become extinct.

30. The author's main purpose in the passage is to:
    F. show that the United States coast was threatened by the enemy in World War II.
    G. explain some of the complexities of deep-sea life.
    H. illustrate the main problems faced by undersea researchers.
    J. gain public support for oceanographic expeditions.

GO ON TO THE NEXT PAGE.

Passage IV

SOCIAL SCIENCE: This passage is from a U.S. Senate report titled "The Constitutional Rights of Children." The passage discusses issues related to rights and responsibilities of both children and parents.

The classic liberal thinkers provided the principles for alleviating the repressed social conditions of the slave, the serf, the woman, for, in effect, assertion of individualism and equality of opportunity. But children were not to be
5   included within these principles. Sir Henry Maine was sure that "they do not possess the faculty of forming a judgment on their own interests; in other words . . . they are wanting in the first essential of an engagement by Contract." And John Locke was clear that the limited capacity
10 of children necessarily excluded minors from participation in the social contract. "Children . . . are not born in this state of equality, though they are born to it." Although Adam was "created" as a mature person, "capable from the first instant of his being to provide for his own support
15 and preservation . . . and govern his actions according to the dictates of law and reason," children lacked a "capacity of knowing that law." Parents were therefore under an obligation of nature to nourish and educate their children to help them attain a mature and rational capacity, "till
20 [their] understanding be fit to take the government of [their] will." "And thus we see how natural freedom and subjection to parents may consist together and are both founded on the same principle."

There is of course no unalterable legal boundary be-
25 tween childhood and adulthood. In different societies and at different times, young people have been accepted into adult society at different ages and children have been variously viewed, and law has differently regulated familial relations at different times. One writer has noted the chang-
30 ing from the early colonial days of this country to the present of the legal regulation of the assumption by the child of an adult economic role. Thus, from the early days till near the end of the 19th century, the economic needs of communities and families in America necessitated early
35 entry of children into the work force. At first, these children were closely restrained by law and custom, whether they lived at home or in an apprentice system in a master's home, and they worked not for their own account but for the account of family or master. Gradually, the law im-
40 posed upon parents some regard and consideration for the child's welfare, especially the obligation to prepare him for assumption of full adult responsibilities. But in the post-Civil War industrialization and the social dislocation accompanying it, social custom and supporting law shifted
45 to a greater requirement of retention of parental control over children for a longer period and to greater protection of family life. Three major institutional changes were legislatively implemented, the juvenile court system, the prohibition of child labor, and compulsory education, all
50 looking toward "external support of the family as the ideal way additionally to prepare children to face life …: bolster the family, leave even the delinquent child in the family—where possible, shield the child from adult roles and responsibilities, and formally educate him, and upward
55 movement could be expected."

The result was an "extension of childhood," with the State "enjoining longer supervision, more protracted education, and the postponed assumption of adult economic roles." The writer notes some elements of reversal of the
60 trend in the second half of [the 20th century] in the context of the middle and late adolescent in particular. The waning of parental immunity from a personal tort [*an injury or wrong done to someone*] action brought by an uneman-cipated child is one example, and another is the
65 passage by many States of medical emancipation laws by which minors are enabled to receive medical treatment without parental consent. . . .

Concomitant with the increased emphasis upon family control and responsibility, common law judges viewed
70 parental rights "as a key concept, not only for the specific purposes of domestic relations law, but as a fundamental cultural assumption about the family as a basic social, economic, and political unit. For this reason, both English and American judges view the origins of parental rights as
75 being even more fundamental than property rights." Parental power has been deemed primary, prevailing over the claims of the State, other outsiders, and the children themselves, unless there is some compelling justification for interference. The primary compelling justification is
80 the protection of children from parental neglect, abuse, or abandonment; statutes proscribing various forms of parental misconduct are found in every State.

"The Constitutional Rights of Children"

31. According to the passage, the principles of equality articulated by the classic liberal thinkers of the past applied mainly to:
    A. minority groups.
    B. women and slaves.
    C. children.
    D. all people of color.

32. In general the laws governing parental responsibility for children in the early 19th century were:
    F. less strict than today's laws.
    G. more strict than present-day laws.
    H. of an altogether different nature.
    J. of about the same degree of strictness.

33. John Locke believed that minors should not share the benefits of equality because young children:
    A. do not know right from wrong.
    B. cannot be trusted to distinguish truth from illusion.
    C. lack understanding of law and reason.
    D. are usually not competent witnesses.

GO ON TO THE NEXT PAGE.

3 3 3 3 3 3 3 3 3 **3**

34. Laws regarding children are sometimes difficult to interpret because:
    F. they keep changing.
    G. previous court decisions do not serve as a reliable guide.
    H. there is no clearcut division between childhood and adulthood.
    J. juveniles who commit serious crimes are increasingly being treated as adult offenders.

35. In making decisions about parent-child relationships, judges are often guided by the principle that:
    A. children and parents are equal in the eyes of the law.
    B. childhood is a special and sacred time of life.
    C. parents' ignorance of the law cannot be excused.
    D. the family unit is the basic unit of society.

36. The passage suggests that laws pertaining to children:
    F. change gradually.
    G. are easy to change when the need arises.
    H. change according to the periodic fluctuations in the economy.
    J. are out-of-date and need to be changed.

37. The "extension of childhood" (line 56) has occurred for all of the following reasons EXCEPT:
    A. children are not expected to go to work at an early age.
    B. children are required to stay in school until they are older.
    C. the courts are severe with parents who do not control their children.
    D. maturity is more difficult to achieve in an increasingly complex society.

38. According to the passage, the responsibilities of modern parents include:
    F. seeing to it that their children are properly clothed.
    G. providing adequate medical care for young children.
    H. preventing their minor children from harming others.
    J. arranging day care, when necessary.

39. Which of the following situations might cause a court to remove a pre-teen child from from the custody of his or her parents?
    A. The child refuses to go to school.
    B. The child is repeatedly left alone while the parents work in another city.
    C. The child keeps company with an older crowd with a reputation for causing trouble.
    D. The home is messy, rundown, and in need of repair.

40. Which of the following is the best interpretation of John Locke's statement that children "are not born in this state of equality, though they are born to it" (lines 11–12)?
    F. All children are created equal, but some are more equal than others.
    G. At birth children do not have the same rights as adults.
    H. The state must be responsible for controlling the rights of children until the children grow up.
    J. Children should not assume that the state will look after their rights.

END OF TEST 3
STOP! DO NOT TURN THE PAGE UNTIL TOLD TO DO SO.

4 4 4 4 4 4 4 4 4 4 4 **4**

Model Science Reasoning Test

35 Minutes—40 Questions

DIRECTIONS: This test consists of several distinct passages. Each passage is followed by a number of multiple-choice questions based on the passage. Study the passage, and then select the best answer to each question. You are allowed to reread the passage. Record your answer by blackening the appropriate space on the answer sheet.

Passage I

The diagram below shows the probable evolutionary relationships of the primates.

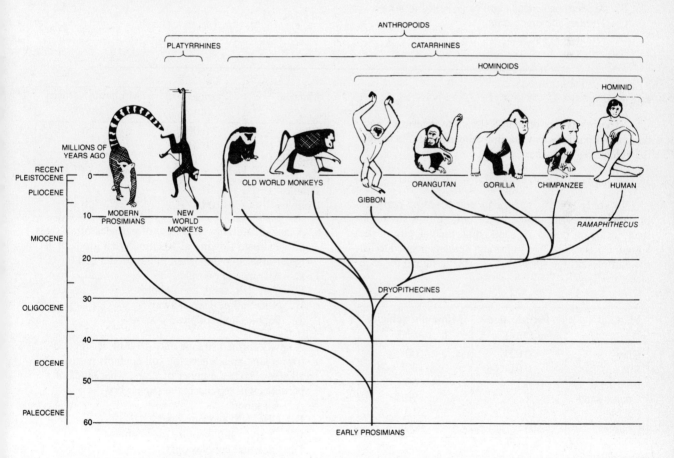

From Helena Curtis, *Biology,* 4 ed. Worth Publishers, New York, 1983.

GO ON TO THE NEXT PAGE.

4 4 4 4 4 4 4 4 4 4 4

1. The most recent common ancestor of human beings and the gorilla lived about:
   A. 10 million years ago.
   B. 19 million years ago.
   C. 25 million years ago.
   D. 33 million years ago.

2. The diagram proposes that the largest group that descended from Dryopithecines is:
   F. the gibbons.
   G. The Catarrhines.
   H. the Hominoids.
   J. the great apes.

3. Two organisms are sometimes said to be closely related if they have a recent common ancestor. By this criterion, which of the following pairs are most closely related?
   A. Old World and New World monkeys
   B. Modern prosimians and New World monkeys
   C. Human and orangutan
   D. Orangutan and gibbon

4. What does the diagram tell us about the relationships of the lemurs, which are the modern prosimians?
   F. Lemurs have existed unchanged for 60 million years.
   G. Lemurs are the ancestors of all primates.
   H. Of all primates, lemurs are most similar to the ancestors of the whole group.
   J. Lemurs have evolved to a greater extent than any of the other primates.

5. *Australopithecus* is a genus of primates, more recent and humanlike than *Ramapithecus*. Of the taxonomic groups named on the chart, which is the smallest to which *Australopithecus* belongs?
   A. Anthropoids
   B. Hominoids
   C. Catarrhines
   D. Hominids

Passage II

Experiments are done in a stream to determine how the size of particles eroded and deposited is affected by the velocity of the water.

Experiment 1

To study erosion, sediments composed of particles of various sizes are placed in the bottom of a stream at many different points. At each point, the velocity of the stream is measured. The minimum velocity needed to lift the particles off the stream bottom is determined for each size particle.

Material	Particle size (mm)	Minimum velocity (cm/s)
Clay	0.001	700
Silt	0.01	180
Fine sand	0.1	60
Coarse sand	1	90
Pebbles	10	210
Cobbles	100	600

Experiment 2

To study deposition, the sediments are dropped into the stream from the surface at various points in the stream. The minimum stream velocity that will prevent the particles from sinking to the bottom of the stream is measured for each size particle.

Material	Particle size (mm)	Minimum velocity (cm/s)
Clay	0.001	20
Silt	0.01	20
Fine sand	0.1	20
Coarse sand	1	30
Pebbles	10	100
Cobbles	100	300

6. A landslide dumps a mixture of particles of all sizes into a stream flowing at 40 cm/s. What kinds of material will be deposited in the stream bed?
   F. All sizes of particles
   G. Clay, silt, sand, and pebbles
   H. None; all will wash away
   J. Pebbles and cobbles

7. A newly formed stream starts to flow at 30 cm/s over a land area where the soil contains particles of all sizes. After a number of years, what kinds of particles will remain in the stream bed?
   A. All kinds
   B. Clay, silt, and fine sand
   C. Coarse sand, pebbles, and cobbles
   D. Clay and cobbles only

8. At a construction site, a quantity of coarse sand finds its way into a stream flowing at 40 cm/s. What happens to it?
   F. It falls to the bottom of the stream and stays there.
   G. It is carried away by the stream and falls to the bottom if the stream speeds up to 90 cm/s.

GO ON TO THE NEXT PAGE.

4 4 4 4 4 4 4 4 4 4 **4**

H. It is carried away by the stream and falls to the bottom if the stream slows down to 25 cm/s.
J. It falls to the bottom of the stream and is then picked up and carried into quieter water.

9. A stream flows at 130 cm/s over soil containing a mixture of all kinds of particles. What kinds of particles will drop to the bottom at a point where the velocity has slowed down to 25 cm/s?
    A. Pebbles and cobbles
    B. Coarse and fine sand only
    C. Coarse sand only
    D. Clay, silt, pebbles, and cobbles

10. Which of the following hypotheses might be advanced to account for the fact that a very large stream velocity is required to lift clay off the bottom of the river?
    F. Clay particles clump together to form lumps the size of cobbles.

G. Clay particles are much larger than sand grains.
H. Rivers always slow down when they flow over clay.
J. Clay particles have a high density, so they drop to the bottom very easily.

11. If similar experiments were done with other materials in other rivers, which of the following outcomes would always be found?
    A. The velocity figures in Experiment 1 would always be larger than the corresponding values in Experiment 2.
    B. The velocity figures would never be larger than 600 cm/s in either experiment.
    C. The velocity figures would never be smaller than 20 cm/s in either experiment.
    D. Medium-size particles are always picked up by the slowest part of the river and carried furthest.

GO ON TO THE NEXT PAGE.

Passage III

The rate of oxygen absorption in fruits is a measure of the ripening process. The graphs below show how this rate is affected, in bananas and avocados, by exposure to various concentrations of the gas ethylene (ppm is parts per million).

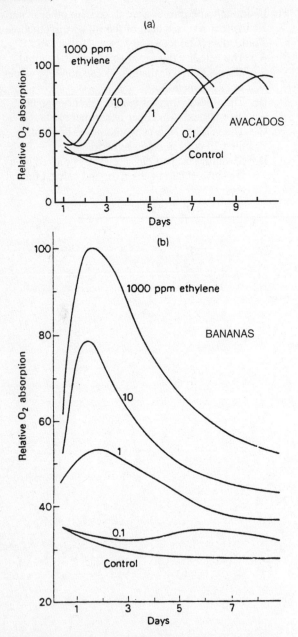

Figure 5.17. Oxygen uptake by developing fruits, and the effect of ethylene gas upon the normal respiratory trends. (a) For fruits which normally show the respiratory climacteric phenomenon (e.g., avacado pear). (b) For non-climacteric fruits such as banana.
(From *The Biochemistry and Physiology of Plant Growth Hormones*, McGraw Hill, 1971.)

12. If the fruits are not exposed to ethylene:
    F. after the first few days, the rate of oxygen absorption is smaller in avocados than in bananas.
    G. absorption of oxygen decreases steadily in both fruits.
    H. in both fruits, oxygen absorption rises to a peak and then drops off.
    J. in avocados, oxygen absorption increases greatly after the first few days.

13. The effect of increasing the exposure to ethylene is to:
    A. increase oxygen uptake in both fruits.
    B. speed up oxygen uptake in both fruits.
    C. increase oxygen uptake for bananas only.
    D. speed up oxygen uptake for avocados only.

14. In what circumstance would both fruits reach about half of their maximum level of oxygen absorption?
    F. On the fourth day with 1 part per million of ethylene.
    G. On the second day with 10 parts per million of ethylene.
    H. On the sixth day with 10 parts per million of ethylene.
    J. On the first day with 50 parts per million of ethylene.

15. A reasonable assumption from the graphs is that:
    A. ethylene causes bananas to greatly increase the total amount of oxygen they absorb in ripening.
    B. concentrations of ethylene above 10 parts per million have little effect on the ripening time of avocados.
    C. the total amount of oxygen absorbed by avocados in ripening is not affected by the ethylene concentration.
    D. bananas are affected more strongly than avocados by the presence of ethylene.

16. The information provided suggests that if a fruit wholesaler wanted to use ethylene to control the ripening of his produce, it would be necessary to:
    F. keep the concentration of ethylene below 10 ppm.
    G. separate the different kinds of fruit into different containers.
    H. test each batch separately with no ethylene.
    J. get the fruit to market promptly after exposure to ethylene.

GO ON TO THE NEXT PAGE.

Passage IV

A chemist is investigating the effect of various kinds and amounts of solutes on the boiling point of a solution.

Experiment 1

Solutions are made of various amounts of glucose dissolved in 1 liter of water, and the boiling point of each solution is measured.

Glucose concentration (g/L)	Boiling point (° C)
0	100.0
100	100.3
200	100.6
300	100.9
400	101.2
500	101.5

Experiment 2

Solutions are made of various solutes (substances dissolved) in water, all with a concentration of 300 g/L. The boiling point of each solution is measured.

Substance	Molecular weight	Boiling point (° C)
Acetaldehyde	44	103.5
Glycerol	92	101.7
Glucose	180	100.9
Sucrose	342	100.5

Experiment 3

Solutions are made of various solutes dissolved in benzene (the solvent), which boils at 80.1° C. All concentrations are 300 g/L.

Solute	Molecular weight	Boiling point (° C)
Butyric acid	88	89.8
Triethylamine	101	88.6
Naphthalene	178	84.8
Cholesterol	387	82.3

17. If 200 g of glucose are dissolved in 500 mL of water, the boiling point of the solution will be:
    A. 100.3° C.
    B. 100.6° C.
    C. 101.2° C.
    D. 101.6° C.

18. Three hundred grams of a substance with a molecular weight of 65 are dissolved in 1 liter of water. The boiling point of the solution will be about:
    F. 103.5° C.
    G. 102.4° C.
    H. 101.7° C.
    J. 100.3° C.

19. For a given concentration and molecular weight of solute, how does the elevation of the boiling point depend on the kind of solvent?
    A. It is the same for all solvents.
    B. It is the same for water and for benzene.
    C. It is more for water than for benzene.
    D. It is more for benzene than for water.

20. The experiments indicate that the boiling point elevation is directly proportional to:
    F. the molecular weight of the solute.
    G. the number of molecules of solute per gram of solvent.
    H. the boiling point of the solvent used.
    J. a combination of solute concentration and molecular weight.

21. In Experiment 3, the solution of butyric acid in benzene boiled at a higher temperature than cholesterol in benzene. A possible explanation is:
    A. the molecules of cholesterol are larger, so they lower the boiling point of the benzene.
    B. the mass of cholesterol in solution was larger than the mass of butyric acid.
    C. cholesterol reacts chemically with benzene, but butyric acid does not.
    D. the butyric acid solution contains more molecules of solute than the cholesterol solution.

22. In trying to determine the nature of a newly discovered substance, a chemist might use experiments of this kind to discover its:
    F. chemical formula.
    G. concentration.
    H. molecular weight.
    J. boiling point.

Passage V

The diagram below represents the forms of energy consumption in an old building, in the design for a new building, and in the actual new building after it was built.

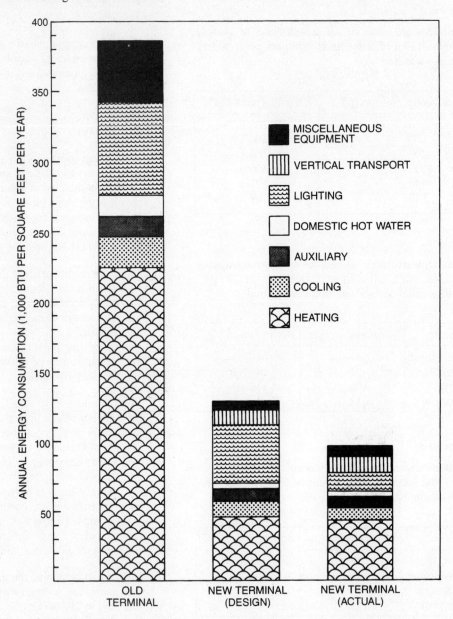

GO ON TO THE NEXT PAGE.

4 4 4 4 4 4 4 4 4 4 4 **4**

23. How effective was the new design in improving the efficiency of energy use?
    A. It reduced the amount of energy used by about 15%.
    B. It was a great improvement, but did not accomplish all that was expected of it.
    C. It was so good that the new building actually performed better than expected.
    D. It was unnecessary, since the new building was so much better than the old one.

24. What service was provided in the new building that was not available in the old one?
    F. Elevators
    G. Fluorescent lighting
    H. Air conditioning
    J. Electronic energy control

25. The difference between the new design and the performance of the actual building might have been due to miscalculation of the energy saving provided by:
    A. insulation.
    B. fluorescent lighting.
    C. air conditioning.
    D. improved boilers.

26. What approach to future problems of design of heating efficiency is suggested by these results?
    F. Since heating is the largest part of the energy cost even in the new building, this design did little to improve heating efficiency.
    G. Design emphasis should be placed on heating because this is the area where the major savings can be made.
    H. Better designs must be sought because this one did not produce a result better than the one achieved in the actual new building.
    J. Little additional research is needed because this design provided the maximum possible saving of heating fuel.

27. Which of the following questions had to be answered before a decision was made as to whether or not to use the new design in constructing the new building?
    A. Should the new building be equipped with air conditioning?
    B. Will the new design improve the efficiency of hot water heating?
    C. Does the actual new building accurately reflect the gains suggested by the design?
    D. Does the new design cost so much more than the old that the fuel saving would not make up the difference?

Passage VI

The purpose of this experiment is to study the rate at which the eyes of guppies become light-adapted.

Experiment 1

Three guppies are kept in daylight conditions at 24° C. They are fed 50 water fleas (*Daphnia*) once a day. The number of *Daphnia* captured in 5 minutes is counted. In six trials, the following results are obtained:
Number of *Daphnia* captured: 35 32 32 36 34 35

Experiment 2

The guppies are kept in the dark at 24° C for a full day. Then a light is turned on. After a measured time delay, 50 *Daphnia* are added to the tank, and the number captured in 5 minutes is counted. The experiment is repeated with various time delays.

Time delay (minutes)	Number captured in 5 minutes
2	0
4	18
6	24
8	33
10	33
12	32

Experiment 3

A similar experiment is done with the guppies, which have been kept at various temperatures. A uniform time delay of 8 minutes is used before the food is added.

Temperature (° C)	Number captured in 5 minutes
15	12
18	18
21	26
24	35
27	34
30	35
33	22
36	9

28. What assumption underlies the design of these experiments?
    F. Guppies are most active when illumination is high.
    G. The ability of guppies to find food depends on their ability to see it.
    H. Temperature affects the ability of guppies to find food.
    J. The eyes of guppies are just like the eyes of people.

GO ON TO THE NEXT PAGE.

29. What was the purpose of Experiment 1?

A. To establish a criterion as to when the guppies' eyes are light-adapted

B. To control any possible effect of temperature

C. To condition the guppies to respond to the presence of *Daphnia*

D. To keep the guppies in healthy condition

30. What was the purpose of the time delays in Experiment 2?

F. To see how long it would take for the guppies to find their food

G. To allow for differences between guppies in their feeding ability

H. To find out how long it takes for the eyes of the guppies to become completely light-adapted

J. To measure the time rate at which guppies find their food under standard conditions

31. What evidence is there that guppies depend solely on their eyesight to find food?

A. Experiment 3 shows that they cannot see well at low temperatures.

B. Experiment 2 shows that, in the first 2 minutes after being kept in the dark, they cannot find any.

C. Experiment 1 shows that they find food very efficiently in daylight.

D. Experiment 2 shows that the rate at which they find food diminishes as the food supply dwindles.

32. A time delay of 8 minutes was selected for Experiment 3 because this is the amount of time required for:

F. the guppies to consume most of the food.

G. the *Daphnia* to become adapted to the tank.

H. the guppies' eyes to become light-adapted at 24° C.

J. the water in the tank to reach a steady temperature.

33. Which hypothesis could NOT account for the results of Experiment 3?

A. Light adaptation is delayed at unusually high temperatures.

B. Guppies are damaged at very high temperatures, and are thus unable to feed well.

C. At high temperatures, *Daphnia* become immobile and more difficult to find.

D. The rate of adaptation to light increases uniformly with temperature.

Passage VII

Two scientists disagree about an important point in the theory of evolution.

Scientist 1

Darwin's theory of evolution by natural selection has a serious flaw. It cannot account for the origin of completely new organs. Consider, for example, the wings of insects. These originate in the embryo as outgrowths of the external skeleton of the thorax. How could such outgrowths have evolved? According to all we know about evolution, they must have started as tiny outgrowths that grew bigger generation by generation until they became functional wings. However, a small, incipient wing is useless; an insect cannot fly with 1% of a wing. Since those tiny wing buds would have no use, they could not contribute to the ability of the insects to survive, and thus could not contribute to the evolution of wings. It has been suggested that these small outgrowths were originally used as gliding surfaces, like the skin flaps of a flying squirrel. This does not solve the problem, however, for a good-sized surface would be needed for gliding; 1% of a surface is as useless for gliding as for flying. Somehow, such a surface must have gradually developed by some means other than natural selection. Natural selection could improve a gliding surface, and turn it into a functional, flapping wing, but it could not invent the surface in the first place. The insect wing is an example of preadaptation, the development of a new structure that subsequently evolves into something useful. Evolution gives us many such examples. Preadaptation surely exists, but it cannot be explained by the theory of natural selection. Explanation of the origin of new, useful structures is an unfinished task of biological science.

Scientist 2

The problem raised by Scientist 1 is not new. Darwin provided the answer a century ago, although at that time there was no real evidence. It all hinges on the meaning of the term *preadaptation*. It does not mean that a new feature arises and then develops for many evolutionary years while it has no function. What it does mean is that an existing structure, developed for one function, can acquire a totally different use. This is undoubtedly how insect wings evolved. Recent studies show that the wings of insects have an important function other than flight; they are temperature-regulating structures. Many insects control their body temperatures by sitting in the sun to warm up. In ancient, primitive insects, an expansion of the thorax exposed more surface. This expansion was promoted by selection, since it allowed for faster and more efficient warmup. Lateral projections provided additional surfaces for temperature regulation. When these projections grew big enough, they acquired a new function; they became useful as gliding surfaces. The ability to glide has developed many times, and it has

GO ON TO THE NEXT PAGE.

4   4 4 4 4 4 4 4 4 4   **4**

sometimes evolved into real, controlled flight. Selection converted the clumsy gliding surfaces of ancient insects into the complex and effective insect wings of today. Preadaptation is simply a shift of function, and is perfectly incorporated into the theory of evolution by natural selection.

34. One of the scientists, but not the other, would agree that:
    F. natural selection results in improved functioning of insect wings.
    G. natural selection can explain the origin of the wings of insects.
    H. insects use their wings to help in temperature control.
    J. insect wings evolved from surfaces previously used for gliding.

35. What evidence does Scientist 2 advance to support her argument?
    A. Tests show that insects use their wings for temperature control.
    B. Darwin provided a competent explanation for preadaptation.
    C. In the development of an insect, the wings arise as outgrowths of the thoracic skeleton.
    D. Many insects use projections from the thorax for gliding.

36. According to Scientist 2, what principle has Scientist 1 overlooked in his argument?
    F. Natural selection can greatly improve the functioning of an organ.
    G. In the evolution of many different flying organisms, gliding always precedes real flying.
    H. New organs can arise even if they have no function at first.
    J. In the course of evolution, an organ can acquire a new function.

37. Which of the following discoveries would support the hypothesis of Scientist 2?
    A. Fossils of insects with primitive wings capable of gliding, but not of flying
    B. A living species of insect that can glide, but cannot fly

    C. A fossil insect with small lateral projections from the thorax
    D. A living insect in which juvenile stages have short wings used only for temperature regulation

38. How should the argument of Scientist 1 be evaluated in terms of its contribution to science?
    F. It is a foolish argument because the question was settled a long time ago.
    G. It is useful to raise the question because it challenges scientists to find evidence for shifts of function.
    H. It wastes valuable time because it has long been established that evolution results from natural selection.
    J. It challenges scientists to find an answer to a perplexing problem for which there is no satisfactory answer.

39. What would the two scientists expect to find in the fossil record?
    A. Scientist 1, but not Scientist 2, would expect to find that functional gliding surfaces appeared suddenly.
    B. Both scientists would expect to find gradual evolution of wings, starting with small projections.
    C. Scientist 2, but not Scientist 1, would expect to find gradual evolution, starting with small projections.
    D. Both scientists would expect to find that there are no fossil insects without some sort of gliding surface.

40. In a recent series of experiments, paper models of insects were exposed to sunshine and to aerodynamic tests in a wind tunnel. Size and wing length were varied to test the concept of:
    F. natural selection.
    G. shift of function.
    H. preadaptation.
    J. evolution.

END OF TEST 4
STOP! DO NOT TURN THE PAGE UNTIL TOLD TO DO SO.

ANSWER KEYS AND ANALYSIS CHARTS

MODEL ENGLISH TEST

1.	D	16.	H	31.	A	46.	F	61.	C
2.	H	17.	D	32.	H	47.	D	62.	G
3.	D	18.	F	33.	D	48.	J	63.	C
4.	H	19.	C	34.	J	49.	C	64.	J
5.	C	20.	H	35.	C	50.	G	65.	C
6.	J	21.	B	36.	G	51.	C	66.	J
7.	B	22.	H	37.	C	52.	F	67.	C
8.	G	23.	B	38.	F	53.	D	68.	J
9.	D	24.	G	39.	D	54.	F	69.	A
10.	H	25.	B	40.	H	55.	B	70.	H
11.	C	26.	H	41.	B	56.	H	71.	B
12.	H	27.	B	42.	F	57.	D	72.	G
13.	A	28.	J	43.	D	58.	G	73.	C
14.	G	29.	A	44.	J	59.	A	74.	H
15.	C	30.	J	45.	A	60.	H	75.	C

Analysis Chart

Skills	Questions	Possible Score	Your Score
Usage/Mechanics			
Punctuation	1, 13, 18, 20, 28, 32, 44, 46, 50, 66	10	
Basic Grammar and Usage	8, 9, 16, 17, 25, 26, 27, 31, 33, 38, 52, 53	12	
Sentence Structure	3, 4, 6, 12, 24, 39, 41, 43, 47, 48, 56, 57, 61, 62, 67, 68, 72	17	
Rhetorical Skills			
Strategy	2, 5, 23, 34, 40, 49, 51, 54, 59, 63, 71, 74	12	
Organization	11, 15, 19, 22, 29, 30, 35, 37, 42, 45, 58, 60, 65, 75	14	
Style	7, 10, 14, 21, 36, 55, 64, 69, 70, 73	10	

Total: 75 _____

Percent Correct: _____

MODEL MATHEMATICS TEST

1.	C	13.	C	25.	B	37.	C	49.	D
2.	H	14.	F	26.	J	38.	K	50.	F
3.	E	15.	A	27.	D	39.	A	51.	C
4.	H	16.	F	28.	J	40.	G	52.	K
5.	C	17.	A	29.	C	41.	D	53.	D
6.	J	18.	J	30.	H	42.	G	54.	H
7.	B	19.	A	31.	D	43.	C	55.	A
8.	F	20.	H	32.	K	44.	K	56.	H
9.	D	21.	E	33.	A	45.	D	57.	D
10.	K	22.	J	34.	K	46.	G	58.	K
11.	E	23.	E	35.	E	47.	D	59.	D
12.	G	24.	G	36.	K	48.	G	60.	J

Analysis Chart

Content Area	Skill Level			Possible Score	Your Score
	Basic Skills	Application	Analysis		
Pre-Algebra Algebra	1, 5, 10, 13, 17, 23, 27, 29	2, 3, 6, 8, 11, 15, 19, 22, 28, 34, 36, 50	12, 16, 24, 30	24	
Intermediate Algebra Coordinate Geometry	7, 14, 21 32, 42, 43, 45	4, 18, 25, 26, 31, 33, 35	40, 44, 49 52	18	
Geometry	38, 48, 51, 53, 56, 57, 58	9, 20, 37, 39, 46, 54, 59		14	
Trigonometry	41, 60	47, 55		4	

Total: 60 _____

Percent Correct: _____

MODEL READING TEST

1.	A	11.	B	21.	D	31.	B
2.	J	12.	J	22.	F	32.	F
3.	A	13.	C	23.	A	33.	C
4.	F	14.	F	24.	G	34.	H
5.	B	15.	A	25.	D	35.	D
6.	H	16.	J	26.	H	36.	F
7.	D	17.	C	27.	A	37.	D
8.	F	18.	H	28.	F	38.	H
9.	B	19.	B	29.	C	39.	B
10.	F	20.	G	30.	G	40.	G

Analysis Chart

Passage Type	Referring	Reasoning	Possible Score	Your Score
Prose Fiction	2, 4, 5, 7	1, 3, 6, 8, 9, 10	10	
Humanities	11, 13, 17	12, 14, 15, 16, 18, 19, 20	10	
Social Sciences	32, 35, 37	31, 33, 34, 36, 38, 39, 40	10	
Natural Sciences	21, 23, 24, 26	22, 25, 27, 28, 29, 30	10	

Total: 40 _____

Percent Correct: _____

MODEL SCIENCE REASONING TEST

1.	B	11.	A	21.	D	31.	B
2.	H	12.	J	22.	H	32.	H
3.	C	13.	B	23.	C	33.	D
4.	H	14.	F	24.	F	34.	G
5.	D	15.	B	25.	B	35.	A
6.	J	16.	G	26.	G	36.	J
7.	A	17.	C	27.	D	37.	D
8.	H	18.	G	28.	G	38.	G
9.	C	19.	D	29.	A	39.	B
10.	F	20.	G	30.	H	40.	G

Analysis Chart

Kind of Question	Skill Level			Possible Score	Your Score
	Understanding	Analysis	Generalization		
Data Representation	1, 2, 12, 13, 23, 24	3, 5, 14, 15, 16, 25	4, 26, 27	15	
Research Summaries	6, 17, 28, 29, 30	7, 8, 9, 18, 20, 31, 32	10, 11, 19, 21, 22, 33	18	
Conflicting Viewpoints	34, 35,	36, 39	37, 38, 40	7	

Total: 40 _____

Percent Correct: _____

Answer Explanations: ENGLISH TEST

1. D Use a comma between the parts of a simple series.

2. H It is important to maintain the established subject—the forces that influence the way a child handles money; the other options are all off the topic.

3. D There is no need for *and* before the adjective clause *that children need to learn.* Choices B and C repeat the error. Choice C is wrong also because the pronoun *whom* is used to refer to a person, and the antecedent here is *principles.*

4. H There is a parallel series of sentences in this paragraph, all employing the infinitive. For this reason, the infinitive *to understand* is correct.

5. C The first sentence of the paragraph is a clear topic sentence that prepares the reader for the series of principles that forms the body of the paragraph.

6. J The antecedent of the pronoun is the plural noun *children* at the end of the preceding paragraph.

7. B The phrase *being as how* is substandard English; the other words create an illogical statement.

8. G The subject of the sentence is the singular noun *rise.*

9. D The pronoun *this* is almost never adequate by itself; the sentence requires a more complete statement. The point made in the preceding sentences is that money is more available.

10. H *Major* is more in keeping with the tone of the passage. The other words do not mean the same as *major* and are less preferable in this context.

11. C The underlined statement is off the topic and so must be eliminated.

12. H The subordinating conjunction *when* forms a logical link with the rest of the sentence; the other options do not.

13. A An introductory adverbial clause, except a very short one, is set off from the main clause by a comma. A stronger mark of punctuation in this place, such as choice D, would create a sentence fragment.

14. G The phrase *material possessions* makes a clear point; *worldly goods* is redundant.

Answer Explanations: ENGLISH TEST (continued)

15. C Paragraph 2 ends with a mention about *pressures,* a train of thought that leads directly to paragraph 5, which begins with the statement *These pressures are strong.* In the same manner, the thought about managing money at the end of paragraph 5 is picked up in the first sentence in paragraph 3; the notion that children need experience in managing money is echoed in paragraph 4, and the emphasis on adults in paragraph 4 is continued in the first words of paragraph 6.

16. H A singular subject—in this case, *police officer*—followed by a phrase such as *in common with, accompanied by, in addition to,* or *together with* takes a singular verb.

17. D To be parallel with the rest of the sentence, this part must begin with the participle *protected,* which modifies the noun *structure.*

18. F A parenthetical expression such as *however* is set off by commas.

19. C This choice is the only one that bears on anatomy.

20. H Compound verbs are not normally separated by a comma.

21. B The words *One after the other* are redundant; the phrase *in turn* means the same.

22. H This sentence has no bearing on the topic of the paragraph or passage and must be removed.

23. B Because the entire passage deals with the great stress placed on the foot, this description of the physical process of using the foot is meaningful.

24. G The word *if* is necessary at this point if the sentence is to be logical. Not all 7-year-old boys weigh 55 pounds.

25. B A present-tense verb is necessary to agree with the other verbs in the sentence.

26. H The subject of the verb is the plural noun *estimates;* the present tense is correct.

27. B When parts of a compound subject are joined by *or* or *nor,* the verb agrees with the nearer part—in this case, *characteristic.* The simple present tense is correct.

28. J The sentence is a simple declarative statement that requires a period.

29. A The figures provided are quite impressive and clearly dramatize the point of the passage.

30. J Paragraph 3 is a more general statement about the foot and should precede the very specific, detailed paragraphs 2 and 4. Note the clue in *During all this walking.*

31. A The subject of the verb *commemorates* is the singular noun *park;* the present tense is correct (note *is* in the same sentence).

32. H Items in a series are separated by semicolons if they contain commas within themselves. This sentence, when correctly constructed, includes a series of direct objects—*meetings, adoption,* and *labors*—the last two of which introduce clauses set off by commas.

33. D To be parallel with the direct objects *meetings* and *labors,* this item must begin with a noun.

34. J The park is the site of Independence Hall, around which most of the historical events described in the passage revolve.

35. C The topic sentence of this paragraph is flawed; the general point it makes is not broad enough to embrace the historical events described. A better topic sentence would be this: *Independence Hall, originally the statehouse for the province of Pennsylvania, was the site of an important event in early American history.*

36. G The word *supervision* is adequate; *overview* is repetitious.

37. C Although Thomas Jefferson figures importantly in the events later described in the passage, where he was in 1736 has no bearing on this paragraph.

38. F The past perfect tense is required in this sentence because the action described took place *before* the past action that is the subject of the passage.

39. D All the actions in the sentence are in the simple past.

40. H The word *Nevertheless* provides the contrast that is needed in a sentence describing an unexpected consequence. The other connective words do not provide the contrast, and so make no sense in the context.

41. B In combination with the word *would, be declared* signals an event in the future; note "not until a year later."

42. F The paragraph, flawed because of a weak topic sentence, presents historical events that occurred in and near Independence Hall. Of the choices given, this is the only one that makes that point.

43. D This is the only correct, complete sentence.

Answer Explanations: ENGLISH TEST *(continued)*

Choices A and B are sentence fragments. Choice C is a sentence plus a sentence fragment.

44. **J** A semicolon joins two main clauses; there is no conjunction. Anything weaker in this spot results in a run-on sentence.

45. **A** The paragraphs are correct as they stand. Since this passage is in chronological order, the sequence is self-explanatory.

46. **F** Items in a series are separated by semicolons if they contain commas.

47. **D** To be parallel with the other clauses in the sentence, this one must maintain the same pattern, *it is a . . . .*

48. **J** The subject of the verb is the plural noun *prolifers;* the present tense is needed.

49. **C** The comma is needed after *Americans* to set off the participial phrase *comprising a majority of Americans.* Otherwise, the sentence can be misread to mean that pro-choice advocates comprise a majority of all Americans who believe that abortion should be legal under certain circumstances, falsely implying that a minority of these Americans are not pro-choice.

50. **G** This phrase is not a digression but rather is information essential to the point being made, and so should not be enclosed in parentheses.

51. **C** This sentence needs to be introduced by a transition that signals the introduction of an example; the other transitions denote contrast *or cause,* and choices B and D result in sentence fragments.

52. **F** The subject of the sentence is the singular noun *group;* the present tense is correct.

53. **D** The word *process* is a noun; it must be described or restated as a noun, not as an adverbial clause.

54. **F** The views of leaders would be useful in this passage about opinions. The information in the other options would be off the topic.

55. **B** The adjective *ill advised* is clear and direct; the other options are colloquial or misleading.

56. **H** The subject of the sentence is the plural noun *programs.* The passage is written in the present tense.

57. **D** The clause *that are beneficial* merely repeats the meaning of the word *positive,* and so should be removed.

58. **G** This sentence has nothing to do with the point of the passage.

59. **A** For the most part, one view of the abortion issue is compared with the other in this passage.

60. **H** Paragraph 2 clearly introduces the topic, and suggests the structure of the passage; paragraph 3 begins with an example of the quality of the thought mentioned at the end of paragraph 2; paragraph 4 presents the other view of the issue, and paragraph 1 sums up the complexity of the issue.

61. **C** The sentence in which this question appears ends with a series of noun objects, in which *comparison of the proposed budget* should be included. Note that the correct choice is the only one that is not a clause.

62. **G** The present perfect tense is required in this sentence because the action referred to extends, at least in its consequences, to the present.

63. **C** The entire passage emphasizes the point that no legislation is more important than the budget.

64. **J** Only the use of the preposition *For* creates a logical, correct sentence; the other choices are substandard English.

65. **C** The statement about traffic on the freeways has no bearing on the point of the passage.

66. **J** Use the comma before a coordinating conjunction linking main clauses.

67. **C** The logic that lies behind each of the options changes the meaning of the sentence dramatically. Only the use of *Because* results in a meaning consistent with the rest of the paragraph.

68. **J** The word *because* here creates an adverb clause that is parallel with the adverb clause that begins the sentence. Also, the other choices either are substandard English (F) or alter the meaning (G, H) of the sentence.

69. **A** *Continually* means "occurring in steady, rapid succession," while *continuously* means "occurring in uninterrupted duration," the latter meaning being preferable in this context.

70. **H** The idea of disputes and stalemates festering borders on a mixed metaphor. More sensible in this very businesslike passage is the use of the term *unresolved.* The other options make no sense in the sentence.

71. **B** The tone and message of the passage seem to be directed at constituents seeking to be informed.

72. **G** When the comparative (here, *larger*) is used for

Answer Explanations: ENGLISH TEST *(continued)*

more than two, it is necessary to exclude from the group the object compared. In the original sentence the expenditures of the Government of California would be included in the group *those of any American governmental jurisdiction ... U.S. Government.*

73. C The word *budget* is what is intended; additional words are distracting.

74. H The passage makes clear in several ways the importance of the state budget as an entity.

75. C Paragraph 3 is clearly the introductory paragraph for this passage. In addition, it refers to early January and the governor's message, two items mentioned also in the first sentence of paragraph 1. Paragraph 2 continues the chronological narrative, and even ends with a closing statement.

Answer Explanations: MATHEMATICS TEST

1. C Only $\frac{x}{2}$ satisfies the definition of a monomial.

2. H Lisa now receives 108% of her previous salary, so $5.67 is 108% of what number? $A = 5.67$, $P = 108\%$, B is unknown. The percent proportion is

$$\frac{108}{100} = \frac{5.67}{B}$$
$$108B = 567$$
$$B = 5.25$$

3. E $5 + 2 \cdot 3^2 = 5 + 2 \cdot 9$ Exponents first.
$$= 5 + 18$$
$$= 23$$

4. H $81x^2 - 36y^2 = 9(9x^2 - 4y^2)$
$$= 9(3x - 2y)(3x + 2y)$$
Always do the greatest common factor first.

5. C $\sqrt{49} = 7$, which is rational.

6. J $\dfrac{(x - y)^2}{y^2 - x^2} = \dfrac{(x - y)(x - y)}{(y - x)(y + x)}$

$\quad = \dfrac{(-1)(x - y)}{y + x}$ Because $x - y$ and $y - x$ are opposites.

$\quad = \dfrac{y - x}{y + x}$

7. B Consecutive terms of a geometric sequence have a common ratio. Only in the sequence 1, 2, 4, 8, . . . is there a common ratio, 2.

8. F $4x - 2[3x - (x + 4)] = 5 - 2(x + 1)$
$$4x - 2[3x - x - 4] = 5 - 2x - 2$$
$$4x - 6x + 2x + 8 = 5 - 2x - 2$$
$$8 = 3 - 2x$$
$$5 = -2x$$
$$x = \frac{-5}{2}$$

9. D Angle ABC is a right angle because a diameter is perpendicular to a tangent at the point of tangency. Angle ADB is also a right angle because it is inscribed in a semicircle. Therefore $\angle DBC$ is complementary to both $\angle ABD$ and $\angle BCD$. Thus $\angle ABD$ and $\angle BCD$ are equal in measure.

10. K $\qquad 7.2\% = 0.072$
$$7.2(10^{-2}) = 0.072$$
$$\frac{72}{100} = 0.72$$
$$(0.08)9 = 0.72$$
$$(0.08)(0.09) = 0.0072$$

11. E $xy^2(x - y) = (-3)(2^2)(-3 - 2)$
$$= (-3)(4)(-5)$$
$$= 60$$

12. G This is a direct-variation-type problem. The proportion is $\dfrac{4}{x} = \dfrac{20}{30} \left(= \dfrac{2}{3}\right)$ $2x = 12$
$$x = 6$$

13. C The associative property of addition allows regrouping of terms.

14. F A pure imaginary number is a complex number with the real part equal to 0. Only $\sqrt{-9} = 3i = 0 + 3i$ is this type.

15. A $\quad 7\frac{1}{4} \qquad 7\frac{3}{12}$ The LCD is 12.

$\quad \underline{-2\frac{5}{6}} \quad \underline{-2\frac{10}{12}}$

$\qquad\qquad\quad 6\frac{15}{12}$ Borrow $\frac{12}{12}$ from the 7.

$\qquad\qquad \underline{-2\frac{10}{12}}$

$\qquad\qquad\quad 4\frac{5}{12}$

16. F This is a work-type problem for which the formula $w = rt$ applies. Since Stan can do the job in 4 hours, his rate of work is $\frac{1}{4}$ of the job per hour. Fred's rate is then $\frac{1}{5}$ of the job per hour. Let $x =$

Answer Explanations: MATHEMATICS TEST *(continued)*

the number of hours it would take to do the job together.

	w	$=$	r	$\cdot$	t
Stan		$\dfrac{x}{4}$		$\dfrac{1}{4}$	x
Fred		$\dfrac{x}{5}$		$\dfrac{1}{5}$	x

The equation is $\dfrac{x}{4} + \dfrac{x}{5} = 1$ (one job completed).

17. A The definition of a composite number includes the phrase "greater than 1."

18. J A special rule about absolute value inequalities allows an immediate translation from $|x + 3| \geq 2$ to

$$x + 3 \geq 2 \text{ or } x + 3 \leq -2$$
$$x \geq -1 \text{ or } x \leq -5$$

19. A Multiply both sides by the LCD, which is 12.

$$12\left(\frac{2x-1}{3} + \frac{x+2}{4}\right) = 12\left(\frac{1}{6}\right)$$
$$4(2x-1) + 3(x+2) = 2$$
$$8x - 4 + 3x + 6 = 2$$
$$11x + 2 = 2$$
$$11x = 0$$
$$x = 0$$

20. H The measure of an angle formed by a chord and a tangent at the point of tangency is half of the intercepted arc. An inscribed angle is also measured by half of the intercepted arc. Therefore $\angle ECB = \angle BAC$.

21. E When completely simplified, the polynomial is
$$27x^6 + \text{(terms of lower degree)}$$
The degree of this polynomial is 6.

22. J Follow the rule for squaring a binomial:
$$(a + b)^2 = a^2 + 2ab + b^2$$
Here
$$(2x - 3y)^2 = 4x^2 - 12xy + 9y^2$$

23. E In quadrant IV, the first component of the ordered pairs is positive and the second is negative. Only $(2, -8)$ is of that type.

24. G $110110_{(two)} = 1(2^5) + 1(2^4) + 0(2^3) + 1(2^2)$
$$+ 1(2^1) + 0(2^0)$$
$$= 32 + 16 + 4 + 2 = 54_{(ten)}$$

25. B The sum of the roots of the quadratic equation
$ax^2 + bx + c = 0$ is $\dfrac{-b}{a}$ and the product is $\dfrac{c}{a}$.
The product of the roots of
$5x^2 - 8x + 7 = 0$ is $\dfrac{7}{5}$.

26. J $8^{-(2/3)} = \dfrac{1}{8^{2/3}} = \dfrac{1}{\sqrt[3]{8^2}} = \dfrac{1}{\sqrt[3]{64}} = \dfrac{1}{4}$

27. D The given expression is the expanded form of 302,470.

28. J First factor each denominator, then use each factor the greater number of times it occurs in any factorization.
$$5a^2b^3$$
$$20ab^4 = 2 \cdot 2 \cdot 5 \cdot ab^4$$
$$15a^3b^2 = 3 \cdot 5 \cdot a^3b^2$$
The LCD is $2 \cdot 2 \cdot 3 \cdot 5 \cdot a^3b^4 = 60a^3b^4$.

29. C The mean of n numbers is found by adding the numbers and dividing by n. The sum of the given numbers is 58, so the mean is 5.8.

30. H Sue is paid 7% only on her sales. Her salary is
$$S = 200 + 0.07t.$$

31. D Multiply the numerator and denominator by the LCD, which is $9x^2$.

$$\frac{9x^2\left(\frac{1}{x} - \frac{1}{3}\right)}{9x^2\left(\frac{1}{x^2} - \frac{1}{9}\right)} = \frac{9x - 3x^2}{9 - x^2} = \frac{3x(3 - x)}{(3 - x)(3 + x)}$$

$$= \frac{3x}{3 + x}$$

32. K The given equation is equivalent to $y + 9 = -2(x + 6)^2$. Compare this to the standard form of such an equation:
$$y - k = a(x - h)^2$$
which has its vertex at (h, k). The parabola's vertex is at $(-6, -9)$.

33. A Multiply both sides by the common denominator, $(x - 3)(x + 3)$. There are, therefore, restricted values 3 and -3.

$$(x - 3)(x + 3)\left(\frac{x^2 + 9}{x^2 - 9} - \frac{3}{x + 3}\right)$$

$$= (x - 3)(x + 3)\left(\frac{-x}{3 - x}\right)$$
$$x^2 + 9 - 3(x - 3) = x(x + 3)$$
$$x^2 + 9 - 3x + 9 = x^2 + 3x$$
$$18 = 6x$$
$$x = 3$$

But since 3 is a restricted value, the solution set is empty.

34. K $\dfrac{2.4(10^{-4})}{6(10^{-2})} = 0.4(10^{-4-(-2)})$

$$= 0.4(10^{-2}) = [4(10^{-1})](10^{-2})$$
$$= 4(10^{-3})$$

Answer Explanations: MATHEMATICS TEST *(continued)*

35. E Substitute the given coordinates into the slope formula.

$$m = \frac{y_2 - y_1}{x_2 - x_1} = \frac{-3 - 8}{-5 - (-5)} = \frac{-11}{0},$$

which does not exist.

36. K During January the Smiths use $0.2(100) = 20$ gallons and have 80 gallons left to begin February. In February they use $0.25(80) = 20$ gallons, so they have $80 - 20 = 60$ gallons left on March 1.

37. C Here is one possible approach. Since $\overline{AE} \perp l$, it is perpendicular to each of the parallel lines. Then $\triangle ACF$ is a right triangle, and, by the Pythagorean theorem, $CF = 8$. Then $\triangle ACF$ is similar to $\triangle ADG$, giving the following proportion:

$$\frac{10}{8} = \frac{24}{DG}$$
$$10DG = 192$$
$$DG = 19.2$$

38. K All of these statements are false.

39. A Angles CBA and CDB are the supplements of the given angles. Their measures are $40°$ and $120°$. Since the sum of the three angels of a triangle is $180°$,

$$m \angle C = 180 - (40 + 120)$$
$$= 180 - 160 = 20°$$

40. G Imagine three containers in which the mixtures could be made.

$$\underbrace{|12 - x|}_{4\%} + \underbrace{|\quad x \quad|}_{100\%} = \underbrace{|\quad 12 \quad|}_{20\%}$$

The equation reflects the fact that the amount of antifreeze does not change as a result of mixing the 4% and 100% solutions.

$$0.04(12 - x) + 1.00(x) = 0.2(12)$$
$$4(12 - x) + 100x = 20(12)$$
$$48 - 4x + 100x = 240$$
$$96x = 192$$
$$x = 2$$

41. D The length of side BC is $\sqrt{5^2 - 2^2} = \sqrt{21}$.

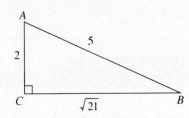

In a right triangle the sine function is

$$\frac{\text{length of opposite side}}{\text{length of hypotenuse}} = \frac{\sqrt{21}}{5}$$

42. G This is a parabola that opens upward and its vertex is $(1, 2)$. Therefore the equation in standard form is

$$y = a(x - 1)^2 + 2$$

Substitute the coordinates $(0, 5)$ into the equation to solve for a.

$$5 = a(0 - 1)^2 + 2$$
$$5 = a + 2$$
$$a = 3$$

The equation is $y = 3(x - 1)^2 + 2$.

43. C Multiply the numerator and denominator by the complex conjugate of the denominator.

$$\frac{(3 - 2i)(2 - i)}{(2 + i)(2 - i)} = \frac{6 - 3i - 4i + 2i^2}{4 - i^2}$$
$$= \frac{6 - 7i + 2(-1)}{4 - (-1)} \quad (i^2 = -1)$$
$$= \frac{4 - 7i}{5} = \frac{4}{5} - \frac{7}{5}i$$

44. K This is a problem of permutations because order is important.

$$_nP_r = \frac{n!}{(n - r)!}$$
$$_6P_6 = \frac{6!}{(6 - 6)!} = \frac{6!}{0!} = \frac{720}{1} = 720$$

45. D Let $x = \log_2 \frac{1}{8}$. Change the equation to its corresponding exponential form.

$$2^x = \frac{1}{8} = \frac{1}{2^3} = 2^{-3} \quad \text{Therefore } x = -3.$$

46. G The ratio of the corresponding linear measures of polygons is the ratio of the square roots of the areas. The ratio of the lengths of the corresponding altitudes is $\frac{\sqrt{9}}{\sqrt{16}} = \frac{3}{4}$.

47. D Coterminal angles are found by adding or subtracting multiples of $360°$ or 2π radians.

$$\frac{75\pi}{4} - \frac{9(8\pi)}{4} = \frac{75\pi}{4} - \frac{72\pi}{4}$$
$$= \frac{3\pi}{4}$$

48. G $CD = 6 - \left(1\frac{2}{3} + 1\frac{1}{4} + 1\frac{1}{12}\right)$
$$= 6 - 4 = 2$$

49. D The vertex of the graph of the equation would locate the time (t) and height (h) of the maximum height. Complete the square to put the equation in standard form.

$$h = -16(t^2 - 4t)$$
$$= -16(t^2 - 4t + 4) + 64$$
$$= -16(t - 2)^2 + 64$$

The vertex is at $(2, 64)$.

Answer Explanations: MATHEMATICS TEST *(continued)*

50. F $\sqrt{54x^4y^5} \cdot \sqrt{2x^2y^4} = \sqrt{108x^6y^9}$
$= \sqrt{(36x^6y^8)(3y)}$
$= \sqrt{36x^6y^8} \cdot \sqrt{3y}$
$= 6x^3y^4 \sqrt{3y}$

51. C Opposite sides of a parallelogram are both parallel and congruent.

52. K Let x be a side of the square. The perimeter of the square is $4x$, and the perimeter of the semicircular region is $2r + \pi r$.
$4x = 16 + 8\pi \qquad x = 4 + 2\pi$

 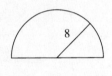

53. D Angles ACB and DCE are vertical angles.

54. H Triangles ABD and CBE are similar, and the corresponding sides have the same ratio.
$$\frac{4}{9} = \frac{x}{5}$$
$$9x = 20$$
$$x = \frac{20}{9} = 2\frac{2}{9}$$

55. A Since the sine is
$$\frac{\text{length of opposite side}}{\text{length of hypotenuse}},$$
$$\sin 25° = \frac{h}{50}.$$

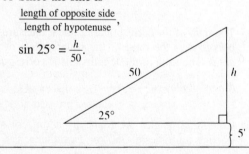

Then $h = 50 \sin 25°$. But the end of the string is 5 feet above the ground, so the total height is $5 + 50 \sin 25°$.

56. H Let $AE = x$; then $BE = 8 - x$. The product of the lengths of the segments of one chord equals the product of the lengths of the segments of the other.
$$x(8 - x) = 2 \cdot 8$$
$$8x - x^2 = 16$$
$$x^2 - 8x + 16 = 0$$
$$(x - 4)^2 = 0$$
$$x - 4 = 0$$
$$x = 4$$

57. D The maximum number of common tangents is 4.

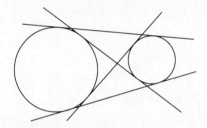

58. K All these statements are true.

59. D Equal chords intercept equal arcs in a circle. Therefore
$$\text{arc } BC = \frac{1}{2}(360 - 2 \cdot 24)° = \frac{1}{2}(312)° = 156°$$
Then
$$\angle BDC = \frac{1}{2}(156)° = 78°$$

60. J The period of the sine function
$$y = a \sin b(x - c) \text{ is } \frac{2\pi}{|b|}.$$
The given function can be written in the form
$$y = -3 \sin 4(x + \frac{\pi}{4})$$
so the period is $\frac{2\pi}{4} = \frac{\pi}{2}$.

Answer Explanations: READING TEST

1. A Souvarine's actions portray his personality. He smokes one cigarette after another, his hand pokes the air nervously, and he "endlessly" strokes Poland, the rabbit. No evidence in the paragraph suggests that B, C, or D is correct.

2. J Lines 21–23 indicate that both men are

Rasseneur's tenants. Since Etienne is a miner and Souvarine an engineman, the other answers are incorrect.

3. A Souvarine deems the international labor movement "just foolishness" (line 54). B and D are incorrect because Souvarine opposes the gradual

Answer Explanations: READING TEST (continued)

change that the movement espouses. Souvarine's outburst against Karl Marx (lines 54–60) eliminates D as a correct choice.

4. F Nothing in the passage alludes to a national labor movement. Pluchart's letters, however, are meant to get information about Montsou, inform Etienne about the movement, and breed discontent among the miners.

5. B Line 37 says that Etienne has a "natural predisposition to rebelliousness." Choice A is not appropriate for Etienne; Souvarine's comments about Marx go right over his head. C is not a reasonable choice because the Workers' International's pursuit of justice is a new concept to him, and since he's not at all interested in personal power, D is not a good answer.

6. H According to lines 62–64, Etienne thinks that Souvarine is just posing as a radical. With regard to choice A, nothing in the passage suggests that Etienne wants to annoy his friend. Nor (choice G) is Souvarine at all funny. While Etienne may not entirely understand Souvarine, he is not afraid of him either (choice J).

7. D Rasseneur raises the issue of paying dues to support the strike in lines 78–80. In the passage, he never alludes to any of the issues raised by choices A, B, and C.

8. F According to lines 70–72 and 82–84, Etienne believes that workers will be given both moral and economic support if they strike. Choices G and J occur to Etienne, but they are not his main reason for advocating a strike. H may be a consequence of a strike, but it is not mentioned in the passage.

9. B Rasseneur is "practical-minded" and "well-established," someone interested in "precise information," traits that suggest he would have more than a passing interest in the consequences of a strike at the mine. Nothing in the passage suggests that A, C, or D is correct.

10. F Souvarine (lines 57–60) advocates violent revolution, Etienne prefers evolutionary change, and Rasseneur seems concerned about protecting the status quo.

11. B The first paragraph of the passage describes Gaudí's revolutionary architectural forms. More specifically, his forms included "all types of animals and plants" (lines 20–21).

12. J "Architecture was regarded as sculpture," according to line 51. Some of the natural shapes that Gaudí used are suggested by lines 71–75.

13. C Line 69 indicates that Gaudí was an artist of the art nouveau period.

14. F Gaudí used animals and plants (lines 20–21), as well as "plantlike ornamentation" (line 55), in his designs for buildings.

15. A Gaudí designed "palaces and villas" (line 43), "housing projects" (line 23), and "a church" (line 46). Libraries are not mentioned in the passage.

16. J A characteristic of Gothic architecture is the use of "mystical and spiritualized forms" (line 35). Spanish architecture combines the pure Gothic and Moorish styles.

17. C The passage says that Catalonia's political climate as well as its prosperous middle class contributed to Gaudí's growth as an architect. The fact that as a Catholic he was "steeped in mystical ideas" (lines 18–19) also influenced Gaudí.

18. H Although architects cannot ignore the prevailing weather conditions at the sites of their buildings, nothing in the passage suggests that climate influenced Gaudí's work.

19. B Lines 26–27 refer to the Moorish influence on the architecture in Europe and Africa.

20. G The ornamentation on a Gaudí structure is powerfully rendered and never fails to be unique and startling to the viewer.

21. D Lines 21–24 state that the food supply decreases as the water level deepens. Hence, the top layers contain the most food.

22. F Scientists used to believe that silence reigned in the deepest ocean waters. That theory no longer holds true, according to the second paragraph.

23. A Lines 1–3 state that many of the animals have gradually become blind because they exist in a world of complete darkness.

24. G Several uses of hydrophones are described in lines 34–44. Searching for unknown species is not mentioned.

25. D Lines 17–21 explain that plants cannot grow in the undersea darkness and that dead and dying plants are eaten before they reach the bottom layers of ocean.

26. H In the battle for food described in lines 24–30, the weaker fish often lose. Therefore, they must wait for long periods of time to eat.

27. A Only this answer is supported by the passage.

Answer Explanations: READING TEST *(continued)*

Oceanographers seem to be making new discoveries all the time.

28. F Repletion means the state of being full or being gorged with food or drink.

29. C The ferocity of the creatures is being emphasized. The other choices may merely call to mind the extinct saber-toothed tiger.

30. G While each of the choices may be valid, most of the passage is devoted to a description of life far below the surface of the sea.

31. B Lines 2–3 of the passage list the people for whom principles for alleviating repression were created. Among those listed are women and slaves.

32. F According to the passage (lines 39–47), over time the laws imposed on parents gradually grew more severe.

33. C John Locke believed that children, unlike the full-grown Adam, lacked the capacity to know "the dictates of law and reason" (lines 15–17).

34. H Laws regarding children vary because there is no distinct line between the end of childhood and beginning of adulthood on which everyone can agree (lines 24–25).

35. D A fundamental assumption in western society is that the family is "the basic social, economic and political unit" (lines 72–73).

36. F As described in the passage, the laws pertaining to children have changed gradually from the early days until the present time.

37. D The passage says that children are not expected to assume the economic roles of adults. They are also required to stay in school for a longer period of time than before. Meanwhile, laws have given parents more responsibility to attend to their children's well-being. Changes in children's maturation is not mentioned in the passage.

38. H Under modern laws, parents are held increasingly liable for personal torts (injuries or wrongs) done by their children to others.

39. B Based on the last paragraph of the passage, courts have the power to interfere in families when parents neglect their children.

40. G John Locke meant that, although a child may be born into a society that enjoys equality, the child is unable to assume equality until later in life.

Answer Explanations: SCIENCE REASONING TEST

1. B Trace the *human* line and the *gorilla* line back to the point where they meet in the early Miocene. The time scale shows that this is at 19 million years ago.

2. H From the point marked Dryopithecines, move upward on the chart to find all the lines that branch out. They are all included within the group marked *Hominoids*.

3. C The *human* and *orangutang* lines diverge from a branching point just over 20 million years ago. For the other pairs, the branching points are as follows: A. 40 million; B 53 million; D 25 million.

4. H Lemurs are classified as prosimians, and this can only be because they are the closest relatives of the ancient prosimians that were the ancestors of the whole order. F is wrong because there is no reason to believe that the modern and the ancient prosimians are identical. G is wrong because the ancestral prosimians were not lemurs, but something similar. There is no reason at all to believe J.

5. D If *Australopithecus* is more humanlike and more recent than *Ramapithecus,* it must lie somewhere between *Ramapithecus* and human, which puts it squarely in the Hominid group.

6. J Experiment 2 shows that particles finer than pebbles will be carried with the current instead of dropping to the bottom when the velocity is under 100 cm/s.

7. A Experiment 1 shows that a stream must flow at 60 cm/s to lift even the fine sand off the bottom.

8. H Experiment 2 shows that coarse sand will not sink to the bottom until the speed of the stream is below 30 cm/s.

9. C Experiment 1 shows that at a speed of 130 cm/s the stream will not pick up clay, silt, pebbles, or cobbles, but only fine and coarse sands. Experiment 2 shows that at 25 cm/s coarse sand will drop to the bottom but fine sand will not.

10. F This would account for the fact that the very

Answer Explanations: SCIENCE REASONING TEST *(continued)*

finest particles are not lifted off the bottom until the speed of the river is quite high. G is wrong because the table shows that clay particles are smaller than sand grains. There is no reason to think that H is true. J is wrong because all the evidence shows that it is the size of the particles that is the pertinent factor.

11. A It is not possible for a river to be flowing too slowly to carry particles along, yet fast enough to lift them off the bottom. B and C are wrong because the experiments do not place limits on the behavior of other kinds of materials. D is wrong because there is nothing in the experiments to indicate how far the particles are carried.

12. J It is the control curves that show what happens if no ethylene is applied; for avocados, oxygen uptake drops for 4 days and then increases to a peak on the ninth day. F is wrong because the graphs do not compare the two fruits, but only give the daily changes for each fruit separately. G is wrong because this is true only for bananas. H is wrong because the control curve for bananas does not rise at all.

13. B In avocados, the peak moves from 6 days to 2 days when the ethylene concentration is increased from 0.1 to 1; in bananas, the peak shows a steady motion to the left as concentration increases. A and C are wrong because the absorption in bananas does not get any greater as concentration increases; it just happens earlier.

14. F On both graphs, the coordinate corresponding to 4 days is about 50 percent. None of the other combinations shows 50 percent at the stated day and concentration for both fruits.

15. B There seems to be a limit on how early avocados can ripen, since there is little difference between 10 ppm and 1000 ppm. A and C are wrong because the graphs give no information about the total amount of oxygen absorbed in ripening. D is wrong because the graphs do not compare the two fruits, but only give information about the behavior of each fruit separately.

16. G Since different fruits respond differently to exposure to ethylene, each would need its own unique treatment. F is wrong because the dosage needed would depend on what the marketer is trying to accomplish. H is wrong because once the properties of each kind of fruit are known, there is no need to keep testing. J is wrong because the graphs provide no information about the durability of the fruit after ripening.

17. C The concentration of 200 g of glucose in 500 mL

of water is the same as 400 g/L; the table for Experiment 1 shows that at this concentration the boiling point is 101.2°C.

18. G Experiment 2 makes it clear that the boiling point elevation, at constant concentration, depends on the molecular weight of the solute. The new substance is made into a solution with the same concentration as the solutions in Experiment 2. The molecular weight of the new substance is about halfway between that of acetaldehyde and that of glycerol, so the boiling point would also be about halfway.

19. D Note that it is the *elevation* of the boiling point that is in question, not the actual boiling point. Naphthalene and glucose have very nearly the same molecular weight. Glucose raised the boiling point of water only 0.9° C from 100.0° C to 100.9° C, while naphthalene, at the same concentration, raised the boiling point of benzene 4.7° C, from 80.1° C to 84.8° C.

20. G This shows most clearly in Experiment 1, where each additional 100 g of glucose in the solution produces a rise of 0.3° C in the boiling point. F is wrong because the boiling point elevation is smaller, not larger, for larger molecules. H is wrong because the boiling point of benzene is lower than that of water, but benzene shows larger elevations. J is wrong because the data do not indicate any such direct proportionality.

21. D With its smaller molecular weight, a given mass of butyric acid has many more molecules than an equal mass of cholesterol. A is wrong because cholesterol does, in fact, raise the boiling point, although to a lesser degree than a substance with smaller molecules will. B is wrong because the experimental design specifies that 300 g was used in both cases. C is wrong because there is no reason to believe there was any chemical reaction; in fact, it is contraindicated because cholesterol follows the pattern of the relationship between molecular weight and boiling point elevation.

22. H Since there is a clear relationship between molecular weight and boiling point elevation, measuring this elevation would make it possible to calculate the molecular weight.

23. C The design predicted a drop of energy consumption from 385 units to 125, but it actually went down to 95. A is wrong because the actual drop was far greater. B is wrong because the design did more, not less, than was expected of it. D is wrong because the new building was based on the revised design.

24. F The item "vertical transport" appears in the new building, but not the old one. G is wrong because the data do not distinguish between different kinds of lighting. H is wrong because the item "cooling" appears in all three bars. J is wrong because no information is given about such an item.

25. B Comparing the design with the actual terminal, it is seen that all the items are about the same in both, except for lighting. This item is much smaller in the actual building than in the design.

26. G The new design lowered the heating cost from 225 units to 45, an enormous saving. F is wrong because it is the total cost of heating, not its fractional part of the total, that is the important datum. H is wrong because the new design drastically reduced the cost of heating, and the design was accurately reflected in the actual building. J is wrong because there is no indication that further improvement is not possible.

27. D If the new design results in a much more expensive building, the difference in cost might not be made up in fuel savings. A is wrong because there are other considerations in the decision. B is wrong because the plan does, in fact, propose improved efficiency in hot water heating. C is wrong because this question cannot be answered until the building is actually built.

28. G This is a test of the time it takes for the eyes of the guppies to become light-adapted; using their ability to find food as a test assumes that they use their eyes to find it. F is wrong because no tests of rate of activity were made. H is wrong because the basic experiment (Experiment 2) did not vary temperature. J is wrong because no comparison with people is made.

29. A The only way to know when the guppies are fully light-adapted is to find out how well they locate their food when their eyes are known to be light-adapted.

30. H This is the basic experiment; when the guppies can find 35 *Daphnia* in 5 minutes, their eyes are light-adapted.

31. B In the dark, all other senses function, but the guppies had to wait for their eyes to become light-adapted in order to find food. A is wrong because Experiment 3 shows only that low temperatures interfere somehow. C is wrong because all the senses of the guppies are functioning in daylight, and there is no evidence to indicate which one is used in finding food. D is wrong because, although the statement is true, it would probably hold no matter how the guppies find their food.

32. H Experiment 2 established a baseline from which temperature variations could be made. F is wrong because the pertinent question is light adaptation. G is wrong because the adaptation of the *Daphnia* is not dealt with anywhere. J is wrong because the tanks were kept steadily at the prescribed temperatures.

33. D The rate of adaptation increased up to a temperature of 24° C, but not above that level. Any of the other choices would be a plausible explanation of the results.

34. G Scientist 2 provides the explanation in terms of natural selection; Scientist 1 does not agree. F and J are wrong because both scientists incorporate these concepts into their theories. H is wrong because Scientist 1 has not committed himself on this issue.

35. A If wings are used for temperature control, it is conceivable that this was the original function of the protowings. B is wrong because a competent explanation is not experimental evidence. C and D are wrong because these points are not in contention.

36. J Scientist 2 uses this principle as her main argument, and Scientist 1 has not mentioned it at all. F and G are wrong because both scientists agree on these points. H is wrong because this is not a principle that Scientist 1 would accept.

37. D This would confirm the priority of temperature control as a function of winglike projections. All of the other choices do not discriminate between the two theories.

38. G Science advances by finding evidence that can be used to settle controversial questions. F is wrong because there is always room for difference of opinion, even in regard to long-established principles. H is wrong because Scientist 1 does not dispute the importance of natural selection; he claims only that it is an incomplete explanation. J is wrong because Scientist 2 has given a satisfactory answer, with evidence to back it up.

39. B Answer B is right, and A and C are wrong, because the two scientists agree that wings evolved gradually from projections out of the thorax. D is wrong because neither theory precludes other kinds of insects.

40. G The experiments must have been designed to test the effectiveness of various body and wing conformations in serving as temperature regulators and also as airfoils. F and J are wrong because the concept of evolution by natural selection is not in question. H is wrong because it is not the *concept* of preadaptation that is being tested, but its *mechanism*.

Index

The following documentation applies if you have purchased
How to Prepare for the ACT, 12th Edition book with CD-ROM.
Please disregard this information if your version does not contain the CD-ROM.

DOCUMENTATION

MINIMUM SYSTEM REQUIREMENTS

- IBM Compatible PC with 486 or higher processor, Intel Pentium or AMD processor recommended.
- Minimum 16 MB RAM, 32 MB RAM and higher recommended.
- Minimum 30 MB free hard disk space.
- CD-ROM Drive, Keyboard, Mouse, and SVGA color monitor.
- Operating system Microsoft® Windows 95/98, with Microsoft® Internet Explorer 4.0 (Version 4.72.2106.8) or higher loaded, or Microsoft® Internet Explorer 5.0 loaded.
- Multimedia sound card and speakers optional.

SOFTWARE INSTALLATION INSTRUCTIONS

1. Insert the Barron's ACT CD into the CD-ROM drive.
2. In the file Explorer (i.e. click right mouse button on **Start** button and select **Explore**), double click on **Setup.exe** in the **D:** directory, where **D** is the letter of your CD-ROM drive.

   Alternatively, click on the **Start** button, choose **Run**, and type **D:\Setup.exe** (where D is the letter of your CD-ROM drive), and then click on the OK button.

3. Follow the instructions on the screen.

   Note: If you encounter any installation problems, please see the solutions under the Help file. The Help file is located at D:\Help\Barrons_ACT.hlp on the CD-ROM, where D is the letter of your CD-ROM drive. Once it is open, click on *Miscellaneous*, and then on *Solutions to Installation Problems*.

USING THE SOFTWARE

1. Run the software just as you would run any other application. Simply click on the Start button, Programs, Barron's Software, and then on **Barron's ACT**.
2. The software contains an integrated learning environment that provides Tutorials, Testing, and Diagnostics. To learn more about it use the online **Help** and read the **How To...** section, which can be directly accessed under the **Help** menu item. You can quickly access Help on anything you see on the screen by pressing the **F1** key on your keyboard.

SOFTWARE FEATURES—SUMMARY

1. Contains an integrated learning environment and provides Tutorials, Testing, and Diagnostics.
2. Tutorial pages are delivered using colorful text, and attractive and illustrative colorful graphics. The tutorial pages are hyper linked to other pages and bookmarks, making navigation easy and convenient.
3. Testing is provided in Simulated and Learning modes. Simulated test mode uses timer controls to simulate actual exam conditions. Learning test mode enables students to focus on the weak areas and solve the questions at their own pace.
4. A variety of users' test responses is saved for later analysis in a built-in database. Typical responses include the answer selected, time taken to answer a question, number of times an answer is changed on a question, etc.
5. Useful diagnostics are provided on completed tests and are displayed in a spreadsheet and graphical chart. These provide the student with insights to strengthen the weak areas and to master the entire subject matter. The student can also view the correct answer to any question in the test with a single click.
6. Built-in utility link to the Windows® calculator is provided for convenience.
7. Easy on-line Help is provided on all aspects of the software. Users can get quick Help on any item on the screen by simply pressing the F1 key on the keyboard.